Ethical, Legal, and Professional Issues in the Practice of Marriage and Family Therapy

S. Allen Wilcoxon
The University of Alabama

Theodore P. Remley, Jr.
Old Dominion University

Samuel T. Gladding
Wake Forest University

Charles H. Huber
New Mexico State University

Upper Saddle River, New Jersey
Columbus, Ohio

Library of Congress Cataloging-in-Publication Data

Ethical, legal, and professional issues in the practice of marriage and family therapy /
S. Allen Wilcoxon ... [et al.]. — 4th ed.
    p. ; cm.
  Rev. ed. of: Ethical, legal, and professional issues in the practice of marriage and family therapy / Samuel T. Gladding,
Theodore P. Remley, Jr., Charles H. Huber. 3rd ed. c2001.
  Includes bibliographical references and index.
  ISBN 0-13-112034-4
  1. Family psychotherapy—Moral and ethical aspects. 2. Marital psychotherapy—Moral and ethical aspects. 3. Family
therapists—Professional ethics. 4. Family therapists—Legal status, laws, etc. I. Wilcoxon, S. Allen. II. Gladding, Samuel T.
Ethical, legal, and professional issues in the practice of marriage and family therapy.
  [DNLM: 1. Marital Therapy—ethics. 2. Family Therapy—ethics. 3. Family Therapy—legislation & jurisprudence.
4. Marital Therapy—legislation & jurisprudence. WM 430.5.M3 E84 2007]
  RC488.5.H8 2007
  174'.2—dc22

                                                                                              2006012077

Vice President and Executive Publisher: Jeffery W. Johnston
Publisher: Kevin M. Davis
Associate Editor: Meredith Sarver
Editorial Assistant: Sarah N. Kenoyer
Production Editor: Mary Harlan
Production Coordinator: Tim Flem/Publishware
Design Coordinator: Diane C. Lorenzo
Text Design: Tim Flem
Cover Design: Candace Rowley
Cover Image: SuperStock
Production Manager: Susan Hannahs
Director of Marketing: David Gesell
Marketing Manager: Autumn Purdy
Marketing Coordinator: Brian Mounts

This book was set in Palatino by Laserwords Private Limited, Chennai. It was printed and bound by R.R. Donnelley & Sons
Company. The cover was printed by The Lehigh Press, Inc.

Pearson Education Ltd.
Pearson Education Singapore Pte. Ltd.
Pearson Education Canada, Ltd.
Pearson Education–Japan

Pearson Education Australia Pty. Limited
Pearson Education North Asia Ltd.
Pearson Educación de Mexico, S.A. de C.V.
Pearson Education Malaysia Pte. Ltd.

10 9 8 7 6 5 4 3
ISBN: 0-13-112034-4

Preface

Although less than 100 years old, the professional practice of psychotherapy has become a major influence in contemporary society. During this time of establishment as a part of most cultures, psychotherapy has broadened its scope of influence to include social, political, and even economic spheres. Clinically, psychotherapy is no longer practiced exclusively on a one-therapist-to-one-client basis. Group therapy efforts have become commonplace in almost every mental health setting. Utilization of technology has even led to the use of technology-based psychotherapy in many locales. The last several decades also have seen the advent of another expansion within the psychotherapeutic field, that of marriage and family therapy.

Many therapists have replaced or supplemented their traditional individual and group models of practice with one emphasizing couples and families as the dominant treatment focus. This is not to suggest that contact with intimate partners and other family members had been completely ignored in previous eras. Rather, couples and family members had always been considered in tandem with, rather than as a component of, an individual client's concerns, and from an individually oriented therapeutic perspective.

As the practice of marriage and family therapy has evolved, supervision and training procedures have become more explicit, replicable, and accessible. Specific theories and techniques have been identified. Broad curricular components for training have been prescribed as required foundational aspects of minimal preparation. Additionally, specific content, goals, and teaching methods for university coursework and professional workshops have been delineated. These materials and strategies all continue to be researched, evaluated, and enhanced. Noticeably lacking before the publication of the first edition of *Ethical, Legal, and Professional Issues in the Practice of Marriage and Family Therapy*, however, were sources addressing "nontherapy" issues necessary to supplement the therapeutic training of marriage and family therapists (Piercy & Sprenkle, 1983). Such issues concern the demonstration of ethical, professional, and competent care on the part of the therapist, regardless of his or her preferred method of intervention or theoretical orientation for work with couples and families. Although not necessarily clinical or theoretical in nature, ineffective management, lack of knowledge, or disregard of such nontherapy concerns may have significant and undesirable effects on the course and outcome of therapy.

The importance of these nontherapy issues was emphasized in an article entitled "Family Therapy May Be Dangerous for Your Health" (Hare-Mustin, 1980), in which the author stated:

> In sum, family therapy may not be in the best interests of individual family members. Family therapists and their clients need to be aware of possible risks to the rights of the individual member. By being required to participate, individuals may have to subordinate their own goals and give up limited confidentiality and privacy. In addition, therapists who idealize the traditional family may foster stereotyped roles and expectations in the family that disadvantage individuals and limit their well-being and mental health. (p. 938)

Although offerings in the professional literature and training opportunities at conferences and workshops have increased in both number and quality, nontherapy issues—particularly ethical, legal, and associated professional concerns—are still underrepresented in relation to their potential impact on the practice of many mental health professionals. The simple fact is that marriage and family therapy differs from individual and group therapy on both conceptual and pragmatic levels. As a clinical practice, marriage and family therapy requires that therapists be adequately prepared to handle controversial issues that are unique to the family perspective. Questions that are difficult in individual and group therapy often become significantly more complicated when a couple or whole family presents itself for services (Margolin, 1982).

The American Association for Marriage and Family Therapy, the professional organization with which most marriage and family therapists are primarily affiliated, specifies graduate-level coursework in "professional studies" as a requirement within its educational requirements for clinical membership. In response to this requirement, courses in "ethical, legal, and professional issues" have been developed and constitute a core component of marriage and family training programs. The first three editions of *Ethical, Legal, and Professional Issues in the Practice of Marriage and Family Therapy* served as a basic text for these courses as well as a primary source for practicing professionals seeking to expand their knowledge of ethical, legal, and professional issues in marriage and family therapy. The current edition of the text is intended to follow and continue this trend as a scholarly and practical reference for emerging marriage and family therapists.

ORGANIZATION OF THE TEXT

This fourth edition has been updated and expanded so that it may continue to serve as a basic resource for both beginning students and practicing professionals. It is divided into four parts. Part I presents a discussion of cultural and value-related issues affecting the practice of marriage and family therapy. Chapter 1 examines the elements of diversity that culturally sensitive marriage and family therapists must encounter and assimilate. Chapter 2 offers a discussion of the multilayered ecology of marriage and family therapy, specifically related to systemic characteristics and the interaction of personal, professional, and institutional values.

Part II addresses ethical issues in marriage and family therapy. Chapter 3 examines foundational ethical principles and traditions that guide all therapists, particularly the beginning marriage and family therapist and the experienced practitioner who is shifting from an individual approach to the more complex systemic view. Chapter 4 discusses ethical issues unique to the contextual nature of marriage and family therapy. Chapter 5 offers a focused illustration of applied principles from the previous chapters by exploring the options and considerations faced by a marriage and family therapist concerning the issue of intimate partner violence. Chapter 6 presents contemporary ethical issues for which some precedent is available, though there is considerable room for interpretation and varied routes of action. Chapter 7 offers a "casebook" of examples with critiques highlighting the *AAMFT Code of Ethics* (American Association for Marriage and Family Therapy, 2001).

Part III considers legal issues in marriage and family therapy. Chapter 8 investigates the roles and relationships of marriage and family therapists within the legal system. Chapter 9 examines relevant family law. Chapter 10, like Chapter 7, is a casebook of examples with critiques discussing the impact of legal issues on marriage and family therapy.

Part IV focuses on professional issues related to the practice of marriage and family therapy. Chapter 11 explores multiple aspects of the professional identity of a marriage and family therapist. Chapter 12 offers another casebook of examples addressing specific professional questions and includes closing comments concerning anticipated trends and issues for the future.

Special attention should be paid to the three casebook chapters: 7, 10, and 12. We recall our days as clinicians-in-training seeking to understand ideas we encountered from our readings. Classroom instructors and clinical supervisors, knowledgeable and skilled from years of experience, provided case examples to illustrate the concepts more clearly. Those illustrations made learning a more concrete experience, from which we emerged much better prepared.

Overall, this book seeks to encourage a greater familiarization and expansion of knowledge relevant to cultural, ethical, legal, and professional issues necessary to supplement clinical training and practice in marriage and family therapy. We hope that you will gain an introductory knowledge of and appreciation for some of the issues you may encounter, and that you will be stimulated to think about your own position as a marriage and family therapist, whether as a primary source of professional identity or professional specialization.

ACKNOWLEDGMENTS

So many persons have contributed, both directly and indirectly, to our personal and professional development and to the writing of this book that it is impossible to thank them all. We thank the majority of them as a group by offering this book as a contribution of social interest that we hope will enhance the lives of mental health professionals and the clients with whom they interact. However, a few individuals need to be singled out for special thanks.

For their constructive suggestions during the preparation of the manuscript, we thank Ken Norem and Sandy Magnuson, University of Northern Colorado; Mary Anne Templeton, Troy University; Mary Hermann, Mississippi State University; and Patricia Stevens, Moorehead State University.

In addition, we especially thank the following reviewers: John J. Benshoff, Southern Illinois University; Michael R. Carns, Southwest Texas State University; Elizabeth B. Carroll, East Carolina University; Joseph M. Cervantes, California State University–Fullerton; Carmen Guanipa, San Diego State University; Tracey Laszloffy, Seton Hill University; Peter A. D. Sherrard, University of Florida; Volker Thomas, Purdue University.

We are particularly indebted to Publisher Kevin Davis, who guided this project at Merrill/Prentice Hall, and Sarah Kenoyer, editorial assistant.

Finally, we thank those who have made personal contributions to our lives.

From Allen Wilcoxon, "I will always appreciate my parents, Helen and Searcy, for impressing upon me the importance of learning and inquiry. I thank my wife, Pat Harrison, for her love, encouragement, and perspective as I have undertaken this task, particularly during my frequent times of frustration and confusion. I also thank our sons, Buz and Andy, for their support and interest throughout this project."

From Ted Remley: "I want to thank my parents, T. P. and Era, for giving me the education necessary to write books. I also appreciate my extended family, close friends, colleagues, and graduate students for tolerating my absences when I write and my crabby disposition when I am trying to make deadlines."

From Sam Gladding: "I am indebted to my parents, Russell and Gertrude, for their attention to teaching me the importance of values at a young age. My wife, Claire, and our children, Ben, Nate, and Tim, have been both understanding and supportive during my times of writing for this book. A family's encouragement and company cannot be valued enough."

REFERENCES

American Association for Marriage and Family Therapy. (2001). *AAMFT code of ethics.* Washington, DC: Author. Available: http://aamft.org/resources/Irmplan/ethics/ethicscode2001.asp

Hare-Mustin, R. T. (1980). Family therapy may be dangerous for your health. *Professional Psychology, 11*, 935–938.

Margolin, G. (1982). Ethical and legal considerations in marriage and family therapy. *American Psychologist, 7*, 788–801.

Piercy, F. P., & Sprenkle, D. H. (1983). Ethical, legal and professional issues in family therapy: A graduate level course. *Journal of Marital and Family Therapy, 9*, 393–401.

About the Authors

S. ALLEN WILCOXON is professor and coordinator of the Program in Counselor Education at the University of Alabama. He is a Licensed Professional Counselor in the states of Alabama and Washington, a Clinical Member and Approved Supervisor with the American Association for Marriage and Family Therapy, and a Nationally Certified Counselor. Dr. Wilcoxon holds a B.A. in Religion and Philosophy from Ouachita Baptist University, an M.A. in Psychology from Stephen F. Austin State University, and an Ed.D. in Counselor Education from East Texas State University (now Texas A & M University–Commerce). His postdoctoral work was at Texas A & M University. He is the author of numerous publications related to marriage and family therapy, clinical supervision, and ethics in mental health care. He is former chair of the Alabama Board of Examiners in Counseling. He is married to Dr. Pat Harrison, Professor of School Psychology at the University of Alabama. Their sons, Buz and Andy, are currently completing their graduate and undergraduate careers, respectively. He enjoys fishing, traveling, and baseball played at any level.

THEODORE P. REMLEY, JR., is a professor of counseling and holds a Batten Endowed Chair at Old Dominion University in Norfolk, Virginia. He is a member of the bar in Virginia and Florida and is licensed as a Professional Counselor in Louisiana, Mississippi, and Virginia, as well as a Licensed Marriage and Family Therapist in Louisiana. He is also a National Certified Counselor. Dr. Remley holds a B.A. in English, an M.Ed., an Ed.S., and a Ph.D. in Counseling from the University of Florida, and a J.D. from Catholic University in Washington, D.C. Dr. Remley is the coauthor with Barbara Herlihy of *Ethical, Legal, and Professional Issues in Counseling.* In addition, he has edited and written books and monographs, book chapters, and numerous articles in professional journals on the topic of legal issues in mental health. He is a former Executive Director of the American Counseling Association and was founding president of the American Association of State Counseling Boards. He has served on the counselor licensure boards in Louisiana, the District of Columbia, Mississippi, and Virginia. Dr. Remley is a former officer of the Mardi Gras Krewe of Orpheus in New Orleans and directs an annual counselor study abroad program in Italy.

SAMUEL T. GLADDING is a professor in and chair of the Department of Counseling at Wake Forest University. He is a Licensed Professional Counselor in the state of North Carolina, a National Certified Counselor, and a National Certified Mental Health Counselor. Dr. Gladding is a Clinical Member and Approved Supervisor in the American Association for Marriage and Family Therapy. Dr. Gladding received a B.A. and M.Ed. from Wake Forest University, an M.A.R. from Yale University, and his Ph.D. from the University of North Carolina at Greensboro. He is the author of numerous publications, including *Family Therapy: History, Theory, and Practice* (4th ed.). He is a past president of the American Counseling Association, a former editor of the *Journal for Specialists in Group Work*, and a past president of the Alabama Association for Marriage and Family Therapy. Dr. Gladding is married to the former Claire Tillson. They are the parents of three children. As a family they enjoy travel, humor, and attending athletic and artistic events.

CHARLES H. HUBER is on the faculty in the Department of Counseling and Educational Psychology, New Mexico State University. A licensed psychologist in the states of Connecticut, Florida, and New Mexico, he also holds diplomas in family psychology and behavioral psychology with the American Board of Professional Psychology. In addition, Dr. Huber is a clinical member and approved supervisor of the American Association for Marriage and Family Therapy and an approved supervisor and fellow of the Institute for Rational Emotive Behavioral Therapy. He maintains a private practice with Associates for Marriage and Family Therapy in Las Cruces, New Mexico. Dr. Huber received his B.A. from Upsala College, M.Ed. and Ed.S. from Florida Atlantic University, and Ph.D. from the University of South Carolina. He has authored or coauthored 10 books, served as editor of several professional journals, and written numerous articles and book chapters. He is active in a number of professional organizations, most recently serving as president of the New Mexico Association for Marriage and Family Therapy. Dr. Huber has been married for over two decades to his partner, Betsy. They and their two children raise and train labrador retrievers as their family hobby.

Discover the Companion Website Accompanying This Book

The Prentice Hall Companion Website: A Virtual Learning Environment

Technology is a constantly growing and changing aspect of our field that is creating a need for content and resources. To address this emerging need, Prentice Hall has developed an online learning environment for students and professors alike—Companion Websites—to support our textbooks.

In creating a Companion Website, our goal is to build on and enhance what the textbook already offers. For this reason, the content for each user-friendly website is organized by topic and provides the professor and student with a variety of meaningful resources. Common features of a Companion Website include:

- **Counseling Topics**—17 core counseling topics representing the diversity and scope of today's counseling field.
- **Annotated Bibliography**—Seminal foundational works and key current works
- **Web Destinations**—Significant and up-to-date practitioner and client sites
- **Professional Development**—Helpful information regarding professional organizations and codes of ethics
- **Electronic Blue Book**—Send homework or essays directly to your instructor's email with this paperless form
- **Chat**—Real time chat with anyone who is using the text anywhere in the country—ideal for discussion and study groups, class projects, etc.

To take advantage of these and other resources, please visit the *Ethical, Legal, and Professional Issues in Marriage and Family Therapy*, Fourth Edition, Companion Website at

www.prenhall.com/wilcoxon

Brief Contents

Contents

NOTE: Every effort has been made to provide accurate and current Internet information in this book. However, the Internet and information posted in it are constantly changing, so it is inevitable that some of the Internet addresses listed in this textbook will change.

Culture and Values: A Beginning Point for Practice Decisions

Being an ethical professional is not independent of being an ethical person.

(Mabe & Rollin, 1986, p. 296)

CHAPTER 1

Values as Context for Therapy

Unlike many texts addressing theoretical aspects of marriage and family therapy, this text focuses on ethical, legal, and professional issues for those in the field. We note this distinction because many of the issues addressed in our text focus on the decisions and behaviors of therapists and how those decisions and behaviors affect the clients they serve. Ultimately, those decisions and behaviors are practical rather than theoretical. Although the most important aspects of therapy concern the welfare of clients, few rules and certainties exist for therapists faced with ethical or legal dilemmas. Similarly, a variety of professional issues affecting marriage and family therapists can be confusing or even divisive among professional peers. This text is fashioned to address, though not necessarily resolve, these ethical, legal, and professional issues.

Marriage and family therapy, indeed, any type of counseling or psychotherapy, cannot be value-free or neutral (Shulte, 1990). "Even trying to avoid a particular value choice by being noncommittal amounts to taking a value position" (Bergin, 1985). Values are a core component of any professional therapeutic endeavor. "As long as one distinguishes between desirable and undesirable change, one is invoking values" (Welfel, 1998, p. 208). Most professional helping organizations build their codes of ethics around values. For example, the National Association of Social Workers (1999) bases its ethical principles on six core values: service, social justice, dignity and worth of the person, importance of human relationships, integrity, and competence. Similarly, the American Psychological Association (2002) features an examination of ethical principles, and the American Association for Marriage and Family Therapy (2001) and the American Counseling Association (2005) employ aspirational introductions for each code section as a framework to emphasize the values espoused and addressed by the entries in that section.

Values are particularly critical to the professional practice of marriage and family therapy. Indeed, the field of marriage and family therapy "recognizes the inescapability and importance of values" (Fowers & Wenger, 1997, p. 153). For instance, assessment and treatment decisions advanced by the different approaches to marriage and family practice reflect the dominant values of clinicians practicing these models (Doherty, 1992). Values are like a compass in that they promote a direction that therapeutic practice may take (Darom, 1988). Therefore, "it is important that marriage and family counselors be in touch with their values" (Kaplan, 1999, p. 13).

Rokeach defined a *value* as "an enduring belief that a specific mode of conduct or end-state of existence is personally or socially preferable to an opposite or converse mode of conduct or end-state of existence" (1973, p. 286). Anthropologists (e.g., Kluckhohn & Strodtbeck, 1961) have identified a great similarity among predominant values orientations found in diverse cultures, suggesting a universal dimension in all human efforts to cope with life's events. These broadly accepted values address a belief in the desirable. An affective component is elicited when this belief is accepted or challenged, and an action component cues behaviors considered congruent or incongruent with the belief (Stuart, 1980).

Our values originate from our experiences within a context, then they *become* the context for our lives. They shape our perceptions of self, others, and the world around us. Our values are the template as well as the reference point for decisions, behaviors, aspirations, expectations, and motivations. Yet our values are unique; they shape our individuality; they address a simple yet compelling question: "Who am I?" Our values emerge from our experiences throughout our lifespan as members of cultural groups who develop, and occasionally amend, our identity. This chapter examines the processes of *acculturation* and *identity development* that create the context for the interaction of values between therapist and client/system in marriage and family therapy. Chapter 2 examines the ways these processes extend beyond personal values and identity of marriage and family therapists to include professional and institutional perspectives and values. However, before examining those issues, we will address the process from which our perspective and our values emerge.

CULTURE, WORLDVIEW, AND IDENTITY

Marriage and family therapists frequently encounter terms such as "pluralism," "multicultural," "diversity," "cultural sensitivity and awareness," and "culturally responsive practice" in a variety of forms and circumstances. Linton (1945) noted that culture is "the configuration of learned behavior and the results of behavior whose components and elements are shared and transmitted by the members of a particular society" (p. 3). Baruth and Manning (2003) described culture as "institutions, communications, values, religions, genders, sexual orientations, disabilities, thinking, artistic expressions, and social and interpersonal relationships" (p. 8). The process of acculturation is a great deal more than simple indoctrination of patterns of behavior. The values and traditions advanced by those persons and agencies who hold a place of significance for an individual (e.g., family, community, religion institutions, etc.) become embraced in a unique way to emerge as one's template for understanding and interpreting interactions and experiences (Ivey, D'Andrea, Ivey, & Simek-Morgan, 2002).

Pedersen (1996) noted that the acculturation process is not uniform within (intra-group) or between (inter-group) cultural groups, meaning that the process of using one's experiences to form one's values is ultimately an *individual* process (p. 237).

Laird (2000) suggested that the intersection of class race, ethnicity, gender, age, and experiences represented the primary bases of intra-group and inter-group differences in acculturation. The term *subculture* has been employed to emphasize the significance of "racial, ethnic, regional, economic, or social community (e.g., gang, drug, gay, elderly) that exhibits characteristic patterns of behavior sufficient to distinguish others in the dominant society or culture" (Baruth & Manning, 2003, p. 9). By contrast, these authors have noted that *intraculture* reflects "a client's educational background, socioeconomic status, acculturation, and urban and rural background. A client may be a member of several subcultures and intracultures . . ." (p. 9). Obviously, a marriage and family therapist may be a member of several subcultures and intracultures. Thus, in the development of one's perspective and values, a variety of elements converge uniquely. Others have addressed these elements in far greater detail than will be attempted in our text (e.g., Baruth & Manning, 2003; Carter & McGoldrick, 2005; Sue & Sue, 1999). We encourage in-depth study of these and other sources to examine further the significant aspects of acculturation, worldview, and psychosocial identity. However, we will briefly examine these aspects as a basis for discussing values in the therapy process.

Gender

Though gender actually begins as a biological distinction, the socialization process of gender-based differences within and between cultural groups has been a basis for substantive commentary and research in professional literature (McCollough, Worthington, Maxey, & Rachal, 1997). Well-entrenched institutional traditions also exist to affect expectations and values distinguished on the basis of gender (Costello, 2004). Gender-based differences are significant factors in the perspectives and values brought to the therapy process by both client and therapist. Feminist literature has led to greater awareness and sensitivity to such traditions and their restrictive options for women (Knudson-Martin, 2001; Vatcher & Bogo, 2001). However, the intra-group and inter-group differences converging into the experiences of each individual indicate that one's perspective and values cannot be accounted for solely on the basis of gender.

Race

Hernandez (1989) noted that race concerns the anthropological aspects of humans related to physical characteristics such as skin and eye color, shape of body features, and similar innate characteristics. As a form of subcultural distinction, race is most often the basis for stereotypical assumptions and institutionalized forms of oppression or privilege (Henderson, 2000). However, a purely anthropological examination of race is far from adequate (Owens & King, 1999). Though race can serve as a significant basis for one's worldview and identity, attributing the development of client or therapist values to race alone is overly simplistic (Constantine, Heather, & Kaing, 2001).

Ethnicity

Discussions about distinctions for ethnic groupings can be complex and varied, though most appear to share the commonality of emphasizing a heritage grounded in nationality, shared socioeconomic and political experiences, and common values. In many instances, ethnicity has an element of economic oppression, though Henderson (2000) has indicated that at different times, all ethnic groups have been the oppressed and the oppressors. In many ways, the intersection of ethnicity and race yields an unavoidable, though not interchangeable, effect on the perspective and values held by all persons. The subcultural and intracultural elements previously noted by Baruth and Manning (2003) further affect the complex nature of values that originate from ethnic origins.

Social Class

The real as well as symbolic value of socioeconomic status is sometimes minimized when considering the perspective and values that emerge in therapy relationships. Atkinson, Morten, and Sue (1998) indicated that the financial considerations related to social class actually pale in comparison to the significance of perceived power or powerlessness, risk or security, and privilege or helplessness associated with social-class distinctions. In some instances, values associated with social class can be even more compelling than gender, race, or ethnicity (Phinney, 2000).

Sexual Orientation

Numerous terms and distinctions have been employed to reflect sexual orientation. MacGillivray (2000) has noted that the terms *gay, lesbian, bisexual, transgender,* and *questioning* have been employed uniformly to describe sexual orientation, although the use of *queer* has had mixed reception in professional literature. *Lifestyle* as a descriptor is rarely employed regarding sexual orientation because of its implied suggestion that sexual orientation is simply a matter of choice. The American Psychological Association (2000) noted that no differences between heterosexual and homosexual groups have been identified on measures of cognitive abilities, self-esteem, and psychological well-being. Though contemporary perspectives on sexual orientation in many social and cultural groups have come to reflect acceptance and support, discrimination and prejudice in social, work, and institutional circumstances continue to be pervasive (Theodore & Basrow, 2000). The perspective and values related to sexual orientation among couples and family members clearly, though not exclusively, affect the interactive nature of marriage and family therapy.

Disability

Middleton, Rollins, and Harley (1999) observed that the struggle for awareness and sensitivity to bias, stereotyping, discrimination, and oppression against persons with disabilities has been a battle no less compelling than that fought in the Civil Rights movement of the 1960s. These authors maintained that coming to value one's identity as a person with a disability during the Disability Rights movement represented both an internal (i.e., intra-group) and an external (i.e., inter-group) battle. As with any attempt at recognition and affirmation, the energy to drive such efforts often stems from focusing on a primary factor of one's identity (i.e., disability) while deemphasizing other factors in one's identity (e.g., race, gender, etc.). Reeve (2000) observed that personal values emerging from one's disability status are compelling to the point of becoming the reference point for defining interactions, even counseling. However, the development of perspective and values present in the therapy relationship cannot be reduced to one's disability status.

Religion

Few aspects of cultural or ethnic groupings are as compelling for its members as the significance of religious traditions and practices. We offer only a note of distinction between *spirituality* and *religion* in that the former is a highly personalized perspective, whereas the latter is a more codified and communal set of beliefs and practices (Elkins, 1990). Readers are encouraged to examine such distinctions in other sources. Unlike many other elements of socialization in distinct groups, such as manners, language, or dress codes, religion has the added impact of sacred rules and reverence for a deity (Kahle & Robbins, 2003). Moreover, religion typically features specialized designations for leaders who interpret rules or scripture, inspire behavior within codes of conduct, arbitrate disputes, perform ceremonies, and console in times of tragedy. Religious beliefs and practices offer an immense array of traditions and derivative values for believers, ranging from sanctuary from oppression (Mahmoud, 1996; McRae, Thompson, & Cooper, 1996) to barriers in overcoming victimization in domestic violence (Foss & Warnke, 2003).

Worldview

In many ways, one's worldview represents more of a composite picture of one's association with a reference group distinguished on the basis of a variety of cultural factors (Sue, 1978), such as those we have examined thus far in this chapter. Worldview is significant in that it reflects *individual* experiences as a member of a reference group, some of which may conform and others of which may diverge from the majority perspective of that group (Lyddon & Adamson, 1992). In this respect, one's worldview represents a phenomenological and epistemological perspective about self in relation to others. Concerning its impact on clients, Baruth and Manning (2003) noted that one's worldview "is an overriding cognitive frame of reference that influences most of his or her perceptions and values" (p. 10). The same can be said for the worldview of therapists. In this respect, the convergence of cultural and group-affiliate factors in one's worldview is an intersection of experiences that is revealed in the perspective and values held by those in the therapy relationship.

Psychosocial Identity

Jones and McEwen (2000) examined the interrelated elements of acculturation and socialization to develop a graphic portrayal of emergent psychosocial identity. Figure 1–1 reveals two aspects of identity development that are of particular importance to marriage and family therapists. The first of these aspects is the contextual nature of one's identity. At the center is the individual who is surrounded by layers of influence, emphasizing the interactive nature of personal development throughout the lifespan. The second of these aspects is the dynamic nature of one's identity. The figure illustrates the motion of various factors and influences that continue to affect identity and values

FIGURE 1–1 Model of Multiple Dimensions of Identity

Note: From "A Conceptual Model of Multiple Dimensions of Identity," by S. R. Jones and M. K. McEwen, 2000, *Journal of College Student Development, 41* (4), p. 409. Copyright 2000 by American College Personnel Association. Reproduced by permission.

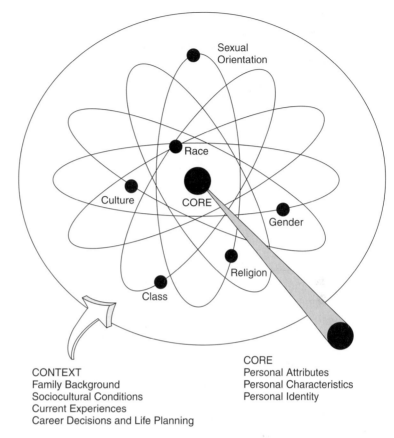

CONTEXT
Family Background
Sociocultural Conditions
Current Experiences
Career Decisions and Life Planning

CORE
Personal Attributes
Personal Characteristics
Personal Identity

held by the individual. This dynamic process suggests coexisting forces that can sustain as well as alter our values and perspectives. These two aspects of the Jones and McEwen (2000) model suggest for the marriage and family therapist that the value-laden interaction of a therapeutic relationship must be honored holistically with an appreciation for the origins of differences as well as the possibility of change.

Psychosocial identity is a partly conscious and largely unconscious sense of self, occurring both in isolation and in relationship to others (Hoare, 1991). Identity is an amalgam of experiences and decisions in which we are both reactive and proactive. Unlike indoctrination that can occur in early life, psychosocial identity is a developmental process that involves both assimilation and an accommodation of experiences in an integrated whole (Robinson, 2005). From such a vantage, our perspective and values are demonstrated in many ways, depending on the dominant elements of our psychosocial identity.

Identity and culture are integrally involved, but one's psychosocial identity is often driven by a focal element of one's acculturation. Consider your response to the question "Who am I?" Our answer to this question often reflects a primary factor from our acculturation. For example, a married, Caucasian heterosexual man employed in an upper-level management position with a U.S. company may answer by saying, "I am a man," "I am a husband," "I am a Caucasian," "I am a heterosexual," "I am a manager," "I am an American," and so on. Although each is accurate, his psychosocial identity may hinge more on some aspects of his acculturation than on others. In another example, a single, Latina lesbian woman employed in an hourly wage retail position as a non-naturalized immigrant may begin by responding, "I am a member of many oppressed groups. Pick one!" Others may even eschew an identity of self-in-isolation to embrace an identity of self-in-collective (e.g., "I am a member of the tribe/group.").

Many models of identity exist as theoretical viewpoints about identity development, including those emphasizing race (Helms, 1990; Ponterotto, 1991; Poston, 1990; Robinson, 2005; Rowe, Bennett, & Atkinson, 1994), gender (Downing & Roush, 1985), and sexual orientation (Sophie, 1985/1986; Troiden, 1989). Readers are encouraged to examine these and other models as examples of theoretical views on the development of a psychosocial identity. Most models feature some commonality in terms of sequential and developmental processes, including: (a) stability and limited awareness, (b) experience and instability through increased awareness, (c) dissonance and discomfort, (d) struggle and reactivity, and (e) resolution and growth.

Marriage and family therapists are uniquely positioned to participate in the change process with individuals, couples, and families. The development of their psychosocial identity is critical in this process, however. In order to be a culturally responsive practitioner, therapists must be aware of their own cultural background and worldview. One approach to understanding one's cultural background is through an *etic* perspective that emphasizes similarities and dissimilarities between one's acculturation and that of others. By contrast, an *emic* approach would focus on one's culture without such comparisons (Draguns, 1989). In either case, a therapist's appreciation for the effects of privilege and oppression from the various factors converging in a client's identity can only emerge from deliberate awareness and sensitivity. In this way, a therapist can appreciate the significance of *perspective* and *values* that affect themselves and their clients in therapy.

PERSPECTIVE, VALUES, AND THERAPY

All human events are guided by the interaction of the perspective and values held by its participants. This interaction of perspective and values determines those aspects of human experience labeled as events, the significance ascribed to those events, and the ways individuals select and pursue goals, as well as the manner in which goal attainment is evaluated. People cannot interact independently of their values, even if those values are not explicit. Professional therapeutic practice is particularly shaped by value interaction among therapists, clients, and institutions.

Institutional representatives of society, including governmental bodies, clinics, hospitals, social services agencies, insurance companies, schools and training centers, and professional associations, formally and informally hold out perspectives and values for professional therapeutic practice. These perspectives define professional therapeutic services, who is eligible to receive them, and who is qualified to offer them. They also decide the conditions under which such services will be financed, whether through direct fee payments, insurance coverage, tax deductions, or other subsidies, and which professionals will be approved for these remunerations. In making these determinations, societal representatives assert their values about the nature of mental illness, marital and family problems, and treatment alternatives (Aponte, 1985).

Values can describe either means or ends to actions. In each case, values determine efforts to make discriminations among alternative courses of actions. Values that prescribe ends contribute to attitudes about all facets of society (Rokeach, 1968). Values that prescribe means provide the basis for professional norms (R. M. Williams, 1968). Professional norms are hierarchically organized (Maslow, 1959) and relate to a series of beliefs about all phases of therapeutic practice (Stuart, 1980). Marriage and family therapists' values thus provide the basis for their professional practice (B. Carter, 1986). Values gained from personal life experiences and professional training interact with and filter societal values about professional practice to influence every therapeutic decision. These decisions may govern who will be offered services, the goals of those services, the procedures used to achieve identified goals, and the criteria by which therapeutically mediated changes are evaluated. A further interaction with clients' values (i.e., the therapeutic process) is framed by and frames the parameters of therapists' values. Thus, this values interaction, or valuing, is an essential aspect in the professional practice of marriage and family therapy. Further discussion of this unique interaction within the multilayered ecology of marriage and family therapy is featured in Chapter 2.

A significant aspect of this interaction of values in therapy for either ends or means concerns clients' initiative for participating in therapy. For many clients, therapy is a question of *crisis*. Are clients experiencing a "crisis of values" or are they experiencing a "crisis of outcomes"? In some cases, clients seek to examine their existing values that may have led to conflict (individual or systemic). Such a crisis of values may reflect new experiences and dissonance with one's existing perspective and values, meaning therapy may be focused on resolution and growth. Other clients seek to affirm existing values and perspective on an issue of conflict, meaning therapy may be focused on trying to secure a preferred outcome, often represented in changes on the part of others. Multiple clients often bring multiple, and possibly conflicting, crises and agendas to therapy. In either case, therapists are faced with determining the role of their own perspective and values addressing these "crises."

In this matter, Napier and Whitaker (1978) have offered a helpful distinction between the "Battle for Structure" and the "Battle for Initiative." Regarding the Battle for Structure, these authors noted that the issues of administration, planning, and management are a component of setting the stage for therapy. This battle concerns elements of informed consent in a therapy contract, a practice statement, or some other means of disclosure to clarify the mutual expectations for therapy. Napier and Whitaker noted that the therapist must "win" the Battle for Structure. By contrast, the Battle for Initiative concerns the motivation, agenda, perspective, and other elements clients bring into therapy. Concerning this battle, these authors observed that the clients must "win" by assuming responsibility for the energy to pursue change. This is not to say that the therapist has no role in such issues. However, imposition of perspective and values of the therapist may suggest that the client's crisis is the "wrong crisis." Thus, the therapist could reduce a client's energy and commitment for change by shaping the crisis to conform to his or her values. This recurring theme of values interaction will be featured throughout the chapters of this book.

The results of this kind of values interaction could be particularly troublesome for a therapist who wants to be a culturally responsive practitioner. Baruth and Manning

(2003) have stated that "Counseling effectiveness will be diminished when the counselor places value judgments on clients' cultures and judges events and situations through his or her identity expectations" (p. 31). Pedersen (1996) has noted that assuming initiatives with clients will derive from presumptions about cultural similarities and differences, which can lead to errors of: (a) overemphasizing similarities, leading to a "melting pot" mindset; (b) overgeneralizing differences, leading to stereotyping; or (c) assuming the need to emphasize *either* similarities *or* differences, leading to devaluation of the uniqueness of each client's perspective and values. Even more troublesome could be the unintended outcome of *pseudospeciation* (Hoare, 1991), a form of oppression that suggests one array of culturally derived value and perspective is superior to others. Thus, the struggle in Napier and Whitaker's "battles" is to determine the extent to which structure and initiative can interact to respect differences in perspectives and values. Toward this end, we offer a discussion of values clarification, the implications of valuing in therapy, and the components of valuing that can affect the practice of marriage and family therapy.

Values Clarification

In an article appropriately entitled, "Counselor: Know Thyself," Hulnick (1977) posited the inescapable need for therapists to clarify their own values if they are to assume a distinct professional identity. Similarly, Pell (1979) concurred with an earlier position asserted by Bergantino (1978) that lack of self-awareness by therapists represented a "fatal flaw." Such self-awareness must entail a clear understanding of the bases on which therapists choose to assume their professional identity. Additionally, for clients facing a "crisis of values," the lack of intentional examination of therapist values may impede their ability to assist such clients.

Values clarification has been suggested as a means for therapists to clarify their professional position (Glaser & Kirschenbaum, 1980). Inherent in the values clarification perspective is the assumption that thoughtfully reflecting on one's beliefs is better than not doing so; that considering alternatives and their consequences is better than not considering them; and that acting consistently with one's most cherished beliefs—one's values—is important.

Values clarification represents a consideration of the process of valuing as opposed to simply identifying the content of values. It is an active process composed of seven subprocesses, each eliciting questions that need to be answered in a developmental sequence (Glaser & Kirschenbaum, 1980):

Choosing Basic Beliefs
1. Choosing from alternatives:
   a. Have a number of alternatives been considered?
   b. Has sufficient time been given to identifying possible alternatives?
2. Choosing after considering consequences:
   a. What are the most valuable aspects of the belief?
   b. What if everyone held the belief?
3. Choosing freely:
   a. How was the belief first procured?
   b. How freely is it now being chosen?

Prizing Basic Beliefs

4. Prizing and cherishing:
    a. Does the belief hold significant importance?
    b. Is it one to be proud of?
5. Publicly affirming, when appropriate:
    a. Is there a willingness to share the belief with others?
    b. Who would it be appropriate to share the belief with?

Acting on Beliefs

6. Acting:
    a. Is the belief one that can be readily acted on?
    b. Is there a willingness to act on it?
7. Acting with a pattern of consistency:
    a. Is the belief one that is typically acted on?
    b. Is there a willingness to consistently act on the belief?

Seymour's (1982) injunction identifying regular values clarification as essential to professional therapeutic practice aptly addresses the importance of this process:

> We do become emotionally invested in our values, we do hold some of them to be unquestionably right, and we do act in counseling in accordance with what we believe. We, as counselors, must be aware of the emotional investment, admit to, and hopefully question those values that have been previously unquestioned, and then examine closely how what we believe influences how we act as counselors. If our values are, in fact, the lenses through which we view the world, then we need to have our vision checked as a part of the selection and training process, and at regular intervals thereafter. (p. 45)

A good example of "checking vision" for marriage and family therapists is the framework of a systemic epistemology. *Epistemology* is a branch of philosophy that investigates the origin, nature, methods, and limits of human knowledge. For the professional practice of marriage and family therapy, the term has come to mean a formal professional worldview—a framework for perspective, thinking, conceptualizing, and valuing (Sauber, L'Abate, & Weeks, 1985). Many hold that the very essence of marriage and family therapy depends on a therapist's choosing, prizing, and acting on certain predominant beliefs of a systemic nature. They posit a systemically oriented epistemology as delineating the difference between doing marriage and family therapy and simply seeing marital partners and family members in the same room and dealing with their individual concerns. For them, systemic epistemology represents the basic core of marriage and family therapy as a professional therapeutic practice. By contrast, others feel that if systemic epistemology, as a professional worldview at least, is no longer acceptable to many marriage and family therapists as a framework for their practice, then the field has come to a crossroads. Should that which has been an intellectually attractive, useful, and dependable theoretical rudder be cast aside (Fish, 1990)?

The perspectives and values associated with the systemic epistemology will be examined more thoroughly in Chapter 2 of our text. However, the differences among marriage and family therapists on this basic issue offer a vivid illustration of the dynamic and interactive nature of perspectives and values affecting therapy, both for the therapist and the client/system. In order to successfully enter into such a relationship, therapists and clients alike are faced with the balance of holding their values but also respecting the values held by others. The process of negotiation exemplifies the true nature of *valuing.*

Negotiation: The Nature of Valuing

The negotiation of values is increasingly central to the professional practice of marriage and family therapy. Today, less is accepted on the strength of tradition and precedent and more is open for debate. Both within the field and in society in general, technological and social changes are occurring at a greater rate than at any previous period. Moreover, people are actively seeking ways to determine the terms of these changes.

One major reason for this progressive acceleration of change has been an explosion in the amount and quality of information available through the media and increased opportunities for education, communication, and travel. All this has led to an escalation in the rate of change among groups and other social network relationships. Traditions, customs, and roles within relationships must contend with mounting pressures to change. They resist, accommodate, mutate, or vanish in this swirl of social movement. In contemporary times, many have gained greater autonomy, flexibility, and power over their own lives and in relation to the rest of society. This phenomenon, although resulting in more choice, has also created more sources of stress. Marriage and family therapy is one of the means societal institutions have identified to assist people in more successfully negotiating this social evolution (Aponte, 1985).

Traditional approaches to exchanges of value-laded issues have promoted a view of reality marked by a *content* rather than a *process* orientation. Put in its most basic terms, there is a "right" way that is usually presented as contrasting to a "wrong" way. The only legitimate response to such an approach is adaptation (Taggart, 1982). A more modern variant of this position is the view that social change is permitted only within the restraints of unchanging social values; the institutions that support and promote these unchanging values must themselves survive without changing (Jantsch, 1980).

This distinction of opposites results ultimately in rigidification of existing professional practice. Values expressed from this perspective are often seen as the only things that last; to tamper with the methods embedded within those lasting values is to risk being accused of seeking to overturn them (Taggart, 1982). Thus, an unnecessary dichotomy is created. *Valuing* suggests that values need not be static entities denoting a right or wrong way; rather, there exists an ongoing negotiation of values resulting in an evolving epistemological process that continually balances between confirmation and novelty. Total confirmation identifies a static, rigid epistemology; for living systems, this equals death. Total novelty, by contrast, identifies a chaotic epistemology; in living systems, this heralds disintegration. Life is a dance between the two (von Weizsacker & von Weizsacker, 1974).

A. Watts (1961) discussed language as a metaphor for the continuing negotiation between novelty and confirmation. A language that becomes too innovative in either time or space is at risk of losing its coherence. A language that stops growing is in danger of becoming a relic. Likewise, valuing suggests an evolving epistemological process of unfolding within the context of negotiating older beliefs, thus ensuring both debate and a common task.

A particularly cogent therapeutic illustration here is the notion of a therapeutic opposition known as resistance. The term *resistance* represents a conceptual wall between the client's and the therapist's values. Traditional views have held that this wall must be broken down for change to occur (Searight & Openlander, 1984). De Shazer (1999) noted how resistance is often used as an explanatory device to account for situations in which clients do not respond to therapeutic interventions in a manner desired by their therapists. Resistance represents attributions made by therapists to account for this "difficulty." Dell (1982) believed this notion was epistemologically mistaken: "People and systems do not resist; they simply are what they are" (p. 22). Likewise, valuing asserts that clients' and therapists' values are not inherently right or wrong, correct or incorrect; they simply are.

As strategically oriented marriage and family therapists have noted, clients traditionally seen as "resistant" by their therapists will be viewed differently by therapists who "go with reality"—therapists who accept clients' values as they are and negotiate their own values with clients' values. Andolfi, Angelo, Menghi, and Nicolo-Corigliano (1983) emphasized a somewhat similar negotiation process, resulting in clients evolving a different "script." In the valuing process of Andolfi and colleagues, a therapist negotiates with a client to emphasize certain values that were previously deemphasized, and at the same time relegates other values to the background. Within the context of the therapist–client negotiation, values evolve with accompanying behavioral changes that are compatible with values changes. Essentially, the therapist and client come together in negotiating a common world of less pain and conflict. Similarly, those embracing a narrative approach will emphasize the importance of respect for the validity and accuracy of the perspective and values held by all members of a system in order to give rise to "new stories" for their futures (Diamond, 2000; White & Epston, 1990). Marriage and family therapists thus can maintain the importance of an epistemology that recognizes the benefits of understanding the shapes and patterns of interaction and simultaneously augments and deepens that understanding. This principle is a must for a culturally responsive therapist.

The Practice Implications of Valuing

For years, therapists have debated whether professional psychotherapy represents art or science. Many marriage and family therapists' opinions are on the side of art, yet their terminology often suggests science. To measure human exchange, couples and families have been compared to the cybernetic working of machines, the organization of solar systems, the interplay of chemical compounds, mathematical equations, and more. The language of science offers a definitive way to describe human functioning. However, it eliminates many of the political and psychological interchanges in human systems as well as peculiarly human qualities—imagination, creativity, and unpredictability (Papp, 1984). It also represents a static value, rather than a valuing perspective for addressing therapeutic change.

As art, the major goal of marriage and family therapy is to negotiate basic perceptions so that participants encounter and consider different perceptions. Through the introduction of the novel or unexpected, a frame of reference is amended and the content of reality is rearranged. This artistic focus does not represent a solely creative act. Something is not created from nothing; rather, there is an uncovering, selection, reshuffling, combination, and synthesis of already existing facts, ideas, and skills (Gladding, 1998a). Valuing as presented in this chapter mirrors the idea of psychotherapy as an artistic endeavor.

One predominant implication of valuing for marriage and family therapists is its affirmation of marital and family relationships as pluralistic and multidimensional. However, as Huntley and Konetsky (1992) stated:

> The areas of family therapy and clinical psychology, in particular, have focused on disturbed family functioning and led professionals to look for pathology in all families and individuals. Additionally, many traits observed in families in treatment become identified as indicators of maladaptive behavior, even though these same traits are observed in people who do not need any psychological intervention. So we are presented with a dilemma. Professionals in the mental health field are looking for any signs of abnormality and are ready to interpret even normal or benign behaviors as symptoms to be treated, and we have a bias toward psychopathology because the families we observe or see in treatment are not healthy, well-adjusted families. (p. 62)

In their educational and clinical training, all mental health professionals have had to address the questions, "What is normal?" and "What is abnormal?" Valuing calls for the full consideration of healthy as well as symptomatic behaviors. The cultural context and worldview of clients strongly affects such circumstances, particularly if an institutional perspective and value "pathologizes" a cultural norm (e.g., expressions of aggression, discomfort with individual initiative, etc.). Dell (1983) proposed that professionals normally behave as if pathology is objective and obvious, when pathology is generally only a projection of their own values and intentions. He noted in this regard:

> When we "see" pathology as having an objective existence in the world, then we are projecting our values about how we think the world ought to be. We have shifted from, "I don't like it to be that way" (an explicit statement of personal values) to, "That's sick; that shouldn't be that way" (a statement that implies that the sickness is objective—independent of the observer's values). (p. 30)

Dell (1983) discussed a number of implications for the professional practice of marriage and family therapy that mirror those implications emanating from a valuing perspective. Four of these include the following: (a) living without objective knowledge, (b) taking personal responsibility, (c) taking responsibility for pathologizing, and (d) accepting what is.

Living Without Objective Knowledge

Dell (1983) asserted that objectivity is impossible. This is not to say, however, that human beings are passive, innocent recipients of information about the world. Rather, "the world bumps up against us and we each have our own reaction to it" (p. 31). Absolute, static values do not objectively exist. A person does not simply receive a system's values; he or she reacts to those values developmentally, based on experiences, some of which affirm a value and some of which create dissonance (T. L. Robinson, 2005).

Even if values did represent an objective, absolute reality, a person could not attain objective knowledge of them. Interaction can only provide one with his or her reaction to them, not how they objectively exist (Maturana, 1978). Thus, valuing represents the "bumping" together of values, with the outcome always being negotiated around any reactions to that collision. The absolute adoption of a value is virtually impossible.

Taking Personal Responsibility

If other systems' values cannot be taken as absolutes, then people must realize some responsibility for their own values. Systems cannot completely determine each other's values and the manner they are acted on. For example, who is responsible for the reader's reaction to a book, the reader or the authors? Does a book determine what a reader's reaction to it will be? Both contribute, but ultimately, as the age-old adage suggests, "Beauty is in the eye of the beholder." Dell (1983) referred to this issue as an epistemological responsibility.

This epistemological responsibility must be contrasted, however, with a more familiar kind of responsibility that occurs in the everyday give-and-take of human interaction. Such a social form of responsibility is also more active: People hold each other responsible for many different things. Valuing posits the fruitlessness of marriage and family therapists' thinking that they can take total responsibility for clients' changing their values. This view is consistent with our earlier discussion on Napier and Whitaker's (1978) ideas about the Battle for Initiative. Both therapists and clients can present and be presented with alternatives, with their ultimate adoptions being a reflection of both since, in the final analysis, they will be personal positions. However, both the therapist and clients are responsible for their alternatives and ultimate adoptions.

Taking Responsibility for Pathologizing

A primary illustration of the implications inherent in therapists' epistemological responsibility is the matter of "seeing pathology." If, as Dell (1983) proposed, we live without objective knowledge, then marriage and family therapists who "see" pathology are projecting certain values. He further asserted:

> We are attached to pathology, I think, because it allows us to disown responsibility for our values. We wish to imply our values are really objective or universal. I believe that many of the protests to my deconstruction of pathology originated in peoples' unwillingness to substitute the personal, "I don't like that," for the objective, "That is sick." (p. 31)

Valuing as a manner of "seeing" is represented by statements such as "I don't like that behavior, view, emotion, and so on"—personal reactions rather than asserted facts. Additionally, in being respectful of the perspective and values of clients, therapists must also accept that some "pathologies" are actually contextualized culturally as accepted traditions and norms.

Accepting What Is

Dell (1983) referred to the idea of "what is, is." He took pains to assert that he was not alluding to an overly optimistic "everything is fine because everything is the way it should be," nor any fatalistic, ideological brainwashing to take no action because "what is, is." Instead, Dell described a distinction many marriage and family therapists already recognize—the difference between Murray Bowen's "taking an I-position" (Bowen, 1978) and not doing so. Dell described this, stating:

> If I say that I dislike something—and explicitly base my dislike on my own values (i.e., take an I-position)—then I am taking responsibility for my disliking. I am not blaming my dislike on an intrinsic wrong or sickness in the object of my dislike. By taking responsibility for my disliking, I am simultaneously accepting myself, i.e., admitting that my feelings are mine, and accepting that the disliked thing is the way it is. Conversely, if I were to refuse to take responsibility for how I should feel by saying, "That's sick," or, "That shouldn't be that way," then I would be refusing to accept both myself and the disliked thing. (p. 64)

From a valuing perspective, "what is, is" does not mean marriage and family therapists should take no action. It means that when marriage and family therapists do seek to change something they don't like, they should take that position from an I-position (i.e., "I don't like that") as opposed to a stance advocating objective pathology (i.e., "You're sick"). Further, "what is, is" means that when taking a position, marriage and family therapists should seek to observe what happens. If the position fails to achieve the intended result, they must identify and accept what has happened: A particular action did not achieve the desired result. For a marriage and family therapist to refuse to accept "what is, is" is to blame the thing (which he or she tried to change) for the therapist's difficulty in changing it. Again, the Battle for Initiative and the context for such a process must be considered by the culturally responsive therapist.

VALUING COMPONENTS

Most discussions of values have tended to focus on content as opposed to process. For example, marriage and family therapists have been urged to be intimately aware of personal and professional values associated with divorce, dual careers, birth control, sexual activities, abortion, child rearing, extramarital affairs, sex roles, and child and spouse abuse (Bird & Sporakowski, 1992; Margolin, 1982; Seymour, 1982). The content of values is obviously important and cannot be ignored. We will devote considerably more attention to these and related elements of personal, professional, and institutional layers of values in Chapter 2 of our text. However, as noted throughout this chapter, values all too often are represented as static stances construed as right or wrong. Valuing proposes that values, the beliefs, the perspective, and the resultant actions they encompass should regularly be reconsidered, reclarified, and renegotiated.

Ivan Boszormenyi-Nagy and his colleagues have been in contrast to those who have predominantly addressed the content of values in marriage and family therapy. They have framed their process-oriented discussions in the context of ethical accountability, stressing that satisfying family relationships requires ethical behavior among family members, that is, consideration of each other's welfare and interests. In describing a type of therapy known as Contextual Family Therapy, family members are facilitated in addressing relational commitments and balances of fairness (Boszormenyi-Nagy & Ulrich, 1981). The aim of the approach is a loosening of static values so family members become better able to shift their intentions and interactions toward more satisfying life experiences. What occurs is the development of a greater balance of fairness and mutual appreciation.

The ethical dimensions at the center of Contextual Family Therapy represent process-oriented elements of equal utility. Employed as *valuing components*, reconciliation of issues of concern can be facilitated. Regardless of the content of values, the use of these process-oriented components allows valuing to generalize to any specific issue arising in marriage and family therapy. We offer these notions not as a preference for the Contextual Family Therapy model but as an informative construct for examining the components of valuing.

Obligation and Entitlement

Valuing begins with recognition of two primary components: the mutual obligations and entitlements within all relationships. These components have been frequently minimized, overlooked, or contested in the professional literature. For example:

> I do my thing and you do your thing.
> I am not in this world to live up to your expectations.
> And you are not in this world to live up to mine.
> You are you and I am me.
> And if by chance we find each other, it's beautiful.

This "Gestalt Prayer," originated by Frederick Perls, represents an overt statement of a value that permeates much of professional therapeutic practice. It is derived from a recognition that many personal and interpersonal problems appear to emanate from destructive and unrealistic obligations in relationships. Consequently, freedom from obligations is sought. Although the intention may be freedom from only *destructive* obligations, the implication in practice has often resulted in encouraging persons to free themselves from all obligations to promote mutuality in interactions (Karpel & Strauss, 1983).

This focus on retreating from relationships with destructive obligations offers little guidance to aid people who want to move back into more or less satisfying, nondestructive relationships. These authors posit that people should take responsibility for themselves instead of trying to get others to take responsibility for their lives. Still, much of what individuals find important in their lives depends on the willingness of people to assume some responsibility for one another.

Karpel and Strauss (1983) expounded on the work of Boszormenyi-Nagy and his colleagues in describing a vocabulary to better comprehend the underlying structure of balanced, fair, mutually satisfying, growth-producing relationships. Karpel and Strauss asserted the inherent presence of obligations in relationships, emphasizing that not all obligations are destructive. They further offered the following illustrations:

- A wife is grateful for her husband's having gone out of his way to purchase something she wanted. She, in turn, offers to make a phone call both of them have been avoiding.
- An adolescent boy feels sad after making fun of his younger sister in front of her peers. He apologizes to her and offers to let her use his previously off-limits MP3 player.
- A young man with severe diabetes feels indebted, literally, for his life, to his sister who donated one of her kidneys for a transplant operation.
- A man feels a sense of debt to his parents for the physical and emotional support they offered him as he built the satisfying, productive life he has come to enjoy.

These illustrations all involve at least one person's obligation based either on the merit of the other person (depending on his or her helpful actions or sacrifices) or the debt of the person (contingent on his or her actions having in some way harmed the other). This valuing component for achieving a balance of fairness relative to obligation is called *entitlement*. Obligation and entitlement represent the ends of a valuing continuum. If it is agreed that one is obliged to another, there follows an agreement that the other is entitled to something.

In any relationship, recognition of obligations and entitlements constantly fluctuates. Fulfilling obligations results in decreasing one's own obligations, yet simultaneously increasing one's entitlement as well as the obligations of others. Ignoring obligations tends to increase one's obligations as well as others' entitlement. "Give and take" underlies most of the valuing process. Examining these processes in the therapy relationship can be of enormous assistance in clarifying the values affecting clients.

Acknowledgment and Claim

Closely related to obligation and entitlement are *acknowledgment* and *claim*. Acknowledgment refers to "the willingness of one party in a relationship to recognize and 'give credit for' the entitlement of the other" (Karpel & Strauss, 1983, p. 34). Acknowledgment calls for a willingness to seek a balance of fairness in a relationship. Withholding acknowledgment in a relationship creates an imbalance. This is so even when such withholding is preceded by a refusal to provide acknowledgment. This second refusal only compounds the initial imbalance. Two examples illustrate withholding of acknowledgment:

- An elderly couple anticipates and makes daily reference to their son's upcoming visit from his distant home. The weekly visits of their daughter who lives locally, however, are ignored or minimized.
- Two young children's efforts to clean up the kitchen receive ridicule and rebuke from their parents when some dishes are accidentally broken in the process.

Resentment and bitterness tend to be evoked by withholding acknowledgment. The likelihood of an in-kind response (concurrent withholding of acknowledgment by the opposite party) is thus increased. Mutual accusation, apathy, mistrust, and stagnation characterize such situations. Additionally, in such circumstances, the Battle for Initiative in therapy may be based on a crisis of outcomes rather than a crisis of values. For example, both partners in a committed relationship may share a value about career stability but may differ in their opinions about whose career may be more important.

Acknowledgment is paired with claim on a valuing continuum for seeking a balance of fairness. Claim refers to "one person's asking for something from the other" (Karpel & Strauss, 1983, p. 35). Examples of claims include the following:

- A woman postpones completing her graduate degree program so she can work to provide income for the family while her husband pursues his professional education. She now requests that the husband assume a greater child-rearing and bread-winning burden so she can complete her own professional educational objectives.

- A single parent, who has provided well for her two teenage children in the past, is temporarily unemployed. She asks that they contribute a portion of their earnings from part-time jobs to support the running of the household during this time of financial crisis.

Claims are not inherently valid. Persons frequently do make unwarranted claims in relationships. Therefore, the willingness of one party to capitulate to unilateral, excessive claims can be as harmful to a relationship as an unwillingness to consider *any* claims (Karpel & Strauss, 1983). Thus, the negotiation of the values held in relationships is successful when a balance can be achieved. Still, therapists must be cognizant of cultural groups and worldviews that do not value balance to avoid the imposition of their own personal perspective and values.

Balance of Fairness

In an ideal sense, beneficial valuing within, between, or among persons is that outcome wherein entitlement/obligation and acknowledgment/claim stand in relative *balance* with each other. There is a balance of fairness. Of course, no perfect, static balance can exist. Any balance of fairness achieved through valuing efforts can and will be altered by a variety of factors. One person may momentarily refuse to acknowledge the contributions of others. His or her entitlement to an acknowledgment may have been inadvertently ignored. Involved parties may have to redefine what they consider a balance of fairness if circumstances drastically alter the entitlement of one or more of them, for example, if one family member becomes seriously injured in an auto accident.

Pursuing a balance of fairness through valuing involves ongoing efforts to consider mutual obligations and entitlements and to make realistic acknowledgments and claims. There is no perfect continuing parity. Seeking a balance of fairness thus requires commitment by all involved to try to correct imbalances. Boszormenyi-Nagy and Ulrich (1981) referred to this as *rejunction*—persons connecting with each other for the purpose of rebalancing fairness in their relationships. This may take the form of willingness to sit in a room together to reassess certain of their values, to surface claims, and to hear one another's sides. This may also call for an acknowledgment of the sacrifice or merit of others, admitting to an obligation (and therefore acknowledging the legitimacy of others' claims) or taking the factors that may limit others' ability to acknowledge certain claims more seriously (e.g., a strong obligation to another relationship, such as a newly married child's significant obligations to his or her new spouse). In these and many other circumstances, the process of attempting balance *must itself* be valued by those participating in the balancing effort. The therapist may introduce a structure for examining these factors, but the initiative to pursue such an outcome can only be fueled by the determination of the participants.

In seeking a balance of fairness through valuing, the question often arises, "Who is to say what is fair and what is unfair?" The answer is rarely simple. Karpel and Strauss (1983) suggested several guidelines to make this determination more manageable. They first asserted the importance of accepting that final word on what constitutes fairness and unfairness in a particular relationship comes from those who are directly involved in the relationship. There are no objective, external criteria to compare against. The only factor that might be introduced is an asserted effort to reassess the balance of fairness. This is not a fixed code with universal application; rather, it is an interchange during which involved members can seek movement forward in the context of the specifics of their relationship. This process is facilitated by asking questions that encourage the consideration of obligations and entitlements and statements of acknowledgment and claim.

The process of give-and-take that this common examination requires—asserting and considering claims, seeking to see another's side, and presenting one's own side—marks the beginning and the most important part of valuing aimed at achieving a balance of fairness. Frequently, this balance is gained in ways quite different from what might have been expected. This is natural because only the participants can truly gauge the meaning of events and considerations for themselves, and even these assessments may significantly change as new factors are introduced into ongoing interactions (Karpel & Strauss, 1983).

A second guideline identified by Karpel and Strauss (1983) for arriving at a balance of fairness involves what they termed *realistic accountability*. This concept suggests that the greatest benefits for all members in a relationship are derived from mutual efforts to carry out reasonable obligations without either shortchanging others or paying excessively or destructively. Realistic accountability encourages persons neither to ignore their entitlement nor to tolerate unreasonable obligations, but rather to look for ways to balance entitlement and obligation. In this sense, realistic accountability proposes that people face obligations in relationships but also puts some ceiling on how much they will ask of themselves and how much they will tolerate being asked by others. The height of the ceiling will be determined by involved members' consideration of obligations and entitlements in the context of their present situation.

Realistic accountability applies equally to all members in a relationship. Thus, a ceiling also exists on the extent to which others can be held accountable. An elderly parent may, for example, desire perfect or total accountability from his or her adult children but should also consider the limitations, lack of resources, and other problems the children face. Put simply, one needs to recognize the importance of judging others' beliefs and actions by the same standard of accountability by which one judges one's own.

So one might ask "Why bother to address the process components of valuing?" A variety of answers can be considered. Emphasizing values at the beginning and throughout the process of therapy is often remedial (Satir, 1972). Stressing the significance of the valuing process also humanizes therapy and the therapist. Highlighting the impact of perspectives and values that promote imbalance and oppression infuses an atmosphere of equity and choice for hopeful change. As we will see in Chapter 12, such hopefulness is essential in overcoming ambivalence in therapy. And, for difficult decisions stemming from ethical dilemmas, legal mandates, or professional obligations, building a relationship that has promoted mutual respect for values, particularly differing values based on cultural distinctions, may assist clients in acknowledging the good-faith efforts of therapists being true to their primary obligation of welfare for clients in the course of addressing those difficulties. This latter benefit is particularly important for the following chapters in our text.

SUMMARY

Valuing has significant implications for the professional therapeutic practice of marriage and family therapy. Valuing is a means by which marriage and family therapists can maintain a systemic worldview while incorporating challenges to it within an evolving epistemology. This chapter discussed practice implications of valuing as well as specific valuing components.

The initial sections of this chapter featured an examination of gender, racial, ethnic, social class, sexual orientation, disability status, and worldview as elements of psychosocial identity. Clearly, the perspectives and values emerging from these factors are complex and unique. Valuing represents a process similar to that suggested by students of ethnicity: Respect for ethnicity involves initial acceptance of cultural differences, polite exploration of those differences, and subtle explanations of how a given ethnic group's customs differ from the larger culture. The marriage and family therapist assumes the role of "culture broker," helping couples and families negotiate the traditional values they wish to retain and discard (McGoldrick, Giordano, Pearce, & Giordano, 1996). Similarly, with respect to gender issues, Pittman (1985) advocated that marriage and family therapists assume a parallel role as "gender brokers":

> As a gender broker, I show initial respect for each person's efforts in playing out the gender role they have been taught, as well as sympathy for the difficulties and limitations they encounter in doing so. I try to make these people aware that they have choices about how and whether they will play out their gender stereotypes, and I am determined that they will get an equal voice in that choice. While I am personally uncomfortable with some of the arrangements my patients choose, I try to make sure that gender issues will never again go unquestioned in their relationship. And, I try to help them realize that whether someone is male or female does not mean that they must be Masculine or Feminine. (p. 31)

The essence of marriage and family therapy as a professional therapeutic practice from this perspective is to participate with persons in relationships so that their interactions within themselves and with each other can move in directions they prefer. The focus of marriage and family therapists is to find out what their clients are trying to conserve and participate in their attempts to conserve it while seeking to maintain that balance of fairness necessary for more satisfying experiences.

Efran and Lukens (1985) proposed that marriage and family therapists do not give "treatment"—something applied like a mudpack—to a waiting, passive organism. They referred to Kelly (1955), who warned against the term *patient*, implying someone who sits patiently, waiting for something to happen or something to be done to him or her. Efran and Lukens stated:

> Families do not start changing at the therapist's office. They are always changing, and the visit to the therapist's office is simply the next step in their process. . . . It is arrogant of us to think that we "control" other people's lives. Even court-adjudicated cases and other so-called "unwilling" clients cannot be sold anything against their will. Because people's structures keep changing as we spend time interacting with them, it seems to us as though they bought something from us that was incompatible with their beliefs. What was bought may have originally been incompatible, but at the point of sale, by definition, there could not have been an incongruity. Neither salespeople nor therapists ever sell their customers anything they do not want. To buy is to want. (1985, p. 72)

From this vantage, the keen observations of Napier and Whitaker (1978) related to the Battle for Structure and the Battle for Initiative are significant for marriage and family therapists. In attempting to balance these elements of therapy, culturally responsive practitioners are also admonished to attend to the possible effects of unexamined values. Of particular importance in this respect are the challenges and barriers to effective therapy noted by Baruth and Manning (2003): (a) erroneous assumptions about cultural differences, (b) stereotyping, (c) unintentional racism and sexism, (d) failure to consider lifespan differences as an element of the therapy relationship, and (e) failing to consider the impact of chronic oppression or institutionalized privilege.

We offer the discussion in this chapter as a preface for considering the systemic and multilayered framework of personal, professional, and institutional perspectives and values that affect marriage and family therapists in their care for clients.

CHAPTER 2

Marriage and Family Therapy: A Framework of Systems and Layers

In Chapter 1, we introduced many of the elements that unite to form one's perspective and values. As we have seen, the process of identity development results from a convergence of factors such as gender, race, culture, ethnicity, social class, sexual orientation, and worldview (Pedersen, 1994). From this process, each person develops values and preferences concerning lifestyle, aspiration, morality, social justice, communicational style, career/leisure, spirituality, traditions, problem solving, and myriad other areas for interacting with those persons and agencies holding similar or differing values (Constantine, Heather, & Laing, 2001; Sue & Sue, 1999).

Christopher (1996) has noted that our values and perspective affect how we think, make decisions, and define events, thus serving as reference points for individual choices. In this respect, accepted personal values, some sacred and some simply habitual, become the test for embracing, rejecting, or negotiating with the values held by others. If our discussion of acculturation, identity, values clarification, and values negotiation had ended with the information presented in Chapter 1, we would have offered only a brief hint of the interactive nature of helping relationships. Chapter 1 focused on the value-laden interactions *between* therapist and clients in the therapeutic relationship. This discussion was provided to emphasize that a culturally responsive marriage and family therapist must be knowledgeable and sensitive to individual differences. In this chapter, we will advance our discussion to consider the more complex nature of this relationship, with particular attention devoted to the sometimes competing considerations affecting marriage and family therapists in decision making related to ethical, legal, and professional issues.

A hallmark distinction between marriage and family therapy and many other forms of mental health services has been the appreciation for *context*. This heritage stems from a simple premise: Therapy does not occur in a vacuum. Regardless of the skill of the practitioner or the initiative of the individual client, the process of change has some form of context for its success or failure. Historically, this context has been grounded in the view of family-as-a-system. In fact, marriage and family therapy occurs within a context of multiple systems (Feldman, 1990; Henggeler & Borduin, 1990; Imber-Black, 1988). Some systems are familial; some systems are social; some systems are legal, regulatory, or organizational; and some systems are not easily categorized. A *systemic perspective* was employed in the early years of describing the context of marriage and family therapy (Nichols & Schwartz, 2004). For some, this perspective represented a framework critical for assessment and intervention, whereas for others, it represented a metaphorical language for describing the complicated nature of family relationships, healthy as well as pathological. Whether as an intervention framework or as a descriptive metaphor, the systemic viewpoint features many of the characteristics discussed in Chapter 1: organization, pattern, heritage, values, and perspective. Similarly, as a reference point for interacting with others, the systemic perspective represents one of many worldviews; consequently, it is a portrayal of values, which may be embraced by some, dismissed by others, and negotiated by many. Therefore, in considering the complex nature of relationships and interactions faced by marriage and family therapists, a systemic epistemology offers at least a useful conceptual structure for discussion.

SYSTEMIC EPISTEMOLOGY

As we discussed in Chapter 1, epistemology is a branch of philosophy that emphasizes the origin, nature, methods, and limits of human knowledge. Anthropologist Gregory Bateson (1979) first addressed epistemology as a professional issue within marriage and family therapy, and others have built on his work. Bateson saw epistemology as rules for making sense out of the world.

Marriage and family therapy as a professional practice initially grew from an intuitive or experiential awareness that families of patients were somehow implicated in the problems being experienced by patients. Patients increasingly came to be viewed by early "family therapists" as family scapegoats rather than as singularly sick individuals. Initially, there was a tendency to flip-flop blame from child to parents or from one marital partner to another. Soon, however, systems theory was discovered as a way to articulate family involvement without simply shifting blame from one individual to others. Eventually, blame, and with it responsibility, was shifted away from the individual altogether and onto the "system" (Cottone & Greenwell, 1992).

The traditional psychotherapeutic perspective has been founded on one's worldview, which was examined in Chapter 1. As we have already discussed, this construct focuses on the individual and on traits or conditions of an individual. As Cottone (1988) stated:

> Traditionally in counseling, individuals are treated primarily as independent entities, having identities all their own and problems bounded to a large degree by their individual identities. Individuals are viewed as having intelligence, skills, abilities, personality traits, interests, self-concepts, mental disturbances, adjustment disorders, etceteras. Counseling goals, likewise, are viewed as primarily "self" oriented. (p. 359)

Regarding this "psychological worldview," Cottone (1991) summarized four general propositions:

1. The focus of study is the individual.
2. Individuals are assumed to possess characteristics and traits, both learned and unlearned, that endure and represent predispositions to act (e.g., interests,

attitudes, self-concepts, disorders). These traits and characteristics can be isolated and influenced in a therapeutic context.

3. Causes can be clearly defined, and symptoms (e.g., inappropriate behavior) and conditions (e.g., disturbance) can be treated directly through a therapeutic relationship.
4. One person can affect change in a second person only to the degree that the first person influences the traits and characteristics or the psychological conditions (internal or external) of the second person.

The *psychological worldview* thus focuses on the individual client. The individual client is viewed as able to be assessed and treated. Interventions attend primarily to the client rather than to social or cultural factors that might be affecting the client.

In the early development of the professional therapeutic practice of marriage and family therapy, more extreme and clear-cut interpretations of systems theory prevailed. The early *systemic worldview* was based primarily on a relational–ecological perspective. Becvar, Becvar, and Bender (1982) expounded on this worldview by stating:

> Previously we studied and treated the person in isolation. Our inquiry consistent with the theoretical models then in use was concerned with the nature of the individual's pathological condition and, in a wider sense, with the nature of the human mind. Consistent with our new models derived from ecology, ethology, cybernetics, systems theory, and structuralism, our inquiry is now extended to include the effects of an individual's behavior on others, their reactions to it, and the context in which all of this takes place. Our focus has shifted from the isolated monad to the relationship among the components or members of a system. We have turned from an inferential study of the mind to a concern with the observable manifestations of relationships. (p. 386)

Cottone (1991) summarized four basic propositions of the "systemic worldview":

1. Relationships represent the focus of study.
2. Relationships can be isolated for study and defined, but only with the understanding that this isolation and definition are relative to the observer and his or her system (relationships) of reference.
3. Causation is circular (nonlinear) within the confines of specified relationships of significance.
4. Therapeutic change occurs through social relationship.

Two additional systemic propositions tended to underlie early family therapists' systemic worldview, particularly in explaining and validating their position in contrast to the traditional psychological worldview dominant at the time. These were: (a) the whole is greater than the sum of its parts, and (b) linear thinking is an epistemological mistake. The first proposition, known as *holism*, asserts that the parts are not as important as the larger system of significance. "Why bother with the individual when it is the family or the system that has overriding influence?" (Cottone & Greenwell, 1992, p. 168). The second proposition, known as *antilinearity*, considers any attempt to identify specific sequences of causation in a linear fashion (A leads to B leads to C) as wasted effort (Fish, 1990).

Early family therapists took great pains to stress this emphasis on the larger context. Hoffman (1981) interpreted this stance by stating:

> To "chop up the ecology" is what one does when one takes the parts and pieces of what one is describing and decides that one part "controls" another or one part "causes" another. (pp. 342–343)

A psychological worldview of linearity is portrayed as resembling, for example, a pair of binoculars that a spectator at a sporting event uses to observe only one player on the field. The spectator can see the player's movements and expressions in fine detail. Yet the drawback of using binoculars eventually becomes clear: The interaction between one player and the others on the field is screened out. The spectator fails to take in the overall action among all participants, particularly important when the primary action of play occurs away from the single player. This oversight was highlighted by those advocating a systemic worldview that calls for widening the spectator's field of vision, so to speak, in an effort to consider the total context.

The systemic worldview was primarily portrayed through the concept of *circularity.* Mental illness had traditionally been perceived in linear terms, with historical, causal explanations given for the distress. Etiology was conceived primarily in terms of prior events—disease, emotional conflict, or learning history—that caused symptoms in the client. Using circularity as a core concept, the systemic worldview represented mental illness not as something that is caused but, rather, something that is part of an ongoing, circular fit. Dell (1982) described this as follows:

> Without reference to etiology or causation, fit simply posits that the behaviors occurring in the family system have a general complementarity, they fit together. Causation, on the other hand, is a specified type of interpretation of fit that considers the observed complementarity to have the form A causes B; for instance, bad parents make their children sick. (p. 25)

Of those who originally addressed the professional impact of this epistemology that included a circular understanding of behavior, Bateson (1979) made a distinction between the world of physical objects and the world of living forms in contrasting linearity and circularity. Linearity applied to the physical world assumes that the world is like a billiard table in which the balls go in one direction when hit. Bateson believed that the world of living things is poorly represented by such a model because it neglects to account for communication and relationships; simple force alone is not enough.

Hoffman (1981) further contrasted linearity and circularity in describing what may occur as a result of kicking a stone compared kicking a dog. In the case of a stone, the energy transmitted by the kick will move the stone a certain distance, depending on the force of the kick and the weight of the stone. But in kicking a dog, the outcome is not so simply predicted. What happens depends on the relationship between the person and the dog. The dog may respond in any number of ways. It may cringe, run away, or bite the person, depending on how the relationship is defined and how the dog interprets the kick. Moreover, the behavior of the dog will send back information that may modify the person's subsequent behavior. If the dog bites, the person will give greater thought before he or she kicks the dog again.

It must be remembered that these basic propositions represent early systemic epistemology. They represented the core components of marriage and family therapy as a unique professional therapeutic practice. By the end of the 1970s, marriage and family therapy had, however, moved from being a radical new approach to becoming an established force within mainstream mental health practice. The 1980s and 1990s ushered in a new stage in which marriage and family therapy's blind spots and biases have been and are being challenged. These challenges have come in a number of forms. Two of the most pointed are the feminist critique of family therapy and the self in the system (Nichols & Schwartz, 2004).

The Feminist Critique of Systemic Epistemology

The feminist critique of systemic epistemology has been characterized as representing a rude awakening (Nichols & Schwartz, 2004). The critique began in the late 1970s when Betty Carter, Peggy Papp, Olga Silverstein, and Marianne Walters formed a coalition called the Women's Project in Family Therapy to "openly and publicly challenge the field's patriarchy and conventional wisdom" (Simon, 1997, p. 60). These feminists and others have called on family therapists to "recognize gender as a central organizing feature of family life and to challenge traditional ways of working which ignore, and therefore reinforce, gender-based power imbalances" (Leslie & Clossick, 1996, p. 253). Such a position is "political" in that it "refers to those processes maintaining or changing power relations within any social or interpersonal system" (Knudson-Martin, 1997, p. 421). Such a position is also ethical in that approaches to gender within marriage and family therapy raise issues that are ethical in nature, such as *beneficence*, *justice*, and *autonomy*, which will be addressed more fully in Chapter 3.

The feminist critique can be summarized by two basic positions. The increasing awareness, if not increasing number, of reported incidents of family violence has led to the first point. Systemic epistemology has been criticized because it often employs circular causality to present violence as serving a functional role in the maintenance of the family system. Bograd (1984) stated:

> Feminist values are clear regarding the allocation of responsibility for wife battering incidents: 1) no woman deserves to be beaten; 2) men are solely responsible for their actions. Careful analysis of prevailing explanatory frameworks of wife battering reveals that there is little logical and empirical support for the prevalent assumption that women provoke men into abusing them. . . . From a feminist perspective, a systemic formulation is biased if it can be employed to implicate the battered woman or to excuse the abusive man. (p. 561)

Those ascribing to this view posit that in either of these circumstances, the systemic principle concerning the stabilizing effect of symptoms would suggest that women prefer battering and men are simply obliging that preference (Knudson-Martin, 2001). In fact, Bograd (1999) argued that the social elements of intimate partner violence are far more complex than a systemic model. Toward this end, Papp noted, "The goal of feminism is not to make villains of men, but to change the social structure that divides men and women and keeps them apart" (Whetstone, 2002, p. 12).

Proponents of this critique also criticize circular causality as it relates to social and cultural context. In particular, patriarchal society is seen as limiting the choices women can make related to possible life roles, and therefore it limits their ability to be causal agents. As Walters, Carter, Papp, and Silverstein (1988) asserted:

> Systems therapy discriminates against women by seeking balance and equilibrium for the family system as a unit, without addressing the unequal access of each individual to choice or role. The pretense that men and women are genderless cogs in the system prevents us from noticing that women are held more responsible than men for making it work, in the family and in family therapy, and that the "complementary" roles, tasks, and rewards of the stable system are allocated by gender, unequally, to its male and female members. (p. 23)

In this regard, the feminist critique is a commentary on the development of a profession that embraces a precept of equality in a social and cultural heritage of inequality, often to the point of oppression. Within specific family units, entrenched cultural traditions promote inequity with expectations of privilege for men. These two points have represented a credible attack on systemic epistemology. In essence, accommodating to this critique calls for a return to linearity (Cottone & Greenwell, 1992). It accentuates the fact that "local" or specific intuitions ought not be swept aside by broader philosophies (Cambien, 1989). One local intuition of concern here is that intimate partner abuse is wrong, that therapists should take action to stop it, and that the abuser is responsible for eliminating the abusive behavior apart from whatever non-physical incitement to abuse may have occurred (Cottone & Greenwell, 1992; Stith, Rosen, McCollum, & Thomsen, 2004). Likewise, a second intuition cautions marriage and family therapists to be more than simply sensitive to gender issues in working with families. Instead, they should assert that issues of gender, or more specifically, patriarchy, permeate therapeutic practice and go on to organize concrete interventions around that understanding (May, 1998). In this respect, the cultural values that define normalcy within the family system may be challenged by the therapist to the extent of resistance and even departure from the relationship. Thus, a sensitive and effective marriage and family therapist must be "feminist-informed" about social application of the systemic view that can oppress and blame (Knudson-Martin, 2002).

Only when we look through this lens of gender can we effectively stop blaming mothers, or stop looking to them to do most of the changing simply because they are the most invested in change or the most cooperative. Only then will we be able to fully counter our unconscious biases toward seeing women as primarily responsible for child rearing and housekeeping, as needing to support their husbands' careers by neglecting their own, as requiring marriage, or at least having a man in their lives. Only then can we stop relying on traditionally male traits like rationality, independence, and competitiveness as our standards of health and stop denigrating or ignoring traits traditionally encouraged in women like emotionality, nurturance, and relationship focus (Giblin & Chan, 1995).

If these two intuitions are lost in, or negated by, systemic epistemology, then feminist intuition argues against the validity of this epistemology (Cottone & Greenwell, 1992). Knudson-Martin (2002) commented, "Persons who criticize the active nature of feminist informed practice may have difficulty fitting feminism's unabashed advocacy of gender equality with the therapeutic role" (p. 31). As Taggart (1989) observed, "By continuing to produce 'family therapy' as if the feminist critique did not exist, family therapy theorists intensify the patriarchal project of presenting as comprehensive and normative that which is partial and atypical" (p. 101). Thus, the philosophical and applied worth of the systemic perspective in professional development of marriage and family therapists can actually promote devaluing women in attempts to enact therapeutic change for those practitioners who are not feminist-informed in their practice.

The Self in the System

A second major challenge to systemic epistemology has been its perceived overemphasis on the family-as-a-system, thereby overlooking the importance of the intrapsychic functioning of the individual. Nichols and Schwartz (2004) described several events that relate to this challenge:

1. Family therapy as a field had grown strong and confident enough to admit it may not have all the answers; intrapsychic considerations may thus be important.

2. The constructivist movement (i.e., therapy occurs when therapists and clients together "co-create" new meanings of experience; Gladding, 2002; Held, 1990) refocused the family therapy field from a primary emphasis on behavioral sequences, in which insight or awareness is discounted, to an emphasis on the meanings that individual family members maintain about each other and their problems.

3. Increasing numbers of psychodynamically trained clinicians have immigrated into the family therapy field as it has established itself in mainstream mental health practice. This has led to an increasing desire for models that bridge the gap between self and system.

4. Popular offshoots of psychoanalysis, notably self-psychology and object relations theory, have evolved in a manner that suggests their compatibility with family therapy.

To use the latter event as a focus of illustration here, object relations theory in essence purports that persons relate to each other in the present partly on the basis of expectations formed by early experience. The past is alive—in memory—and significantly affects a person's present existence. Mental images, called internal objects, are formed during early childhood interactions with significant others. As adults, individuals' reactions to others depend to a large degree on how much those persons resemble one's internal objects rather than on the actual characteristics of the persons in the present.

Applied to family therapy, object relations theorists posit that dysfunctional patterns of behavior among family members are maintained by the internal object relations of family members. Through a process of projective identification, the images of certain internal objects are projected onto other family members. Therapy involves interpreting these projections to the family so that family members can be more aware of the unseen forces behind their patterns and be better able to change them.

Nichols and Schwartz (2004) noted that some family therapists have advocated giving up systems theory and replacing it with object relations as the foundation for family therapy. Others seek to use both, keeping them separate and using them sequentially or to complement each other. Still others look to integrate the psychodynamic concepts and systems theory. For example, the efforts of Bowen (1978) promote an initial point of understanding systemic interrelations through the significance of differentiation of self and detriangulation from unhealthy systemic patterns. Similarly, other models (e.g., social constructionism) emphasize the importance of individual reality to validate each member of the system as a prelude to change. Even in experiences and expressions of spirituality, marriage and family therapy cannot account for all aspects of change and growth through a systemic perspective (Kahle & Robbins, 2003). In these and other cases, the professional perspective and values of the marriage and family therapist seeking to integrate a practice model of self-in-the-system with family-as-a-system require diligent and complex conceptualization efforts.

Evolving Epistemology

The circular emphasis within systemic epistemology reflects a viewpoint that individuals are not unrelated atoms motivated only by internal urges and instincts; rather, they are parts of larger systems that exert considerable influence on their thoughts, feelings, and actions. Nonetheless, couples and families are composed of individuals, an understanding that tended to be minimized or ignored by early systemic writers in their zealousness to assert their perspective. It is little wonder that challenges to this worldview such as those just discussed eventually appeared and were followed by comments like G. D. Erickson's (1988):

> None of the major human problems of our era can be adequately addressed by, or treated within, a systemic paradigm. . . . [T]he neglect of social context and persons qua persons is inherent in the theory and noncorrectable. (p. 226)

Inherent in any discussion of epistemology, however, is also the issue of evolution. The belief that patterns of connectedness are dynamically unfolding rather than structurally based is at the heart of the matter (Taggart, 1982). Structural, fixed worldviews propose an ultimate, objective knowledge. Evolutionary worldviews emphasize that knowledge can never be entirely stabilized. Brown (1977) proposed that the only permanent aspect of science is the process of research, and it is only the current consensual agreement of the scientific community that determines the research findings that have validity, not the findings themselves. Thus, one discovery sets the stage for another, like the ever-widening ripples occasioned by the proverbial pebble thrown into the pond.

M. P. Nichols's (1987a) admonition relative to the need for openness to continuing discovery aptly summarizes the need for an evolving epistemology by marriage and family therapists:

> Over the past 30 years we have learned that there is a vast range of difficulties which respond quickly to family therapy interventions. At the same time, all family therapists know that many problems don't yield to our most ingenious methods. Clearly family treatment is not a cure-all for all the problems people bring to us. As we continue to examine our practices and note where what we do doesn't work, we need to deepen our ability to listen to our clients and explore the forces that keep them stuck. . . . Unless we do, we may find that, rather than continuing to expand, the boundaries of our understanding will begin to constrict. (p. 85)

The evolution of systemic epistemology, just as with any attempt to conceptualize the complexity of human behavior, will be affected dynamically by infusing scientific discovery with social sensitivity to promote revision. In this process, only one certainty exists: There are always exceptions. A model that can fully address all aspects of a phenomenon is not a model; it is a law, such as the various laws of physics. Epistemology is philosophical in origin, perhaps even more metaphorical than scientific at times. Systemic epistemology should never be viewed as nor sought to become recognized as law.

At this point, we must reemphasize the importance of valuing as a component of the therapeutic relationship as it was presented in Chapter 1 of our text. The process of valuing suggests that when therapist and client come together, they can negotiate a new, common system containing elements of both perspectives as well as unique properties arising from their interaction. Similarly, when traditional systemic epistemology is challenged, it need not be discarded; instead, a new context should be negotiated that contains those challenges. As M. P. Nichols (1987a) stated:

> We do not have to choose between a theory of persons and a theory of persons in relationship. We may need both the wide-angle lens of interactional view and the ability to use the magnifying glass of individual psychology when necessary. (p. 85)

As we also discussed in Chapter 1, the process of respecting divergent values and negotiating those values has practice implications for marriage and family therapy. This process is no less significant for a systemic epistemology and the challenges that confront it than it is for the interactions between family members or between therapists and clients. Additionally, systemic epistemology reminds us that other systemic bodies or agencies external to the therapy relationship organize around values concerning significant issues such as power to control access to services, definitions, causes, and remedies related to abnormal behavior, and responsibility for the change process in therapy. These will be examined in the next section of this chapter.

Personal reference points for valuing are significant in this process. However, unlike family members or even an individual client, therapists are affected by more than their personal reference points of acculturation, identity, perspective, and values. The multiple systems affecting the practice of marriage and family therapy actually create a type of ecology representing three layers of contextual reference for therapists: (a) personal, (b) professional, and (c) institutional.

For purposes of this text, we will refer to the convergence of acculturation, identity, and perspective across these contextual layers using the term *values*. We have selected this term to distinguish the result of a variety of processes affecting a therapist's development, such as mentoring, education, acculturation, supervision, and regulation. These processes are both internal and external in nature, but they result in the values that direct decision making as it relates to ethical, legal, and professional issues. The following discussion features an examination of the separate and interactional aspects of *personal values*, *professional values*, and *institutional values* affecting marriage and family therapists.

CONTEXTUAL LAYERS OF VALUES

Personal Values

Much of the process involved in the development of *personal values* has been examined previously in Chapter 1. From this earlier discussion, we know that each of us has a sense of self that is strongly influenced by acculturation in our rearing and development. We develop our identity to answer the question "Who am I?" by emphasizing or deemphasizing characteristics and qualities we have come to embrace as significant or reject as unimportant. For example, many people in Westernized cultures place great value on attributes such as efficiency, problem solving, competitiveness, and self-reliance. By contrast, those acculturated to embrace deliberation, emergent solutions, noncompetitiveness, and collaboration may view such traditional Westernized values as pushy and even oppressive (Ivey, D'Andrea, Ivey, & Simek-Morgan, 2002). Similar aspects of our personal development and identity formation lead to perspectives about those who share our frame of reference and those who differ from it. From these experiences, we develop a frame of reference for our personal values as a means of self-assessment and accountability.

As we also discussed in Chapter 1, assimilation and accommodation of perspectives and values for each individual is a developmental process across one's lifespan. For some, personal values that emerge in early life are sustained with limited challenge and with limited revision. For others, encountering those with differing personal frames of reference requires considerable personal exploration to amend our perspective and our values (Carter & McGoldrick, 2005). Costello (2004) has noted that *cultural awareness* challenges one's insular personal perspective, often creating dissonance that can only be resolved by introducing greater cognitive complexity for understanding and interacting with other persons and systems. Throughout our text, you will note that we maintain that such sensitivity and awareness is essential for a culturally responsive marriage and family therapist.

The development of personal values for marriage and family therapists is no different than for any other person. Our value perspectives reflect our notions about right–wrong or good–bad distinctions. Gender-referenced expectations, problem-solving and conflict-resolution approaches, parenting styles, expressions of intimacy and sexuality, appreciation for racial and ethnic differences, views on money and socioeconomic status, the necessity for non/conformity, use of alcohol or drugs, work ethic, displays of violence, and even views on time and efficiency are all significant aspects of the personal values one develops *before* becoming a marriage and family therapist. From a rather exhaustive review of literature, Richards, Rector, and Tjeltveit (1999) concluded that therapists cannot refrain from introducing their personal values and perspectives into the therapy relationship. Personal values for marriage and family therapists are therefore significant foundational elements for their relationships with clients, peers, and institutions. However, because of the professional role one assumes as therapist, personal values cannot be the only source for direction in the therapeutic relationship. To do so could possibly relegate therapy to a status of simple indoctrination and exploitation in which a therapist imposes values on clients. Or, as Holmes (1996) stated, "when psychotherapy becomes certain of itself or its values, it ceases to be psychotherapy and becomes something akin to proselytizing religion" (p. 272). In the same way that Costello (2004) described the importance of cultural awareness in the development of a more cognitively complex perspective, the contextual layers of values do not allow the marriage and family therapist to simply rely on personal values as the basis for interaction with clients. To balance such possibilities, marriage and family therapists encounter a second layer of development related to *professional values*.

Professional Values

As we saw in Chapter 1, marriage and family therapy is not value-free. Such an expectation would require a capitulation to the values of the client/system or simple mechanistic approaches to the special yet risky relationship of therapy. Values are a core component of any professional therapeutic endeavor. Edwards and Bess (1998) advocated *therapeutic neutrality* as a position of retaining one's personhood without exploiting clients. Developing a perspective of values within a therapy relationship derives from a process of acculturation, education, and regulation that goes beyond the development of individual values. Sue et al. (1998) suggested this developmental process occurs not only at personal levels and professional levels but also at an institutional level that affect mental health systems of service.

Because marriage and family therapists must address distinctions between personal and professional elements of their lives, it would seem that the origin of such decisions requires a balance between personal values and *professional values*. In many ways, marriage and family therapists engage in an internal dialogue featuring the dual and sometime conflicting questions "Who am I?" and "What do I do?" The development of professional values for marriage and family therapists reflects knowledge and experiences acquired through relationships with other professionals related to ethical propriety, accepted practices, legal constraints, and even therapeutic tradition (Nelson & Jackson, 2003). Academic programs, clinical supervision, mentoring, and various other means of orientation and training converge to promote a form of professional socialization for marriage and family therapists. Just as with personal socialization in a cultural group, professional socialization is strongly influenced in mentoring relationships (Beresin, 2004). Covan (2000) has even suggested the nature of the mentor–protégé relationship compels professional veterans into "social reproduction" (p. 11) in the next generation of practitioners. Additionally, in their continued development, marriage and family therapists are faced with professional and social issues that require renewed examination of their personal values and professional values as the socialization process continues.

Think for a moment about the elements that establish and sustain the professional values of marriage and family therapists. We are exposed to codes of behavior. We are taught the value of scientific methodology and rigor. We are exposed to models of healthy-family functioning as well as pathological family patterns. We explore changes based on notions of equality and power and the capacity to gauge complex circumstances. We learn what it means to "be a professional" through a process of gatekeeping and guidance, not unlike any other profession. We develop professional identity based on shared values especially toward clients, professional peers, and even self-policing in much the same way personal values emerge at the layer of our personal development (Stern, 2000). Such a statement coincides with Phinney's (2000) observation that a component of successful acculturation is represented in "group identity formation" (p. 29) with those of a particular group.

The foundational elements of professional values are established through completion of specialized education, adherence to an established code of ethics, development of competence in supervised practice, learning and following legal precedents affecting practice, and good-faith efforts toward client care and welfare. By contrast, when people make assumptions about their ability to be a practitioner because they are innately skilled as listeners and problem solvers, they believe they can rely primarily on intuition and personal values and skip the developmental processes leading to professional values. In such cases, we are reminded of the adage "Be less worried about one who is troubled by difficult questions than one who is unaware that the questions even exist."

A compelling need for balance emerges when one considers the overlapping issues of "Who I am" and "What I do." For marriage and family therapists, the interplay between personal values and professional values suggests such considerations are inseparable but not equivalent. For example, consider the impact of one's personal values and perspective about the meaning of work and career. This personal point of reference affects one's professional socialization and values in the role of a marriage and family therapist. Valuing work as an activity and a means to an end differs greatly from valuing work as an aspect of professionalism and identity. Similarly, personal values about the significance of formal education and learning differ greatly for individuals. For some, completing the educational requirements at any level is a matter of "jumping through hoops" established by external agencies in order to qualify for employment. For others, educational experiences are valued as initial steps in an evolving career. The professional identity of marriage and family therapists often hinges on perceiving the completion of an academic degree as one element or as *the* element of professionalism. For many, demonstrating professional values is represented in continuing education, professional affiliation and service, securing formal credentials, and even political efforts on behalf of the field. We posit that professional values based on the completion of an academic program may not promote valuing the group identity formation Phinney (2000) discussed. Other elements of professional identity and values are noted in Chapters 11 and 12, which provide information related to accreditation, professional affiliation, licensure/certification, and other issues of professional practice.

As we examine professional issues that affect marriage and family therapy, some readers may be more inclined to consider the narrow elements of *task* and *activity*, whereas others may consider the larger elements of *identity* and *perspective*. Neither is an improper vantage and both typically coexist for most practitioners. However, our personal values set the stage for our view of professionalism, but our professional values often inform our personal values. Once again, the balance of "Who I am" and "What I do" becomes significant in our professional socialization. Addressing this point with straightforwardness and candor, Whitaker and Keith (1981) noted, "We do not simply do marriage and family therapy; we are marriage and family therapists" (p. 202).

Regardless of one's theoretical and applied orientation, marriage and family therapists have a heritage of considering aspects of systemic epistemology. Thus, professional values held by therapists typically feature an appreciation for a broad perspective that includes awareness of differences *within* the therapeutic relationship as well as those *beyond* the therapeutic relationship. Such a perspective includes the multilayered ecology of external agencies and bodies affecting therapy. Thus, organizations and agencies within this ecology are significant contextual factors in overall efforts to promote the welfare of clients, since such organizations operate according to values designed to achieve outcomes preferred by those institutions. This means that most marriage and family therapists encounter, learn about, and expect to be influenced by "extra-therapeutic" agencies promoting *institutional values*.

Institutional Values

Sue et al. (1998) noted that many mental health professionals serve clients while attending to external constraints and requirements that greatly affect the delivery and support of therapy. These authors maintained that therapists interact frequently with regulatory, administrative, and managerial organizations that often reflect an "ethnocentric monocularism" (p. 14) that promotes conformity and standardization. They further commented that such a perspective institutionalizes policies, practices, programs, and structures that often serve as impediments and barriers to service recipients who are not of European-American cultural origins. In this respect, they wrote:

> Rugged individualism, competition, mastery and control over nature, a unitary and static conception of time, religion based on Christianity, separation of science and religion, and competition are a few of the values and beliefs indicative of this orientation. (p. 19)

A variety of organizational systemic structures affect marriage and family therapists in their relationships with couples and families. Such institutions include: (a) legal systems, (b) managed care systems, (c) practice settings, (d) medical systems, (e) regulatory bodies (e.g., licensure boards), and (f) delivery and management systems (e.g., technology-based systems). These and similar institutions formally and informally pursue initiatives that affect both the personal and professional values of marriage and family therapists. As one encounters and becomes more immersed in learning the procedures, formats, and rules that direct such organizations, one comes to recognize that the objectives of these "extra-therapeutic" agencies and entities actually reflect *institutional values.* In an era of tremendous interactivity between therapists and such outside systems, assuming that one can rely on personal and professional values as the basis for understanding and administering practice decisions may be shortsighted. Further, failing to understand the ways in which values promoted by such organizations may be dissimilar and even contradictory to personal/professional values of the therapist may be myopic or even naïve. To be sure, institutional values have substantial effects on both the marriage and family therapist and the families they serve.

Social psychologists have addressed issues of personal/professional identity and how we interact with larger systems and organizations affecting our work. van Knipper and van Schie (2000) discussed "work-group identification" and "organizational identification" (p. 138) in a manner that connoted professional socialization in the former and institutional socialization in the latter. Further, these authors indicated that the work-group identification appears to be more predictive of values within an organization than organizational identification. From these findings, one might conclude that institutional acculturation may have minimal impact on the professional work of marriage and family therapists when the work-group identity is with other therapists rather than with an external agency or body. However, Bryan, Barnett, Hester, and Relyea (2003) noted that "organization-based self-esteem (OBSE)" (p. 791) was a significant factor in one's allegiance to larger organizations, even to the extent of amending personal and professional values in favor of organizational values. From this finding, it would seem that for some, the powerful influence of institutional values and perspectives cannot be dismissed in the multilayered ecology of marriage and family therapy. Whether one views institutions external to the therapy process as ancillary necessities, adversarial obstacles, or sources for developing identity and demonstrating organizational loyalty, one cannot deny that institutions infuse their values in a powerful way for marriage and family therapists.

For example, the institutional values within managed care agencies may specify types of therapy, who is eligible to receive those services, who is qualified to offer them, what confidential information is required for authorization, and even a time frame in which specific outcomes must be achieved. Similarly, legal institutions may specify participation requirements, disclosure requirements, and even requirements that may place the therapist in a role that conflicts with that of being a therapist (e.g., reporting suspected victimization of a minor). Practice settings may espouse an institutional value that may profoundly affect therapy efforts (e.g., a specified number of closed cases per month, extended waiting periods for certain categories of clients, etc.). Even governmental bodies enact legislative mandates reflective of institutional values that require specific actions by therapists. The enactment of the Health Insurance Portability and Accountability Act (HIPAA) of 1996, for example, has had a substantial effect on the management of electronic storage and dispersal of confidential client information. In making these determinations and enacting such policies, institutional representatives assert institutional values about the nature of mental illness, marital and family problems, and treatment alternatives (Aponte, 1985).

The evolution of these various institutional entities actually reflects development of rules, standards, procedures, and even hierarchical recognition of professional and nonprofessional participants in the systems (e.g., gatekeepers, managers, auditors, support staff, etc.). Seasoned marriage and family therapists will likely recognize the sense of "fighting the system" clients often describe in therapy. For many families, their personal worldview affects expectations for therapy, thus "fighting the system" may even be perceived as another example of oppression (Sue et al., 1998). In much the same way, marriage and family therapists may feel the oppressive nature of some institutions affecting therapy services. Professional socialization of marriage and family therapists even emphasizes the necessity of complying with paperwork requirements, regular reports, agency policies, and similar procedural aspects of institutionalized design as an element of one's professional role.

A more pronounced effect of institutional culture and values emerges when marriage and family therapists find themselves in the role of institutional affiliate or even representative, thereby embracing and espousing the expressed values of the institution. In some instances, cultural or ethnic heritages of clients may reflect great value differences when compared with those of an institution. For example, some families' cultural values allow for aggressive expression in disagreements (e.g., a teenage son confronting a peer student in a classroom). However, in defying expectations of self-control from educational or legal systems, these families may find themselves "fighting the system." Even more disturbing may be their sense of "fighting the therapist" who advocates those institutional values of self-control. This example does not infer that acting on behalf of the safety of others is improper. However, care and attention should be given to such circumstances, since the therapist may be unaware of the value attributed by clients to an institutional course of action that simply reflects standard operating procedure. For many, the imposition of such a standard procedure represents a struggle with personal values. For instance, a family with a common value about the importance of privacy may be overwhelmed and even resistant to sharing information with external agencies (e.g., managed care gatekeepers) in order to qualify for insurance coverage for services. Similarly, the sense of fighting or acquiescing to "the system" is also present for the therapist who values, personally and professionally, a systemic perspective, but who faces the requirement of a diagnostic procedure that reinforces an identified patient as "sick" so that the family can qualify for insurance reimbursement. Standard operating procedure for the institution is crisis for the family; standard paperwork for the agency is personal and professional conflict for the therapist. In a presentation entitled "Brief Therapy: A Multicultural Perspective," Wilcoxon (2004) even examined the institutionalized oppression of some cultural groups through an imposed pace in therapy that stemmed from managed care practices.

Though somewhat less apparent, the utilization of technology in data management, assessment, and even as a therapeutic delivery system reflects inherent institutional values affecting society-at-large and therapists in particular. If readers doubt such a claim, consider how often we encounter difficulties in the service sector when a representative states "I'm sorry, but the computer won't allow me to do what you want to do. You'll have to find another way." As a tool for speed, accuracy, and data management, technology has been a force of unparalleled success in contemporary society. However, the institutional values associated with the use of technology within and between agencies (as well as a means of serving clients) have created specialized terminologies, exacting procedures, intimidating obstacles, and depersonalized environments. Years ago, Ibrahim (1985) prophetically addressed this issue by observing that the therapeutic community had

> . . . been struggling to serve its constituents effectively and ethically in a culturally pluralistic society and trying to resolve and overcome issues involving age, social class, handicaps, race, and sex differences. Now, the profession needs to consider how human rights concerns can be integrated in the profession's advancement toward incorporating advanced technology into its ongoing philosophical and practical assumptions.(p. 135)

Similarly, Baltimore (2000) suggested that a variety of concerns may develop in the use of technology-assisted practice and Internet delivery of services to clients. Many practitioners rely on computer-assisted administration and scoring of standardized tests/surveys. Many also refer clients to various Web sites for therapy resources. Jencius and Sager (2001) observed that the use of "cybercounseling" (p. 295) has introduced significant concerns for practitioners (e.g., client identity, consent, interstate commerce, varying state regulations and statutes, etc.). These and related practice issues will be examined more fully in Chapter 6. However, as a force for expressing institutional values, technology seems to reflect two significant institutional (and Westernized) values in contemporary marriage and family practice: efficiency and access.

One could easily overlook the implicit nature of institutional values affecting marriage and family therapists. However, one need not be in practice very long until one hears or states "That is the only way it can be done in our setting." When considering the impact of an institutional value on the development of a marriage and family therapist, one might ask at what point does complying with standard procedure become "organization-based self-esteem" (p. 791), described by Bryan, Barnett, Hester, and Relyea (2003). Having examined the contextual layers of personal, professional, and institutional values, we can now consider the ways in which they interact to affect marriage and family therapists.

Convergence and Interactivity of Layers

When considering the impact of personal, professional, and institutional values, one can likely conclude they are interactive but also convergent as one functions in various roles associated with those layers. Simultaneously, one can be a woman/wife/mother responding to personal values, a therapist/colleague/supervisor responding to professional values, and an employee/provider/licensee responding to institutional values. As with any process, the evolution of values developmental and change is inevitable. New experiences and insights affect personal values; new discoveries and paradigms affect professional values; and new objectives and procedures affect institutional values. However, the evolution of any value array for a marriage and family therapist requires an attempt to integrate, if possible, the new with the old. If such integration is not possible, therapists are often faced with "identity dissonance," an outcome when one identifies with two cultures that feature conflicting values or expectations (Costello, 2004, p. 139). However, a unique element of such dissonance for the marriage and family therapist is the overarching expectation that our decisions must be informed primarily by considering the best interests of clients. We certainly should not be expected to abandon our personal values, but we do not have the luxury of allowing those values to dominate our professional judgments, decision making, and practices. Similarly, while we may be affiliated with an array of institutions, our allegiance to clients must inform our institutional representation or allegiance. Therefore, we are compelled to address the difficult issues emerging from Costello's notions of dissonance within the ecology of marriage and family therapy. This topic will be examined more thoroughly in later chapters of our text.

The interactive and convergent nature of the multiple layers of values reflects a variety of characteristics similar to those of any system. Each is associated with established roles and rules that have evolved from traceable origins. Each has a capacity for change and resistance to change. Each has feedback procedures for detecting conformity and error. Perhaps the most illustrative systemic characteristic for this convergence within the multi-layered ecology of marriage and family therapy is that of boundaries. Minuchin (1974) described boundaries as being either rigid (i.e., exclusive), diffuse (i.e., undefined), or clear (e.g., defined but inclusive). Marriage and family therapists who refuse to acknowledge and interact across the multiple layers of values would prefer rigid boundaries of separateness. In this regard, the balancing act between "Who I am" and "What I do" would suggest categorical distinctions that may be naïve, unproductive, and potentially problematic for clients as well as the therapist. To the opposite extreme, interacting with this systemic and layered framework from a vantage of diffuse boundaries could lead to confusion, indefiniteness, and indecision, none of which serve either the client or the therapist. Only by interacting with clear boundaries of permeability and appreciation for the complex and often conflictual nature of the multilayered ecology can the therapist successfully determine the best choices for serving couples and families while minimizing the effects of dissonance. We will discuss various models of decision making in Chapter 3 of our text.

When considering the interrelationships between the various layers of values, consistency across the layers for some practice issues can be addressed with little concern for conflict or dilemma. For example, in the case of client resistance, if the personal, professional, and institutional layers of values support patiently waiting until the client's resistance is successfully overcome, limited concern would arise. However, if the personal values of the practitioner support patience, the professional values of the practitioner support a strategy of pressure (e.g., a therapeutic paradox), and the organizational values of the work setting support rapid compliance, these conflicting values interact to create a dilemma for the practitioner. In such situations, the therapist would be faced with multiple considerations, as he or she realizes that favoring one action could effectively discount other actions. These circumstances are not uncommon. Therapists must give considerable forethought and often must seek consultation from others in addressing such situations. Decision making in marriage and family therapy is rarely as simple as following a predetermined rule. Consequently, therapists must continually examine the values represented within and between these various layers.

A similar process of balancing competing values across layers arises for therapists as they examine the legal issues affecting their practice. In this respect, personal values about law as being rules for conformity may often lead practitioners to believe in the primacy of legalism over therapy considerations. For some, decisions driven primarily by legal considerations can often support a view of duality (e.g., right–wrong, good–bad, embraced–eschewed, etc.). By contrast, one's personal values leading to a view that law is instructive but not compelling may result in examining professional dilemmas in shades of grey with multiple sensible choices. Perhaps the most accurate depiction of the respective position of these two vantages is in balance, although a significant distinction between personal values and professional values may exist when the marriage and family therapist is faced with legally compulsory actions (e.g., mandatory reporting of abuse, etc.). In such instances, the value expressed by the legal institution for the safety considerations of others disallows competing personal or professional values of loyalty or advocacy for clients that might result in seeking a compromise among a variety of possible alternatives.

Danginger, Patterson, and Welfel (2001) reported that significant quandaries emerged for therapists when faced with conflicting personal/professional issues versus institutional issues in managed mental health care. Specifically, these authors noted that the oppressiveness of compliance demands from managed care agencies had the effect of imposing values on practitioners that were dissonant with their personal and professional values. Of particular concern for these authors was the loss of confidence in external agencies in terms of protection of client confidentiality. Applebaum (2002) noted similar concerns about privacy with technological access to client records, despite the intention of HIPAA legislation. In this matter, Applebaum noted, "Although the new federal regulations offer patients some additional protections . . . they also mark a retreat from reliance on patient consent and open up records to previously unauthorized uses, among them law enforcement investigations and marketing and fundraising by health care organizations" (p. 1818). Once again, the institutional values of efficiency and access juxtapose with the professional values of confidentiality. In this regard, marriage and family therapists are compelled to examine ways in which these competing concerns may be reconciled. These issues will be revisited in Chapter 6.

A final example may emerge from one's professional values to embrace social constructionism in practice models such as narrative therapy (Anderson & Goolishian, 1988; Gergen,1991). This approach is a widespread contemporary method of engaging in a collaborative process of change with clients that is nonhierarchical and somewhat elusive in description. However, one must take care not to expect collaboration, equity, and patience from institutions founded on acculturated values such as accountability, imposed pace of changes, or similar hierarchical processes. This is not to say that the narrative model abdicates these values but, rather, the tendency to minimize imposition of leadership in therapy by its proponents may emerge in value conflicts reflecting differences between professional and institutional objectives.

SUMMARY

This chapter has focused primarily on the internal struggles that may occur for marriage and family therapists. In our discussion of the systemic epistemology, we have even identified elements of conceptual dissonance (e.g., feminist critique, self-in-the-system, etc.) that require the marriage and family therapist to be conscientious about values negotiation in the course of therapy. We have examined the layers of personal, professional, and institutional values as a context for discussing the multilayered nature of family therapy and the various ethical, legal, and professional considerations that may surface for therapists. As we have noted, the dynamic interactions across these layers requires diligence on the part of therapists to examine how they affect efforts to support the welfare of clients. We have noted that at times those interactions may be consistent and at times they may be conflictual.

We have discussed how marriage and family therapists are not compelled to abandon their personal values but also that they cannot rely solely on their personal perspective as the basis for serving couples and families. Rather, we have discussed how therapists must embrace professional values because of the special and powerful nature of the therapeutic relationship. We have noted that many of the "extra-therapeutic" institutions affecting marriage and family therapy reflect values of compliance (e.g., managed care systems, legal systems, etc.) or even unintended (though significant) oppression for clients (e.g., technological systems). We have also noted that institutional values may occasionally create dissonance for a practitioner.

In these two introductory chapters, we have discussed the contextual elements that affect both client and therapist as they enter and proceed in a therapy relationship. We offer these comments at this point in the text because the complex nature of decision making related to ethical, legal, and professional issues in marriage and family therapy begins and ends with values. This is not to ignore the primacy of the therapist's obligation to the welfare of clients. Rather, it is to emphasize that in attempting to execute responsibly that obligation, much is open to interpretation by the therapist, and that interpretation occurs within the ecology of marriage and family therapy. In the next five chapters, we offer a discussion of the ethical elements of that obligation.

Ethical Issues in Marriage and Family Therapy

The training of the family therapist requires attention to ethical issues as well as to techniques. Self-awareness and social responsibility are important parts of the professional ethics of therapists. By being demanding of ourselves in our professional role, we may be able to be more reasonable toward our patients.

(Fieldsteel, 1982, p. 267)

CHAPTER 3

Promoting Ethical Practice: Foundational Principles and Traditions

Ethics is concerned with the conduct of human beings as they make moral decisions. These decisions reflect judgments that lead to action, and they involve the use of words known as moral predicates: "ought," "should," "right," "good," and their opposites (Brandt, 1959). Unlike a discipline such as mathematics, ethics is normative rather than factual. "Ethical thinking is not simply a matter of black and white categorization" (Herlihy & Corey, 1996, p. 297). That is, ethics address principles that ought to govern human conduct rather than those that often do govern it (Daubner & Daubner, 1970). Therefore, ethical reasoning, judgment, and decision making involve a "complex interplay of morals, values, and priorities" (Cottone & Tarvydas, 1998, p. 122). Similarly, Ford (2001) noted that expressions of morality and ethics emerge in special relationships such as those involving mental health professionals. As discussed in Chapter 2, marriage and family therapists must consider this interplay as being related, at least in part, to cultural and value differences within the multilayered framework of therapy. When considering the complexity of ethical decision making, we must be mindful that such complexities exist for both the therapist and the clients involved in those decisions.

Although *morality* is sometimes thought of as synonymous with *ethics*, the distinction between the two terms is critical. Barry (1982) defined ethics as "the study of what constitutes good and bad human conduct, including related actions and values" (p. 4). Barry recognized the difficulty of maintaining a separation between ethics and morality, and he proposed restricting the terms *moral* and *morality* to the conduct itself, whereas the terms *ethical* and *ethics* should be employed for the study of moral conduct or a code a person follows. Mowrer (1967) likewise reported finding the two terms used interchangeably but cautioned that morals definitively refers to the goodness or badness of behavior, whereas ethics represents an objective inquiry. For our purposes, readers may want to consider that the interplay between personal values and professional values is relevant for examining ethics and morals as indicated by Ford (2001). In this respect, Ford noted that the primary purpose of intentional and ethical actions in mental health services elevates practitioners' decisions beyond simple moral exercises to the status of accountable care.

Ethics address questions that have no ultimate answers yet are important in planning, justifying, and carrying out decisions. Consider the following situation:

> A woman initially presented herself for individual therapy, seeking to resolve a number of personal conflicts, only one of which was the state of her marriage resulting from an extramarital affair in which she was engaging. Later, her husband accompanied her to therapy for conjoint efforts. The woman was still engaged in the affair, and it was obvious to the therapist that this involvement impeded progress with her husband. She demanded, however, that the therapist maintain the confidentiality of what was discussed during the individual sessions.

Should the therapist respect the individual confidences of one marital partner when doing so clearly impedes those goals overtly agreed to by both? Ethics offers guidance in answering such a question. However, ethics are primarily concerned with helping the *therapist* decide what is right, not with getting *clients* to do what is believed to be right (W. T. Jones, Sontag, Beckner, & Fogelin, 1977). Again, we urge marriage and family therapists to consider the impact of cultural distinctions about morality that may affect such questions. In most respects, ethical standards and traditions affecting marriage and family therapists concern the behavior of the therapist to uphold the rights and promote the welfare of clients they serve individually and or collectively. However, such an apparently clear dictum can sometimes yield conflict and confusion.

VIRTUE ETHICS AND PRINCIPLE ETHICS

Freeman, Engels, and Altekruse (2004) observed, "There is nothing so practical as good theory" (p. 164) as a reference point for ethical decision making. In this respect, ethical practice in the mental health fields has tended to emphasize the application of ethical principles to situations involving a dilemma. Although these dilemmas take a variety of forms, they typically involve the competing rights and responsibilities of therapists, clients, and institutions. In such dilemmas, some therapists are most concerned with following the law and their codes of professional ethics so that they will stay out of trouble. Other therapists, although they are also concerned with the law and their profession's code of ethics, further take into account what is best for their clients. In many ways, the professional values of marriage and family therapists emphasize the practical elements of ethical propriety as only a beginning point in ethical decision making.

A. E. Jordan and Meara (1990) made a distinction between what they term *principle ethics* and *virtue ethics*. As the basis for ethical judgments, principle ethics emphasizes the use of objective, rational standards, rules, or universal codes. Principle ethics focus on acts and choices in an impartial manner and lead a person to answer the question "What shall I do?" Virtue ethics, on the other hand, emphasize the use of historical "virtues" and the development of individuals' character. Virtue ethics focus subjectively on the qualities, traits, and habits of the person carrying out the action or making the choice and leads the person to answer the question "Who shall I be?" As we discussed in Chapter 2, finding the balance between "Who I am" and "What I do" often introduces a quandary for therapists.

Simply stated, principle ethics reflects established societal or professional standards and prompts the question "Is this choice or action consistent with the norms?" Virtue ethics prompts the question "Is this the best thing to do?" If virtue ethics predominates, ethical awareness is a constant, even in the absence of an ethical dilemma (Corey, Corey, & Callanan, 2003).

Therapy is a human endeavor; the therapist cannot help but be involved as a person. For example, Wylie (1989) viewed the human factor as critical in the therapist and then raised the crucial question "Is he or she honest, trustworthy, sensitive, knowledgeable, courageous, open-minded, modest, and rigorously self-reflective?" (p. 33). Likewise, Hundert (1987) asserted that personal experiences "must and should influence our moral experience within our professional life" (p. 843). Thus, the personal values of the therapist have a substantial influence on decisions in the professional role of being a marriage and family therapist. These authors asserted the essential importance of virtue ethics. Commenting on the merger of this delicate balance, we earlier noted the observation by Mabe and Rollin (1986) that "Being an ethical professional is not independent of being an ethical person" (p. 296).

Virtue ethics and principle ethics, however, are not mutually exclusive. Therapeutic training traditionally has sought to set limits on the influence of personal identity, seeking to integrate the personal and the professional. So it is with virtue ethics and professional ethics. Both are important elements in promoting ethical practice.

> A 35-year-old male sought therapy to address longtime sexual difficulties with women he dated. He attributed the problems to his experience of being sexually abused as a child. The perpetrator was his now-deceased stepfather. The therapist was aware of a sex therapist in the city who was well known for successful work with victims of abuse but chose not to refer the client.

Although the therapist in this case illustration could legally and ethically justify seeing this client, it might be more "virtuous" to refer him to the expert (Corey et al., 2003). When an ethical dilemma faced by a marriage and family therapist can be resolved with the retention of both principle ethics and virtue ethics, clarity often emerges in the decision. However, such instances are not always the rule for practitioners. One must also not ignore the potential impact of institutional objectives and derivative values discussed in Chapter 2 when facing an ethical dilemma. For example, the values promoted in the therapist's practice setting may be reflected in an agency objective of serving a high volume of clients for financial purposes, which could also enter into the decision of the therapist who might refer a client to someone in another agency. Again, few decisions are clear-cut and prescribed when therapists consider virtue ethics and principle ethics in their practice decisions.

A. E. Jordan and Meara (1990) concluded their discussion by stating, "The ideals . . . must include conscientious decision-making, but they must also include virtuous deciders, who emphasize not so much what is permitted as what is preferred" (p. 112). In this respect, attempting to integrate personal and professional values, rather than view them as distinct categories, is a significant task in the development of the marriage and family therapist.

The personal and professional values developed by the therapist urge attention to both principle ethics and virtue ethics to demonstrate that ethical decision making is more than a simple rule-governed compliance with a legalistic set of laws. The considerations in such decisions will be examined in a later section of this chapter. However, broad philosophical principles serve as a point of origin for such decisions. Five principles applied by Beauchamp and Childress (2001) to biomedical ethics have been recommended as specifically relevant to overarching considerations in psychotherapy: autonomy, beneficence, nonmaleficence, justice, and fidelity.

Autonomy is the principle that all human beings have the right to make decisions and act on them in an independent fashion. *Beneficence* is the principle that one must actively attempt to benefit another in a positive manner. The principle that one must avoid causing harm to another is *nonmaleficence*. *Justice* is the principle that all individuals should be treated fairly; equals must be treated as equals, and unequals must be treated in a way most beneficial to their specific circumstances. *Fidelity* is the principle of commitment to keep promises, uphold the truth, and maintain loyalty.

Although our discussion now moves to professional codes of ethics, which are rooted in principle ethics, therapists are urged to embrace a virtuous view—their own sense of what is right—as they interpret and apply the principles of these codes if they are to achieve the best ethical practice possible. We will begin by examining some of the general elements of professional ethical codes, followed by a discussion of decision making, and conclude the chapter with a review of selected foundational ethical principles and traditions.

PROFESSIONAL CODES OF ETHICS

"The establishment of ethical guidelines is relatively new" to the helping professions; the first code of ethics was established by the American Psychological Association in 1953 (Neukrug, Lovell, & Parker, 1996, p. 98). The first American Association for Marriage and Family Therapy (AAMFT) code of ethics was approved by the membership in 1962 (Brock, 1998). Ethical codes are important because they set the standards of expected conduct for a society or subgroup. A code of ethics for a profession is meant to "enhance, inform, expand, and improve" members of the profession's "ability to serve as effectively as possible those clients seeking their help" (Zibert, Engels, Kern, & Durodoye, 1998, p. 35). Thus, a significant component of professional socialization of values for marriage and family therapists is their immersion into the understanding and application of these ethical codes.

Universal aspects of ethical codes among the professions have been identified by Van Hoose and Kottler (1985). These codes reflect concerns and define basic principles that "ought" to guide professional activities. They provide a position on standards of practice to aid members in deciding how to act when conflicts arise. They assist in clarifying professionals' responsibility to clients and society. They give society some guarantee that professionals will demonstrate a sensible regard for the mores and expectations of the society. Finally, they give professionals themselves a means of safeguarding their freedom and integrity.

With regard to this last point, Van Hoose and Kottler (1985) posited that codes of ethics aid professionals in dealing with potential dangers from three groups: government, professionals, and the public:

1. Codes of ethics are designed to protect the profession from the government. All professions desire autonomy and seek to avoid undue interference and regulations by lawmakers. Professional codes assert a self-regulatory stance.

2. Codes of ethics offer protection to a profession from potential self-destruction occasioned by internal discord in the absence of such areas of common agreement. For example, it is unethical to entice colleagues' clients to leave them. Such a standard enables professionals to live in harmony.
3. Codes of ethics protect professionals from the public. Professionals who act according to accepted professional codes have some protection if sued for malpractice.

With respect to the mental health professions, the first two statements require little explanation; the last can be clarified in light of recent litigation, which will be discussed in Part III. Again, one must consider the multilayered ecology of therapy reflected in institutional values for various systems (e.g., the legal system) that affects therapists' decision making, since such decisions affect themselves and their clients far beyond the boundaries of the therapy relationship. We will examine this matter briefly in a subsequent section of this chapter.

Ethical codes are adopted by professional associations as a means of offering norms relative to the conduct of their members to ensure that the members properly represent the profession. As noted in Chapter 2, the professional socialization of the marriage and family therapist includes indoctrination about precedents and traditions of practice. Throughout this developmental process, therapists are expected (by the larger professional group) to implement practices consistent with the ethical code. Such self-regulation through established ethical codes involves both informal and formal discipline. *Informal discipline* is seen in the subtle or overt pressure colleagues exert on one another in the form of consultations about practices and referrals of clients. *Formal discipline* is seen in the power exercised by professional associations in publicly criticizing or censuring members and, in extreme cases, barring violators from membership. Although this threat of formal discipline does have some influence on professionals who are not members of their representative professional associations, an association's code of ethics is binding only on its actual members. Consequently, sanctions can be imposed only on those violators who are members of the association. Formal disciplinary actions for departures from ethical practice or code that emerge for marriage and family therapists licensed by state licensure bodies reflect more legally based consequences. These issues will be discussed later, in Chapters 7 and 11.

Since this chapter is devoted to examining foundational principles and traditions related to ethical behavior, we offer a comparison of codes from five mental health disciplines: (a) the American Association for Marriage and Family Therapy, (b) the American Counseling Association, (c) the American Psychological Association, (d) the National Association of Social Workers, and (e) the International Association of Marriage and Family Counselors. Some readers may have exclusive membership in one of these associations, and others may have multiple memberships, thus requiring careful attention to differences ranging from nuances to substantive disagreements. Regardless of one's professional membership and affiliation, comparisons across disciplines can often enlighten and expand our appreciation for elements of virtue and principle that may be overlooked.

Codes of ethics provide the bases from which responsibilities of professionals are articulated. A code of ethics represents the consensus of a large number of reputable members of a profession (Scalise, 2000). As such, it demands primary attention from those seeking to practice in an ethical manner. Generally speaking, ethical codes encompass aspirational precepts that reflect a plane of thought and behavior beyond legalism. Thus, the majority of codes are more informative than instructive, though some entries are quite specific and directive in nature. In a later section of this chapter, we will examine a variety of broad precepts. However, as an example of a specific ethical directive that offers accompanying broad implications, consider the circumstances of the following case:

> A male therapist has been working for several months with a couple seeking a divorce. He finds the wife attractive and exciting. He is aware that she has similar feelings toward him and would like to become involved with him socially and sexually. Because of his desire to become intimate with her, he often finds it difficult to concentrate during therapy sessions.

Standards set by the codes of ethics of a number of major professional associations can offer relatively explicit guidance in such a case. Some of these standards are listed in Table 3–1. However, beyond the principle ethics prohibiting sexual intimacies with clients, the virtue ethics of strained attentiveness and possible bias favoring the wife may compromise the quality of care demonstrated by the therapist. Utilization of various remedies to ensure fairness and quality care (e.g., supervision, co-therapy, referral, etc.) may be necessary on the part of the therapist determined to reflect such virtue ethics.

These standards imply that the therapist's considerable influence must be properly used. The creation of this type of dual or multiple relationship with a client (both therapeutic and intimately personal/sexual) is clearly unethical (Brock, 1998). However, codes of ethics frequently offer only general philosophical guidance for conceptualizing and responding to conflicts. It is not their purpose to recommend specific behaviors in limited situations. If it were, codes would become voluminous, lack broad-based support,

TABLE 3–1 Ethical Considerations Regarding Sexual Relationships with Clients

American Association for Marriage and Family Therapy (2001)
"Sexual intimacy with clients is prohibited."

American Counseling Association (2005)
"Sexual or romantic counselor–client interactions or relationships with current clients, their romantic partners, or their family members are prohibited."

American Psychological Association (2002)
"Psychologists do not engage in sexual intimacies with current therapy clients/patients."

International Association of Marriage and Family Counselors (2005)
"Marriage and family counselors do not harass, exploit, coerce, or manipulate clients for personal gain. Couple and family counselors avoid whenever possible multiple relationships, such as business, social or sexual contacts with any current clients or their family members."

National Association of Social Workers (1999)
"The social worker should under no circumstances engage in sexual activities or sexual contact with current clients whether such contact is consensual or forced."

and infringe on the role of the individual professional in ethical decision making (Huston, 1984). Stude and McKelvey (1979) shared this belief by noting:

> They [codes of ethics] are statements of principle, which must be interpreted and applied by the individual or group to a particular context. They present a rationale for ethical behavior. Their exact interpretation, however, will depend on the situation to which they are being applied. (p. 453)

In situations of clear duty, ethical decision making would appear to be a matter of simply following rules. However, larger and shared philosophical ideologies distinguish professionalism from citizenship or a personal code of behavior. From these overarching ideologies, marriage and family therapists must examine ethical dilemmas with breadth. In so doing, difficult circumstances ultimately entail difficult decisions on the part of therapists. Thus, we will examine various approaches to ethical decision making.

ETHICAL DECISION MAKING

Therapists must have a clear process for understanding ethical decision making if they are to act ethically (Cottone & Tarvydas, 2003; Garcia, Cartwright, Winston, & Borzuchowska, 2003; Stevens, 1999; Van Hoose, 1980). Such an understanding should allow therapists to critically evaluate and interpret their professional code of ethics (Freeman et al., 2004). Furthermore, it should guide therapists in integrating virtue ethics by helping them analyze feelings as appropriate or inappropriate bases for ethical behavior (Ford, 2001). There are several models for understanding and enacting the processes of ethical decision making. We will mention only a few and will elaborate on two, because of their specific relevance to marriage and family therapy.

The first model of ethical decision making is offered by Kidder (1995). According to Kidder, ethical decisions are (a) end-based, (b) rule-based, or (c) care-based. Stevens-Smith (1997a) explained:

> End-based thinking, or utilitarianism, asserts the greatest good for the greatest number drives the ethical decision-making process. In rule-based thinking, one relies on obligations to a set of codes or principles, regardless of outcome. Care-based thinking is committed to the Golden Rule: Do unto others as you would have them do unto you. (p. 251)

In this respect, the Kidder model reflects the multiple considerations reflective of a synthesis of principle ethics and virtue ethics. As a decision-making schema, this approach offers broad guidelines to inform therapists about the type of outcome they wish to achieve in addressing an ethical question.

The Kitchener Model

A second model of ethical decision making that we will examine has been advanced by Kitchener (1986), who synthesized the work of Rest (1983) in identifying four major psychological processes underlying applied ethics in psychotherapy. Ethical decision making, according to Kitchener, demands proficiency in all four processes.

Process 1: Interpreting a Situation as Requiring an Ethical Decision
This process involves the ability to perceive the effect of one's actions on the welfare of others. Several relevant research findings have important implications here. First,

many people have difficulty interpreting the meaning of even simple situations. Sometimes failure to intervene in a situation calling for ethical action may be attributable to a misunderstanding about what is actually occurring. Such instances are particularly relevant considerations for marriage and family therapists at an early point in their professional development, such as in graduate school or during postgraduate supervised work as a prelicensed practitioner. Thus, a lack of knowledge or inexperience can impede an interpretation of an ethical dilemma.

Individuals also differ in their ability to be sensitive to the needs and welfare of others (S. H. Schwartz, 1977). For example, Welfel and Lipsitz (1984) estimated from a number of research studies that between 5% and 10% of mental health practitioners are substantially insensitive to the ethical dimensions of their work. Such insensitivity could be reflective of practitioner impairment or developmental egocentrism. Or such insensitivity could be based on a failure of the therapist to consider the cultural distinctions affecting self and the client system.

The ability to infer the effect of one's actions on others as well as to infer others' needs develops with age and experience. In many ways, the maturation of the therapist is a key component of his or her ability to identify a situation that requires an ethical decision. In other words, knowing a question exists is prerequisite to answering the question.

A social situation also may arouse a strong emotional response before there is time to reflect on it (Zajonc, 1980). Thus, to interpret a situation, persons must understand their feelings about it. In this respect, the personal and professional values of the therapist may come to bear in this process.

Process 1 depends on therapists' developing ethical sensitivity and empathy. This development is essential to effective therapy. Therapists always must be aware that their actions have real ethical consequences that can help, but also can potentially harm others. Virtue ethics and principle ethics interact to establish a central framework for professional behavior and responsibility. This framework provides guidance in identifying situations in which an ethical decision is needed (e.g., confidentiality in therapy).

Process 1 further emphasizes the fact that feelings may not always be good guides for ethical action. For example, the therapist who breaks confidentiality to prevent serious harm to the client or another person will feel bad. On the other hand, the therapist would feel worse if the client or another person suffered unduly for the sake of maintaining confidentiality. In an ethical dilemma such as this, a lesser harm is balanced against a greater harm. As Nozick (1968) asserted, such situations ought to leave therapists with feelings of dissatisfaction and regret that, to make the most ethical decision, they had to violate other ethical responsibilities. Ethical action does not always feel good nor does it always lead to choices that are "good" in an absolute sense. Certainly, some decisions mandated by legislation or legal precedent will often prompt negative feelings on the part of the marriage and family therapist.

Process 2: Formulating an Ethical Course of Action

It is not enough to be aware that an ethical situation exists. One must also be able to integrate various considerations into an ethically justifiable course of action. Process 2 underscores the need for fundamental ethical guidelines. In proposing a model for ethical reasoning, Kitchener (1984a, 1985) distinguished between the *intuitive level* and the *critical-evaluative level* of ethical justification.

The intuitive level of ethical justification addresses immediate feeling responses to situations. It affords a basis for immediate action that is necessary in some situations (e.g., dealing with a suicidal client). However, in many situations, intuitive responses alone are not appropriate (e.g., when intuition leads to sexual relations with clients). Additionally, intuitive level justification may reflect cultural biases or even oppression when therapists practice with a personal and professional worldview of entitlement to impose an agenda.

The critical-evaluative level of ethical justification is composed of three tiers. At the first tier, an ethical course of action can be judged by formal ethical rules (e.g., one's professional code of ethics). For example, therapists can receive ready guidance regarding sexual contact with clients from their code of ethics. If the ethical standards of such a code are insufficient, movement to a second tier is in order. This tier encompasses more general and fundamental ethical principles that serve as a foundation for formal codes of ethics. For example, therapists might justify a particular standard in their ethical code by citing underlying principles (the right to make one's own decisions or the need to respect the rights of others to make free choices). The third tier of critical evaluation is that of ethical theory. Many ethicists (Abelson & Nielson, 1967; Baier, 1958; Ford, 2001; Toulmin, 1950) have posited that, when principles are in conflict, ethical actions should emanate either from what one would want for oneself or significant others in the same circumstances or from what would produce the least amount of avoidable harm. In this respect, the ethical principles of *beneficence* and *nonmaleficence* weigh heavily in formulating an ethical course of action.

Process 3: Integrating Personal and Professional Values

It is possible for persons to know what they "should" do ethically (Process 2) but decide against taking ethical action because of competing values and motives. Process 3 emphasizes that how individuals decide to act is heavily influenced by factors such as ambition, money, and self-interest. Research and ordinary observation have consistently shown that persons do not always do what they think they "should" do, but rather respond to personal values and practical considerations in determining what they actually "would" do (T. S. Smith, McGuire, Abbott, & Blau, 1991). For example, a therapist who knows that a colleague is acting unethically may, because of friendship or loyalty, decide not to intervene. In the end, such a decision may actually sustain a common belief among consumers that members of the therapeutic community fail to "police the profession," thereby lending tacit support for unethical behavior on the part of a colleague (Ford, 2001).

One explanation for the degree of congruence between what therapists believe to be correct and their willingness to carry out this action is the concept of *personal consistency* (Blasi, 1980). Blasi proposed that lack of personal consistency "does not simply indicate the situational specificity of traits but suggests expediency and opportunism" (p. 6). Professional ethical conflicts encountered by therapists frequently do involve issues of expediency and opportunism. For example, it is simpler (i.e., more expedient) not to report the inappropriate professional actions of a colleague and thereby to avoid possible confrontation and recriminations (T. S. Smith et al., 1991). In many ways, the lack of personal consistency can reflect a lack of integration of the layers of values noted in Chapter 2.

Process 3 also emphasizes the impact of virtue ethics on ethical decision making. The gap between understanding and implementation of ethical behavior is a function not only of how much a therapist knows about principle ethics (e.g., professional ethical standards, "the letter of the law") but also of the degree to which a therapist possesses or lacks virtue ethics (e.g., honesty and personal integrity, a willingness to follow "the spirit of the law").

Process 4: Implementing an Action Plan

Perseverance, resoluteness, and character are elements of virtue ethics that are also involved in acting on any decision (Rest, 1982). Process 4 addresses therapists' need to develop and maintain their virtue ethics, particularly a sense of ethical responsibility. It is not enough to be aware of and concerned about ethical issues, nor even to think wisely about them. Professional practice requires that therapists take responsibility for their actions and the consequences of those actions. In this respect, failing to follow through on good intentions reflects a "decision-by-indecision" on the part of the therapist.

An important aspect of assuming responsibility is the ability to tolerate the ambiguity that accompanies ethical decision making. Therapists must understand that few absolute answers exist; certainty is frequently impossible. At the same time, ethical reasoning can be precise and can in many cases resolve dilemmas. In more difficult situations, it can at least identify the precise nature of the dilemma.

The Keith-Spiegel and Koocher Model

A third model of ethical decision making derives from the work of Keith-Spiegel and Koocher (1998). These authors offer a somewhat more pragmatic approach to practice-based ethical decision making, emphasizing evaluations of possible choices and potential outcomes emerging from those choices. Specifically, their model progresses in the following sequence.

Step 1: Describe the Parameters

First, therapists should identify the circumstances with which they have been presented. Any time a decision must be made, these authors admonish the practitioner not to act with haste, but rather to consider elements of the situation by a careful assessment and identification of the whole picture. In some instances, therapists may consider a circumstance in isolation rather than as a part of the context that may be affected by a decision. This initial step is particularly significant for marriage and family therapists who embrace a systemic perspective in their work, who seek personal consistency, and who attempt to be culturally responsive in their professional efforts.

Step 2: Define the Potential Issues

In this step, the authors encourage a very broad and comprehensive examination of possible issues emerging from the assessment conducted in Step 1. At times, therapists may be persuaded that a difficult situation is related to only a limited range of considerations (e.g., confidentiality, etc.) when the issue may be considerably more complex (e.g., duty to warn or protect, etc.). From such a simplistic perspective, the therapist may address the "task" of an ethical dilemma but may neglect the "processes" associated with completing a task.

Step 3: Consult Legal and Ethical Guidelines

In attempting to address an ethical dilemma, these authors encourage therapists to be exhaustive in examining legal precedents, practice traditions, specific instructions in codes of ethics, and related applications of these factors. In this respect, knowledge and awareness of common concerns addressed by legal and ethical precedents is essential, not to mention a relevant component of continued professional socialization and development on the part of the therapist. For example, a therapist who views a duty-to-protect circumstance as simply being a matter of determining to whom they should disclose such information misses the complexity of balancing public protection, client welfare, legal precedent, and ethical tradition. In essence, few ethical decisions are simple.

Step 4: Evaluate the Rights, Responsibilities, and Welfare for All

A significant aspect of the Keith-Spiegel and Koocher model is the deliberateness of examining the rights, responsibilities, and welfare of all parties involved in a decision. Certainly, almost any ethical practitioner will consider the rights and welfare of clients when making an ethical decision. In some instances, however, therapists may assume responsibilities that go beyond their duties, even to the point of compromising the ethical principle of *autonomy*. A therapist assuming responsibility for an action with no legal rule or ethical directive may be expedient, but actually may be taking on a responsibility that should fall to the client. For example, consider the circumstance of a husband and wife scheduled for a conjoint marital session. The husband arrives on time but has a problem with his automobile. The wife has phoned 15 minutes after the scheduled beginning of the session to say her office meeting ran well beyond its scheduled time. The husband indicates that he is concerned about being able to pick up his son from basketball practice, which he knows is along the route taken by the therapist when she is leaving the office. Offering a ride to the husband and retrieving the child may be expedient, and from the perspective of the therapist's personal socialization, a sign of politeness. However, if the nature of marital conflict between the partners concerns chronic patterns of inflexibility in scheduling and prioritizing, to do so may actually promote rather that confront this pattern. The husband does not have a right to expect a ride; the son's welfare is not in danger; and the wife has a functional vehicle. In such a circumstance, a decision to emphasize responsibility within the family system may be ethical as well as therapeutic.

Step 5: Generate Alternate Decisions

For this step, practitioners are instructed to engage in brainstorming possible solutions for the dilemma. In some instances, a limited number of options exist; in others, an array of possibilities may be available. As with any procedure for creating possible solutions to a circumstance, one should think broadly. Additionally, one should also consider the impact of perceived stress, even panic, that would preclude a remedy that is sometimes overlooked: Consider waiting. In some instances, delaying a decision may be an appropriate strategy, though decision-by-indecision should be avoided in time-sensitive circumstances.

Step 6: Enumerate the Consequences of Each Decision

Perhaps Steps 6 and 7 in the Keith-Spiegel and Koocher model are the most specific of ethical decision models. Purposeful consideration of the potential aftermath of a decision is a step many therapists may neglect. In fact, when possible, considering the potential "consequences of consequences" of a decision will prompt the therapist to take an extended view of a dilemma. One caution must be addressed in this step: Few difficult decisions have no unpleasant consequences. Being overwhelmed by objectionable outcomes makes professional decisions difficult, though no less compelling.

Step 7: Estimate Probability for Outcomes of Each Decision

Probable outcomes concern both pleasant and unpleasant consequences associated with the dilemma. In this step, the probability of possible outcomes may rely on the actions taken by others (e.g., parents, external agencies, other therapists, etc.). Thus, when considering such estimates, one must factor the ability and willingness of others to act in concert with the actions of the therapist. This is not to say that the therapist must assume total responsibility for an action, as was discussed in Step 4. However, reliance on others to make commitments, pursue a timely schedule, and act as agreed upon should be factored into the estimate of probability for an outcome with a decision.

Step 8: Make the Decision

Finally, once the assessment, precedents, and estimates have been considered, a decision must be made. As noted earlier, a decision to defer on an action is a deliberate decision within this model. Otherwise, a chosen action within a specified time frame with thorough consideration for the possible outcomes is a pragmatic approach to decision making. Though actions following this or any other model will not provide certainty in maximizing benefits and minimizing liabilities, the sequential nature of this model may assist therapists in a good-faith attempt to resolve difficult situations. Remember: No decision models are foolproof.

Other authors have also noted significant elements of the decision-making process, such as Welfel's (1998) notation to develop ethical sensitivity prior to actually encountering the presenting dilemma; Stadler's (1986) advice to identify possible competing principles in the early stage of examining the dilemma; and the admonition by Corey et al. to consult with colleagues prior to taking action.

To make solidly grounded ethical decisions, it is important to refer to one's professional code of ethics (Cottone & Tarvydas, 2003). However, one must also identify basic ethical concepts that can serve both as a supplement to the code and as additional sources of guidance in ethical decision making. Van Hoose (1980) summarized a general rule for therapists faced with ethical decisions:

> The counselor or psychotherapist is probably acting in an ethically responsible way concerning a client if (a) he or she has maintained personal and professional honesty, coupled with (b) the best interests of the client, (c) without malice or personal gain, and (d) can justify his or her actions as the best judgment of what should be done based upon the current state of the profession. When these four components are present, ethically responsible behavior is likely to be demonstrated. (p. 11)

Tymchuk et al. (1982) drew a similar conclusion from their survey of psychologists. They found a low consensus of opinion about the ethics of situations that were either not addressed by the Ethical Standards of Psychologists (American Psychological Association, 1981) or not of immediate concern to the psychologists. Those authors called for a model of ethical conceptualization as an adjunct to the code.

In 1982, Margolin cautioned that insufficiencies in the Ethical Standards of Psychologists (American Psychological Association, 1981) as they applied to practitioners of marriage and family therapy were not being fully appreciated. Almost a decade later, Patten, Barnett, and Houlihan (1991), in a review of the literature on ethics in marriage and family therapy, echoed Margolin's comments in asserting that the same insufficiencies still remain. With the exceptions of the AAMFT Code of Ethics (American Association for Marriage and Family Therapy, 2001) and the Ethical Code for the International Association of Marriage and Family Counselors (International Association of Marriage and Family Counselors, 2005), similar insufficiencies can be found in the codes of ethics of other professional associations whose members engage in the practice of marriage and family therapy. These codes have been established in and reflect an atmosphere in which traditional individual and group therapy models predominate.

The generality inherent in codes of ethics on such topics as nondiscrimination, client welfare, confidentiality, and informed consent can make ethical decision making difficult when a therapist is dealing with individual clients. The difficulties are compounded when the primary treatment unit consists of a couple or multiple family members. Even more complicated is the consideration of the multilayered ecology of values affecting ethical practice on the part of the marriage and family therapist. The balance of this chapter addresses ethical decision making in relation to these thorny topics, first from a therapist–individual client perspective and then from a therapist–couple/family perspective.

DIVERSITY, NONDISCRIMINATION, VALUES, AND ALLEGIANCES

We begin our examination of traditions and foundational ethical principles embedded in selected mental health codes by revisiting some elements from Chapters 1 and 2. Readers will recall that Chapter 1 provided a discussion of diversity, and Chapter 2 offered an examination of layers of values. Both of these spheres of human experience have substantive effects on the work of marriage and family therapists. However, one might ask, "Are these addressed in any of the codes of ethics?" The answer is a resounding "Yes!"

A discussion of ethical propriety beginning with these elements of the therapeutic relationship is somewhat unusual. Many such discussions begin with the more obvious admonitions concerning client welfare (which we will consider in the next section). However, attitudes and ideologies regarding the primacy of human dignity and respect for differing values are significant preexisting conditions on the part of any therapist before she or he ever even forms a therapeutic relationship. Discussions of these concerns, grounded in a review of relevant professional literature, have already been offered in the previous two chapters. Therefore, we will only briefly address the entries offered in professional ethical codes concerning these important matters affecting marriage and family therapists.

Nondiscrimination and Respect for Diversity

Readers will recall the discussion in Chapter 1 about the various elements affecting our psychosocial identity, our perspective, and our values. The physical, environmental, developmental, and historical elements of one's circumstance and place create complexities for therapists to consider when attempting interventions with individuals, couples, and families. The various disciplines feature great commonality regarding nondiscrimination and respect for diversity, as noted in Table 3–2.

TABLE 3–2 Ethical Considerations Regarding Nondiscrimination and Respect for Diversity

American Association for Marriage and Family Therapy (2001)
"Marriage and family therapists provide professional assistance to persons without discrimination on the basis of race, age, ethnicity, socioeconomic status, disability, gender, health status, religion, national origin, or sexual orientation."

American Counseling Association (2005)
"Counselors do not condone or engage in discrimination based on age, culture, disability, ethnicity, race, religion/spirituality, gender, gender identity, sexual orientation, marital status/partnership, language preference, socioeconomic status, or any basis proscribed by law."

"Counselors communicate information in ways that are both developmentally and culturally appropriate."

American Psychological Association (2002)
"In their work-related activities, psychologists do not engage in unfair discrimination based on age, gender, gender identity, race, ethnicity, culture, national origin, religion, sexual orientation, disability, socioeconomic status, or any basis proscribed by law."

International Association of Marriage and Family Counselors (2005)
"Marriage and family counselors respect cultural diversity. They do not discriminate on the basis of race, gender, disability, religion, age, sexual orientation, cultural background, national origin, marital status, or political affiliation."

"Marriage and family counselors recognize that each family is unique. Couple and family counselors do not promote bias and stereotyping regarding family roles and functions."

National Association of Social Workers (1999)
"Social workers should not practice, condone, facilitate, or collaborate with any form of discrimination on the basis of race, ethnicity, national origin, color, sex, sexual orientation, age, marital status, political belief, religion, or mental or physical disability."

In examining these codes, it is evident that attention is devoted to the pluralistic nature of contemporary society and contemporary families. Sensitivity for differences is clearly reflective of the ethical principles of *beneficence, justice,* and *autonomy* discussed earlier in this chapter. Additionally, the principle and virtue ethical vantages clearly emerge to inspire and instruct marriage and family therapists in these matters.

Personal Values, Institutional Values, and Legal Precedence

Chapter 2 offered an examination of systemic epistemology, including criticisms, as well as a discussion of the multiple layers of values affecting marriage and family therapists. Specifically, this discussion featured an examination of the convergence and divergence of personal, professional, and institutional values affecting therapeutic relationships.

The ethical codes selected for examination in our text are not without commentary on these issues. For example, Table 3–3 offers substantive and consistent remarks about

TABLE 3–3   Ethical Considerations Regarding Personal Values and Preferences of the Therapist

American Association for Marriage and Family Therapy (2001)
"Marriage and family therapists are aware of their influential positions with respect to clients, and they avoid exploiting the trust and dependency of such persons."

"Marriage and family therapists do not use their professional relationships with clients to further their own interests."

American Counseling Association (2005)
"Counselors are aware of their own values, attitudes, beliefs, and behaviors and avoid imposing values that are inconsistent with counseling goals and respect for the diversity of clients, trainees, and research participants."

American Psychological Association (2002)
"Psychologists are aware of and respect cultural, individual, and role differences . . . Psychologists try to eliminate the effect of biases based on those factors. . . ."

International Association of Marriage and Family Counselors (2005)
"Couple and family counselors examine personal biases and values."

National Association of Social Workers (1999)
"Social workers also should be aware of the impact on ethical decision making of their clients' and their own personal values and cultural and religious beliefs and practices. They should be aware of any conflicts between personal and professional values and deal with them responsibly."

the need for awareness of our personal values when assuming the powerfully influential role of a marriage and family therapist. Even if one's professional identity may be in affiliation with an adjacent discipline, one can appreciate the admonitions of other groups about the care needed in managing the impact of personal values on others.

Chapter 2 also featured a discussion about convergence and divergence among the layers of values. When personal, professional, and institutional values and traditions coincide (such as in the previous discussion about sexual relationships with clients), therapists are not faced with conflicts about appropriate behavior. However, sometimes therapists may face conflicts between these layers of values. Table 3–4 shows that ethical codes do not fail to take into account circumstances of disagreement and angst.

Readers will recall that Chapter 2 offered a view that legal precedence, whether in case law or statutory law, is a form of institutional values that can conflict with personal, professional, or even other institutional considerations. In this respect, a common thread among the ethical codes is the responsibility to inform institutions of conflicts with ethical traditions and attempt to resolve such conflicts by retaining allegiance to the code of one's profession. Regarding both personal values and value conflicts, the philosophical foundations of *beneficence, justice, autonomy,* and *fidelity* come to the forefront of decisions and practices.

As we indicated previously, the discussion of these aspects of ethical decision making focused on the contents of selected mental health codes, since references to professional literature were offered in Chapters 1 and 2. The remaining sections of this chapter include a review of both professional literature and relevant ethical codes.

TABLE 3–4 Ethical Considerations Regarding Conflicts Between Ethics and Laws or Institutions

American Association for Marriage and Family Therapy (2001)
"Marriage and family therapists comply with the mandates of law, but make their commitment to the AAMFT Code of Ethics and take steps to resolve the conflict in a responsible manner."

"Marriage and family therapists remain accountable to the standards of the profession when acting as members or employees of organizations. If the mandates of an organization . . . conflict with the AAMFT Code of Ethics, marriage and family therapists make known to the organization their commitment to the AAMFT Code of Ethics and attempt to resolve the conflict in a way that allows the fullest adherence to the Code of Ethics."

American Counseling Association (2005)
"If ethical responsibilities conflict with law, regulations, or other governing legal authority, counselors make known their commitment to the ACA Code of Ethics and take steps to resolve the conflict. If the conflict cannot be resolved by such means, counselors may adhere to the requirements of law, regulations, or other governing legal authority."

"If the demands of an organization with which counselors are affiliated pose a conflict with the ACA Code of Ethics, counselors specify the nature of such conflicts and express to their supervisors or other responsible officials their commitment to the ACA Code of Ethics. When possible, counselors work toward change within the organization to allow full adherence to the ACA Code of Ethics."

American Psychological Association (2002)
"If psychologists' ethical responsibilities conflict with law, regulations, or other governing legal authority, psychologists make known their commitment to the Ethics Code and take steps to resolve the conflict. If the conflict is unresolvable via such means, psychologists may adhere to the requirements of the law, regulations, or other governing legal authority."

"If the demands of an organization . . . conflict with this Ethics Code, psychologists clarify the nature of the conflict, make known their commitment to the Ethics Code, and to the extent feasible, resolve the conflict in a way that permits adherence to the Ethics Code."

International Association of Marriage and Family Counselors (2005)
"Marriage and family counselors do not engage in actions that violate the legal standards of their community."

"Marriage and family counselors specify the nature of conflicts between work requirements and other demands of an employing organization and the relevant codes of ethics. Employment and consultation of couple and family counselors should not compromise ethical standards."

National Association of Social Workers (1999)
"Instances may arise when social workers' ethical obligations conflict with agency policies or relevant laws or regulations. When such conflicts occur, social workers must make a responsible effort to resolve the conflict in a manner that is consistent with the values, principles, and standards expressed in this Code."

"Social workers should not allow an employing organization's policies, procedures, regulations, or administrative orders to interfere with their ethical practice of social work. Social workers should take reasonable steps to ensure that their employing organizations' practices are consistent with the NASW Code of Ethics."

CLIENT WELFARE

The codes of ethics of all major professional associations affirm that a therapist's primary responsibility is to the client. Consistent with our earlier discussion, the needs of clients, not therapists, take first priority in the therapeutic relationship. Embedded in any discussion of client welfare is the assumption that the therapist is competent to provide professional services for the needs of clients. Also implied is that therapeutic relationships should be maintained only as long as clients are benefiting from them or until a referral is indicated. Finally, ethical attention to client welfare cannot be assured in instances in which a therapist's ability is compromised or hindered. These and related matters will be considered in our discussion of client welfare.

A review of the various professional ethical codes in Table 3–5 reveals that the primacy of the clients' welfare is unquestionably clear. Corey et al. (2003), however, raised several cogent questions that tend to cloud this simple assertion:

- What criteria should be used to determine whether a client is benefiting from the therapeutic relationship?
- What should be done if a client reports that she or he is benefiting from therapy but the therapist is unable to identify any signs of progress?
- What courses of action are available to the therapist who believes that a client is seeking only to purchase friendship and has no intention of pursuing therapeutic change?

These and other questions call upon a marriage and family therapist to weigh a variety of ethical principles when faced with determining a course of action. As was noted previously, these principles are *autonomy, beneficence, nonmaleficence, justice,* and

TABLE 3–5 Ethical Considerations Regarding Client Welfare

American Association for Marriage and Family Therapy (2001)
"Marriage and family therapists advance the welfare of families and individuals. They respect the rights of those persons seeking their assistance, and make reasonable efforts to ensure that their services are used appropriately."

American Counseling Association (2005)
"The primary responsibility of counselors is to respect the dignity and promote the welfare of clients."

American Psychological Association (2002)
"In their professional actions, psychologists seek to safeguard the welfare and rights of those with whom they interact professionally and other affected persons, and the welfare of animal subjects of research."

International Association of Marriage and Family Counselors (2005)
"Members demonstrate caring, empathy, and respect for client well-being. They promote safety, security, and sense of community for couples and families."

National Association of Social Workers (1999)
"Social workers' primary responsibility is to promote the well-being of clients."

fidelity (Beauchamp & Childress, 2001). Such complex principles often have varying interpretations and can even conflict in their application. Using the decision-making models advocated by Kidder (1995), Kitchener (1986), Keith-Spiegel and Koocher (1998), or others, marriage and family therapists may attempt to clarify the factors affecting their efforts at promoting client welfare, including attempts to demonstrate principle ethics and virtue ethics. When our energies are devoted to such an elusive task, the professional values of the therapist are informative, though interactive, with both personal and institutional values.

Ethical decision making for client welfare can sometimes appear to be quite clear. In instances where measurable progress is being made toward established therapy goals, the therapist may actually have data to verify efforts on behalf of client welfare. In other circumstances, client welfare may not be so apparent. For example, when a couple is working slowly to overcome resistance in trusting one another to address a chronic difficulty, determining client welfare may be a more difficult proposition. In some situations, the complexity of factors converging to affect decisions by the practitioner may even appear to be at odds with the broad ethical principles advanced by Beauchamp and Childress (2001). Such an example is offered in Chapter 5, related to circumstances of intimate partner violence. For the present discussion, however, a variety of issues that relate to client welfare are highlighted.

Therapist Competence

Though sometimes considered in other frameworks, an essential element of client welfare is therapist competence. *Competence* involves the infusion of knowledge, skill, professional judgment, scientific acumen, and supervised experience into the capacity for marriage and family therapists to care for the clients they serve reasonably and reliably. Against this backdrop, one must ask, "How could an incompetent therapist possibly assure client welfare?"

Verified by graduate educational performance, professional examinations, and rigorous review by professional and regulatory bodies, competence is a dynamic aspect of ethical propriety (Corey et al., 2003). Sustaining competence requires continued professional development involving new findings and techniques. Sustaining competence relies on peer review, supervision, or consultation with other professionals to maintain sharpness and focus. Clients must inherently trust the competence of their marriage and family therapist in order to risk disclosures, dialogue, and change. Competent marriage and family therapists are far more than simple technicians. Rather, competence is reflected in the therapist's skill in assessing, planning, intervening, managing, and terminating clients. Thus, the competence of the therapist is integral in ensuring client welfare. A review of relevant ethical codes concerning therapist competence is provided in Table 3–6.

Due Care

If a therapist is sued for malpractice, he or she will be judged in terms of actions appropriate to other therapists with similar qualifications and duties. Ethical standards of the profession will be a probable basis for comparison (Corey et al., 2003). If therapists act in good faith, they are not likely to be found responsible for a client's lack of progress or mistake in judgment on their part, if the mistake is the kind a "careful and skillful" therapist could make (Anderson & Hopkins, 1996).

TABLE 3–6 Ethical Considerations Regarding Therapist Competence

American Association for Marriage and Family Therapy (2001)
"Marriage and family therapists do not diagnose, treat, or advise on problems outside the recognized boundaries of their competence."

American Counseling Association (2005)
"Counselors practice only within the boundaries of their competence, based on their education, training, supervised experience, state and national credentials, and appropriate experience."

American Psychological Association (2002)
"Psychologists provide services, teach, and conduct research only within the boundaries of their competence, based on their education, training, supervised experience, or appropriate professional experience."

International Association of Marriage and Family Counselors (2005)
"Marriage and family counselors do not attempt to diagnose or treat problems beyond the scope of their training and abilities. They do not engage in specialized counseling interventions or techniques unless they have received appropriate training and preparation on the methods."

National Association of Social Workers (1999)
"Social workers provide services and represent themselves as competent only within the boundaries of their education, training, license, certification, consultation received, supervised experience, or other relevant profesional experience."

The application of the "careful and skillful" test originated in medical ethics, representative portions of which have been made into law. Physicians are expected to display behavior suitable to their profession related to *due care*:

> The law imposes on [physicians who undertake] the care of a patient the obligation of due care, the exercise of an amount of skill common to [their] profession, without which [they] should not have taken the case, and a degree of care commensurate with this position. (61 Am. Jur. 2d)

Further commentary concerning due care by physicians is offered in this regard:

> Physicians also have a duty to act in good faith and advise patients regarding the best possible treatment: [Physicians occupy] a position of trust and confidence as regards [their] patient, and it is [their] duty to act with the utmost good faith; if [they know] that the treatment adopted by [them] will probably be of little or no benefit, and that there is another method of treatment that is more likely to be successful, which [they have] not the training or facilities to give . . . [they] must advise [their] patient. (61 Am. Jur. 2d)

Most mental health professionals are familiar with the idea of "basic care" or "reasonable care" which we will equate with the term "due care" throughout our text. From this perspective, due care concerns reflect a prevalent array of practice decisions employed by therapists. This principle is far more specific to therapy services than the administrative emphasis of the Battle for Structure (Napier & Whitaker, 1978) discussed earlier in Chapter 1. Rather, due care involves elements of professional care such as monitoring benefit, referral, and termination. By contrast, due care also involves a lack of professionalism in instances such as abandonment and neglect. The standards from the ethical codes of other professional associations reflective of due care considerations are listed in Table 3–7.

TABLE 3–7 Ethical Considerations Regarding Due Care

American Association for Marriage and Family Therapy (2001)
"Marriage and family therapists continue therapeutic relationships only so long as it is reasonably clear that clients are benefiting from the relationship."

"Marriage and family therapists assist persons in obtaining other therapeutic services if the therapist is unable or unwilling, for appropriate reasons, to provide professional help."

"Marriage and family therapists do not abandon or neglect clients in treatment without making reasonable arrangements for the continuation of such treatment."

American Counseling Association (2005)
"Counselors do not abandon or neglect clients in counseling."

"If counselors determine an inability to be of professional assistance to clients, they avoid entering or terminating counseling relationships. Counselors are knowledgeable about culturally and clinically appropriate referral resources and suggest these alternatives. If clients decline the suggested referrals, counselors should discontinue the relationship."

"Counselors terminate a counseling relationship when it becomes reasonably apparent that the client no longer needs assistance, is not likely to benefit, or is being harmed by continued counseling."

American Psychological Association (2002)
"Psychologists terminate therapy when it becomes reasonably clear that the client/patient no longer needs the service, is not likely to benefit, or is being harmed by continued service."

International Association of Marriage and Family Counselors (2005)
"Marriage and family counselors have an obligation to withdraw from a counseling relationship if the continuation of services would not be in the best interest of the client or would result in a violation of ethical standards. If the counseling relationship is no longer helpful or productive, couple and family counselors have an obligation to assist in locating alternative services and making referrals as needed. Marriage and family counselors do not abandon clients. They arrange for appropriate termination of counseling relationships and transfer of services as indicated."

National Association of Social Workers (1999)
"Social workers should terminate services to clients and professional relationships with them when such services and relationships are no longer required or no longer serve the clients' needs or interests."

"Social workers should take reasonable steps to avoid abandoning clients who are still in need of services."

"Social workers should refer clients to other professionals when the other professionals' specialized knowledge or expertise is needed to serve clients fully or when social workers believe that they are not being effective or making reasonable progress with clients and that additional service is required."

FIGURE 3–1 Interactivity of Competence and Due Care

Complementary Elements: Competence and Due Care

Competence concerns the ability of the marriage and family therapist to provide services with *beneficent* intentions for client welfare. Due care concerns the obligations of the therapist to provide competent services to clients by initiating, continuing, limiting, and redirecting. How can one expectation not directly complement the other?

We maintain that a marriage and family therapist who fails to embrace fully the professional duties associated with either of these aspects of client welfare will inevitably jeopardize client welfare. Figure 3–1 graphically demonstrates the complementary nature of these ethical expectations. From both our discussion and this figure, readers can deduce that client welfare involves careful attention to sustained competence and vigilant care for clients. However, marriage and family therapists must be fully in command of their faculties in order to execute these complementary elements of client welfare.

Impairment

The capacity of the marriage and family therapist to demonstrate competence and due care in attending to client welfare is compromised in circumstances of impairment. Practitioner impairment was once viewed as being primarily reflective of alcohol or substance abuse (Annas, 1978; Bissell, 1983; Laliotis & Grayson, 1985; McCrady, 1989; Thoreson, Nathan, Skorina, & Kilburg, 1983). In more contemporary times, however, therapist impairment has come to be a cause for concern related to physical, mental, or emotional distress (Emerson & Markos, 1996; Herlihy, 1996; Kottler & Hazler, 1996; Reamer, 1992).

Marriage and family therapists are susceptible to a variety of developmental or environmental stressors that can affect their ability to sustain their best performance. Any expectation of faultless work is unreasonable for therapists, particularly in relation to temporary, acute difficulties. However, more chronic patterns of lethargy, distraction, indifference, or intoxication on the part of a therapist can place the welfare of clients in serious jeopardy (Sheffield, 1998). Ethical codes have come to reflect appreciation for and admonition about therapist impairment, as evidenced in Table 3–8.

When considering the subtle as well as obvious elements of ethical practices concerning client welfare, marriage and family therapists should remember that such matters are grounded in a great deal more than an attitude of *nonmaleficence* or doing no harm. Rather, the interrelationship between competence and due care, coupled with

TABLE 3–8 Ethical Considerations Regarding Impairment

American Association for Marriage and Family Therapy (2001)
"Marriage and family therapists seek appropriate professional assistance for their personal problems or conflicts that may impair work performance or clinical judgment."

American Counseling Association (2005)
"Counselors are alert to the signs of impairment from their own physical, mental, or emotional problems and refrain from offering or providing professional services when such impairment is likely to harm a client or others. They seek assistance for problems that reach the level of professional impairment, and, if necessary, they limit, suspend, or terminate their professional responsibilities until such time it is determined that they may safely resume their work."

American Psychological Association (2002)
"Psychologists refrain from initiating an activity when they know or should know that there is a substantial likelihood that their personal problems will prevent them from performing their work-related activities in a competent manner."

"When psychologists become aware of personal problems that may interfere with their performing work-related duties adequately, they take appropriate measures, such as obtaining professional consultation or assistance, and determine whether they should limit, suspend, or terminate their work-related duties."

International Association of Marriage and Family Counselors (2005)
"Marriage and family counselors do not undertake any professional activity in which their personal problems might adversely affect their performance. Instead, they focus on obtaining appropriate professional assistance to help them resolve the problem."

National Association of Social Workers (1999)
"Social workers should not allow their own personal problems, psychosocial distress, legal problems, substance abuse, or mental health difficulties to interfere with their professional judgment and performance or to jeopardize the best interests of people for whom they have a professional responsibility."

"Social workers whose personal problems, psychosocial distress, legal problems, substance abuse, or mental health difficulties interfere with their professional judgment and performance should immediately seek consultation and take appropriate remedial action by seeking professional help, making adjustments in workload, terminating practice, or taking any other steps necessary to protect clients and others."

attention to any hint of impairment, serve as the standard for principled and virtuous ethical practice. When applied to the complexity of marriage and family therapy, reflecting multiple client perspectives, client welfare is often severely tested for therapists facing situations such as marital dissatisfaction, disputes in blended families, child custody conflicts, and addiction or abuse of drugs and alcohol. These and similar presenting concerns will be discussed in later chapters of the text.

CONFIDENTIALITY

The single most widely recognized ethical issue in the practice of psychotherapy is confidentiality, which is "often referred to as the cornerstone of ethics" (Kaplan & Culkin, 1995, p. 336). Confidentiality had its genesis in the physician–patient relationship in the 16th century, when physicians began to realize that contagious diseases were being spread by persons who feared that detection of their affliction would condemn them to social isolation (Slovenko, 1973). More recently, confidentiality has become intertwined with legal constraints dictated by state and federal legislation and court decisions regarding privileged communication and privacy. However, the terms *confidentiality, privileged communication,* and *privacy* should not be used interchangeably, because they have different though interrelated meanings.

S. H. Erickson (1998) defined confidentiality in this way: "Confidentiality is the ethical responsibility required of all national counseling organizations and some state licensing boards that nothing disclosed within the counseling session will be revealed to another person without the client's expressed consent" (p. 223). Denkowski and Denkowski (1982) identified two reasons for maintaining confidentiality in psychotherapy:

1. Confidentiality protects clients from the social stigma frequently associated with therapy.
2. Confidentiality promotes vital client rights, integral to therapists' professed concern for the welfare of clients.

Confidentiality is maintained as a standard by the ethical codes of all professional therapy organizations. Relevant standards from the codes of ethics of several professional organizations are listed in Table 3–9.

Little else in psychotherapy commands as much agreement as the belief that therapists have a responsibility to safeguard information obtained during the treatment process. Confidentiality is considered to be essential for a satisfactory therapist–client relationship. Therapists' professional training and emergent values in this matter have traditionally emphasized a stern but simplistic admonition about the sanctity of psychotherapeutic confidentiality with references to principles stated in professional codes of ethics (R. L. Smith, 1999).

From the perspective of the legal system, confidentiality is generally viewed as a narrowly drawn exception to the principle that all relevant information should be available to judicial decision makers (Gumper & Sprenkle, 1981). Further, state and federal legislation as well as court decisions have increasingly mandated disclosure of information in certain situations and imposed penalties for noncompliance, most notably in instances of child abuse. Likewise, procedures for disclosure of therapy information in educational settings must be determined in accordance with the Family Educational and Privacy Rights Act of 1976. Maintaining confidentiality in the treatment of minors with alcohol or drug abuse problems may also not be possible after the first interview, as mandated by the Confidentiality of Alcohol and Drug Patient Records Act of 1975 (DePauw, 1986). Hence, a thorough understanding of the concepts of privileged communication and privacy is prerequisite to offering and maintaining client confidentiality. Particularly relevant in this matter is the need for marriage and family therapists to clarify the limits of confidentiality in the therapeutic relationship prior to or at the beginning of therapy.

TABLE 3–9 Ethical Considerations Regarding Confidentiality

American Association for Marriage and Family Therapy (2001)
"Marriage and family therapists have unique confidentiality concerns because the client in a therapeutic relationship may be more than one person. Therapists respect and guard confidences of each individual client."

American Counseling Association (2005)
"Counselors aspire to earn the trust of clients by creating an ongoing partnership, establishing and upholding appropriate boundaries, and maintaining confidentiality."

American Psychological Association (2002)
"Psychologists have a primary obligation and take reasonable precautions to respect confidential information obtained through or stored in any medium, recognizing that the extent and limits of confidentiality may be regulated by law or established by institutional rules or professional or scientific relationship."

International Association of Marriage and Family Counselors (2005)
"Marriage and family counselors recognize that trust is the foundation of an effective counseling relationship. Professional counselors maintain appropriate boundaries so that clients reasonably expect that information shared will not be disclosed to others without prior written consent . . . Clients have the right to know the limits of confidentiality, privacy, and privileged communication."

National Association of Social Workers (1999)
"Social workers should protect the confidentiality of all information obtained in the course of professional service, except for compelling professional reasons."

To the extent allowed in state statutes and other legal precedents, clients are typically afforded the right to consent in regulating the disclosure of confidential information in a therapy relationship. This situation is particularly compelling in applying the ethical precept of confidentiality when posed with legal attempts to offset this cornerstone of psychological care. In such cases, privileged communication is a significant consideration for therapists.

Privileged Communication

Privileged communication is "a legal right which exists by statute and which protects [clients] from having [their] confidences revealed publicly from the witness stand during legal proceedings without [their] permission" (Shah, 1969, p. 57). Where privileged communication laws apply, therapists are prevented from testifying in court about clients without their consent (Glosoff, Herlihy, & Spence, 2000). If a client waives this privilege, a therapist has no grounds for withholding information. The privilege belongs to the client and is meant for the protection of the client, not the therapist (Corey et al., 2003). It is important to note that privileged communication for the therapist–client relationship is not legally supported in all states (Bray, Shepherd, & Hays, 1985). Further, even when clients have not waived their right, privileged communication can be subject to exceptions such as those listed in Table 3–10.

TABLE 3–10 Exceptions to Unwaived Rights to Privileged Communications

- When the therapist is acting in a court-appointed capacity—for example, to conduct a psychological examination (DeKraai & Sales, 1982)
- When the therapist makes an assessment of foreseeable risk of suicide (Schultz, 1982)
- When the client initiates a lawsuit against the therapist, such as for malpractice (Denkowski & Denkowski, 1982)
- In any civil action when the client introduces mental condition as a claim or defense (Denkowski & Denkowski, 1982)
- When a client is under the age of 16 and a therapist believes that the child is the victim of a crime—for example, incest, child molestation, rape, or child abuse (Everstine et al., 1980)
- When the therapist determines that the client is in need of hospitalization for a mental or psychological disorder (DeKraai & Sales, 1982; Schultz, 1982)
- When criminal action is involved (Everstine et al., 1980)
- When information is made an issue in a court action (Everstine et al., 1980)
- When clients reveal their intention to commit a crime or when they can be assessed as "dangerous to society" or dangerous to themselves (DeKraai & Sales, 1982; Schultz, 1982)

Note. From *Issues and Ethics in the Helping Professions* 6th edition by Corey/Corey/Callanan. © 2003. Reprinted with permission of Wadsworth, a division of Thomson Learning: www.thomsonrights.com. Fax: 800 730-2215.

Gumper and Sprenkle (1981) examined the potential repercussions of privileged communication laws for psychotherapy. They reported a wide variation in legal statutes, and this variation presents particular problems for marriage and family therapists. Dominant among the problems that arise is the question "Who owns the right to waive privilege in marriage and family therapy?" Gumper and Sprenkle specifically reemphasized that ownership of this privilege—and therefore the right to waive it—resides *with the client*, not the therapist.

Margolin (1982) addressed this question in discussing the case of a New Jersey couple seen in conjoint marital therapy by a psychologist:

> When the couple, who were seen in marital therapy, decided to divorce, the psychotherapist was subpoenaed by the husband's lawyer to testify in court about statements made during the conjoint therapy sessions. Since the wife refused to waive privilege, the therapist refused to testify. On the basis of psychologist–patient privilege in New Jersey, the wife's confidentiality would not have been protected. The judge decided to rule to protect the wife's confidentiality, however, on the basis of laws in that state for marriage counselors. (p. 793)

Margolin noted similar cases involving psychiatrists. She reported cases in which courts in New York and Tennessee upheld privilege but a Virginia court denied the psychiatrist that protection. As reported by Herrington (1979), the Virginia judge ruled that "when a husband and wife are in a counseling session with a psychiatrist . . . there is no confidentiality because statements were made not in private to a doctor, but in the presence of the spouse" (p. 1).

The model for statutory privilege provisions that apply in psychotherapeutic contexts was drawn from and has largely concerned one-to-one (e.g., attorney–client, husband–wife, clergy–penitent, etc.) relationships. Most privileged communication statutes tend to be ill-defined for situations in which two or more clients are seen simultaneously (Benke, 1998). In some states, for example, the presence of a third party is construed to mean that necessary confidentiality is lacking and the therapist–client privilege is accordingly deemed lost or waived (Gumper & Sprenkle, 1981). Questions also arise as to whether privilege applies to client-to-client communications. Because some states extend privilege to persons who aid in the delivery of personal services and are present during the uttering of confidential information (e.g., nurses, medical technicians), a liberal interpretation of privilege statutes can identify family members as agents of the therapist (Bersoff & Jain, 1980; Nagy, 2000), though such interpretations may not always be reliable unless specified statutorily.

Gumper and Sprenkle (1981) argued that in states where statutory protection of communications in multiperson therapies is unclear, marriage and family therapists should take the position that the "client" is the couple or family as a unit. Rather than identifying family members as agents of the therapist, they recommend claiming that third-party limitations on privilege do not apply because only one client (the couple or family) is present. However, lacking definitive legislation on these issues, marriage and family therapists cannot comfortably assume that existing privilege statutes protect the confidentiality of communications in their work with couples and families.

Legal protection against court-compelled disclosure of therapy communications is thus qualified and particularly flawed with respect to marriage and family therapy. Given this cloudy mixture of protection and compelled disclosure, Gumper and Sprenkle (1981) offered several practical suggestions to therapists for preparing themselves to confront this issue:

1. Whatever their credentials, therapists should acquaint themselves with the particular privilege provisions of their state. It is insufficient to simply know that "some kind of privilege statute" exists.
2. In marriage and family therapy, especially when divorce may be a real possibility, therapists would be wise to obtain a written agreement from all parties not to make or seek court disclosures of therapy communications. Courts may differ in the enforcement of such agreements, but when they have been entered into, efforts to obtain court disclosures are more likely to be restrained, that is, stopped by restraining order.
3. If contacted by an attorney, a therapist should advise the attorney that a written release signed by the participating clients is necessary before the therapist can give out information. The conversation should be one-way (i.e., the therapist can ascertain but not divulge information) until such a release is obtained. Details about the pending proceeding and the attorney's plan for involving the therapist might be elicited, and such information could be helpful in arriving at a position on the disclosure issue.
4. A therapist who decides to take a position of nondisclosure with an attorney should do so firmly and persistently, but without the loud indignance of a crusader seeking to protect therapist–client confidentiality. Most attorneys are conditioned to react to such a militant stance in an adversarial manner. A calm, reasoned approach, emphasizing the therapist's duty as opposed to the attorney's, is less likely to polarize the parties. This calmer approach will allow the

attorney not to lose face and potentially conclude that the therapy information is not worth the effort necessary to obtain it.

5. Subpoenas should be viewed as the formal commencement, not the conclusion, of any disclosure controversy. A therapist should not testify without a subpoena, but conversely, the therapist also need not testify simply because a subpoena is present. When subpoenaed, a therapist should have or obtain sufficient time to carefully consider ethical and legal obligations before making any decision regarding disclosure. Unless steps are taken to have a subpoena canceled or limited by the court, the therapist must respond by being present at the hearing in question. The therapist or the therapist's attorney can, however, still make arguments against testifying or providing records or reports. If a subpoena requiring a court appearance is presented on short notice, the therapist should simply notify the court representative of when the subpoena was received and request time to consult legal counsel.

6. Ideally, therapists should maintain their own independent legal counsel. This policy is especially important when the therapist is subpoenaed and the client is not represented by counsel in the proceeding, when the therapist perceives her or his ethical or legal interests to be at odds with the client's, or when interests conflict between clients who are marital partners or family members.

In states that do feature legal privilege for marriage and family therapists, the specific language of the statute must be examined. Additionally, the therapist may want to present the language of the statute to the court as a matter of information that may have considerable effect on the nature of disclosures from the therapy relationship. In such cases, the court may recognize that privilege compels the therapist to maintain confidentiality and rule accordingly. Even in instances of compelling statutory language concerning privileged communication, however, therapists will encounter situations demanding action on behalf of clients to preserve their safety. Such a duty to protect will be examined later in this section. Considerable complexity emerges in considering the nature of privacy when applied to therapy practices.

Privacy

Privacy with regard to psychotherapy has been defined as "the freedom of individuals to choose for themselves the time and the circumstances under which the extent to which their beliefs, behavior, and opinions are to be shared or withheld from others" (Siegel, 1979, p. 251). More simply stated, privacy is the "right of persons to choose what others may know about them and under what circumstances" (Stadler, 1990, p. 102). "Privacy not only deals with communications . . . but also relates to the disposal of records, not being identified in a waiting room, tape recordings, use of credit cards for billing, use of computer services for scoring of tests or billing, and other documentary or business activities" (Cottone & Tarvydas, 2003, p. 66). The concept of privacy is addressed by the Fourth Amendment to the U.S. Constitution, that portion of the Bill of Rights that protects a person's home against illegal search and seizure by the government. A rich tradition of case law concerns the application of the basic principle of this amendment to a wide range of contemporary issues. In effect, persons are protected against invasion of their privacy by their government or by the agents of government.

Everstine et al. (1980) raised important questions about preserving privacy:

- To what extent should psychological or emotional states be protected from the scrutiny of others?
- Who may intrude on persons' privacy? Under what circumstances and by what means should this decision be made?

These questions are particularly important when managed care agencies and other third-party payers attempt to gain access to therapy information about clients or when therapists are bound by law and/or professional codes of ethics to break confidentiality (e.g., in child abuse cases in which clients pose a serious danger to themselves or others). By contrast to some legal decisions and legislative outcomes that have created exceptions to confidentiality and privacy, the Health Insurance Portability and Accountability Act (HIPAA) of 1996 has further validated consumer rights for privacy outside these exceptions, especially regarding electronic storage and transmission of private information. Privacy questions are somewhat less important in circumstances involving professional consultation, tape recording, and third-party observation or supervision of therapeutic activities. In fact, the issue of privacy even involves practitioners who also teach courses, offer workshops, write books and journal articles, and give lectures. Aside from institutional applications of privacy, assumptions about privacy are significant considerations for marriage and family therapists. Dilemmas concerning trust may emerge in instances in which legal duty or practice traditions typically involve intrusions by others. Once again, the multilayered framework affecting the therapeutic relationship must be considered by the marriage and family therapist when offering descriptions of the extent to which privacy can be retained.

Therapists should maintain a current record of third-party reimbursement requirements (such as insurance or similar managed mental health care information) to apprise clients of the kinds of information that will need to be released, particularly diagnostic labels, and who may have access to the information. When they understand the requirements, many clients choose to assume self-responsibility for therapy fees (i.e., they themselves pay), for example, when employers have access to reimbursement requests. Therapists who seek professional consultation and supervision or who utilize case examples from their clinical work in teaching and writing should obtain clients' consent beforehand or take adequate measures to ensure that clients' identities are disguised (Corey et al., 2003).

A rather curious tension has evolved in terms of privacy concerns for clients and the institutional procedures and traditions that emerge in the use of technology. As an overarching principle, professional values for the marriage and family therapist urge respect for client privacy. By contrast, an overarching principle of institutional values for those employing technological adjuncts to therapy and case management is access to and exchange of private client information (Remley & Herlihy, 2005). Though not inherently in opposition to one another, the values associated with each of these principles may come into conflict with one another unless therapists take great care to avoid such difficulties. Here again, the significance of the HIPAA legislation represents an institutional value supporting limited and authorized privacy for client information.

In addressing the question "Whose agent is the therapist?" Shah (1970) noted that in some governmental agencies and institutions, the therapist is not primarily the client's agent. In these situations, therapists are faced with acculturation conflicts between professional obligations to clients and institutional obligations to their agency or work setting. Shah maintained that potential conflicts should be clarified before beginning diagnostic or therapeutic relationships. Denkowski and Denkowski (1982) supported Shah's position in contending that therapists must inform clients of potential breaches of confidentiality reflective of the values of an institutional culture. They also urged that therapists go further to assure "that all reasonable steps be taken to restrict the legally sanctioned dissemination [of] confidential client information to its bare minimum" (p. 374). Still, while attempting to guard the privacy of the relationship, therapists must be cognizant of the multilayered nature of that relationship. Additionally, therapists may encounter circumstances in which compelling legal precedents overwhelm considerations of confidentiality and privacy. Such is the case in instances in which therapists have a duty to protect.

The Duty to Protect

All professional organizations in the Western world whose members practice psychotherapy have taken the position that certain information must be revealed when there is clear and imminent danger to an individual or to society. Essentially, therapists have a duty to protect (Felthous, 1999). Consistent with this ethical position are legal mandates from legislation and court decisions. These and related issues will be discussed beginning in Chapter 8.

Addressing therapists regarding their duty to protect, Knapp and VandeCreek (1982) wrote: "Psychotherapists need only follow reasonable standards in predicting violence. Psychotherapists are not liable for failure to warn when the propensity toward violence is unknown or would be unknown by other psychotherapists using ordinary skill" (pp. 514–515). These authors cautioned therapists not to become intimidated by clients' statements of potential hostility. Not every impulsive threat is evidence of imminent danger. In their opinion, recent behaviors are the best predictors of future violence. In cases of likely danger, in addition to warning potential victims, Knapp and VandeCreek suggested that therapists also consider alternatives that could defuse the situation and, simultaneously, satisfy their ethical or legal obligations. They particularly recommend that therapists consult with professionals having expertise in dealing with potentially violent persons and that they document all steps taken. Others have offered suggested guidelines for duty-to-protect circumstances (Burkemper, 2002; Costa & Altekruse, 1994). Remley and Herlihy (2005) have noted that the urge to protect must be tempered with caution not to overreact in instances of possible need for action to protect. Learning to balance therapy intentions with legal duties is a significant aspect of professional development for marriage and family therapists.

Corey et al. (2003) offer a set of procedures for therapists to follow if they determine that a client poses a serious danger of violence to others:

1. Therapists should inform their clients of the possible action they must take to protect a third party in situations in which violence might be inflicted on that party.
2. When a client makes threats against others, everything observed and stated in the session should be documented.
3. The therapist should inform his or her supervisor in writing of any serious threat.

4. The therapist should consult with colleagues qualified to offer opinions on how to proceed. This consultation should be documented.
5. The police and other proper authorities should be alerted.
6. The intended victim must be notified; in the case of a minor, her or his parents also should be notified.

These authors further emphasized the need for therapists to consider issues of risk management when considering a duty-to-warn-or-protect circumstance (Monahan, 1993).

Therapists have an obligation to inform clients that the duty to protect exists (Burkemper, 2002; Everstine et al., 1980). Further, clients should be told that therapists also have a "duty to report" suspected instances of child abuse, incest, and other actions that constitute a threat to others as well as to clients themselves. Everstine et al. (1980) aptly summarized therapists' overall obligations in matters of privacy: "Although a therapist, a person is still a citizen and he or she must protect and contribute to the common good. As a private citizen, the person of good conscience will not hesitate to warn an intended victim" (p. 836). Likewise, the person of good conscience would not hesitate to prevent the continuation of child abuse, incest, or other forms of violence. In this regard, both principle ethics and virtue ethics may affect the therapist's decision. Additionally, the ethical principles of *nonmaleficience* and *justice* combine with practice traditions and legal obligations (Chaimowitz, Glancy, & Blackburn, 2000). In this way, the therapist's personal, professional, and institutional values often align to support the care and safety of both clients and others.

Online practice of marriage and family therapy has introduced significant revisions in procedures related to confidentiality and the duty to warn or protect (Remley & Herlihy, 2005). In such circumstances, regardless of the locale of the client, therapists have an obligation to warn or protect the welfare of both clients and, in some instances, the public at large. Yet to be determined by statute or case law in such circumstances are the guidelines for actions taken by the therapist related to this duty. A therapist providing Internet therapy from State X (hereafter designated as the "state of origin") to clients in State Y (hereafter designated as the "state of destination") faces significant and troublesome issues that need to be addressed in the informed consent procedures. For example, if the requirements in the state of origin compel the therapist to inform local authorities in a circumstance of duty to warn or protect, but no such obligation exists for the clients in the state of destination, the therapist may be forced to break confidentiality and risk legal action. Similarly, if privileged communication exists for therapists in the state of origin but not in the state of destination, which legally governs the protection of confidential information when the delivery system is technological? More specific discussion of these and related concerns will be examined in Chapter 6 of our text. As we proceed through this chapter, however, another significant foundational principle and tradition affecting therapy relationships must be examined: informed consent.

INFORMED CONSENT

Basic to ethical psychotherapeutic practice is the assurance that clients are adequately informed of their rights and responsibilities. For most clients, the therapeutic setting is new. They present themselves for assistance and unquestioningly accept what the therapist says or does. Little thought is given to the possible discomfort to be endured as well as to the considerable effort necessary to gain therapeutic benefits. Clients need to know what will be expected of them, what they may expect from the therapist and therapy, and generally what their rights as clients are. "This information should be given to clients in a package that includes an acknowledgment sheet that can be signed and returned to you" (Kaplan & Culkin, 1995, p. 335). It is ethically incumbent on therapists to inform and educate clients. Only when clients understand and act on their rights and responsibilities can therapists facilitate positive movement within the therapeutic process. One should always remember the adage that "participation is not consent" regarding psychotherapy services. Additionally, special circumstances and factors affect informed consent, including multicultural sensitivity and clarity (Palmer & Kaufman, 2003) as well as clinical supervision (Cobia & Boes, 2000; McCarthy & Sugden, 1995).

Informed consent actually reflects on the intentionality of the therapist. To begin, the issue of consent is significant for clients as well as therapists, in that it is a process of structure about mutual expectations in the therapy process. Further, to the extent that clients have the sense of being fully informed about the nature of the relationship, trust that the therapy process will be respectful, open, and deliberate often can be established. From a practical vantage, informed consent addresses issues related to financial obligations, scheduling, documentation and records, and similar administrative concerns in the therapy relationship. Additionally, for clients who may be engaged in therapy through a sense of obligation, coercion, or absolution, the choice aspect of informed consent can be empowering or clarifying. Consistent with the objectives of HIPAA legislation, informed consent establishes an expectation that clients or consumers will be notified of all actions related to disclosures of confidential information concerning their therapy.

As we noted in Chapter 1, the acculturation and worldview of clients has a significant effect on the therapy relationship. In terms of informed consent, varying expectations may exist among clients, such as a prescriptive model of instruction, a consumerism perspective on receiving services whenever a need arises (e.g., unscheduled drop-in visits), or simply an opportunity for airing complaints. As an example, an initiative to provide preventive medical services to women in a developing nation faced obstacles when the women's husbands refused to give consent for such services. Clearly, marriage and family therapists should be vigilant in addressing cultural differences, even to the point of clarifying those differences at the initial stage of therapy (Palmer & Kaufman, 2003).

The codes of ethics of all the major professional organizations whose members engage in the practice of psychotherapy require that clients be given adequate information to make informed choices about entering and continuing a therapeutic relationship. The responsibility of therapists to educate clients in this regard is referred to as the ethical issue of informed consent. Relevant standards from the codes of ethics of several professional organizations are listed in Table 3–11.

Hare-Mustin, Marecek, Kaplan, and Liss-Levenson (1979) outlined three types of information clients should have in order to make informed choices about entering into and continuing therapy: (a) the procedures, goals, and possible side effects of therapy; (b) the qualifications, policies, and practices of the therapist; and (c) other available sources of help. Most therapists who recognize the need to educate clients about their rights and responsibilities employ some form of written document to introduce and record the implied contract that consent for treatment represents. Two such types of written communications are the therapeutic contract and the professional disclosure statement.

TABLE 3–11 Ethical Considerations Regarding Informed Consent

American Association for Marriage and Family Therapy (2001)
"Marriage and family therapists respect the rights of clients to make decisions and help them to understand the consequences of these decisions. Therapists clearly advise the clients that they have the responsibility to make decisions regarding relationships such as cohabitation, marriage, divorce, separation, reconciliation, custody, and visitation."

American Counseling Association (2005)
"Counselors have an obligation to review in writing and verbally with clients the rights and responsibilities of both the counselor and the client. Informed consent is an ongoing part of the counseling process, and counselors appropriately document discussions of informed consent throughout the counseling relationship."

American Psychological Association (2002)
"When psychologists conduct research or provide assessment, therapy, counseling, or consulting services in person or via electronic transmission or other forms of communication, they obtain the informed consent of the individual or individuals using language that is reasonably understandable to that person or persons except when conducting such activities without consent is mandated by law or governmental regulation or as otherwise provided in this Ethics Code."

International Association of Marriage and Family Counselors (2005)
"Marriage and family therapists promote open, honest and direct relationships with consumers of professional services. Couple and family counselors inform clients about the goals of counseling, qualifications of the counselor(s), limits of confidentiality, potential risks and benefits associated with specific techniques, duration of treatment, costs of services, appropriate alternatives to marriage and family counseling, and reasonable expectations for outcomes."

National Association of Social Workers (1999)
"Social workers should provide services to clients only in the context of a professional relationship based, when appropriate, on valid informed consent."

Therapeutic Contracts

The purpose of a therapeutic contract is to clarify the therapeutic relationship. Providing information and obtaining agreement through the use of a contract defines therapy as a mutual endeavor to which therapists contribute their professional knowledge and skills and clients bring a commitment to work. In this respect, the use of a therapeutic contract (or a practice statement) represents Napier and Whitaker's (1978) dual battles for structure and initiative already discussed in Chapter 1. The development of a contract encourages all concerned parties to specify relevant goals, expectations, and boundaries (Hare-Mustin et al., 1979).

Most therapeutic contracts consider such issues as the specific therapeutic approach and procedures to be employed, the length and frequency of sessions, the duration of treatment, the cost and the method of payment, provisions for cancellation and renegotiation of the contract, the extent of each party's responsibilities, and the degree of confidentiality. Areas actually covered by any contract may vary according to a therapist's orientation and the inclination of the client. Haslam and Harris (2004) suggested that the variability of therapeutic contracts primarily lies in the detail and specificity of content. These authors also noted that many elements of a therapy contract may be peculiar to the practice setting (e.g., billing practices, differential costs for court appearances, records retention, supervisory arrangements, etc.). Most important, however, is the fact that concrete, identifiable ground rules are decided on in advance and endorsed with signatures before the hard work of therapy begins.

Everstine et al. (1980) outlined a sample document incorporating the basic elements of informed consent in contract form. An adapted version of this document is illustrated in Figure 3–2.

FIGURE 3–2   A Therapeutic Contract

Mary E. Spates, Ph.D.
Licensed Psychologist (Connecticut No. 472)
62 Broadway, Suite 401
Bridgeport, Connecticut 06602
203/268-7899

PART I: *Your Rights as a Client*

1. You have a right to ask questions about any procedures used during therapy; if you wish, I will explain my usual approach and methods to you.
2. You have the right to decide *not* to receive therapeutic assistance from me; if you wish, I will provide you with the names of other qualified professionals whose services you might prefer.
3. You have the right to end therapy at any time without any moral, legal, or financial obligations other than those already accrued.
4. You have a right to review your records in the files at any time.
5. One of your most important rights involves confidentiality: Within certain limits, information revealed by you during therapy will be kept strictly confidential and will not be revealed to any other person or agency without your written permission.
6. If you request it, any part of your record in the files can be released to any person or agency you designate. I will tell you, at the time, whether or not I think releasing the information in question to that person or agency might be harmful to you in any way.
7. You should also know that there are certain situations in which I am required *by law* to reveal information obtained during therapy to other persons or agencies *without your permission.* Also, I am not required to inform you of my actions in this regard. These situations are as follows: (a) if you threaten grave bodily harm or death to another person, I am required by law to inform the intended victim and appropriate law enforcement agencies. (b) If a court of law issues a legitimate subpoena, I am required by law to provide the information specifically described in the subpoena. (c) If you reveal information relative to child abuse and neglect, I am required by law to report this to the appropriate authority; and (d) if you are in therapy or being tested by order of a court of law, the results of the treatment or tests ordered must be revealed to the court.

PART II: *The Therapeutic Process*

One major benefit that may be gained from participating in therapy includes a better ability to handle or cope with marital, family, and other interpersonal relationships. Another possible benefit may be a

FIGURE 3–2 *Continued*

greater understanding of personal goals and values; this may lead to greater maturity and happiness as an individual. Other benefits relate to the probable outcomes resulting from resolving specific concerns brought to therapy.

In working to achieve these potential benefits, however, therapy will require that firm efforts be made to change and may involve the experiencing of significant discomfort. Remembering and therapeutically resolving unpleasant events can arouse intense feelings of fear, anger, depression, frustration, and the like. Seeking to resolve these issues between family members, marital partners, and other persons can similarly lead to discomfort, as well as relationship changes that may not be originally intended.

PART III: *Fees and Length of Therapy*

1. I agree to enter into therapy with Mary E. Spates, Ph.D. for _____ one-hour sessions during the next _____ weeks.
2. I agree to pay _____ for each completed one-hour session. Payment may be made by me or by a third party when billed.
3. I understand that I can leave therapy at any time and that I have no moral, legal, or financial obligation to complete the maximum number of sessions listed in this contract; I am contracting only to pay for completed therapy sessions.

Client(s): _____

_____

_____

Therapist: _____ *Date:* _____

Note. From "Privacy and Confidentiality in Psychotherapy" by L. Everstine, D. S. Everstine, G. M. Heymann, R. H. True, D. H. Frey, G. H. Johnson, and R. H. Seiden, 1980, *American Psychologist, 35,* pp. 828–840. Copyright 1980 by the American Psychological Association. Adapted by permission of the publisher and authors.

Hare-Mustin et al. (1979) advocated contracts as an integral part of therapy. However, these authors cautioned that therapists should first resolve certain questions before beginning this practice:

- How much should the contract specify?
- What should be done if the therapist has personal or moral concerns about clients' goals?
- What should be done with clients who are unable to be specific about their goals?
- How should therapists respond to clients who refuse to agree to a contract?

It is impossible to specify all that might occur during the course of therapy. Most therapists feel that providing clients with an understanding of the broad outlines is sufficient. They seek to offer only the assurance of a degree of predictability about potential processes and procedures. However, therapists should anticipate obstacles or misunderstandings in the therapy or in aspects of the therapy relationship that should be addressed in their informed consent. For example, a therapist faced with an unpaid balance for services with a former client may assume the use of a collection agency would be a fair and common remedy for any consumer who has failed to meet a financial obligation. In this respect, clients are not simply any consumer because of the confidential nature of the therapy relationship. Similarly, actions such as telephone or e-mail contact between sessions, missed appointments, court appearances, bartering, supervision of therapy, and other aspects of therapy are not uncommon considerations for redress in informed consent. Wear (1999) noted that many people view the sharing of contractual information in informed consent as a matter of simply completing a task with broad brushstrokes. He further indicated that many clients are actually confused but embarrassed to clarify misunderstandings, often adding further distress in initiating their services. Hare-Mustin et al. (1979) also posited that procedures at odds with clients' values should be specified. Clients should be clearly apprised if any aversive techniques or physical contact is planned or if the use of medication is expected. Therapists who follow up on clients should secure their permission in the contract to do so, even if this follow-up might bias future responses.

Practices such as sexual relations with clients are unethical and remain so even if agreed to by clients. Some have argued that treatments objected to by many therapists, such as primal scream or "tickle" therapy, should be permitted if clients freely agree to their use with full knowledge of potential risks and benefits. It must be remembered, however, that there is initial inequity in the bargaining power between clients and therapists in that many clients' vulnerability opens them to manipulation; thus, such contracts are likely unconscionable (Schwitzgebel, 1975, 1976). The essential component of informed consent should guide in all elements of formal disclosure to clients; that is, clients are entitled to adequate information to make a choice. To the extent that this component is threatened, the capacity to consent is compromised, often to the detriment of client welfare.

Clients occasionally present goals that are neither appropriate nor desirable but are instead detrimental to the best interests of the clients themselves or others. Halleck (1976) proposed that "therapists try to change behaviors they believe should be changed and be reluctant to change behaviors they view as understandable or socially acceptable" (p. 167). He cited the case example of a woman who wanted to eliminate feelings of possessiveness and jealousy, yet whose current life circumstances suggested that these feelings were entirely appropriate and that what she lacked was the ability to better cope with being oppressed.

When clients' goals are at odds with therapists' personal or professional values, the potential consequences of working toward goals sought by clients should be examined. If therapists feel that they cannot agree with clients' expressed goals, they should not work with those clients. For example, a couple's goal of establishing an open marriage or pursuing a form of power inequity may be personally and professionally incompatible with the values of the therapist. Still, Palmer and Kaufman (2003) pointed out that many differences are cultural in origin and may be examined successfully with deliberate attention and discussion. Whether based on personal preferences, clinical experience, or research findings, practitioners who find themselves in a situation that requires them to provide services when a fundamental disagreement exists in client goals and therapist values actually may reflect a circumstance of non-negotiable values. Recall that in our discussion about the principle of valuing and values negotiation from Chapter 1, we noted that circumstances may simply arise in which an impasse does not allow for meaningful compromise. Referral to another therapist or source of assistance should then be offered (Hare-Mustin et al., 1979).

Therapists must negotiate with clients who are unable to be specific about their goals. These clients challenge therapists to help them translate vague complaints into concrete concerns. For such clients, an initial therapeutic goal might be to explore what prevents them from being specific about their desires with more definitive behavioral goal setting to follow. Outside-session tasks such as keeping records and diaries can encourage specificity. Time limits on therapy may also provide an incentive to set goals. Therapists who allow clients to stay in therapy without specific goals only increase the ambiguity of treatment efforts and deprive clients of the benefits inherent in pursuing a sought objective. Additionally, such an approach may not serve the principle of client welfare. Often, clients having a brief interruption in such a pattern of therapy may return with new clarity and focus. Again, Napier and Whitaker's (1978) observations about the Battle for Initiative become cogent concerns at this point.

For some clients, negotiation and establishment of a therapeutic contract may be threatening. Certain clients may reject a contract because they suspiciously see it as benefiting only the therapist. For these clients, considerable orientation to the idea may be necessary. This orientation, however, must be presented in a manner that retains clients' right to refuse (Hare-Mustin et al., 1979). C. E. Rosen (1977), using a sample of more than 900 clients in a study investigating reasons why clients relinquish their rights, found that when clients were not informed of their right to refuse, all signed away their rights to privacy. By contrast, when informed that such an option existed, only 41% signed. This finding is not to say that clients will feel a sense of empowerment or rebellion by refusing. Rather, when faced with threatening and uncertain arrangements at the outset of therapy, clients may want to minimize their risks. Again, such perceived risks may have some, if not most, of their origins in cultural differences (Palmer & Kaufman, 2003).

In this discussion of therapy contracts as one approach to securing informed consent from clients, we have examined a variety of elements that may be considered for the language of such documents. A second approach to informed consent is the use of a professional disclosure statement.

Professional Disclosure Statements

A number of authors have advocated a written professional disclosure statement as a means of meeting informed consent provisions of codes of ethics (Gill, 1982; S. J. Gross, 1977; J. L. Swanson, 1979; Winborn, 1977). Professional disclosure statements take many forms, but essentially they entail a process of introducing prospective clients to a therapist's qualifications, the nature of the therapeutic process, and administrative procedures relating to time and money. An adaptation of Winborn's (1977) professional disclosure statement illustrated in Figure 3–3 provides a model.

Besides contributing to the ethical objective of gaining clients' informed consent, a professional disclosure statement also yields developmental benefits for practitioners. Creating such a statement clarifies aspects of one's professional values related to practices and identity. To accomplish such an outcome, personal beliefs, values, strengths and weaknesses, and objectives pertaining to therapeutic relationships must be examined. By concisely stating who they are and what they are trained to do, therapists

FIGURE 3–3 A Professional Disclosure Statement

David Morgan, M.S.
Licensed Marriage and Family Therapist (Florida No. 475)
Child Guidance Clinic
181 Atlantic Avenue
Orlando, Florida 33310
904/342-7658

Some Things You Should Know About Your Therapist and Therapy

Since therapy is conducted in a number of different ways, depending on the therapist and his or her orientation, this description has been prepared to inform you about my qualifications, how I view the therapeutic process, and what you can expect from me as your therapist.

My Qualifications. I received my graduate degree from Florida State University with a major in Marriage and Family Therapy. I have been employed as a therapist for more than 8 years, the past 6 years here with the Child Guidance Clinic. I am a licensed Marriage and Family Therapist in Florida. I am also a Clinical Member and Approved Supervisor in the American Association for Marriage and Family Therapy. I have written over 30 articles for professional journals and coauthored 2 books relating to marriage and family therapy.

The majority of my experience has been working with couples and families. While I do see individuals alone, especially children, I attempt to involve the entire family where appropriate and when possible. I have worked with individuals, couples, and families experiencing a wide range of problems. My training and experience provide me with the ability to assist with concerns that range from children's poor school achievement to marital problems and family hostility, as well as social skills training and alleviating fears, anxiety, and depression.

I am not a physician and cannot prescribe or provide any medication, nor perform any medical procedures. If medical treatment is indicated, I can recommend a physician and in certain situations, I have worked in concert with and under the supervision of a psychiatrist.

The Therapeutic Process. Marriage and family therapy is a learning process that seeks for you and your marital partner, parents, and/or other family members or significant persons to better understand yourself and others and the interactions that occur between and among you. Additional goals include achieving better functioning as a couple and/or family so that healthy interactions are established and greater satisfaction is attained. Further, by gaining a more harmonious relationship with significant persons around you, individual concerns can be more effectively and efficiently dealt with.

There are several steps in the therapeutic process. First, we will need to spend some time exploring the problems that have brought you to therapy. I need to get to know you, how you view yourself, and how you and significant persons in your life interact. You will likely come to understand your situation better as we proceed in this manner. Obviously, we need to discuss things openly and honestly. My responsibility at this point in the therapeutic process is to listen, to assist you to communicate with me and others who may take part in the therapy, and to provide an environment of trust so that all present can interact freely and speak what is on their mind.

All of our sessions will, of course, be confidential to persons outside of the therapy. Therapy will likely involve the participation of family members and/or other significant persons. I do not guarantee confidentiality among participants in the therapy, although I would use my professional discretion in disclosing communications related to me. My professional code of ethics prevents me from discussing what is said during sessions with anyone other than participants in the therapy or releasing any records without your/their permission. The only exceptions to this are if someone is in danger of being harmed or if the law explicitly states that confidentiality provisions do not apply.

FIGURE 3–3 *Continued*

> After we have explored and developed sufficient background to proceed, we will decide upon specific goals and objectives. We will then develop a treatment plan outlining how these goals will be achieved. Such a plan will likely require strong efforts, and feelings of discomfort inherent in change will be experienced. We will regularly evaluate progress in terms of whether the plan is effective in attaining the desired objectives, comparing progress with the situation when therapy began. Treatment efforts will conclude when the sought-after goals are sufficiently achieved. This will be determined through mutual agreement among the participants, including myself as therapist.
>
> *Fees and Length of Therapy.* Therapy sessions are normally for one hour. Depending upon the nature of the presenting problems, sessions are held one or two times per week. It is difficult to initially predict how many sessions will be needed. I will be better able to discuss the probably number of sessions after we have explored and gained some background into the situation—usually after two or three sessions. I will verbally discuss fees with you as the Child Guidance Clinic operates on a *sliding scale* fee structure, meaning the cost of sessions varies according to the clients' yearly income.
>
> *Please Ask Questions.* You may have questions about me, my qualifications, or anything not addressed in the previous paragraphs. *It is your right* to have a complete explanation for any of your questions at any time. Please exercise this right.

define a set of competencies and an approach identifying them as unique providers of beneficial human services. As Gill (1982) put it:

> Are we shrinks, faith healers, or gurus whose mystical understandings of the universe magically transform problems into solutions? Or, are we trained specialists who utilize a set of skills and a body of knowledge to help people cope with normal life problems? If we are the latter, we should be able to describe who we are and what we do. (p. 444)

Gill (1982) suggested that putting into writing one's approach to the therapeutic process is a particularly demanding experience. As a way of facilitating therapists' preparation of this part of the professional disclosure statement, Gill has synthesized a set of questions from the recommendations of a number of professional disclosure advocates (S. J. Gross, 1977; J. L. Swanson, 1979; Witmer, 1978):

- What do you believe is the purpose of psychotherapy?
- What do you believe helps persons lead more satisfying lives?
- What should clients expect as a result of engaging in therapy efforts?
- What is your responsibility during therapy?
- What are the responsibilities your clients can be expected to assume during therapy?
- What is your primary therapeutic approach, and what are the general intervention strategies that emanate from that approach?
- What types of presenting problems have you been most effective in assisting clients with in the past?
- Under what circumstances might clients be offered referral to another source of assistance?
- How do you handle the confidential nature of the therapeutic relationship?

The process of assuring informed consent, whether through a therapeutic contract or a practice statement, accomplishes two significant tasks at the outset of a marriage and family therapy relationship. Clients are oriented to the process of therapy, including realistic expectations of the therapist, the necessity of intentional effort by the client, and the possible impact of the multilayered ecology affecting therapy. The second task involves the real work of a therapist: integrating personal, professional, and institutional acculturation into a meaningful holistic form that is understandable to clients and informative in therapy. Such a task should not be undertaken casually or capriciously.

Haslam and Harris (2004) coined the phrase "informed consent documents" or ICDs (p. 359) as a catchall phrase regarding both disclosure statements and therapy contracts. Braaten, Otto, and Handelsman (1993) inquired among groups of both former clients and new clients concerning the most important and least important issues addressed in informed consent. They found that personal characteristics about therapists were most important, whereas appointments, treatment alternatives, and confidentiality information were least important for both groups. Later, Braaten and Handelsman (1997) investigated congruence between participants who were currently in therapy, those who had been in therapy, and those with no therapy experiences. Their findings indicated the issues of congruence in terms of importance concerned confidentiality, inappropriate techniques, and risks of alternative treatments. In a qualitative study examining an array of ICDs, Haslam and Harris (2004) identified seven conceptual categories and definitions as well as two stylistic or salient observations judged as consistently critical for ICDs. A summary of these findings is noted in Figure 3–4.

From these results, they noted that great consistency existed among ICDs in terms of basic areas needing discussion with clients. Additionally, they indicated that "business or personal tone" (p. 372) was a critical issue in terms of style. By contrast, these authors determined that the greatest variance among documents concerned the nature of detail regarding clinical orientation, training, personal features, and approach to the consent process, noting such variance is reflective of creativity and individuality that makes ICDs less rigid and mechanical. Thus, procedures to assure informed consent seem to have an array of commonalities but still leave room for individual style differences.

Along with informed consent, a variety of other foundational ethical considerations exist for therapists. As a final topic of discussion in this chapter, we examine the complexity of therapeutic considerations in serving multiple clients, a circumstance quite common to practicing marriage and family therapists.

MULTIPLE CLIENT CONSIDERATIONS

Indoctrination to North American culture promotes a highly individualistic viewpoint; each person's rights take precedence. Consequently, multiple clients, such as those in marriage and family therapy, can create dilemmas for therapists. In some situations, an intervention that serves one member's best interest may be countertherapeutic to another. Indeed, the very reason why couples and families seek out professional assistance is that they have at least differing experiences and narratives (Zimmerman & Dickerson, 1996), if not conflicting goals and interests (Margolin, 1982). Consider the following illustration:

Two parents come to family therapy with their 17-year-old son. They seek to have their son acquiesce more readily to their directives, invoking a rather rigid "honor

FIGURE 3–4 Findings on Informed Consent

Conceptual Categories and Definitions

1. *Title of Documents*: What the therapist actually called their documents
2. *Person-of-the-Therapist Information*: Items that therapists disclosed about themselves that were personal in nature. This section was divided into two categories:
   a. *Personal Professional Information*: Therapist's education, credentials, licensure, experience, services offered, and areas of specialty.
   b. *Theory or Philosophy of Therapy*: Items that described the therapist's theoretical orientation and/or religious background (including explaining a systemic approach to practice).
3. *The Process or Nature of Therapy*: Items related to the therapist's conceptualization about the "nuts and bolts" of the therapy process, such as information that orients the client to the treatment process and the structure of therapy.
4. *Confidentiality*: Two main subcategories:
   a. *Standard exemptions* in which confidentiality *must* be compromised (i.e., suicide, homicide, child abuse, etc.);
   b. *Other situations* in which it *may* be compromised (i.e., insurance and court interactions, outside consultations).
5. *Issues Related to Insurance*: Items specifically related to dealing with insurance companies, such as the division of responsibility for setting up reimbursement or how to obtain preauthorization
6. *Fee Structure*: Items related to the financial relationship with the client, such as charges for specific services, payment expectations, policies on unpaid debts, etc.
7. *Office Information/Emergency Procedures*: Items related to hours of operation, after-hours access to therapist, and emergency procedures.

Stylistic or Salient Observations

1. *Tone of Document*:
   a. Formal and official in tone ("The client will . . .") vs. more personal in tone ("Dear client").
   b. The use of first person and third person when referring to the client and/or therapist.
2. *Length of Document*: How long and detailed the document was and impact on client perceptions of the therapist or the services he/she renders.

Note. From "Informed Consent Documents of Marriage and Family Therapists in Private Practice: A Qualitative Analysis" by D. R. Haslam and S. M. Harris, 2004, *American Journal of Family Therapy, 32*(4), 359–374. Copyright 2004 by Taylor & Francis, Inc. Reprinted by permission.

thy father and mother" dictum. The son's actions as described during the therapy are not destructive, but he has been actively disobedient.

Achieving the parents' goal of having their son respond more readily to their commands might ease the parents' tension as well as perhaps provide secondary benefits for their marriage. The son, however, is at a developmental life stage at which he is attempting to launch himself from the family. Achieving the parents' goal would not be necessarily advantageous to the son's overall development. From a long-term vantage point, some parents may worry that disobedience will escalate into impulsivity or criminality. Perhaps this concern is an overreaction for the child; perhaps this concern is prophetic. In either case, for circumstances reflecting such escalation, the considerations of the therapist and family become complicated by the multilayered and systemic framework affecting the therapy relationship, such as legal system, school system, or other systems. The therapeutic relationship may reflect valuing patience and tolerance toward the son, but the objectives of the larger institutions may value conformity, imposed or otherwise. Obviously, the ethical principles of *autonomy, beneficence,* and *justice* can converge to create sizable difficulties when serving multiple clients.

Marriage and family therapists must strive to see that the status of one partner or family member does not improve at the expense of the other partner or another family member. This objective is not entirely unique to marriage and family therapy (Margolin, 1982). Persons in individual therapy can also make changes that cause discomfort to, or conflict with, the desires of significant others. Individually oriented therapists are always wise to encourage clients to explore the potential consequences of their actions on those around them (Wilcoxon, 1986). What sets marriage and family therapists apart, however, is their commitment to promote the welfare of each family member (Kaslow, 1986). Through direct involvement with all members, marriage and family therapists are able to assess how each member's actions affect the others. Thus, marriage and family therapists take on more responsibility for exercising judgment about the welfare of more than one individual. Equally significant in such judgments, however, is the effect of institutional values that may require the therapist to "pathologize" an individual member in order to permit services (e.g., in a managed care system, etc.). In such situations, the ethical principle of *justice* must be considered by the therapist.

The marriage and family therapist can respond to this dilemma of conflicting interests by identifying the marital or family system, rather than a single individual, as the "client." The various ethical codes we have been considering throughout this chapter address the issues of identity, rights, and service to multiple clients in Table 3–12. Such a stance should be a natural outgrowth of the therapist's theoretical position and professional values. The therapist who is an advocate of the system avoids becoming an agent of any one marital partner or family member. Working within a framework that conceptualizes change as affecting and being affected by all family members, marriage and family therapists define problems and consider plans for change in the context of the entire family. Consider the following situation:

> A couple presents themselves for therapy stating opposite goals. She wants divorce counseling; he is seeking to save or improve the marriage.

The system advocate works to define the couple's problem as a relationship concern, seeking to help them establish and pursue relationship goals. Whether marriage enhancement or divorce is the ultimate result, reorganizing their relationship interactions so that they can problem solve more effectively can only be in the best interests of both.

Functioning as a system advocate suggests a knowledge that often goes beyond the specific and sometimes self-centered goals of the individual members (Margolin, 1982). Functioning as a system advocate occasionally even has the paradoxical effect of actually creating greater variance between the aims of the therapist and those of marital partners or family members. Most couples and family members enter treatment wanting to change their partner or a specific family member's behavior or attitude. "If only he/she/they would change" is likely the most frequent complaint communicated to therapists. The system advocate's problem definition and goal orientation are at odds with those of some couples and families and must be reconciled when they are unacceptable.

TABLE 3–12 Ethical Considerations Regarding Multiple Clients	*American Association for Marriage and Family Therapy (2001)* "In the context of couple, family, or group treatment, the therapist may not reveal any individual's confidences to others in the client unit without the prior written permission of that individual." *American Counseling Association (2005)* "In couples and family counseling, counselors clearly define who is considered 'the client' and discuss expectations and limitations of confidentiality." *American Psychological Association (2002)* "When psychologists agree to provide services to several persons who have a relationship (such as spouses, significant others, or parents and children), they take reasonable steps to clarify at the outset (1) which of the individuals are clients/patients and (2) the relationship the psychologist will have with each person." *International Association of Marriage and Family Counselors (2005)* "Marriage and family counselors have an obligation to determine and inform counseling participants who is identified as the primary client. The marriage and family counselor should make clear when there are obligations to an individual, a couple, a family, a third party, or an institution." *National Association of Social Workers (1999)* "When social workers provide services to two or more people who have a relationship with each other (for example, couples, family members), social workers should clarify with all parties which individuals will be considered clients and the nature of social workers' professional obligations to the varous individuals who are receiving services."

For example, therapists preferring a postmodern perspective may address such schisms as differing realities rather than competition (Freeman & Combs, 1996). Marriage and family therapists should clearly communicate the nature of their commitment as system advocate. Informed of the therapist's stance as advocate of the system, most marital partners and family members generally understand and accept this position, although during therapy they may at times seek to solicit the therapist as a personal ally (Margolin, 1982). Should such attempts prove successful for one member of the family, the position of the therapist can empower other members of the system to create an imbalance and a threat to ethical treatment reflective of *justice*.

Although the stance of system advocate works well in the majority of instances, it does not eliminate the problems of conflicting interests. In certain circumstances, such as care for a victim in an abusive intimate relationship, the immediate course of action recommended calls for the overt primacy of individual needs. The system is not set aside, but it is given an apparent secondary focus, as it is when the welfare of an individual member is in jeopardy. It still is, of course, in the best interests of all members of the system to prioritize the welfare of a member in jeopardy. In addition to clinical considerations, there are also laws that require certain actions to be taken when the welfare of an individual is in danger. For example, in a case of child neglect or abuse, child abuse reporting laws require therapists to inform authorities if they learn that a child is suffering from neglect or being abused, regardless of the negative consequences likely to be incurred for future family treatment efforts.

Margolin (1982) summarized the complex responsibilities of therapists seeking to promote optimal client welfare from a system advocate's position:

> Attempting to balance one's therapeutic responsibilities toward individual family members and toward the family as a whole involves intricate judgments. Since neither of these responsibilities cancels out the importance of the other, the family therapist cannot afford blind pursuit of either extreme, that is, always doing what is in each individual's best interest or always maintaining the stance as family advocate. (p. 790)

Framo (1981) offered the commonsense, but perhaps understated, conclusion that "part of the skill of the therapist resides in finding the appropriate balance between the conflict of goals and expectations of all family members as well as those of the therapist" (p. 143). Of particular significance in such circumstances is the interaction between personal values and professional values in the development and maturation of therapists. Novice therapists are often confronted with the intuitive sense of failing to demonstrate *beneficence* in the face of conflicting goals among family members. In such situations, their personal values may drive an impulse toward rapid action to rescue or minimize discomfort on the part of clients. However, failure to tolerate periods of painful growth can actually represent an agenda of value and pace that reflects his or her preferences rather than affirming the value of believing in the ability of the system to emerge with new organization. In some cases, such actions may be assistive, though for some systems, the imposition of a pace of change or outcome may be viewed as another form of cultural oppression that is institutionalized through the therapy relationship. Additionally, marriage and family therapists encountering conflicting goals from members of family systems should also remember that some systems are organized to sustain conflict and inefficiency.

SUMMARY

From their professional socialization and development, therapists must be well versed in the theory and procedures of the therapeutic approaches they advocate. They must also be able to recognize and respond to ethical issues directly affecting the delivery of services and public acceptance of those services. One way of doing so is to have a clear understanding of ethical decision making. Such an understanding allows therapists to critically evaluate and interpret their professional code of ethics. Furthermore, it guides a therapist in expressing her or his personal values as a human being as well as a professional by allowing the analysis of feelings as appropriate or inappropriate bases for ethical behavior. Certainly the complex interactivity of personal, professional, and institutional values of the therapist will impact those decisions.

This chapter has emphasized the importance of principle ethics and virtue ethics, not as a means of procuring definitive guidelines for professional conduct, but rather as a way of becoming aware of options for ethical decision making. Promoting ethical practice frequently involves ambiguity, not simple choices between right and wrong or good and bad. Optimal outcomes more often than not contain elements of both extremes. The challenge is not only to identify an ethical position to take but also to consciously apply that position.

We presented and discussed the foundational ethical principles of *beneficence, nonmaleficence, justice, autonomy,* and *fidelity* that serve as guides to both principle and virtue ethics for psychotherapists. Additionally, we emphasized diversity, values, conflicting directives, client welfare, confidentiality, informed consent, and multiple client considerations as significant ethical concerns in any form of psychotherapy. These and related ethical considerations require special and deliberate attention, and they will be examined further in later chapters. Chapter 5 offers an illustrative discussion of applied principles, decision making, and related considerations using the example of intimate partner violence. Chapter 6 features a discussion of other challenging contemporary issues for consideration by today's marriage and family therapists. Chapter 7 provides an opportunity to gain greater expertise by offering case examples and critiques from the AAMFT Code of Ethics (American Association for Marriage and Family Therapy, 2001).

Now that we have examined the foundational and traditional principles of ethical propriety common to all psychotherapy practices in this chapter, we will build on this discussion in Chapter 4, which offers a view of these and other ethical considerations that are particularly unique to the practice of marriage and family therapy.

Unique Ethical Considerations in Marriage and Family Therapy

As we continue our examination of ethical issues in marriage and family therapy, let us review our earlier discussions from the text. Chapter 1 addressed the elements and processes of acculturation and identity development with particular attention devoted to the impact of values in the therapy relationship. Chapter 2 offered a discussion of the systemic epistemology, including criticisms related to gender and cultural stereotypes, as well as the multilayered ecological framework for marriage and family therapy. In particular, this chapter emphasized the convergence and divergence of personal, professional, and institutional layers of values.

Chapter 3 featured a discussion of values, morals, and traditions related to decision making in ethical dilemmas in therapy. This chapter also included information about principle ethics and virtue ethics and highlighted foundational ethical principles and their application in the most basic ethical concerns in psychotherapy (e.g., client welfare, confidentiality, informed consent, multiple clients, etc.). Chapter 4 continues this discussion with particular emphasis on the unique elements of marriage and family therapy when considering ethical quandaries.

SYSTEMIC AND INTERACTIVE: VIEWS ON COMPLEXITY

The discussion of systemic epistemology in Chapter 2 offered a beginning point for this chapter. Almost any historical review of marriage and family therapy will emphasize early conceptual adoption of a systemic perspective in reaction to traditional linear models of development, pathology, and change (Gladding, 2002). This revolutionary (and evolutionary) viewpoint developed into explanations and models of causation and intervention, bolstered by lines of empirical inquiry and organizational affiliation (more discussion on this evolution is offered in Chapter 11).

Readers will recall the examination of acculturation and identity development in Chapter 1. In a very real way, these processes occurred for the field of marriage and family therapy in the early years of its development. Many practitioners found resolution for the dissonance between their personal and professional values, which emphasized the importance of familial interactions, and traditional professional and institutional values that emphasized individual responsibility and change. Specialized language and terminology peculiar to the field was promulgated. Early advocates for the novelty of marriage and family therapy were sometimes viewed as renegades, and some even experienced professional oppression by traditionalists. Disagreements across applied lines of psychotherapy prompted entrenchment of differences and the emergence of something like cultural enclaves, which led some practitioners to separate and then reaffiliate with others who shared their perspective and values (Baruth & Manning, 2003).

M. P. Nichols and Schwartz (2004) called this period "the golden age" of family therapy (p. 41), when icons became spokespersons for the emergence of a new field, and systemic perspective was at its foundation. As we saw in Chapter 2, however, the systemic epistemology has drawn criticism from various quarters. Coincidental with these criticisms has been the evolution of marriage and family therapies to include postmodern epistemologies and viewpoints. These and other developments reveal that systemic epistemology is a conceptual schema with tremendous practical value in application. It is not, however, a law of science such as gravity or thermodynamics.

Our text is not meant to focus on discussions of conceptual differences in models of marriage and family therapy; however, readers are reminded that marriage and family therapy is not simply a treatment approach. It is a way of understanding human behavior and conceptualizing problems—how symptoms develop and how they are resolved. Marriage and family therapy has traditionally viewed the transactions between individuals rather than each individual's characteristics as the primary therapeutic focus (Sluzki, 1978). Even when attention focuses on a single person, that person's actions are analyzed in terms of how they affect and shape the actions of other members of the relationship system, as well as how other members' actions reciprocally affect and shape the individual's original actions. In this respect, the use of the term *systemic* in Chapters 4, 5, 6, and 7 is intended to emphasize the *complex* and *interactive* nature of marriage and family therapy, rather than to advance an epistemology that would suggest individuals are unaccountable for their actions or that victims of violence in intimate partner relationships seek to sustain their pain, with reference to the discussion in Chapter 5.

Marriage and family therapy contrasts with an individually oriented view of psychological functioning in adopting a systemic framework that emphasizes interdependence between and among persons, information exchange, and circular feedback mechanisms (Gladding, 2002). Individuals' symptomatic behaviors are viewed within an interpersonal context in which they currently function. Further, these symptoms are seen as serving a regulating, stabilizing, and communicating function in that context (Feldman, 1990; O'Shea & Jessee, 1982). When observing partners' and family members' interactions, marriage and family therapists consider effects rather than intentions. The effects *of* behaviors *on* behaviors and the way interpersonal sequences are organized become the primary focus of observation, not the personal motivation of those parties (Sluzki, 1978).

Marriage and family therapists do not deny the existence of individual motivation or intention. Rather, the inferences that can be drawn from assertions about persons' intentions or inner motivations simply are of secondary importance for purposes of diagnosis and treatment. The use of a systemic perspective for understanding and modifying the way couples and families interact requires therapists to focus on certain clinical considerations at the expense of others. The therapist must guide clients to selectively attend to and act on relevant variables, while giving lesser regard to other variables.

The selective clinical attention and actions called for in adopting a systemic perspective cause therapists to confront long-standing social, cultural, and even religious assumptions. From a sociocultural vantage, marriage and family therapists are often at odds with North American ideology and legal tradition, which emphasize individual self-sufficiency, value individual responsibility and accountability, and sanction individual rights over group preferences. From a religious vantage, Judeo-Christian tradition incorporates strong limits for the behavior of couples and families as well as profound assumptions about how marital and family organizations should proceed. Notable examples include "Honor thy father and thy mother" and "Thou shalt not commit adultery." Even from the postmodern vantage of individual construction of personal reality, the complexity of involving multiple internal and external points of reference in marriage and family therapy requires one to conceptualize multidimensionally.

When a therapist proposes to see the couple or family unit as the focus for therapeutic efforts, she or he must consider the many deep-seated beliefs they may confront as well as the professional ethics involved in doing so. These confrontations create conflicts that are concrete reflections of the clash among the practice of marriage and family therapy, individually oriented theories of psychological disturbance and treatment, and value traditions (social, cultural, or religious) that espouse individualism or prescribe marital and family mores. Some major ethical dilemmas stemming from a therapeutic focus on the couple or family unit as the "client" include issues of problem definition, participation in therapy, the role of the therapist as a direct and active change agent, the use of paradoxical procedures, agency triangulation, power inequities, and diverse or nontraditional families. However, before discussing these specific examples, we offer a view of two foundational principles of ethical propriety.

FOUNDATIONAL ETHICAL PRINCIPLES IN MARRIAGE AND FAMILY THERAPY

In Chapter 3, we introduced several ethical principles and foundational ethical considerations for mental health practice, regardless of the theoretical orientation, professional identity, or practice setting of the practitioner. However, when considered within the interactivity of marriage and family therapy, such principles often take on even greater complexity. In this regard, we offer a discussion of two such examples: confidentiality and informed consent.

Confidentiality in Marriage and Family Therapy

All therapists must inform clients in individual therapy of the limits of confidentiality. Marriage and family therapists have the same responsibility. Moreover, they have an additional obligation toward marital partners or other family members: They must decide what confidentiality means for the couple or family group and how it will be maintained. Generally speaking, issues of confidentiality unique to marriage and family therapy are in two areas: (a) secrets, and (b) changes from systemic to individual formats.

Karpel (1980) noted that families tend to have three types of secrets: (a) shared family secrets known to and kept by all members, (b) internal family secrets known to and kept by some family members, and (c) individual secrets known to and kept by individual members. Vangelisti (1994) observed that family secrets fell into different types of categories: (a) taboo topics, (b) rule violations, and (c) conventional secrets. *Taboo topics* refer to actions that, if known socially or to uninformed family members, could embarrass or liable the perpetrator (e.g., extramarital affairs, illegalities, addiction, etc.). *Rule violations* concern breaking accepted norms of conduct related to behavior (e.g., sexual activity, drinking, etc.). *Conventional secrets* include conversational topics (e.g., academic success, health, conflicts, religion, etc.) that may be more reflective of social discretion and privacy. When working with couples and families, one will likely encounter some form of secret. Farber and Hall (2003) also suggested that disclosures to therapists may even relate to elements such as cultural and gender distinction.

Margolin (1982) identified two standard but opposing positions on maintaining confidentiality with regard to secrets that may be taken by therapists working with couples and families. One position calls for therapists to treat each partner or family member's confidences as though that person were an individual client. Information obtained during a private session, in a telephone call, or from written material is not divulged to a spouse or fellow family member. Therapists adhering to this position often arrange for sessions with individual family members to actively encourage the sharing of "secrets" to better understand what is occurring within the relationship system. The therapist then works toward a goal of enabling that individual to disclose therapeutically relevant information in the couple or family session. However, should the individual client elect not to do so, the therapist still upholds the individual's confidentiality.

An alternate position adopted by marriage and family therapists is that of nonsecrecy. The therapist discourages the sharing of information that might lead to, or maintain, an alliance between the therapist and one family member or between individual family members. Therapists subscribing to this approach generally avoid receiving individual confidences by conducting only conjoint or family sessions. However, this safeguard can prove insufficient. Unless clients are informed of a nonsecrecy policy when they initiate therapy and are able to adequately consider its consequences, many will seek to influence the therapist using secrets.

Some therapists select an intermediate position between these two options. These therapists inform clients that information shared in individual sessions, over the phone, through written messages, or by similar means may be divulged as the therapist determines to be in accordance with the greatest benefit for the couple or family. They simply reserve the right to use their professional judgment about whether or not to maintain individual confidences (Corey et al., 2003). This intermediate approach creates greater responsibility for therapists who select it. Identifying information as ultimately helpful or hurtful places an increased burden on therapists' clinical abilities. Such is the nature of attempting to promote *beneficence* in therapy services. The ethical principles of *autonomy* and *fidelity* may also come into play when making such decisions. Vangelisti, Caughlin, & Timmerman (2001) noted that the criteria for revealing family secrets are not grounded in a set of clear rules. They further observed that, unfortunately, learning after the fact that such a decision to disclose was unwise typically cannot be offset with even the best intentions. The consequences of maintaining or divulging information in an untimely or what might be perceived as an inappropriate manner can cause an abrupt, premature termination of therapy as well as a souring toward future psychotherapeutic assistance of any kind. Brendel and Nelson (1999) noted that a therapist "is held directly responsible for directing the flow, or lack thereof, of sensitive information disclosed" (p. 113), creating a potential legal consideration to supplement the ethical principles affecting such decisions. A derivative of this intermediate position is to require the waiver of confidentiality restrictions by family members as a stipulation for initiating a therapy relationship. Such a decision could serve to assist the therapist in avoiding contentious conflicts between family members about disclosures from therapy in instances of subsequent litigation (e.g., divorce, child custody, etc.).

Karpel (1980) critiqued a number of ethical and practical considerations confronting therapists seeking to select a position with regard to handling marital and family secrets. In this critique, which is especially perceptive concerning this intermediate position, Karpel advocated a distinction between *secrecy* and *privacy* in terms of how relevant information is to those unaware of it. For example, a traumatic episode in one's childhood, now reasonably well resolved and not significantly affecting the present relationship, would be considered private. The client might at some time decide to share this history with his or her partner or children but does not owe it to them to do so. Similarly, intimate details of a marital partner's previous love relationships that have no important implications for her or his current relationship are private, not secret. In contrast, a spouse engaged in an extramarital affair maintains a secret in the sense that it involves deception as well as a violation of trust. Likewise, parents who withhold the fact that a child is adopted might violate that child's right to a complete self-definition and identity. The typology noted by Vangelisti (1994) can help determine if a specific circumstance involves a taboo topic, a rule violation, or a conventional secret. For these and similar circumstances of disclosure, marriage and family therapists must pay particular attention to their personal values as well as to their professional values in order not to impose a predetermined agenda that may not yield an expected outcome for client welfare.

Karpel advocated a policy of "accountability with discretion." A therapist would share or withhold information based on his or her clinical judgment involving (a) a consideration of the relevance of the material for the person who is unaware of it, (b) an attempt to perceive the situation as much as possible from the perspective of the person who is unaware, and (c) a sensitivity to the timing and consequences for the person who is unaware.

> This means, to use an everyday expression, trying to "put yourself in the other person's shoes," trying to understand what they need and what they are owed. It also means that when a decision to share is made, it takes the other's situation and likely reactions into account. For example, one does not reveal a secret that is likely greatly to upset the other in the midst of his/her surprise birthday party or when s/he is already in crisis due to an unrelated situation. This stance clearly reflects . . . a respect for individuation, an effort to maximize trust and trustworthiness in relationships, and an attempt to balance the two fairly. (Karpel, 1980, p. 298)

Karpel supported his stance of "accountability with discretion" by arguing that therapists who agree to keep secrets collude with secretholders and thereby betray the trust of unaware members while enhancing the potentially destructive power of secretholders. Karpel warned that although keeping secrets may be a well-intentioned attempt to protect the unaware members, this stance carries significant risk. The secret information may unexpectedly be revealed, resulting in negative consequences for the individuals, the relationship, and the therapy. Karpel acknowledged that therapists' need to know relevant information for diagnostic and treatment purposes and their obligation to maintain trustworthiness frequently come in conflict. He proposed a solution that involves discussing the dangers posed by special confidences with the couple or family in the initial session and asking them to agree on the direction the therapy will take:

> The therapist might describe the likely decrease in effectiveness that occurs when something important is known in therapy that can't be discussed. Having explained this, s/he can ask how they would like this to be handled. It can also be made clear, if they sanction such confidences, that this arrangement may become unworkable at some point. If so, the therapist will tell them so and they will have to choose between disclosure and termination. (Karpel, 1980, p. 305)

Following Karpel's lead in this matter, Fall and Lyons (2003) summarized the considerations therapists must consider by noting the following:

1. Make sure that your clients understand the nature of counseling and its inherent risks,
2. Make accurate assessments of boundaries within the family, and,
3. Be prepared to assess the impact of the disclosure of the system. (pp. 284–285)

Another factor that complicates confidentiality obligations is a change in the format of therapy, specifically when individual therapy is replaced by marriage or family therapy. Margolin (1982) raised a number of critical issues to address when considering such a change:

> How does the therapist handle the information that he or she has obtained during individual therapy? One possibility is to obtain the individual client's permission to use such information, when necessary, in the conjoint sessions. If permission is not granted, however, that information must be kept confidential, a resolution far from desirable for the therapist who prefers not maintaining individual confidences in conjoint therapy. Even if the client permits the information to be shared, this permission has been granted after the information was obtained. Does the client remember all that she or he has confided under the previously assumed condition of confidentiality? Would that person have responded differently in individual therapy if it were known from the outset that such information would be available to the spouse? (p. 791)

Karpel (1980) used two case examples to illustrate what he refers to as "reparative strategies" for therapists to employ in responding to a change in format from individual to marriage and family therapy.

CASE 1

Mrs. T. is a 35-year-old, childless, married woman. She comes self-referred to an outpatient mental health clinic requesting an appointment for herself. She complains of some anxiety and depression, which she attributes to long-standing marital problems. She reveals that she has carried on a secret three-year affair with her husband's married brother. She is inflexible in her request for marital therapy, her insistence that the affair never be revealed to her husband, and her refusal to give it up. There are no indications of suicidal or homicidal ideation or intent. (Karpel, 1980, p. 303)

In this case, it was recommended that the therapist communicate to the woman the extent to which her requests are incompatible. Improving her marital relationship requires building greater trust and reciprocity. She is unwilling to give up a competing relationship that violates both. She is also unwilling to discuss it. The therapist was advised to offer the woman additional individual sessions to explore her feelings about the situation with the hope that this additional counseling would help her decide on a course of action incorporating more realistic goals.

CASE 2

Mr. and Mrs. L. seek psychiatric help for problems involving their 9-year-old son who is described as being withdrawn and depressed, with a poor relationship with his father. Mr. L. is a successful architect who is heavily involved in community affairs. There are two teenage children. As part of a routine family evaluation, the parents are seen together and separately. In her individual meeting with the therapist, Mrs. L. impulsively discloses that in the past her husband has been involved in homosexual extramarital affairs. He has not done so for several years, although she says she remains somewhat jealous and anxious about this recurring. She immediately regrets having disclosed this and asks the therapist not to reveal his knowledge to her husband. She makes a persuasive argument that her husband might be able to tolerate the therapist's knowing this once he knew and trusted the therapist more but that finding out at this early stage would almost certainly drive him and therefore the family from treatment. (Karpel, 1980, p. 303)[1]

In this second case, it was recommended that the therapist communicate the potential importance of informing the husband of the disclosure. Therapy may eventually reach a point where the therapist must revisit the issue with the wife unless she is able to inform her husband of her disclosure or he spontaneously discloses relevant facts in therapy. The therapist must clearly communicate that treatment efforts can go only so far if significant information is withheld.

The situation in this latter case example allows for a gradual, less rigid approach. The therapist's insistence, for ethical and practical reasons, that the disclosure eventually be shared remains unchanged. The circumstances and timing of this sharing, however, are negotiable.

As one considers the application of confidentiality and its derivatives (i.e., privacy, privileged communication, duty to protect), it becomes apparent that for therapists to demonstrate both principle ethics and virtue ethics in serving families and couples, they must be deliberate in disclosing relevant information to clients. Professional as well as institutional traditions of marriage and family therapy emphasize clients' fundamental rights to information relevant to their welfare and the expectations they may have for therapy. Such information is addressed through procedures of informed consent.

---

[1]*Note:* From "Family Secrets: I. Conceptual and Ethical Issues in the Relational Context: II. Ethical and Practical Considerations in Therapeutic Management," by M. A. Karpel, 1980, *Family Process, 19*, p. 303. Copyright 1980. Reprinted with permission.

Informed Consent Concerns in Marriage and Family Therapy

A primary concern in marriage and family therapy is that procedures for informed consent be conducted with all persons who participate in treatment efforts, including those who may join therapy at a later time (Margolin, 1982). This concern is especially pertinent because risks and benefits for individuals tend to be much different in marriage and family therapy than in individual therapy. Consider the following example:

> A couple sought treatment for marital problems. In the process that ensued, the wife recognized her unwillingness to expend the effort necessary to eventually gain the satisfaction she wanted from the marriage, and so she stated her rational desire to seek a divorce. The husband reacted to his wife's statement with a verbal attack upon the therapist for allowing this outcome to occur: "Therapy was supposed to save our marriage!"

Clients need to be forewarned that marriage and family therapy can lead to outcomes viewed as undesirable by one or another of the participants, for example, the wife's decision to divorce. Other examples of change unanticipated by some family members may include revising a power inequity between partners, disclosing victimization of a partner or child, or confronting familial patterns that enable the maintenance of a chemical or alcohol dependency.

Similarly, marriage and family therapy may not always be in the perceived best interests of individual marital partners or family members. Priority placed on the good of the couple or family as a whole calls for individuals at times to subordinate personal desires that are not congruent with the overall goals. The following case example illustrates this point:

> Parents of a 15-year-old son and a 17-year-old daughter complained of the teenagers' unwillingness to follow their directives unquestioningly. Interaction during the initial evaluation session showed that the parents were excessively authoritarian and the youths' actions were normal developmental strivings. As therapy progressed, the parents eventually came to realize that their "overparenting" was a major part of the presenting problem; they nevertheless experienced significant anguish in allowing their son and daughter to take on greater self-responsibility.

Different family members can benefit unequally from therapy, at least in terms of the immediate changes resulting from treatment efforts that are aimed at enhancing the overall functioning of the family. A significant aspect of inequality is the acculturation of clients within a social structure in which such inequities are traditionally accepted. Similarly, clients who are socialized to believe that group membership is more valuable than individual autonomy may encounter considerable difficulties within the contextual format of marriage and family therapy. For traditionally Westernized therapists, such cultural perspectives may be overlooked or even discounted, reflecting the possible imposition of therapist values rather than the emergence of a new understanding for the family system (Palmer & Kaufman, 2003).

Hare-Mustin (1980) urged that therapists recognize their responsibility for minimizing the risks in marriage and family therapy and share this recognition with therapy participants. She suggested that these objectives are best accomplished by clearly stating the goals that the therapist plans to pursue. Marital partners and family members should be encouraged to question these goals so that they can better identify how their individual needs align or contrast with overall goals of the marital or family relationship. Therapists must be explicit about the extent to which individual goals are incompatible with the relationship goals, need to be subordinated to the relationship goals, or are simply unacceptable to the marital partner or other family members. A common misperception among novice therapists is that establishing goals is a simple *prelude* to therapy when, in fact, establishing goals *is the beginning* of therapy (M. P. Nichols & Schwartz, 2004).

Although general procedures for informed consent in marriage and family therapy appear basic, therapists need to consider carefully how well their primary therapeutic orientation matches their informed consent practices. This question is most relevant in determining the degree of specificity in information presented (Margolin, 1982). Most marriage and family therapists offer an overview of objectives (e.g., more satisfactory family functioning, clearer communications) as well as the format that sessions will take (e.g., length and frequency of sessions, approximate duration of treatment efforts). More precise information, however, may be detrimental to some types of treatment efforts, such as Strategic Therapy, for example, in which the therapist attempts to mobilize oppositional tendencies of participants through paradoxical interventions (Haley, 1976; Stanton, 1981).

Most marriage and family therapists advocate certain "maneuvers" that indirectly limit fully informed consent and free choice about therapy (Margolin, 1982). For example, in relating benefits to be expected from treatment efforts, therapists cannot ethically guarantee positive change. However, most therapists do express optimism about the potential outcome of treatment to reduce participants' anxiety, raise their expectations, and increase their persistence in pursuing established goals (Jacobson & Margolin, 1979).

Another such therapeutic maneuver involves certain explanations and interpretations offered to partners and family members. Several major marriage and family therapy approaches advocate reframing or relabeling behaviors and interactions in ways that do not reflect a couple's or family's current reality but rather facilitate their interactions in more efficient and effective ways. Relabeling two partners' constant arguments as evidence of "your persistence in seeking to communicate clearly with each other" introduces a positive goal orientation where hostility is present. The likelihood of the couple's pursuing a common course of future action will be greater if they accept the therapist's reframing of their interaction, even if it is seen by an objective observer as an inaccurate description of an actual occurrence.

More than a simple therapeutic maneuver, some practitioners embrace theoretical models reflective of an intergenerational perspective to understanding and changing unproductive familial patterns (Bowen, 1978; Framo, 1981). For these therapists, informed consent about efforts to convene family members in an intergenerational session or to involve adult siblings may require specific discussion and lengthy preparation prior to engaging members for such services. However, as Framo stated "I've heard every excuse in the world, but I can say that one session with the family of origin is as powerful as all other sessions combined in the treatment regimen" (American Association for Marriage and Family Therapy, 1985). Based on such a statement, therapists should take particular caution in informed consent procedures prior to an intergenerational session.

Bray et al. (1985) proposed that marriage and family therapists have a responsibility to inform family members about the nature of the procedures they will use, the more probable consequences of these procedures, alternative treatments, and the risks of therapy. However, they do not view it as realistic to discuss every possible risk. They recommend that family members be informed of those risks they might find important in deciding whether or not to consent to treatment.

Margolin (1982) summarized marriage and family therapists' need for balance between informed consent and appropriate therapeutic action:

> Thus, even though clients deserve an accurate portrayal of therapy in informed consent procedures, complete objectivity and openness may not be possible. At the same time that families need factual information to make an informed decision about therapy, they also need the therapist's support, encouragement, and optimism for taking this risky step. An overly enthusiastic discussion of alternatives to therapy or overly detailed explanation of the risks of therapy may convince the client that the therapist does not want him or her in therapy. (p. 795)[2]

As one can see, even in addressing foundational elements of ethical propriety, the interactive nature of marriage and family therapy introduces considerable complexity for the practitioner. Other similar practical examples can be found in the ethical practice of marriage and family therapy.

DEFINING THE PROBLEM

In the typical interaction occurring in the opening phase of most marriage and family therapy efforts, either one member of a dyad or family is presented as the "identified patient" or an individual coming alone requests assistance. The therapist who defines the problem as one of relationship makes an assumption that immediately raises an ethical issue (Fieldsteel, 1982). The therapist has taken on the obligation of imposing a new set of values and beliefs on the individual or members of the relationship system. The couple, family, or individual seeks therapeutic assistance for a specific concern; the therapist implicitly or explicitly informs them that they must put aside their beliefs and adopt those of the therapist. As we discussed in Chapter 2, such an intervention could represent a point of divergence in personal values of clients versus professional values of the therapist.

Most therapists assume the right to define clients' presenting problems in terms of their own therapeutic orientation. They make this assumption with the belief that, as owners of greater psychological knowledge and professional qualifications, they have the prerogative to assert themselves without violating their clients' rights. Because most clients accept the perceived role inequality between client and professional, they tend to accept therapists' assertions as actual fact. Although this redefinition of clients' problems is not limited to marriage and family therapy, it is more dramatic in this kind of therapy (Fieldsteel, 1982). This point is illustrated by certain therapeutic definitions in the treatment of schizophrenic disorders, particularly the premise that weaning from both institutional and family caregiving will stimulate the "identified patient" to develop skills necessary for independent community living. Dincin, Selleck, and Streicker

---

[2]*Note:* From "Ethical and Legal Considerations in Marriage and Family Therapy," by G. Margolin, 1982, *American Psychologist, 7*, pp. 790, 791, 793, 795. Copyright 1982. Reprinted with permission.

(1978) took a family therapy tack common in the management of schizophrenia in their work with parents of schizophrenic offspring:

> The consistent message of the agency is that the greatest love parents can show . . . is to allow and encourage the child to separate from the parental home. We believe that living at home is usually counterproductive to long-term growth and that psychological damage occurs when parents are unwilling or unable to "let go." (p. 599)

Madanes (1983) demonstrated a similar stance in her work using a Strategic Family Therapy approach:

> Parents typically avoid defining the family hierarchy as one in which they have power over their offspring. They do so because . . . they are afraid to do the wrong thing and harm the youth, because they are afraid they are to blame and wish to do no more harm. . . . The therapist must respond with various counteracting maneuvers to keep the parents in charge. (p. 216)

Terkelsen (1983), in contrast, questioned the degree to which family interaction contributes to the etiology of schizophrenia, a position that has dominated contemporary family therapy even in the absence of solid empirical confirmation. He held that sociogenic models of schizophrenia and their attendant assumptions may be not only incorrect but even harmful to families. He foresaw the potential for similar harm to the relationship between families and clinicians and has indicated a need for more research in this area.

Terkelsen described the dilemmas he encountered in 10 years of work with families that had schizophrenic offspring. He was trained in "a tradition that assumed madness to be an interpersonal affair" (p. 192). In early sessions with families, he had attuned himself to abstract from family members' reports only those interactional phenomena representative of parental pathogenicity that would "explain" the individual pathology. Treatment sessions constituted efforts to cloister the identified patient, to separate her or him from the rest of the family, with the belief that it was the family interaction that maintained the patient's pathology. The usual result was a sense of alienation as he found family members unwilling or unable to conform to his theoretical formulations.

In commenting on Terkelsen's experience, Grunebaum (1984) proposed that therapists' first and foremost task is to understand and share the pain of parents and other family members who find themselves in such a predicament. He identified this understanding as a precondition necessary for family members to open themselves to alternative explanations of their circumstances. Family members focus on the identified patient because they do not know how to cope with the manifestations of mental illness in any other way. Grunebaum offered a case example involving a 25-year-old woman with mild retardation and her parents:

> Now it would appear to many clinicians that these parents needed to be reassured that their daughter was not suicidal, that she was highly unlikely to commit suicide, and that by responding to her slightest threats, they were responding to a manipulation on her part. In fact, the daughter would leave the community placements, wander around for a few hours and then call home. Her parents would then immediately come and get her. Reassurance about suicide had been given before and fallen on deaf ears. . . . The parents then left the room and the staff continued the discussion. Present were the three nurses who had been on call for such cases. They included the two nurses responsible for community placements and one nurse from the ward from which the patient had been discharged. The latter, who knew the patient well, did not

believe the patient was suicidal. She stated that she did not think the patient should have been readmitted. The other two nurses were equally clear that they were responsible for the patient and if she expressed suicidal thoughts or feelings, she had to be hospitalized. They were willing to delegate that responsibility to someone else but not to "take a chance." They turned to the ward nurse and asked, "Can you promise she won't kill herself?" (1984, pp. 422–423)

These three nurses, trained mental health professionals, were unwilling to put their roles in interacting with the woman at risk by allowing her to determine her own well-being. Yet they had just suggested that the woman's parents should take that very risk and assume the responsibility of not letting themselves be manipulated by their daughter's threats.

Grunebaum (1984) proposed that families who appear to interfere with attempts to foster the independence of the identified patient are sometimes making positive moral choices, even though these choices involve capitulating to manipulation or intimidation at the hands of the schizophrenic member. He theorized that many of these individuals suffer from disruption of fundamental neurobiological processes. Their insistence on being taken care of by their family is often a "default position," because their experiences in the community often are characterized by impossible challenges, humiliating failures, and rejection by others. So they may view life with their family as the one respite from the continual agony of constant defeat.

Terkelsen (1983) summarized his own discussion and Grunebaum's comments by noting:

> If, under these circumstances, the family permits the patient to manipulate his or her way back into a dependent status, perhaps the family has come to feel that enough is enough. . . . If, . . . and I speak as a family therapist to family therapists—we lose sight of this sensibility, we will also have lost contact with the very people whose burden we seek to alleviate. (p. 427)

If the perspective for problem definition emphasizes client welfare and safety such as that of the previous example, persuasive arguments can be fashioned to defend the logic presented by the various authors cited in the discussion. However, such examples may be more the exception than the rule in marriage and family therapy. Consider an example with less dramatic overtones. A newly blended family presents for family therapy due to transitional difficulties such as the disciplinary expectations of the biological parent compared to those of the stepparent and the divided loyalties of the children reflected in requests to greater access to the noncustodial parent. Is this a circumstance with a "neurobiological basis"? Probably not. Is this a circumstance that presents a threat to client safety? Not at this time. Is there an identified patient? Possibly. Is this circumstance reflective of a variety of individual realities conversing in a novel and underdeveloped system? Almost certainly. Is it likely that the therapist might implicitly or explicitly view and examine the situation in a manner that might differ from some of those divergent realities? Yes. Even for the therapist embracing a narrative approach to intervention (White & Epstein, 1990), affirming respect for differing realities among family members represents professional value for an interactional and systemic context rather than a psychological and linear context. Efforts at collaborating and negotiating between new spouses as well as among children and parents does not negate the importance of the individual but, rather, requires perspective-taking and valuing as discussed previously in Chapter 1. By its very nature, the selection of a focal point for therapy efforts is a statement of problem definition. When working with an individual client, this circumstance is difficult at best. When working with a system of clients, the situation requires some imposition of parameters by the therapist (Ford, 2001).

There is little doubt that couples, families, and individual clients present themselves for therapy because they are experiencing a sense of distress and desire to gain relief. They seek professional assistance because they attribute power to therapists on the basis of their clinical knowledge and skills. It is thus critical that therapists recognize the difference between appropriate professional judgment and biased personal power. By redefining presenting problems as relationship rather than individual issues, therapists ask members of relationship systems to sacrifice, at least temporarily, their autonomy. The therapist who imposes a specific problem definition on a relationship system can do so only with the cooperation of the members of that system. Often, however, therapists must ask themselves if this cooperation is obtained under circumstances that could realistically be construed as involving clients' "informed consent."

Marriage and family therapists have an ethical obligation to help the members of a relationship system seeking treatment to understand what is involved in the therapist's definition of their presenting concern. Reasons why such a definition is therapeutically beneficial and what it will demand of them should be provided (Fieldsteel, 1982). Couples, families, and individuals may be labeled "resistant" or "poor therapy risks" for many reasons, as we have discussed previously in Chapter 1. Therapists have a further ethical obligation to examine how their expectations and biases may lead to fulfillment of these prophecies (Hines & Hare-Mustin, 1978). This statement is not meant to suggest that empirical evidence and clinical experience should be ignored. Characteristics of certain clients, especially as they interact in relationship systems, are highly suggestive of a poor therapeutic prognosis. Rather, therapists must be cognizant of the long-term significance of the definitions they impose and the extent to which these definitions follow from an inability to deal with beliefs and value systems different from their own.

COMPLICATIONS IN CONVENING THERAPY

Most families do not seek therapeutic assistance by specifically requesting relationship therapy. Although this behavior pattern is changing as public awareness of marriage and family therapy as a treatment option increases, typically, one partner or family member seeks an appointment. Marriage and family therapists have a critical task during this initial "presession" contact: to promote the assembling or convening of significant familial or extrafamilial members for the upcoming first session. This convening session is especially important because (a) an adequate relationship assessment requires the presence of all significant members of that relationship, (b) convening as a dyad or total family symbolically expresses the systemic or relationship nature of the presenting problem and its potential treatment, (c) it becomes increasingly more difficult to bring in absent members as therapy progresses, and (d) convening represents the first test of a therapist's ability and commitment to effectively manage relationship resistance (Teismann, 1980).

This desire by marriage and family therapists to engage all significant members of a relationship system raises the ethical issue of voluntary participation (Margolin, 1982). Obviously, coercion of reluctant members by their marital partner, family members, or the therapist is unethical. However, therapists should encourage reluctant members to participate in at least the initial evaluation session to investigate what therapy may entail.

Therapists should also pay attention to what may be contributing to this reluctance, such as general anxiety, insistence on individual treatment for the identified patient, lack of effort on the part of the initiating members or the therapist, denial of any existing problem, or covert maneuvering by the participating member to exclude the reluctant member.

The most common ethical dilemma raised by the convening process involves the therapeutic policy of many marriage and family therapists to refuse treatment unless all significant members of a relationship system become involved. Should willing members seeking assistance go untreated because one individual refuses to participate? This issue is particularly problematic for therapists employed in public agencies where withholding services is not only ethically but legally and politically questionable, given that they are tax-supported, legally mandated to serve those requesting help, and often funded on the basis of how many clients they serve (O'Shea & Jessee, 1982). Additionally, from our discussion of institutional objectives and values in Chapter 2, one could surmise that some settings would prefer billable hours of service to clients over the professional value of convening family members. In such instances, marriage and family therapists may be faced with divergent values affecting their service to clients. By contrast, therapists who insist on convening strategies may be assisting the couple or family in offsetting institutional values about individual pathology and treatment approaches.

In a real way, the decision by a therapist to attempt to convene absent family members in the therapy process reflects elements of problem definition. Regardless of the specific applied model employed by the practitioner, espousing an interactional perspective for therapeutic change would seem to require efforts to convene relevant members of the system. From Chapter 1, readers will recall the discussion of Napier and Whitaker's (1978) ideas about the Battle for Initiative and the Battle for Structure. These authors refer to the convening process in marriage and family therapy as an element of the Battle for Structure in that it is an overt or covert attempt by a couple or family to control and resist change by dictating the terms of therapy. More often than not, the absent member or members are contributors to the symptom being presented and thus crucial to accurate identification of and intervention in the problem. Napier and Whitaker asserted that therapists' ability to convene all significant relationship members is a necessary factor in achieving successful treatment outcomes and "winning" this battle.

O'Shea and Jessee (1982) argued that withholding treatment in the Battle for Structure does not constitute a refusal to provide mental health services. Instead, they described it as an "insistence on providing services appropriate to the nature of the difficulty, and thus, it is a responsible, competent, professional practice" (p. 6). They compare a therapist who withholds treatment to a physician who orders tests and prescribes medication based on what is appropriate to a patient's illness or injury, not on what the patient might want.

Teismann (1980) argued against the withholding of treatment in the Battle for Structure on the grounds that doing so denies services to motivated marital partners and family members and risks the creation of an implicit alliance between the therapist and the nonparticipant. He identified two types of strategies, short of refusing or withholding services, for involving reluctant members of a relationship system: *enforcing* and *enabling*. He labels a strategy as enforcing when therapists mobilize referral agents to exert pressure on relationship systems to convene for therapy as a total system. Rather than directly requesting reluctant members to come to therapy, therapists indirectly do so through the referral source. Enforcing, if it is used in an authoritarian manner, can be tantamount to coercion.

However, enforcing done in a proactive manner, as opposed to a reactive manner, allows for greater freedom of choice to all involved. Enforcing requires preplanning and a prereferral agreement between therapists and referral agents. For example, a physician may make family therapy a prescribed part of medical treatment. Juvenile court services may offer family therapy as an alternative to prosecution or sentencing, with the stipulation of total family participation. Employee assistance program referral sources can similarly provide options such as marital or family therapy to workers whose personal problems affect their jobs. It is even possible for referral agents to be present at the initial evaluation session to explain the reasons for the referral and reconfirm the marital partners' or family members' right to refuse treatment. Although potentially negative consequences may result, the understanding that there is an alternative course of action is critical to therapists' ethical practice.

Teismann (1980) explained enabling from two perspectives. In the first method of enabling, the therapist works to increase the attractiveness of attending. Essentially, therapists who use this enabling strategy seek to decrease the threat a reluctant member perceives from participation in therapy and simultaneously to persuade the member that there is something to be gained personally from participating. The therapist must first make contact with the reluctant member, preferably in a face-to-face meeting. To alleviate reluctant members' anxiety about the unknown that therapy represents, therapists might provide a verbal outline of the process, photocopies of relevant articles from popular magazines, or a referral to former clients willing to make themselves available to share their experience in marriage and/or family therapy. Frequently, if the therapist offers a simple description of expectations, potential experiences, and probable effects, this direct approach will sufficiently relieve many reluctant members' anxiety. In interacting with the reluctant member, the therapist also should seek to increase the attractiveness of attending by appealing to and confirming the individual's strength and potential and focus on his or her position and special importance in the relationship system. For example, the therapist can point out to a reluctant father that his son needs a strong and able male role model that only he can readily offer. Or a wife can be told that her husband needs someone with the courage and tenacity to temporarily, at least, take charge of the disorganization he is experiencing in his life. Such proposals frequently provide reluctant members with a sense of purpose that leads them to participate in therapy.

The second form of enabling involves decreasing the attractiveness of being absent from therapy. Often, reluctant members offer rationalizations for declining to participate in therapy. Therapists can use the members' own reasoning to emphasize the additional problems they potentially foster by not attending. For example, one man believed that his wife had "serious personal problems" that required individual attention. The therapist agreed and added that the husband may have underestimated the seriousness of the problems and that the help of both the husband and other family members would likely prevent the problem from worsening. In another case, a reluctant parent voiced concern that a family should not "hang out its dirty laundry" for all (meaning the therapist) to see. The therapist replied with full agreement and went on to note that therapy appeared to be a last resort to stop the trend, because the dirty laundry was already visible at the child's school (through truancy) and to the police (through marijuana possession).

Wilcoxon and Fenell (1983) suggested a therapist-initiated letter for engaging a non-attending spouse in marital therapy. Given to the participating member as a homework assignment, the letter not only acts as an enabling strategy for engaging the reluctant member but also offers a structured task for the couple to complete in their home. This task facilitates clarification of their intentions regarding their marriage as well as the marital therapy process. Figure 4–1 provides a sample letter.

FIGURE 4–1   Letter to Engage a Non-Attending Spouse

(Date)

Mr. John Jones
111 Smith Street
Anytown, USA 00000

Dear Mr. Jones,

As you may know, your wife, Jill, has requested therapy services for difficulties related to your marriage. However, she has stated that you do not wish to participate in marital therapy sessions.

As a professional marriage therapist, I have an obligation to inform each of you of the possible outcome of marital therapy services to only one spouse. The available research indicates that one-spouse marital therapy has resulted in reported increases in marital stress and dissatisfaction for both spouses in the marriage. On the other hand, many couples have reported that marital therapy which includes both spouses has been helpful in reducing marital stress and enhancing marital satisfaction.

These findings reflect general tendencies in marital research and are not absolute in nature. However, it is important for you and Jill to be informed of potential consequences which might occur through marital therapy in which only your spouse attends. Knowing this information, you may choose a course of action which best suits your intentions.

After careful consideration of this information, I ask that you and Jill discuss your options regarding future therapy services. In this way, all parties will have a clear understanding of one another's intentions regarding your relationship.

As a homework assignment for Jill, I have asked that each of you read this letter and sign in the spaces provided below to verify your understanding of the potential consequences to your relationship by continuing one-spouse marital therapy. If you are interested in joining Jill for marital therapy, in addition to your signature below, please contact my office to indicate your intentions. If not, simply sign below and have Jill return the letter at our next therapy session. I appreciate your cooperation in this matter.

Sincerely,

Therapist X

We verify by our signatures below that we have discussed and understand the potential implications of continued marital therapy with only one spouse in attendance.

Attending Spouse _____ Date _____

Non-Attending Spouse _____ Date _____

Note. From "Engaging the Non-Attending Spouse in Marital Therapy Through the Use of Therapist-Initiated Written Communication" by A. Wilcoxon and D. Fenell, 1983, *Journal of Marital and Family Therapy, 9,* 199–203. Copyright 1983 by the American Association for Marriage and Family Therapy. Reprinted by permission.

When enforcing or enabling efforts at convening all significant relationship members have been unsuccessful, therapists still can choose to treat the marital partner or family members who do want therapy rather than offer the ultimatum of no therapy. However, Patten, Barnett, and Houlihan (1991) cautioned that the decision to conduct individual therapy for relationship issues may result in less than optimal outcomes. They cited empirical findings in the professional literature supporting systemic intervention as opposed to traditional, single-client intervention for relationship issues (Gurman & Kniskern, 1981; Wohlman & Stricker, 1983):

1. Family therapy is at least as effective as individual therapy for most clients' complaints and leads to significantly greater durability of changes made.
2. Specific forms of family therapy are significantly more effective than individual interventions in addressing certain complaints (e.g., structural family therapy in addressing substance abuse).
3. The presence of both parents (particularly noncompliant fathers) in family therapy significantly improves the chances for successful therapeutic outcomes.
4. With marital complaints, therapy with both spouses present is nearly twice as effective as individual therapy with one spouse.
5. Relationship treatment not conducted within a conjoint or systemic format may promote negative therapeutic effects (e.g., problem exacerbation rather than problem resolution).

These findings indicate that change to a relationship, although less than optimal, is still possible if key relations and dynamics are identified and interventions are planned and executed from a systemic perspective. From a postmodern vantage, one might argue that an effort to convene all parties is a metaphorical expression of respect for differing realities, an endorsement of hope for cooperative change, and a verification of the therapist's notions of power equity, a particularly valuable commodity for marriages built on misogyny and gender inequity (Downing & Roush, 1985; Knudson-Martin, 2001). When a couple or family is resistant to convening together, the therapist can focus on individual change within the static relationship system to bring about change (P. Watzlawick, Weakland, & Fish, 1974).

For example, a very motivated 33-year-old woman, after gaining awareness that her unconditional caretaking perpetuated her husband's substance abuse, agreed to spend the night in a motel whenever he came home drunk. She left him a note explaining that she had been hurting him with her caretaking, that she wanted to stop doing so, and that she would return the next day. This strategy effectively interrupted a basic interaction sequence symbolic of the system's dysfunction. It further redefined the problem as residing in the wife and thus enabled her to initiate change in herself and simultaneously to introduce change into the relationship. Wilcoxon (1986) and Kaslow (1986) have taken differing positions on whether or not informed consent is necessary in instances wherein change in one marital partner may be anticipated as possibly distressing to the other partner. Regardless of one's position on this and related ethical matters, the significance of convening is unique to the practice of marriage and family therapy.

In clarifying whether or not a partner or particular family member needs to participate in therapy efforts, therapists must be able to identify the extent to which each member of the relationship will be expected to participate. For example, some members may attend sessions in the role of observer simply to learn enough about the therapeutic process so that they will not impede its progress. Therapists with a strong preference for convening all members of a relationship system should inform persons seeking assistance that other therapists do not necessarily share this view (Margolin, 1982). A list of competent referral sources should then be made available. The ethical issue is not so much a question of whether therapists have a definition of what is conducive to optimal psychological functioning as whether they can acknowledge their professional views and be willing to be flexible in offering options to persons seeking help.

THE THERAPIST AS AGENT FOR CHANGE

As we consider the notion of therapist as agent for change, two foundational assumptions must be verified. The first assumption is about the nature of therapy: Therapy is *about* change. Different models of theory and intervention feature distinct perspectives concerning the origin of problems and expected outcomes from the application of that model. However, all models emphasize that therapy is geared toward change rather than maintenance and status quo. A second assumption is about the nature of the therapy relationship: The relationship is *special*. Because this special relationship is grounded in an expectation of change, the therapist assumes obligations related to change. Napier and Whitaker's (1978) discussion about the Battle for Structure and the Battle for Initiative suggests these obligations require attention to the parameters of therapy and energy in therapy. As an agent of change, therapists may take on any number of roles in addressing this obligation. Some therapists prefer the role of teacher; some prefer the role of catalyst; some prefer the role of collaborator. However, regardless of the role selected by the therapist, the expectation is to utilize the special relationship of therapy for change.

A related element in the change process is a distinction between the *power to control* and the *power to influence*. As you will see in Chapters 8, 9, and 10, some legal obligations for therapists involve taking steps to control the possibility of danger to self or others based on information from the therapy relationship. However, power to control is not the typical basis of change embraced by marriage and family therapists. By contrast, the power to influence is more typically associated with the professional traditions and values embraced by therapists. From this perspective, the knowledge, experience, skill, competence, and energy of the therapist is employed on behalf of individuals and families. You will recall the discussion of the ethical principles advocated by Beauchamp and Childress (2001) in Chapter 3. For each of these principles, the power to influence as an agent of change represents respect for the self-determination of family members to utilize or reject the special nature of the therapy relationship as a venue for change. The power to influence is not simply a matter of inspiration and suggestion by the therapist, however. Rather, influence may involve assertiveness, intrusion, maneuvering, or even directiveness on the part of the therapist. Otherwise, the therapy relationship will likely replicate the patterns that occur outside therapy, which would negate the special nature of the relationship and hinder the prospects for meaningful change.

All couples and families enter therapy with their own idiosyncratic styles of communicating with implicit patterns of meaning and relationship rules embedded in what can appear to an outsider as unimportant, insignificant, conventional interactions (F. Watzlawick, Beavin, & Jackson, 1967). Such idiosyncrasies may be family-specific or cultural in origin. Therapists beginning therapy with a couple or family are not privy to the special importance that many of these interactions have within the relationship system. This lack of familiarity puts therapists at an immediate disadvantage, not unlike that of a person seeking entry into a secret organization without benefit of the required password (O'Shea & Jessee, 1982). The therapist must decipher the relationship's communication style and gain access to the meanings and rules employed by the members of the system. Only then can the therapist accurately assess, intervene with, and ultimately facilitate change within the couple or family.

The importance of marriage and family therapists' functioning in an active, directive manner has been clearly stressed by a majority of family therapy approaches (M. P. Nichols & Schwartz, 2004). To be effective, marriage and family therapists need to be influential. Although therapists' influence and power are a recognized part of individually oriented therapies, the means by which marriage and family therapists achieve such a position characteristically stands in ready contrast. Marriage and family therapists recognize the necessity of asserting power. In describing the movement from an individual to a marriage and family therapy perspective in her practice, Wachtel (1979) suggested that the more reflective and insight-oriented stance common in individual therapy is influential only because of the traditional nature of the therapeutic contract and is conferred largely as a result of clients' seeking to alleviate personally felt distress. She found that it was difficult to share more control over the content and direction of sessions with family members because her position with them was of less authority and centrality than with an individual client. The importance of assuming an active position of power to gain influence became readily evident as her experience with couples and families increased.

Most marriage and family therapists are direct about their role as agents of change. For example, family theorist and therapist Salvador Minuchin expressly described his own Structural Family Therapy as a "therapy of action." Minuchin (1974) wrote that families are organized around the specific functions of their members. The power of the therapist is considered to be the primary means of bringing about change: "Change is seen as occurring through the process of the therapist's affiliation with the family and his [or her] restructuring of the family in a carefully planned way, so as to transform dysfunctional transactional patterns" (p. 91). Other marriage and family theorists and therapists convey similar messages, as is evident from the titles of their major writings (e.g., Virginia Satir's *Peoplemaking*, 1972, and Jay Haley's *Changing Families*, 1971). Postmodern approaches to marriage and family therapy cast a somewhat different view on the assertion of authority by the therapist in the process of change (Freeman & Combs, 1996). Still, serving as a collaborator or advocate or facilitator, marriage and family therapists assert their power to influence in problem definition, pursuit of goals, and selection of techniques.

Corey et al. (2003) raised several ethical considerations about the power- and action-oriented approach advocated by most marriage and family therapists:

- Should therapists impose their control on couples and families?
- Should the primary responsibility for defining how change should occur rest with the therapist as opposed to with the individual marital partners or family members?

Similarly, in asserting the power to influence as an agent of change, marriage and family therapists need to be *competent* and *current* regarding practices and skills they employ in pursuit of change, as was discussed in Chapter 3 and will discuss later in Chapter 12. In these and related questions, it is instructive to refer to the ethical principles noted by Beauchamp and Childress (2001). Therapists asking themselves, "Is this effort beneficent in nature?" or "Do these directives support justice, autonomy, and fidelity?" can assist in clarifying good-faith efforts for employing the special nature of the therapy relationship for change.

As one can infer, the power of the therapist is a vital component in marriage and family therapy and in itself is not inherently a negative force. When that power is misused, however, questions of ethical misconduct emerge. The major potential for misuse of a therapist's power is generally evidenced when it encourages a client's dependence. Some therapists establish their power and influence in a marital or family relationship system at the cost of reducing the adaptive autonomy of family members. Fieldsteel (1982) has pinpointed the ethical dilemma confronting therapists who assume an inordinate share of responsibility for change in relationship systems: "There is a danger that the role of the therapist as a more active agent for change may shift the responsibility for the direction of change from the patient to the therapist" (p. 262). In such instances, the therapist may be moving from the power to influence into the power to control.

A related issue involves marital partners and family members who attribute to therapists magical qualities to effect changes in their marital or family functioning. This mystification process tends to intensify clients' dependence and reduces clients' ability to assert their rights in the therapy process (Hare-Mustin et al., 1979). Stensrud and Stensrud (1981) proposed that some therapists unintentionally teach clients to be powerless instead of teaching them to trust themselves. They described this powerlessness as a "learned state of generalized helplessness in which clients (a) believe they are unable to have an impact on their environment, and (b) need some external force to intercede on their behalf" (p. 300). Stensrud and Stensrud cautioned that clients can develop self-fulfilling prophecies, whereby expectations of powerlessness evolve into regular experiences of powerlessness. They urge therapists to relate to clients in ways that maintain client self-responsibility—by regularly challenging clients to actively participate throughout the entire therapeutic process. Consider the following therapist's actions:

> A marriage and family therapist in a family services agency devoted many more hours to her position than she was expected to and overtaxed herself by taking on an inordinately large caseload. She frequently let sessions run overtime and encouraged clients to call her at home at any time. Couples and families were maintained much longer in therapy with her than with her colleagues. Her former clients had a recidivism rate that was significantly higher than that of her colleagues' clients.

This therapist clearly has an obligation to examine the ways she established and misused her power base to keep clients so dependent. Redekop (1995) posited that therapists must "confront the question of how their own beliefs and behaviors influence persons who seek therapy" (p. 316). Similarly, White (1993) stated:

> Therapists can challenge the idea that they have an expert view by continually encouraging persons to evaluate the real effects of the therapy in their lives and relationships, and to determine for themselves to what extent these effects are preferred effects and to what extent they are not. The feedback that arises from this evaluation assists therapists in squarely facing the moral and ethical implications of their practices. (p. 57)

Wachtel (1979) proposed that as the therapist's role is demystified, clients become more active. In discussing therapists' actions in this regard, she suggests that they openly and explicitly communicate their preferences. This explicit communication leaves clients knowing more clearly what is going on and where they stand. They may still feel pressure and anxiety in response to a therapist's expectations, but they are potentially in a much better position to differentiate their own preferences from those of the therapist. Fieldsteel (1982) affirmed the power of marriage and family therapists as agents of change. She urged that they not delude themselves into thinking that therapy is an egalitarian, democratic relationship, especially at the outset. Rather, Fieldsteel called for this egalitarian relationship to be a goal toward which therapists should work, much as this relationship becomes one of the major goals of child rearing. However, as we will see in the next section of this chapter, inequities in couple and family relationships may represent major obstacles to an egalitarian outcome in therapy.

Another major ethical dilemma confronting marriage and family therapists is occasioned by the priorities they set: Relationship change is primary, and individual change, although possibly equal, is more likely secondary. O'Shea and Jessee (1982) suggested that therapists confront a central, ethical dilemma when they accept the notion that the symptomatic individual serves a homeostatic, protective, stabilizing function in his or her relationship system. This premise has been challenged and qualified by feminist commentary (Featherstone, 1996; Knudson-Martin, 2001; McLellan, 1999), though primarily for assumptions about the functional nature of a victim role in domestic violence (Gondolf, 2002; Vatcher & Bogo, 2001). Otherwise, a focus on contextual elements of problem definition and change appears to be relatively uniform among marriage and family therapies. Still, O'Shea and Jessee (1982) raised the question of how much distress or risk one member should tolerate for the sake of long-term benefit to the greater marital or family relationship system.

It has been repeatedly recognized that many couples and families manifest a rigid scapegoating pattern toward one or more members and select specific members to bear the brunt of systemic discomfort. Therapists attempting to intervene can expect symptoms to escalate accordingly. To counteract this rigid homeostatic balance, it may be necessary to increase individual distress to a crisis level to facilitate a fundamental change in how the relationship system operates (Hoffman, 1981). However, O'Shea and Jessee (1982) asserted:

> The therapist who attempts to precipitate a structural shift in the system by tolerating or deliberately intensifying the distress in the system does so in opposition to the medical ethic and cultural expectation that helping professionals should relieve rather than prolong suffering. Clearly, a physician, despite the use of anesthetics, often inflicts immediate pain on the patient in the process of restoring a more global and long-term health. In systems therapy, however, the distress must at times be amplified before the family is motivated to change its dysfunctional avoidance behavior patterns. The therapist must, as it were, overcome the self-anesthetizing effect of the family's dysfunctional interactions by getting the family to experience the full thrust of anxiety and tension. (p. 12)

Several examples can serve to illustrate this ethical dilemma. The common and mostly necessary legal response in cases of child abuse is to protect the victim by removing the abused or abusing member from the home. Marriage and family therapists are likely to view the abusing or abused member as being affected by a contextual pattern within the family system. From this therapeutic perspective, optimal treatment might call for the inclusion of the whole family for the sake of a more important and likely lasting change: a change in the basic family functioning. The potential risks inherent in such a path are obvious (Kemp, 1998). In addressing such a circumstance, Rosen, Matheson, Stith, McCollum, and Locke (2003) suggested that a period of de-escalation in "time-out" could be beneficial.

The presenting of destructive behaviors such as suicidal potential makes treatment decisions even more precarious. Therapists who emphasize the importance of having a primary impact on the relationship system face a trade-off between conservatively safeguarding the suicidal client through immediate hospitalization, thus reinforcing the system's scapegoating process, and risking self-harm to the identified patient by denying the necessity of hospitalization in favor of outpatient treatment of the entire relationship system (Langsley & Kaplan, 1968). Marriage and family therapists prepared to accept this risk to the identified patient for the sake of a more meaningful and important relationship change also should be prepared to receive censure by individually oriented colleagues. However, precautions such as including all members of a relationship system in the evaluation and treatment of an identified patient exhibiting suicidal symptomatology may reveal that what appears as a mild suicidal risk when seen in isolation is actually more serious when viewed within the context of a lethal relationship system (Richman, 1979).

Others have taken a somewhat different approach in attempting to enact relationship change by beginning with individual change as a precursor to more systemwide changes. Historically, Bowen (1978) urged differentiation of self as a step in systemic change. More recently, McGoldrick and Carter (2001) advocated coaching as a means of individual change with systemic benefits. As an extension of Bowenian principles, this approach features an emphasis on individual client change with an eye on contextualization. Similarly, Skowron, Holmes, and Sabatelli (2003) advanced the idea that to be truly interdependent in the family system, individual members had to face personal stress and evolve toward differentiation. For these and similar models, stress of the individual still serves the good of the familial relationships.

Less dramatic ethical confrontations in this regard frequently occur within the confines of the therapy hour when marriage and family therapists encourage direct expression of negative feelings and evoke and escalate confrontations among members of relationship systems. Minuchin and Fishman (1981) offered a representative case example in which the therapist purposely uses mocking and inflammatory language to describe the static behavior patterns into which a married couple has fallen and the unspoken attitudes they hold about the relationship, thereby provoking them to articulate their problems:

> **[Wife]:** In the last five years I said to myself the only way not to be hurt is to try to be more like him, and I did. I tried to be like that. I tried to say, "I don't care. I don't need anybody." But I don't want to be like that anymore! I really want to be like I used to be, and then I found that I couldn't, that I have really changed. It's hard when somebody reaches out to you. The normal thing would be to respond. I find that I'm not quite able to do that. It happened before: He touched me and I don't know what to do.

> **Minuchin:** That is saying again that you want to sit on your shit!

>> The therapist's pressure produces a response in the wife. . . . "That is saying that you want to sit on your shit" is not a challenge to the dynamics of the wife but rather a reiteration of the demand for a transformation of the spouse subsystem.

[Wife]: But then he'll stick a knife in my back. (To husband.) If I drop my defenses when you feel like it, you'll withdraw and you'll start throwing little needles at me, and I don't know when it's going to happen.

Minuchin: Milt, she is throwing you a lot of nonsense. She is saying, "Love me, but don't do it because I will kick you in the balls." She is saying to you, "Hold me," and pushing you away. Don't listen to her.

[Wife]: Is that true? Is that what I have been doing all these years?

[Husband]: Well, I felt that before, too.

[Wife]: Why didn't you tell me that?

[Husband]: I'm not a talker, but you push yourself away. I know in the past I felt you preferred to be unhappy.

[Wife]: I don't know what to say. I don't know what to do next. I don't want to be unhappy like this.

[Husband]: Well, the problem in the past—why I didn't tell you things—was because you get angry when you're criticized. Any kind of criticism on what you are or what you do gets a very strong reaction from you.

> The insistence of the therapist on stressing the system in the direction of changing the family members' perspectives in relation to each other produces a transformation of the spouse subsystem. The wife now takes the patient position, not as an isolating technique, but as a request for help. This change in the wife is complemented by the response of the husband.[3]

The degree to which potential risk to an identified patient or to other members should be tolerated for the sake of improved functioning in the total system also raises the problem of deterioration effects in marriage and family therapy. Gurman and Kniskern (1978) identified an important distinction between *deterioration* and *relapse*. They defined deterioration as a negative change or escalation of symptoms during treatment. In contrast, relapse is a negative change occurring between post-treatment and follow-up in the direction of the pretreatment level of functioning. Thus, the risk of deterioration poses a more serious ethical dilemma for therapists than relapse, because relapse suggests that treatment was ineffective but not necessarily harmful (O'Shea & Jessee, 1982).

Although deterioration effects are a concern for individually oriented therapists as well as marriage and family therapists, the latter incur a greater obligation because the scope of their responsibility must be expanded to include multiple members of a relationship system. Further, the position of marriage and family therapists as active, directive agents of change increases the likelihood that they could precipitate deterioration. Gurman and Kniskern's (1978) review of research on deterioration in marriage and family therapy clearly indicates this possibility. They identified a therapist's levels of functioning as dominant among those factors that could contribute to deterioration effects by stating:

> In summary, the available evidence points to a composite picture of deterioration in marital-family therapy being facilitated by a therapist with poor relationship skills who directly attacks "loaded" issues and family members' defenses very early in treatment, fails to

---

[3]*Note:* Reprinted by permission of the publisher from *Family Therapy Techniques* by Salvador Minuchin and H. Charles Fishman, pp. 188–189, Cambridge, MA: Harvard University Press, Copyright © 1981 by the President and Fellows of Harvard College.

intervene in or interpret intra-family confrontation in ongoing treatment, and does little to structure and guide the opening of therapy or to support family members. Such a style is even more likely to be counter-therapeutic with patients who have weak ego-defenses or feel threatened by the nature or very fact of being in treatment. . . . [T]he therapist seems clearly to occupy a central role in most negative treatment outcomes. (p. 14)

Attempting to alter the predominant mode of interaction within a couple or family, promoting change in one member of the system, or seeking change in an area of the total relationship's functioning is likely to evoke new or increased distress or dysfunction in the system, at least temporarily. Therapists who encourage the enhancing of distress and intensification of symptomatology within the therapy hour must be concerned with the continued occurrence of these actions when the session ends. Marital partners or other family members may suffer from embarrassment, anxiety, and loss of respect in the eyes of their mate or other members of the system when they are pressured to make disclosures in session (Hines & Hare-Mustin, 1978). Angry outbursts and strong feelings may be provoked in marital and family sessions; if they are not resolved in the session, they can lead to increased hostility and bitterness.

Therapists who do not address this possibility run the risk of promoting premature termination from therapy, not to mention marital and family dissolution (Mace, 1976). Hines and Hare-Mustin (1978) suggested "inoculation" to guard against potential marital or family disintegration resulting from the direct facilitation of increased stress in the system. By this term, these authors noted therapists should alert members during the initial stage of therapy to the stresses that can likely be expected in resolving their problems. This procedure also alleviates much of the ethical conflict occasioned in therapists' escalating symptomatology and distress in the interest of potential outcome. However, therapists must ultimately learn to weigh the safety and immediate well-being of individual members of a relationship system against effective treatment strategies for the overall system. As we noted in Chapter 1, Boszormenyi-Nagy (1974) identified this ultimate goal as "a restoration of balanced reciprocity of fairness" in marriage and family relationships. Despite such noble egalitarian goals, however, marriage and family therapists must be attentive to inherent or emergent inequities that become evident in the context of their work with couples and families.

INEQUITIES IN POWER AND OPPORTUNITY

As we noted in the beginning of this chapter, we employ the terms *systemic*, *interactional*, and *contextual* in a way to emphasize the unique nature of relationships in marriage and family therapy. In Chapter 2, however, we identified some difficulties that emerge from a purely systemic view of causality and change in marriage and family therapy. Chief among these difficulties are erroneous assumptions about equity in power, opportunity, and hopefulness among all members of the system. In a real way, a factory has many of the characteristics of a system. When compared to factory management, however, the labor force of a factory does not have equal access and power. This inherent inequity gave rise to the development of labor unions in the later years of the 19th century. By contrast, families do not have external organizations such as labor unions to empower its members to demand preferred outcomes. External bodies such as legal or judicial authorities typically act to protect rather than to empower. However, therapists must also recognize that external bodies and traditions (e.g., doctrine of religious groups, cultural/ethnic heritages, etc.) may have familial inequity as a foundational value for the couple or family. Thus, to assume equity in therapy efforts with couples and families could be faulty from the outset.

One may make assumptions about equity within the context of multiple clients when those clients are members of a therapeutic group. A review of the history of family therapy reveals that much was learned and extrapolated about the nature of family relationships by examining group therapy (Gladding, 2002). To be sure, the dynamic complexity of group process is powerful and unique to group composition. Additionally, the capacity for change appears to be strengthened among group members as a result of group identity (Gladding, 2004). However, substantive differences exist between groups and families. Group members typically do not have a preexisting history of experiences and rules, or the power of enforcement, as does a family. The impact of those outside the therapy group often is minimized in sessions, though the impact of extended family often is emphasized by some models of family therapy (Bowen, 1978). Members of a therapy group rarely face threats of possible retaliation for offenses in group sessions, but these risks can be a real concern for spouses and family members. In fact, promises of safety in therapy sessions can offer only false assurances in families with violent predilections. Thus, the fact that a couple or family convened for a session may appear to be in similar circumstances to the beginning of group therapy, but assurances and assumptions of equity cannot be reliable in marriage and family therapy.

In the feminist critique of family systems, elements of marriage and family therapy conceptualization and practice were exposed for vestiges of sexism ranging from blaming mothers for the problems of their adult children to emphasizing the child-rearing role of mothers to marginalizing career preferences of women (C. M. Anderson, 1995; Costello, 2004; Laird, 2000). Gender-bound stereotypes socialized in Western cultures tend to promote expectations about women as dependent, unambitious, overly emotional, and self-sacrificing as a means of validation. According to Betty Carter, "marital therapy that ignores sexism is like rearranging the deck chairs on the Titanic" (Carter, 1986, p. 19). As we will see in Chapter 5, the proliferation of intimate partner violence has led to a form of "patriarchal terrorism" (M. P. Johnson, 1995, p. 285) in which victimized women fear for their lives and those of their children. Against this backdrop, to convene a family or a couple for marriage or family therapy with the hope of promoting an atmosphere of equity in power and opportunity can be naïve and disingenuous. As we noted in Chapter 3, the concept of *therapeutic neutrality* may actually contribute to faulty assumptions about equity, since this concept surmises that similarly respectful and supportive attitudes toward men and women will create and sustain "a level playing field" within the family system.

In an earlier section of this chapter, we noted the uniqueness of convening as an element in marriage and family therapy. When considering this issue in the context of possible inequities, a pattern emerges related to gender distinctions. Butcher, Rouse, and Perry (1998) suggested that gender-based differences may exist related to problem recognition and seeking treatment, with women appearing to be more sensitive and willing than men. However, these authors focused their efforts on individual therapy. In their efforts to examine any differences between husbands and wives in seeking treatment for marital therapy, Doss, Atkins, and Christensen (2003) reported that both husbands and wives rated the efforts of the wife as more active than the efforts of the husband.

These authors further stated, "Because of the dyadic nature of seeking marital therapy, it is possible that much of our clinical work with couples involves a spouse that simply does not see the need to be in therapy" (p. 175). Thus, an inequity in initiative or commitment may be a significant factor in marital therapy, particularly for women when they view both the social obligations and the remedy opportunities as offering severely restricted options for change.

In the earlier discussion of informed consent, we identified another form of inequity in family therapy: the power of children to initiate and enact changes. Certainly, the importance of leadership and decisiveness by parents for purposes of safety and management in a household requires such inequities in most cultures. Although attractive in principle, egalitarian parenting styles often are not supported in research findings. In some families, inequity emerges not through parenting styles but through the parentification of a child. In such instances, a child is elevated in power and responsibility to assume duties more typically associated with parents. Jurkovic (1997) observed that in single-parent families, the parentification of an older child is not uncommon, if only for the simple purpose of having additional decision-making assistance with younger children. Similarly, in conflictual marriages, the parentification of a child as an ally or to assist in triangulating a spouse is also common. Finally, Jurkovic (1997) has indicated that assumption of an inordinate measure of responsibility for familial welfare is quite typical when parentified children become adults, marry, and become parents. Thus, some traditional as well as nontraditional family structures may feature inequities of power, duty, and opportunity related to parentified children or when those children move into adulthood. Marriage and family therapy approaches that involve the inclusion of children are unique when compared to other forms of intervention, though notions of equity can be illusory. More so, the significance of an adult who sustains patterns of parentification as a spouse or parent becomes more apparent in the context of marriage and family therapy.

For marriage and family therapists who embrace a postmodern approach to their work, appreciation for and attentiveness to individual realities and self-in-the-system is critical to affirming respect for each family member. In such models, constructions of realities differ for each member. Additionally, efforts to collaboratively seek a mutually satisfactory remedy to a conflictual circumstance hinges upon valuing individual differences and preferences. Despite this perspective, however, the dynamic forces of family life, the history of family development, and the socialized and institutionalized disparities affecting women makes the uniqueness of marriage and family therapy a setting in which inequities of power and opportunity must be acknowledged as a matter of ethical propriety. Failure to do so may even serve to sustain and further entrench disparities among family members.

PARADOXICAL PROCEDURES

According to Haley (1976), two major types of interventions are possible in marriage and family therapy: (a) interventions in which therapists direct clients with the expectation of compliance, and (b) interventions in which therapists direct clients with the expectation of noncompliance. The latter type of intervention specifically suggests the purpose of a paradoxical procedure: The couple or family changes by rebellion or noncompliance. For example, Hoffman (1981) cited the case of a wife whose constant jealous questioning of her husband only reinforced the husband's reticence toward her. This reticence in turn reinforced her jealousy. A paradoxical procedure was employed to disrupt this destructive sequence of behavior. The wife was directed by the therapist to redouble her jealous questioning. The expected result was achieved when the wife rebelled against the task, which led to a resolution of the presenting problem.

The use of paradox has been a central and frequently controversial topic in marriage and family therapy (Keim, 2000). Proposing that a couple or family continue dysfunctional patterns of behavior with the suggestion that these interactional sequences have a benevolent function constitutes a therapeutic intervention that seems contradictory to the couple's or family's expressed desire for problem resolution. Paradoxical procedures are designed to block or change dysfunctional sequences by using indirect and seemingly illogical means. They "encourage" rather than confront symptoms and objectionable behaviors. They are used instead of direct attempts to introduce change when it is assumed that the couple or family cannot or will not comply with the therapist's advice or persuasion (M. P. Nichols & Schwartz, 2004). Paradoxical procedures thus can require selective disclosure to marital partners and family members by the therapist.

Regardless of their therapeutic orientation, all therapists selectively highlight certain facts and ignore, deemphasize, or avoid others. Although such behaviors constitute selective disclosure (or distortion) of information, the ethical issue that arises involves whether or not therapists are actually deceiving or harming clients (O'Shea & Jessee, 1982). Haley (1976) proposed that ethical prescriptions requiring therapists to disclose to clients everything they sense about them are naïve and that therapists who are unwilling to draw a boundary between themselves and their clients and insist on sharing all not only risk failure but also risk doing harm. Haley maintained that the marriage and family therapist should function as a trained expert, not an equal partner.

In contrast, others (Fisher, Anderson, & Jones, 1981; O'Shea & Jessee, 1982) have stated that paradoxical procedures are effective precisely because they do represent the actual situation the couple or family is experiencing. These procedures embody each marital partner's or family member's phenomenological experience of being involved in a dysfunctional system. P. Watzlawick et al. (1974) were quite explicit in this respect in defining change that occurs through reframing. They identified this process as an attempt to alter "the conceptual and/or emotional setting or viewpoint in relation to which a situation is experienced and to place it in another frame which fits the facts of the same concrete situation equally well or even better, thereby changing its entire meaning" (p. 95). In other words, the meaning attributed to the situation is altered or redefined, and therefore, its consequences change as well. Such a paradoxical directive brings covert patterns of interaction to the surface; the family responds by choosing either to continue or stop the problematic sequences. In either case, the problematic style of interaction now falls within the family's control.

However, some paradoxical procedures are directives given to clients without an explicit explanation or rationale. For instance, Hoffman (1981) described a therapist's telling a depressed wife to become more subservient to her husband. Not surprisingly, the wife rebelled in defiance of the therapist's directive. According to Hoffman, the paradoxical directive unbalanced a dysfunctional complementary balance in the marital relationship, which then became more functionally symmetrical. Previously, the husband and wife had been balanced in a relationship in which he was one-up and she was one-down. By requesting that she put herself even further down (which she had been doing almost daily), the therapist provoked a rebellion, and the couple was able to establish a relationship characterized by greater equality. In discussing this case illustration offered by Hoffman, however, M. P. Nichols and Schwartz (2004) questioned why this outcome should have resulted as Hoffman presented it. Why did the couple not simply reestablish the same complementary relationship?

This question raises an added ethical concern: Therapists can never be sure how a relationship system will absorb and respond to a given intervention (Selvini-Palazzoli, Boscolo, Cecchin, & Prata, 1978). O'Shea and Jessee (1982) proposed that out of the wide range of possible interventions, the use of paradoxical procedures in particular "comes close to being based on faith" (p. 11). Gurman (1978) further asserted that paradoxical reframing and interactional tasks used without explanation or education may at times prolong the couple's or family's dependence on the therapist, preventing the relationship system from developing its own coping mechanisms. O'Shea and Jessee (1982) indicated the appropriateness of paradoxical procedures that are factual from the couple's or family's frame of reference and are truly systemic—procedures that include and affect all members of the relationship system and that employ language or metaphor in harmony with members' subjective experience of their marital or family life. With such paradoxical procedures, the couple or family will more likely identify with the task, change in a more functional manner, and experience the change under their own direction (Selvini-Palazzoli et al., 1978).

Fraser (1984) made a strong case for the use of paradox as a primary procedure in marriage and family therapy. In doing so, he stated:

> For a therapist to look for "a paradox," and then decide whether to do or not to do the supposed paradoxical action is a contradiction in itself. Seeing an action as paradoxical implies that it is contradictory to an accepted body of beliefs. If these beliefs are the guiding premises of the therapist, then choosing to perform the perceived paradoxical action implies the need to question or alter the very principles which guide the therapist's action. System-based intervention should ideally evolve from consistent employment of system theory and a subsequent description of system patterns. Consequent choice of therapeutic action should thus make "sense" to the therapist from within the theory. (p. 370)

Paradoxical approaches also can be employed in other ways. From Figure 4–1 on page 101, you will recall the use of a letter by Wilcoxon and Fennell (1983) as a means of convening non-attending spouses in marital therapy. In this same publication, these authors offered an alternative paradoxical content for their letter (Figure 4–2; see italicized content). In both cases, the letter served as an attempt to convene marital partners and to secure informed consent. In the paradoxical version, however, the authors posed the idea that a less straightforward content could activate both partners to action. Thus, a paradoxical approach to Napier and Whitaker's (1978) Battles for Structure (i.e., informed consent and convening) and Initiative (i.e., energy for change) could support Fraser's (1984) preceding statement about "guiding premises of the therapist." A subsequent study by Wilcoxon and Fennell (1986) addressed differences in rates of engagement and convening with non-attending spouses by comparing the straightforward letter in Figure 4–1 with the paradoxical letter in Figure 4–2. Their findings indicated support for the former.

FIGURE 4–2   Letter to Engage a Non-Attending Spouse—Paradoxical Content

---

(Date)

Mr. John Jones
111 Smith Street
Anytown, USA 00000

Dear Mr. Jones,

As you may know, your wife, Jill, has requested therapy services for difficulties related to your marriage. However, she has stated that you do not wish to participate in marital therapy sessions.

As a professional marriage therapist, I have an obligation to inform each of you of the possible outcome of marital therapy services to only one spouse. The available research indicates that one-spouse marital therapy has resulted in reported increases in marital stress and dissatisfaction for both spouses in the marriage. On the other hand, many couples have reported that marital therapy which includes both spouses has been helpful in reducing marital stress and enhancing marital satisfaction.

These findings reflect general tendencies in marital research and are not absolute in nature. However, it is important for you and Jill to be informed of potential consequences which might occur through marital therapy in which only your spouse attends. Knowing this information, you may choose a course of action which best suits your intentions.

I want you to know that I appreciate your decision not to attend counseling sessions thus far, since I am certain that you feel doing so is your own best effort to maintain your marriage at its current level of satisfaction for both yourself and Jill. In fact, there is even a possibility that the research findings noted above might not apply in your marriage.

As a homework assignment for Jill, I have asked that each of you read this letter and sign in the spaces provided below to verify your understanding of the potential consequences to your relationship by continuing one-spouse marital therapy. If you are interested in joining Jill for marital therapy, in addition to your signature below, please contact my office to indicate your intentions. If not, simply sign below and have Jill return the letter at our next therapy session. I appreciate your cooperation in this matter.

Sincerely,

Therapist X

We verify by our signatures below that we have discussed and understand the potential implications of continued marital therapy with only one spouse in attendance.

Attending Spouse _____ Date _____

Non-Attending Spouse _____ Date _____

Note. From "Engaging the Non-Attending Spouse in Marital Therapy Through the Use of Therapist-Initiated Written Communication" by A. Wilcoxon and D. Fenell, 1983, *Journal of Marital and Family Therapy, 9,* 199–203. Copyright 1983 by the American Association for Marriage and Family Therapy. Reprinted by permission.

Paradoxical procedures are clearly unethical if they are used as a spur-of-the-moment ploy based on limited data. Ethical, responsible use of a paradox requires a therapist's competency and experience gained from a thorough understanding of the role of the symptom within the relationship system, a theoretical or therapeutic approach conducive to the use of paradox, and sufficient clinical supervision and continuing consultation (Fisher et al., 1981). For example, Madanes (1980) concluded that certain steps are necessary for the use of paradoxical procedures in alleviating relevant psychiatric problems in children. She described a specific six-step process emanating from a Strategic Family Therapy orientation:

1. The problem should be clearly defined and specific goals set.
2. The therapist should conceptualize the problem (to him- or herself only) as one in which the child is protecting one or both parents or a relative through his or her symptoms. (This conceptualization depends on the therapist's theoretical orientation.)
3. The therapist must plan to intervene in offering the parents a directive that they will give their child; other family members potentially participate in auxiliary ways. The directive must include a prescription:
   a. To have the problem.
   b. To pretend to have the problem.
   c. To pretend to help the parents.
4. The directive should be practiced in the session before being carried out at home.
5. In the session following the one in which the directive is given, the therapist must obtain a report on the performance of the directive and then continue to prescribe the same directive.
6. As change occurs and the presenting problem behavior begins to disappear, the therapist should drop the issue of the symptom and terminate therapy or begin dealing with other problem behaviors in the same or different ways. Credit should always be given to the parents for their child's improvement.

Madanes' six-step process encompasses a clear, conceptual rationale for the choice of, as well as the content of, a paradoxical procedure ethically considered and employed (Rohrbaugh, Tennen, Press, & White, 1981).

For some, the use of paradoxical procedures represents a form of deception and manipulation that questions the ethical principle of *fidelity*. By contrast, others may conclude that paradoxical procedures are good-faith, though possibly confusing, means of stressing a well-established pattern in a family that may eventually free its members for change. As we saw in our earlier discussion concerning marriage and family therapists as agents of change, the intentional introduction of stress is not an uncommon, or unethical, element of the change process for couples or families. Thus, it would seem that the use of forms of therapeutic paradoxical prompts therapists to consider the ethical principle of *beneficence* as well as the issue of virtue ethics in considering whether such procedures are "therapeutic."

TRIANGULATION

Triangulation as used in the marriage and family therapy literature has been defined as "the process by which a dyadic emotional system encompasses a third system member for the purpose of maintaining or establishing homeostatic balance" (Sauber, L'Abate, & Weeks, 1985, p. 172). Bowen (1978) asserted that two-person emotional systems become unstable in the face of conflict and stabilize by forming three-person systems or triangles. In general, the concept of triangulation has been used to describe interactional problems within the context of a marital or family system or within the therapy setting itself. Once again, the contextual nature of marriage and family therapy often convenes multiple family members in the therapy relationship to create unusual dynamics and unusual ethical dilemmas such as triangulation. For example, a therapist may become "triangulated" in a conflict between two marital partners, as in the following case illustration:

> A couple with increasing marital difficulties presented themselves for therapy. Immense hostility was clearly evident between the pair almost immediately when the wife voiced her opinion that therapy "was a waste of time." The husband remained after the conclusion of the initial evaluation session to complain about his wife's unwillingness to "try." The therapist, a relative novice, felt good that the husband was open in confiding further information and was reinforced in fantasizing about rescuing the couple—or at least the husband, who was more open and accepting of the therapist's assistance.

The emerging triangulation process will be destructive to all three paired relationships: the therapist and wife, the wife and husband, and the therapist and husband as well. Triangulation here represents two close and two distant poles (Figure 4–3).

If the therapist sympathizes with the husband, that will alienate the wife even further. It also makes it less likely that the husband will do anything directly to work out his complaints with his wife. Although this triangulation process may give the therapist the illusion of being close to the husband, it is at best a false intimacy. Defending the wife offers no better solution. That alternative only moves the therapist from the husband to the wife and widens any gulf between them. As long as the triangulation continues, personal and direct one-to-one interactions cannot develop between the couple. Any boundary violation in any form of therapy can be problematic, but a boundary violation leading to triangulation involving the therapist represents the infusion of personal needs of the therapist into the relationship. More compelling, however, is the introduction of exploitive inequity that could actually do harm to one or both family members or spouses in the triangle.

FIGURE 4–3 Triangulation Involving the Therapist

Note. From "Agency Triangles: Problems in Agency–Family Relationships" by D. Carl and G. J. Jurkovic, 1983, *Family Process, 22,* 441–451. Copyright 1983 by Blackwell Publishers. Reprinted by permission.

Even though marriage and family therapy involves individuals who display symptoms in the larger context of their marital or family system, couples and families themselves are part of a larger social–cultural system. Thus, the concept of triangulation can extend beyond the boundaries of the couple–therapist or family–therapist relationship system (Gladding, 2001). This is a fact often neglected by marriage and family therapists, even though they ironically address triangulation in the context of the couple or family relationship system. Unwittingly, many therapists become part of dysfunctional triangles created by the very sources that refer couples and families to them for help (Carl & Jurkovic, 1983). The ethical dilemmas presented can be troublesome. Bowen (1978) addressed one part of this problem:

> In periods of very high tension, a system will triangle in more and more outsiders. A common example is a family in great stress that uses the triangle system to involve neighbors, schools, police, clinics and a spectrum of outside people as participants in the family problem. The family thus reduces the tension within the inner family, and it can actually create a situation in which the family tension is being fought out by outside people. (p. 479)

Therapists allowing themselves to become triangulated in such situations show little regard for the self-reliance of couples and families and their ability to grapple effectively with their own difficulties, an approach that raises the ethical issue of encouraging unnecessary client dependency. Additionally, such an approach clearly begs the question of virtue ethics on the part of the marriage and family therapist.

Therapists must avoid assuming a superior position in relation to couples and families by excessively helping them cope with service systems. Hoffman and Long (1969) asserted that therapists who act as "social brokers" or "advocates" in expertly mediating couple–agency or family–agency relations may become "too omnipotent a figure" in the couple's or family's affairs. In such cases, the inequity in the therapy relationship is reflected in the subordination of family members to the power and control of the therapist. Though some cultures may support such outcomes, the ethical pursuit of *autonomy* for clients is compromised to the extent that a family's growth and efficacy is impeded. This issue is particularly compelling for advocates of a postmodern model of intervention that values collaboration within the therapy relationship. Carl and Jurkovic (1983) offered a case illustration in this regard:

> Ms. James, a single parent whose 6-year-old was not participating at school . . . complained that the teacher did not understand her daughter, Angela, and even feared that the teacher was physically abusing her. With [the] mother's permission, the therapist visited the teacher at school where he learned that Angela was behaving in a listless and immature manner in the classroom. It was questionable whether she would be promoted to the next grade. Also of serious concern to the teacher was that Angela's mother did not have confidence in her teaching, although she had more than fifteen years' experience. All of the ingredients for an agency triangle were present. Both mother and teacher were complaining to the therapist about the other and clearly seeking a coalition with him. To avoid becoming part of the problem, the therapist "detriangulated" himself in a subsequent session in which he met with both the family and the teacher in the child's classroom. The strategy simply was to encourage mother and teacher to talk directly to one another and to agree on a plan for helping Angela. After a number of angry false starts in which Ms. James and the teacher attempted to speak through Angela first and then through the therapist, which he stopped, they were able to make eye contact and to air their differences directly to each other. In the process,

the mother learned that the teacher had Angela's best interests at heart, and the teacher came to some understanding of the mother's fears and stressful life situation. With additional prompting by the therapist, they clarified how each could appropriately help Angela in view of their different roles and also ways in which they could collaborate. (pp. 448–449)

The most respectful and productive stance by the therapist was to encourage Ms. James to deal directly with her daughter's teacher. Therapists can normally leave this task to a couple or family themselves or, if necessary, coach marital partners or family members on how to assert themselves when seeking services as well as how to protect themselves from unwarranted agency intrusions. By creating a context in which Ms. James was able to work out her concerns with the teacher in a one-to-one manner, the therapist not only aided her in resolving the current problems but also prepared her to better cope with similar future difficulties.

Bowen's (1978) comments emphasize triangulation initiated by family members. Carl and Jurkovic (1983) also addressed the actions of helping agents who inadvertently triangulate families. They proposed the addition of a corollary to Bowen's axiom concerning the instability of two-person system conflicts: "The relationship between an agency and a family is unstable under stress and will tend to form a three-party system, often with another agency, to diffuse the stress" (p. 442). Such interagency conflicts frequently develop after difficulty arises between an agency and a couple or family (as client). Some third agency is then pulled in as an attempt to divert the original conflict. Hoffman and Long (1969) termed this predicament a systems dilemma, describing it as follows:

> These systems seldom act collaboratively, and are more often than not in conflict with one another. As a result, a person may be caught in a paradoxical situation in a family which is in turn caught in paradoxical situations within the systems designed to help the family or person. (p. 241)

Couples and families enter therapy in many ways: referrals from family service agencies, schools, clergy, and courts; cross-referrals within mental health centers; and self-referrals. The kind of "paradoxical situation" alluded to by Hoffman and Long frequently develops when an agency refers a couple or family to another agency (e.g., a marriage and family therapist). The couple or family may have challenged the agency to be more helpful or act differently in some manner, or the agency may have felt the need for support services to carry out its functions, perhaps because its own efforts had been unsuccessful. The nature of this referral process can have a powerful effect on the therapeutic process and outcome (Selvini-Palazzoli et al., 1978).

For example, family service agencies may refer a family for therapy to "fix up" parents so that they can become "fit" to regain custody of their children. A court may refer a couple to therapy as a required precursor to potential divorce proceedings. Schools regularly refer children because they are acting out or doing poorly in the classroom in the belief that problems in their home environment constitute primary contributors. As we discussed in Chapter 2, the objectives and values of an institution can blend or conflict with the personal or professional layers of values held by the marriage and family therapist. If the values of an institution conflict with the personal values of the family, however, the therapist can easily be cast into a position of "choosing sides." Carl and Jurkovic (1983) suggested that all of these situations have a common denominator: an "agenda" from the referral source that figures prominently in the development of agency triangulation. They illustrate this issue in discussing day treatment program referrals:

> Another intrasystem dilemma occurs when a day program in a mental health center refers a client family for treatment in the hope of making the client a "better-adjusted part" of the day program. Since many systems' interventions rely on reframing problems and inducing change in ways that make clients less dependent upon supporting agencies, conflictual program goals provide ample opportunity for a triangle. The day program wants a more cooperative "member." The systems therapist wants no "member" at all. The family can stay the same so that all concerned remain involved. These different "agendas" derive, of course, from the guiding philosophy, rules, procedures, and objectives of the agency. As stress develops between the agency and its charges (whether they be day program participants in a mental health center, students in the classroom, parolees, etc.), the agency may direct the client and his or her family to some other agency—often a therapist. The therapist's orientation frequently conflicts with that of the agency, and unless the two collaborate effectively, an agency triangle can result. (p. 444)[4]

In accepting referrals from agency sources, therapists are immediately faced with an ethical dilemma. The couple or family as client is entitled to expect certain things from the therapist, particularly to put their interests above all others' interest. Couples and families as clients derive intrinsic benefits from the assurance that the therapist has a commitment to helping them. All these circumstances change when a third party enters the picture. The quality of the relationship between the therapist and a couple or family is irrevocably altered once the self-contained structure of that relationship is no longer intact, which inevitably is the case when agency referrals incorporate agendas emanating from the referral source. Although the therapist–couple or therapist–family relationship is not necessarily invalidated and the couple or family will not stop receiving adequate services, the nature of the relationship is different.

Bourne (1982) summarized the ethical dilemma in a biblical allusion: "No [one] can serve two masters." This principle is at the heart of the ethical issue therapists must confront in addressing agency triangulation. Carl and Jurkovic (1983) proposed a number of guidelines for therapists to prevent agency triangulation:

1. Therapists must include themselves and other nonfamily members, agencies, and institutions as parts of the presenting problem needing treatment. The unit of treatment thus becomes the larger "suprasystem" incorporating the couple–therapist–agency or family–therapist–agency.
2. The identification of these parts requires an ecological assessment that extends beyond the boundaries of the immediate couple or family relationship system to include other interacting systems. (Note: Carl and Jurkovic propose that this assessment is a point at which potential agency triangulation can be detected.)
3. After conducting such an assessment, therapists' further strategies should incorporate cooperation with relevant agencies. Successful collaboration that does not limit therapists' ability to maneuver requires them to join skillfully with other helping agents without taking a one-up position and without implying that

---

[4]*Note:* From "Agency triangles: Problems in agency–family relationships," by D. Carl and G. J. Jurkovic, 1983, *Family Process, 22,* pp. 444, 448–449. Copyright 1983. Reprinted with permission.

these agents are part of the unit of treatment. These collaborative efforts should begin early in the therapy process, preferably at the point of referral.

4. Although it is best for couples and families to handle problematic agency contacts themselves, there will be times when therapists may want to block or redirect subversive agency actions, especially if the couple or family is under significant stress. Particularly at a time when publicly funded services are declining, therapists who work with couples and families receiving such services will have to resolve any quandary created by encouraging these relationship systems to be more self-reliant in the face of harsh economic realities.

5. Therapists should always be aware of their limited power to control other agency interventions and policies. At minimum, adverse agency actions can often be reframed in the interest of the couple or family. Or inventive therapists can seek out other facets of the agency operation that might offer therapeutic opportunities. For example, in special education settings, the development and updating of Individualized Education Plans require that parents meet regularly with school staff. If not invited, therapists can ask to attend these meetings to offer input as a part of family therapy efforts.

6. Therapists must perceive themselves as active, not passive, participants in any agency triangulation process. They may even be the primary precipitators of such processes. Therapists who refer couples or families for other services—psychological testing, medication, tutoring, and so on—must be clear about the purpose of the referral. Is it to help the couple or family or to alleviate the therapist's own discomfort? If the former, then it is necessary to coordinate therapeutic efforts with other service providers and to reach agreement on areas of responsibility and control. Therapists' discomfort, on the other hand, is best addressed through consultation with a clinical supervisor or colleague.

OTHER UNIQUENESSES IN MARRIAGE AND FAMILY THERAPY

From our discussion in Chapter 1, readers should be reminded that as agents of change, marriage and family therapists should strive to be culturally responsive practitioners. In this respect, a variety of relevant uniquenesses exist in the practice of marriage and family therapy. For example, our earlier discussion concerning stress as an element of the process of change may not necessarily be understood consistently among all cultural groups. Of particular regard in this matter are those people whose cultural heritage has promoted an expectation that the therapy process will result in relief and comfort rather than added stress. Similarly, although many Westernized clients may be comfortable with assertiveness and even conflict within the therapy relationship, those of non-Westernized backgrounds may find conflict and expressiveness within the family to be troublesome, disrespectful, or inappropriate.

Our earlier discussion in Chapter 2 concerning institutional objectives and values is also significant in considering unique elements of marriage and family therapy. Consider a circumstance in which a teenage girl has elected to drop out of high school. In some situations, institutions (e.g., schools, courts, etc.) may require that she return to school until she has reached an age at which she can legally make such a choice.

However, her cultural heritage may be one in which such a decision is both typical and even endorsed. In this situation, the problem definition and related goals for therapy may reflect conformity. Since the institutional values may conflict with the personal values of the family, conformity may actually be perceived as another form of oppression. In traditional individual psychotherapy, such a situation may be troublesome. Within the context of family therapy, however, parents may perceive admonishment in the presence of their children, resulting in embarrassment and resistance.

Other uniquenesses in marriage and family therapy emerge from nontraditional family structures and organizations. Though quite common, single-parent families are still socialized as being nonrepresentative of the Westernized ideal of family structures. Similarly, blended families, although common, have unique challenges, and family therapy with a blended family introduces unique circumstances for the therapist. Same-gender couples continue to encounter social and political barriers for acceptance and recognition. Same-gender parents face a variety of challenges that emerge in the context of family therapy. Additionally, mixed-racial or mixed-cultural families introduce differences in both social and intercultural traditions and expectations that emerge in the context of family therapy.

From these and various other examples, one can note that diversity in family structures and backgrounds can introduce unique challenges for the marriage and family therapist. As we noted in Chapter 1, valuing and respecting differences on the part of the therapist is critical with all couples and families but particularly those with uniqueness in structure and heritage. From the vantage of ethical considerations, marriage and family therapy introduces a unique context for encountering both traditional and nontraditional family structures and compositions that requires therapists to attend to personal biases or reference points of conventionality. Additionally, marriage and family therapists must develop competencies for working with such diverse families through continuing education, consultation, and supervision. Finally, nontraditional families require marriage and family therapists to think expansively about the applied meaning of foundational ethical principles such as *beneficence*, *nonmaleficence*, *autonomy*, *justice*, and *fidelity* as well as virtue ethics in decision making and practice.

SUMMARY

Marriage and family therapy, as opposed to individually oriented psychotherapy, considers the couple or family as an active, whole unit. This view represents a conceptual change in therapeutic thinking: Relationship systems are seen as rule-governed, organic wholes rather than as collections of individuals interacting according to the dictates of their separate personalities. This point of view—thinking about relationship systems instead of individuals—requires that special ethical as well as theoretical dilemmas be confronted. Solutions to such dilemmas cannot necessarily be derived from individually oriented psychotherapeutic experiences.

Marriage and family therapists are faced with the challenge of coping with a plethora of thorny ethical issues that impinge on their work; they must deal with far more potential ethical conflicts in their clinical decision making than most individually oriented therapists because of the increasingly complex nature of their work (Morrison, Layton, & Newman, 1982). The ethical concerns addressed in this chapter raise questions that need to be answered by marriage and family therapists:

1. In what ways are the foundational ethical principles unique for the practice of marriage and family therapy?
2. In what ways are principle ethics and virtue ethics unique for the decision-making process in marriage and family therapy?
3. Can therapists automatically assume the right to define couples' and families' presenting problems in terms of their own therapeutic orientation?
4. How much concerted effort (or pressure) can therapists exert in convening all significant familial or extrafamilial members for therapy sessions?
5. Should willing individual marital partners or several family members seeking assistance go untreated because one individual refuses to participate?
6. Should therapists impose their control on couples and families? If so, to what extent should they impose it in seeking change in the relationship system?
7. How much intrasystem stress should be introduced or allowed to materialize in the pursuit of change?
8. What are the ethical implications inherent in employing paradoxical procedures?
9. How can the impact of working with couples and families within the larger context of service agency impingements be ethically pursued?
10. What other nontraditional family structures or dynamics exist to present unique ethical concerns for marriage and family therapists?

Abroms (1978) asserted that ethical behavior on the part of the therapist requires more than good intentions based on personal bias and subjectivity. If therapeutic ethics involves a determination of what therapists ought to do to provide maximum benefit for the greatest number of persons, then marriage and family therapy as a treatment of relationship systems instead of individuals in relative isolation appears to be the most ethical and integrated of approaches (O'Shea & Jessee, 1982). Still, such an approach requires attention to the unique ethical dilemmas that emerge in marriage and family therapy. In Chapter 6, we offer a discussion of selected contemporary ethical issues faced by practitioners, supervisors, and researchers. As we examine those issues in Chapter 6, we encourage readers to return to this chapter and reconsider the ways in which the unique framework of marriage and family therapy affects ethical decision making and practice. In an attempt to demonstrate the interactive nature of cultural diversity, worldview, multiple layers of values, ethical propriety, and the unique nature of marriage and family therapy, however, first we offer Chapter 5 as an illustration of the considerations marriage and family therapists will encounter if faced with a situation involving intimate partner violence.

Intimate Partner Violence:
An Illustrative Example

At the conclusion of Chapter 4, we discussed the complexity of ethical decision making while attending to concerns such as diversity and pluralism, emergent layers of values, foundational principles, ethical traditions, and the unique aspects of marriage and family therapy. Chapter 6 will offer an examination of selected contemporary ethical issues and Chapter 7 will feature a casebook approach to considering the implications of the AAMFT Code of Ethics (2001).

This chapter offers one an in-depth example in which we apply the array of elements marriage and family therapists may consider when faced with an ethical dilemma. We have not selected an easy or simple issue; rather, we have selected an issue with great complexity and possible uncertainty for marriage and family therapists: intimate partner violence. In reviewing a variety of ethical considerations related to this topic, we hope to offer a view that consolidates our earlier discussions and that prompts similar thought for the remaining two chapters concerning ethical practices in marriage and family therapy. We also offer these comments with an intentional grounding in relevant professional literature rather than reliance on intuition or personal preferences.

INTIMATE PARTNER VIOLENCE: AN OVERVIEW

The terms *domestic violence* or *intimate partner violence* (IPV) have emerged in the professional literature as descriptors of chronic as well as episodic patterns of abuse, ranging from harsh criticism to aggressive brutality, between adults in intimate relationships (Danis & Lockhart, 2003). For purposes of this chapter, we will use these terms interchangeably, although IPV has become the more common term for describing abusive relationships among both married and unmarried couples. Distinguished from criminal acts that may occur between strangers, such as assault, battery, or other similar crimes, IPV concerns perpetrating hostility of a more hidden nature (M. P. Johnson, 1995).

Unlike other forms of aggression, IPV often features the unfortunate yet compelling elements of intergenerational and gender-specific traditions promoted within a family or a community (Bevan & Higgins, 2002; J. Brown, 2004).

Acts such as child abuse or elder abuse are actually forms of domestic violence, though they are typically distinguished in duty-to-warn and duty-to-protect legal mandates that compel action on the part of therapists in order to protect those who may be unable to protect themselves (Buttell, 2001). The distinction between adult partner victimization and child abuse or elder abuse has been the myth of equality among adults; that is, that an adult *could* choose to leave the relationship, should one wish to do so, unlike less powerful children or aged adults. Over time, however, findings have indicated that such equity does not exist, particularly regarding the options for alternate living arrangements available to victims (Kurri & Wahlstrom, 2001; Sharman, 2001). Originally described as "wife-beating," domestic violence initially concerned violence perpetrated by a husband against his wife. From this background emerged the term *battered wife syndrome* or similar references to chronic yet inescapable victimization (Holtzworth-Munroe & Stuart, 1994). In more contemporary times, views on IPV have been amended to reflect other relationships (e.g., cohabitation, same-gender couples, etc.).

IPV is a complex and multifaceted condition for marriage and family therapists to encounter. Holtzworth-Munroe and Stuart (1994) identified three dimensions of domestic violence as the basis for distinguishing subtypes of offenders. They noted offenders differ according to *severity of violence* (e.g., shoving, severe brutality, etc.), *generality of violence* (i.e., violence toward partner or toward others), and *presence/absence of psychopathology/personality disorders*. Within this framework, a single unitary view of IPV is unlikely. Similarly, M. P. Johnson and Ferraro (2000) identified two types of intimate violence: (a) male power and dominance, and (b) mutual conflict between partners. Although the first of these two types coincides with the long-standing notions of battered-wife syndrome, the second suggests a more reciprocal pattern of conflict within a relationship. However, these authors were quick to point out that despite such a pattern of conflict between partners, the majority of such circumstances led to the wife as the victim. M. P. Johnson (1995) offered an insightful view of the multidimensional nature of IPV related to *patriarchal terrorism* and *common couple violence*. The former represents an omnipresent and chronic pattern of dominance and maltreatment involving both violent and nonviolent means of control, while the latter is more episodic, situation specific, and more likely to include both partners, though more severe expressions continue to be associated with males. From these few works, one can see that IPV can have a number of faces, but all are scarred in some ways.

As with most any circumstance of oppression or harmful acts toward another person, speculation about causes of IPV have been offered in the professional literature. Thus far, no single cause has yet been identified (Holtzworth-Munroe, Meechan, Herron, Rehman, & Stuart, 2000). Instead, discussions of the origins of domestic violence consider co-occuring or contributing factors and conditions that may promote or sustain such patterns. These factors appear to be both psychological/experiential and environmental in nature. Chang and Saunders (2002) indicated that a history of child abuse, antisocial tendencies, and a predilection toward expressing anger in violent ways appeared to be common among victimizers. Bevan and Higgins (2002) observed that a variety of types of childhood maltreatment contributed to tendencies of violence; including: (a) physical abuse, (b) psychological maltreatment, (c) sexual abuse, (d) neglect, and (e) witnessing violence. J. Brown (2004) speculated that from chronic childhood experiences such as these, the development of shame as a significant aspect of domestic violence should not be discounted. Other variables such as unemployment, poverty, stress, suicidal ideation, and homelessness also have been noted as co-occuring factors in IPV (Danis & Lockhart, 2003; Gerlock, 2001).

Data from the Centers for Disease Control (2003) regarding IPV indicate that 5.3 million incidents are reported annually in the United States. These incidents result in nearly 2 million injuries and nearly 1,300 deaths per year. Additionally, a complete picture regarding the incidence of IPV will likely never be known, since decisions not to report are common among victims, due to fear of retaliation or possible harm to others (e.g., children).

A growing awareness of the prevalence of abuse and violence in families began in the 1970s. Before that time, "intimate partnerships" were "believed to emanate from higher virtues like romantic love, affection, or a natural unity of interest" and thus were "exempt from considerations of justice" and ethics (Jory, Anderson, & Greer, 1997, p. 401). However, contextual therapists brought the concept of justice with its ethical implications into the field of marriage and family therapy especially through the writings of Boszormenyi-Nagy (e.g., Boszormenyi-Nagy & Sparks, 1973). The focus in this approach was the intergenerational nature of justice, in which justice was defined as the "long-term preservation of an oscillating balance among family members, whereby the basic interests of each are taken into account by the others in a way that is fair from a multilateral perspective" (Boszormenyi-Nagy & Ulrich, 1981, p. 160).

In examining the considerations relevant for marriage and family therapists in ethical actions concerning IPV, we offer an applied view of the issues discussed in previous chapters. To begin this discussion, we posit that marriage and family therapists, as well as their clients, have cultural and value heritages that affect their viewpoints concerning IPV. A review of Chapters 1 and 2 may be in order to assist with the following section of this chapter.

DIVERSITY, SYSTEMIC, AND VALUE CONSIDERATIONS

Perhaps the most distinguishing characteristic of IPV is its contextual framework within familial and social cultures. A notable pattern of intergenerational repetition has emerged from the literature to suggest that many who resort to violence in instances of domestic disagreement or frustration believe it is both allowable and even deserved (Danis & Lockhart, 2003; McCloskey, Treviso, Scionti, & Posson, 2002). Anecdotal stories appear in popular literature and movies suggesting that a "new victim" of domestic violence will "simply have to learn that it's the way things are done around here" or "It was the same for me with your father, so get used to it."

Research concerning aspects of *diversity* and distinction has bolstered the notion that marriage and family therapists must consider these dimensions when working with clients who are dealing with IPV (May, 1998). Significant considerations have been identified for dimensions such as gender (Carney & Buttell, 2004; Henning, Jones, & Holdford, 2003), race (Buttell & Carney, 2004; Sharman, 2001), and ethnicity and national origin (Fulcher, 2002; Kasturirangan & Williams, 2003; Lee, 2003; McCloskey et al., 2002). Similarly, others have identified considerations such as religion (Foss & Warnke, 2003), sexual orientation (Kaschak, 2001; Peterman & Dixon, 2003; A. Robinson, 2002), and disability (Hassouneh-Phillips & Curry, 2002) as critical aspects of IPV. Though psychiatric conditions or forms of emotional impairment may contribute to IPV, the acceptability of episodic or chronic aggression among some groups is not uncommon (Pedersen, 1996; Thomas, 1998). Such patterns and customs compel marriage and family therapists to consider heritage and social circumstances of clients as significant factors in avoiding the nondiscrimination elements of ethical codes previously noted in Table 3–2 on page 55. If a question exists for ethical propriety on the part of marriage and family therapists encountering IPV, does such a question pit concerns about victimization against respect for heritage and social or family custom (C. Williams, 1999)?

The discussion about *valuing* from Chapter 1 is also relevant for marriage and family therapists facing an IPV circumstance. An interpretation of the principle of "accepting what is" may suggest that restraint and tolerance are in order for the culturally responsive therapist. "After all," the therapist may conclude, "I am not at liberty to force a value or a choice on clients simply to feel better about my place in this relationship." However, a more complete picture emerges when the therapist considers the "balance of fairness" between *obligation* and *entitlement*, particularly in terms of *freedom from destructive obligations.* From this more complete vantage point, the valuing efforts among participants in marriage and family therapy, including the therapist, appear to indicate that respect for differences does not equate with tacit acceptance of victimization.

Chapter 2 featured an examination of *systemic epistemology.* As was noted, the systemic viewpoint continues to have considerable influence on conceptual and applied aspects of marriage and family therapy. However, the *feminist critique* offered in this review specifically emphasized domestic violence as a circumstance in which, if applied in a mechanistic fashion, the systemic perspective suggests that the victim seeks and desires violence for the sake of stability. In this regard, the systemic perspective on the "balance of fairness" and the obligation–entitlement interaction could focus on the element of *balance* rather than the element of *fairness.* It is this point with which feminist-informed authors disagree mightily. In a related discussion of possible exceptions to systemic epistemology, those emphasizing *self-in-the-system* suggested that viewing one's self as "one among many" failed to acknowledge individual uniqueness. Such a position could serve to sustain the oppressive nature of IPV, particularly when a victim considers other options as beyond reasonable hope. When considering these two points regarding domestic violence, marriage and family therapists espousing a systemic viewpoint should take great care in examining unintended consequences of a logical syllogism leading to the conclusion that the victim rationally chooses to stay in a violent relationship.

Chapter 2 also featured a discussion of *multiple layers of values* affecting marriage and family therapists. The *personal values* of the therapist may be particularly important when confronting various aspects of IPV. A therapist may find such behavior to be unacceptable and may seek an outcome consistent with his or her preferences. The personal values of the therapist may clash with those of the client or family, however, particularly if the victimization is sustained in cultural or familial origins. By contrast, a therapist impaired by an unresolved history of victimization with an intimate partner may minimize its significance or may over-identify with the victim to the extent of undertaking a personal crusade for justice. As one can see, decisions deriving from the personal layer of values held by the marriage and family therapist may be complex and even interrelated with those of the family.

At the *professional layer of values*, a significant consideration for the therapist may be a hierarchy of duties. Attending to concerns about *client safety* and *therapist role* (e.g., neutrality, noncoercion, etc.) generally coexists in a balanced manner in therapeutic relationships. In instances of IPV, however, duties related to client safety may outweigh duties related to therapist role. Such is the case in instances of duty-to-warn or duty-to-protect obligations on the part of a therapist. For some, becoming an advocate for client safety may be the more compelling personal and professional value. However, such a role may impede, if not clash with, the role of therapist should he or she act in a manner that could be inequitable toward other members of the family, particularly the victimizer.

Institutional values associated with social custom, legal precedent, and even risk management in liability may converge or conflict with personal or professional layers of values. For example, a marriage and family therapist who wants to reserve the primacy of the "therapist" role may face conflicting institutional mandates for advocacy or even referral in cases of domestic violence. By contrast, all three layers may support insistence that the victim seek safety, a role that could clearly threaten a subsequent therapist function with both the victim and the victimizer.

A recurring discussion in previous chapters has concerned the Battle for Structure and the Battle for Initiative (Napier & Whitaker, 1978). Thus far, our examination of elements related to ethical considerations in circumstances of IPV has focused on elements of values and roles. A clear distinction between these battles often is not realistic in instances of IPV, however. To manage therapy by requiring victim and victimizer to convene in order to win the Battle for Structure could possibly enrage the victimizer and endanger the victim. To consider the Battle for Initiative to be fully the responsibility of all parties could be based on an erroneous assumption of equity in power and control, which research literature conclusively demonstrates does not exist (Danis & Lockhart, 2003; Gerlock, 2001; Kurri & Wahlstrom, 2001). Similar to many conceptual notions, a neat package of distinction is frequently impossible. However, ethical principles, traditions, and codes can be informative in terms of decisions and actions.

PRINCIPLES, TRADITIONS, AND UNIQUENESSES

Chapter 3 offered a distinction between principle ethics and virtue ethics on the part of marriage and family therapists. As was discussed, principle ethics primarily address the question "What do I want to do?" whereas virtue ethics primarily address the question "Who do I want to be?" In many ways, the circumstance of IPV merges these questions, since, absent a legal mandate, therapists' actions define who they want to be.

Some findings have evolved from studies of IPV circumstances suggesting that a victimized partner should be encouraged by the therapist to leave the abusive relationship (Betancourt, 1997; Roberts, 1996; Stith et al., 2004). But the issue is often complicated by the acculturation of the victim or victimizer to the extent that a pattern of violence is viewed as normal or expected (Bograd, 1999; Kasturirangan & Williams, 2003; Sharman, 2001). Ethically, a recommendation of separation creates a dilemma: Should the therapist encourage the victim to leave the relationship? On one side of the question is respect for one's self-determination and an assumption that the victim possesses sufficient psychological competence to act in his or her own best interests. On the other side is the conviction that the experience of the victimization cycle sufficiently justifies compromising the client's autonomous functioning. The five principles of Beauchamp and Childress (2001) can guide therapists in deciding what action would best serve the standard of primacy of the client's welfare.

Beneficence promotes the notion that therapists confer benefits and promote clients' well-being. The literature describing chronic patterns of IPV often notes that separation from the victimizer will maximize a victim's psychological growth, facilitate a more objective assessment of the relationship, and reduce the immediate potential of injury or death:

> Only after women feel protected from another assault, can they begin to deal with the reality of the battering situation. (L. Walker, 1981, p. 88)

> The symbiotic dependency bonds must be broken and each partner taught independence and new communication skills. (McG Mullen & Carroll, 1983, p. 34)

> Marriage counseling cannot proceed while the wife is living in fear. (Wentzel & Ross, 1983, p. 427)

Beneficence compels that benefits and harms be balanced; that is, positive outcomes must be weighed against the risks (Beauchamp & Childress, 2001; Bograd & Mederos, 1999). Studies have shown that victims of IPV, most frequently battered women, who leave the batterer and go to a shelter where help is available have far greater success in overcoming the emotional and motivational deficits induced by the feelings of helplessness they experience while remaining at home (Ehrensaft & Vivian, 1996; L. Walker, 1984). Less success in overcoming these feelings of helplessness has been reported when victims remain with abusive partners and try to change the relationship to one with minimal violence (Flax, 1977; Greenspun, 2000). Because the benefits outweigh the harms, a therapist could assert the value for a victim to leave the relationship.

The principle of *nonmaleficence* is epitomized by the adage "above all, do no harm." Not encouraging a victim to leave circumstances that are certainly dangerous appears to violate this principle. Although a therapist may not be inflicting the harm personally, he or she is allowing clients to return unchallenged and unaided to a setting in which they will probably be abused in the future (Goldner, 1999; L. Walker, 1984; Wentzel & Ross, 1983).

The principle of *justice* demands that clients with equal needs not be discriminated against through either a therapist's incompetence or denial of treatment. However, clients with unique needs that require special interventions are entitled to unique treatment (Freeman, Engels, & Altekruse, 2004; Huston, 1984). Intimate partners victimized by domestic violence display unique characteristics and needs because of the psychological reactions concomitant to living in a violent environment. Some authors have compared victims of IPV to hostages who are unable to escape life-threatening or identity-threatening situations characterized by social isolation and dependency, and who then form deep attachments to their captors as a form of "patriarchal terrorism" (M. P. Johnson, 1995, p. 285). Because of this trauma, they are unable to assess their real plight or risk; the perpetrator's intermittent but persistent abuse has destroyed their subjective realities (Graham, Rawlings, & Rimini, 1988; Painter & Dutton, 1985). Justice, therefore, lends support to acting on behalf of a victimized partner.

Fidelity emphasizes the importance of therapists' faithfulness and loyalty to clients. L. Walker (1981) reported that battered women generally believe that their batterer's charm will seduce anyone, even professionals: A "battered woman may misinterpret any attempt at developing a therapeutic alliance with the batterer" (p. 85). Victimized clients must be assured that the therapist will be loyal to them above any connection to the victimizer or to the unconditional maintenance of the marriage (Vatcher & Bogo, 2001). Fidelity also demands that therapists be truthful with clients, suggesting that the therapist has an obligation to inform a victimized client of research findings indicating that it is dangerous and not psychologically helpful to return to the batterer (Goldner, 1999; Graham, Rawlings, & Rimini, 1988; Huston, 1984).

The ethical dilemma created by potential infringement of the client's *autonomy* is less easily resolved. Autonomy proposes that an individual has a right to make her or his own decisions if those decisions do not violate the rights of others. Consider the entries in the various ethical codes relative to autonomy and rights to choice noted in Table 5–1.

To tell a client to leave home can be viewed as an infringement of her or his autonomy. It also can be argued that respect for the autonomous functioning of the victim is vital because of the vulnerable and dependent nature of the victim, particularly given the inherent transference aspects of the therapist–client relationship. Transference issues with battered women tend to include withholding anger from or being overly compliant with persons of authority (Heppner, 1978; McG Mullen & Carroll, 1983; Stith et al., 2004). Therapists must be cautious not to misuse their position as the object of the transference phenomenon by being overly directive with these clients (Huston, 1984).

TABLE 5–1 Ethical Considerations Regarding Client Rights to Autonomy and Self-Determination

American Association for Marriage and Family Therapy (2001)
"Marriage and family therapists respect the rights of clients to make decisions and help them to understand the consequences of these decisions."

American Counseling Association (2005)
"Counselors encourage client growth and development in ways that foster the interest and welfare of clients and promote formation of healthy relationships."

American Psychological Association (2002)
"Psychologists are aware that special safeguards may be necessary to protect the rights and welfare of persons or communities whose vulnerabilities impair autonomous decision making."

International Association of Marriage and Family Counselors (2005)
"Marriage and family counselors respect the autonomy of the families with whom they work. They do not make decisions that rightfully belong to family members."

National Association of Social Workers (1999)
"Social workers promote clients' socially responsible self-determination. Social workers seek to enhance clients' capacity and opportunity to change and to address their own needs."

The right of individuals to autonomy can be affected by their level of psychological competence. An individual whose psychological competence is limited is unable to make consistent rational judgments (Beauchamp & Childress, 2001). Mills (1985) described battering victims' debilitating use of minimization (e.g., "compared to others, my problems are small") to mistakenly justify their circumstances and to allow them to tolerate violent marriages. Similarly, Ferraro and Johnson (1983) described how women "rationalized" being abused—by saying such things such as "I asked for it," "He's sick," and "He didn't injure me"—and demonstrate how these rationalized accounts prevent the women from seeking help. Gondolf (2002) noted that such patterns may be reflective of self-deception to avoid further emotional deterioration and loss of self-worth, particularly in a perceived circumstance of inescapable danger.

L. Walker (1979) described victimized partners as experiencing a form of learned helplessness because of a consistent and well-reinforced message that nothing they can do will change their situation. Because victimized partners consequently can become immobilized, they may be considered as having limited psychological competence and therefore in need of someone to assist them to get out of what they see as a "hopeless" situation (Huston, 1984). In such a situation, the marriage and family therapist is faced with a compelling question: Is this victim capable of an autonomous decision?

Victims of IPV also can be immobilized by a state of extreme fear. Symonds (1979) cited research findings indicating that many victims of violent crimes become reduced to an infantile obedience to and cooperation with their attacker. Symonds suggested that a victimized woman who follows this response pattern "experiences terror which traumatically infantilizes her" (p. 169). Heppner (1978) reported that such victims often remain in abusive relationships out of fear of the consequences of leaving. These and many other findings suggest that victims of domestic violence, both male and female, are in need of directive assistance (e.g., Greenspun, 2000; Vatcher & Bogo, 2001).

In Chapter 4, we examined a variety of ethical concerns unique to the practice of marriage and family therapy. One such topic concerned the nature of secrets in couple or family relationships. For some, IPV may represent a *taboo topic* that is not to be addressed by either those in the system or those outside the system, such as a therapist. Thus, an effort by a marriage and family therapist to discuss domestic violence may be rejected on the basis that it is "too personal" or "not the reason we've come to see you." Despite such boundary-setting by clients, therapists are generally expected to examine other issues of safety (e.g., suicidal ideation, intentions to harm others, etc.) in the course of therapy. For some, failing to consider IPV, despite protests of a taboo by one or more parties, may represent a struggle over virtue ethics.

A related discussion in Chapter 4 concerned the nature of *triangulation* in marriage and family therapy. Some therapists may elect to sacrifice neutrality associated with their role as a therapist in favor of assisting a victim to find safety. In such cases, the likelihood of perceived triangulation of the victimizer by the victim and the therapist could be formidable, possibly to the point that a referral to another therapist would be in order.

To this point, we have considered applied aspects of the previous chapters of our text regarding therapists faced with a situation of IPV. Both professional literature and practice traditions offer insights about the various considerations the practitioner faces. At some point, however, the therapist must consolidate the available information and make a good-faith decision. Otherwise, a delay in decision making reflects decision-by-indecision, an approach of passivity clearly in conflict with the active nature of *beneficence*.

DECISION-MAKING MODELS AND OPTIONS FOR RESOLUTION

Marriage and family therapists are increasingly being asked to intervene in cases of domestic violence (Bograd & Mederos, 1999; Eisikovits, Edleson, Guttmann, & Sela-Amit, 1991). Yet family therapy is at odds with traditional approaches in its determination that problems exist not in a single individual but between and among family members. This basic tenet of family therapy has been interpreted by many to imply that neutrality on the part of the therapist should be the norm in cases of domestic violence.

> Violence can draw the therapist into taking charge of others' lives, a role that does not enhance the process of therapy. Violence also draws in helping systems to protect the "inno-cent" and "powerless" members of the family. Such a band-aid approach does not begin to resolve the issues which lead to violence. Quite to the contrary, it seems to perpetuate them. (Combrinck-Graham, 1986, p. 69)

The clinical debate about what type of approach is most appropriate in cases of domestic violence has tended to be narrowly limiting, couched in terms that argue for one approach at the exclusion of another (Eisikovits et al., 1991). Some have suggested that standardized approaches to evaluation and intervention can assist in resolving ethical dilemmas faced by marriage and family therapists (Miller, Veltkamp, Lane, Bilyeu, & Elzie, 2002; Stith, Rosen, & McCollum, 2002). Most approaches to best practice in intervention appear to emphasize separation of the victim from the victimizer for a period of time, followed by psychoeducational approaches to skills building and resocialization (Greene & Bogo, 2002; Goldner, 1999; Shapiro, 1986) and possible multiple couple therapy (Stith et al., 2004). One could argue that a clearer decision could be made by knowing that a standardized procedure would yield a reliable and positive outcome. However, such certainty is not the case, even when a standardized approach is employed.

Buttell (2001) proposed that, despite efforts of compassion and understanding in therapy, many chronic victimizers may not have established the stage of moral development even to desire ending violence in domestic conflict. In addition, possible cultural and familial traditions may create a situation in which some abusers do not believe that a problem exists. Concerning decision-making matters encountered by therapists faced with circumstances of domestic violence, Kurri and Wahlstrom (2001) noted that the morality of counseling involves a curious balance of advocating for client rights to choose versus a "normative and public ethic" that advocates "prescribing the ideal of a good life" (p. 188). In their discussion, these authors noted that the tension between these two positions appears to stem from the perceived weakness of the victim who might otherwise choose a more desirable situation. In other words, Buttell (2001) seemed to ask if some victimizers possessed the moral compass for change, whereas Kurri and Wahlstrom (2001) appeared to suggest that therapy with a weak and confused victim obliges the therapist to choose "the better life" on behalf of the client. These two entries in the professional literature converge to form the crux of this ethical dilemma: What assurances exist about the aftermath of a therapist's decisions? Is there hope for rehabilitating the victimizer? Does the therapist have an obligation to prescribe "the ideal of a good life" for the victim?

In Chapter 3, we encountered models of ethical decision making. Kidder (1995) noted that *end-based decisions* involve the greatest good for the greatest number; *rule-based decisions* involve meeting obligations to a code, regardless of the outcome; and *care-based decisions* involve demonstrating compassion for a unique situation.

From these options, the therapist who emphasizes a rule-based approach may conclude that the primacy of code derivatives such as client autonomy, nondiscrimination, and restraint in imposing personal values are best served by acceptance of the taboo designation of IPV with clients, thereby avoiding its consideration. Such a position could be bolstered by the previous comments offered by Buttell (2001) and Kurri and Wahlstrom (2001). By contrast, the therapist may conclude that the end result of greatest good to the greatest number would stem from preserving options for future changes and thus would advocate for compromising neutrality to ensure client safety. A similar outcome could derive if the therapist takes a care-based approach that emphasizes respect for the uniqueness of the circumstance, including unique co-occurring psychological, environmental, and cultural factors, but insists upon valuing freedom from destructive obligations.

Chapter 3 also featured a discussion of the *four processes* associated with Kitchener's (1986) decision-making model for ethical dilemmas. *Process 1* of this model concerns sensitivity, knowledge, and perceptiveness to interpret that a situation requires an ethical decision. Despite many persistent questions and uncertainties surrounding IPV, its prevalence among a wide array of relationship patterns and the systemic (even intergenerational) nature of the harm it can cause would seem to prompt a principled and virtuous therapist to action. *Process 2* of the Kitchener model concerns the formulation of an ethical course of action. Kitchener emphasized an *ethical course of action* since actions reflecting intuition at the personal layer of values may not be supported as ethical at the professional or institutional layers of values. In the case of IPV, any course of action selected by a therapist should be examined critically against ethical codes, foundational principles, and ethical theory. For each of these tiers, a decision to support safety for the victim seems justified.

Process 3 of the Kitchener model concerns the integration of personal and professional values in a decision. According to Kitchener, this process is particularly critical because one must address inequities and imbalances in imprecise decisions. Think for a moment: What creates a dilemma? In circumstances with obvious issues and established procedures, clarity is not a problem; no dilemma exists. When faced with competing obligations, values, perspectives, and traditions, however, the lack of clarity can stymie even the most informed and experienced professional. Kitchener accentuated the term *integration* for this process to convey the necessity of commitment to action rather than a simple exercise in logic and deduction.

Process 4 of the Kitchener model concerns the end product of the model: action. Acting without the commitment of Process 3 may leave one open to dissuasion. However, commitment to a course of action will not offset ambiguity or even the risk of repercussions. Taken together, these two processes suggest that once a therapist examines his or her role in the balance of fairness concerning IPV, advocating for client safety is justifiable and grounded.

From the previous examination, it appears that many elements of ethical tradition and rules, reciprocal valuing in the therapy relationship, and decision-making frameworks favor the systemic inequity of acting to ensure safety for the victimized partner. However, what actions should be taken? In the majority of circumstances, encouraging the victim to leave the violence is indicated. But what then? Decisions rarely occur in a vacuum and rarely fail to lead to consequences, anticipated and otherwise. A signifi-cant aspect of ethical action is the aftermath of such decisions.

TREATMENT ALTERNATIVES

It seems ethically justifiable to encourage a partner in a violent intimate relationship to leave that relationship if the victim is judged to have limited psychological competence because of the severity of the circumstances. Whether it is ethically justifiable to force one to leave or to deny treatment should they refuse to leave is questionable (Rosen et al., 2003). As was discussed in Chapter 3, most ethical codes admonish the practitioner to discontinue therapy when benefit appears to have ended. As an interpretation of Kidder's rule-based approach to decision making, a decision to deny therapy unless the victim leaves the relationship may appear justified. By contrast, demanding that a client relocate from a residence or else be denied therapy could be interpreted as abandonment, since the potential for benefit in future therapy efforts may be jeopardized. Forcing someone to leave can also amount to an overt violation of the right to autonomy. If an initial effort is unsuc-cessful, the therapist might better maintain a position of respect for autonomous decision making. In discussing wives whose marriages involve domestic violence, Wolf-Smith and LaRossa (1992) asserted, "Respecting the choices that women make is an integral part of the counseling/therapeutic process. Victims must always know that there are people ready and willing to listen to them and assist them" (p. 329). Huston (1984) proposed that a therapist then should adopt more of a "maternalistic" treatment stance:

> Maternalism as the recommended treatment approach for battered women can be defined as offering a nurturing, directive stance at early stages of the client's development and an accep-tance of more autonomy at later developmental stages. This approach recognizes that battered women as clients move through developmental stages of growth in objectively understanding their battering relationships. The women demonstrate different needs at different stages, and treatment must vary accordingly. . . . This stance is congruent with feminist treatment beliefs, because it acknowledges a deep respect for the autonomous functioning of the individual and yet recognizes the unique needs of specific populations and developmental tasks. (p. 831)

Entries in the feminist literature have pointed out that paternalism can be a debili-tating mode of interaction with many women, reinforcing the predominant societal con-ditioning that made them passive and dependent (Goldner, 1999; Greenspun, 2000; Sue et al., 1998; Vatcher & Bogo, 2001). The maternalistic alternative espoused by Huston involves initial assertion but recognizes the potential need to patiently await develop-mental movement toward increased independence, positive self-worth, and autonomous action. For some therapists, such a decision may even represent a struggle between per-sonal values and professional values on behalf of a client's welfare. In this respect, the dilemma may be related to the Battle for Structure versus the Battle for Initiative. How-ever, these dual battles are founded on an assumption of competence on the part of both client and therapist, an assumption that is questionable at best for a victim of IPV.

To address this controversy, the use of ethical judgment by mental health profes-sionals must be an integral part of treatment planning. Employing a guiding concept of neutrality has much to offer from an ethical standpoint. It ensures that all family mem-bers are treated as self-reliant, responsible individuals whose autonomy is recognized and respected (Willbach, 1989). However, Willbach also asserted that ethically aware marriage and family therapists actively utilize their perception of who is right and who is wrong in a family in which domestic violence is present. In doing so he noted:

> An ethically aware approach to psychotherapy points to the flexible utilization of different techniques and modalities. Because family therapy developed in opposition to a tradition of individual therapy, the limits of its appropriate use have rarely been explored, as if to do so would run the danger of conceding valuable ground to the enemy. In fact, when a potentially actively violent abuser and the abused person are in the same family, family therapy may be generally contraindicated. (p. 50)

It is valuable to recognize that Willbach employs the qualifying term *may* in considering contraindications for family therapy in cases of IPV. Family therapy certainly has a function in the treatment of such circumstances. Willbach affirmed this function, though with due consideration given to four interrelated clinical positions as a means of ensuring ethical practice:

1. The overt goal of therapy should be the complete cessation of intrafamily violence whenever it is present.
2. When intrafamily violence is the therapeutic focus, neutrality should not be a primary therapeutic procedure.
3. Therapists should use their ethical judgment in asserting individual responsibility for violent behavior.
4. Family therapy is contraindicated unless the violent family member is able to contract for nonviolence (i.e., formally agree not to use violence).

The Cessation of Violence

Among the behaviors that can contribute to harm, marriage and family therapists ought to especially strive toward eliminating violence and make a priority of eliminating it whenever it is present. Willbach (1989) offered a strong statement for this position:

> Violence is qualitatively different from other actions, in that the harm it causes is not capable of being controlled by the person harmed ("sticks and stones . . ."). Secondly, violence, in its most extreme manifestation, results in death, a most unquestionable harm. Lesser degrees of violence have a greater probability of leading to death, either accidentally or as the result of willful escalation, than does the infliction of emotional suffering. Thirdly, physical injury is a particularly blatant and obvious type of harm. For these reasons, violence is an especially condemned form of harm in our broader community's moral standards as embodied in the legal system. (p. 47)

The Contraindication of Neutrality

Marriage and family therapists are trained to highlight the interactive nature of family members' behaviors. For example, Sluzki (1978) stated:

> The positions of "victim" and "victimizer" are the result of a punctuation in the sequence of events, that is, of an arbitrary decision on the part of one or both participants about who leads and who follows. . . . Except perhaps in the very early stages of parent–child relationships, there is no totally passive, victim-like position in interpersonal situations within small systems. All members are contributing parties to the interactional sequences, the behavior of

each member being induced and in turn inducing the other. At the most, in certain circumstances one of the actors appears to be the victim. (pp. 377–378)

Although this "powers of the weak" perspective (Janeway, 1980, p. 4) is quite valid, Willbach (1989) proposed that it is a conceptualization oversimplified in its application to cases of domestic violence. Violence signals a breakdown in the very bedrock of family life, a family's willingness to take responsibility for the safety of its members, cautioned Mathias (1986), who quoted family therapist Betty Carter's admonishment: "To stop domestic violence you must intervene in the system in a dramatic way. . . . Putting the abuser in jail may not be therapy, but data shows it gets his attention and stops the violence." (p. 27)

Willbach (1989) called for a more pragmatic model of systems theory in working with cases of domestic violence. This model assumes family relationships to be interactive, but unequally so as a consequence of gender and power differentials in that

> it takes a certain amount of money to feed, clothe and house young children. . . . The victim is constrained by these material limitations in reacting to the activity of the victimizer. Coercive power is based, to a large extent, on the effective control of material realities. (pp. 45–46)

Thus, advocacy, rather than neutrality, must be employed to equalize interactions before a pure systems approach is considered.

Individual Responsibility

Some marriage and family therapists have addressed the importance of taking responsibility in cases of domestic violence, but with the proviso that neither partner should be blamed: "Violence invariably translates into victim and aggressor, right and wrong, good and bad. . . . To transcend this viewpoint is a difficult task for the therapist, yet to be fully effective, it is necessary to do so" (Shapiro, 1984, p. 118). "If the worker did think the husband to blame, she or he would not be able to help him. One of the basic tenets for therapeutic practice is freedom from judgements" (Geller & Wasserstrom, 1984, p. 39). Willbach (1989) identified such a position as illogical:

> If the batterer is found responsible for the violence, then, unless there are mitigating factors, such as diminished mental capacity, he [or she] is also to blame for the violence. In the normal case, it is contradictory to affirm the former and deny the latter, even if these therapists feel it would be less emotionally problematic to work with blameless perpetrators. (p. 49)

According to Bograd (1986), cases of IPV demand that marriage and family therapists "take unapologetically value-laden stands" (p. 47). He further stated:

> Most family therapy training discourages us from advocating for just one member of a couple. . . . But when there is violence, what is good for the system is often not good for the more victimized partner. For such couples, the most crucial intervention may be giving a strong, unequivocal message about who is responsible for the violence. (p. 47)

Krugman (1986) likewise recommended that family therapists "give a clear message that the hitter is responsible for [the] hitting and that rationalizations like 'she [or he] provoked me' or 'I couldn't help it' are not acceptable" (p. 42).

In cases of mutual violence, therapists' judgments of responsibility can be critical. A victim's violent behavior in most cases of IPV is reactive and defensive

(Kemp, 1998; Saunders, 1988). The differences between aggressive and defensive behaviors need to be accentuated and the aggressor held accountable (Willbach, 1989).

Contracting for Nonviolence

A number of marriage and family therapists have recommended family or conjoint sessions without qualification in cases of IPV (Madonna, 1986; W. C. Nichols, 1986; Weidman, 1986) or have offered only vague criteria as contraindications, such as the presence of "severe violence" (Bagarozzi & Giddings, 1983, p. 11; Gelles & Maynard, 1987, p. 272). Willbach (1989) strongly advocated the ability to contract for nonviolence as an essential criterion to employ in determining treatment modality. He likened such a contract to those used in cases of suicidal behavior in which the possible consequences are so ethically unacceptable that the therapist simply has to oppose it and intervene to stop it.

Bograd (1986) likewise recommended contracting for nonviolence in cases of domestic violence. Adherence to the contract establishes a safe context that enables systemic interventions to proceed more readily; the consequences of violating it constitute a powerful therapeutic intervention. Clinical evidence suggests that abusive men require strong external pressures as motivation to seek treatment. The threat by their partner to leave or the partner's actually leaving has been viewed as the most effective pressure in this regard (Roberts, 1996; Saunders, 1984). If a person is unable to contract or adhere to contract terms, however, then individual issues become primary and must be dealt with before relationship or contextual issues (Willbach, 1989).

Stith et al. (2004) also described an alternative approach that excluded the use of couple therapy. In a situation of power dominance by one partner over another, a model founded on equitable opportunity to change and request changes is unsound. In instances in which partners want to remain together, however, interventions that promote safety, reeducation, and support are vital. Following a brief respite of separation, these authors emphasized the use of multicouple therapy to accomplish these ends, noting significant reductions in aggression. In this approach, the context of violence can be considered among group members as well as individual couples in a way that avoids a linear view while promoting accountability and opportunity for more equitable change.

These and other alternative methods are important considerations for marriage and family therapists who encounter circumstances of IPV. A decision to imbalance a stable, though harmful, relationship by promoting safety for the victim is not an end but, rather, a step in the therapy process. In such instances, the therapist may have to assume an advocate role and relinquish the opportunity to return to a therapist role, based on the perpetrator's perception of triangulation. However, therapists who exchange neutrality for protection can have some assurances that subsequent interventions may be successful with other practitioners should therapy be reinitiated.

SUMMARY

In this chapter, we have made an effort to present a thorough examination of a significant and complex ethical dilemma faced by many marriage and family therapists. In attempting to address the multiple ethical concerns discussed in the initial chapters of this text, we have presented a discussion of the considerations in a circumstance of intimate partner violence.

The struggles of addressing personal values and appropriate ethical actions are difficult and even isolating for marriage and family therapists. In instances such as intimate partner violence, we urge review of relevant professional literature, assessment of ethical and legal precedents, and consultation with colleagues or supervisors. However, we strongly support the contention of Pope and Vasquez (1999) that therapists must ultimately choose a course of action that reflects cognizance of human suffering.

In Chapter 6, we offer a brief review of significant contemporary ethical issues faced by marriage and family therapists. As you consider these issues, we suggest that you return to the framework of this chapter as well as previous chapters to contemplate possible courses of ethical action.

CHAPTER 6

Contemporary Ethical Issues

Few marriage and family therapists take their responsibilities lightly. This weight is particularly heavy when a therapist is operating with a sense of uncertainty about what direction their professional care should take.

The scope of ethical issues faced by marriage and family therapists continues to widen. This expansion reflects a growing awareness among practitioners that their resources for decision making when faced with ethical concerns are limited. One element of this ambiguity is due to the general, nonspecific nature of the ethical guidelines provided by professional organizations and bodies (Green & Hansen, 1989). However, another major contributor is the lack of precedent for handling many contemporary ethical issues.

This chapter offers a look at some selected contemporary ethical issues faced by marriage and family therapists. The choice of these issues is not intended to suggest an exhaustive or definitive list. Rather, these topics are examined because of the relative frequency of their occurrence or the complexity of their impact upon both the therapist and the client system. Additionally, the discussion of these issues offers a view into the considerations the therapist faces when examining an ethical quandary, similar to our discussion of intimate partner violence in Chapter 5.

As you examine these issues, be mindful of the discussions from earlier chapters in our text. Questions you may wish to consider are: (a) What cultural and contextual concerns exist for this issue? (b) What possible convergence or divergence surfaces among the layers of values affecting this issue? (c) What foundational ethical principles and traditions impact upon this issue? (d) What is unique about this issue for the practice of marital and family therapy? and (e) What are the elements of decision making that should be considered in attempting to resolve this ethical issue?

For your consideration, we offer a discussion regarding: (a) use of technology in marriage and family therapy, (b) implications of diagnosis, (c) considerations in managed mental health care, (d) conflicts arising from dual or multiple relationships, (e) Acquired Immune Deficiency Syndrome (AIDS) and the therapist's duty to protect, and (f) ethical considerations in publications efforts.

TECHNOLOGY

The growth of technology has been phenomenal in the last three decades. Technology that has "had the most impact on a therapy practice are voice mail, personal computers, e-mail, pagers, answering machines, and hand-held audio recording devices" (Caudill, 1999, p. 20). Electronic connections and transmissions truly have revolutionized the sending and receiving of information and have important ethical implications for any type of therapeutic relationship. Technology can be used well or abused in therapeutic relationships.

Contemporary marriage and family therapists need some awareness of the technology that can be employed in their professional practice. Many options exist for the use of technology in therapy, whether as ancillary or primary methods of care for clients. The following discussion addresses technology as: (a) a practice resource, (b) an information management system, and (c) a primary therapeutic modality. A final discussion is offered concerning ethical issues and implications for the use of technology in marriage and family therapy.

Technology as a Practice Resource

Marriage and family therapists have historically relied on the use of homework or suggested activities between scheduled therapy sessions. The rationale for such activities has been that they extend the intentions of therapy sessions and create opportunities for autonomous discovery and insight for clients. For example, the use of journaling or bibliotherapy is not uncommon among practitioners who want to supplement themes or intentions of therapy sessions. With the access to information available in Web-based technologies, some therapists have begun to recommend a Web site as a supplemental information resource for clients between therapy sessions, not unlike recommended reading or homework. Just as with recommended reading or similar information resources, however, therapists should exercise care in scrutinizing the content of Web sites to verify that they supplement the in-session work in a consistent and positive way.

Another technology-based resource involves on-line queries and assessments. Kier and Molinari (2004) described the popularity of "Do-It-Yourself (DIY) Testing" options available on-line that permit consumers to investigate medical concerns. By entering information about physical symptoms and following a prescribed pathway of questions, such services offer users an array of possible diagnoses and recommendations for medical referrals. These authors noted that developments in the use of DIY technologies for assessment of psychological disorders had emerged with features similar to those for users seeking information about medical problems. They noted that enormous risks and hazards currently exist for users of these services, such as lack of informed consent and potential misuse or misinterpretation of results. Similarly, Wall (2004) advocated for cautious utilization of on-line assessment services, particularly related to accountability and oversight as well as data storage and transmission. Over time, such concerns may be addressed adequately, though presently they merit caution and scrutiny by consumers and practitioners. With developments that address these and related concerns, on-line services of this type may become reliable resources that may be ancillary to marriage and family therapy.

For the marriage and family therapist, technological resources are abundant and varied to support their skills and competence. Ample on-line opportunities can be found for professional development, many of which include instruction in the use of technology in therapy practice. On-line graduate courses and curricula exist for more formal methods of continuing education or even pursuit of advanced degrees. Technology-based supervision is not uncommon and on-line consultation has come to be utilized in many isolated areas with limited professional colleagues or specialists (Coker, Jones, Staples, & Harbach, 2002; Nickelson, 1998). Additionally, a number of on-line journals exist for self-directed professional development, such as *CyberPsychology and Behavior* and the *Journal of Technology in Counseling*. Both the content and format of these and similar Web-based publications offer therapists useful technological resources for their practices.

Thus, for both clients and for therapists, technological resources exist to supplement marriage and family therapy. Technology has also become a mainstay for the management of information in therapy.

Technology in Information Management

There are few contemporary agencies or private practices that do not utilize technology as a primary means of information management. Identity information, standardized forms, diagnostic and treatment data, billing, progress notes, and archival records are among the many forms of client records that create databases for therapy practices. Such records are often stored electronically in a self-contained agency server. An option for larger volumes of client records is an off-site database designed with specialized encryption procedures to limit access to only authorized persons.

Electronic transmission of client data is often a standard operating procedure for interagency exchanges of information involving other practitioners or managed care agencies. Entire or partial client records may be forwarded almost instantaneously to third parties via networked electronic pathways. The electronic transmission of client information using fax machines is even more prevalent.

For some, technological management of client information may seem to be simply a form of an electronic filing cabinet. However, any user of contemporary technology is aware of unsolicited intrusions into personal e-mail accounts and similar networked databases, from unwanted and annoying spam to destructive "electronic viruses." Just as the safeguards of locked filing cabinets are customary for therapy offices, such safeguards are typical for electronic information systems, though some may contend that the latter type of security is more reliable than the former. We will address some unique ethical issues related to these and other information management concerns following a discussion of technology as a primary modality for marriage and family therapy.

Technology as Therapeutic Modality

Web therapy, cybercounseling, e-therapy, and a host of other terms have emerged in recent years to describe the use of on-line technology for mental health services

(Duncan & Watts, 1999). Unlike the previous discussions of technological supplements to marriage and family therapy, these practices concern using technology-based interventions as the *primary* modality for therapy services. In this regard, a number of options and considerations exist for marriage and family therapists.

A significant distinction in the use of on-line technology concerns time or immediacy in the exchanges of information between users. Some technology employs a *synchronous* format, meaning "real time" exchanges between those involved in the interaction. Examples of synchronous technologies are telephone or video sessions in which interactions are immediate and most similar to face-to-face interactions. By contrast, an *asynchronous* technology format describes delayed exchanges between those involved in the interaction; that is, time will elapse between sending and receiving information. Perhaps the most common example of asynchronous technology is an e-mail correspondence.

One form of synchronous interaction is a *chat room* in which two or more users may interact from different locations at a predetermined on-line site. *Instant messaging* (IM) is a similar form of synchronous interaction between users with many of the features of a chat room, though not necessarily used within a predetermined site or time frame. A third form of synchronous interaction is *video conferencing*, which allows for face-to-face exchanges through an electronic medium. Unlike chat rooms and IM, video conferencing includes nonverbal cues and spoken exchanges, though the cost for such systems is considerably greater than the text-only formats of chat rooms and IM. For this reason, the most common form of synchronous on-line therapy service is through the use of a chat room, and the most common form of asynchronous on-line therapy services is through the use of e-mail (Maheu & Gordon, 2000).

On-line therapy services do not necessarily require advanced equipment for the therapist or the client to interact. Most home computers with high-speed or even dial-up Internet services can allow consumers to access therapy opportunities. Researchers have noted that using technology-based services as the exclusive method of therapy can be efficient, cost-effective, and convenient for both clients and practitioners (Riemer-Reiss, 2000).

Many have concerns that the lack of access to "in-person" interactions between therapist and client creates difficulties and possibly compromises the effectiveness of therapy, however. Addressing this concern, Day and Schneider (2002) compared process and outcome variables across three modalities of therapy (face-to-face, synchronous video, and synchronous audio) for 80 clients. They reported that "differences in process and outcomes among the three treatments were small and clinically promising" (p. 504).

The ethical concerns noted in Chapters 3 and 4 are substantive for any approach to marriage and family therapy. However, these foundational and traditional ethical concerns typically have been addressed in customary, and generally reliable, ways in face-to-face therapy. By contrast, some specific and unique considerations are presented to marriage and family therapists utilizing technology for either ancillary or primary functions in the therapy relationship.

Ethical Issues in the Use of Technology

The use of technology in marriage and family therapy is fraught with ethical concerns (Duncan & Watts, 1999). Those who want to use technology in the course of therapy should consider that the process is more potentially perilous than it appears. Years ago,

Ibrahim (1985) noted great concern about the possible "dehumanization" and potential "violation of human rights" that might transpire from the anticipated explosion in the use of technology for mental health services (p. 135). Similarly, Early and Hulse (1986) observed that the emergence of a "technological society" could "create an environment" (p. 334) of concerns that responsible professionals should foresee and address, particularly for value-related aspects of technology and therapy. In a virtual environment of technological exchanges, one can appreciate the initial skepticism about possibly minimizing the significance of interpersonal relationships, the emotional growth of clients, and even the worth of human interaction, all of which might be tied to the mechanistic nature of technology-assisted care. Thus, as a beginning point for considering the ethical use of technology, marriage and family therapists are encouraged to be vigilant in retaining the humanity of the therapy relationship.

From our discussion in Chapters 1 and 2, we can surmise that therapists who want to be ethically principled and virtuous in using technology with clients should consider the potential for cultural pitfalls when using high-tech media. Think for a moment about some of the proclaimed advantages of technology: speed, efficiency, and convenience. Although these advantages and other factors may be desirable for many who use technology, they are clearly associated with a Westernized approach to gathering information and solving problems. Could such an approach be troublesome for non-Westernized clients or families who do not share the same attitudes toward speed and efficiency? Similarly, are these characteristics reflective of institutional values (e.g., managed care agencies) that could have a repressive impact upon some clients? Also, what about clients whose familiarity with, access to, or competence in the use of technology is limited? Is it still beneficial to use technological methods in either a primary or an ancillary role in therapy for such clients? Could the technological environment promote a form of discrimination, repression, or even "violation of human rights" noted by Ibrahim? These and similar notions are worth consideration for culturally responsive marriage and family therapists contemplating the use of technology in their practices. Each of these issues is relevant whether technology is employed in an ancillary or a primary role in the therapy relationship.

A closely related consideration regarding the advantages of technology is the atmosphere it promotes for therapy. In an environment emphasizing speed, efficiency, and convenience, unintended consequence may emerge when technology is the modality for therapy services. For instance, clients are often restricted to a 200-word limit in chat room formats (and even less text can be sent in IM exchanges). With such limitations, some may not be able to explain their situation adequately, especially if it involves multiple family members. Even more compelling is the expectation clients may have for the nature of therapy. As most practicing marriage and family therapists know, therapy is a *process* that often involves patience and deliberation. Despite the contemporary era emphasizing brief forms of therapy and managed care constraints, therapy is often difficult, slow, nonlinear, and even inconvenient. By contrast, technology-based therapy may come to be viewed by clients as an array of *tasks* that involve a *formula for immediate results*. This type of "add-water-to-create-therapy" view should be addressed as a matter of ethical care on the part of the therapist, since such expectations may be unrealistic or changes may not be durable. This is not to say that technology-assisted therapy is inappropriate. Rather, it is unique and requires deliberate attention on the part of marriage and family therapists. In this respect, *beneficent* attention to client welfare may be threatened by approaches that fail to address fully any vital contextual issues of distress, that may minimize aspects of the change process, or that exclude members of the system.

An aspect of deliberate attention for the ethical practice of marriage and family therapist is informed consent. In Chapters 3 and 4, we examined the multiple considerations a practitioner should address to ensure that clients are fully and formally informed about the expectations for therapy. Because informed consent can have contractual characteristics for all parties, clarity and thoroughness are crucial. You may recall from previous chapters that issues related to informed consent involve items such as client rights, authority to consent, services and restrictions concerning minors, confidentiality and legal exceptions, fee structure, and emergency procedures. Such items are related to the *due care* obligations of the therapist. Additional items in informed consent documents include information about the training and competence of the therapist, philosophical statements about therapy foci, expectations for non-therapy activities (e.g., court appearances, interactions with third parties, etc.), and disclosures about supervision (if present) or consultation. Such items are related to the *competency* obligations of the therapist. Kanani and Regehr (2003) noted that the informed consent process is complicated for face-to-face therapy, but it is even more complicated for on-line therapy services. For example, in face-to-face therapy, the identity of the client and his or her authority to consent to services is typically not at issue. By contrast, the therapist must address any uncertainties about the identity and age of the client in informed consent procedures for on-line relationships. Similarly, full disclosure of presenting problems is vital for effective care, and it is sometimes difficult even in face-to-face therapy; the process is amplified for on-line work.

A particularly important aspect of informed consent for on-line services is the disposition of text exchanges. In many ways, the record of text exchanges is analogous to recordings of therapy sessions. In what ways will the array of text interactions be handled? Will they be retained in full on each end of the interaction? Will they be destroyed? Will they be entered into client records and thus be subject to possible compulsory disclosure in court? Will they be utilized in supervision? Deliberate attention to such matters in informed consent procedures is important and appropriate for the unique medium of cybertherapy.

Another unique aspect of e-therapy services concerns the procedure for addressing confidentiality. Because of the potential for unauthorized access to confidential exchanges via networked electronic media, confidentiality is far less reliable than in traditional face-to-face arrangements (Jencius & Sager, 2001). Full disclosure of this possibility should be a mainstay in informed consent procedures for on-line therapy. Utilization of encryption methods, arrangements for secure chat rooms, and similar efforts by the therapist to ensure a secure exchange of information are common in e-therapy.

A typical element of informed consent involves procedures for addressing emergency situations. Clients receiving in-person therapy often receive information about contacting either the therapist or an emergency service such as a hospital or other agency. Emergencies or unscheduled contacts require deliberate attention in informed consent procedures for on-line therapy (Frame, 1997). For example, if an e-therapist employs an asynchronous format such as e-mail, delays in sending and receiving information could cause substantial and potential serious problems. What if an actual emergency circumstance existed and the therapist did not access the message until some time later? What if a duty-to-warn circumstance had emerged? What if intimate partner violence had occurred? Delays in responding to clients, even in emergency situations, are not uncommon in face-to-face marriage and family therapy; thus emergency procedures and provisions for back-up assistance are customary. Arrangements for situations that may require immediate attention must be addressed by the cybertherapist as a matter of due care in informed consent. However, the standard of such due care for on-line services has not yet evolved to address common procedures in the same way it exists for in-person care.

In a related example, a cybertherapist using a synchronous format such as a chat room may promote an expectation of more immediate accessibility on the part of clients, even to the point of intrusiveness and violating the personal boundaries of the therapist. As with in-person therapy, the nature of limited boundaries to distinguish impatience from emergencies should be addressed in informed consent procedures.

Another unique aspect of using technology in therapy concerns the straightforward nature of information. In text-only services (e.g., e-mail, chat room, etc.), the inability to access nonverbal cues on the part of the therapist may be of critical importance. Consider the following text statement: "Some day I think I'm going to kill my husband." As a text-only comment by a wife, such a statement could reflect emotions ranging from mild frustration to malice, which nonverbal cues might clarify. In addressing this issue to clarify the intent of the wife, the efficiency of on-line therapy could be lost and a rhythm of dialogue could be interrupted.

Or, consider a circumstance in which the presenting concern for the client or family involves social isolation and shyness? In such a circumstance, the medium of technology could actually serve to *sustain* such patterns, particularly if they are not discussed deliberately by the marriage and family therapist. Once again, we note that items of concern should not dissuade therapists from using technology for ancillary or primary purposes in therapy. Rather, the uniqueness of the medium creates considerations not traditionally addressed by professional custom.

For consumers, assessing the competence of the therapist is critical for promoting trust and confidence in the therapy relationship. Face-to-face interactions typically promote an atmosphere of assurance about the competence of the therapist. By contrast, an on-line consumer may have difficulty even verifying the identity of the therapist, not to mention his or her competence as a practitioner. In situations in which the therapist is involved in formal supervision arrangements, face-to-face discussions about this issue (sometimes even involving the supervisor) are customary to ensure full disclosures about access to client information. If an e-therapist is being supervised by a superior, it is important to provide the consumer or client with careful and clear description of the supervision arrangements before therapy is even initiated. Obviously, for e-therapists under supervision, their supervisors should be competent in the use of e-therapy as well as in supervision of e-therapy delivery services.

Competence in on-line therapy also requires attention to the technological aspects of the medium. Due care in both the content *and format* of cybertherapy is a reasonable expectation of clients who must place their trust in the practitioner *and* the medium. Thus, clients should be assured of the technical ability of their on-line therapist as well as his or her therapeutic skills. For purposes of informed consent about practice competency, therapists may even encourage on-line clients to verify their credentials with licensure boards, certification bodies, or similar professional agencies. Once again, the issues of informed consent are equivalent in face-to-face therapy and on-line therapy. However, the procedures for addressing these issues may differ appreciably.

Ethical attention to technology as a means of information management is also particularly important for contemporary marriage and family therapists. One area of tremendous concern in the use of technology in therapy involves storage and retrieval of confidential information. The electronic transformation of data "has greatly increased the complexity of issues related to confidentiality" (Bonnington, McGrath, & Martinek, 1996, p. 156). Computerized records are subject to potentially less security than records kept under lock and key. "The availability of client records through computerized transmission and storage in national data banks creates a nightmare for both clients and clinicians" (Stevens-Smith, 1997b, p. 54). In fact, Freeny (1995) has stated that "computers and confidentiality may be incompatible" (p. 37). Even faxing information to a managed mental health care provider or to a supervisor can have profound ethical implications and ramifications. E-mails, chat room exchanges, and faxes are not protected by federal law in the same way that items carried by the United States Postal Service are protected. Thus, if someone who is not the intended receiver reads information that has been transmitted electronically, a client's integrity and confidentiality would be compromised.

The passage of legislation leading to the Health Insurance Portability and Accountability Act (1996), or HIPAA, has been particularly significant related to diligent attention in electronic storage, receipt, and transmission of client data. HIPAA legislation compels health-related practitioners as well as associates (e.g., staff, etc.) to secure authorization from clients concerning all relevant aspects of information management. For example, under HIPAA regulations, a practice setting that utilizes an off-site database for retaining confidential records must secure client authorization for such arrangements. Similarly, the electronic transmission of client information (including fax transmissions) must be discussed and specifically authorized by clients. Procedures for archival retention of records, destruction of records, and similar activities could all be subject to the extension of HIPAA regulations. Thus, informed marriage and family therapists should be aware of revisions and applications of such legislation and how it will affect their use of technology for information management.

In using technology as a resource to support face-to-face therapy efforts, practitioners should be attentive to the skill and access required of clients for whom they have made such a recommendation. This issue is particularly important if the therapist requires utilizing a particular Web site as a component of therapy. Therapists should also give some scrutiny to recommended Web sites. As a resource for practice, therapists should devote attention to the quality of on-line instruction as well as professional development opportunities in which they participate.

Baltimore (2000) noted the need for standards to assist in the provision of on-line therapy services. Entries in the ethical codes of the mental health disciplines listed in Chapter 3 reveal increased awareness of the role of technology among professional groups. A code of ethics for "WebCounseling" developed by the National

Board for Certified Counselors, Inc. (2001) also offers instruction and cautions for practitioners to consider when they employ technology-assisted methods. Using these standards as a point of reference, Heinlen, Welfel, Richmond, and Rak (2003) surveyed 136 practitioner Web sites that utilized chat rooms or e-mail services. These authors specifically examined the extent to which practitioners' Web sites reflected compliance with NBCC standards and how well they provided details about practitioner credentials. Eight months later, they noted that more than one-third of these sites were no longer in operation and that the majority of these closed sites had been developed by noncredentialed providers. They also reported that credentialed professionals provided significantly greater compliance with the NBCC standards than their noncredentialed counterparts. From these findings, one might conclude that credentialed practitioners attending to aspects of ethical care were even more successful in sustaining their on-line practice.

The use of technology as a supplemental or primary medium for therapy as well as for information management poses a variety of unique ethical concerns for marriage and family therapists. Aside from those issues already noted in this chapter, other aspects of on-line practice include licensed therapists practicing across state lines, care for the inclusion of all significant members of a family system, and derivatives of the Battle for Structure and the Battle for Initiative (Napier & Whitaker, 1978). For some, cybercounseling and marriage and family therapy may be ethically, if not legally, incompatible. For others, the use of technology may be most appropriate in specific situations, such as following up with a client family or working with a family member who cannot come to in-office sessions because of extenuating circumstances (e.g., disability, prolonged absences, etc.). Certainly, the ethical principles of *nonmaleficence, justice,* and *fidelity* must be addressed carefully when technology is a part of therapy with couples and families (American Association for Marriage and Family Therapy, 1999).

THE DIAGNOSTIC AND STATISTICAL MANUAL OF MENTAL DISORDERS AND ITS USE IN MARRIAGE AND FAMILY THERAPY

The Diagnostic and Statistical Manual of Mental Disorders—Text Revised (4th edition), known as the DSM-IV-TR (American Psychiatric Association, 2000), and its immediate predecessors have had an enormous impact on mental health disciplines. The DSM "made available for the first time, diagnostic criteria that people could agree upon, based on descriptive features, rather than speculations about etiology" (Wylie, 1995, p. 25). Thus, the DSM nomenclature has come to be accepted as the common standard of language for most mental health researchers and clinicians. Indeed, most marital and family therapy educational programs train their students in the DSM if for no other reason than to be able to communicate with other professional specialists (Denton, Patterson, & Van Meir, 1997).

"Like many other classification systems, the DSM focuses on 'mental' disturbance that occurs within individuals, and relational conditions are outside this domain" (Simola, Parker, & Froese, 1999, pp. 225–226). Therefore, the use of the DSM raises several ethical concerns for marriage and family therapists. Denton (1989) discussed four of these concerns: (a) incompatibility of orientations, (b) the stigma of diagnosis, (c) misrepresentation of diagnoses, and (d) competence to diagnose.

Incompatibility of Orientations

Although there are many approaches to the practice of marriage and family therapy, nearly all share a common basis in general systems theory, that is, an emphasis on the interactions between and among persons. In contrast, the DSM has as its basis an emphasis on the individualistic notion of a "mental disorder."

Thus, no matter what may be occurring in a client's family or social contexts, any distress she or he experiences is assumed within the DSM paradigm to be due to a dysfunction within the individual. This assumption is in direct conflict with marriage and family therapists' belief that such distress is due, partially or primarily, to dysfunction within the entire family system. Stevens-Smith (1997a) expressed the dilemma this conflict creates for marriage and family therapists. She noted that marriage and family therapists who work within an agency or interagency structure, or who are dependent in other ways for third-party payments requiring DSM diagnoses, frequently find themselves in an ethical conflict concerning how to define a presenting problem. This conflict is particularly acute for family systems "purists," such as Haley (1987), who believe that individual and family approaches are inherently incompatible. A therapist who conceptualizes a child's behavior as only one link in a circular chain of interactions with other members of the family will have to diagnose an individual "mental disorder" to ensure reimbursement from insurance coverage. The discussion in Chapter 2 concerning contextual layers of values is pertinent for the ethical aspects of this contradiction. In this respect, the institutional layer of values may conflict with one's personal or professional values in a manner that reflects substantive differences about etiology and treatment of systemic versus individual difficulties.

A second incompatibility between the DSM and marriage and family therapy lies in where they locate a presenting problem. The DSM promotes the view of an "identified patient." By contrast, marriage and family therapy focuses on shared responsibility, that is, the concept that family problems involve everyone in the family. When they enter family therapy, however, most family members understand and communicate their presenting concerns only from their own perspective, the same individually oriented approach reflected in the DSM toward mental disorders. Children typically complain, "My father is too strict" or "My mother is unfair," while their parents in contrast protest, "She just won't listen" or "He's so self-centered." Again, if DSM diagnosis is required in the workplace or if managed care reimbursement is sought, marriage and family therapists will probably find themselves supporting family members' views that there is a scapegoat on whom to focus their complaints.

Denton (1990) observed that, in practice, most experienced marriage and family therapists generally recognize that a "pure" family systems approach is too indefinite for describing complex problems. A number of marriage and family therapy writers have advocated a reconceptualization of the "systems" perspective that incorporates the interaction among different systems levels. For example, Coyne and Anderson (1989) proposed that marriage and family therapists give due consideration in their practice to the interaction between the health care delivery system and family system as well as to the interaction between the individual system and family system. Melito (1988), M. P. Nichols (1987a, 1987b), and R. Schwartz (1987) have all stressed the role of the individual within the family system.

Marriage and family therapists whose conceptualization of systems theory includes more than just the family system and incorporates the individual, family, and larger social systems as different system levels interacting with each other will likely find greater compatibility between their views and the DSM. On the other hand, family systems "purists" may struggle to manage this incompatibility harmoniously in their explanations to family members. Once again, the persuasiveness of institutional layer of values may affect the professional layer of values for the marriage and family therapist. To this extent, the concept of personal consistency noted in Chapter 3 must be addressed and resolved for the individual practitioner. From the vantage point of virtue ethics, some practitioners may even reconsider a decision to seek managed care reimbursement as well as their place of employment if an individual diagnosis is a requirement in the workplace.

The Stigma of Diagnosis

Marriage and family therapists need to be acutely aware of how DSM diagnoses might be perceived by family members as well as how they might be used by others. DSM diagnoses can serve useful therapeutic purposes. Providing an individual diagnosis (e.g., Major Depression) for one family member may alleviate criticism of that member, because her or his social withdrawal can be seen as "illness" and not "noncaring" (Denton, 1989). Accepting that a family member is experiencing an "illness" also can facilitate family members' participation in family therapy; they will be less likely to feel blamed when a family systems conceptualization of their circumstances is offered (C. M. Anderson, Reiss, & Hogarty, 1986).

Although a DSM diagnosis may reduce unhelpful blaming, it also can be perceived mistakenly as an excuse to keep an individual from accepting responsibility. For example, a physically abusive spouse might seek to excuse his or her violent attacks by claiming to have "Intermittent Explosive Disorder" (Denton, 1989). Individual diagnoses also can induce persons who are diagnosed to become resigned to certain conditions; these persons subsequently may begin to despair, or their actions may become self-fulfilling prophecies (Corey, Corey, & Callanan, 1998). Such diagnoses can also damage family members' perceptions of the individuals and family interactions with them.

Honos-Webb and Leitner (2001) offered a detailed case study to illustrate the potential for DSM diagnoses to "exacerbate clients' symptoms and inhibit the healing process in psychotherapy" (p. 37). Specifically, these authors noted that, for some, the use of a diagnosis actually may become an internalized construct to the extent that it becomes a dominant view of self for clients. Additionally, they observed that such an outcome could even impede the therapy process, since clients may view their prospects for successful change as limited or unattainable.

In considering the stigma of diagnosis, culturally responsive marriage and family therapists also should be aware of the biases that may be embedded in diagnostic practices when applying the DSM. In some instances, issues ranging from language and tradition differences to ageism, sexism, or even disregard for disability status may be significant prejudicial factors related to misuse of the DSM. In many ways, the DSM may emphasize a Westernized model of mental health and pathology that may not be shared across cultural groups (Hardy & Laszloffy, 1992; Jordan & Stevens, 1999; Thomas, 1998).

Another ethical quandary arises over the potential uses to which the information in a diagnosis might be put. For example, the revelation on a job application that applicants have received mental health treatment or a diagnosis of a mental disorder might preclude their being considered for a position because of the continuing stigma attached by many to mental and emotional disorders and their treatment. A diagnosis might be used to impede clients in custody hearings or other legal proceedings or might prevent them from obtaining insurance.

Denton (1989) recommended that the most ethical way to approach the potential problems imposed by the stigma of diagnosis is to discuss the risks directly with clients and their family members. Marriage and family therapists should address, as part of their informed consent procedures at the beginning of therapy, both the benefits and the risks of releasing diagnostic codes.

Misrepresentation of Diagnoses

Many marriage and family therapists are somewhat uninformed about the rationale of managed care agencies and the way they work. One agency executive has addressed psychiatrists on this point:

> A . . . problem is the willingness of some psychiatrists to put an insurance-acceptable diagnosis on a condition that is not considered a covered diagnosis. Examples of this category include the problems of living: floundering marriages, trouble raising children. . . . We can understand why a person would go to an analyst to get rid of such unpleasant or unwanted human behavior . . . but insurance was never intended to cover this type of 'non-psychiatric problem.'
>
> Medical insurance should only be asked to cover medical mental disorders. Insurance is meant to pay for the sick, not the discontented who are seeking an improved lifestyle. We need your help in differentiating between those who have mental disorders and those who simply have problems. (Guillette, 1979, p. 32)

This lack of knowledge can lead to what Packer (1988) has termed "insurance diagnosis" (p. 19). Pressure from both clients and therapists themselves to obtain health insurance reimbursement increases the possibility that a diagnosis will be misrepresented and that a DSM diagnosis will be applied when none of the family members actually meets the criteria.

For an illustrative example, let us consider Meg and Kevin. They have been married for 21 years. In the past 4 years, their two children have entered young adulthood and have progressively separated from the home. Meg and Kevin are once again a couple alone and find themselves somewhat aimless. They seek the assistance of a marriage and family therapist to renew the "spark" they once had. Neither reports experiencing any major distress.

All the diagnostic classifications in the DSM have criteria that must be met in order for a specific diagnosis to be given. Diagnosis of a reimbursable mental disorder might be difficult to justify in Meg and Kevin's case. A nonreimbursable V Code classification (e.g., V62.89 Phase of Life Problem or Other Life Circumstance Problem) appears more appropriate. Yet some marriage and family therapists and clients do not see misrepresentation of diagnosis as a serious concern. They justify "insurance diagnosis" by noting that premiums have been paid and therefore reimbursement is deserved—despite the fact that the client may not have a covered condition (Denton, 1989, 1996).

Obviously, in many cases, one or more family members can clearly meet the criteria for a DSM diagnosis of mental disorder. When none do, the offer of a misrepresented "insurance diagnosis" constitutes fraud (Packer, 1988). The comments of Wilson (1985) apply just as much to marriage and family therapists as they do to physicians:

> The falsification of records or case reports to protect the patient's access to treatment undermines the credibility of the profession itself as well as the individual physician. . . . It is also unethical for the physician to collude with the patient to obtain, fraudulently, insurance reimbursement to which the patient is not entitled. (p. 63)

Most clients find it relatively easy to locate a clinician who will provide a coverable diagnosis when it is not justified (Packer, 1988). Marriage and family therapists have an obligation—one that may be economically difficult but is still ethically clear—not to misrepresent diagnoses. Again, the interactivity of professional and institutional layers of values, as well as the personal values of clients versus those of the therapist, can introduce some significant dilemmas concerning the representativeness of a DSM diagnosis.

Competence to Diagnose

Standard 3.11 of the *AAMFT Code of Ethics* (American Association for Marriage and Family Therapy, 2001) states:

> Marriage and family therapists do not diagnose, treat, or advise on problems outside the recognized boundaries of their competence.

According to a research study in 1999 by William Doherty, only 13% of the 352,535 mental health professionals in the United States "were specifically taught marital therapy as a part of their professional training" (K. S. Peterson, 1999, p. D2). Thus, most marriage and family therapists received their training in other disciplines (e.g., counseling, psychiatry, psychology, social work) in which the study of psychopathology and the use of the DSM were required portions of the training program. As a consequence, assessing individual symptoms and assigning DSM diagnoses are fully within their realm of competence. Similarly, as we will see in Chapter 11, clinical membership in the American Association for Marriage and Family Therapy (AAMFT) requires curricular experiences emphasizing psychopathology. As with therapy, however, competence to diagnose is not static and requires diligent attention to new developments and diagnostic criteria in postgraduate continuing education.

Denton (1989, 1996) asserted the responsibility of marriage and family therapists to be able to recognize and appreciate the significance of serious individual symptoms and syndromes so that they can be dealt with or the person can be appropriately referred. Although many symptoms may be exacerbated by systemic factors, a variety of psychiatric conditions require competent diagnostic skills on the part of the therapist to avoid possibly dire outcomes. These include clinical depression and suicidal ideation (Hirschfeld & Goodwin, 1988) as well as schizophrenia (Black, Yates, & Andreasen, 1988).

Marriage and family therapists who have not had adequate or updated training in psychopathology or abnormal behavior and the use of the DSM therefore should make every effort to increase their level of competence by acquiring the appropriate skills and knowledge. Then they will be better equipped to address with due care some of the possible ethical challenges occasioned by the interaction of the DSM and marriage and family therapy.

Christensen and Miller (2001) reported that one significant struggle for marriage and family therapists who participated in their qualitative investigation was the dilemma of "fudging on diagnosis at times" and resolving diagnostic versus reimbursement dilemmas that "were not entirely consistent with the therapy case" (p. 513) in order to serve clients in need. Such a quandary is not uncommon and represents the interrelationship between diagnostic decision making and managed mental health care.

MANAGED MENTAL HEALTH CARE

Until the 1980s, health care was generally financed by traditional major medical insurance. In such a fee-for-service delivery system, the provider of services submitted a bill to the insurance company and was paid by the company for services rendered after a deductible balance was paid by the consumer. However, since then the traditional insurance system has given way to managed health care and mental health care delivery systems. This revolution has transformed the delivery of mental health services in the private sector. Fueled by sweeping cost-containment efforts, this revolution has brushed aside almost all resistance from the various mental health care provider professions. The resulting system in place today is called managed mental health care (MMHC), and it involves a service delivery system that is driven more by costs than by client needs. The familiar fee-for-service system has been replaced by a system in which costs are controlled by placing limits on the amount and type of services, by monitoring services intensely, and by changing the nature of services (Coleman, 2003; Foos, Ottens, & Hill, 1991; Lawless, Ginter, & Kelly, 1999).

A variety of models exist for MMHC (e.g., employee assistance programs, utilization review, preferred provider organizations, etc.). Each model incorporates greater or lesser intrusiveness into the procedures of treatment. Additionally, each model involves various means of addressing cost containment, specifying acceptable practitioners for reimbursement, and similar procedures.

Haas and Cummings (1991) raised several questions that prospective service providers (i.e., therapists) should consider before participating in an MMHC program:

- Who takes the risks? (That is, who pays additional costs?)
- How much does the plan intrude into the relationship between client and service provider?
- What provisions exist for making exceptions to the rules?
- Are there referral resources if clients' needs exceed the plan's benefits?
- Does the plan provide assistance or training to help service providers achieve treatment goals?
- Is the plan open to input by providers?
- Are policyholders clearly informed of the limits of benefits?

The following discussion extends Haas and Cummings's responses and considers the ethical implications of each of the questions.

Risk Taking

As a reference point for discussing ethical treatment of issues related to MMHC, one must understand that to do so involves addressing a balance of *therapy concerns* and *business concerns.* Similar to the previous discussion about the use of the DSM for purposes of fee reimbursement in diagnostic decisions, many aspects of contemporary marriage and family therapy relate to financial considerations. In this respect, therapists can be faced with the divergence of professional values related to therapy practices and institutional values related to economic practices (even if the institution is the private practice of the therapist). Marriage and family therapists are typically compassionate professionals concerned about human conflict and pain. They are also citizens and consumers in need of reliable income for their lifestyle, ambitions, and futures. Thus, the interplay between principle ethics and virtue ethics discussed in Chapter 3 becomes pertinent for many decisions about MMHC. One must realize that considering the business aspects of marriage and family therapy is not unethical, however, as long as reasonable due care is afforded to clients still in need of services.

Traditionally, insurance companies have taken the risk of paying for unforeseen expenses for client services. Plans have generally factored in the probability of particular treatment needs. If clients need more treatment, however, insurance plans usually reimburse for some of the cost of those additional needs. In some MMHC programs, a portion of this added cost has been shifted to the client. If the client needs treatment past a certain predetermined point, the client becomes liable for the cost of that treatment. Thus, the risk of additional financial obligation in such circumstances is borne by the client.

In other MMHC programs, a portion of the added cost is shifted to the service provider. If costs exceed a set limit, or if referral for ancillary treatment is required, the service provider's reimbursement is reduced or eliminated. In such circumstances, the risk of additional financial obligation is borne by the therapist.

One potential ethical concern that can emerge in such a circumstance is the tendency for service providers to "hoard resources" (Morreim, 1988). Some view such actions as accounting procedures that allow for a more continuous flow of financial support for the therapist. In this way, service providers enact a business decision based on their reluctance to refer or extend treatment if it costs them too much. The ethical quandary in this respect concerns the priority of a business decision versus a therapy decision. In such a circumstance, *beneficence* and *justice* are key ethical considerations for the service provider.

Intrusion into the Therapeutic Relationship

Traditional fee-for-service insurance plans provided substantial contractual freedom. A client expresses a need for a service, selects a service provider from among existing alternatives, and has some degree of participation in the treatment-planning process. This process calls for an expression of loyalty on the part of the service provider. The provider has the freedom to accept or decline working with the client, to select that treatment method in which he or she is most competent, and then to honor his or her commitment to treat the client until the presenting complaint is resolved, an appropriate referral is made, or the client discontinues treatment. The therapeutic relationship is characterized by free-dom and responsibility: freedom to provide treatment as the service provider sees fit and responsibility primarily to the client, not the managed care agency. Some have argued that such an arrangement offers incentives to provide more treatment than is necessary (Nel-son, Clark, Goldman, & Schore, 1989). Others have contended that it also emphasizes that the primary loyalty of the service provider is to the client (Haas & Cummings, 1991).

In contrast, service providers who agree to participate in an MMHC incur obligations not only to clients but to the MMHC program as well. For example, if a provider's practice includes too many clients whose treatment involves cost overruns, the MMHC program's financial viability, if not its existence, is threatened. In turn, the service provider's finan-cial viability likewise would be threatened. Therefore, how service providers balance their loyalty to clients with their responsibilities as an agent of the MMHC program becomes a critical ethical issue (Stevens-Smith, 1997a, 1997b). In some ways, the dynam-ics of *triangulation* discussed in Chapter 4 may apply to such arrangements. Additionally, the discussion in Chapter 1 regarding the *balance of fairness* in valuing is a pertinent ref-erence point for the therapist. One important method that practioners can use to manage the balance of obligations ethically is through the use of clear and thorough informed con-sent procedures with clients. This approach will be considered later in this chapter.

Exceptions to the Rules

Certain clients' conditions or circumstances call for treatment beyond the prevailing norm. Some MMHC programs employ a method called *capitation* to pay for such treatment. Under a capitated system, the MMHC provider agrees, within certain para-meters, to deliver all the mental health services required by a given population for a fixed cost per member or employee. In a capitated system, the MMHC provider assumes financial risk for a given population because the payment to the provider is the same regardless of the amount of service offered (Richardson & Austad, 1991).

Continuing treatment past a certain point is primarily a financial consideration and a built-in risk. Other MMHC programs employ a noncapitated system wherein services are simply limited to a specific number of sessions or to a preset cost per case. In such noncapitated systems, the temptation for a service provider to change a diagnosis or description of treatment for a particular client who has exceeded the benefits but requires continuing treatment is always present and represents a poten-tially recurrent ethical conflict. This issue has already been discussed previously regarding misrepresentation of a diagnosis.

It would seem that the ethical principle of *fidelity* would be pertinent for the mar-riage and family therapist involved in a situation of cost capitation. This is not to say that clients should be privy to all business aspects of a therapist's practice. However, truthful representation of business procedures affecting therapy practice is supported in codified ethical standards (American Association for Marriage and Family Therapy [AAMFT], 2001) as well as in notions about virtuous ethical practice.

Referral Resources

Marriage and family therapists, like all providers of mental health services, have a respon-sibility to offer treatment until a presenting complaint is resolved, an appropriate referral is made, or the client or clients discontinue treatment. To do otherwise is to abandon clients, which is clearly unethical according to the AAMFT Code of Ethics (AAMFT, 2001).

Although this same code calls for marriage and family therapists to devote a portion of their professional activity to services for which there is little or no financial return (i.e., pro bono service), the key question becomes "Can I avoid abandoning my clients without going bankrupt?" (Haas & Cummings, 1991). Thus, to provide continuing treatment to clients whose benefits have been exhausted, referral frequently may be necessary. Are appropriate referral resources available? It may present significant ethical conflict for most marriage and family therapists to provide extensive pro bono service if such resources are not available. Certainly aspects of the Battle for Initiative (Napier & Whitaker, 1978) must be addressed in such circumstances to ensure continued client commitment and need. Similarly, revisions may be made in aspects of the Battle for Structure, such as alternate scheduling of sessions, use of self-help activities or groups, or even technology-based services. The key to ethical treatment in such instances is responsible and effective due care. Virtuous ethical practice does not require the therapist to threaten his or her professional and financial livelihood, an outcome that could actually impede care to other clients served by the therapist.

Short-Term Treatment and Therapist Competence

Mental health services under an MMHC plan must be delivered within the parameters of the plan, which typically limit the number of sessions or allowable treatment costs. Time limitations and monetary constraints dictate that marriage and family therapists working under such a plan be proficient in brief, time-limited therapy. Treatment plans have to be formulated rapidly and must include specified goals and number of sessions (Foos et al., 1991).

Most clinicians resent having their practices subjected to external control (Zimet, 1989). Short-term treatment approaches are not simply a form of long-term treatment squeezed into a briefer time period. Marriage and family therapists who are not trained in brief therapy and yet who work under an MMHC plan that demands short-term, cost-effective treatment are more likely to be dissatisfied with the treatment they can offer. Consequently, their clients may be similarly dissatisfied with their treatment. The treatment is more likely to be less structured and therefore less effective. Further, these therapists are more likely to lack faith in their ability to obtain positive outcomes from brief treatment, resulting in a pessimism that is covertly, if not overtly, communicated to their clients (Budman, 1989). Toward this end, Sperling and Sack (2002) argued that traditional psychodynamic treatment is essentially at odds with treatment conducted in MMHC frameworks.

As we have indicated, brief-therapy modalities are not simply abbreviated forms of the long-term therapy approaches to which most clinicians were exposed in graduate school (Gladding, 1998b; Sperry, 1989). Brief-therapy modalities entail their own framework of skills and assumptions. Budman and Gurman (1988) presented compelling theoretical arguments that brief, time-sensitive treatment can offer benefits that, in many cases, are superior to therapy that has no time constraints. Furthermore, they have shown that repeated "doses" of brief therapy have the same effect as, or even a better effect than, one dose of long-term treatment.

The widespread use of brief approaches to intervention in MMHC is not without criticism as well as support. Dermer, Hemesath, and Russell (1998) observed that solution-focused therapy had not been systematically examined regarding feminist issues. To begin, these authors questioned many of the foundational notions of this brief-therapy approach, such as "change is constant," "emphasizing positive solutions," and "families are competent and are experts in their choices of goals and solutions" (p. 248). In circumstances such as intimate partner violence or sexual victimization, these notions could actually minimize the significance of the power inequity between partners while also supporting denial and even urging acquiescence on the part of the victim in order to "move beyond this incident." In this way, the institutional values of speed and brevity within the MMHC system actually could promote the maintenance of threatening or even harmful situations for victims. By contrast, Lee, Uken, and Sebold (2004) reported that a solution-focused approach to treatment in instances of domestic violence yielded only a 16.7% recidivism rate among 90 offenders over a six-year period of monitoring.

Huber (1998) observed that the use of short-term therapy approaches within an MMHC framework posed concerns for complex client complaints, particularly for those who may require longer-term services. One aspect of this issue is the comfort level of clients with the rapid pace of short-term care. Wilcoxon (2004) observed that brief therapy, just as any other therapy approaches, occurs in interaction with the cultural and value traditions of clients. But what if clients' cultural and value traditions do not embrace the Westernized view of a rapid pace and an action-oriented (rather than contemplative) approach to change? What if behaviors traditionally labeled by therapists as "client resistance to change" are more accurately reflective of "client resistance to pace"? What if an imposed rate of change in the therapy process is viewed as simply another form of oppression against clients from a minority group? These and similar issues of cultural and value traditions addressed in Chapters 1 and 2 should be considered as ethical aspects of culturally responsive marriage and family practice within the framework of MMHC.

In addition to possible hazards related to brief therapy, marriage and family therapists who are not competent in brief therapy as a distinct modality should probably avoid involvement in an MMHC program (Haas & Cummings, 1991). Likewise, MMHC programs ought to select only service providers competent to offer short-term mental health treatment, or they ought to make provisions for selected service providers to receive training to gain competence in employing a short-term treatment model.

Input by Service Providers

MMHC programs have encouraged the development and use of clinical decision-making aids (e.g., diagnosis-specific treatment protocols). Such procedures are grounded in a contemporary emphasis on "best practice" methods for therapy. The majority of these aids are relatively newer to mental health care than to physical health care. They assist in controlling costs by promoting a standard quality of care, and they can be readily examined in utilization review.

One of these clinical aids, the *algorithm*, is an outline of a methodology (usually represented in graphic form) or a prescribed procedure for diagnosis and treatment.

Algorithms assist service providers in making sound clinical decisions and in providing efficient care, thereby protecting against possible claims of negligence. However, they also tend to homogenize treatment (Grumet, 1988). Unfortunately, research into the utility and effectiveness of algorithms on the nature and quality of mental health care has been sparse (Cohen, 2003; Coleman, 2003; Richardson & Austad, 1991). Given the proliferation and support of such approaches by MMHC programs, it is essential that service providers have frequent and formal means of offering input not only about the overall MMHC plan but also about those therapeutic decisions they promote. Otherwise, the service provider becomes only an employee as opposed to a mental health professional treating clients (Haas & Cummings, 1991). In this respect, aspects of institutional identification and valuing discussed in Chapter 2 could conflict with personal as well as professional layers of the therapist's values. Additionally, one may want to consider the basis for Napier and Whitaker's (1978) discussion about the necessity of the therapist "winning" the Battle for Structure, namely to retain administrative and management control of therapy to avoid clients gravitating toward old patterns and arguments. If the Battle for Structure is an essential aspect of administrative control on the part of the therapist, at what point does the therapist acquiesce to the control of the MMHC agency? Additionally, what is the "therapeutic cost" of such a decision?

Keefe, Hall, and Corvo (2002) surveyed practitioners from social work, psychiatry, and psychology regarding clients they served using an MMHC framework. Respondents indicated that 39% of their caseload encompassed managed care clients and that nearly one-third of those clients had been denied reimbursement for ongoing therapy services. These authors further reported that 42% of the managed care clients served by the respondents and who had been denied reimbursement reentered therapy at a later time with exacerbated symptoms. From these findings, they noted that these and similar data should be compelling to managed care agencies as a matter of principle. However, they also noted the limited opportunity many providers have to influence revisions in agency policies and practices.

Informed Consent

All the disciplines within the mental health field are clear on the issue of informed consent. Prospective MMHC clients should be given full information about the benefits to which they are entitled as well as the limits of treatment as the clinician envisions them.

As noted before, marriage and family therapists working under an MMHC program have inherently divided loyalties to both the MMHC program and to clients. It is critical that marriage and family therapists avoid being caught in the middle, having to explain benefit limitations to naïve clients after the benefit limits have been reached (Haas & Cummings, 1991). Supporting this belief, Pomerantz (2000) provided a stimulating array of observations in an article entitled "What If Prospective Clients Knew How Managed Care Impacts Psychologists' Practice and Ethics?" In this publication, the author offered a straightforward and thorough discussion about the need for full disclosure on the part of practitioners concerning the unique business aspects of their practice in conjunction with a managed care agency. Additionally, issues of confidentiality discussed in the preceding section of this chapter also are relevant for disclosure concerning the storage and distribution of client data (electronic and otherwise) from MMHC facilities.

Acting Ethically as an MMHC Service Provider

Third-party payment arrangements consistently raise ethical concerns, and ethical dilemmas are a price a therapist has to pay if he or she decides to participate in the managed care marketplace (Golden & Schmidt, 1998). We have noted a variety of concerns pertinent to a marriage and family therapist who elects to be an MMHC provider. One such concern involves the accurate representation of a client when formulating a treatment plan. The temptation might be to try to justify an individual diagnosis when seeing a couple or family (Bonnington, Crawford, Curtis, & Watts, 1996), but such a ploy could be a misrepresentation of the family therapist's client—that is, the couple or family—and could be unethical.

An equally difficult dilemma for family therapists who participate in MMHC programs is in regard to divided loyalties. The ethical principle of *fidelity* (Beauchamp & Childress, 2001) demands that marriage and family therapists as professionals must be loyal to those with whom they have a contractual relationship. Therefore, marriage and family therapists who agree to MMHC participation should believe in the service philosophy and procedures the MMHC endorses (Huber, 1995). Likewise, if a marriage and family therapist agrees to work with a certain client, she or he should be loyal to that client's interests.

Other concerns we have emphasized involve informed consent and full disclosure regarding financial constraints in managed care, intrusion into the therapy process by MMHC agencies or representatives, referral and pro bono care, and initiatives by therapists to influence agency policies and practices regarding financial and treatment exceptions. Additionally, we have emphasized the therapist's cognizance of competence to use brief-therapy methods as well as cultural and value issues associated with those methods. J. A. Cohen (2003) noted that, despite the value of cost-containment strategies to assure at least minimal access to mental health services, managed care is a business approach to a therapy function. He further noted that, although these paradigms to consumer care may converge in many ways, they may also diverge in a manner that creates conflict.

Christensen and Miller (2001) noted that two significant issues permeated the decisions of the therapists participating in their study of practices involving managed mental health care. The first issue was that "these therapists had to accommodate more hassles that were brought on by managed care guidelines" (p. 513), particularly concerning paperwork and regulations. The second issue was one previously addressed in this chapter: paradigm differences in DSM categories and a systemic view. They concluded by stating, "In an effort to contain costs, managed care companies have overreacted by creating policies that compromise the quality of care and strain the ethical boundaries of therapists" (p. 513).

Subprinciple 6.1 of the AAMFT Code of Ethics (American Association for Marriage and Family Therapy, 2001) calls for marriage and family therapists to remain accountable to the standards of the profession when acting as members or employees of organizations. One such standard is that marriage and family therapists should avoid relationships that could impair professional judgment or increase their risk of exploitation. In MMHC participation, the most likely conflict would be between the demands of the MMHC plan (e.g., that reimbursement for treatment cease beyond a specified point regardless of the client's need) and the ethical responsibility of the marriage and family therapist to provide for needs of a client who requires continuing treatment (e.g., that the welfare of the client be considered above all other concerns). Should the demands of MMHC participation conflict with a marriage and family therapist's code of ethics, that therapist should attempt to bring the conflict to the attention of the relevant parties and seek to resolve it. Establishing and maintaining support systems of informed colleagues to help generate alternatives through open discussion in such circumstances can be of immeasurable assistance.

Should the conflict remain unresolved, however, the marriage and family therapist should consider temporarily withdrawing from active participation as an MMHC service provider and pursue resolution in other ways (e.g., through professional, organizational, and/or legislative advocacy efforts on behalf of consumer-clients). To do otherwise would risk colluding with either the client or the MMHC to the detriment of the other (Haas & Cummings, 1991).

An emerging option for third-party reimbursement in the health care industry is *consumer driven health care* (CDHC). This new approach is designed to increase the freedom and autonomy of patients by permitting them to make decisions about such issues as the nature of diagnostic procedures (e.g., X-ray or CT scans) or the provider of medical advice (e.g., a specialist in a group of practicing specialists or a generalist in independent practice). In most MMCH approaches, such decisions are determined by a representative of a managed-care agency. The driving force behind CDHC is to allow consumers to have greater freedom and oversight regarding the costs of their own care. However, such freedom also includes greater responsibility for consumers making those choices.

Though promising, CDHC is not without possible difficulties, particularly regarding ethical considerations related to the standard of due care. Extensions of CDHC into mental-health services have not yet been fully implemented. Thus, ethical considerations by marriage and family therapists in the provision of services to clients utilizing this model will be discussed in the future. However, just as with any derivative of managed care, CDHC is likely to present unique challenges to therapists in the ethical areas of informed consent, confidentiality, clinical record-keeping, competence, and coordination of services with professional peers.

MULTIPLE OR DUAL RELATIONSHIPS

Multiple or *dual relationships* are those in which marriage and family therapists assume two roles simultaneously with a person or persons engaging their professional assistance (Herlihy & Corey, 1992). These roles may both be professional in nature, such as therapist and supervisor, or a combination of professional and nonprofessional, such as therapist and friend or therapist and lover. "Dual relationships are problematic because they are (a) so pervasive, (b) difficult to recognize at times, (c) sometimes unavoidable, (d) sometimes harmful but may also be beneficial, and (e) the subject of conflicting advice" (B. Pearson & Piazza, 1997, p. 91). In addition, multiple relationships may cause a therapist to lose impartiality as well as impair the therapist's professional judgment (McGrath, Browning, Martinek, Beck, & Culkin, 1995). The ethical codes of mental health professions prohibit or warn of the dangers of relationships involving *simultaneous* but competing relationships. Some professions offer additional commentary about *sequential changes* in relationships such as relationships with former clients. As an initial point of discussion regarding multiple relationships, we will examine portions of selected entries from the codes and standards of ethics from various professional associations concerning both simultaneous and sequential relationships involving therapists, clients, and others.

Ethical Codes and Multiple Relationships

Citations from selected mental health disciplines have been emphasized in previous chapters for purposes of comparison and contrast. These discussions have included codes of ethics and standards from the American Association for Marriage and Family Therapy (2001), the American Counseling Association (2005), the American Psychological Association (2002), the National Association of Social Workers (1999), and the International Association for Marriage and Family Counseling (2005).

Many commonalities exist across each of these associations in language and emphases concerning multiple or dual relationships. For example, all associational codes and standards indicate that dual or multiple relationships may be harmful, may be exploitive, and should be avoided if possible, though not all such relationships may be avoidable. Additionally, these professional codes and standards clearly prohibit sexual or intimate relationships with current clients and all offer commentary about sexual or intimate relationships with former clients. The admonition against sexual relationships between therapists and clients has already been noted in Chapter 3 of our text. Despite this apparently clear sanction, one of the most frequent ethical violations reviewed by ethics committees involves dual relationships, particularly sexual intimacy between therapist and client (Ethics Committee of the American Psychological Association, 1988), a phenomenon a former president of the American Psychological Association termed a "national disgrace" for his profession (Cummings, 1985).

As previously noted, not all dual relationships can be avoided, nor are they all necessarily harmful (Keith-Spiegel & Koocher, 1998; Kitchener, 1988). In a survey of rural physicians, Purtilo and Sorrel (1986) identified the overlapping of professional and personal relationships as a major ethical issue that these physicians consistently faced. Professionals who live and work in small or rural communities may be unable to avoid blending roles with clients. For instance, when there is only one marriage and family therapist in a community with only one grocery store (whose owner has sought therapy services), unless the grocer and his or her family go without treatment when treatment is needed *or* the therapist travels an inordinate distance to purchase groceries, a dual relationship may be almost impossible to avoid. Or, what if in that same community, the therapist and the client have children involved in the same activity (e.g., a school sports team, a community drama guild, etc.)? Should the clients go without care *or* should the therapist require his or her child to withdraw from the activity?

As we discussed in Chapter 3, ethical codes reflect the interpretation and application of foundational ethical principles for a profession. Many commonalities exist across professions in the language and emphases. However, some differences emerge in the language and emphases of the mental health regarding multiple relationships. Chapter 7 features an examination of all the standards in the AAMFT Code of Ethics (2001), thus we offer the following summary of selected portions of the remaining codes and standards from professional associations we have considered in earlier portions of our text. These selections are intended to serve as a point of comparison and stimulation for marriage and family therapists seeking an expansive view and understanding about the ethical issues associated with multiple or dual relationships.

American Counseling Association (2005)

The code of ethics for the American Counseling Association (ACA) offers considerable commentary about multiple relationships. Excerpts from these standards state the following (italics added for emphasis):

> A.5.a: "Sexual *or romantic* counselor–client interactions or relationships with current clients, *their romantic partners, or their family members* are prohibited."
>
> A.5.b: "Sexual *or romantic* . . . relationships with former clients, *their romantic partners, or their family members* are *prohibited for a period of 5 years* following the last professional contact."
>
> A.5.d: ". . . *a counselor–client non-professional interaction with a client or former client may be potentially beneficial.* . . . Examples of potentially beneficial interactions include but are not limited to attending a formal ceremony (e.g., a wedding or graduation); purchasing a service or product provided by a client or former client (excepting unrestricted bartering); hospital visits to an ill family member; mutual membership in a professional association, organization, or community."
>
> A.9.3: "Counselors understand the challenges of *accepting gifts from clients and recognize that in some cultures, small gifts are a token of respect and showing gratitude.* . . ."
>
> F.9.c: "*If students request counseling or if counseling services are required as part of a remediation process, counselor educators provide acceptable referrals.*"
>
> F.10.c: "Counselor educators do not serve as counselors to current students *unless this is a brief role associated with a training experience.*"

From these entries, you will note recognition of the hazards of a therapist's involvement with partners or family members of current clients, the significance of token gifts in some cultural groups, and notations about conflicts in student–educator relationships involving counseling. The fact that the ACA code of ethics includes guidelines concerning beneficial nonprofessional interactions or relationships is a formal acknowledgement that not all dual relationships are harmful, though they can still be complicated. Additionally, the ACA code provides direction concerning relationships with former clients, their partners, or their family members less than 5 years after the conclusion of the professional relationship.

American Psychological Association (2002)

The code of ethics for the American Psychological Association (APA) also addresses a variety of aspects concerning dual or multiple relationships. Excerpts from these standards state the following (italics added for emphasis):

> 3.05(a): "A multiple relationship occurs when a psychologist is in a professional role with a person and . . . (2) at the same time is in a relationship *with a person closely associated with or related to the person* . . . or, (3) *promises to enter into another relationship in the future with the person or a person closely associated with or related to the person.* . . . *Multiple relationships that would not reasonably be expected to cause impairment or risk exploitation or harm are not unethical.*"
>
> 7.05(a): "When . . . *therapy is a program or a course requirement,* psychologists responsible for that program allow . . . *such therapy from practitioners unaffiliated with the program.*"

7.05(b): *"Faculty who are or who are likely to be responsible for evaluating students' academic performance do not themselves provide that therapy."*

10.05: "Psychologists do not engage in sexual intimacies with individuals *they know to be close relatives, guardians, or significant others of current clients/patients."*

10.07: "Psychologists do not accept as therapy clients/patients persons *with whom they have engaged in sexual intimacies."*

10.08: "Psychologists do not engage in sexual intimacies with former clients/patients for *at least two years* after cessation or termination of therapy."

As with the counselors and the ACA code, psychologists accountable to the APA ethical code are not to enter into relationships with others involved with a current client or patient. Significant notations appear related to persons "associated with" a current client, "promises" of future relationships, and students receiving services from professionals not affiliated with an academic program. An important phrase concerning sexual intimacies with others is "they know to be," which reflects recognition of inadvertent relationships as well as the duty for the practitioner, rather than the client, to monitor dual relationships. The specific notation about not entering into a professional relationship with a person with whom one has had a previous sexually intimate relationship is an emphatic statement about an obviously potential difficulty. Unlike the five-year prohibition in the ACA code, the APA code reflects a two-year period of no sexual intimacy with former clients or patients. Finally, the statement concerning reasonableness in multiple relationships reflects recognition that to imply all multiple relationships are unethical is to create unrealistic barriers for consumers to secure professional services.

International Association of Marriage and Family Counselors (2005)

The code of ethics for the International Association of Marriage and Family Counselors (IAMFC) features standards about multiple relationships similar to those of ACA and APA. One notable exception to this is in Standard 1.9, which states ". . . Couple and family counselors avoid *whenever possible* multiple relationships, such as business, social, or sexual contacts with any current clients or their family members. Marriage and family counselors should *refrain generally from nonprofessional* relationships with *former clients and their family members* because termination of counseling is a complex process" (italics added for emphasis). This admonition appears to suggest that the therapeutic relationship is such than any sequential role change could be harmful to even former clients or their family members. This issue is addressed later in this section of our chapter, as it differs from the specified periods noted in both the ACA and APA codes.

Additionally, Standard 1.14 of this code states, ". . . *Culturally sensitive counselors recognize that gifts are tokens of respect and gratitude in some cultures.* Marriage and family counselors may receive gifts *or participate in family rituals that promote healthy interaction* and do not exploit clients." In this standard, the explicit nature of the guidance provided for practitioners offers aid concerning cultural sensitivity and even participation in family rituals that may arise from those cultures.

National Association of Social Workers (1999)

The code of ethics for the National Association of Social Workers (NASW) features standards about multiple relationships similar to those of the other professions discussed thus far. The NASW code prohibits sexual intimacies with current clients, relatives, and others affiliated with clients. The NASW code also clearly addresses the fact that multiple relationships should be avoided but may be unavoidable. Similar to the APA code, the NASW code prohibits therapy with a former intimate partner. Similar to the IAMFC code, the NASW code offers no specified time period for possible intimacies with former clients. However, the NASW code offers some distinct differences in comparison to other codes (italics added for emphasis):

> 1.06: "Social workers should not engage in dual or multiple relationships . . . (and) *are responsible for setting clear, appropriate and culturally sensitive boundaries. . . ."*
>
> 1.09(b): ". . . Social workers—*not their clients, their client's relatives, or other individuals with whom the client maintains a personal relationship—assume the full burden for setting clear, appropriate, and culturally sensitive boundaries."*
>
> 1.10: "Social workers *should not engage in physical contact with clients when there is a possibility of psychological harm to the client as a result of the contact. . . ."*

From these entries, one can note some unique features of the NASW code, primarily in emphasizing the duty of the professional, rather than another party, to clarify boundaries and manage multiple relationships. Additionally, the sensitivity to cultural differences is recognized formally in this code. Finally, the NASW code offers even greater clarity about possible misinterpretations of physical contact as a portrayal of a multiple relationship.

From this brief review of selected code entries from professional associations, one can see that great care has been taken to emphasize the complex and potentially harmful nature of multiple relationships. Even though one may be a member of one or more of these groups, the information from peer professional associations can serve to assist in ethical sensitivity and decision making to avoid possible exploitation or harm to clients in multiple relationships.

So where is the line between those relationships that are clearly unethical and those that are acceptable if handled with due care and caution? Kitchener (1988) offered three guidelines based on role theory that can be used to differentiate between dual role relationships that will probably lead to unethical behavior and those that are less likely to be problematic. Specifically, she proposed guidelines related to: (a) compatibility of expectations, (b) divergence of obligations, and (c) the power and prestige differential. We will examine each of these in following sections of our discussion. Additionally, we will offer a brief commentary about other specific issues involving multiple relationships. Finally, appropriate action emanating from the contemporary literature on this topic is suggested within the context these guidelines and discussions create.

Compatibility of Expectations

As the difference between the expectations of the therapist and client increases, the potential for misunderstanding and harm increases. Consider the following example:

> Jacob has seen Dr. P. in her private practice for weekly sessions over the past two months following his divorce. During the most recent sessions, Jacob has asked questions about Dr. P.'s personal relationships. Dr. P. senses that Jacob is interested in pursuing a social relationship outside of therapy with her and raises the issue with him. Jacob confirms her suspicion. Dr. P. states that it would be unethical for her to pursue such a relationship with him.

Herlihy and Corey (1992) and Welfel (1998) stressed the importance of clear expectations regarding the therapeutic relationship. They noted that when therapists' expectations are unclear, clients' expectations are likely to be even more unclear. A survey by Borys (1988) suggested that the majority of responding therapists avoided social relationships with clients. However, the intimacy of the therapeutic relationship can readily lead clients to expect a "special type of friendship" and to invite their therapists to participate in their lives outside of therapy. When such incompatible expectations are allowed to continue, the potential increases for multiple relationships that promote compromising or unethical behaviors, possibly to the point of harm but certainly compromising the ethical principle of fidelity in the therapy relationship.

In the preceding case illustration, Dr. P. was very clear in her expectations for the therapeutic relationship once she suspected that her client may not have been. In the future, she might proactively forestall such potential problems by including a clear policy on social relationships as part of the informed consent information provided to clients when they enter therapy. However, one may never be able to anticipate all forms of attraction or interest shown toward the therapist by clients (e.g., proposed business opportunities, invitations to participate in civic activities, etc.).

Divergence of Obligations

As the divergence between the obligations imposed by different roles increases, the potential for divided loyalties and loss of objectivity increases. Consider the following example:

> Karen is a single parent experiencing significant difficulties with her two teenage daughters. She requests that Dr. K., her neighbor, see her and her daughters in family therapy. Dr. K. declines Karen's request and suggests several marriage and family therapists in the community whom she might contact. Karen implores Dr. K. to reconsider, maintaining that her daughters are more likely to agree to therapy with him because they know and like him.

The professional literature contains many cautions regarding seeing friends and acquaintances in therapy. Keith-Spiegel and Koocher (1998) put forth the position that conducting therapy with friends or acquaintances as clients potentially involves mixed allegiances and misinterpretation of motives. Likewise, Kitchener and Harding (1990) proposed that therapeutic relationships and friendships differ in function and purpose. Herlihy and Corey (1992) characterized the roles of therapist and friend as generally divergent:

> Because being a counselor as well as a friend to the same person creates a dual relationship, there is always the possibility that one of these relationships will be compromised. It may be difficult for the counselor to switch roles from friend to professional and to confront the client for fear of damaging the friendship. It may also be problematic for clients, who may hesitate to talk about deeper struggles for fear that their counselor/friend will lose respect for them. Counselors who are tempted to enter a counseling relationship with a friend might do well to ask themselves whether they are willing to risk losing the friendship. (p. 137)

In the preceding case illustration, the primary obligation of Dr. K. is to promote the welfare of Karen and her daughters. It would be very difficult for Dr. K. to carry out his professional responsibilities to Karen and her daughters as clients while simultaneously attempting to maintain his relationship to them as friends. Necessary confrontations, the need for addressing intimacies or trauma, distractions in therapy by mixing social chats in sessions, or disappointment and frustration over expected but unrealized closeness are all possible areas of concern that may emerge by mixing personal with professional roles.

Power and Prestige Differential

As the difference in power and prestige increases between the roles of therapist and client, the potential likewise increases for exploitation on the part of the therapist and an inability on the part of clients to remain objective about their own best interests. Consider the following example:

> A marriage and family therapist terminates therapy with a couple deciding to amicably divorce. The divorce becomes final one month after the last session is held. The therapist and former wife happen to meet at the party of a mutual acquaintance shortly thereafter and begin an intimate relationship. When questioned by a colleague, the therapist states that the relationship was instituted after termination of therapy.

Ryder and Hepworth (1990) posited that differences in power and status, not specifically dual relationships, encourage exploitation. Kitchener (1992) described this differential:

> Acknowledged or not, therapists because of their prestige and personal characteristics and because of transference issues often have considerable power over their clients. This power does not necessarily end with the end of therapy and may limit a former client's ability to make clear, rational, and autonomous choices about entering into a relationship with a former therapist. (p. 147)

As we noted previously, professional codes typically address intimate relationships with former clients. In some codes, specific periods of time are indicated, but for others the principle of "once a client, always a client" is the rule. The marriage and family therapist in the preceding case illustration would be acting in violation of the AAMFT Code of Ethics Subprinciple 1.5, which prohibits sexual intimacy with former clients for two years following termination of therapy. Perhaps of more consequence, however, is the fundamental ethical principle that many scholars argue applies in such situations (Beauchamp & Childress, 2001; Kitchener, 1984b; Stadler, 1986): Agreeing to work with persons in therapy implies a contract to help them. To harm those whom one has agreed to help undermines the foundation of the profession (Kitchener, 1984b).

When the therapeutic relationship ends, does the therapeutic contract end? Some maintain that sexual relationships with former clients have harmful consequences for most clients (Vasquez, 1991). Although few would suggest that therapeutic contracts ought to carry a lifelong obligation, it is equally implausible to suggest that the formal ending of a contract should entitle a therapist to engage in activities with a former client that will undo the benefits that therapy promoted. Additionally, as we noted in the earlier discussion concerning managed care, many clients will return to their former therapist for therapy, thereby causing even greater potential for distress. The fundamental ethical principles of helping clients and doing no harm to clients would be violated (Kitchener, 1992). Marriage and family therapists are cautioned to proceed with particular care should they ever consider entering into an intimate relationship with a former client, even two years or more after the termination of therapy.

Other Forms of Multiple Relationships

Aside from sexual, romantic, and business forms of interaction, other related circumstances exist as multiple relationships in marriage and family therapy. We believe these specific issues can be examined within the framework of Kitchener's (1988) guidelines in our discussion of appropriate ethical actions. Consider the following example:

> Dr. Smith has just met Kevin, a 32-year-old referral from the county probation office. Kevin is involved in therapy as part of his sentence for embezzling funds from his former employer, a local investment agency. After Kevin has offered his account of the circumstances leading to his conviction, Dr. Smith says, "You know, Kevin, in some ways you're the victim of a flaw in the legal definition of embezzlement. But our local senator happens to be fighting for a revision of this law. Are you a voter? Would you consider affiliating with the National Party? If so, you could help yourself therapeutically as well as legally. We'd all even be working together." Dr. Smith goes on to say that Kevin is the eighth client this week with whom he's found the opportunity to share this kind of information, and that he is certain Kevin, along with these other clients, will benefit from their decision to support the senator's reelection as well as the election of other candidates in his party.

Most any marriage and family therapist would be appalled by Dr. Smith's actions. One interpretation of his statements would be that they represent intrusion of a personal agenda and personal bias. Another interpretation might be that his agenda and bias has evolved beyond intrusion and into an actual role that competes with his role as therapist: Dr. Smith is functioning as a recruiting activist. Additionally, he has merged his view with his therapy work to the extent that he suggests therapeutic gain for those who agree.

As we discussed in Chapter 2, difficulties sometimes emerge in managing personal preferences and beliefs in therapy relationships. However, admonitions to acknowledge such preferences and to avoid imposing them on clients are noted throughout various ethical codes. Essentially, one aspect of professionalism is the creation of personal boundaries for therapy relationships, such as avoiding intimate or even friendship relationships with clients we have discussed previously. In Dr. Smith's case, such boundary violations have evolved beyond an episodic and inadvertent intrusion of his personal agenda. He is now a habitual zealot for a personal issue with the opportunity to share his view to the point of exploitation while he serves as a therapist.

The role of "political activist" is likely not very common in therapy relationships. The role of "religious activist" may be more common, however. In this respect, we maintain that marriage and family therapists who assume the religious activist role of "believer" or "disciple" in habitually imposing their views on clients may be exploiting them in a manner no less troublesome than a political activist.

Like other mental health disciplines, marriage and family therapy has come to acknowledge appreciation and respect for the significance of spirituality as a component of the human condition. As we noted in Chapter 1, spirituality and religion encompass an aspect of psychosocial identity that is essential to many. However, exploration of spirituality may differ greatly from promotion of religious values and traditions specific to a faith doctrine, particularly if such an emphasis is not anticipated by the client. Of course, such an emphasis might be expected if a client seeks out a pastoral counselor clearly associated with a specific church or faith-based setting. Even so, Smith and Smith (2000) have noted that ethical dilemmas certainly may emerge when professional helpers also serve as clergy.

M. R. Hill (2001) observed that family therapists involved with religious communities in roles such as congregational leaders, institutional employees, or even community members encounter potentially troublesome (as well as beneficial) dual relationships in practicing their faith. O'Dell (2003) noted that the intersection of spirituality and the therapy relationship need not be inherently problematic, though problems may emerge in either dramatic or subtle ways. For clients who have no affiliation with a faith community, attempts to "convert" unbelievers to one's faith has some similarity with attempting to convert a client to one's political party or to join one's social club. Those who utilize their powerful relationship to meet personal needs for finding converts are exceeding the traditional role of therapist. Or, as O'Dell has noted, "It is not the therapist's job to prioritize for the client which spiritual values they will uphold and in what order" (p. 28).

Another issue related to multiple or dual relationships involves conflicting or exploitive outcomes when marriage and family therapists simultaneously or sequentially function as therapist and evaluator. For example, a therapist engaged in therapy activities while also working to provide a forensic evaluation for mental competence has roles that are at cross purposes. Similarly, a therapist involved in a custody evaluation for a client may actually find herself or himself criticizing a client in court. For this reason, AAMFT and most other professional associations offer advice or prohibition against such role conflicts.

As a final issue, we note that marriage and family therapists may have multiple affiliations and allegiances to a variety of professional groups or agencies. For example, a marriage and family therapist may simultaneously be a Clinical Member of the AAMFT, a member of the NASW, a Licensed Marriage and Family Therapist, and a Certified Play Therapist. In this circumstance, the therapist would have a duty to four sets of ethical codes, not to mention state statutes, regarding due care and competent practice. As we have noted in the earlier reviews of various ethical codes and standards, one may find differences or perhaps even conflicts concerning multiple relationships that emerge from these various affiliations. Thus, the therapist should take great care in addressing any discrepancies that may come to light in his or her professional duties.

Taking Appropriate Action

The potential for a dual or multiple relationship to promote harm increases to the extent that therapist–client expectations become increasingly incompatible, role obligations become increasingly divergent, and the power differential enlarges. In contrast, when therapist–client expectations are clearly defined and compatible, role obligations convergent, and the power differential is small, there is much less danger that harm will ensue (B. Pearson & Piazza, 1997).

In marriage and family therapy, multiple relationships can triangulate, especially if such a relationship exists for one member of a client system but not for all members. As we noted from our review of various ethical codes and standards, in academic or supervisory settings, risky or harmful multiple relationships involving therapy and faculty or supervisors may be exploitive or even harmful for students or supervisees. Additionally, naïve or uninformed students or supervisees may view such practices as appropriate models which they may employ in their practices. Exploitive dual relationships are also often public portrayals of unprofessional behavior, thereby affecting the image of marriage and family therapy with both peer professionals and public consumers. This issue will be addressed later in Chapter 12.

Marriage and family therapists have a special obligation to promote the welfare of the clients with whom they work. Consequently, even in relationships in which there is minimal danger of harm, they are ethically bound to exercise due care. Therapists exercising due care would be sensitive to potential role conflicts and work to minimize their impact should they occur. Thus, marriage and family therapists must be cognizant of the potential for harm in any dual relationship, even when they determine that the potential for harm is minimal. They must be vigilant in their continued education to learn about new perspectives on multiple relationships. They must also be attentive in informed consent and other procedures (e.g., supervision) to address possible multiple relationships and react with candor should they develop in the course of therapy.

AIDS/HIV AND THE DUTY TO PROTECT

Acquired immune deficiency syndrome (AIDS), caused by the human immunodeficiency virus (HIV), is one of the most serious epidemics of this century. "Persons with HIV-positive status, compared to those with other diseases, tend to be seriously stigmatized in contemporary society" (Huber, 1996, p. 55). Researchers do not know how long it may take to find a cure for or an immunization against the disease, or even if it will be possible to do so. Unlike other sexually transmitted diseases that typically produce visible lesions or blisters, the HIV infection frequently produces no apparent symptoms for months or even years. Thus, many persons living with HIV/AIDS (PLWHA) are sometimes not diagnosed until they exhibit evidence of AIDS through the onset of unusual infections or cancers. Studies suggest that within seven years after infection, 30% of HIV-positive persons will develop AIDS, and another 40% will have other opportunistic illnesses associated with HIV infection (Allen & Curran, 1988). As of 2005, the Centers for Disease Control reported that the total cases of HIV/AIDS reported in the United States had eclipsed the one million mark.

The spread of AIDS has given rise to questions regarding the limits of confidentiality within the therapeutic relationship. Do marriage and family therapists have a duty to warn a potential victim when a client discloses that she or he has tested HIV-positive and has an identifiable sexual or needle-sharing partner who is unaware of the infection? A study by Kegeles, Catania, and Coates (1988) indicated that 12% of homosexual or bisexual men being tested for HIV said that they would not tell their primary sexual partners if they tested positive, and 27% said that they would not contact their previous partners. Almost one-fifth of the sample reported that they had been engaging in high-risk sexual relations with nonprimary sexual partners. In a similarly focused study (Elias, 1988), approximately 35% of single, sexually active heterosexual males stated that they had lied about past sexual behaviors to female partners. Furthermore, 20% reported that they would lie about being HIV-positive. Thus, it cannot be assumed that HIV-positive individuals will be open and honest with others about their sexual habits or infectious state.

As practicing mental health professionals, do marriage and family therapists face ethical decisions concerning the unique nature of AIDS? Does any duty exist for therapists concerning the potential harm that may come to an unknowing partner of a client who has disclosed an HIV-positive condition? Gray and Harding (1988) reviewed the limits of confidentiality with HIV-positive clients in light of accepted ethical and legal practices. They advocated procedures to increase clients' responsibility for informing their sexual partners. Should a client refuse to do so, however, Gray and Harding proposed that the therapist take action to protect potential victims. Responding to Gray and Harding's position, Kain (1988) emphasized the needs of the HIV-positive client in asserting that the therapist's primary responsibility is to help clients deal with issues such as abandonment, rejection, and loneliness, as well as, perhaps, reasons for not informing their partners of their condition. These and similar findings pose the crux of the ethical dilemma for marriage and family therapists: If we are unable to act ethically on behalf of both the client and the potential victim, whom and how do we choose?

In examining the reasons HIV-positive women decided to disclose their HIV status to family members, Kimberly, Serovich, and Greene (1995) found a six-step framework for understanding the process of deciding. Each step included a proposed counseling intervention:

1. Accepting and adjusting to the diagnosis (counseling intervention—information and education)
2. Evaluating personal disclosure skills (counseling intervention—emphasis on pros, cons, difficulties, and strategies of disclosure)
3. Taking inventory of who should be told (counseling intervention—highlighting the issue of family boundaries)
4. Evaluating potential recipients' circumstances, such as health and age (counseling intervention—addressing feelings of guilt, anxiety, and sadness for telling some family members and not others; developing plans for disclosure)
5. Anticipating reactions of recipients, such as anger, support (counseling intervention—clarification of possible reactions)
6. Motivation for disclosure, such as desire for support or obligation (counseling intervention—defining personal needs and identifying family members most likely to meet those needs)

Although disclosing to family members may not be the same as disclosing to sexual partners, Kimberly et al. (1995) provided a model that may be used in understanding the HIV-positive client and how the client can be helped in making a decision regarding disclosure. This process has important ethical implications that can be translated to both family and society.

A more legally oriented ethical approach to dealing with HIV-positive clients is taken by Melton (1988) and S. H. Erickson (1998), who proposed that the ethical dilemma involving therapists' obligations to their clients and third parties relative to

AIDS bears an apparent resemblance to the question regarding the duty to protect third parties from violent behavior by a client believed to be dangerous. The question of what to do in such situations was answered in the Tarasoff decision (*Tarasoff v. Regents of the University of California*, 1976). According to the Tarasoff decision, confidentiality within psychotherapy is to be valued highly, but it should never be regarded as absolute:

> A therapist is not to be encouraged routinely to reveal such threats since such disclosures could seriously disrupt the patient's relationship with the therapist and with the person threatened. On the contrary, the therapist's obligations to the patient require that he [or she] not disclose a confidence unless necessary to avert danger to others, and even then that he [or she] do so discreetly and in a fashion that preserves the privacy of the patient to the fullest extent compatible with the prevention of a threatened danger. (p. 337)

Schlossberger and Hecker (1996) made recommendations based on the Tarasoff ruling and went further in addressing the ethics of disclosure. According to Schlossberger and Hecker (1996), when there is "no legal duty to warn . . . and the information is not expressly protected from disclosure by law, therapists must struggle with the ethical aspects of disclosure" (p. 34). Among the relevant ethical factors therapists must consider are "respecting autonomy, maintaining integrity, benefiting clients, and fostering responsibility" (p. 35).

Lamb, Clark, Drumheller, Frizzell, and Surrey (1989) and Knapp and Vande-Creek (1990) encouraged therapists dealing with confidentiality in an AIDS-related therapeutic situation to employ criteria resulting from Tarasoff: (a) the presence of a fiduciary relationship, (b) the identifiability of a victim, and (c) the foreseeability of danger. They then offer further recommendations about taking appropriate action; these are discussed next.

A Fiduciary Relationship

The first criterion is whether or not a *fiduciary* relationship—a relationship of special trust—is present between therapist and client. This relationship is inherent when a therapist agrees to work with a client. In doing so, the therapist assumes special responsibilities for the client's behavior that are not a part of everyday relationships.

Identifiability

According to the second criterion, the duty to protect extends only to identifiable victims and not to all persons whom a client could potentially harm. With HIV-positive clients, only identifiable sexual or needle-sharing partners such as spouses or monogamous lovers would be included. The duty to protect would not necessarily extend to casual sexual or drug partners unless they were readily identifiable.

Foreseeability

According to the third criterion, the danger must be foreseeable before the duty to protect is invoked. Knapp and VandeCreek (1990) identified the issue of foreseeability as the most difficult to ascertain for therapists working with HIV-positive clients. Research has not defined all the risk factors involved in HIV transmission. With this in mind, Knapp and VandeCreek offered direction in classifying low-risk behaviors that do not appear to give rise to a duty to protect, high-risk behaviors that clearly give rise to such a duty, and intermediate-risk behaviors for which the duty to protect may be present but the foreseeability of danger to others is less apparent.

Low-Risk Behaviors

Current evidence suggests that transmission of HIV infection cannot occur through food, tears, urine, or insect bites. Isolated reports of transmission through kissing, human bites, or tattoos have been made but not confirmed (Castro et al., 1988). Thus, casual nonsexual contact and simply living together should be considered low-risk behaviors and should not be the basis for any breach of confidentiality.

High-Risk Behaviors

Unprotected sexual contacts and sharing of needles are the primary modes of HIV transmission. Knapp and VandeCreek (1990) proposed that therapists assess the presence of high-risk behaviors in the context of establishing and enhancing a therapeutic relationship, because a primary goal of psychotherapeutic efforts is to empower clients to be responsible for their own well-being and that of another.

Intermediate-Risk Behaviors

Knapp and VandeCreek identify the greatest difficulty in determining foreseeability as involving HIV-positive clients who engage in "safe sex" but do not inform their partners of their infection. Although barrier contraceptives can reduce the risk of infection ("Condoms for Prevention," 1988), maximum protection occurs only when both partners know the risks (Kaplan, Sager, & Schiavi, 1986).

> The vulnerable partner has to make the final decision whether to continue sexual relations, engage in only completely safe sex such as parallel or mutual masturbation, or discontinue the sexual relationship completely. A unilateral decision to protect the partner through use of barrier contraceptives by a person who has already shown a lack of adequate concern in concealing the fact of the infection cannot be viewed as an acceptable resolution. This would deny the partner's right to decide what risks are acceptable. (Knapp & VandeCreek, 1990, p. 163)

Other Factors and Considerations

From the previous discussion of client risk factors, one can see that the ethical dilemma of unauthorized disclosure is multifaceted and far more complex than a decision of "to tell or not to tell." In some ways, the decision-making risks for the therapist, as well as the continuation of therapy, interact with the behavioral risks of the client. Huber (1996) advocated the preference for client-initiated disclosure as a way of preserving the therapy relationship as well as a means of promoting support from family and others. Britton (2000) noted that because of the tremendous medical advances in the treatment of HIV/AIDS, jeopardizing the supportive nature of therapy for the client, and possibly others, must be a significant consideration in disclosure decisions. Chaimowitz, Glancy, and Blackburn (2000) observed that a decision to break confidence by warning those who could potentially be infected critically alters the therapy relationship in a manner not unlike disclosures to authorities about suspected abuse or neglect of minors or elders. In such cases, the disclosing therapist is often viewed as no longer being a reliable resource and even being an adversary. Still, one can argue that a client with an apparent intent on harming another person forces the therapist to address virtue ethics involving whom she or he wants to be as a person.

Pais, Piercy, and Miller (1998) offered some revealing findings concerning the interactive nature of therapy in affecting the perceptions of the therapist in disclosure decisions. Using fictitious vignettes of HIV-positive clients with a national survey of 309 marriage and family therapists, these authors reported that decisions for disclosures to others were associated with both client variables as well as therapist variables. Specifically, they reported that therapists were more likely to break confidence when the vignettes portrayed clients who were male, young, gay or African-American. Additionally, these authors reported that therapists who were more likely to break confidence were older, female, less experienced with gay and lesbian clients, Catholic, very religious, and practicing in urban settings. From these findings, one can surmise that, in the absence of a clear mandate for action, risk behaviors as well as client and therapist characteristics may affect unauthorized disclosure decisions.

As noted previously, an alternate perspective on decisions about unauthorized disclosures can be gained from a legalistic framework (Erikson, 1998; Melton, 1988). As Schlossberger and Hecker (1996) observed, the interchangeable application of Tarasoff is not clear for HIV-positive clients. Mandatory decisions about required disclosures are not featured in the ethical codes of professional associations. Because practitioners may be subject to retaliatory legal action, Chenneville (2000) emphasized the importance of a decision-making model that derived from individual state laws relative to professional duties, confidentiality, privileged communications, and protection of others. Such legal derivatives may be found in both licensure laws and other state statutes defining special professional relationships.

Burkemper (2002) reported on the decision-making considerations of 177 marriage and family therapists when faced with two ethical quandaries of unauthorized disclosures: (a) reporting suspected child abuse, and (b) preventing HIV transmission. In this qualitative approach, she distinguished between *lower-level decision components* such as "personal/therapeutic response," "professional ethics," and "legal considerations/laws of the state" (pp. 204–205) and *higher-level decision components* such as the principles of beneficence, nonmaleficence, autonomy, justice, and fidelity. The author reported that reliance on the lower-level components of professional ethics and legal considerations were most common in decisions related to suspected child abuse, whereas professional ethics were the preferred lower-level component affecting decisions related to HIV transmission. In terms of higher-level decision components, nonmaleficence was the preferred guideline for both scenarios, though the order of importance of other higher-level components differed for the two scenarios. Specifically, Burkemper noted that "The order of the remaining principles in the HIV scenario was fidelity, justice, autonomy, and beneficence" (p. 209), reflecting the dilemma of wanting to avoid harm while also retaining confidentiality. She concluded that relying on personal or therapeutic feelings for the HIV scenario "may reflect the lack of an entrenched legal stance, or therapist knowledge of State law, and resulting confusion concerning the violation of confidentiality in the HIV scenario" (p. 209). From these reported findings, it seems that marriage and family therapists addressing the issue of unauthorized disclosures about HIV/AIDS risks must rely on considered judgment, since few specific statutory or code mandates currently exist to instruct professional duty. Certainly, deliberate and appropriate actions are to be expected on the part of the practitioner.

Taking Appropriate Action

"A therapist should not be encouraged routinely to reveal such threats . . . unless such disclosures are necessary to avert danger to others" (*Tarasoff v. Regents of the University of California*, 1976). Less intrusive means of diffusing risks should always be considered before making an exception to confidentiality. Depending on the level of risk for transmission, clients' voluntary disclosure of their HIV status (and the processes that go with deciding on disclosure as outlined by Kimberly et al., 1995) should be a more or less immediate focus of therapy.

In making a final determination, factors such as the client's credibility, perceived degree of concern for the identifiable partner, and overall sense of social responsibility must be taken into account (Silva, Leong, & Weinstock, 1989). In some situations, however, certain clients may act in ways that meet the criteria of a duty-to-protect case. Clinical experience with physically assaultive clients provides direction for making a necessary disclosure. Additionally, it is always helpful to include a formal statement about criteria for disclosure in the informed consent or therapy contract document presented to the client at the initiation of the therapy relationship.

PUBLICATIONS

The importance of the publication of professional literature is an area vital to marriage and family therapists. Published research is a means by which therapists can (a) share information, (b) promote themselves, and (c) succeed in academia (K. D. Jones, 1999). Yet, the ethical code of the AAMFT addresses the ethics of publishing in only four articles under Section 6—Responsibility to the Profession (American Association for Marriage and Family Therapy, 2001). These subprinciples (6.2, 6.3, 6.4, and 6.5) address general concerns that frequently arise in publishing and that are vital to marriage and family therapists.

In subprinciples 6.2 and 6.3, the issue of crediting those who contributed to a research or publication effort is raised. Although it may seem straightforward to assume that participants who contributed the most to a publication should be listed first, such is not always the case. To avoid ethical dilemmas in multiple authorship, Goodyear, Crego, and Johnston (1992) suggested the use of an informed consent process before entering a publishing endeavor. In such a process, the roles, duties, and expectations of each participant should be spelled out. Likewise, in student/faculty publications, potential ethical problems arise because of the unequal status of the participants. K. D. Jones (1999) proposed that in these situations, a student author should be listed first if he or she has contributed the most to the publication. Such a listing places students on an equal footing with faculty, and it also models appropriate ethical behavior.

In subprinciple 6.4, the AAMFT code addresses plagiarism and the giving of proper credit to sources. The perils of plagiarism may seem relatively easy to avoid, but in fact, they are not, because of the pressure to perform and contribute to the field. Thus, marriage and family therapists who write must observe copyright laws and the temptation to promote an idea of another as their own. Adhering to subprinciple 6.4 means exercising the principle of fidelity, that is, upholding truth and maintaining loyalty. Likewise, in subprinciple 6.5, the same principle of fidelity comes into play in the guideline that directs marriage and family therapists who publish to take reasonable precautions "to ensure that the organization" that "promotes and advertises" their books and materials do so "accurately and factually."

SUMMARY AND CLOSING COMMENTS

Marriage and family therapists are well aware that they will constantly be challenged to address ethical concerns in their work. One means of doing so is to look to a professional code of ethics for guidance. Such a code, however, is a finite document that can cover only a limited number of issues. To a great extent, historical factors influence what is incorporated into any code of ethics. Significant changes in society can result in a code that omits issues of current concern or contains gaps in its discussion of those issues.

A limited range of topics are covered in a code, and because a code approach is usually reactive to issues already developed elsewhere, the requirement of consensus prevents a code from addressing new issues and problems at the "cutting edge" (Mabe & Rollin, 1986, p. 295).

Although these matters are eventually addressed by revision committees that meet periodically to bring a code of ethics up to date, professionals must look to the literature and consult with colleagues to find precedents on which to base their decisions until the guidelines are revised. This chapter addressed six contemporary ethically sensitive areas. In our discussion of these items, we have emphasized the practical as well as the conceptual aspects of: (a) technology, (b) diagnosis, (c) managed mental health care, (d) multiple relationships, (e) AIDS/HIV, and (e) publications.

Though the discussion concerning these matters features considerable topic-specific issues, we want to reiterate that ethical decision making for these and similar ethical dilemmas must begin with sensitivity and respect for clients. Additionally, attempts to resolve ethical dilemmas involve respect for legal precedents and practice traditions. Marriage and family therapists should always be cognizant that their decisions affect both clients and peer professionals.

As an overarching principle, we strongly urge therapists to consider a preemptive approach to ethical concerns. Though it would be impossible to predict all ethically challenging circumstances, many dilemmas, including those noted in this chapter, have been identified and discussed in professional literature. Thus, a well-prepared marriage and family therapist continues professional development through continual study and education. Additionally, once a therapist has determined a likely routine course of action for a recurring ethical dilemma, a formal and expressed notation in his or her informed consent statement offers clarity for the therapist and the client. In this way, therapists can help educate consumers about risks, expectations, limitations, and duties affecting the therapy relationships such as the first five topics covered in this chapter. Only then can consumers make fully informed choices about the care they can expect to receive and the actions they can antici-pate from their therapists (Newman & Bricklin, 1991). In a similar fashion, profes-sional colleagues addressing issues in publication may resolve possible emerging ethical quandaries through a preemptive and formal approach similar to an informed consent or authorship agreement.

It may be easy to overlook any of the ethical dilemmas mentioned in this chapter unless a marriage and family therapist is attuned to present concerns and issues. Therefore, therapists should stay abreast of current events and advancements and con-tinuously query themselves and others regarding the proper course of action to take in novel situations.

In the next chapter, our final chapter related to ethical issues in marriage and family therapy, we offer two forms of discussion. The first discussion concerns the investigation and adjudication process guiding formal charges of ethical impropri-ety. This process offers protection for consumers while policing the profession in a manner respective of due process. The second discussion in Chapter 7 features a case-study approach to the application of the AAMFT Code of Ethics (2001) using various demonstration scenarios. In this way, we will attempt to identify clusters of applicable ethical standards for resolving the featured case scenarios.

Ethical Accountability: A Casebook

Several professional association ethics committees have published books on their respective codes of ethics (e.g., American Counseling Association's *Ethical Standards Casebook*, Herlihy & Corey, 1996; American Association for Marriage and Family Therapy's *Ethics Casebook*, Brock, 1998; American Psychological Association's *Ethical Conflicts in Psychology*, Bersoff, 1995). Codes of ethics are, by nature, general and often debatable. These texts represent a consensus from reputable professionals and assist practitioners in understanding how best to apply the principles the codes represent.

Two primary professional affiliations for marriage and family therapists are the American Association for Marriage and Family Therapy (AAMFT) and the International Association of Marriage and Family Counselors (IAMFC). These organizations have promulgated the AAMFT Code of Ethics (American Association for Marriage and Family Therapy, 2001) and the Ethical Code for the IAMFC (International Association of Marriage and Family Counselors, 2005). Both associations maintain an ethics committee. Operating under the AAMFT bylaws, the AAMFT ethics committee interprets its code of ethics, considers allegations of violations of the codes made against association members, and, if the case is heard by Judicial Council, adjudicates the charges against the member.

Both the AAMFT and IAMFC have published an ethical casebook for the practice of marriage and family counseling (Brock, 1998; Stevens, 1999). A casebook approach to examining ethical dilemmas has great appeal for novice and veteran practitioners alike, since it relies on the presentation of a multifaceted case and provides a subsequent discussion of the applicable ethical standards and codes that can be employed for decision making. This chapter, using a casebook format, represents our analysis of the selected standards within the AAMFT Code of Ethics through consultation with relevant professional colleagues. Actions recommended within each case illustration were developed in a similar manner. The AAMFT Code of Ethics and specific cases follow an overview of the structure and functioning of AAMFT's Ethics Committee.

ADJUDICATION OF ETHICAL COMPLAINTS

The Ethics Committee is composed of six members appointed by the president of AAMFT. Five are AAMFT Clinical Members and one is a "public member," representing the interests of potential clients, consumers of marriage and family therapy services. The committee ordinarily meets once a year in person and by conference call whenever there are three or more cases to be deliberated. The Procedures for Handling Ethical Matters (American Association for Marriage and Family Therapy, 1992b) codify the manner in which the Ethics Committee and associated bodies address ethical complaints raised against AAMFT members. Figure 7–1 graphically describes the five major steps (each with substeps) in handling complaints of unethical behavior by AAMFT members.

FIGURE 7–1   Decision Tree for AAMFT Ethics Cases

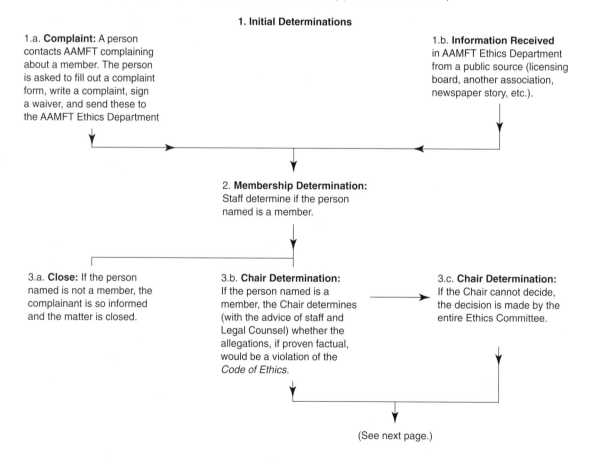

Decision tree: AAMFT Ethics Cases

AAMFT follows a process of five major steps (each with sub-steps) in handling complaints of unethical behavior by AAMFT members, Approved Supervisors, applicants for membership or the Approved Supervisor designation, or recently resigned members or Approved Supervisors (hereafter, member). After steps I, III, IV, and V, the process may be closed or may proceed to the next step.

1. Initial Determinations

1.a. **Complaint:** A person contacts AAMFT complaining about a member. The person is asked to fill out a complaint form, write a complaint, sign a waiver, and send these to the AAMFT Ethics Department

1.b. **Information Received** in AAMFT Ethics Department from a public source (licensing board, another association, newspaper story, etc.).

2. Membership Determination: Staff determine if the person named is a member.

3.a. **Close:** If the person named is not a member, the complainant is so informed and the matter is closed.

3.b. **Chair Determination:** If the person named is a member, the Chair determines (with the advice of staff and Legal Counsel) whether the allegations, if proven factual, would be a violation of the *Code of Ethics.*

3.c. **Chair Determination:** If the Chair cannot decide, the decision is made by the entire Ethics Committee.

(See next page.)

FIGURE 7–1 *Continued*

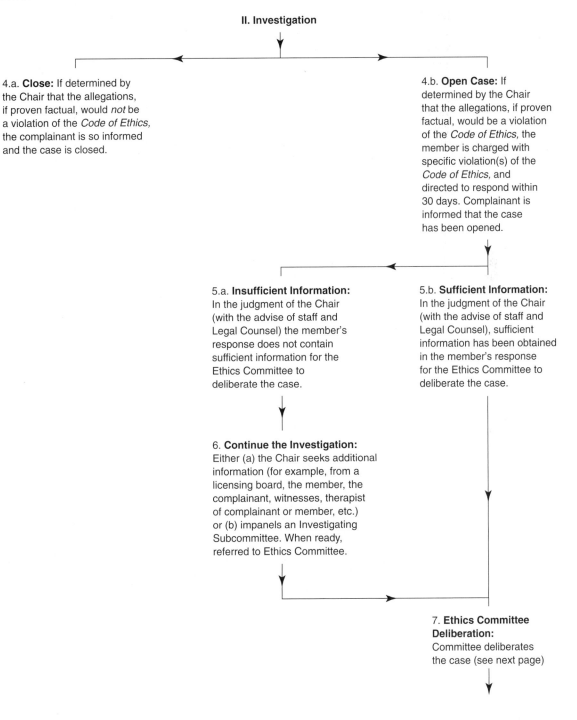

II. Investigation

4.a. **Close:** If determined by the Chair that the allegations, if proven factual, would *not* be a violation of the *Code of Ethics,* the complainant is so informed and the case is closed.

4.b. **Open Case:** If determined by the Chair that the allegations, if proven factual, would be a violation of the *Code of Ethics,* the member is charged with specific violation(s) of the *Code of Ethics,* and directed to respond within 30 days. Complainant is informed that the case has been opened.

5.a. **Insufficient Information:** In the judgment of the Chair (with the advise of staff and Legal Counsel) the member's response does not contain sufficient information for the Ethics Committee to deliberate the case.

5.b. **Sufficient Information:** In the judgment of the Chair (with the advise of staff and Legal Counsel), sufficient information has been obtained in the member's response for the Ethics Committee to deliberate the case.

6. **Continue the Investigation:** Either (a) the Chair seeks additional information (for example, from a licensing board, the member, the complainant, witnesses, therapist of complainant or member, etc.) or (b) impanels an Investigating Subcommittee. When ready, referred to Ethics Committee.

7. **Ethics Committee Deliberation:** Committee deliberates the case (see next page)

FIGURE 7–1 *Continued*

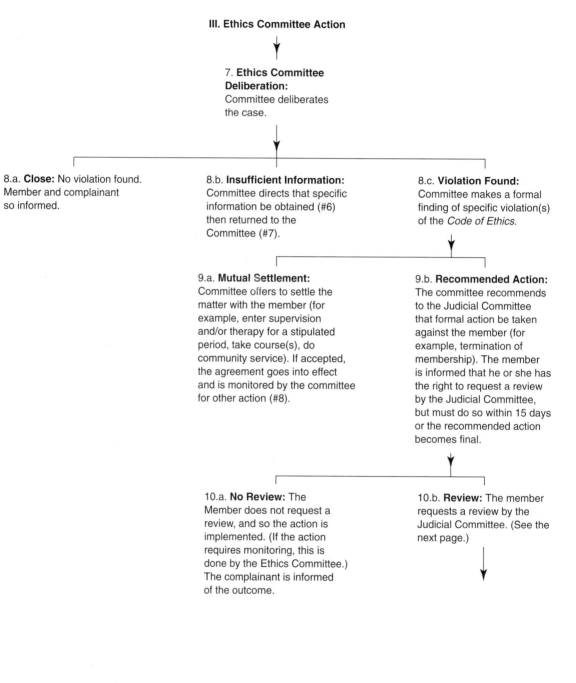

III. Ethics Committee Action

7. Ethics Committee Deliberation:
Committee deliberates the case.

8.a. Close: No violation found. Member and complainant so informed.

8.b. Insufficient Information: Committee directs that specific information be obtained (#6) then returned to the Committee (#7).

8.c. Violation Found: Committee makes a formal finding of specific violation(s) of the *Code of Ethics*.

9.a. Mutual Settlement: Committee offers to settle the matter with the member (for example, enter supervision and/or therapy for a stipulated period, take course(s), do community service). If accepted, the agreement goes into effect and is monitored by the committee for other action (#8).

9.b. Recommended Action: The committee recommends to the Judicial Committee that formal action be taken against the member (for example, termination of membership). The member is informed that he or she has the right to request a review by the Judicial Committee, but must do so within 15 days or the recommended action becomes final.

10.a. No Review: The Member does not request a review, and so the action is implemented. (If the action requires monitoring, this is done by the Ethics Committee.) The complainant is informed of the outcome.

10.b. Review: The member requests a review by the Judicial Committee. (See the next page.)

FIGURE 7–1 *Continued*

IV. Review by Judicial Committee

10.b. **Review:** The member requests a review by the Judicial Committee.

11. **Hearing:** An in-person hearing is scheduled before a Hearing Panel of the Judicial Committee. Chair of the Ethics Committee serves as prosecutor, and member presents case. Witnesses may be called.

12.a. **Close:** No violation found. Member and complainant so informed.

12.b. **Violation Found:** The Hearing Panel fully or partially upholds the findings of the Ethics Committee and orders action(s) to be taken. The member is informed that he or she has a right to appeal to the AAMFT Board of Directors, but only if the Judicial Committee's *Procedures* were violated in such a way as to prevent a fair hearing, and must do so within 15 days or the order becomes final.

13.a. **No Appeal:** The member does not appeal so the action is implemented. (If the action requires monitoring, this is done by the Ethics Committee.) The complainant is informed of the outcome.

13.b. **Appeal:** The member appeals to the Board of Directors (See the next page.)

FIGURE 7–1 *Continued*

V. Appeal to the Board

↓

14. **Appeal:** The Board reviews the information submitted by the member and the Judicial Committee to determine whether the *Procedures* were violated.

↓

15.a. **Upholds Judicial Committee Decision:** The Board finds no violation of the *Procedures.* The action ordered by the Judicial Committee is implemented. (If the action requires monitoring, this is done by the Ethics Committee.) The member and complainant are informed of the outcome.

15.b. **Remands to Judicial Committee:** The Board finds that the *Procedures* were violated and orders a new hearing before a Hearing Panel of the Judicial Committee (Return to #11.)

Engelberg (1985) summarized this process with the following commentary:

> Cases consist of complaints brought against AAMFT members for violating the AAMFT Code of Ethical Principles. Complaints may be brought against an AAMFT member by another AAMFT member, or nonmember therapists, by clients, by members of the public, and by the Ethics Committee itself. Once a complaint is made, the AAMFT national office first determines whether the charged professional is an AAMFT member. If confirmed, the complaint is forwarded to the Chair of the Ethics Committee. The Chair then makes a determination whether the complaint, if proven, states a claim under the Code. If so, a case is opened and the complainant (if a client) is sent a waiver of the client–therapist privilege. Upon receipt of the signed waiver, a letter is written to the charged member, requesting a response. The case may be decided through further written communications between the Ethics Committee and the charged member. On occasion, the Ethics Committee impanels an investigating subcommittee before which the charged member has a right to appear. (p. 16)

High (2005) further clarified that "the Complainant completes the waiver of privilege/authorization to release information as part of the initial complaint filing and not as a separate step, should the chair decide not to charge."

Cases are often disposed of through a process of agreement called "settlement by mutual consent." If settlement by mutual consent is unable to be agreed upon, the Ethics Committee can recommend to the AAMFT Judicial Council that final action be taken against a member. Any proposed settlement or final action recommended by the Ethics Committee can include a requirement that the charged member seek therapy or obtain supervision. The Ethics Committee also is authorized to propose revocation of a member's approved supervisor status and, in most serious cases, termination of membership. Charged members may appeal Ethics Committee recommendations for final action; appeals are made to the independent Judicial Committee. At that point, the Ethics Committee is, in effect, prosecuting the complaint, and the Judicial Committee makes the final ruling on the matter.

The presence of the Ethics Committee exemplifies AAMFT's commitment to protect consumers of marriage and family therapy services from unethical practices without violating the rights of AAMFT members. However, the Ethics Committee does not serve simply as a reactive body; proactive functions are of equal importance. The Ethics Committee also serves as a consultation source for members of the association for an opinion relative to a course of action. For example, what decision should a marriage and family therapist who is concerned with possible confidentiality violations make when considering a request to appear on a television program aimed at common problems of couples in marital therapy? Thus, the actions of the Ethics Committee are primarily constructive and educational; they are problem solving and adversarial only when the occasion arises.

THE AAMFT CODE OF ETHICS

Principle 1: Responsibility to Clients

Marriage and family therapists advance the welfare of families and individuals. They respect the rights of those persons seeking their assistance, and make reasonable efforts to ensure that their services are used appropriately.

1.1 Marriage and family therapists provide professional assistance to persons without discrimination on the basis of race, age, ethnicity, socioeconomic status, disability, gender, health status, religion, national origin, or sexual orientation.

1.2 Marriage and family therapists obtain appropriate informed consent to therapy or related procedures as early as feasible in the therapeutic relationship, and use language that is reasonably understandable to clients. The content of informed consent may vary depending upon the client and treatment plan; however, informed consent generally necessitates that the client: (a) has the capacity to consent; (b) has been adequately informed of significant information concerning treatment processes and procedures; (c) has been adequately informed of potential risks and benefits of treatments for which generally recognized standards do not yet exist; (d) has freely and without undue influence expressed consent; and (e) has provided consent that is appropriately documented. When persons, due to age or mental status, are legally incapable of giving informed consent, marriage and family therapists obtain informed permission from a legally authorized person, if such substitute consent is legally permissible.

1.3 Marriage and family therapists are aware of their influential positions with respect to clients, and they avoid exploiting the trust and dependency of such persons. Therapists, therefore, make every effort to avoid conditions and multiple relationships with clients that could impair professional judgment or increase the risk of exploitation. Such relationships include, but are not limited to, business or close personal relationships with a client or the client's immediate family. When the risk of impairment or exploitation exists due to conditions or multiple roles, therapists take appropriate precautions.

1.4 Sexual intimacy with clients is prohibited.

1.5 Sexual intimacy with former clients is likely to be harmful and is therefore prohibited for two years following the termination of therapy or last professional contact. In an effort to avoid exploiting the trust and dependency of clients, marriage and family therapists should not engage in sexual intimacy with former clients after the two years following termination or last professional contact. Should therapists engage in sexual intimacy with former clients following two years after termination or last professional contact, the burden shifts to the therapist to demonstrate that there has been no exploitation or injury to the former client or to the client's immediate family.

1.6 Marriage and family therapists comply with applicable laws regarding the reporting of alleged unethical conduct.

1.7 Marriage and family therapists do not use their professional relationships with clients to further their own interests.

1.8 Marriage and family therapists respect the rights of clients to make decisions and help them to understand the consequences of these decisions. Therapists clearly advise the clients that they have the responsibility to make decisions regarding relationships such as cohabitation, marriage, divorce, separation, reconciliation, custody, and visitation.

1.9 Marriage and family therapists continue therapeutic relationships only so long as it is reasonably clear that clients are benefiting from the relationship.

1.10 Marriage and family therapists assist persons in obtaining other therapeutic services if the therapist is unable or unwilling, for appropriate reasons, to provide professional help.

1.11 Marriage and family therapists do not abandon or neglect clients in treatment without making reasonable arrangements for the continuation of such treatment.

1.12 Marriage and family therapists obtain written informed consent from clients before videotaping, audio recording, or permitting third-party observation.

1.13 Marriage and family therapists, upon agreeing to provide services to a person or entity at the request of a third party, clarify, to the extent feasible and at the outset of the service, the nature of the relationship with each party and the limits of confidentiality.

CASE 1

A female client had been seeing a male marriage and family therapist for over a year to resolve issues emanating from her divorce. When sexual desires between her and the therapist were mutually conveyed and then acted on, the therapist immediately terminated the therapeutic relationship. No referral was recommended, nor was there any time spent addressing the termination. They continued a socially and sexually intimate relationship for the next six months. The woman eventually broke off the relationship when she began to experience the same emotional difficulties that originally led her to initiate therapy following her divorce.

Analysis

Subprinciples 1.3, 1.4, 1.5, 1.9, 1.10, and 1.11 all come under consideration in this case. The therapist was correct in terminating the therapeutic relationship. By not assisting the client to obtain other therapeutic services when he decided he was no longer able to offer professional help, however, the therapist abandoned the client therapeutically. At the very least, the therapist could have prepared a list of resources that he could have mailed or discussed with the client. A more serious ethical consideration was the therapist's lack of cognizance relative to the influence he had with the client, which suggests an exploitation of her vulnerable position. The issue of sexual intimacy is a flagrant ethical violation, as was the therapist's use of his professional position to advance his own sexual interests.

CASE 2

A marriage and family therapist with a national reputation as an expert in the area of fathers who have sole custody of their children was recommended by a lawyer to a father engaged in a custody case. The father wrote to the therapist, who resided in a neighboring state, and requested any relevant information that the therapist might be able to provide to him. The therapist replied that some materials could be sent for a specified fee. The therapist also offered his services as an expert witness to the father for a fee, which included travel expenses. The father wrote back to the therapist, expressing anger at the therapist for "soliciting" him.

Analysis

Subprinciples 1.3 and 1.7 are of primary consideration in this case. Although the father claims that the therapist sought to further personal financial interests, nothing directly proves this allegation. Similarly, nothing explicitly suggests that the therapist sought to exploit the father's request or create any dual therapeutic–business relationship, particularly because a relationship could not be considered as expressly present. The therapist was reasonable in requesting compensation for offering services to the father.

CASE 3

A couple sought marital therapy from a female marriage and family therapist. The therapist saw the couple conjointly and also in concurrent individual sessions for several months. The couple eventually decided on divorce and terminated their participation in therapy. Several months after the divorce was finalized, the wife discovered that her former husband and the therapist were seeing each other socially and had in fact become quite intimate. The wife confronted the therapist, charging her actions to be unethical. The therapist replied that she had not entered into a social relationship with the woman's former husband until some time after professional contact between them had ended. The therapist further responded that she had sought peer consultation with two other marriage and family therapists immediately after meeting the husband at an open social affair; afterward, he had telephoned her in pursuit of further social contact. Both therapists consulted recommended a hiatus of several months before accepting any social invitation from the husband. The therapist stated she had communicated this to the husband and followed through with her colleagues' recommendations.

Analysis

Subprinciples 1.3 and 1.7 are of primary concern in this case. Although the therapy had ended before the inception of the therapist's close personal relationship with the husband, concern must be raised in the case of a marriage and family therapist becoming socially and emotionally involved with a former client. Did the therapist exploit her professional position and enter into a dual relationship to further personal interests? Based on the therapist's pursuit of peer consultation and follow-through with regard to the professional cautions offered, it appears that the therapist acted in a conscientious, ethically aware manner. Still, we offer a caveat: Although the extent of the intimacy shared between the therapist and her former client is not specified, Subprinciple 1.5 does clearly state that sexual intimacy with former clients is prohibited for two years following termination of therapy.

CASE 4

A 16-year-old sought the assistance of a marriage and family therapist working in a Catholic Services Center regarding her discovery that she was pregnant. The girl communicated her desire to obtain information and professional assistance in making a decision to either terminate her pregnancy by abortion or offer the child for adoption. The therapist, a strong "pro-life" advocate, provided the girl with factual information and assisted her in contacting relevant referral sources to further investigate the available options. The therapist also, with the girl's permission, convened family therapy efforts to include the girl's parents and boyfriend in the decision making. At no time did the therapist personally advocate one option over the other.

Analysis

Subprinciples 1.8 and 1.10 are of particular relevance in this case. The therapist displayed exemplary diligence in the respect shown this teenage girl. Despite strong personal views, the therapist sought only to assist the girl in arriving at a fully considered decision. Providing direct referral to both adoption and abortion services for concrete information and convening the boyfriend and parents in family therapy exhibited further evidence of the therapist's efforts to help the client fully comprehend the consequences of her options.

Principle 2: Confidentiality

Marriage and family therapists have unique confidentiality concerns because the client in a therapeutic relationship may be more than one person. Therapists respect and guard the confidences of each individual client.

2.1 Marriage and family therapists disclose to clients and other interested parties, as early as feasible in their professional contacts, the nature of confidentiality and possible limitations of the clients' right to confidentiality. Therapists review with clients the circumstances where confidential information may be requested and where disclosure of confidential information may be legally required. Circumstances may necessitate repeated disclosures.

2.2   Marriage and family therapists do not disclose client confidences except by written authorization or waiver, or where mandated or permitted by law. Verbal authorization will not be sufficient except in emergency situations, unless prohibited by law. When providing couple, family, or group treatment, the therapist does not disclose information outside the treatment context without a written authorization from each individual competent to execute a waiver. In the context of couple, family or group treatment, the therapist may not reveal any individual's confidences to others in the client unit without the prior written permission of that individual.

2.3   Marriage and family therapists use client and/or clinical materials in teaching, writing, consulting, research, and public presentations only if a written waiver has been obtained in accordance with Subprinciple 2.2, or when appropriate steps have been taken to protect client identity and confidentiality.

2.4   Marriage and family therapists store, safeguard, and dispose of client records in ways that maintain confidentiality and are in accord with applicable laws and professional standards.

2.5   Subsequent to the therapist moving from the area, closing the practice, or upon the death of the therapist, a marriage and family therapist arranges for the storage, transfer, or disposal of client records in ways that maintain confidentiality and safeguard the welfare of clients.

2.6   Marriage and family therapists, when consulting with colleagues or referral sources, do not share confidential information that could reasonably lead to the identification of a client, research participant, supervisee, or other person with whom they have a confidential relationship unless they have obtained the prior written consent of the client, research participant, supervisee, or other person with whom they have a confidential relationship. Information may be shared only to the extent necessary to achieve the purposes of the consultation.

CASE 5

A marriage and family therapist working within an employee assistance program in a large company received a complaint from an employee who, with his wife and children, was seeing the therapist. The employee alleged the therapist had discussed aspects of the employee's family life, as revealed during therapy sessions, with the executive vice president in charge of the employee's department. He recalled signing a release of information allowing the therapist and the department vice president to communicate about his progress, but alleged that the information shared was of a strictly personal nature and not job-related.

Analysis

Subprinciples 2.1 and 2.2 are of primary concern in this case. Although the client had signed a waiver, it is obvious that there was some misunderstanding about the exact terms of the waiver. Whether the therapist or the client was unclear cannot be identified from the facts presented. However, it is a therapist's responsibility to provide clients with a copy of the waiver and to fully explain its terms, confirm the clients' understanding, and then act accordingly when communicating information.

CASE 6

A marriage and family therapist received a referral of a 19-year-old client who was a niece of the referral source, a physician. The client's parents lived in another city, and the physician initiated the referral on the request of his brother and sister-in-law, who were concerned about their daughter's adjustment in establishing herself away from home for the first time. Some months later, the physician contacted the therapist with the complaint that the therapist had refused to give the client's parents any indication of her well-being, despite the fact that they had made phone calls and written letters to the therapist, all of which had gone unanswered. The therapist replied that the client was an adult who requested that no information about her participation in therapy be communicated to anyone.

Analysis

Subprinciples 2.1 and 2.2 are of primary consideration in this case. It is clear that the therapist was responding to the client's request according to these two ethical standards. However, the issue of the therapist's obligation to the client's family as well as to the referral source is raised in this case. The client specified that no information about her participation in therapy be divulged. Although it would have been prudent for the therapist to have asked the client to consider communicating with her parents, she still might have chosen not to do so. The therapist could be considered to have some responsibility to the client's parents because of their repeated attempts to contact the therapist. A brief return call or letter might have been appropriate, simply explaining in a general sense that no information about clients could be communicated ethically without their expressed permission, not even confirmation as to whether or not a specific person is or is not a client. A similar stance might have been taken with the referral source as well after the client had made her wishes regarding strict confidentiality known to the therapist.

CASE 7

A new secretary was hired by a marriage and family therapist. The therapist provided an orientation to the position, addressing the importance of confidentiality, but only in a general sense. A few days after the orientation, an attorney contacted the office with regard to a couple with whom the therapist had previously worked. The attorney requested information about the couple's participation in therapy efforts, indicating she was representing one of them in a divorce suit. She further noted that she would subpoena the records if she was unable to get the information requested over the telephone. The therapist was unavailable at the time, and, deciding that the information would eventually be available to the attorney anyway, the secretary provided the requested details.

Analysis

Although Subprinciples 2.1 and 2.2 are relevant, of dominant concern is Subprinciple 2.4. The therapist did not display sufficient attentiveness to the training of the secretary concerning responsibilities for the maintenance and communication of client records. Support staff must be trained in the importance of confidentiality and in the appropriate management of case files. The secretary should have been instructed explicitly not to reveal information regarding persons presently or previously receiving services or the nature of any services they received in response to inquiries made by phone, letter, or in person. Such inquiries or related questions should always be reviewed by the therapist before final action is taken.

CASE 8

A marriage and family therapist received a telephone call from a husband whose wife and adult children were being seen together with him in family therapy because of his alcohol abuse. The husband requested that information about his progress be communicated to his employer. The therapist was aware that the husband's job was in jeopardy but declined his request, explaining that all family members must agree to the release of information on their mutual participation in therapy. The husband became angry, stating that his job was on the line and that he was the one with the problem, not his family. The therapist reiterated the ethical importance of mutual consent and then requested that the husband gather the family members together, stop by the therapist's office, and sign a waiver. The therapist explained that then the information could be forwarded as requested.

Analysis

Subprinciple 2.2 is quite explicit in respect to the circumstances in this case. Without a waiver from each family member, the therapist is obliged ethically not to disclose the information. Although the client made a logical argument for his request, marriage and family therapists must be attuned to the fact that the "client" in the therapeutic relationship is the family, which calls for mutual consent for a waiver. The therapist acted in full ethical accord in this case.

Principle 3: Professional Competence and Integrity

Marriage and family therapists maintain high standards of professional competence and integrity.

3.1 Marriage and family therapists pursue knowledge of new developments and maintain competence in marriage and family therapy through education, training, or supervised experience.

3.2 Marriage and family therapists maintain adequate knowledge of and adhere to applicable laws, ethics, and professional standards.

3.3   Marriage and family therapists seek appropriate professional assistance for their personal problems or conflicts that may impair work performance or clinical judgment.

3.4   Marriage and family therapists do not provide services that create a conflict of interest that may impair work performance or clinical judgment.

3.5   Marriage and family therapists, as presenters, teachers, supervisors, consultants and researchers, are dedicated to high standards of scholarship, present accurate information, and disclose potential conflicts of interest.

3.6   Marriage and family therapists maintain accurate and adequate clinical and financial records.

3.7   While developing new skills in specialty areas, marriage and family therapists take steps to ensure the competence of their work and to protect clients from possible harm. Marriage and family therapists practice in specialty areas new to them only after appropriate education, training, or supervised experience.

3.8   Marriage and family therapists do not engage in sexual or other forms of harassment of clients, students, trainees, supervisees, employees, colleagues, or research subjects.

3.9   Marriage and family therapists do not engage in the exploitation of clients, students, trainees, supervisees, employees, colleagues, or research subjects.

3.10 Marriage and family therapists do not give to or receive from clients (a) gifts of substantial value; or (b) gifts that impair the integrity or efficacy of the therapeutic relationship.

3.11 Marriage and family therapists do not diagnose, treat, or advise on problems outside the recognized boundaries of their competencies.

3.12 Marriage and family therapists make efforts to prevent the distortion or misuse of their clinical and research findings.

3.13 Marriage and family therapists, because of their ability to influence and alter the lives of others, exercise special care when making public their professional recommendations and opinions through testimony or other public statements.

3.14 To avoid a conflict of interests, marriage and family therapists who treat minors or adults involved in custody or visitation actions may not also perform forensic evaluations for custody, residence, or visitation of the minor. The marriage and family therapist who treats the minor may provide the court or mental health professional performing the evaluation with information about the minor from the marriage and family therapist's perspective as a treating marriage and family therapist, so long as the marriage and family therapist does not violate confidentiality.

3.15 Marriage and family therapists are in violation of this Code and subject to termination of membership or other appropriate action if they: (a) are convicted of any felony; (b) are convicted of a misdemeanor related to their qualifications or functions; (c) engage in conduct which could lead to conviction of a felony or a misdemeanor related to their qualifications or functions; (d) are expelled from or disciplined by other professional organizations; (e) have their licenses or certificates suspended or revoked, or are otherwise disciplined by regulatory bodies; (f) continue to practice marriage and family therapy while are no longer competent to do so because they are impaired by physical or mental causes, or of the abuse of alcohol or other substances; or (g) fail to cooperate with the Association at any point from the inception of an ethical complaint through the completion of all proceedings regarding that complaint.

CASE 9

A marriage and family therapist had given court testimony contradicting the testimony of a second marriage and family therapist in a child custody action brought by one parent against the other. The marriage and family therapist hired by the father was upset and very concerned about the ethical implications of the testimony of the mother's marriage and family therapist. The therapist's concerns emanated from the fact that the therapist hired by the mother had seen the child alone during the actual therapy sessions, communicated with the mother only very briefly before and after those sessions, and had never met with the father, yet testimony was given relative to the entire family's functioning. In contrast, the therapist hired by the father had seen the entire family together in therapy for several months.

Analysis

Subprinciples 3.11, 3.13, and 3.14 present the primary ethical issue in this case. The marriage and family therapist hired by the mother appears to have based court testimony solely on hearsay. This therapist might have given reliable testimony relative to the child's current functioning, but the ability to accurately evaluate total family functioning solely from the communications of the child or through brief encounters in a waiting room with the mother is a questionable practice. This therapist should be strongly urged to seek supervision from a marriage and family therapist with significant experience in family evaluation, especially before agreeing to act as an expert witness to provide similar court testimony.

CASE 10

A psychiatrist raised questions about the ethical conduct of a marriage and family therapist employed by the clinical group to which he acted as psychiatric consultant. The psychiatrist alleged that the therapist's use of intensification procedures with the family of a young boy whom he was psychopharmacologically treating for hyperactivity was having a harmful effect on his client's condition. The psychiatrist portrayed the boy as experiencing undue harassment from his parents as a result of the family therapy sessions. The therapist responded by conveying to the boy's parents that the psychiatrist had some questions about the family therapy, requesting the parents' consent to communicate with the psychiatrist in this regard. With the parents' consent, the marriage and family therapist explained to the psychiatrist the specific nature of the procedure, anticipated side effects, and the likelihood of greater improvement as a result of its use.

Analysis

Subprinciples 3.5 and 3.8 are of direct concern in this case. The psychiatrist's inquiry was reasonable, given his apparent linear perception of his client's condition. The therapist responded conscientiously in asking the parents' permission to consult with the psychiatrist and then seeking to educate the psychiatrist on relevant ramifications of the procedures in question. The therapist presented not only the potential positive attributes of the procedures but also anticipated side effects. At no time, however, does it appear that the therapist engaged in any action that would encourage unwarranted harassment of the boy.

CASE 11

A marriage and family therapist had seen a client for a number of therapy sessions when he realized that his intimate feelings toward her were excessive and potentially harmful in their effect on the therapeutic relationship. He sought consultation from a senior colleague who recommended that the therapist refer the client to another therapist and consider the probability of similar situations occurring in the future. The therapist followed through with the suggestions of the consultant and entered into personal therapy to address his own needs in more appropriate ways. Concurrently, he also contracted with the senior colleague whom he had consulted to provide regular supervision of his work until the time his personal concerns were adequately addressed.

Analysis

Subprinciple 3.2 states that marriage and family therapists seek professional assistance when personal issues might negatively affect their clinical practice. When he became aware of his inappropriate feelings, the therapist in this case acted with ethical promptness in consulting a senior colleague. His further actions of pursuing personal therapy and contracting for supervision are evidence of proper ethical practice.

CASE 12

A young woman asked a marriage and family therapist if she could attend a therapy session with her parents, who were seeing the therapist to resolve their marital discord. The woman conveyed that she was feeling very depressed over her parents' conflicts and sought desperately to help them in any way she could. The parents had expressed strong feelings of anger and resentment about their daughter's continuing interference in their lives. Without considering the possible negative impact of the daughter's presence during a session or forewarning the daughter of her parents' intense hostility, the therapist agreed (with the parents' consent) to allow the daughter to attend the next session. The parents verbally attacked her and she responded immediately by crying hysterically and running out of the session.

Analysis

This case highlights the importance of preparing family members who join in the therapy some time after it has begun with other family members. Not preparing the daughter for a possible negative reaction by her parents in this case suggests a violation of Subprinciple 3.8. The daughter communicated to the therapist that she was in a depressed mental state when she made her request to participate in therapy with her parents. The therapist should have recognized that this vulnerability, combined with the fact that the parents had conveyed intense hostility toward their daughter during sessions, could create a context for harassment of the daughter. Although the harassment came directly from the woman's parents, the therapist indirectly facilitated its occurrence, particularly by not preparing the daughter for its possible emergence in the therapy session.

Principle 4: Responsibility to Students and Supervisees

Marriage and family therapists do not exploit the trust and dependency of students and supervisees.

4.1 Marriage and family therapists are aware of their influential positions with respect to students and supervisees, and they avoid exploiting the trust and dependency of such persons. Therapists, therefore, make every effort to avoid conditions and multiple relationships that could impair professional objectivity or increase the risk of exploitation. When the risk of impairment or exploitation exists due to conditions or multiple roles, therapists take appropriate precautions.

4.2 Marriage and family therapists do not provide therapy to current students or supervisees.

4.3 Marriage and family therapists do not engage in sexual intimacy with students or supervisees during the evaluative or training relationship between the therapist and student or supervisee. Should a supervisor engage in sexual activity with a former supervisee, the burden of proof shifts to the supervisor to demonstrate that there has been no exploitation or injury to the supervisee.

4.4 Marriage and family therapists do not permit students or supervisees to perform or to hold themselves out as competent to perform professional services beyond their training, level of experience, and competence.

4.5 Marriage and family therapists take reasonable measures to ensure that services provided by supervisees are professional.

4.6 Marriage and family therapists avoid accepting as supervisees or students those individuals with whom a prior or existing relationship could compromise the therapist's objectivity. When such situations cannot be avoided, therapists take appropriate precautions to maintain objectivity. Examples of such relationships include, but are not limited to, those individuals with whom the therapist has a current or prior sexual, close personal, immediate familial, or therapeutic relationship.

4.7 Marriage and family therapists do not disclose supervisee confidences except by written authorization or waiver, or when mandated or permitted by law. In educational or training settings where there are multiple supervisors, disclosures are permitted only to other professional colleagues, administrators, or employers who share responsibility for training of the supervisee. Verbal authorization will not be sufficient except in emergency situations, unless prohibited by law.

CASE 13

A licensed marriage and family therapist in private practice expanded her practice by opening satellite offices in a number of surrounding communities. She hired several school counselors on a part-time basis to assist her in offering family therapy services. None of the school counselors had any formal family therapy training. All listings and literature associated with the satellite offices claimed that the offices were owned and staffed by a licensed marriage and family therapist. The therapist had, however, made arrangements to meet weekly with each of her employees.

Analysis

Subprinciple 4.4 is of direct concern in this case. The marriage and family therapist appears to have sought to expand her practice more on an economic than an ethical basis. If the satellite offices are identified as offering services from a licensed marriage and family therapist, then the therapist should endeavor to employ licensed marriage and family therapists. Employing school counselors to offer services relevant to their training and demonstrated competencies is ethical and appropriate as an adjunct to family therapy services. Permitting these individuals to hold themselves as family therapy providers, even though under the supervision of a trained, experienced marriage and family therapist, represents unethical practice, not to mention its possible illegality under state licensure statutes. It is therapists' ethical responsibility to state clearly the purposes of services being offered to prospective clients, being very careful to label providers appropriately so consumers can accurately pursue desired services, and all providers can be accountable for their various professional activities.

CASE 14

A professor in a graduate marriage and family therapy training program maintained a part-time private practice in addition to his university responsibilities. The professor had a reputation among colleagues and students as an outstanding clinician as well as academician. Occasionally, students in the program requested marital or family therapy services from the professor through his private practice. The professor was conscientious in explaining that such services could be obtained at the university's counseling center at minimal cost for students and their families. Some students, however, insisted, and the professor agreed to provide them the therapy services requested.

Analysis

The therapist in this case appears to be cognizant of his influential position with respect to students in the training program. His advocacy of the university's counseling center appropriately conveys this cognizance. However, he had obligations to his academic position that might create conflicts should issues of a problematic nature arise in therapy. For example, information might be shared in therapy suggesting that the student should be prevented from pursuing an internship that incorporated direct client work. The student might seek to immediately pursue that kind of internship, maintaining that information shared within the therapy be kept confidential. Or, although the student might not be ready for an internship from an academic perspective, the therapist's sympathy for the student's family circumstances generated during therapy could encourage a biased academic assessment. Subprinciples 4.1 and 4.2 call for marriage and family therapists to avoid multiple relationships that could impair their judgment and indicate that they should not provide therapy to current students. The therapist in this case seems to have entered such a multiple relationship.

CASE 15

Several faculty members from a university training program in marriage and family therapy expressed concern to the department head about one graduate student who received satisfactory grades in his didactic coursework but exhibited extremely poor relationship skills with family members as well as individual clients in the program's in-house practicum placement. The department head did not follow up on faculty concerns, as the student had an acceptable overall grade point average.

Analysis

Subprinciples 4.4 and 4.5 are relevant here. Even though he is still a student, by allowing the student to provide services to family and individual clients when he was reportedly not currently competent to do so is of concern. It is critical that marriage and family therapy educators and supervisors assist students in securing remedial assistance when needed. Also of critical importance is the potential need to screen from further training those individuals who are unable to provide competent services following reasonable remediation efforts.

Principle 5: Responsibility to Research Participants

Investigators respect the dignity and protect the welfare of participants in research and are aware of federal and state laws and regulations and professional standards governing the conduct of research.

5.1 Investigators are responsible for making careful examination of ethical acceptability in planning studies. To the extent that services to research participants may be compromised by participation in research, investigators seek the ethical advice of qualified professionals not directly involved in the investigation and observe safeguards to protect the rights of research participants.

5.2 Investigators requesting participants' involvement in research inform participants of all aspects of the research that might reasonably be expected to influence willingness to participate. Investigators are especially sensitive to the possibility of diminished consent when participants are also receiving clinical services, or have impairments which limit understanding and/or communication, or when participants are children.

5.3 Investigators respect each participant's freedom to decline participation in or to withdraw from a research study at any time. This obligation requires special thought and consideration when investigators or other members of the research team are in positions of authority or influence over participants. Marriage and family therapists, therefore, make every effort to avoid multiple relationships with research participants that could impair professional judgment or increase the risk of exploitation.

5.4 Information obtained about a research participant during the course of an investigation is confidential unless there is a waiver previously obtained in writing. When the possibility exists that others, including family members, may obtain access to such information, this possibility, together with the plan for protecting confidentiality, is explained as part of the procedure for obtaining informed consent.

CASE 16

An advertisement was placed in the university and city newspapers by a marriage and family therapy graduate student and her major professor for the purpose of recruiting volunteer families to take part in a "Family Mediation Project." The research involved having half of the families subjected to "very uncomfortable circumstances" when they took part in the research (i.e., the family would be kept waiting a long time before being seen, the temperature in the waiting room would be raised, there would be only two seats in the waiting room). The other half of the families would not experience these uncomfortable circumstances. Both groups would take part in family mediation with a trained therapist following their respective circumstances. The study was intended to test the efficacy of certain mediation techniques with families under stress.

Analysis

A study such as this raises several potential ethical problems, given the information offered in the scenario. Subprinciples 5.1 and 5.2 are especially relevant. In research with human subjects, investigators must take special care when planning a study to avoid inflicting physical, psychological, or social harm on the subjects. Minimally, this would include consent procedures so that subjects are fully informed of the purpose of the study and the possible risks. In studies in which some information is withheld or subjects are given misinformation because it is essential to the investigation, corrective action must be taken as soon as possible following completion of the study. Whether family members in this study would be informed that some will experience "very uncomfortable circumstances" is unclear; further, there is no indication of any debriefing procedures to address any negative effects of those who do experience "uncomfortable procedures." Finally, all studies involving human subjects should be reviewed by a "human subjects committee" or "internal review board" before being implemented to ensure that research participants' rights are safeguarded.

CASE 17

A couple participated in a research project conducted by a marriage and family therapy doctoral student. The couple filed a complaint with the university after their participation in the project. The complaint stated that they were deceived by the student regarding the requirements of their participation, and they suffered undue stress as a result. The project did incorporate deception because participant couples were led to believe that the purpose was to rate a videotape of another couple's interaction, when the dependent variable was actually their reaction to having experienced a two-hour delay before viewing the tape. The couple was thoroughly debriefed following their participation according to procedures incorporated in the project, which had been previewed and approved both by the student's doctoral committee members and the university's Human Subjects Research Committee.

Analysis

Subprinciple 5.1 maintains that marriage and family therapists are responsible for making careful examination of ethical accountability in planning studies. The student's preparatory actions in seeking the preview and approval of relevant bodies suggest she took adequate precautions to minimize any stress reactions participant couples might experience. If a significant number of the participant couples from the study had complained that they had experienced excessive stress as a result of their participation in the study, however, it would be ethically incumbent on the student to consider revision of her procedures in consultation with her doctoral and university research committees. Although the potential impact of the findings may be considerable, the welfare of participants must be the primary concern.

CASE 18

A marriage and family therapy professor was teaching an undergraduate course in family relations. The professor was conducting a study that required subjects to complete a family inventory. The inventory results would be compared with subjects' behavior in small-group interaction activities held during class. Participation was mandatory, as the study was related to the course content.

Analysis

Subprinciple 5.3 is particularly applicable in this case: Participation in research must be voluntary. Further, investigators who are in positions of authority over participants such as this professor must show due care in potentially asserting their influence. Even if participation in this study was not overtly mandatory, the professor's position could influence some students to participate even though they would rather not (e.g., because of fear of receiving a lower grade, etc.). In a situation such as this, the professor might conduct the study, as it is related to course content, but offer another equally valuable way to contribute to the class for those choosing not to participate in the study (e.g., a paper and/or presentation). Subprinciple 5.4 may be applicable in this case as well, depending on the manner in which inventory results are shared or not shared during class. If they are to be shared, it is critical that participants understand the content of what may be shared and provide their written permission to do so. Again, many such issues are typically addressed in proposal form in a review by a human subjects research committee or a similar oversight body.

Principle 6: Responsibility to the Profession

Marriage and family therapists respect the rights and responsibilities of professional colleagues and participate in activities that advance the goals of the profession.

6.1 Marriage and family therapists remain accountable to the standards of the profession when acting as members or employees of organizations. If the mandates of an organization with which a marriage and family therapist is affiliated, through employment, contract or otherwise, conflict with the AAMFT Code of Ethics, marriage and family therapists make known to the organization their commitment to the AAMFT Code of Ethics and attempt to resolve the conflict in a way that allows the fullest adherence to the Code of Ethics.

6.2 Marriage and family therapists assign publication credit to those who have contributed to a publication in proportion to their contributions and in accordance with customary professional publication practices.

6.3 Marriage and family therapists do not accept or require authorship credit for a publication based on research from a student's program, unless the therapist made a substantial contribution beyond being a faculty advisor or research committee member. Coauthorship on a student thesis, dissertation, or project should be determined in accordance with principles of fairness and justice.

6.4 Marriage and family therapists who are the authors of books or other materials that are published or distributed do not plagiarize or fail to cite persons to whom credit for original ideas or work is due.

6.5 Marriage and family therapists who are the authors of books or other materials published or distributed by an organization take reasonable precautions to ensure that the organization promotes and advertises the materials accurately and factually.

6.6 Marriage and family therapists participate in activities that contribute to a better community and society, including devoting a portion of their professional activity to services for which there is little or no financial return.

6.7 Marriage and family therapists are concerned with developing laws and regulations pertaining to marriage and family therapy that serve the public interest, and with altering such laws and regulations that are not in the public interest.

6.8 Marriage and family therapists encourage public participation in the design and delivery of professional services and in the regulation of practitioners.

CASE 19

A marriage and family therapist discovered to his dismay that the publisher with whom he had contracted had changed the subtitle of his book to one that conflicted with the AAMFT Code of Ethics (American Association for Marriage and Family Therapy, 2001). The subtitle was altered by the publisher during editing to promise "a guarantee of family happiness" to the reader. The therapist immediately contacted the publisher on learning of the subtitle change and was informed that the first printing of the book would have to stand as is; no changes could be made until a second printing was initiated sometime in the future, depending on the book's sales.

Analysis

Subprinciple 6.5 is of direct concern to the author in this case. Although the relevant prepublication contact between the author and publisher is not clear, the author does appear to have taken timely and appropriate action on learning of the subtitle change. Unfortunately, this case illustrates the limited control authors sometimes have when dealing with publishers and suggests a need for the marriage and family therapist to assume a more assertive stance with regard to editorial changes. Ethically, the author should have required his consent to any changes made before actual publication of the book to ensure its accuracy.

CASE 20

In a graduate course in marriage and family therapy theory, the instructor assigned students an extensive analysis of dominant figures in the field as their major project. The instructor required that the projects become the permanent property of the department and asked that any student desiring feedback attach a photocopy of his or her paper, which was returned to them with comments. Later the instructor used the materials submitted by the students in preparing an article that was accepted and eventually published in a leading journal. No mention of the students' contribution was made.

Analysis

The instructor's actions in this case appear questionable with regard to Subprinciples 6.2, 6.3, and 6.4. This is particularly true if the instructor used any students' original ideas in writing the article. If this is the case, proper credit was ethically due to the students. Further, the students whose projects were used in the preparation of the article would have significantly contributed to its contents, and thus publication credit was ethically due them.

CASE 21

A marriage and family therapist employed by a county agency recognized that understaffing had become a serious problem. As demands for services increased, therapists were being asked to carry excessive caseloads, which caused the quality of services being delivered to deteriorate. Further, more and more student interns were being recruited by the agency's administration to meet new requests for services at a time when staff members' increased caseloads allowed less time for supervision of the interns' work. This was done in lieu of hiring additional full-time experienced professionals.

Analysis

Subprinciple 6.1 is most relevant for the marriage and family therapist experiencing this dilemma. Although the therapist should expect the agency administration to recognize and respond appropriately to concerns about the quality of services, it is ultimately the therapist's responsibility to inform the administration and other relevant sources of the ethical standards that apply. In this instance, the therapist would be ethically bound to make concerns about understaffing known to the administration. Depending on the response the therapist received, further action might include identifying relevant staff involved in the delivery of services and proposing that they organize to assess the present needs for direct client services, staffing, supervision, and other agency functions. Additionally, agency administration may take an even more proactive stance in asserting that these needs be more adequately and ethically addressed.

Principle 7: Financial Arrangements

Marriage and family therapists make financial arrangements with clients, third-party payors, and supervisees that are reasonably understandable and conform to accepted professional practices.

7.1 Marriage and family therapists do not offer or accept kickbacks, rebates, bonuses, or other remuneration for referrals; fee-for-service arrangements are not prohibited.

7.2 Prior to entering into the therapeutic or supervisory relationship, marriage and family therapists clearly disclose and explain to clients and supervisees: (a) all financial arrangements and fees related to professional services, including charges for canceled or missed appointments; (b) the use of collection agencies or legal measures for non-payment; and (c) the procedure for obtaining payment from the client, to the extent allowed by law, if payment is denied by the third-party payor. Once services have begun, therapists provide reasonable notice of any changes in fees or other charges.

7.3 Marriage and family therapists give reasonable notice to clients with unpaid balances of their intent to seek collection by agency or legal recourse. When such action is taken, therapists will not disclose clinical information.

7.4 Marriage and family therapists represent facts truthfully to clients, third-party payors, and supervisees regarding services rendered.

7.5 Marriage and family therapists ordinarily refrain from accepting goods and services from clients in return for services rendered. Bartering for professional services may be conducted only if: (a) the supervisee or client requests it, (b) the relationship is not exploitative, (c) the professional relationship is not distorted, and (d) a clear written contract is established.

7.6 Marriage and family therapists may not withhold records under their immediate control that are requested and needed for a client's treatment solely because payment has not been received for past services, except as otherwise provided by law.

CASE 22

A family initiated therapy services with a marriage and family therapist. In completing a written intake form, the parents indicated that they had mental health benefits as part of their insurance coverage. When they requested information with regard to the therapist's fees, they were told not to be concerned, as insurance would cover the costs.

Analysis

Subprinciple 7.2, which clearly states that a therapist's fee structure should be disclosed to clients at the onset of treatment, is of specific concern in this case. Adherence to this standard allows clients to make a fully informed choice regarding the pursuit of treatment. The client is not the insurance company or any other third-party payor. Consequently, the family (parents in the present case) must be informed of the session fees before being rendered services. This ethical obligation still stands, even though services are paid for by a third party.

CASE 23

A marriage and family therapist was frequently called on by a group of pediatricians to provide family therapy services in cases where family dynamics appeared to be negatively affecting children's physical conditions. In return, the marriage and family therapist regularly referred families to this particular medical group because of their enlightened position on the value of family therapy for their patients.

Analysis

Violation of Subprinciple 7.1 is the major concern in this case. The primary ethical question revolves around the presence of any formal agreement regarding compensation for referrals. Although the marriage and family therapist accepted referrals from the group and made referrals in turn, the facts suggest that this was done due to the professionals' mutual confidences in each other, not because a specific agreement had been made to offer remuneration in return for referrals. Thus, the marriage and family therapist's actions represent appropriate ethical practice.

CASE 24

A marriage and family therapist had been working with a family whose insurance benefits expired. Both she and the family recognized the need for further sessions to achieve the goals they had mutually established. The family could not, however, afford to pay the therapist's fees.

Analysis

Subprinciple 7.2 calls for marriage and family therapists to disclose their fees to clients at the beginning of services. The preamble for Principle 7 states that financial arrangements with clients should be reasonably understandable. In establishing a fee agreement with this family, it does not appear that the limitations of insurance benefits were considered, or at least discussed. Such possibilities should be addressed with clients at the onset of services with alternative courses of action (e.g., referral, pro bono sessions, etc.) that might be pursued if the need for continuing therapy exceeds the benefit period.

Principle 8: Advertising

Principle 8 concerns professional advertisements and announcements. This principle, its subprinciples, and relevant illustrations are featured in Chapter 12.

CLOSING REMARKS

We have offered a casebook approach to examining the application of the *AAMFT Code of Ethics* in this chapter. Our attempt has been to illustrate the application of the codes related to a variety of case scenarios. This chapter also concludes our examination of ethical issues related to the practice of marriage and family therapy. Therefore, we offer a few final comments concerning Chapter 7 as well as the coming chapters.

From our discussion concerning multiple relationships in Chapter 6, you will recall the examination of the AAMFT ethical code along with similar codes from other professional groups. In that discussion, we noted subtle as well as significant differences in the language and admonitions of those codes. The comments in Chapter 7 reflect *only* the AAMFT codes, though many professionals hold multiple concurrent memberships in other professional groups. Consequently, we strongly encourage readers to examine the ethical codes of all of their professional affiliate groups for direction and assistance when they encounter an ethical quandary. In those instances of inconsistencies, we strongly recommend consultation or supervision for assistance.

We would also remind readers of the comment in Chapter 3 concerning the dynamic nature of ethical codes. Changes in legal precedents, emerging traditions, research findings, and overall social-political insight often converge to bring about changes in the ethical conduct for a profession. For example, some groups have come to address difficult issues such as right-to-die decisions (ACA, 2005) within the scope of their codes of ethics. Thus, the discussions of the various scenarios in this casebook chapter may differ over the years, requiring vigilance and attentiveness in remaining current about the content of ethical codes.

Chapters 8, 9, and 10 offer examinations of legal precedents and issues that affect contemporary practices in marriage and family therapy. From our discussion in Chapter 2, you will recall the distinctions between personal, professional, and institutional layers of values. In Part III, we emphasize the interrelationship between institutional and professional layers, along with providing a somewhat lessened emphasis on personal layer. Such is the nature of attending to legal obligations. In some ways, when compared with the often elusive nature of ethical judgments, legal precedents can offer greater clarity, though no less difficulty, for marriage and family therapists faced with compelling issues concerning care for their clients and management of their practices. We hope our remarks concerning ethical issues have laid a foundation for a thorough examination of the remaining discussions in our text regarding legal and professional issues for the practice of marriage and family therapy.

Legal Issues in Marriage and Family Therapy

Law and therapy go hand in hand. What are some of the obvious areas in which legal input would be essential to the therapeutic or counseling process? When should the therapist be sensitive to legal issues? What problems can exist where therapy and law must co-exist? Can a therapist afford to be ignorant of the law? Can such ignorance ever be excused?

(Bernstein, 1982, p. 10)

CHAPTER 8

The Marriage and Family Therapist: Roles and Responsibilities Within the Legal System

Contemporary public policy has evolved from a progressive merger of legal principles and social science conceptualizations. As with most mergers, these two factions have come to pursue similar ends. For years the legal system has sought to maintain the family as the primary building block of the social order. Likewise, over the past century, mental health professionals became increasingly influential in helping to create laws aimed at facilitating healthy, stable family functioning (Mulvey, Reppucci, & Weithorn, 1984). Today, the knowledge and assistance of legal services and mental health professionals are inextricably linked to most aspects of public policy, so much so that there is presently an active use of the legal system to promote goals deemed desirable by the mental health profession and vice versa.

Marriage and family therapists need to know the law (Riley, Hartwell, Sargent, & Patterson, 1997). For instance, marriage and family therapists are regularly called as expert witnesses to assist the legal system; effective testimony requires familiarity not only with marital and family issues but also with the legal issues in question and the process by which they will be decided. Similarly, the principles on which judgments of professional legal responsibility and liability are based have seen many changes in recent years. Marriage and family therapists must keep abreast of these changes to protect themselves and their clients. For example, familiarity with relevant law allows therapists to make more sophisticated decisions about when confidentiality applies as opposed to circumstances mandating disclosure of information (e.g., child abuse, suicidal threat).

Involvement with the legal system calls for conceptual changes by many marriage and family therapists. In contrast with professionals from other disciplines, marriage and family therapists may find movement into legal matters more difficult because of their philosophy and methods. Most marriage and family therapists' training is heavily influenced by goal-oriented notions of "what should be"; as a result, they are often unprepared for the "what is" emphasis of the courtroom. The legal system aims not at helping clients progress and become better but rather on reaching a fair decision that solves a practical and immediate problem, one that can be applied to similar situations in the same way in the future. The philosophy of the courtroom process frequently contradicts the therapy process (Woody & Mitchell, 1984).

Methodologically, the major therapeutic role of marriage and family therapists is helping individuals and families to function better. In legal proceedings, marriage and family therapists' primary role is simply to tell the truth. The attorneys' role is to promote their particular client's interest within the boundaries of the law and rules of the court. The attorney is not there to discover the truth; the court will determine the truth by weighing all evidence within the context of an adversarial struggle between attorneys. Marriage and family therapists are placed in the middle, and sometimes they mistakenly interpret an opposing attorney's activities as a personal attack against themselves or the best interests of their client. This makes it difficult to remain objective in an atmosphere that accentuates any tendency, conscious or unconscious, for personal bias as well as actual abuse of behavioral science data.

Many of the pressures potentially confronting therapists in these circumstances can be relieved if therapists acquire an understanding of the law and the legal system relevant to marriage and family therapy issues. Therapists do not have to possess the knowledge of an attorney in these matters; rather, they should have a basic comprehension of legal processes and procedures, information necessary to pursue elementary legal research efforts, and access to an attorney when legal advice is required.

Ruback (1982) asserted that marriage and family therapists may assume three major roles within the legal system: (a) a source of information leading to intervention by the state, (b) a resource for therapy services, and (c) an expert witness. Following an introduction to the basics of legal education, this chapter considers each of these roles as well as the increasingly pertinent issue of marriage and family therapists' professional liability under the law. A bibliography of recommended resources at the end of the chapter provides a more extensive exploration of the topics addressed.

LEGAL EDUCATION

Marriage and family therapists need to be familiar with the basics of legal research so they can educate themselves in matters relevant to their professional practice. Shea (1985) asserted that researching a particular point amid the expanse of the law is generally not beyond the ability of the competent layperson. For marriage and family therapists—legal "laypersons"—several distinctions are of particular concern.

Common Law

Common law is the fundamental law of the United States. Derived from English Common Law, its authority stems from tradition and usage, not from legislation. Common law is regarded as expressing "the usage and customs of immemorial antiquity" common to the people of England. Conceptually, common law represents the belief that law does not have to be derived only from written sources (Reed, 1985). American law in the 1800s took pride in its common law arrangement. In the 1900s, legislation modified and often supplemented the common law, a trend that has continued.

Constitutional Law

The U.S. government and each of its states and territories have a constitution. Constitutions provide basic principles that cannot be violated by other types of law.

Statutory Law

Statutory law consists of those laws passed by a legislative body, such as a state legislature or Congress, and signed into law. Statutory laws exist in each of the 50 states, in the U.S. territories, and at the federal level. The statutes are binding only in the jurisdiction where they were passed.

Administrative (Regulatory) Law

Administrative agencies have grown rapidly in this country, beginning with the New Deal legislation of the 1930s. At that time it became clear that Congress and state legislatures could not effectively promulgate the rules required to regulate all areas of government control. Highly specialized areas required knowledge and time beyond the limits of the average legislator. Consequently, the U.S. Congress and state legislatures passed laws delegating broad rule-making authority to specialized agencies (Knapp, Vandecreek, & Zirkel, 1985).

Case Law (Court Decisions)

Case law is a body of legal decisions that, when taken collectively, create rules for decision making. Typically, statutes prescribe certain legal principles. Legislation, however, is frequently written in broad terms, and thus courts apply, interpret, and fill in the intricacies in the statutes. Courts consider a statute and its legislative history and then decide what the legislators actually intended. Court opinions take into account any bearing that higher laws (such as the state or federal constitution) may have on the interpretation of the statute in question (Knapp et al., 1985).

Many nuances enter the process. A determination must be made as to whether federal or state law applies. In general, state law must be considered first; if a federal issue is raised, such as a constitutional right or a conflict between states, then federal law will come into play. Depending on the nature of a case, a federal court may apply a state law, even when considering a federal issue (Woody & Mitchell, 1984).

Case law accumulates on the basis of *stare decisis* (let the decision stand). Under this doctrine, when a court interprets and applies common law, statutes, and/or regulations to the facts of a case, that court and lower courts in the same jurisdiction are bound to apply that precedent to future cases with similar facts (Kempin, 1982). Other courts may regard such decisions, depending on their number and reasoning, as persuasive, albeit not binding. Reed (1985) described this process:

> The fashion in which one case governs another is elusive of description. In retrospect, the process is seen to constitute a form of logic, but a logic which often deals with principles that are imperfectly expressed, even in the court's opinion in the case at hand. Indeed, merely because a case has been decided in a given direction and because a legal principle applying to the case has been enunciated, the law on the point is, by no means, necessarily established. The saying, "Hard cases make bad law," illustrates a common failing of judges to overgeneralize a legal principle in rationalizing a case which, because of its one-sidedness, is

easy to resolve. But one case does not establish the law; others come along which test declared legal principles and, consequently, lead to refinement.

Typically, case law originates with a case; for example, in Oklahoma, the Supreme Court in that State formulates a legal principle that will be considered binding in Oklahoma (until it is successfully challenged). But the lawyers in an adjoining state might say that they are from Missouri and that they, themselves, have to test such a finding in their own courts. (A precedent in a neighboring state is bound to carry some weight in a jurisdiction, but it is not binding as precedent.) Missouri, with a somewhat similar fact situation as that in the Oklahoma case, will be likely to deal with the Missouri facts in the light of the decided case from Oklahoma, but may find different conclusions and somewhat different case law.

Ultimately, several states, and perhaps even the courts of the Federal system, will formulate principles dealing with the same type of related cases, and a "weight of opinion" will have been achieved. The weight of opinion, expressed in differing ways and perhaps binding with somewhat differing nuances in different states, is considered to be the law. If the original decision on a case, as in Oklahoma, should, in retrospect, be seen as countering the trend of opinions, it is likely that that viewpoint will be challenged in the original state. The highest appellate court may overrule its original opinion, usually in some face-saving manner, or the state may continue in a maverick status with respect to that particular legal point. The trend is for some homogeneity to evolve over the various states and over Federal jurisdictions. The process of this evolution takes place over time and over several regions.[1]

Cases may be decided in the trial, intermediate, appellate, or highest court levels within the state or federal system. Although the nomenclature may vary from one jurisdiction to another, the typical designations for various court levels are listed in Figure 8–1.

Trial courts determine facts in disputes and apply appropriate rules of law. In the trial court, parties first appear, witnesses testify, and other evidence is presented. The losing party on the trial level may appeal the decision to an appellate court. Appellate courts do not hear new testimony, but rather, they determine if the law was properly applied at a lower level in the court system. A higher level of appeal is typically available, depending on the issue, as a matter of right (the legal privilege due each person as a citizen) or as a result of an upper court's discretion. It is important to note that even a minor change in the facts can change the decision of the court.

An understanding of five component parts is helpful in interpreting court decisions (Shea, 1985):

1. *Facts.* The facts of a case form the basis for a court's decision. In a jury case, it is the jury who decides what are the facts; in a nonjury case, it is the trial judge who makes these determinations.
2. *Issue.* An issue of a case is its decisional focus. The parties attempt to focus a judge's attention on the issues of a case most favorable to their position. Ultimately, the judge decides what the issues in a case are regarding his or her decision.
3. *Rule.* A rule is a statement of the law that is applied to the facts. Often rules are incomplete or ambiguous, requiring the court to interpret them. Such an interpretation then becomes a rule in that it is a statement of law developed by the court. The rule of a decision, especially of an appellate court, serves as a precedent. Once a rule is stated in a decision, only that court or a higher court may alter it.

---

[1]*Note.* From "The Origin and Functions of American Law," by J. M. Reed, in *Law and Ethics: A Guide for the Health Professional* (pp. 4–5), edited by N. T. Sidney, 1985, New York: Human Sciences Press. Copyright 1985 by Human Sciences Press. Reprinted with permission.

FIGURE 8–1 Typical Court Names in Federal State Systems

Note. From "Legal Research Techniques: What the Psychologist Needs to Know" by S. Knapp, L. Vandecreek, and P. Zirkel, 1985, *Professional Psychology: Research and Practice, 16,* pp. 363–372. Copyright 1985 by American Psychological Association. Reprinted by permission of the author.

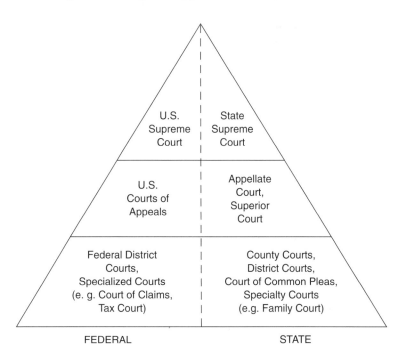

FEDERAL   STATE

4. *Holding.* The holding of the decision is its outcome, the result of the rule applied to the facts, and who wins or loses.
5. *Dicta.* In a decision, a court may discuss rules that are not directly related to the facts of present case. When a court states a rule that is not necessary for deciding a case, the rule is referred to as an *obiter dictum.* Dicta (plural) provide guidance but do not constitute binding precedent for lower courts.

Criminal vs. Civil Law

Although their basic purposes are similar, that is, to promote social order and to provide a system of dispute resolution, civil and criminal law differ in one significant way. Civil law pertains to acts offensive to individuals, criminal law to acts offensive to society in general. The ultimate remedy for harms inflicted in violation of criminal laws is punishment of the violator in the name of the state. Civil law provides a framework within which claims by one party or parties against another are adjudicated before a court. In civil law, the remedy is some compensation to the victim (Keary, 1985).

Marriage and family therapists who seek to supplement their therapeutic expertise with specific legal understandings should become familiar with the major types of legal sources. Woody and Mitchell (1984) offered an orientation for doing so, as illustrated in Figure 8–2.

This orientation should provide sufficient information to enter a law library. Law libraries are maintained by law schools, whose official policies vary; however, most will give permission for legal research by professionals such as marriage and family therapists. State, county, and city law libraries, although intended for judges and lawyers, are generally available to the public. Their collections are probably less extensive than a good law school library, but most civic law libraries are quite willing to provide assistance to

FIGURE 8–2   An Orientation to Legal Research Sources

It would be unrealistic to expect the human services professional to acquire the same facility at locating and understanding legal information as would be commonplace for the legal scholar. On the other hand, the human services professional can supplement his or her behavioral or health science expertise with legal ideas, albeit in a somewhat rudimentary fashion. The human services professional can achieve an adequate orientation by becoming familiar with the major types of legal sources. This fundamental orientation can be augmented by guidance from a professional legal librarian.

United States Supreme Court decisions are reported by official and unofficial reporters. The official reporter, created by statutory authority, is the *United States Supreme Court Reports* (cited as U.S.). The unofficial reporters, products of commercial publishers, are the West Publishing Company's *Supreme Court Reporter* (S.Ct.) and the Lawyers Co-operative Publishing Company's *Lawyers' Edition of United States Supreme Court Reports* (L. Ed. or L. Ed. 2d). All these editions are authoritative as to text, but the unofficial versions may also contain supplemental information (such as summaries of the attorneys' arguments or abstracts on specific legal points). If a Supreme Court case has not yet appeared in these publications, it might be found in *United States Law Week* (U.S. L.W.), a looseleaf service.

Decisions on cases from the U.S. Courts of Appeals appear in the *Federal Reporter* (F. or F.2d). U.S. District court decisions appear in the *Federal Supplement* (F. Supp.) and *Federal Rules Decision* (F.R.D.).

State court decisions (except in a few states) are disseminated by an official state reporter, such as *Michigan Reports* (Mich.) or *California Reports* (Cal., Cal.2d, or Cal.3d). There will also be a regional reporter, such as *Northwestern Reporter* (N.W. or N.W.2d), which includes important cases from Michigan, Wisconsin, Minnesota, Iowa, North Dakota, South Dakota, and Nebraska.

Contrary to popular belief, not all court cases are published. That is, most cases at the federal level are published (especially those decided by the U.S. Supreme Court or a U.S. Court of Appeals); at the state level, most jurisdictions publish appellate decisions, but other cases (for instance, those decided at the trial level) may not be published unless they have special legal importance. Cases that are unreported elsewhere (as well as recent cases that have not yet appeared in the various reporters) may sometimes be found in separately paginated "advance sheets," in "looseleaf services" (such as the *Criminal Law Reporter,* the *Family Law Reporter,* or the *Labor Law Reporter*), or in legal periodicals.

Federal statutes appear, among other sources, in the *Statutes at Large* (these "session laws" are arranged in the order in which they are enacted); this source (cited Stat.) also includes congressional resolutions, select presidential proclamations, and treaties and other international agreements. *The United States Code* (U.S.C.) is published by the U.S. Government Printing Office and is the primary authority on final legislative law.

Federal administrative rules and regulations appear in the *Federal Register* (Fed. Reg.). The *Code of Federal Regulations* (C.F.R.) cites (by title and section) all federal administrative rules and regulations, except Treasury materials. Federal administrative decisions are published by various agencies, such as the Federal Trade Commission and the National Labor Relations Board.

State statutes—for example, the *Arkansas Statutes Annotated* (cited Ark. Stat. Ann.)—are published in bound volumes periodically. In between issues, a statute may be eliminated, amended, or added, and will be found in supplemental editions. It is always necessary to check in the back of a bound volume to see whether a "pocket supplement" reflects any revision of a statute.

Municipal and county ordinances appear in many forms but are usually confined to local distribution. The variations in form preclude detail herein. In general, however, these ordinances are similar in form to the statutes.

Legal research is blessed with encyclopedic sources. For example, the *American Law Reports* (A.L.R., A.L.R.2d or A.L.R.3d) include selected cases and annotations on specific subjects, along with historical background, current law, and probable future developments. Similarly, the *Corpus Juris Secundum* (C.J.S.) series cites case authority; presents a researched summary of the law, and so on. *Words and Phrases* contains more descriptive and extensive definitions than the well-known *Black's Law Dictionary.*

FIGURE 8–2 *Continued*

An often-used legal research method is to "Shepardize" a case—that is, to use *Shepard's Case Citations* to follow the judicial history of a targeted case, learn the contemporary status of the case, locate other cases that have cited it, and acquire research leads (such as where to look in *American Law Reports*). The *Shepard* volumes are divided by jurisdiction. Statutes may also be researched in *Shepard's United States Citations,* and law review articles may be located in *Shepard's Law Review Citations.* Municipal charters and ordinances may be cited in *Shepard's Ordinance Law Citations.*

Legal materials follow a special referencing or citation system. For example, cases are cited as follows (with minor variations in type style used in different publications):

Tarasoff v. Regents of the University of California, 17 Cal.3d 425, 551 P.2d 334, 131 Cal. Rptr. 14 (1976).
("Cal.3d" is the third series of *California Reports,* the state reporter for California Supreme Court cases; "17" is the volume where the *Tarasoff* case is reported, and "425" is the first page where the case appears. "P.2d" is the *Pacific Reporter,* the regional reporter for California state court cases; and again, "551" is the volume number and "334" the first page where the case appears. "Cal. Rptr." is *West's California Reporter,* an unofficial reporter for California court cases.

Muller v. Oregon, 208 U.S. 412, 415 (1908).
("U.S." is *United States Supreme Court Reports,* and "415" is the page where a specific quoted passage, presumably just cited in the text, appears. If the case has previously been cited, this citation may appear as "*Muller v. Oregon,* 208 U.S. at 415.")

Driver v. Hinnant, 356 F.2d 761 (4th Cir. 1966).
("F.2d" is *Federal Reporter,* publisher of U.S. Court of Appeals cases; "4th Cir." indicates that the case was heard by the U.S. Court of Appeals for the Fourth Circuit.)

Greenberg v. Barbour, 332 F. Supp. 745 (E.D. Pa. 1971).
("F. Supp." is the *Federal Supplement,* reporter for U.S. District Court Cases; "E.D. Pa." indicates that the case was heard by the U.S. District Court for the eastern district of Pennsylvania.)

In addition, books, periodicals, newspapers, statutes, legislative materials, and other specialized materials are cited in prescribed ways. An authoritative source for learning legal citations is *A Uniform System of Citation* (12th ed., 1976), created by law review groups at Columbia, Harvard, Pennsylvania, and Yale (distributed by the Harvard Law Review Association, Gannett House, Cambridge, Massachusetts 02138).

Note. From "Understanding the Legal System and Legal Research" (pp. 30–33), by R. H. Woody & R. E. Mitchell. In *The Law and Practice of Human Services* by R. H. Woody (Ed.). 1984, San Francisco: Jossey-Bass. Reprinted by permission.

nonlawyers. Local bar associations can be contacted for the location of these libraries. Private law libraries provide another research source. Larger law firms and office complexes catering to attorneys often have fairly extensive libraries. Access may prove more difficult, however (Shea, 1985). Finally, many university, college, and public libraries have good legal collections.

In most locations, law librarians are available to assist researchers, including marriage and family therapists. Furthermore, many attorneys typically welcome the opportunity to give free advice for bona fide research efforts; such contacts frequently facilitate future referral relationships. In addition, colleges and universities, public and private agencies, and various professional organizations regularly sponsor seminars, symposia, and workshops on relevant legal issues.

THE MARRIAGE AND FAMILY THERAPIST AS A SOURCE OF INFORMATION

Marriage and family therapists have an obligation to provide information leading to intervention by the state. The two most frequently encountered situations in which therapists need to serve as sources of information involve their duty to protect third parties from actions by a client believed to be dangerous (R. E. Watts, 1999) and statutes requiring the reporting of child abuse and neglect. Both of these requirements can pose painful professional dilemmas for therapists, as discussed in earlier chapters on ethical obligations. The present discussion, however, highlights only the legal obligations.

Confidentiality, Privileged Communication, and Records

Because clients have an expectation of privacy when they receive marriage and family therapist services, and because marriage and family therapists have an ethical duty to keep confidential the information they learn in therapy sessions, a legal duty exists for marriage and family therapists to maintain the privacy of their clients. Of course there are many exceptions to the duty to keep therapy information private. Some exceptions, for example, include when the client has been determined to be a danger to self or others, when the client has requested that private information be provided to a third party, when child abuse or neglect is suspected from information learned by therapists, or when a court orders that confidential information be disclosed. If a marriage and family therapist inappropriately discloses confidential information about a client and that client can prove that he or she was damaged in some way by that disclosure, the client has a legal foundation for holding the therapist accountable for any damages he or she suffered as a result of the disclosure.

Privileged communication is a legal concept. As with other legal concepts, it is impossible for marriage and family therapists to know the law adequately enough to practice without the advice of an attorney. When legal questions arise related to confidentiality or privileged communication, it is essential that marriage and family therapists obtain the advice of a lawyer. Marriage and family therapists who are employed can request legal advice from their immediate supervisor, who then has the legal obligation to provide it. Marriage and family therapists who are in private practice must pay for the legal advice they need by consulting with an attorney.

If a state legislature or the federal government passes a law that makes a particular relationship privileged, then a court cannot order that information from that relationship be revealed during the litigation of a lawsuit. All privileged communication statutes have exceptions. The most notable exception is instances of suspected child abuse or neglect, in which therapists are required by law to report their suspicions to state authorities. In most states in which marriage and family therapists are licensed by their state, there is a privileged communication statute that has been passed. However, in some states the clients of marriage and family therapists do not enjoy statutorily privileged relationships with their therapists.

Statutes that grant privilege to relationships provide the legal protection to recipients of professional services, not to the professionals themselves. As a result, it is the responsibility of clients to assert their privilege in court if their privacy is being challenged. If clients cannot be located, however, then the professionals must assert the privilege on behalf of their clients. Clients may waive their privilege if they choose to. As a result, if clients sign a form waiving their privilege, then therapists will have to disclose private information that otherwise might have been protected in court proceedings.

Subpoenas for testimony or records of marriage and family therapists must be dealt with carefully. Because client information may be privileged, therapists cannot produce information in response to a subpoena if the information is privileged. On the other hand, if the information is not privileged, then therapists must comply with the subpoena and produce either the testimony or record. Because state and federal statutes and case law determine whether information is privileged, and whether exceptions exist to any privilege, it is essential that marriage and family therapists obtain legal advice before complying with subpoenas they receive. Therapists should provide their attorney with full information regarding the client relationship, should point out any state statute they are familiar with that might grant privilege, and should follow their advice of their attorney.

Records kept by marriage and family therapists that include private information related to their clients come under the same confidentiality and privileged communication protections as verbal information. Most marriage and family therapists work in settings in which they must comply with the federal law known as the Health Insurance Portability and Accountability Act (HIPPA). This law specifies steps that must be taken to ensure client privacy and includes civil and criminal penalties for therapists who do not comply. A copy of the HIPAA rules and modifications are located at 45 CFR Part 160 and Part 164, Subparts A and E on the United States Government's Office of Civil Rights Web site, http://www.hhs.gov/ocr/hipaa. Agencies that employ therapists are responsible for compliance with HIPAA, but marriage and family therapists in private practice must develop forms and procedures for themselves that ensure that they meet the law's requirements. There are a number of commercially developed HIPAA compliance packages that private practitioners can purchase.

The Duty to Protect

In 1976, the California Supreme Court handed down a decision in *Tarasoff v. Board of Regents of the University of California* that signaled a trend toward protection of the public's safety in preference to client confidentiality in psychotherapy. The case involved a client who threatened during therapy to kill his girlfriend and did so two months later:

> In August 1969, Prosenjit Poddar, a voluntary outpatient at the student health service on the Berkeley campus of the University of California, informed his therapist, a psychologist, that he was planning to kill a young woman. He did not name the woman, but as was established later, the psychologist could have easily inferred who she was. The murder was to be carried out upon the woman's return to the university from her summer vacation. Following the session during which this information was given, the therapist telephoned the campus police, requesting that they observe Poddar for possible hospitalization as a person who was "dangerous to himself or others." The therapist followed up his telephone call with a formal letter requesting assistance from the chief of the campus police. The campus police did take Poddar into custody for the purpose of questioning, but later released him when he gave evidence of being "rational." Soon afterward, the therapist's supervisor asked the campus police to return the letter, ordered that the letter and the therapist's case notes be destroyed, and directed that no further action be taken to hospitalize Poddar. No warning was given to the intended victim or her parents. The client, understandably, did not resume therapy. Two months later Poddar killed Tatiana Tarasoff. Her parents filed suit against the Board of Regents of the university, several employees of the student health service, and the chief of the campus police plus four of his

officers for failing to notify the intended victim of the threat. A lower court dismissed the suit, the parents appealed, and the California Supreme Court upheld the appeal and later reaffirmed its decision that failure to warn the intended victim was irresponsible. (*Tarasoff v. Board of Regents of the University of California*)

In *Tarasoff*, the court held that a therapist who knew, or by the standards of his or her profession, should have known, that his or her client posed a threat to another, had a duty to exercise reasonable care to protect the intended victim. Several other courts in jurisdictions outside California have since adopted the *Tarasoff* reasoning, subsequently further narrowing and refining it.

Three factors emanating from the *Tarasoff* decision have come to embody the findings regarding therapists' duty to protect. First, the court noted that generally one person does not have a duty to control the conduct of another. However, an exception to this was established for instances in which one person has a "special relationship" either to the person whose conduct needs to be controlled or to the foreseeable victim of that conduct. This special relationship must be found to exist in the factual context of the case. In *Tarasoff*, the court held that the therapist–client relationship met the test of being a special relationship.

The second condition required to create a duty to protect is a determination that a client's behavior "needs to be controlled." Again, in the factual context of *Tarasoff*, the court found that the client, Prosenjit Poddar, was a threat. It was noted, however, that determining if an individual's conduct needs to be controlled is frequently a difficult prediction to make.

There is no definitive formula for determining if an individual is at risk for violence, but Beck and Baxter (1998) have suggested that both internal (related to the person's thoughts, perceptions, feelings) and external (related to environmental or other situations that exist outside the individual) factors must be considered in assessing a person's potential for violence. These authors cautioned that a client has the potential for dangerousness if he or she (a) is angry; (b) has a motive, either delusional or realistic, for harming someone; (c) drinks (Rice & Harris, 1995; J. W. Swanson, 1993); or (d) is now or has been delusional, especially if the delusions involve influence or control. Kausch and Resnick (1998) have declared:

> Risk factors for violence include a past history of violence, young age (early 20s), gender (male), lower social class, low intelligence quotient (IQ), major mental illness, organic brain disorder, a history of violence, suicide attempts, a history of prior criminal acts, access to lethal weapons, and use of drugs and alcohol. (p. 334)

In *Tarasoff*, the court identified a "reasonableness" test as the standard for determining if a client's conduct could result in a threat to a third person. In determining reasonableness, the court considered within the context of the specific case "that reasonable degree of skill, knowledge, and care ordinarily possessed and exercised by members of (that professional specialty) under similar circumstances" (*Tarasoff v. Board of Regents of the University of California*, 1976, p. 345). The court further pointed out within that standard, opinions might differ and thus therapists are free to exercise judgment without fear of liability: "Proof aided by hindsight, that he or she judged wrongly is insufficient to establish negligence" (p. 345).

The third and final condition that gave rise to the duty to protect was a "foreseeable" victim. Tatiana Tarasoff, although not specifically named by the client, was readily identifiable as the proposed victim. Thus, the facts of *Tarasoff* satisfied the three conditions creating a duty to protect for the therapist: a special relationship, a reasonable prediction of conduct that constituted a threat, and a foreseeable victim.

In *McIntosh v. Milano* (1979), a New Jersey court ruled on a factual situation similar to that found in *Tarasoff* and similarly addressed a therapist's duty to protect:

> In this case, the client was an adolescent boy referred by a school counselor to the therapist, a psychiatrist. The boy informed the therapist of several fantasies he had including a fear of others, being a hero or important villain, using a knife to threaten those who might intimidate him, and having sexual experiences with Kimberly, the girl living next door to him. The boy also informed the therapist of having shot at Kimberly's car with a BB gun when she left for a date and showed the therapist a knife he had bought. The therapist was well aware of the boy's possessive feelings for Kimberly. The boy further told the therapist that he wanted Kimberly "to suffer" as he had and showed anger when Kimberly moved out of her parents' home. He was hateful toward Kimberly's boyfriends and upset when he could not obtain her new address. The boy killed Kimberly. Although the therapist had spoken to his client's parents on a number of occasions about their son's relationship to Kimberly, he never addressed the issue with either Kimberly or her parents.

Lane and Spruill (1980) asserted that dangerousness cannot be accurately predicted and that errors in making this decision are likely. The prediction of dangerousness in *Tarasoff* did not seem to be a questionable factor. Based on the testimony of another psychiatrist, dangerousness was not a question in *McIntosh v. Milano* but rather considered a fact based on a violent act (firing a weapon at Kimberly's car) and on the therapist's statement that his client had admitted fantasies of violence and feelings of retribution. The client also had verbalized threats toward Kimberly and her boyfriends. The court pointed out that "a therapist does have a basis for giving an opinion and a prognosis based on the history of the patient and the course of treatment" (*McIntosh v. Milano*, 1979, p. 508). In *Davis v. Lhim* (1988), the Michigan Supreme Court specified factors that should be considered by a mental health professional in seeking to determine if a client might act on a threat to a third party. These included the client's clinical diagnosis, the manner and context in which the threat was made, the opportunity to act on the threat, a history of violence, factors provoking the threat and if threats are likely to continue, the relationship with the potential victim, and the client's response to treatment.

In *Thompson v. County of Alameda* (1980), the court was asked to decide if there was a duty to protect the parents of a child who was murdered by a released juvenile offender. The juvenile had been in the custody of Alameda County and confined to an institution. He was known to have "latent, extremely dangerous and violent propensities regarding young children and that sexual assaults upon young children and violence connected therewith were a likely result of releasing (him) into the community" (p. 72). Within 24 hours of his temporary release to his mother, the boy killed a child who lived a few doors away. The foreseeability of the victim was the predominant question. The court referred to the language of *Tarasoff* and held that although the victim need not be directly named, he or she must be "readily identifiable." The court thus refused to impose liability on the involved county officials for failing to give a blanket warning to all neighborhood parents, the police, or the juvenile's mother.

Although the courts in other states have similarly declined to impose liability in the absence of an identifiable victim (*Brady v. Hopper*, 1983; *Leedy v. Hartnett*, 1981), the Vermont Supreme Court in *Peck v. Counseling Service of Addison County, Inc.* (1985) ruled that a mental health professional who knows that a client poses a risk to an identifiable person or group has a duty to protect that person or group. Other courts (*Hedlund v. Superior Court*, 1983; *Jablonski v. United States*, 1983) have held that the duty to protect extends to "foreseeable" victims who may not be specifically identifiable but nevertheless would be probable targets if the threatening client were to become violent or carry through on threats. For example, in *Hedlund v. Superior Court*, a woman was assaulted in the presence of her child by a client who had threatened to harm her. The mother alleged that the child had sustained "serious emotional injury and psychological trauma" as a consequence. The California Supreme Court held that a duty to "exercise reasonable care" needed to be fulfilled, which would have been satisfied by warning the mother that both she and her child might be in danger (Corey et al., 1993).

Although generally no legal obligation is imposed on a person to control the conduct of another, there is an exception. When an individual has a special relationship to either the one whose conduct needs to be controlled or to the intended victim of that conduct, the law imposes a duty to protect the victim (Serovich & Mosack, 2000). This is particularly relevant for marriage and family therapists because their relationship with their clients fulfills this "special relationship" condition. Given this, marriage and family therapists are expected to apply a standard of reasonableness in determining a threat posed by clients' conduct. It is important to remember that reasonableness is not a fixed concept but a standard comparing an individual therapist to others in the same profession with similar knowledge, skills, and training. Finally, when these two conditions occur and there is an intended victim or victims who are foreseeable, the marriage and family therapist has a duty to protect that victim or be liable under the law for negligence.

In an article entitled "*Tarasoff*: Ten Years Later," Fulero (1988) proposed that the issues raised by the *Tarasoff* decision were likely to continue to generate litigation, legislation, and controversy for some time into the future. Fulero strongly urged that clinicians seek consultation whenever necessary to clarify the soundness of their professional practices. As discussed earlier, a marriage and family therapist would not be liable for any negative outcome unless his or her actions fell below a reasonable standard of care. We advocate the position presented by Fulero, that marriage and family therapists should be competent relative to assessing and dealing with dangerousness as well as maintain a current understanding of statutes and case law in their own states.

Ginsberg (2004), in his article "*Tarasoff* at Thirty: Victim's Knowledge Shrinks the Psychotherapist's Duty to Warn and Protect," concluded, "*Tarasoff* has been both nexus and naysayer for American psychotherapy, but it appears that it has the potential to make the field of psychotherapy better through the holding's steady and reasoned limitation in the courts and emergence as a decision with tangible clinical benefits."

When the *Tarasoff* case was first announced, many marriage and family therapists were dismayed because they believed that the entire concept of privacy of clients would be compromised. Developments in the intervening 30 years, however, have demonstrated that mental health professionals can accommodate the exception of compromising the general rule of privacy when it is determined that clients are a danger to themselves or others. To find out more about this issue, we suggest that readers investigate some of the controversy within the legal profession in its ongoing debate about whether or not lawyers should be ethically required to report clients who threaten to harm others (Walther, 2005).

McIntosh and Cartaya (1992) have suggested that there is a trend in case law to acknowledge the difficulty of predicting aberrant behavior. Although this is a welcome development, marriage and family therapists must strive to protect others from the acts of dangerous clients.

Child Abuse and Neglect

There are no reliable statistics regarding the exact extent of child abuse and neglect in the United States. This uncertainty is likely caused by inconsistencies in definitions of child abuse and neglect, variations in reporting laws from state to state, and the different methods of data collection commonly used. Nevertheless, the U.S. Advisory Board on Child Abuse and Neglect (1990), established by Congress to evaluate the nation's effectiveness in accomplishing the purposes of the Child Abuse Prevention and Treatment Act of 1974, declared that the problems still present relative to the treatment and prevention of child abuse and neglect in this country are so extreme as to constitute a national emergency. L. Davis (1991), for example, estimated that one in four girls and one in seven boys are sexually abused by the time they reach the age of 18.

Therapists are cautioned, however, to avoid discrimination against clients who live in poverty. Bullock (2003) states that because statutory definitions of child neglect often reflect poverty-level living conditions, and because indigent individuals accused of child abuse and neglect are not guaranteed legal counsel, persons living in poverty often are discriminated against in the legal system that seeks to protect children from harm.

The Child Abuse Prevention and Treatment Act of 1974 (PL 93-247) defines abuse and neglect as follows:

> Physical or mental injury, sexual abuse or exploitation, negligent treatment, or maltreatment of a child under the age of eighteen or the age specified by the child protection law of the state in question, by a person who is responsible for the child's welfare, under circumstances which indicate that the child's health or welfare is harmed or threatened thereby.

Although a clarifying definition, because child abuse is not a federal crime, federal law does no more than make money available to the states that meet its reporting guidelines and other qualifications, such as agreeing to set reporting standards. Thus, state definitions become very important as they provide the basis for abuse and neglect as a crime within a particular jurisdiction. Although state laws vary, most use a combination of two or more of the following elements in defining child abuse and neglect: physical injury, mental or emotional injury, and sexual molestation or exploitation. Fischer and Sorenson (1985) noted that although some states have separate definitions for abuse and neglect, others do not. They asserted that it was unimportant to be able to distinguish between abuse and neglect:

> The time and effort spent in trying to distinguish between abuse and neglect serves no useful purpose. A child may suffer serious or permanent harm and even death as a result of neglect. Therefore, the same reasons that justify the mandatory reporting of abuse require the mandatory reporting of child neglect. (p. 183)

All states require reporting child abuse and neglect to the proper authorities, particularly if physical injury is present. Other aspects of mandatory reporting laws may differ from state to state. For example, in Pennsylvania, therapists are required to file a report if their client is a child who has been abused; if their client is the abuser, however, the mandatory reporting law does not apply. New York state law requires that therapists report abuse whether they learn of it from a child in therapy, from an abuser in therapy, or from a relative. Maryland law requires therapists to report both present and past cases of child abuse that have been revealed by adult clients in therapy (Corey et al., 1993).

State statutes mandating that marriage and family therapists report cases of suspected child abuse or neglect vary substantially in their content. As a result, it is imperative that therapists read and understand the exact language of the reporting statutes that govern mandatory reporting in their states. Volumes containing the language of state statutes are available in all public and educational libraries, and statutes for all states can be found on the Internet.

When reading the language for their state statute that mandates suspected child abuse reporting, therapists should make the following determinations: (a) which categories of professionals must make suspected abuse or neglect reports; (b) whether reports are required only for current abuse or for suspected past abuse as well; (c) if there are statutes that require reporting suspected abuse or neglect of adults who are elderly, developmentally disabled, residents of institutions, or otherwise vulnerable; (d) whether reporting suspected abuse or neglect to a therapist's supervisor is sufficient to satisfy the law or whether a therapist must make direct reports to child protection agencies; (e) if oral reports must be followed by written reports; (f) the types of specific information that must be included in reports; and (g) circumstances under which reports must be made.

To be eligible for federal funds under the Child Abuse Prevention and Treatment Act, states must grant immunity to reporters. All states have complied with this requirement and therefore provide immunity by law from civil suit and criminal prosecution that might arise from the reporting of suspected child abuse or neglect. Such immunity applies to all mandatory or permissible reporters who act "in good faith." In many states, good faith is presumed; therefore, the person seeking to sue a reporter has the burden to prove that the reporter acted in bad faith. Clearly, any marriage and family therapist who, mandated by law, acts in good faith in reporting suspected cases of abuse or neglect is immune from suit.

No state requires that the reporter be absolutely certain before filing a report of abuse or neglect. It is sufficient that the reporter has "reason to believe" or "reasonable cause to believe or suspect" that a child is subject to abuse or neglect. As noted with respect to the duty to protect, the standard applied is what the reasonable person (professional) would believe under similar circumstances. As abuse rarely occurs in the presence of witnesses and because the protection of children is the primary purpose of reporting laws, reporters are not held to unduly rigorous standards as long as they act in good faith. Some states even require one to report when he or she "observes the child being subjected to conditions or circumstances which would reasonably result in child abuse or neglect" (Fischer & Sorenson, 1985, p. 184).

Marriage and family therapists are trained observers of children and their interactions with significant adults. There are, however, various symptoms that should alert therapists that some form of abuse or neglect is taking place. Table 8–1 lists some of the most

TABLE 8–1   Physical and Behavioral Indicators of Child Abuse and Neglect (CA/N)

Type of CA/N	Physical Indicators	Behavioral Indicators
PHYSICAL ABUSE	Unexplained Bruises and Welts: —on face, lips, mouth —on torso, back, buttocks, thighs —in various stages of healing —clustered, forming regular patterns —reflecting shape of article used to inflict (electric cord, belt buckle) —on several different surface areas —regularly appearing after absence, weekend, or vacation	Wariness of Adult Contacts Apprehensiveness When Other Children Cry Behavioral Extremes: —aggressiveness —withdrawal Fear of Parents Fear of Going Home
	Unexplained Burns: —cigar, cigarette burns, especially on soles, palms, back or buttocks —immersion burns (sock-like, glove-like, doughnut shaped on buttocks or genitalia) —patterned like electric burner, iron, etc. —rope burns on arms, leg, neck or torso	Reports of Injury by Parents
	Unexplained Fractures: —to skull, nose, facial structure —in various stages of healing —multiple or spiral fractures	
	Unexplained Lacerations or Abrasions: —to mouth, lips, gums, eyes —to external genitalia	
PHYSICAL NEGLECT	Consistent Hunger, Poor Hygiene, Inappropriate Dress Consistent Lack of Supervision, Especially in Dangerous Activities or for Long Periods Unattended Physical Problems or Medical Needs Abandonment	Begging, Stealing Food Extended Stays at School (early arrival and late departure) Constant Fatigue, Listlessness, or Falling Asleep in Class Alcohol or Drug Abuse Delinquency (e.g., thefts) Statements That There Is No Caretaker
SEXUAL ABUSE	Difficulty in Walking or Sitting Torn, Stained, or Bloody Underclothing Pain or Itching in Genital Area Bruises or Bleeding in External Genitalia, Vaginal, or Anal Areas Venereal Disease, especially in Preteens	Unwilling to Change for Gym or Participate in Physical Education Class Withdrawal, Fantasy, or Infantile Behavior Bizarre, Sophisticated, or Unusual Sexual Behavior or Knowledge

TABLE 8–1   *Continued*

Type of CA/N	Physical Indicators	Behavioral Indicators
	Pregnancy	Poor Peer Relationships Delinquency or Running Away
		Reports of Sexual Assault by Caretaker
EMOTIONAL MALTREATMENT	Speech Disorders Lags in Physical Development Failure to Thrive	Habit Disorders (sucking, biting, rocking, etc.)
		Conduct Disorders (antisocial, destructive, etc.)
		Neurotic Traits (sleep disorders, inhibition of play)
		Psychoneurotic Reactions (hysteria, obsession, compulsion, phobias, hypochondria)
		Behavior Extremes: —compliant, passive —aggressive, demanding
		Overly Adaptive Behavior: —inappropriately adult —inappropriately infant
		Developmental Lags (mental, emotional)
		Attempted Suicide

Source. From *The Educator's Role in the Prevention and Treatment of Child Abuse and Neglect,* by D. D. Broadhurst, 1979, Washington, D.C.: National Center on Child Abuse and Neglect, U.S. Department of Health, Education and Welfare, Publication No. 79-30172.

common indicators of child abuse and neglect. These signs are only indicators that should alert marriage and family therapists to the possibility of abuse or neglect, of course. They do not prove the existence of abuse or neglect. The therapy setting provides further clues to confirm suspicions of abuse or present satisfactory explanations for a child's condition.

Marriage and family therapists have criminal liability, usually at a misdemeanor level, for failure to report suspected abuse or neglect in the overwhelming majority of states. The penalty might range from a low of a 5- to 30-day jail sentence and/or a fine of $10 to $100 to a high of a year in jail and a fine of $1,000. Criminal prosecution for failure to report a case of child abuse or neglect usually occurs after a child has been seriously injured or murdered and a later investigation reveals that a mandated reporter knew or should have known that abuse was occurring.

Fischer and Sorenson (1985) attribute this lack of enforcement to the fact that state laws sometimes require a "knowing" or "willful" failure to report. They note the difficulties involved in proving, beyond all reasonable doubt, that someone knowingly or willfully failed to report. For example, a limited-license psychologist in Michigan was prosecuted for failure to report suspected child abuse. Part of the psychologist's defense was the argument that the Michigan reporting law (i.e., "reasonable cause to suspect") was vague and not objective. The psychologist was ultimately acquitted at a jury trial (Kavanaugh, 1989).

Concern has been expressed by Brown and Strozier (2004) regarding the statutory requirement that marriage and family therapists report cases of suspected abuse. They found in a survey research project that when mental health professionals hear in a counseling session that abuse or neglect may have occurred, they focus so intently on that issue that they forget other important counseling issues that are present in the counseling relationship.

THE MARRIAGE AND FAMILY THERAPIST AS REFERRAL RESOURCE

As a referral resource, marriage and family therapists are called on by the courts for informational as well as therapeutic intervention assistance. Primarily within the juvenile justice system and in civil actions addressing issues ranging from adoption to divorce to child custody, marriage and family therapists assume the role of referral resource. This referral resource role reflects a growing recognition of marriage and family therapists' expertise in offering preventative as well as rehabilitative services to youthful offenders and their families. Likewise, it has long been recognized that every civil action reflects the failure of a relationship. The parties involved are not capable of satisfactorily resolving their own disputes. All things considered, it is almost always more advantageous for two disputing parties to come to their own resolution rather than run the risk of losing control of their situation by having a third party (judge or jury) decide for them. This is in addition to the costs and time involved with a court encounter (Sidley & Petrila, 1985). Marriage and family therapists have thus taken on the roles of treatment specialist, particularly within the juvenile justice system, and mediator in averting civil court actions.

The Treatment Specialist

Evans (1983) described the role of mental health professionals aiding the courts within the criminal justice system as that of treatment specialist. Marriage and family therapists have the clinical and academic training as well as the experience and are currently acting in some capacity as treatment specialists predominantly within the juvenile justice system. Marriage and family therapists also take a similar role in civil hearings relative to cases involving divorce, child custody, visitation, and so on.

Diagnostician

A primary function of marriage and family therapists within the juvenile system is to provide diagnostic evaluations for rehabilitative decisions. Although judges make the final decisions about what will happen to a youthful offender, information made available through evaluations of identified youths and their families has a heavy impact on those decisions.

Initially the court must decide if it has jurisdiction to act; that is, it must decide if the youth falls within a prescribed statutory classification. Although there is variance from state to state, typical statutory classifications and dispositional alternatives in which marriage and family therapists can provide diagnostic input within the juvenile justice system include juvenile delinquency, having been identified as a person in need of supervision

(PINS), and child abuse and neglect cases (Kissel, 1983). The role of marriage and family therapists in each of these situation is described in turn, and then the role they play as diagnosticians in civil hearings involving child custody and visitation is discussed.

Juvenile Delinquency

Juvenile courts generally have jurisdiction over youth accused of committing a crime if they are under 18 years of age on the date of the commission of the act. Some state laws treat children as adults if they are age 13 or older and are charged with murder, forcible rape, robbery while armed, first-degree burglary, or assault with intent to commit any of the aforementioned crimes (Guggenheim, 1979). State laws sometimes specify that juveniles age 15 and over at the time of the offense who are charged with a felony, as well as juveniles age 16 or over who have previously been committed to an institution and are charged in a new delinquency petition for any offense, may be transferred to the appropriate criminal division for trial.

The court's relationship to youthful offenders is a meld of providing for "the best interests of the child" along with protection for the community. The court can decide to dismiss a youth, that is, grant an outright dismissal of the charge. This motion might be considered when a minor offense is charged against a first offender and court supervision of the child is perceived as unnecessary. A consent decree can also be granted by the court and may be entered if the youth has not been previously adjudicated a delinquent by the court, or if such adjudication has been sealed (is not available to the court). Under a consent decree, a juvenile is put on probation for up to six months without a finding of guilt. Thus, the court provides supervision without stigmatization. After successful completion of the specific terms of the decree (therapy, community work hours, restitution, etc.), the original petition is dismissed. If the conditions of the decree are violated, the original petition may be reinstated and the juvenile then may be forced to stand trial.

Person in Need of Supervision

A PINS is typically a youth who is habitually truant from school without justification or is habitually disobedient of the reasonable and lawful commands of his or her parents, guardians, or other custodians and is thus ungovernable and in need of care and supervision. When parents and social agencies are unable or unwilling to find a solution for a troubled or troublesome child, it is in society's interest to try, through its legal system, to prevent crime and delinquency through an attempt at rehabilitation, rather than wait to punish a juvenile until after a crime has been committed.

The court normally has at its disposal an array of social services as well as traditional judicial remedies. Referral to court is not meant for children with inconsequential discipline problems at home or minor school difficulties. Only when youths are at risk of becoming delinquent should this step be taken. The court has considerable leeway when fashioning a plan for disposition. Youths typically are placed in facilities for delinquents only if they have been adjudicated as a PINS more than once.

Child Abuse and Neglect

The primary aim of the court is to preserve the family bond unless such preservation endangers the welfare of a child. Consequently, when abuse and neglect allegations are brought before it, the court attempts to arrange dispositions that permit parents to maintain custody of their children unless such custody is harmful to the child. The judge also can order families to seek medical, psychiatric, or other treatment services if parents want to maintain custody of their child.

If the court finds that placement with the parents is not possible, then relatives, other qualified individuals, or commitment to an agency charged with foster placement will be sought. When more than one child is involved, courts generally prefer to keep siblings together to preserve whatever family bonds remain as well as to ease the transition to an alternative home environment. The court also can free a child for adoption by termination of parental rights in severe cases. It is important to know, however, that unless abused or neglected children also are found to be delinquent, they cannot be committed to or confined in an institution for delinquent children.

Child Custody and Visitation

In Domestic Relations Courts throughout the country, disputes between parents and, increasingly, grandparents (Thompson, Tinsley, Scalora, & Parke, 1989) concerning custody and visitation are commonplace. Sanders (2004) noted that mental health professionals should be aware that few families today are "traditional," and often third parties who are not biological parents are being evaluated for their fitness to parent children. It is difficult for the court to determine child custody and visitation both at the time of a divorce and when the terms of the settlement are reviewed for potential amendment. The testimony presented by the two parents is obviously weighted toward what each one wants. The standard employed by the court is what constitutes "the best interests of the child(ren)." To help make this determination, the court often relies on the testimony of an evaluator representing the child(ren) and the court, not the parents (Stevens-Smith & Hughes, 1993).

Therapists should be aware that some professionals believe that there is no scientific evidence to prove that the process a child custody evaluator uses will lead to correct recommendations regarding the best interests of a child of divorce, and that it may even be unethical for a mental health professional to provide an opinion regarding who would be the best parent when there is no scientific foundation for doing so (Tippins & Wittmann, 2005). Bricklin and Halbert (2004) suggested, however, that certain psychological tests increase the scientific credibility afforded to child custody evaluations.

As a diagnostician in child custody evaluation cases, the marriage and family therapist conducts an assessment, offers a detailed view of the family dynamics, and provides recommendations regarding the form of custody and/or visitation in a report addressed primarily to the judge and attorneys. Although the specifics of law and expectations for such reports vary among jurisdictions, most reports are expected minimally to include recommendations about the structure of how decisions should be made, the primary residence for the child(ren), and the amount of time to be spent with each parent. Other recommendations might include such things as the need for therapy by family members. Typically, the attorneys and parties use the report as a fulcrum to leverage further discussion. If the parties cannot reach agreement, however, the report and its recommendations can become a central focus of the court in its decision making (Lebow, 1992).

Lebow (1992) proposed guidelines for marriage and family therapists to consider in systemically evaluating custody disputes. These are offered in Figure 8–3. In addition,

FIGURE 8–3 Some Guidelines for Custody Evaluation

1. Don't try to do this without special training.
2. Establish your independence. If you conduct an evaluation at the behest of one party, you are likely to be treated as biased and of limited credibility. Always look to be appointed by the judge or at the agreement of both parties.
3. Develop at least a cursory understanding of the law about custody and visitation in your state.
4. Get in writing the parameters of your role and an agreement about who pays your fee.
5. See parents alone, children alone, and each parent with children. Pay a home visit if you can.
6. Always balance. Never do something with one parent you are not prepared to do with the other.
7. Listen with an open mind, while remembering the power of personal construction.
8. Encourage the presentation of simple information, like police reports, that confirms or disputes the occurrence of events.
9. Employ standardized tests. Not only can these offer valuable information, they increase credibility considerably.
10. Don't try to be a detective or the judge.
11. Make recommendations that promote the long-term welfare of children. In almost all cases, our knowledge base tells us this involves the inclusion of both parents in some shape or form in the children's lives.
12. Remember the focus of your evaluation: a recommendation for custody and visitation that is in the best interest of the children.
13. Look to research data whenever it is possible to support your recommendations.
14. If you can't decide about something, say so.
15. Make your recommendation clearly. Always speak to custody, residence, visitation, and other needs of the family (e.g., therapy . . . always explain why you are deciding what you are deciding).
16. Be prepared for cases to take a long time to reach resolution through the court. Although some court systems are quite quick to adjudicate matters, many are slow; even when the court itself moves for speed, lawyers may move slowly. Take thorough notes that will help you recall your process a year or two later. Take comfort in the fact that in most jurisdictions, 80%–90% of these cases settle before trial.
17. If asked or subpoenaed to appear before the court for deposition or trial, cooperate; but know and assert your rights. You usually can establish a good amount of control over scheduling. Answer questions as best you can. Don't try to answer questions you can't.
18. Employ a lawyer to help you prepare for testimony. Court appearances should only be undertaken with careful preparation.
19. Know thy biases. These cases pull for massive countertransference. Some parents are truly monstrous; many are in the process of using their children as self-objects in the pursuit of their battles with their spouses. Gender bias also needs to be explored.
20. Use every opportunity to explicate and promote a systemic viewpoint. Lawyers, judges, and others who work in the area of family law are the first and often most influential contact point for a wide array of distressed families. Typically, their training offers them little background in systemic understanding or the role of marital and family therapists. The evaluator is perfectly positioned to educate these professionals about family systems, not only specifically about the cases served but also with regard to others.

Source. Reprinted from Volume 23 Number 2 of *Family Therapy News,* Copyright 1992, American Association for Marriage and Family Therapy. Reprinted by permission.

L. Hunter (2005) has called for the development of practice standards in the area of child custody evaluations by professional associations of mental health professionals.

Resource Expert

A second major function of marriage and family therapists serving in the role of treatment specialist is that of resource expert. Courts are continually in need of information regarding referral resources, particularly for use in the disposition of youths and their families. Identification and categorization of referral resources require knowledge of treatment modalities and a constant updating of information on the facilities providing treatment. To the court, it is the quality of the information and the credibility of the treatment specialist that are crucial. Evans (1983) asserted that the following information regarding referral resources should be submitted to the court: (a) information describing the "primary" program being recommended, (b) the relationship of the program to the court, and (c) information about other available programs.

"Primary" Program Characteristics

The treatment specialist should be prepared to offer his or her "primary" recommendation given the circumstances of the case and his or her understanding of the way the recommendation will fit with available referral resources. This includes a detailed description of the services offered by the recommended program, the clients served, the referral procedure, the cost and duration of structured programs, funding sources and location, the director or contact person, and the telephone number.

The Relationship of the Facility to the Court

It is important that the recommended program establish and maintain contact with the court, probation department, or other relevant personnel. Will the program's facilitators accept court referrals that require them to report back to the court and possibly make court appearances? There may also be questions of payment, the acceptance of juvenile offenders, and the ethical implications of accepting a court-ordered referral.

An Inventory of Other Available Programs

An up-to-date list of other available programs should include some subjective and evaluative comments regarding the reputation, outcome of program involvement, and treatment modality used, in addition to the typical objective data described for the primary recommendation. With some youthful offenders, the court may be highly sensitive to security issues, for example. Thus, if the court sees a need for a secure facility that is fully accredited and licensed, a program that meets these criteria on the list of alternatives may override the therapist's recommendation of an innovative drug program that seemed ideal and which was the primary recommendation to the treatment specialist.

Treatment Provider

The third function of marriage and family therapists as treatment specialists involves providing direct treatment services to families and their individual members at various points during the court process. Shrybman and Halpern's (1979) summarization of a child abuse–related hearing process in juvenile court illustrated a successful method for handling intervention times in such a setting:

> Utilizing the instance of a complaint of abuse and neglect, said complaint can be initiated by the filing of a petition (written complaint) in the juvenile court alleging that a child has been abused or neglected. The petition may be written and filed by the county attorney, the juvenile probation officer, and/or county social worker according to state law and local court procedures. (Some states allow anyone to file a petition alleging a child has been abused or neglected.)

In emergency situations in which there is imminent danger to the child in remaining with the parent(s), the child may be removed from the custody of the parent(s) and placed in protective custody pending the outcome of the juvenile court proceeding. This decision may be made by the police, juvenile probation, child protective services, and/or a physician, depending on state law. Whenever a child is placed in protective custody, a petition must be filed in juvenile court, usually within 24 to 48 hours, and a hearing must be held soon thereafter (usually within 48 to 72 hours, depending upon state law), to allow a judge to review the decision.

There must be an evidentiary trial in which the state must prove to a judge that a child has been abused or neglected. Unless the parent(s) admit to abusing or neglecting their child, it is necessary to call witnesses to substantiate the allegations of abuse or neglect. This is called an *adjudicatory hearing* and normally occurs from two to six weeks after the initial petition is filed. Because dependency (the idea that the child is in need of services that the parent[s] cannot provide and therefore is dependent upon the state to see that they are provided) is technically a civil rather than criminal issue, the state need not prove abuse or neglect beyond a reasonable doubt, only by a preponderance of evidence, a somewhat lower standard of proof.

Child abuse and neglect proceedings are usually "bifurcated proceedings," meaning the decision about what should be done with the child occurs in a separate hearing from that which determines whether the child is, in fact, abused or neglected. A dispositional hearing, analogous to the sentencing hearing in a criminal case, may occur on the same day as the adjudication hearing or it may be held at another time, sometimes weeks later. The dispositional hearing generally focuses on those recommendations made to the judge regarding the appropriate order for the child. An important point to understand regarding the disposition order is that the court has leverage over parents only by its jurisdiction over their child. Thus, the court cannot directly enforce its orders against parents of a child by fines, imprisonment, or threats of either. The court can, however, after finding that a child has been abused or neglected, order that the child remain in the home of the parents on the provision that the entire family participate in therapy efforts. If the parents fail to comply, the court can then order the child removed from the home and placed in a foster home or other care setting.

In some states, no review hearings are held. In others, they are an integral part of the hearing process. After a child has been declared dependent by the court, the court retains jurisdiction over that child until the child reaches adulthood or until the dependency status is ended by the court. In order to measure the progress of the case and determine any need to modify a previous order, courts will generally hold periodic hearings to review the case every six months to a year.

In their function as treatment providers, marriage and family therapists work closely with the court and associated state social service personnel to formulate and facilitate families' follow-through on treatment plans designed to protect their children and improve the family situation with the primary purpose of preserving the family system. Intervention can come at any point in the process, beginning with the initial petition and concluding with a successful treatment outcome culminated with dependency status being terminated by the court at a follow-up hearing sometime subsequent to the disposition order.

Mediation

For some time, marriage and family therapists have had fundamental questions about the legal system's response to families experiencing divorce. Therapists who have seen family conflicts exacerbated by courtroom experiences have sought alternatives to the traditional procedures for legally dissolving marriages. The central issue raised has been the adversarial orientation embedded within the very structure of the court system.

Trained to operate within this adversarial system, divorce lawyers typically see their job as getting the best possible settlement for their particular client, while remaining relatively unconcerned about the impact of the settlement on the entire family system. Nor do they see their role as including helping a family to negotiate the emotional minefield of divorce. Law schools do not pretend to prepare their students to appreciate the psychological dilemmas divorcing families must face. Although family law constitutes a primary component of most law programs, there is rarely more than a passing reference to the personal and family trauma involved or to the effect of divorce on children (Vroom, 1983).

Mediation is used increasingly as an alternative to court action (Hahn & Kleist, 2000). A cooperative dispute resolution process in which a neutral intervener helps disputing parties negotiate a mutually satisfactory settlement of their conflict, mediation stresses honesty, informality, and open and direct communication. It also facilitates emotional expressiveness, attention to underlying causes of disputes, reinforcement of positive bonds, and avoidance of blame (Deutsch, 1973; Felstiner & Williams, 1978). Many lawyers believe, however, that individuals seeking a divorce must have attorneys involved in a fair mediation process (N. J. Foster & Kelly, 1996; Gangel-Jacob, 1997).

According to proponents, mediation relieves court dockets that are clogged with divorce and child custody actions, reduces the alienation of litigants, inspires durable consensual agreements, and helps families to resume workable relationships even though the parents are legally divorced. Further, the process itself is significantly less traumatic and less costly to the participants (Blades, 1984; DelCampo & Anderson, 1992). Comparisons of mediation and court adjudication have shown that mediation encourages settlement, generates a higher degree of user satisfaction, improves communication and understanding in families, results in more cooperative coparenting, and reduces the incidence of divorce relitigation (J. Pearson & Thoennes, 1982). Conciliation courts in many states offer mediation as a court-related service for families with parents seeking divorce. The family sits down with a mediator to resolve disputed areas rather than have a judge impose a resolution. For years, the Family Court System in Australia has used such court-related mediation services as the primary method of working out visitation, child custody, spousal maintenance, and child support questions (McKenzie, 1978).

In actual practice, divorce and family mediation can look much like couples counseling or family therapy. As in family therapy, husband and wife sit together in a room with a third person who facilitates their communication (although some mediators may see each party separately and perform a kind of "shuttle diplomacy"). When appropriate, children are brought into the decision making. There are some differences between mediation and family therapy, however. The primary difference is that the mediator begins with the understanding that it is the clear intention of the family to physically break up (Vroom, 1983). The task of the mediator is then to create an environment in which productive negotiation in areas of conflict can occur.

Generally, the mediation process is viewed as progressing in stages such as the following:

1. Setting the stage by providing a neutral setting, introducing oneself as a mediator, establishing ground rules, and gaining the disputants' commitment to mediation.
2. Defining the issues by eliciting facts and expression of needs, desires, and feelings.
3. Processing the issues by managing emotions, encouraging empathy, narrowing differences, exploring solutions, and maintaining positive momentum.
4. Resolving the issues by offering concessions, evaluating alternative solutions, and tentatively coming to an agreement.
5. Formalizing an agreement that is realistic and positively framed; details are specified in a concrete, understandable manner to ensure implementation by all concerned (DelCampo & Anderson, 1992; New Mexico Center for Dispute Resolution, 1990).

This type of stage conceptualization is used by virtually all the practitioners who have developed and published model approaches to divorce and family mediation. For example, Kessler (1978) emphasized the need to systematically progress from the beginning to final stage. Rules need to be established at the beginning to create a secure atmosphere and avoid the violation of "unspoken" rules by either party at critical moments later in the mediation. Processing and resolving issues prior to their proper definition may result in wasted energy. Kessler clearly defines specific mediator goals, focuses, and techniques appropriate to each mediation stage.

M. Black and Joffee (1978) outlined a stage approach to mediation comparable to Kessler's, although they also delineated a division of labor for attorney–mental health professional teams. With the attorney focusing on settlement details and the mental health professional dealing with emotional and communication issues, the team helps families to simultaneously achieve a legal and psychological divorce.

Milne (1978), a social worker, outlined a very specific procedure that involves extensive information gathering and emotional ventilation prior to the generation of a mediation settlement. Believing that emotional issues are at the root of most custody battles, Milne advocated instructing each disputant to prepare an autobiography and spend one mediation session reviewing the marriage and the decision to divorce. During following sessions, the parties describe existing and desired custody and visitation arrangements. The mediator also meets with the children and communicates the information to the parties. The mediator then solicits resolution proposals from the parties and helps them combine these proposals and/or generate new ones.

In contrast, Coogler (1978), a lawyer with training as a therapist, identified economic issues as underlying most custody battles. His model calls for extensive information gathering on financial matters and property issues. After an orientation to the mediation process, the disputants work out a temporary arrangement regarding child and financial issues. Next, they do homework that involves identifying assets and preparing budgets and income statements. Subsequent sessions are devoted to dividing property and generating acceptable maintenance and child support arrangements. Custody and visitation matters are tackled last. Each party submits two property settlement plans: one in the event they receive custody, the other in the event they do not. The goal of the process is to prevent children from becoming pawns in their parents' financial battles. The resolution of financial issues is believed to lead to resolution of emotional issues.

Another mediation model was developed by Haynes (1981), a social worker with experience in labor mediation. Haynes also offered a stage approach. Initially, the process is explained and basic data on the marriage and impending divorce collected. The parties then meet with the mediator individually to assess their areas of agreement and disagreement, power relationship, communication style, and potential divorce adjustment. The mediator also seeks to balance the couple's power relationship by educating the weaker party about negotiation strategies, divorce finances, and the adjustment process. The mediator then meets with the parties jointly to identify points of agreement and narrow the issues in dispute. The parties are then separated, and the mediator uses shuttle diplomacy techniques to relay trial proposals, encourage trade-offs, and suggest compromises. The parties are brought together again when it seems they have reached a settlement.

DelCampo and Anderson (1992) proposed that adversarial court proceedings only produce increased stress among already stressed families. They cited Kass (1990) and Gardner (1989) in asserting that such adversarial proceedings encourage family members to turn against each other and force win-lose situations. Although the court may order a decision, its decision does not necessarily stop the fighting and disagreements. Instead, the conflict frequently becomes intensified, particularly over the long term. As DelCampo and Anderson stated, "Only the disputing family members can fully resolve their conflicts" (p. 77). Mediation offers families a setting in which this can occur.

THE MARRIAGE AND FAMILY THERAPIST AS EXPERT WITNESS

Recognition by the courts that family influences play a significant part in determining litigants' behavior has expanded the role of marriage and family therapists to encompass that of expert witness. For many marriage and family therapists, however, the courtroom may be an unfamiliar environment with different ground rules and basic assumptions. Testifying as an expert witness may require the therapist to reconsider the situational role demands normally encountered in therapeutic settings. Although marriage and family therapists have the knowledge and expertise necessary to serve in courts as expert witnesses, they should attend training seminars and read materials on the topic (e.g., Gould, 1998; Weikel & Hughes, 1993) before accepting cases.

Brodsky and Robey (1972) identified the ideal role of the expert witness as "that of a detached, thoroughly neutral individual who simply and informatively presents the true facts as he sees them" (p. 173). Likewise, others have asserted that the position of the mental health professional as expert witness should be to strive to be impartial, free from prejudice, and not act as an advocate for either side (Bromberg, 1979; MacDonald, 1969; Slovenko, 1973). The expert witness is specifically defined as one who "formulate[s] a presented opinion in court based on [his or her] specialized knowledge" (Remley, 1991, p. 39). When a marriage and family therapist is called on to testify as an expert witness, he or she is explicitly appointed by the court to prepare and provide a professional opinion relative to the case in question emanating from his or her specialized knowledge.

The Rules of Evidence

Understanding the rules of evidence employed in the courtroom is the most fundamental issue that marriage and family therapists must consider. These rules have evolved to promote the goals of the law, specifically, to facilitate a fair trial. The marriage and family therapist can tailor a therapeutic plan to the needs of clients; if one intervention does not produce the desired results, intervention efforts can be redirected. Courts cannot afford this luxury. They must solve presenting problems in a timely manner, and the solutions must be applicable to persons with similar problems. A court reaches a solution to a problem on the basis of presented evidence. The rules of evidence, therefore, are of utmost importance because they determine what will be allowed to come before the court. No professional function in the legal system can occur without an allegiance to the rules of evidence (Woody & Mitchell, 1984).

Almost anyone who is "professionally acquainted with, skilled, or trained in some science, art, trade, and thereby has knowledge or experience in matters not generally familiar to the public" can serve as an expert witness (Schwitzgebel & Schwitzgebel, 1980, p. 238). The expert witness may offer opinions or inferences and may respond to hypothetical questions, in contrast with the lay witness, who must have had direct contact with the action or expression—otherwise, the testimony would be hearsay and not admissible.

The expert witness may be allowed to offer testimony based on indirect observation. For example, many jurisdictions will allow a professional to testify about data collected by another professional who is part of a team effort; in a child custody case, for example, a marriage and family therapist may be allowed to cite a home visitation report made by a child services worker. Usually, however, any source of information, such as the child services worker, is expected to be personally available for testimony to accommodate cross-examination by the attorney for the party being testified against (Woody & Mitchell, 1984).

Opinion testimony must be directly aligned with the issue in question and must include a concrete description of facts. Opinion evidence also must be such that the state of the present scientific body of knowledge permits a reasonable opinion to be asserted by an expert (Cleary, 1972). Examining attorneys will frequently preface or summarize their questioning of an expert witness by asking, "Have you derived or formed an opinion based on your professional knowledge and with a reasonable degree of professional certainty?" Because experts must be qualified by a judge before they testify, expert witnesses are usually asked to cite their qualifications relevant to their professional knowledge on the subject and to enter a copy of their professional credentials into the court record.

Hypothetical questions comprise another area where experts may be allowed to testify without firsthand, observation-based knowledge of the parties involved (Woody & Mitchell, 1984). Judges are free to decide whether or not to allow testimony based on hypothetical facts that closely parallel the characteristics of the parties or circumstances of the current case. If such testimony were erroneously admitted, however, it would present the probable basis for an appeal. For example, a judge could be led to believe that certain data were obtained through normally accepted data collection methods of a profession and therefore qualified as an exception to the hearsay rule. If the methods were not commonly used, however, the information would definitely be hearsay. And if a case were determined based on that evidence, an appeal would be in order.

Some jurisdictions allow reports to be submitted as evidence, whereas others will not allow reports unless the author is available for in-court cross-examination (or is available for cross-examination under oath via a deposition). There are some exceptions, such as illness, incapacitation, and death. Cross-examination, however, maintains strong traditional importance:

> For two centuries, common law judges and lawyers have regarded the opportunity of cross-examination as an essential safeguard of the accuracy and completeness of testimony, and they have insisted that the opportunity is a right, and not a mere privilege. . . . And the premise that the opportunity of cross-examination is an essential safeguard has been the principal justification for the exclusion generally of hearsay statements, and for the admission as an exception to the hearsay rule of reported testimony taken at a former hearing when the present adversary was afforded the opportunity to cross-examine. Finally, state constitutional provisions guaranteeing to the accused the right of confrontation have been interpreted as codifying this right of cross-examination. (Cleary, 1972, pp. 43–44)

Courtroom Testimony

An expert witness generally testifies at the request of a representative attorney, although an expert can be requested to give testimony by both attorneys or by the court. Irrespective of the basis of the expert's entry into a case, however, testimony should reflect expertise, preparation, and perhaps most importantly, complete candor. Sidley and Petrila (1985) outlined a slate of strategies applicable to marriage and family therapists serving as expert witnesses.

Preparation

The successful presentation of testimony depends to a large degree on the willingness of the witness and requesting attorney to prepare for court. There are a number of preparatory steps that expert witnesses should concern themselves with.

1. Provide the requesting attorney with a written list of qualifications; for example, include information about education, years in practice, publications, and other pertinent information that demonstrates familiarity with the subject of the upcoming testimony.
2. If the testimony will involve a particular client, review and become familiar with the client's records. Particularly be aware of the frequency of sessions with the client.
3. Acquire at least a rudimentary understanding of the legal issues involved in the case. This information can be most readily obtained from the requesting attorney.
4. Insist that the requesting attorney take the time to prepare and discuss the questions he or she intends to ask on direct examination. The attorney should also assist in anticipating and discussing questions that are likely to be asked on cross-examination. Issues of information protected by confidentiality or privilege particularly need to be addressed at this time.
5. If you are going to testify for the first time as an expert witness, visit a court in session in advance and observe the examination and cross-examination of a number of witnesses.

Direct Examination

The requesting attorney presents his or her side of a case through direct examination of the expert witness. The goal of the requesting attorney and expert witness on direct examination is to present the technical aspects of the case in layperson's terms so that the judge and, when present, jury may understand. In direct examination, the attorney cannot "lead" the witness; that is, the witness must testify without the aid of suggestions from the attorney conducting the examination. Preparation by expert witnesses before court appearances is essential for success (Taylor, 2004). This is one example of why precourt preparation is so valuable. In-court considerations are also of paramount importance as well.

1. The expert witness must remember that the judge or jury is the ultimate decider of what is "fact" in a given case. Thus, in presenting testimony to the fact finder, the witness may enhance effectiveness and credibility by carefully attending to his or her courtroom image.
   a. Arrive on time.
   b. Concentrate on courtroom etiquette, especially in addressing the judge as "Your Honor."
   c. Dress conservatively and neatly.
   d. Maintain a generally serious demeanor; do not talk about the case in hallways, restrooms, or other public places.
   e. Avoid displaying nervous mannerisms (e.g., wringing hands or pencil tapping).

2. The manner in which the expert witness listens and responds to the requesting attorney's questions is similarly important.
   a. Listen carefully to each question, and be certain that you understand the question. If necessary, request that the question be repeated.
   b. Directly and simply, in appropriate layperson's language, answer the question asked and then stop. Do not volunteer information.
   c. Address the judge or jury when responding, rather than the attorney who asked the question. Never forget that it is the jury or judge who weigh the testimony.
   d. Speak clearly, slowly, and sufficiently loud so all present can hear, remembering that the court reporter is recording the proceedings. "Yes" and "no" responses must be spoken, not given as head shakes.
   e. Questions should never be answered in a joking or arrogant manner.
   f. Pointedly avoid exaggeration and misrepresentation in answering.
   g. Answers should be given as confidently as possible; avoiding using words such as "perhaps" or "possibly."
      (1) Mere speculation or possibility is usually not relevant to a legal decision, which demands at least a preponderance of the evidence. This means that any proposition presented should be more probably true than not. Therefore, in any situation involving less than certainty in an expert witness's testimony, the expert must be prepared to give a reasonable appraisal of how probable the proposition is. The usual, still ambiguous standard sought is "to a professional certainty."
      (2) Qualifying words like "possibly" suggest uncertainty and lack of confidence.
   h. If the answer to a question is unknown or can only be estimated, clearly state such qualification when answering. The expert witness is only human, and fact finders appreciate an honest recognition of this point.

    i.   Avoid looking at the examining attorney or judge in a manner that suggests seeking their assistance.

    j.   When an objection is made by the nonexamining attorney, stop until the court or that attorney indicates it is acceptable to continue.

Cross-Examination

After direct examination, in which the expert witness has usually been questioned in a sympathetic manner by the requesting attorney, the opposing attorney cross-examines the witness. During cross-examination, the opposing attorney will attempt to discredit the expert witness by asking leading questions and framing questions in a manner that requires a "yes" or a "no" answer favorable to that attorney's position on the case. The opposing attorney generally will seek to test the credibility of both the substance of the expert's testimony and the expert as well.

Common methods of attempting to discredit the expert witness include the following:

1. Challenging the thoroughness of an evaluation by asking if the examiner was aware of certain facts when performing an evaluation. Sometimes, certain facts that may bear on the expert's opinion surface only during the court proceedings. It is, of course, perfectly reasonable on cross-examination to ask if those facts change the expert's opinion, as indeed they might. The requesting attorney calling the expert should apprise him or her of those facts; otherwise, the opposing attorney may take the expert by surprise, with potentially disastrous consequences for the requesting attorney's case.
2. Challenging the witness by the use of treatises giving an opinion contrary to that of the witness.
3. Challenging the witness by attempting to demonstrate that his or her viewpoint, as presented on direct examination, is either internally inconsistent or has changed over time.
4. Challenging the expert by attempting to show that he or she is incompetent because of a lack of necessary training or experience. Although this will not serve to disqualify the expert after having been qualified previously, it may reduce the value in the fact finder's eyes of any testimony given. For example, the cross-examiner may deliberately ask obscure questions from the witness's field.
5. Challenging the expert by attempting to show that he or she has a financial interest in the outcome of the case.

The opposing attorney may ask one or more trick questions in an effort to discredit the expert witness. Examples include:

1. "Have you talked to anyone about this case?" A response of "no" is easily disproved, because inevitably the witness has discussed the case with others, normally including the requesting attorney for whom he or she has already testified. A response of "yes" may lead the opposing attorney to suggest that the witness was told what to say. The best response is to simply acknowledge that the case was discussed. If the cross-examiner persists, the witness can mention that he or she was advised only to tell the truth.

2. "Are you being paid to testify in this case?" This question implies that the expert's testimony is for sale. An appropriate answer to this question is, "I am not being paid to testify. I am being compensated for time I have spent on this case and for my expenses associated with it."

The expert who is undergoing cross-examination must remember that his or her demeanor and style of presentation are even more important on cross-examination than on direct examination. Further considerations in this regard include the following:

1. Above all, remain calm and answer the opposing attorney's questions in a courteous manner. Avoid becoming upset or angry on the witness stand. A cross-examiner who is able to provoke an expert to an emotional display has scored a major triumph.
2. Ask to have a question repeated if it is not clearly understood.
3. Indicate when a "yes" or "no" answer is insufficient and that an explanation is necessary by responding, "That requires more explanation than a simple 'yes/no' answer." (Remember that the cross-examiner will attempt to restrict the witness to "yes" or "no" answers.)
4. Refrain from asking the judge if you must answer a given question. If the question is improper, the requesting attorney should object to it. Remember that the court proceedings are primarily orchestrated by the attorneys. If the attorney who requests the expert's presence is at all competent, he or she will know better than the expert whether to object to a question or allow it to be presented to the expert without challenge. It is advisable for the expert and the requesting attorney to discuss in advance how to deal with such questions on cross-examination.

Redirect Examination

After cross-examination is concluded, the requesting attorney who originally called the expert witness will have the opportunity to redirect examination. This gives that attorney and the witness the opportunity to offer clarification on any points made by the opposing attorney during cross-examination. A further round of cross-examination may follow the redirect examination.

Marriage and family therapists must prepare themselves for the emotional experience of having their opinions discredited and their credentials questioned. Lawyers have at their disposal professional materials designed to assist them in attacking the testimony of mental health experts (e.g., Becker, 1997; Hagan, 1997; Ziskin, 1995). Marriage and family therapists are advised to take the time to prepare themselves sufficiently before making themselves available for expert testimony.

Systemic Understandings and Expert Testimony

Meyerstein and Todd (1980) asserted that marriage and family therapists who can transfer their systemic understandings from the therapy context to the courtroom significantly enhance their effectiveness as expert witnesses. These authors paralleled the courtroom context with a family environment. For example, they noted the unique physical arrangement evident in a courtroom that immediately and graphically conveys the hierarchy of positions and nature of the contest. Likewise, the activities of the courtroom are governed by rules that possess their own internal logic and order; the system is based on a theory predicating that the truth will emerge from the oppositional presentation of the best arguments that can be made for each side of the conflict.

Meyerstein and Todd (1980) proposed that marriage and family therapists enter the courtroom and redefine the setting as simply a different kind of system. Although different, it is still a system in which certain predictable phenomena occur. The therapist's task is to apply available information and transfer it to the interactional skills within the court context. Particularly valuable strategic suggestions in this regard included redefining the problem and dealing with resistance.

Redefining the Problem

Perhaps the key technique of a skilled marriage and family therapist is the art of redefining the problem, or reframing (P. Watzlawick et al., 1974). The therapist challenges the couple's or family's view of a problem and presents an alternative explanation of the same set of facts in a way that facilitates change through a shift in context. By using reframing, the witness should feel free to engage in a persuasive teaching and advocacy of his or her position (Brodsky & Robey, 1972). This often entails elaboration, systematic repetition, and intensification of ideas using commonsense examples familiar to laypersons to illustrate concepts clearly.

Meyerstein and Todd (1980) described the case example of a marriage and family therapist called to give testimony as an expert witness in a civil commitment suit filed against an adult male by his parents. The prosecutor portrayed the defendant as insane and beyond rehabilitation. He advocated for an indefinite commitment to a state institution, suggesting a belief that contextual family and community factors were irrelevant both to the defendant's emotional disturbance and his treatment. The therapist as expert witness sought to provide a clearer, more encompassing contextual view:

> **Question:** Are you saying that the blame can't really be placed on either side?
>
> **Answer:** All of them participated in this situation and the outcome was a result, but it's not really one party's fault. The parents have a good deal of love for both their boys, but in their parenting approach they had been so lenient with them that they never put any regulation on them, and they were so worried about their welfare that they could never leave them alone. If he was six or eight I would say that he was a bad boy, that he was disobedient, stubborn and childish. He's not six or eight or 10, but 29. Perhaps he should be seen as an ungrateful son. No doubt, in recent events the defendant equally participated in maintaining the closeness in the family which became detrimental to his and the parents' growth. The defendant has continued to reinvolve his parents and they comply. There is no question . . . the difficulty separating has been a two-sided thing. (p. 47)

The therapist viewed her task as illustrating an interactional picture of the problem by highlighting, in a sympathetic manner, participation of family members in maintaining the defendant's problem. Furthermore, the witness used developmental analogies to reframe the behavior in question from "sick" to "immature" and "disobedient" to construct a more normalized and, thus, treatable view of the disability.

Dealing with Resistance

The marriage and family therapist is no stranger to the strategic handling of resistance in therapy situations. The most effective path is to go with resistance initially and then redirect it. This skill is particularly relevant during cross-examination in the courtroom setting as well. The cross-examining attorney ordinarily has a well-practiced repertoire consisting of clever phrasings. The grammatical logic of these phrases are intended to create doubt and rejection of the expert witness's testimony in the minds of the judge or jury. Any discrepancy uncovered in the testimony given may cause the witness to redouble efforts at explaining apparent inconsistencies. Backtracking and correcting misimpressions may leave the witness looking flustered and defensive.

A common tactic used by cross-examining attorneys in this regard is to ask questions that begin, "Would you be surprised if I were to tell you that . . . ?" Meyerstein and Todd (1980) offered the following example taken from a right-to-treatment suit on behalf of mental hospital patients:

> **Question:** So, would you assume that the people in the higher staff positions are basically unfamiliar with the community based programs, that sort of orientation?
>
> **Answer:** I would suspect that, yes.
>
> **Question:** Would it surprise you if I were to tell you that [the hospital superintendent] is a former Executive Director of [a] community mental health center?
>
> **Answer:** Yes, that would surprise me.
>
> **Question:** Would it surprise you to know that he was a consultant to the Department of Health, Education, and Welfare, in community mental health, from 1970 to '74?
>
> **Answer:** Based on the operation he's running at [the mental hospital], that surprises me a great deal. (pp. 49–50)[2]

Being opaque and calling the questioner's bluff with a calm "Yes, that would surprise me" obviously is preferable to equivocating and attempting to reconcile apparent inconsistencies. And, if the cross-examining attorney does procure contradictory evidence to compromise the witness, it is still possible for the witness to have an opportunity to explain on redirect examination. The expert witness should pursue proper preparation to be sure of his or her facts and conclusions.

PROFESSIONAL LIABILITY UNDER THE LAW

Always implicit, and frequently explicit, in legal discussions regarding the practice of marriage and family therapy is the concept of therapists' responsibility and professional liability. Most legal authorities agree that if a therapist is to act legally, then he or she must behave responsibly. Responsible behavior seems clearly to be at least a necessary, if not a sufficient, condition for legal behavior (Widiger & Rorer, 1984). Legally, therapists have a responsibility to communicate to their clients an honest representation of their skills and methods, along with the conditions of treatment, fees, appointment schedules, and any special obligations incumbent on either the therapist or client. Clients' informed consent

---

[2]*Note.* From "On the Witness Stand: The Family Therapist and Expert Testimony," by I. Meyerstein and J. C. Todd, 1980, *The American Journal of Family Therapy, 8*(4), pp. 47, 49–50. Copyright 1980. Reprinted with permission.

should always be obtained. The understanding that develops during the initial contacts becomes, in effect, an unwritten agreement. (The terms of therapy may be established in a written document as well.) Each party has a responsibility to abide by the agreement. If the agreement is breached, the remedy may be legal action (Van Hoose & Kottler, 1985). Marriage and family therapists' major areas of legal responsibility and thus liability are centered on civil liability, including contract law, unintentional torts or malpractice, and intentional torts (Lifson & Simon, 1998; Remley & Herlihy, 2001; Schultz, 1982).

Contract Law

Contractually, marriage and family therapists' legal responsibility to their clients and thus their liability comes from a conception of the therapist–client relationship as a fiduciary one. *Black's Law Dictionary* (1968) says a *fiduciary* relationship "exists where there is a special confidence reposed in one who in equity and good conscience is bound to act in good faith and with due regard to interests of one reposing the confidence" (p. 753). Anderson and Hopkins (1996) suggested that a fiduciary relationship fosters the highest level of trust and confidence.

A fiduciary relationship is, in essence, based on trust; the therapist, as fiduciary of the client's trust, cannot serve his or her own needs in preference to those of the client. Schultz (1982) stated that a therapist is not strictly a fiduciary because the commonly called-for requirement of absolute candor is normally not present: "The therapeutic privilege—instances where the therapist withholds information in the interest of the patient and the treatment—may contraindicate it; and the maintenance of early rapport, so that later confrontations may be handled, also cuts into the degree of candor that best serves the patient" (pp. 12–13). Despite this concept of therapeutic privilege, the therapeutic relationship is still a fee-for-services relationship. It has implied contractual elements and legal responsibility and thus liability is present through contract law.

Schultz (1982) raised a number of situations in which therapists might be liable under contract law. For example, the fee-for-services aspect of the therapeutic relationship can be construed as a situation in which the therapist has a compelling personal interest that takes precedent over the client's interest, that is, preserving his or her income. A marriage and family therapist who recommends that a couple or family not terminate treatment or that the frequency of sessions be increased without a sound therapeutic rationale could be open to a charge of fiduciary abuse. Likewise, the therapist who tells clients that treatment will be successful can be sued for breach of warranty if the predicted outcome does not occur. Reassurances should always be couched in probabilistic terms. Therapists who hold themselves out as guarantors of success can be held to that, even though it is not a normally expected responsibility.

Marriage and family therapists can carry out their legal responsibilities more definitively by the use of explicit, written contracts specifying roles and duties. They can shape such contracts to accurately reflect what they can provide for a fee. At the same time, however, precisely because of their clarity, expressed contracts can make breach of contract or warranty easier to prove (Malcolm, 1988). Moreover, reducing the complexity involved in the therapeutic enterprise to the confined context of an explicit contract may reinforce clients' tendency to view the relationship solely in terms of the conditions described in the contract, therefore increasing the likelihood of litigation (Schultz, 1982). The client can point to the contract and say, "We didn't get what we paid for." On the other hand, research has indicated that clients want information about their prospective counselors (Braaten, Otto, & Handelsman, 1993) and that clients perceive counselors who provide information as being more expert and trustworthy (Walter & Handelsman, 1996).

Although contractual liability is potentially a source of litigation, it is a relatively infrequent approach to legal liability for psychotherapeutic dissatisfaction (Hendrickson, 1982; Schultz, 1982). Primary liability has been through tort liability.

In general, tort liability is a civil wrong that does not arise out of contractual liability (Hendrickson & Mangum, 1978). Torts arise out of a responsibility to protect individuals from harm resulting from socially unacceptable behavior. A *tort* is a type of harm done to an individual in such a manner that the law orders the person who inflicts the harm to pay damages to the injured party. Torts may be intentional or unintentional.

Unintentional Torts: Malpractice

Corey et al. (1984) defined *malpractice* as "the failure to render proper service, through ignorance or negligence, resulting in injury or loss to the client" (p. 229). In order to prove malpractice, four key elements must be shown to be present (Prosser, Wade, & Schwartz, 1988; Schultz, 1982):

1. A therapist–client relationship was established.
2. The therapist's conduct fell below the acceptable standard of care.
3. This conduct was the cause of an injury to the client.
4. An actual injury was sustained by the client.

Professional Relationship

The existence of the therapist–client relationship is usually the easiest of the four elements to prove; normally, a bill for the therapist's services is sufficient evidence. Casual conversations could be interpreted by courts as professional relationships if marriage and family therapists listen to a person's personal problems and offer advice regarding the situation.

Standard of Care

Establishing the acceptable standard of care in a given case is more difficult. First, there are numerous schools within the psychotherapeutic community advocating different treatment approaches to the same presenting problem, so almost any treatment activity will probably be endorsed somewhere. In writing on tort liability, Prosser (1971) clarifies this, however, in stating:

> A "school" must be a recognized one with definite principles, and it must be the line of thought of at least a respectable minority of the profession. In addition there are minimum requirements of skill and knowledge as to both diagnosis and treatment, particular in light of modern licensing statutes which anyone who holds himself out as competent to treat human ailments is required to have, regardless of his personal views. (p. 163)

Schultz (1982) highlighted two situations in which therapists might not be judged according to the tenets of a particular school: (a) if the therapist does not profess membership (if, for example, he or she advocates a professional eclecticism), he or she will then be held to the standard of care of a therapist "in good standing" who will be called on to testify as an expert witness in the case; and (b) if the approach is so innovative that the therapist is the only person capable of expert testimony, then his or her testimony will be held to a general standard of reasonableness, as evaluated by the judge and/or jury. Obviously, marriage and family therapists who adhere to a particular school carry less liability in that the scope of a standard of care is clarified. Such clarity will aid those therapists falling within the scope, but it may hurt when practices employed are at odds with the school's principles or with commonsense expectations; innovation could appear as negligence.

Traditionally, the standard of care for psychotherapeutic practice has been based on what other practitioners in the same geographical area would do under similar circumstances. This is still the predominant frame of reference; however, because information has become increasingly more accessible, this "locality rule" is being replaced by national standards of practice. In addition to expert testimony, published professional standards are allowed as a yardstick in a number of states, particularly if they are standards of a school or group with whom the therapist identifies.

Once a standard of care has been determined, the plaintiff must show that a breach of this standard occurred, in that the therapist did not exercise (a) the minimally accepted degree of knowledge or skill possessed by other practitioners, or (b) the minimally accepted degree of care, attention, or diligence exercised in the application of that knowledge or those skills.

Proximate Cause

Once a breach of standard of care has been shown to have occurred, then that breach must be proved to be the proximate cause of the injury. Proximate cause is considered to be a cause that produces the injury in question in a natural and continuous sequence, unbroken by any independent intervening causes. Thus, the breach must be the direct cause of the injury.

Proximate cause is easiest to prove if the acts and the injury in question are closely related in time. As the time between act and injury increases, the opportunity for intervening variables to intercede increases. States arbitrarily set statutes of limitations on negligence cases, thereby setting a limit on liability. It is important to know the statute of limitations in one's own jurisdiction and whether it is dated from the day of the actual injury or of the discovery of the injury. It also should be noted that a minor's right to sue begins when he or she comes of age, so that a therapist might be sued by a child's parents, or, depending on the age of the child and statute of limitations, some years later by the child, now an adult.

The major defense against allegations of malpractice is the concept of contributory negligence on the client's part as an intervening cause, breaking the chain of causality between the therapist's acts and the injury. What must be proved is that the client's acts fell below the level of self-care that the average person would have exercised under the same or similar circumstances. This defense is not normally applicable to children or to clients whom a judge has declared mentally incompetent.

Injury

If proximate cause is proved, an injury must have resulted from it. Strupp, Hadley, and Gomes-Schwartz (1977) offered a partial list of negative effects:

1. Exacerbation of the presenting symptoms (including increased depression, inhibitions, extension of phobias; increased somatic difficulties; decreased self-esteem; paranoia; obsessional symptoms; guilt; decrease in impulse control).
2. Appearance of new symptoms (including severe psychosomatic reactions, a suicide attempt, development of new forms of acting out, disruption of previously perceived stable relationships).

3. Client misuse or abuse of therapy (settling into a dependent relationship, increased intellectualization with concomitant avoidance of action, therapy as a place to ventilate and rationalize hostility, increased reliance on irrationality and "spontaneity" to avoid reflection on real-world limits).
4. Clients' overextending themselves in taking on tasks before they can adequately achieve them, possibly to please the therapist or due to inappropriate directives, leading to failure, guilt, or self-contempt.
5. Disillusionment with therapy, leading to feelings of hopelessness in getting help from any relationship.

Other negative effects often cited by plaintiffs as injuries emanating from psycho-therapeutic malpractice include damages due to reliance on a therapist's directives leading to divorce, job loss, economic loss, emotional harm, suicide or death of a third party, and self- or nonself-inflicted injuries (Schultz, 1982).

Damages

If the four key elements of malpractice are proved, then damages will be awarded to the plaintiff. The standard of proof in civil cases is a "preponderance of the evidence." Numerically, this would mean at least a 51% to 49% split of the evidence in favor of the plaintiff, a lower standard than the criminal standard of "beyond a reasonable doubt." Damage can be of two types, either compensatory for the injury or punitive as punishment for wanton or reckless acts. Compensatory damages generally consider past earnings lost, future earnings lost, pain and suffering, restitution to undo the damage, and/or the cost of the therapy itself (Schultz, 1982).

Intentional Torts

A number of difficulties arise when plaintiffs seek to prove the four elements in a malpractice action. These difficulties center primarily on the inherent vagueness in the elements of standard of care and proximate cause. Barring gross misconduct, the large range of treatment options allows for great latitude in acceptable care. Also, because the "natural" course of "mental illness" is a still uncertain conception, it is difficult to prove that a therapist's action or inaction caused an alleged injury; the injury might just as easily be explained as a natural consequence of the illness. This vagueness of the elements of proof in negligence cases invites more suits than other tort actions but, at the same time, makes them harder for plaintiffs to win. In contrast, the relative clarity of the elements of proof for intentional torts makes them easier to prevent but harder to defeat in court when reality-based allegations are made (Schultz, 1982).

Generally, expert testimony is not required in cases involving intentional torts. The questions raised are ones that demand clear-cut "yes" or "no" answers as opposed to variable assessments of acceptability or proximate causation. The major intentional tort actions normally filed are discussed in the following paragraphs.

Battery

Schwitzgebel and Schwitzgebel (1980) stated with regard to battery:

> The unconsented touching of a person gives rise to a legal action in tort, even though that touching as a treatment is for the welfare of the patient and actually benefits the patient. . . . If the person consents to the touching, then there is no battery. (p. 274)

The standard of care is not a question in battery. Although the act must be willful on the part of the therapist, it does not have to be based on proving intent to harm the client. Proximate cause, injury, and most importantly, lack of informed consent are the elements needed to be proved in this tort. It should be noted, however, that consent obtained without imparting adequate information nullifies the consent. Therapists must fully explain treatment procedures and any possible adverse or negative consequences that may result from clients' participation. The reasoning of this requirement is that clients who know the risks involved in certain procedures would elect not to participate. Sex therapy represents an area of potential liability of particular relevance for marriage and family therapists.

Defamation

Black's Law Dictionary (1968) defines *defamation* as "The offense of injuring a person's character, fame, or reputation by false and malicious statements" (p. 505).

Defamation may be oral, as in slander, or written, as in libel. It must be made public, and it must be injurious to the reputation of the plaintiff. There are three avenues of defense in this tort (Schultz, 1982): (a) An absolute bar to liability is that the statement is true; (b) an informed consent to release the information would indicate that the plaintiff had no reason to bar the information from being made public; and (c) the defendant can invoke the doctrine of "qualified privilege," or overreaching social duty to release the information. *Berry v. Moensch* (1958) elaborated on this latter point in setting forth the following four conditions:

1. The information must be presented in good faith and not in malice.
2. There must be a legitimate social duty to release the information.
3. The disclosure must be limited in scope to what is necessary to discharge the duty.
4. The disclosure must be only to the appropriate parties with a right to know.

Marriage and family therapists who act in a professional manner and are cautious about client information communicated to third parties will generally be protected from defamation actions because of the doctrine of qualified privilege (Hopkins & Anderson, 1990).

Invasion of Privacy

Invasion of privacy is a violation of the right to be left alone. It requires that private facts be disclosed to more than a small group of persons and that the information must be offensive to a reasonable person of ordinary sensibilities (Schultz, 1982). Invasion of privacy can be distinguished from defamation in that even complimentary statements can be considered an invasion of privacy and such invasion need not require publication of the information, only an intrusion into an individual's private spheres. It is the fact of the invasion itself that is the question in this tort, regardless of the intent or negligence. The certain defense in this tort action is informed consent by the client.

Invasion of privacy requires unreasonable or offensive conduct. Schultz (1982) identified a number of examples in this regard:

A therapist who makes phone calls to a patient's place of work, identifying himself as a therapist, or who sends bills and correspondence to a patient, with an identification of his relationship to the patient, might give grounds for an invasion of privacy action. The

> presence of nonessential staff in treatment settings has been viewed as an intrusion on the patient's seclusion. The patient has an absolute right to refuse to be interviewed as a "case conference." (p. 11)

It is obviously important, not only from an ethical standpoint, but also from a legal one, that therapists maintain client confidentiality carefully. The implications for this tort reach into office practices such as record keeping as well as the professional realms of research, training, and supervision.

Infliction of Mental Distress

The tort of infliction of mental distress normally requires outrageous conduct by the defendant. The harm done is the infliction of emotional pain, distress, or suffering. Schwitzgebel and Schwitzgebel (1980) noted that most cases have required the existence of physical injury resulting from the distress as well.

Malicious Prosecution and False Imprisonment

The tort of malicious prosecution is relatively difficult to prove, as it requires the plaintiff to prove malicious intent on the part of the plaintiff or prosecutor of the underlying case. Even grossly destructive behavior can occur without the requisite malice (Schultz, 1982). False imprisonment normally is brought as an action when the sufficiency of an examination or treatment are questionable, particularly in cases of involuntary commitment (Schwitzgebel & Schwitzgebel, 1980). The injury in both of these torts is usually deprivation of liberty.

Diligence and a reasonable belief on the part of the therapist that a client may be harmed or harmful should serve as adequate protection against this tort action. Completeness in examinations and regular evaluations should be standard procedure so any necessary confinement is kept to a required minimum.

Professional Liability Insurance

Therapist–client relationships resulting in court action, although infrequent, are always possible, with subsequent risks to the contemporary marriage and family therapist (Appleson, 1982). Certainly such risks can be minimized by acting responsibly and in concert with the ethical standards of the profession and accepted practices within the field. Although the risk can be minimized, it cannot be eliminated, and insurance coverage is therefore advisable (Hendrickson, 1982).

It is important to remember that even a marriage and family therapist who is innocent might still be sued. Bennett, Bryant, VandenBos, and Greenwood (1990) estimated that costs including legal fees, expenses such as telephone calls and photocopying, expert witness fees, transcript fees, and court costs can amount to approximately $20,000 in a typical lawsuit; and this amount does not even consider the million or more dollars that could theoretically be awarded to a plaintiff if a suit is lost.

Professional liability insurance is necessary for most marriage and family therapists to pay the costs of litigation, should they be sued, as well as to pay any damages, should a court find liability. Some states have indemnification statutes that provide that state or private institutions pay for damages and legal fees of employees at the end of litigation. Insurance is advisable for these professionals as well. Because litigation frequently can be drawn out over several years, professional liability insurance will prevent these therapists from having to use their own personal assets to pay legal expenses during the litigation.

In purchasing professional liability insurance, it is critical that therapists carefully consider the kinds of policies and coverages available. For example, there are typically two very different types of policies: claims-made policies and occurrence-based policies. Occurrence-based policies cover a therapist against any claims that may be filed for acts that occurred during the policy period covered, even if the therapist is no longer insured by that policy or the insurance carrier who provided it. In simple terms, the insured is covered forever for acts that occurred during the policy coverage period. This form of coverage is generally more expensive than claims-made policies.

Claims-made policies protect the insured against a claim only if he or she is covered at the time the alleged act occurred and has been continuously insured with that same carrier up to the time the claim is filed (Bennett et al., 1990). This means that if an annual policy is not renewed, even if the therapist is no longer in practice (e.g., retired), any subsequent claims will not be covered. Bennett et al. (1990) commented on this more specifically:

> If you are insured under an employer's claims-made policy, you are in effect tied to that employer forever, even if you stop working for the employer. If you have chosen a claims-made policy, it may be necessary to purchase a special kind of coverage to protect you after you retire, stop working, change jobs, or change insurance carriers. The cost of this special coverage—referred to as tails, riders, or reporting endorsements—could offset any savings achieved when you chose the claims-policy. You buy the tail to cover a particular period of time . . . between 1 and 5 years and even longer. (p. 107)

Although most insurance carriers offer occurrence-based coverage, many are attempting to switch their clients to claims-made coverage. It is important to note, however, that the average time lapse between events precipitating a malpractice claim and the claim report is 2 to 3 years; some suits have been brought 10 years after the events on which they are based occurred (Bennett et al., 1990).

Professional liability insurance is available through most national and regional professional associations. The American Association for Marriage and Family Therapy, American Psychological Association, American Counseling Association, and others offer a group liability insurance plan for members. Again, as with any insurance, the policy should be studied and exclusions should be noted and considered by any therapist comparing available liability coverage.

SUMMARY

Legal roles and responsibilities have become more important in the practice of marriage and family therapy as consumer advocacy and stress on accountability have grown along with changes in judicial attitudes toward mental health professionals. These roles and responsibilities influence every aspect of practice and must be addressed by all marriage and family therapists.

The courts are finding an increasing number of uses for the opinions, recommendations, and therapeutic resources offered by marriage and family therapists—as a source of information leading to needed intervention by the state, as a resource for therapy services, and as expert witnesses. It is clear that training in this psycholegal interface must be a significant part of marriage and family therapy training. Relative to other participants in the courtroom drama, marriage and family therapists will otherwise be underprepared, however expert they are in clinical confines. The legally naïve therapist will likely experience frustration and embarrassment at the hands of a skilled and well-prepared attorney within the adversarial system of the court. Moreover, his or her responsibility to best serve clients' welfare may be seriously compromised in the process because of improper preparation.

The previous five chapters of this book addressed ethical responsibilities incumbent on marriage and family therapists. There is a strong relationship between ethics and the law. Codes of ethics reflect statements by professions with respect to acceptable standards of practice; they outline members' basic responsibilities. Ethically responsible therapist behavior relating to client welfare, confidentiality, and especially informed consent not only maintain professional standards but help avoid unnecessary legal actions.

Van Hoose and Kottler asserted one major reason for the professional codes of ethics is to protect the profession from governmental regulation. Ethical codes foster professions' internal regulation of themselves rather than risk being regulated by governmental bodies. A therapist's failure to follow the published code of his or her primary professional association may result in disciplinary action and/or expulsion from that group. Van Hoose and Kottler (1985) noted, however, that:

> Professional societies have no legal power per se, and their standards, however appropriate, may be unenforceable without statutes to back them up. Thus, laws may become necessary to prevent practice by unqualified persons, to prevent abuses, to protect the general public and the professions from charlatans and quacks, and to discipline offenders. (p. 70)

Ultimately, ethical responsibilities thus equate with legal responsibilities; neither can be ignored. Marriage and family therapists need to educate themselves with regard to both. Chapter 9 looks specifically at family law and Chapter 10 provides case examples and critiques that offer further opportunities to expand one's knowledge base in this area.

RECOMMENDED RESOURCES

Bennett, B. E., Bryant, B. K., VandenBos, G. R., & Greenwood, A. (1990). *Professional liability and risk management.* Washington, DC: American Psychological Association.

Cohen, R. J., & Mariano, W. E. (1982). *Legal guidebook in mental health.* New York: The Free Press.

Coogler, O. J. (1978). *Structured mediation in divorce settlement.* Lexington, MA: D. C. Heath.

Gould, J. W. (1988). *Conducting scientifically crafted child custody evaluations.* Thousand Oaks, CA: Sage.

Haynes, J. M. (1981). *Divorce mediation. A practical guide for therapists and counselors.* New York: Springer.

Hopkins, B. R., & Anderson, B. S. (1990). *The counselor and the law.* Alexandria, VA: American Counseling Association.

Lifson, L. E., & Simon, R. I. (Eds.). (1998). *The mental health practitioner and the law.* Cambridge, MA: Harvard University Press.

Remley, T. P., Jr., & Herlihy, B. (2007). *Ethical, legal, and professional issues in counseling* (second edition). Upper Saddle River, NJ: Prentice Hall.

Reppucci, N. D., Weithorn, L. A., Mulvey, E. P., & Monahan, J. (Eds.). (1984). *Children, mental health and the law.* Beverly Hills: Sage.

Schultz, B. M. (1982). *Legal liability in psychotherapy.* San Francisco: Jossey-Bass.

Sidley, N. T. (Ed.). (1985). *Law and ethics: A guide for the health professional.* New York: Human Sciences Press.

Stevens-Smith, P., & Hughes, M. M. (1993). *Legal issues in marriage and family counseling.* Alexandria, VA: American Counseling Association.

Woody, R. H., & Associates. (1984). *The law and the practice of human services.* San Francisco: Jossey-Bass.

CHAPTER

9

Family Law

When legal problems arise within the therapeutic context, clients usually are advised to consult with an attorney. Yet there can be several significant stumbling blocks in gaining meaningful assistance simply by telling clients, "This is a legal problem—see a lawyer." Some lawyers may not be aware of, may not understand, or may not even care about relevant psychosocial or psychiatric difficulties underlying a legal problem. Consulting an attorney could initiate the involvement of marital partners or family members in a bitter adversarial process, resulting in the reversal of therapeutic efforts. Once begun, litigation could become difficult to channel directly or to accomplish in a manner conducive to the treatment goals that were originally sought (Bernstein, 1982).

Marriage and family therapists need to be familiar with these stumbling blocks and the law that affects couples and families if they are to work effectively with cases requiring the input of both legal and therapeutic objectives. Many problems that couples and families present for therapy have legal implications that cannot be ignored. Therapists must be able to effectively address both legal and therapeutic problems when they exist in tandem. Marriage and family therapists should recognize and understand relevant legal issues—not to practice law, but rather to provide basic, therapeutically relevant information—and to refer or seek consultation appropriately. Bernstein (1982) summarized this position most aptly:

> Ignorance of the law may be an excuse in the malpractice area in the sense that therapists are not liable for failure to offer legal advice nor would they be liable for failure to refer a client to an attorney. But, certainly, effective therapy must at least consider the options that are allowable and involve these options in the therapeutic process. (p. 100)

This chapter presents an overview of relevant issues in family law. However, contemporary family law in the United States is far too complex a subject to detail in depth in a single chapter. Changes in the law are constantly occurring, individual states have different rules and procedures, and courts can interpret the meaning of the law in contrasting ways. When applicable, the primary references employed for the information presented in this chapter are "uniform" acts put forth by professional bodies for the purpose of providing common provisions for state legislatures. For example, the Uniform Marriage and Divorce Act was promulgated by the National Conference of Commissioners on Uniform State Laws in 1971. The American Bar Association approved this act and recommended it for passage by the states in 1974. Acceptance by the American Bar Association does not imply that the act has been equally accepted by all state legislatures; however, it does provide the model most frequently used by states to revise or prepare their own statutory provisions. To clarify specific laws in their own state, marriage and family therapists must consult that state's statutes and cases. With regard to particular legal problems, therapists are urged to consult an attorney who specializes in family law. For a more thorough presentation of the issues addressed in this chapter, consult the bibliography of recommended resources at the end of the chapter.

MARRIAGE AND COHABITATION

The two major forms of legal marriage are *ceremonial marriage* and *common-law marriage*. Ceremonial marriage is performed in a ceremony before a religious or civil authority, and common-law marriage results from partners living together as husband and wife for a specified minimum period of time without having participated in a marriage ceremony. For both forms of marriage, partners must have the legal capacity to enter into a contract and actually have made an agreement to marry (Clark, 1974).

Most marriages are ceremonial marriages. In the majority of states, there is no specified procedure for the ceremony, although most require witnesses (usually at least two) and that a marriage license has been obtained and recorded in the appropriate civil office. Section 203 of the Uniform Marriage and Divorce Act (Bureau of National Affairs, Inc., 1982) outlined this licensing procedure:

> When a marriage application has been completed and signed by both parties to a prospective marriage and at least one party has appeared before the (marriage license) clerk and paid the marriage license fee of ($. . . .), the (marriage license) clerk shall issue a license to marry and a marriage certificate form upon being furnished:
>
> (1) satisfactory proof that each party to the marriage will have attained the age of 18 years at the time the marriage license is effective, or will have attained the age of 16 years and has either the consent to the marriage of both parents or his guardian, or judicial approval; (or, if under the age of 16 years, has both the consent of both parents or his guardian and judicial approval); and
> (2) satisfactory proof that the marriage is not prohibited; and
> (3) a certificate of the results of any medical examination required by the laws of this State.

Requirements relating to subsection 2 prohibiting marriage have been the subject of significant judicial scrutiny. The Supreme Court has established persons' marital choice as a fundamental right: "The freedom to marry has long been recognized as one of the vital personal rights essential to the orderly pursuit of happiness by free men" (*Loving v. Virginia*, 1967). The Supreme Court held in *Loving* that the state of Virginia could not prohibit interracial marriage between whites and members of other races because such racial classifications violated the equal protection clause of the Fourteenth Amendment and because marriage is a basic right:

> Marriage is one of the "basic civil rights of man," fundamental to our very existence and survival. To deny this fundamental freedom on so insupportable a basis as racial classification embodied in these statutes, classifications so directly subversive of the principle of equality at the heart of the Fourteenth Amendment, is surely to deprive all the state's citizens of liberty without due process of law. The Fourteenth Amendment requires that the freedom of choice to marry not be restricted by insidious racial discriminations. Under our Constitution, the freedom to marry, or not to marry, a person of another race resides with the individual and cannot be infringed by the state.

Given that the right to marry is fundamental, the extent to which states may infringe on that right has been incorporated in a number of judicial decisions. For example, in *Zablocki v. Redhail* (1978), the Supreme Court held a Wisconsin statute as unconstitutional. The statute required state residents who were under a court order to support minor children not in their custody to prove, before being permitted to marry, that the children were not likely to become public charges. In a similar stance, the Court of Appeals of California ruled against prison officials who sought to prevent prisoners from marrying (*In re Carrafa*, 1978). *In re Carrafa* affirmed the right to marry as a fundamental one, especially considering that many of the civil rights normally available to citizens convicted of criminal action may be curtailed.

Because the right to marry is a basic one, states can significantly interfere with this right only in the presence of a "compelling state interest" (Glendon, 1976). Prohibitions against bigamy and close incestuous marriage have been upheld consistently.

Although the federal government passed the Defense of Marriage Act (1996), which supports states in refusing to allow same-sex marriages or refusing to acknowledge such marriages performed in other jurisdictions (Polikoff, 1993), and most state courts have held that gay and lesbian marriages can be prohibited, two state supreme courts (Hawaii and Vermont) have held that denying the right to marry to gay and lesbian couples violates the constitutions of those states (*Baehr v. Lewis*, 1993; Sneyd, 2000; Thompson-Schneider, 1997). In addition, the Vermont legislature has passed a law creating "civil unions" available to gay and lesbian couples that are equivalent to marriages (Sneyd, 2000). Although many authors have argued that gay and lesbian marriages should be permitted because gay and lesbian individuals are discriminated against if they are not given the protections and benefits available to heterosexual citizens (Eskridge, 1993; N. D. Hunter, 1991; Thompson-Schneider, 1997), Kovacs (1995) has added another argument suggesting that the children of gay and lesbian couples need to be protected by allowing their parents to marry.

The National Gay and Lesbian Task Force has provided an analysis of the differences among gay and lesbian marriages, civil unions, and domestic partnerships (2005). There are 1,138 federal laws and policies that protect married persons but do not protect individuals who are in civil unions or living as domestic partners. These federal laws and policies include social security, family medical leave, federal taxation, and immigration legislation. Federal protections are one of the reasons advocates for gay and lesbian marriage have rejected compromises such as civil union and domestic partner laws. Portability is another important issue. At this time, only Vermont confers civil unions on partners, and no other state has recognized the legality of these civil unions. On the other hand, all states recognize the marriages of other states.

Clearly, the structure of the family in America has dramatically changed since the 1970s. In a parallel process, the nature and functions of marriage as a legal and social institution have seen a similar evolution. Although this evolution is ongoing, particular patterns can be discerned. A family based on marriage is still perceived as the most desirable and productive unit of society, although no longer necessarily the most stable. Procreation may continue to be a predominant purpose of marriage, but other forms of productiveness are being increasingly recognized; for example, the financial or educational advancement of both partners by joint effort. With such ends in view, parties to a marriage are paying closer attention to the economics of the relationship than they might have in the past. Thus, marriage can be viewed as a partnership similar to a commercial arrangement created to pool resources for speculative investment, or as a co-ownership of present and future property similar to a business partnership for profit (Weyrauch & Katz, 1983).

As a result, prenuptial agreements have taken on increased importance and recognition. A *prenuptial agreement* is a contract made by a couple before their marriage in order to modify certain legal repercussions that would otherwise occur as a result of marrying (Krause, 1977). In the past, such agreements were a rare practice confined to the elderly and rich who sought to preserve their assets. Prenuptial agreements today are being entered into by many couples attempting to articulate their mutual expectations. Reversing the common-law principle that contracts between husband and wife interfered with the marital commitment and were therefore not recognized, courts are tending to accept the validity of prenuptial agreements even if they contemplate and regulate the possibility of future divorce or dissolution of a marriage. The courts are increasingly leaving the nature and terms of marriage to the parties themselves rather than imposing restrictions by a formal pronouncement of policy by the state (Weyrauch & Katz, 1983).

This increased acceptance of prenuptial agreements by the courts has particular relevance for marriage and family therapists. Religious mandates frequently call for couples contemplating marriage to seek premarital counseling from the clergy. Likewise, many couples considering marriage, especially for a second or third time, sensibly seek therapeutic input (from marriage and family therapists) prior to entering into marriage to address potential problems they may encounter. In this era of the blended family, individuals who may have entered an early marriage basically unencumbered are more cautious when approaching second or third relationships, carefully considering legal and property rights before, during, and perhaps even following the marriage, should it end in divorce. Bernstein (1982) characterized these possible circumstances in stating:

> One can easily picture the typical American family of "your" children, "my" children, and possibly "our" children. Then there is your property before marriage, my property before marriage, and our property during marriage. Then, in a later marriage there are children and grandchildren as well, often former spouses, and business or financial arrangements and obligations of various degrees of complexity. Likewise, there might also be items of inheritance from either side of the family that can cause ownership problems. One can easily envision two parties immediately prior to marriage who have real and personal property, children, insurance, family obligations, and perhaps properties secured by substantial debts. (p. 96)

Couples entering into marriage should be forewarned about the legal complexities and potential consequences arising from their union in the same manner as they need to understand and address emotional and developmental tasks. Therapists who participate in premarital therapy efforts with couples should present legal issues that may impinge on their emotional well-being. The possibility of preparing a prenuptial agreement should accompany such a discussion. Each party may clearly desire the marriage. One or both partners, however, may fear the real or imagined hazards inherent in negotiating finances and other sources of contractual conflict during this sensitive time. One or both partners may be so enamored that emotion overrules thought that should be given to realistic, concrete planning for the future.

Bernstein (1982) proposed that, at minimum, each party entering into marriage should prepare an inventory of their present assets. He recommended an accompanying prenuptial agreement that can then provide that, in the event of divorce, each partner will leave the marriage with the property they brought into it. Furthermore, the ownership, control, and characterization of property gained during the marriage also can be fixed. Thus, each partner can be secure in understanding that the interest in his or her property and monies earned from that property during the marriage remain personal, individual, and apart from that of his or her spouse. Finally, a full review of each party's insurance and estate plan should be made so that each party can be comforted by the knowledge that loved ones will not be isolated and that prior family expectations and obligations will be respected.

Most states require that prenuptial agreements be in writing. Ruback (1984) reported that prenuptial agreements that concern the transfer of property before a marriage have generally been considered valid, although federal tax consequences were applicable. Similarly, agreements relating to the distribution of property on the death of one spouse also have been validated generally assuming there was full disclosure of the spouse's financial circumstances at the time of the contract and the other spouse was fairly provided for. Ruback cautioned, however, that prenuptial agreements relating to the distribution of property and support obligations that a partner would receive in the event of a divorce have been struck down by the courts as being against the public policy of state. This suggests that such agreements encourage divorce.

To assist attorneys in drafting premarital agreements that will withstand later legal challenges, Belcher and Pomeroy (1998) have developed the following suggestions: (a) Each partner should have his or her own attorney who will give independent advice on the terms of the agreement. (b) Enough time should be allowed to draft and negotiate the agreement before the wedding to avoid the appearance of duress. (c) Each partner should fully disclose his or her assets and obligations rather than asking a partner to waive the disclosure requirement. (d) Personal obligations such as requiring a partner to live in a particular location after the marriage should be avoided. (e) Any marital rights that are waived, such as a probate homestead or serving as a personal representative, should be clearly specified rather than waived with a general statement. (f) Recitals (which include, among other things, that the agreement is freely and voluntarily entered into without duress or undue influence, each partner is represented by independent legal counsel, and full disclosure of assets and obligations have taken place) should be read by each partner and his or her lawyer before execution of the document.

Weyrauch and Katz (1983) advocated the increasing importance and acceptance of prenuptial agreements as they relate to potential divorce settlements. They cited *Posner v. Posner* (1979) as a leading case in support of the proposition that parties should be able to regulate incidents of marriage breakup. According to the viewpoint alluded to as background for the case, such regulation was traditionally identified as against public policy; the conception of marriage as a personal relationship entered into for life made any contemplation of divorce seem an impairment to the marital intent. Also noted was the traditional notion of the state as a third party to the marriage contract, intervening with party autonomy. In its final decision, the court stated:

> We cannot blind ourselves to the fact that the concept of the "sanctity" of a marriage—as being practically indissoluble, once entered into—held by our ancestors only a few generations ago, has been greatly eroded in the last several decades. This court can take judicial notice of the fact that the ratio of marriages to divorces has reached a disturbing rate in many states; and that a new concept of divorce—in which there is no "guilty" party—is being advocated by many groups and has been adopted by the State of California in a recent revision of its divorce laws providing for dissolution of a marriage upon pleading and proof of "irreconcilable differences" between the parties, without assessing the fault for the failure of the marriage against either party. With divorce such a commonplace fact of life, it is fair to assume that many prospective marriage partners whose property and familial situation is such as to generate a valid antenuptial agreement settling their property rights upon the death of either, might want to consider and discuss also—and agree upon, if possible—the disposition of their property and the alimony rights of the wife in the event their marriage, despite their best efforts, should fail.

Prenuptial agreements concerning obligations and duties during marriage also are becoming increasingly common. These agreements attempt to regulate areas such as sexual practices, finances, and religious upbringing and education of children. These latter agreements, however, have been rarely enforceable because of courts' increasing reluctance to intrude in ongoing marriages (Ruback, 1984).

Given this shifting emphasis toward marriage as a legal partnership with a corresponding acceptance of prenuptial agreements, marriage, except in the formal legal sense as a symbol, has been increasingly viewed as decreasingly necessary. Although the practice of living with someone of the opposite sex without being married is old, it has become more commonly practiced in contemporary society over the past several decades (Glendon, 1980).

Mahoney (2005) reported that 35 municipalities have enacted domestic partner ordinances that give status to cohabiting partners. In addition, the states of Hawaii, Vermont, California, New Jersey, and Maine have passed domestic partnership laws that apply to the entire state. Each domestic partner ordinance and law have different provisions related to giving legal status to the relationship and the partners' legal relationships with third parties and the government. Most of the domestic partner laws provide benefits to partners of government employees, and some extend the definition of domestic partners to same-sex couples.

Lavori (1976) offered a number of reasons to explain the increase in cohabitating couples:

1. The desire by couples to avoid the sex-stereotyped allocation of roles associated with marriage.
2. The feeling that unless children are involved, marriage is unnecessary or irrelevant.
3. A lack of readiness to commit oneself completely.

4. The idea that one cannot predict how he or she will feel in the future and so promises should not be made that potentially cannot be kept or may not promote desirable outcomes.
5. The desire to avoid the legal involvement and expense inherent in a possible divorce.
6. A conscientious objection to marriage on the part of some couples.
7. The belief that legal sanction of a relationship is irrelevant and meaningless.

Corresponding to this increase in cohabitation among couples has been a trend for individuals to seek court action when the relationship ends to divide property that was obtained during the period of cohabitation (Cruchfield, 1981). This was exemplified in the well-publicized case of *Marvin v. Marvin* (1976) in which the California Supreme Court held that the cohabiting couple, actor Lee Marvin and his partner, could make an express contract affecting their property rights as long as sex was not part of the consideration for the agreement. In responding to the question of precedence in legal theory and practice set by *Marvin v. Marvin*, Weyrauch and Katz (1983) concluded:

> An express contract of cohabitation is not likely to raise serious problems; courts will be increasingly inclined to enforce well-drafted ones. Since one of the many functions of express contracts of cohabitation is to refute any presumption of marriage, as well as limit judicial discretion, express contracts may become an alternative available to the literate American middle classes. That is, if they choose not to protect themselves by formal marriage, they will be able to protect themselves through written contractual stipulation. (p. 204)

Not all states have followed the decision handed down in *Marvin v. Marvin*. Where they have not, however, the general trend has been to incorporate concepts from other areas of the law to address the obvious fact that a legal remedy is often needed to divide property obtained by couples cohabitating without being married. Such borrowed concepts include implied contract, implied partnership, and constructive trust (Douthwaite, 1979; Hennessey, 1980). The position of the prudent practitioner of marriage and family therapy in all of these instances is a recommendation to formalize relationship interests whether through ceremonial marriage or legal contract. Even if this recommendation is not followed, however, equitable legal remedy still might be available, although the ultimate outcome would probably be less certain, and the process would likely require more effort to secure a successful decision.

PARENT–CHILD RELATIONSHIPS

Ruback (1984) identified five frames of reference for considering parent–child relationships under the law: legitimacy, paternity, adoption, surrogate parenthood, and abortion.

Legitimacy and Paternity

Legitimate children are those who are held as having a "full legal relationship" with both of their parents (Krause, 1977). Generally, the marital status of the parents determines legitimacy of children. Because of the importance of identifiable and stable family relationships for society, the law presumes that children born to married women are the offspring of their husbands (Ruback, 1984).

Children identified as illegitimate were, until relatively recently, denied benefits relating to such things as support, inheritance, and wrongful death claims. Although discrimination is still present to some degree in cases of legitimacy determination, the Supreme Court has offered judicial opinions that have struck down most legislation denying benefits to nonmarital children. For example, in *Trimble v. Gordon* (1977), the Supreme Court ruled as unconstitutional an Illinois statute that allowed illegitimate children to inherit only from their mothers, not from their fathers. Similarly, the Supreme Court found in *Weber v. Aetna Casualty & Surety Co.* (1972) that there is no justifying state interest for denying workers' compensation benefits to the dead father's unacknowledged, illegitimate children. In *Gomez v. Perez* (1973), the Supreme Court decided that illegitimate children are guaranteed a right of support from their father in striking down a Texas statute that granted legitimate children a judicially enforceable right to support from their natural fathers but denied that right to illegitimate children. In its decision, the court stated:

> Once a State posits a judicially enforceable right on behalf of children to needed support from their natural fathers there is no constitutionally sufficient justification for denying such an essential right to a child simply because its natural father has not married its mother. For a State to do so is "illogical and unjust."

Different states vary in the types of proceedings used to make paternity determinations. Some states settle paternity issues in civil proceedings. Other states determine paternity as an adjunct to a criminal proceeding. As a result of contrasting types of proceedings, various standards of proof and presumptions of paternity are employed. Section 4 of the Uniform Parentage Act (Bureau of National Affairs, Inc., 1976) is that portion of the act dealing with the ascertainment of parentage and provides a common statutory framework that has been presented to the states by the National Conference of Commissioners on Uniform State Laws:

(a) A man is presumed to be the natural father of a child if:
  (1) he and the child's natural mother are or have been married to each other and the child is born during the marriage, or within 300 days after the marriage is terminated by death, annulment, declaration of invalidity, or divorce, or after a decree of separation is entered by a court;
  (2) before the child's birth, he and the child's natural mother have attempted to marry each other by a marriage solemnized in apparent compliance with law, although the attempted marriage is or could be declared invalid; and,
    (i)   if the attempted marriage could be declared invalid only by a court, the child is born during the attempted marriage, or within 300 days after its termination by death, annulment, declaration of invalidity, or divorce; or
    (ii) if the attempted marriage is invalid without a court order, the child is born within 300 days after the termination of cohabitation;
  (3) after the child's birth, he and the child's natural mother have married, or attempted to marry, each other by a marriage solemnized in apparent compliance with law, although the attempted marriage is or could be declared invalid; and
    (i)   he has acknowledged his paternity of the child in writing filed with the (appropriate court or Vital Statistics Bureau);
    (ii) with his consent, he is named as the child's father on the child's birth certificate; or
    (iii) he is obligated to support the child under a written voluntary promise or by court order;

(4) while the child is under the age of majority, he receives the child into his home and openly holds out the child as his natural child; or

(5) he acknowledges his paternity of the child in a writing filed with the (appropriate court or Vital Statistics Bureau), which shall promptly inform the mother of the filing of the acknowledgment, and she does not dispute the acknowledgment within a reasonable time after being informed thereof, in a writing filed with the (appropriate court or Vital Statistics Bureau). If another man is presumed under this section to be the child's father, acknowledgment may be effected only with the written consent of the presumed father or after the presumption has been rebutted.

(b) A presumption under this section may be rebutted in an appropriate action only by clear and convincing evidence. If two or more presumptions arise which conflict with each other, the presumption which on the facts is founded on the weightier considerations of policy and logic controls. The presumption is rebutted by a court decree establishing paternity of the child by another man.

Section 12 of this same Uniform Parentage Act identifies evidence courts can be expected to employ relating to paternity cases:

(1) evidence of sexual intercourse between the mother and alleged father at any possible time of conception;

(2) an expert's opinion concerning the statistical probability of the alleged father's paternity based upon the duration of the mother's pregnancy;

(3) blood test results, weighted in accordance with evidence, if available, of the statistical probability of the alleged father's paternity;

(4) medical or anthropological evidence relating to the alleged father's paternity of the child based on tests performed by experts. If a man has been identified as a possible father of the child, the court may, and upon request of the party shall, require the child, the mother, and the man to submit to appropriate tests; and

(5) all other evidence relevant to the issue of paternity of the child.

In paternity suits, a judgment that a man is a child's father usually incorporates an order that the father pay periodic support for the child. Also included may be an order for the father to pay the mother's expenses for the pregnancy and birth, as well as expenses incurred in prosecuting the paternity suit (Krause, 1977).

Adoption

Adoption is the legal process by which children acquire parents other than their natural parents and parents acquire children other than their natural children (Clark, 1968). In the event of adoption, the rights and duties between a child and his or her natural parents are ended and replaced by rights and duties between the adoptive parents and the child. All states permit adoption of children and minors (Krause, 1977).

Most adoptions of children by nonrelatives are supervised and take place through adoption agencies. Private adoptions are legal in certain states; however, some contact with a public child welfare agency is still required before a legal adoption can occur. The extent of this required contact varies. Some states merely require that parents provide notification of the prospective adoption to the appropriate regulatory agency. In other states, the agency investigates the prospective parents. In still others, it totally controls the adoption process. Criminal prosecution is possible in some states if an adoption takes place without the requisite agency involvement, particularly if the natural parents receive compensation beyond what is required for medical, legal, and appropriate administrative expenses (Krause, 1977).

Despite the threat of criminal prosecution, there is an extensive black market in "desirable" (usually meaning healthy and white) babies. Likewise, independent adoptions, where available, also are steadily increasing. It is often more advantageous for natural mothers to participate in a private adoption as opposed to public adoption. The former process is often viewed as less demeaning, and mothers who give their children up for public adoption are not likely to be reimbursed for medical and living expenses as they are with private adoptions. Further, the natural parent can occasionally meet the adopting parents, a practice that is almost impossible in public adoptions (Ruback, 1984).

Two points currently lack clarity with regard to the adoption: (a) the rights of a nonmarital father in proceedings by others to adopt his children, and (b) an adoptee's right to know the identity of his or her natural parents. The Supreme Court in *Stanley v. Illinois* (1972) held that an unwed father was entitled to notice and a hearing concerning the disposition of his children. A major factor in this decision, however, was the fact that the father had lived with the children in a de facto family unit (Krause, 1977). Following *Stanley,* the Supreme Court extended constitutional protection to unwed fathers in the adoption process in the case of *Caban v. Mohammed* (1979). In *Caban,* the Court considered the constitutionality of a New York law that permitted an unwed mother but not an unwed father to block the adoption of their children by withholding consent. In this case, the unwed father challenged the adoption of his two natural children by their natural mother and stepfather without his consent. The Supreme Court struck down the New York law in stating:

> The effect of New York's classification is to discriminate against fathers even when their identity is known and they have manifested a significant paternal interest in the child. The facts of this case illustrate the harshness of classifying unwed fathers as being invariably less qualified and entitled than mothers to exercise a concerned judgement as to the fate of their children.

Several years later, the Supreme Court again ruled on unwed fathers' rights in *Lehr v. Robertson* (1983). In *Lehr,* the Court found that the mere existence of a biological link is insufficient to merit constitutional protection. An unwed father must demonstrate a full commitment to the responsibilities of parenthood by coming forward to participate in the rearing of his child. It is this exhibited interest and personal contact that allow him protection under due process. Given these decisions by the Supreme Court, many states have statutes that require some form of notice be given to unwed fathers before their children can be adopted. The exception to this general rule, however, is when the father never had or sought custody or did not exhibit interest in their children's well-being (S. E. Friedman, 1992).

Courts and state legislatures have long recognized that ensuring the sealing of adoption records serves a number of vital interests. These include (a) preventing natural parents from interfering with adoptive parents' raising of the adoptee, (b) protecting the adoptee from the potential stigma of illegitimacy, and (c) protecting the natural parents from the unwanted intrusion that might arise in the event of the sudden appearance of their natural child. Virtually every state provides that records relating to adoptions are confidential and can be examined only on establishing good cause and after securing judicial approval (S. E. Friedman, 1992). Although adoptees have instituted constitutional challenges to sealed records laws on the theory that they have a right to know their origins, these challenges have tended to be rejected by the courts (e.g., *In re Roger B.,* 1981).

In response to these court decisions, some states have implemented voluntary registries that authorize the release of sealed records in the event that both the natural parents and the adult adoptee consent. One drawback, however, is that these acts typically do not allow the solicitation of a person's registration. An alternative response has been the enactment of what are termed *consent statutes.* Under these statutes, an adult adoptee may request a state agency to locate his or her natural parents, and once identified, seek their consent to be identified to their natural child (S. E. Friedman, 1992).

Surrogate Parenthood

Recent years have seen a pronounced increase in the number of instances in which only one member of a marital dyad is the natural parent of their child (Ruback, 1984). With regard to artificial insemination of the mother from a donor who is not the husband, presumptions as to legitimacy and paternity are relatively clear. Section 5 of the Uniform Parentage Act (Bureau of National Affairs, Inc., 1976) precisely specifies:

(a) If, under the supervision of a licensed physician and with the consent of her husband, a wife is inseminated artificially with semen donated by a man not her husband, the husband is treated in law as if he were the natural father of a child thereby conceived. The husband's consent must be in writing and signed by him and his wife. The physician shall certify their signatures and the date of the insemination, and file the husband's consent with the [State Department of Health], where it shall be kept confidential and in a sealed file. However, the physician's failure to do so does not affect the father and child relationship. All papers and records pertaining to the insemination, whether part of the permanent record of a court or of a file held by the supervising physician or elsewhere, are subject to inspection only upon an order of the court for good cause shown.

(b) The donor of semen provided to a licensed physician for use in artificial insemination of a married woman other than the donor's wife is treated in law, as if he were not the natural father of a child thereby conceived.

In re Adams (1990) represented an Illinois case brought by a woman seeking to dissolve her marriage and obtain financial support for her child conceived in Florida by artificial insemination during the marriage. Her husband contested the claim for child support on the grounds that the Illinois Parentage Act, modeled on the Uniform Parentage Act, required the written consent of the husband to establish paternity. Both parties agreed this had never been given. In its finding, the Illinois Appellate Court found that even though the written consent of the husband was absent, 35 other facts contested the husband's current disclaimer of parental responsibility (e.g., the husband taking an active part in selecting the child's name, his never objecting to his designation on the child's birth certificate as the father, his listing the child as a dependent on the couple's federal income tax return).

Clearly, identifying parenthood is difficult when a surrogate mother bears the child of a father whose wife is unable to do so. Major questions arise regarding financial considerations, possible criminal penalties, and the unenforceability of the contracts between the parties (Ruback, 1984). Financial considerations involve the surrogate mother's medical expenses (including prepregnancy, medical, and psychological screening) and compensation to her for the pregnancy. Paying the surrogate mother for her services can make the procedure a crime in some states where statutes have been enacted outlawing payments to parents for their consent to an adoption of their children.

Handel and Sherwyn (1982) asserted that these statutes are likely unenforceable because of their vagueness and the fact that they may violate constitutional guarantees of privacy.

A potentially more volatile concern is the question of surrogate mothers who ultimately decide to keep their children. To overcome this possible circumstance, prospective parents and surrogate mothers often sign contracts prior to the pregnancy designed to allay this problem. Handel and Sherwyn (1982) caution, however, that such contracts probably are unenforceable. The Uniform Status of Children of Assisted Conception Act (USCACA), promulgated in 1988, has been approved by the American Bar Association. The act provides two basic options for states considering its implementation. Option one provides that surrogate mother agreements must be approved by a court if they are to be held valid. The second option voids all surrogate motherhood agreements. Walton reported in 1996 that courts have consistently ruled against surrogates who carried a child to term who later wanted to keep the child, or even gain visitation rights.

Another area of parenthood that is still legally unsettled is donor egg in vitro fertilization (IVF). In donor egg IVF, an egg that has been removed from one woman is fertilized and then implanted in another woman. The birth mother then carries and gives birth to a child who is not genetically related to her. In donor egg IVF, the donor's role ends when the egg is retrieved, and the mother who gives birth performs most of the creation process. The donor has no emotional ties to the child, which might develop during gestation.

Henry (1994), after reviewing the law related to donor egg IVF, concluded that no model statutes, actual state statutes, or case law have given any legal rights to or imposed any legal responsibilities on women who provide donor eggs that result in a later birth. Birth mothers are sometimes protected in statutes from unwanted interference from the donor. All existing U.S. statutes establish the birth mother as the natural and legal mother.

Abortion

Roe v. Wade (1973) represented a landmark Supreme Court decision on the subject of abortion. In it, the Court examined the state's interests in regulating abortion. The Court held that during the first three months of pregnancy, a mother's right to privacy is paramount and the state has no compelling interest that outweighs this right; during the second three months, the state has a compelling interest in the mother's health and therefore can establish reasonable regulations for the abortion procedure; during the last three months, the state has a compelling interest in safeguarding the life of the fetus. Thus, the Supreme Court asserted that the state can regulate and even ban abortion. However, in *Doe v. Bolton* (1973), a companion case to *Roe v. Wade*, the Court declared unconstitutional a Georgia statute that was too restrictive of abortion. Among other things, this law required that abortions be performed only in accredited hospitals and only after approval by a hospital abortion committee.

The Supreme Court addressed the issue of whether or not consent from a woman's husband or parent is required prior to an abortion being performed in *Planned Parenthood of Central Missouri v. Danforth* (1976). The Court held that both adult and minor women have a constitutional right to reproductive privacy; no spousal or parental consent is thereby necessary for the woman to procure an abortion. However, the Court also suggested that the constitutional right may be restricted in the case of minors. Justice Blackmun, writing for the Court, described the right as extending to the "competent minor, mature enough to have become pregnant." Shortly thereafter, however, he further noted that "not every minor regardless of age or maturity may give effective consent for the termination of her pregnancy."

Thus, the extent to which a state might involve parents in their child's reproductive decision was left unsettled in *Planned Parenthood of Central Missouri v. Danforth* (1976). In *Bellotti v. Baird (II)* (1979), the Supreme Court held that although a state may require parents' consent as one form of access to abortion, an alternative, either a judicial or administrative proceeding, must be available to the minor woman who is reluctant to approach her parents. If she demonstrates that she is "mature and competent to make the abortion decision" to the satisfaction of a judge or other state decision maker, she must be allowed to act independently. Even if she fails to establish her capacity to make a mature decision, the abortion should be authorized if it is determined to be in her best interest.

In *Planned Parenthood Association v. Ashcroft* (1983), the Supreme Court affirmed the revised parental consent clause of *Bellotti v. Baird (II)*. Although this represents an avenue to abortion for the minor woman who does not want to seek parental permission, it still offers a forbidding path to the teenager who lacks experience or knowledge of legal procedures. A requirement that minors pursue a legal remedy to prove their ability to make an abortion decision potentially can lead to delayed decisions (and hence more risky abortions), illegal abortion, and an increased incidence of unwanted childbirth (Torres, Forest, & Eisman, 1980).

These Supreme Court decisions have established that states may not require that minor women must have parental consent to obtain an abortion. Notice to parents of any abortion, however, may be an acceptable restriction. In *H. L. v. Matheson* (1981), the Supreme Court held constitutional a Utah law requiring physicians to give notice to parents when performing an abortion on a minor. The Court suggested several significant state interests were served by the statute. These included encouraging pregnant minors to seek advice from their parents, preserving the integrity of the family, and protecting the adolescent. The assumption that all informed parents will respond in a manner beneficial to their daughter's interests has been questioned. Although many parents may be supportive, it seems equally plausible that others will respond negatively (Scott, 1984).

The Supreme Court reconsidered the abortion issue again in 1989 in *Webster v. Reproductive Health Services* (1989) in upholding a Missouri statute restricting the availability of publicly funded abortion services. The Missouri statute also required physicians to test for fetal viability at 20 weeks, two-thirds of the way through the second trimester of a pregnancy. Furthermore, the preamble of the Missouri statute expressed the intention of stopping abortions. The Court stated that the language in the preamble was not binding on anyone, and the public funding of abortion services has never been constitutionally protected. This decision highlighted that states do have the right to regulate abortions (Hopkins & Anderson, 1990).

After reviewing the *Planned Parenthood of the Blue Ridge v. Camblos* (1998) decision, McLaughlin (1999) concluded that the U.S. Supreme Court "still requires parental consent, parental notification, or judicial bypass for minors seeking an abortion, thus infringing on this very private right of a minor's autonomy" (p. 150). The U.S. Supreme Court's position on abortions for minors has been consistent since 1980 (Vitiello, 1999).

Commenting on the policy issues surrounding minors' legal rights to an abortion, Ehrlich (2003) proposed that legislators and judges consider the following changes in our laws and court decisions that would improve the rights of pregnant minors: (a) to require counseling from a professional, rather than parental permission; (b) to give a preference to pregnant minors being required to consult with professionals (such as marriage and family therapists) rather than parents; (c) and to retain the option of bypassing permission requirements if ordered by a judge.

PARENTAL RIGHTS AND RESPONSIBILITIES

The area of primary legal impact on parents' rights and responsibilities relative to their children are those state statutes that address child maltreatment: neglect and abuse. Rosenberg and Hunt (1984) characterized legal issues in cases of child maltreatment as "an evolving attempt to balance the often competing interests of state, parent, and child" (p. 83). They described the interests of the state and the child as requiring that children be protected from serious harm, such as might result from abuse or neglect. Parent and child interests require that the family be free from unnecessary intrusion by the state. In circumstances in which parents act in ways inconsistent with their children's best interests, the state can assume the role of parent in protecting children's welfare, thereby overriding parental authority. There has been ongoing debate, however, as to the state's ability to provide alternatives that are as good or better than children's own family situations (S. E. Friedman, 1992; Mnookin, 1973; Wald, 1976, 1982).

The state's right to intrude on a family derives from two distinct sources: its police power and the concept of *parens patriae*. The police power is the state's inherent power to prevent its citizens from harming one another as well as its mandate to promote all aspects of the public welfare. *Parens patriae* is the limited paternalistic power of the state to protect and promote the welfare of certain individuals (e.g., children) who lack the capacity to act in their own best interests (Rosenberg & Hunt, 1984). The state's exercise of *parens patriae* over children, however, is limited: It is used solely to further the best interests of children. Before intervening, the state must show that children's parents or guardians are either unfit, unable, or unwilling to care for them (Mnookin, 1973).

Determining this unfitness has been a controversial issue, becoming associated with and further delimiting *parens patriae* by the "void for vagueness" doctrine. As applied herein, this doctrine concerns potential infringement of parents' due process rights, and it is composed of three distinct, yet related, components that provide the basis for judicial consideration (D. Day, 1977). The concept of "fair warning" comprises the primary component of the doctrine and requires that a statute be worded clearly so that parents are given adequate notice of what behaviors are considered illegal. The second component, an antidiscretionary element, concerns the potential for arbitrary judicial enforcement of ambiguously worded statutes. The third component considers if a component is too broad; that is, there is a strong potential that legal as well as illegal behavior might be prosecuted.

Alsager v. District Court of Polk County, Iowa (1975) was a precedent-setting family law case that illustrated the importance of the void for vagueness doctrine as well as the tension between the state's *parens patriae* interests and parents' autonomy. In this case, the Supreme Court of Iowa acted "in the best interest of the child" to terminate the parents' rights with respect to five of the six Alsager children. The stated grounds for doing so were that the parents "substantially and continuously or repeatedly refused to give the child necessary parental care and protection" and that they were "unfit parents by reason of . . . conduct . . . detrimental to the physical or mental health or morals of the child."

The parents successfully appealed this initial decision; the appeals court held that the evidence presented in the termination proceeding was insufficient to warrant severing the parent–child relationship. For example, evidence entered into the proceedings identified that the parents "sometimes permitted their children to leave the house in cold weather without winter clothing on, allowed them to play in traffic, to annoy neighbors, to eat mush for supper, to live in a house containing dirty dishes and laundry, and to sometimes arrive late at school." The decision to order the initial temporary removal of the children from the home was based on a 20-minute visit by a probation officer who found that the only occupants at that time included the mother and her youngest child, who was less than a year old. Further, following the children's removal from the home, they spent the next five years in a total of 15 separate foster homes and 8 juvenile home placements. The decision to terminate the parental rights was determined to have failed to provide the children with increased stability or improved lives.

Although few would argue that severe, purposefully inflicted physical injury or a clear diagnosis of failure to thrive constitutes abuse in the first instance and neglect in the latter, the majority of reported abuse and neglect cases fall somewhere along a continuum of "potential" child maltreatment. The importance of clearly defining and delineating instances of abuse and neglect was aptly noted by Wald (1975) in considering psychological harm to children emanating from abusive and neglectful caretaker behaviors:

> While emotional damage to a child should be a basis for intervention in some cases, it is essential that laws be drafted in a manner consistent with our limited knowledge about the nature and causes of psychological harm. Intervention should not be premised on vague concepts like "proper parental love," or "adequate affectionate parental association." Such language invites unwarranted intervention, based on each social worker's or judge's brand of "folk psychology." Although such language might clearly apply to parents who refuse to hold, talk to, or engage in any contact with their children, it could also be applied to parents who travel a great deal and leave their children with housekeepers, who send their children to boarding school to get rid of them, or who are generally unaffectionate people. (pp. 1016–1017)

Ruback (1984) proposed that court procedures are usually in the best interests of allegedly abused or neglected children. In child protective court proceedings in most states, involved children are provided representation by an independent agent, an attorney or lay guardian *ad litem* ("in a lawsuit") appointed by the court. This party represents the child's interests as opposed to those of the parents or the state. Prior screening tends to eliminate the majority of cases that do not belong in court and often acts as a precipitant for families to seek therapeutic assistance and/or change their potentially destructive interactions. Court proceedings generally are dismissed when there is insufficient evidence of abuse or neglect, when the child is in no danger of further harm, if the harm from potential state intervention outweighs any dangers posed by the parents, when a mature child asks that a petition be dismissed, or if the parents voluntarily accept treatment (Besharov, 1982).

"Voluntary" acceptance of treatment services is frequently the result of pressures from professionals to "take advantage" of these services in lieu of threatened court action (Rosenberg & Hunt, 1984). Furthermore, most families who proceed through court action find participation in treatment to be embodied in consequent court orders, particularly in cases in which children are temporarily removed from their parents' custody. Thus, these families' contact with marriage and family therapists is common.

If a court does find that parents have abused or neglected their children, several options are available. The children may be temporarily or permanently removed from the custody of their parents. If so, a temporary or permanent guardian (an individual or a state or private agency) is appointed to take responsibility for the child's well-being. Although it depends on the facts present in individual cases, parents do not necessarily lose their parental rights (e.g., visitation) when a guardian is appointed. In severe cases of abuse or neglect, however, the state may initiate proceedings to terminate parents' rights to the custody of their children and permit the children to be adopted (Chemerinsky, 1979).

ANNULMENT AND DIVORCE

A marriage can be terminated in three ways: death, divorce, or annulment. Because the overwhelming majority of unsuccessful marriages are dissolved through divorce as opposed to annulment, the former will be given the greater emphasis, but first we will provide a brief overview of the latter.

Annulment

Annulment is a declaration by the court that for reasons existing at the time of a marriage, the marriage was invalid from its inception. Common grounds for annulment include factors affecting parties' ability to enter a legal contract (such as fraud, duress, insanity, and immaturity) and factors about the parties' marriage proscribed by law (such as incest or bigamy). The traditional difference between court actions initiated for annulment and those initiated for divorce is that the grounds for annulment must have occurred prior to the marriage, such as preexisting insanity or fraud, usually combined with an allegation that marital consent had been impaired as a result. In contrast, divorce conceptually requires grounds that occurred after the marriage.

Weyrauch and Katz (1983) reported that requests for annulment have tended to become increasingly rare and frequently involve cases in which one party, because of strong feelings, is particularly aggrieved. Allegations necessary to obtain an annulment can be difficult to adequately prove to a court's satisfaction. For example, in *Larson v. Larson* (1963), the Appellate Court of Illinois ruled that the plaintiff, the husband, had not clearly and definitively satisfied the burden of proving that his wife was insane at the time of their marriage even though she had numerous inpatient hospitalizations during their 10 years of marriage. In commenting on this case, Weyrauch and Katz (1983) emphasized that insanity as used for purposes of an annulment action is not necessarily identical with common psychiatric conceptions of mental illness. Specific complications in this case surrounded the psychiatric classification of schizophrenia.

Because of the difficulty in obtaining annulments and to avoid the need for filing new complaints, many attorneys are inclined to combine requests for annulment with alternative requests for divorce. There are situations, however, wherein obtaining an annulment as opposed to a divorce can be critical. Examples include efforts to receive a pension or Social Security benefits from a preexisting marriage.

Divorce

Many couples initially seek therapy in the hope of preserving and enhancing their marriage. The result of therapeutic efforts is often a more vibrant, healthier marriage. By contrast, however, therapeutic efforts also can create an increased awareness in one or both partners that the costs of maintaining the marriage greatly outweigh the potential benefits. Should this be the case, the therapist involved with the couple leading up to their decision to divorce is then often excluded from the divorce proceedings as the couple seeks legal assistance. It is important that marriage and family therapists work with couples past the point of deciding to divorce; a couple must be prepared to deal with the win–lose legal process they are about to enter.

Most couples, particularly those seeking an amicable divorce, seldom consider in advance that they might be thrust into a bitterly competitive struggle. Although they have heard stories about divorce and custody battles, they may have agreed not to let it happen to them. After all, they may say, "We've gone through enough pain," or "We've got to work things out peacefully for the children's sake." Perhaps they even worked out an agreement in advance to address everything they thought was necessary. What they did not realize is that the legal system they are entering is by its nature adversarial and can work against their well-intentioned, cooperative endeavors. Coogler (1978) addressed this issue:

> The lawyer, as an advocate, is required to represent, or advocate, solely the interest of his client. He cannot represent both parties, as is commonly supposed. The lawyer represents his client within the "light of his professional judgment." But the client's interest is always perceived as being in opposition to the interests of the other party. The lawyer cannot and does not regard the parties as having a common problem which he or she will help resolve. (p. 7)

Lawyers are ethically bound to represent their own particular client to the best of their abilities, regardless of the effect it might have on the other party. As a result, each tends to push his or her own client to win every possible advantage (Haynes, 1981). The retaining of one attorney leads to the retaining of a second for the unrepresented partner. These circumstances certainly do not support the give and take required to gain a mutually satisfying settlement. Furthermore, much of the decision making is taken out of the couple's hands.

The battle between attorneys normally occurs outside of the courtroom. If attorneys cannot agree on an out-of-court settlement, however, the matter goes before a judge who makes the final decision. Unless they are prepared to individually and assertively push for a concerted and active involvement, neither husband nor wife will have much of an effect on the outcome. This lack of involvement often leaves both partners dissatisfied and angry at the court, the attorneys, and even more antagonistic toward each other. These potentially bitter and hostile responses frequently continue long after the marriage is legally ended, not because of the fact that it did end, but because of the way it ended. The resulting negative effects can be devastating, especially for children (Hammond, 1981; Schoyer, 1980).

Traditionally, obtaining a divorce required that one party be at fault. The original fault grounds were adultery and physical cruelty. These were later expanded to include habitual drunkenness, willful desertion, mental cruelty, and conviction of a felony. Because the assumption was that only the innocent party was entitled to a divorce, if it could be proved that both parties were at fault, neither one could receive a divorce. This reasoning, called the *doctrine of recrimination,* made contested divorces difficult to win. Proof of collusion between the two parties also was sufficient to bar the action for a divorce. This action was based on the state's interest in protecting marriages (Ruback, 1984).

Recent years have evidenced a significant trend away from requiring fault in divorce actions. Almost every state allows for some type of no-fault divorce, although traditional fault ground may still be alleged. The grounds in these no-fault actions are best represented by Section 305 of the Uniform Marriage and Divorce Act (Bureau of National Affairs, Inc., 1982):

> (a) If both of the parties by petition or otherwise have stated under oath or affirmation that the marriage is irretrievably broken, or one of the parties has so stated and the other has not denied it, the court, after hearing, shall make a finding whether the marriage is irretrievably broken.
> (b) If one of the parties has denied under oath or affirmation that the marriage is irretrievably broken, the court shall consider all relevant factors, including the circumstances that gave rise to filing the petition and the prospect of reconciliation, and shall:
>   (1) make a finding whether the marriage is irretrievably broken; or
>   (2) continue the matter for further hearing not fewer than 30 nor more than 60 days later, or as soon thereafter as the matter may be reached on the court's calendar, and may suggest to the parties that they seek counseling. The court, at the request of either party shall, or on its own motion may, order a conciliation conference. At the adjourned hearing the court shall make a finding whether the marriage is irretrievably broken.
> (c) A finding of irretrievable breakdown is a determination that there is no reasonable prospect of reconciliation.

Although finding fault is no longer required, in most states, divorce is not immediately granted merely on the parties' filing a petition. Many states have a mandatory minimum waiting period after the action is filed before the court may grant a divorce. Further, there normally must be some evidence to support the finding that the marriage is irretrievably broken (Freed & Foster, 1981). In addition, in many states, courts have at their discretion the ability to require couples to attend counseling and conciliation sessions. The stated purpose of these barriers to automatic divorce is to avoid hasty dissolution of marriages. For liberalized divorce procedures, the barriers might also still be viable and remain intact (Ruback, 1982). Such statutes that delay but do not deny access to divorce have been ruled as constitutional, the assumption being that the delay is reasonable and the state has legitimate interests protected by the requirements (Strickman, 1982). For example, in *Sosna v. Iowa* (1975), the Supreme Court upheld Iowa's requirement of a year's residency in the state for a divorce action. This requirement could be justified in several legitimate ways, other than budgetary considerations or administrative convenience (e.g., confirming that the party seeking divorce had sufficient contact with the state before important questions such as child custody were decided by the courts; Ruback, 1984).

The requirement of counseling and conciliation sessions prior to the granting of divorce has obvious implications for marriage and family therapists. For example, an Iowa statute allows judges the power to require parties to participate in conciliation efforts conducted by the domestic relations division of the court or its representative.

Orlando (1978) reported that, in those areas in which required conciliation counseling outcome has been studied, a majority of participating couples reconcile and stay together for at least a year. Even when reconciliation was impossible, however, the required counseling was successful in reducing the number of custody disputes and contested divorces. Others have disputed the value of required conciliation efforts, suggesting them to be expensive, to have a low probability of success, and to generate overexpectations due to the shortage of trained personnel (Krause, 1977).

Given that no-fault divorce is the avenue of choice for most divorcing couples, problems relative to divorce tend to center almost completely on matters relating to property and children. Thus, marriage and family therapists seeking to prepare couples to address issues amicably, yet assertively, relative to their divorce proceedings need to be aware of matters relating to spousal maintenance (alimony) and the division of property as well as custody and support of dependent children.

Spousal Maintenance

Although newspaper headlines are sometimes made by alimony awards, even in 1981 only about 14% of all divorces involved alimony (U.S. Bureau of the Census, 1981). Moreover, the amount of alimony awarded is relatively small. Statutory guidance is provided in most states for awarding alimony; however, some states provide no clear guidelines beyond considering the "wife's needs" and the "husband's ability to pay" (Ruback, 1984). Section 308 of the Uniform Marriage and Divorce Act (Bureau of National Affairs, Inc., 1982) offers a common denominator for marriage and family therapists to consider concerning alimony awards:

(a) In a proceeding for dissolution of marriage, legal separation, or maintenance following a decree of dissolution of the marriage by a court which lacked personal jurisdiction over the absent spouse, the court may grant a maintenance order for either spouse, only if it finds that the spouse seeking maintenance:

   (1) lacks sufficient property to provide for his reasonable needs; and
   (2) is unable to support himself through appropriate employment or is the custodian of a child whose condition or circumstances make it appropriate that the custodian not be required to seek employment outside the home.

(b) The maintenance order shall be in amounts and for periods of time the court deems just, without regard to marital misconduct, and after considering all relevant factors including:

   (1) the financial resources of the party seeking maintenance, including marital property apportioned to him, his ability to meet his needs independently, and the extent to which a provision for support of a child living with the party includes a sum for that party as custodian;
   (2) the time necessary to acquire sufficient education or training to enable the party seeking maintenance to find appropriate employment;
   (3) the standard of living established during the marriage;
   (4) the duration of the marriage;
   (5) the age and the physical and emotional condition of the spouse seeking maintenance; and
   (6) the ability of the spouse from whom maintenance is sought to meet his needs while meeting those of the spouse seeking maintenance.

Required alimony payments generally end with the death of the supporting ex-spouse or with the remarriage of the supported ex-spouse. In some states, alimony can be discontinued with the submission of proof that the supported ex-spouse is cohabitating with a person of the opposite sex. Further, permanent or open-ended alimony awards are declining significantly, probably reflecting the belief that alimony should be used to obtain education and training leading to self-sufficiency (i.e., rehabilitative alimony). In most states, alimony is paid only for a brief period of time (typically no more than five years) after the divorce (Sack, 1987). Increasingly, however, the trend among states is away from alimony and toward a division of property. Alimony is being seen as a supplement to the division of property occurring on divorce (Ruback, 1984).

Division of Property

One of two basic systems of marital property rights are usually operational in divorce proceedings: common law and community property (Krause, 1977). In those states where common-law property rights laws are present, each spouse separately owns the property that he or she brought into the marriage and that came to him or her during the marriage by personal income, interest, or dividends from separate property; by inheritance; or through gifts. Problems arise in deciding on the division of property primarily in regard to property bought during the marriage with money from both spouses but with the title taken in the name of only one spouse or property purchased with money from only one spouse but with the title taken in the name of both spouses. Courts frequently have difficulty deciding who owns what property. They attempt to answer this by reconstructing the parties' intent at the time the property was purchased (Ruback, 1984).

As is the case with spousal maintenance, statutory guidelines available to judges with regard to the division of marital property have been relatively unclear. Most often those factors taken into account relate to an evaluation of marital assets (Connell, 1981). Section 307, Alternative A of the Uniform Marriage and Divorce Act (Bureau of National Affairs, Inc., 1982) provides a common set of considerations for adoption in this regard:

(a) In a proceeding for dissolution of a marriage, legal separation, or disposition of property following a decree of dissolution of marriage or legal separation by a court which lacked personal jurisdiction over the absent spouse or lacked jurisdiction to dispose of the property, the court, without regard to marital misconduct, shall, and in a proceeding for legal separation may, finally equitably apportion between the parties the property and assets belonging to either or both however and whenever acquired, and whether the title thereto is in the name of the husband or wife or both. In making apportionment the court shall consider the duration of the marriage, any prior marriage of either party, any antenuptial agreement of the parties, the age, health, station, occupation, amount and sources of income, vocational skills, employability, estate, liabilities, and needs of each of the parties, custodial provisions, whether the apportionment is in lieu of or in addition to maintenance, and the opportunity of each for future acquisition of capital assets and income. The court shall also consider the contribution or dissipation of each party in the acquisition, preservation, depreciation, or appreciation in the value of the respective estates, and as the contribution of a spouse as a homemaker or to the family unit.

(b) In the proceeding, the court may protect and promote the best interests of the children by setting aside a portion of the jointly and separately held estates of the parties in a separate fund or trust for the support, maintenance, education, and general welfare of any minor, dependent, or incompetent children of the parties.

In contrast to states in which common-law property statutes operate, courts in states emphasizing community property rights rule that all property coming to spouses during their marriage belongs equally to the husband and to the wife. On divorce, community property is divided equally between the two spouses. Courts are, however, free to divide the community property as they see fit (Ruback, 1984). Section 307, Alternative B of the Uniform Marriage and Divorce Act (Bureau of National Affairs, Inc., 1982) seeks to offer a set of common considerations relative to the division of marital property for jurisdictions in which community property laws are in effect:

> In a proceeding for dissolution of the marriage, legal separation, or disposition of property following a decree of dissolution of the marriage or legal dissolution by a court which lacked personal jurisdiction over the absent spouse or lacked jurisdiction to dispose of the property, the court shall assign each spouse's separate property to that spouse. It shall also divide community property, without regard to marital misconduct, in just proportions after considering all relevant factors including:
>
> (1) contribution of each spouse to acquisition of the marital property, including contribution of a spouse as homemaker;
> (2) value of the property set apart to each spouse;
> (3) duration of the marriage; and
> (4) economic circumstances of each spouse when the division of property is to become effective, including the desirability of awarding the family home or the right to live therein for a reasonable period to the spouse having custody of any children.

Ruback (1984) reported two important contemporary developments regarding the division of marital property. The first relates to property "earned" but not received during the marriage; this includes pensions and training, the latter especially through a formal education. With regard to pensions, particularly in states with community property laws, the trend has been to give the spouse (generally the wife) a property interest in the husband's pension proportional to the amount of the pension earned during the marriage (Krause, 1977). An exception has been made for military pensions. In *McCarty v. McCarty* (1981), the Supreme Court held that these pensions are controlled by federal law, not state property laws.

The second type of property earned, but not received, during the marriage is a professional degree, normally obtained by one spouse while the other works to pay for the education and support the dyad during the schooling period. Several state courts have held that the spouse who worked has an equitable interest in the value of the professional degree. For example, in *Reen v. Reen* (1981), a Massachusetts probate and family court held that a wife who sacrificed her own education and the prime child-bearing years of her life to put her husband through dental school and orthodontic training was entitled to part of the value of the degree in orthodontia.

CHILD CUSTODY AND SUPPORT AFTER DIVORCE

In the past, parents usually entered divorce proceedings believing that single-parent custody with tightly regulated visitation rights was the only option. Parents, angry with each other particularly given the potential hostility emanating from the adversarial legal process, frequently used custody controversies over children to provide an outlet for their anger. In the past, most states gave physical custody only to mothers and put sole responsibility for child support on fathers. Times have changed, however. Mothers are working and fathers are mothering. Parenting roles have lost their gender identity as parents are increasingly becoming equally involved in raising their children, though their children are likely spending greater amounts of time in the care of others. Likewise, the male's image as breadwinner has been considerably blemished by the developing evidence that women have been and are providing substantially to the support of the family. These developments have had a significant impact on child custody and support determinations in divorce proceedings.

Child Custody

Ruback (1984) proposed that child custody after divorce is best seen as a continuing problem rather than a one-time determination. He partitioned the issue into initial determinations and changes in custody.

In the past, initial custody decisions have been based on a conceptualization termed "the tender years doctrine," which was an assumption that preadolescent children benefit most from being with their mother because only their mother could provide the particular nurturance they needed during their "tender years." Mothers were generally awarded custody of younger children unless ruled by the court to be "unfit." The term *unfit* referred to moral fitness. It was and occasionally still is an attack on a mother's morals and represented the only successful way of overcoming the tender years presumption. Children beyond their tender years were presumed to benefit more from being in the custody of their same-sex parent, thus fathers were awarded custody of sons and mothers custody of the daughters. Exceptions usually occurred only in cases in which courts were reluctant to separate siblings (Krause, 1977).

In the past several decades, the tender years doctrine has been officially discarded by the courts or legislatures in most states (Freed & Foster, 1981). Replacing it is the "best interests of the child" standard. Section 402 of the Uniform Marriage and Divorce Act (Bureau of National Affairs, Inc., 1982) offers guidelines delineating the best interests standard:

> The court shall determine custody in accordance with the best interest of the child. The court shall consider all relevant factors including:
>
> (1) the wishes of the child's parent or parents as to his custody;
> (2) the wishes of the child as to his custodian;
> (3) the interaction and interrelationship of the child with his parent or parents, his siblings, and any other person who may significantly affect the child's best interest;
> (4) the child's adjustment to his home, school, and community; and
> (5) the mental and physical health of all individuals involved.
>
> The court shall not consider conduct of a proposed custodian that does not affect his relationship to the child.

Although the tender years doctrine has been superseded in most states by the best interests standard, judges still tend to have a bias to determine that children's best interests are served by awarding custody to their mother. Other problems that arise in the application of the best interests standard include children's natural unwillingness to express a preference for one parent and thereby offend the nonchosen parent, and judges' subjectivity and/or lack of professional training regarding adjustment, interactional, and mental health variables. The best interests standard also requests that judges ignore conduct of a parent that does not affect his or her relationship with the child. This provision was included to discourage parties from spying on each other to prove marital misconduct (usually sexual) for use as evidence in a custody case. Some authors have suggested, however, that marital misconduct often is paralleled by poor parenting practices. Such misconduct might include serious emotional problems, habitual drunkenness, adultery, and gross immorality (Weiss, 1979).

In determining child custody under the best interests standard, judges often need to rely on the advice of experts. Marriage and family therapists' testimony in this regard can be very persuasive. Frequently, parents seek the services of marriage and family therapists, as do the courts themselves. For example, if testimony is rendered by a marriage and family therapist asserting that a child's emotional needs would be best met by one parent over another, or that the parent's marital behaviors did not affect his or her parenting practices, the parent whose case is strengthened by the therapist's testimony obviously will have a better chance to be awarded custody. If the testimony is perceived to be objective, it could have even more impact on the outcome. In fact, expert testimony regarding the emotional needs of a child is generally superior to the expressed wishes of the child (Kazen, 1977).

Mnookin and Weisberg (1995) have distinguished between physical and legal custody. In initial custody determinations, four forms of legal custody are available today: sole custody, split custody, divided custody, and joint custody (Folberg, 1984):

1. *Sole custody* is still the most common form of custody determination after divorce. One parent is awarded sole legal custody of the child, with visitation rights allowed to the noncustodial parent. The noncustodian, by informal agreement, may have a voice in important decisions affecting the child, but ultimate control and legal responsibility rest with the custodial parent.

2. *Split custody* is a custody award of one or more of the children to one parent and the remaining children to the other. Courts tend, however, to generally refuse to separate siblings unless there are compelling reasons. Intense hostility or competition between siblings may be one such reason. Another reason might be the inability of either parent to care for all of the children at once.

3. *Divided custody* allows each parent to have primary custody of the child for a part of the year or every other year. This form of custody is also referred to as *alternating custody*. Each parent has reciprocal visitation rights under this arrangement, and each exercises exclusive control over the child while the child remains in his or her custody. Courts tend to most often award divided custody that provides for residence with one parent during the school year and the other during vacations. When parent's homes are separated by greater geographical distances, making frequent visitation impossible, divided custody is generally an approved award. In contrast, courts also have tended to award divided custody on the grounds that both parents live in close proximity. In these cases, this proximity was seen as minimizing the strains that divided custody might place upon children (Folberg & Graham, 1979).

4. *Joint custody* goes beyond the concept of divided custody and also may be referred to as *shared parenting, shared custody,* or *concurrent custody.* Both parents retain legal responsibility and authority for the care and control

of their child, much as in an intact family unit. The parent with whom the child is residing at a specific moment must make immediate, day-to-day decisions regarding discipline, diet, emergency care, and so on. Both parents in joint custody awards have an equal voice in their child's education, upbringing, religious training, nonemergency medical care, and general welfare. Joint custody is applicable most often for situations in which parents are able to give priority to their children's needs, are willing to negotiate differences, and can arrange their life-styles to accommodate their children's needs.

Joint custody awards are controversial (Kramer, 1994). Some state courts have stated a preference for joint custody (*In re Marriage of Kovash*, 1993), but other state courts have determined that joint custody should be avoided (*Petrashek v. Petrashek*, 1989).

How children and their parents react to the aftermath of divorce and initial custody determinations is relevant to the law in that any problems that children experience may initiate and thus affect judgments concerning modifications of custody. The primary consideration in calling for a custody change is proof that there have been substantial changes in the custody situation that affect the welfare of the child and that have arisen subsequent to the initial award of custody (Ruback, 1984). What constitutes sufficient evidence to justify a decision to alter an initial custody determination varies from state to state. Furthermore, changing societal values have created a mirroring change in what constitutes an unfit parent. For example, although the appeals court in one state approved a change in custody because the mother was cohabitating with a man who was not her husband (*Sims v. Sims*, 1979), in other states, such behavior is not likely to result in a change in custody. Correspondingly, a parent's homosexuality has traditionally been a bar to custody. More recently, however, many courts are requiring evidence confirming a connection between the parent's homosexuality and likely harm to the child before deciding custody (Guernsey, 1981).

Interstate custody disputes are more common. Direct attempts to alter custody decisions by seeking proof that substantial changes have occurred following the initial award emanate from violations of prior determinations of custody. Increasing mobility is a reality in American society. In 1981, over 47% of the population moved at least once within the past five years (U.S. Bureau of the Census, 1981). Thus, many divorced parents are moving to different states. Noncustodial parents have kept their child after a visitation period has ended, or simply snatched their child from the custodial parent's home and taken him or her to a second state and entered a court action there to change custody.

Before the adoption of the Uniform Child Custody Jurisdiction Act (UCCJA) by the vast majority of the states, it was relatively easy for an abducting parent to find a court in a second state that would not enforce a first state's custody decree. The reasons for this were based in states' sovereignty issues, judicial jurisdictional contradictions, and the fact that child custody decrees are never final (S. N. Katz, 1981). The UCCJA was designed to prevent conflicting custody decrees in two or more states. To ensure that only one state makes an official custody determination, the act requires that parties notify the courts of any pending custody proceeding in another state and that the courts involved determine the more appropriate forum, so that the actual custody determination will be made in only one court. Thus, the predominant emphasis of the

UCCJA is that only one state and one court will make a final judgment. Since being drafted and approved by the American Bar Association in 1968, the UCCJA has been enacted in varying forms by every state (S. E. Friedman, 1992).

The federal government became deeply involved with the enforcement of child custody decrees with the enactment of the Parental Kidnapping Prevention Act of 1980 (PKPA). The PKPA establishes rules to decide jurisdictional disputes that arise in inter-state custody disputes. Under the PKPA, every state court is required to enforce custody orders entered by other states that were issued consistently with this act. The scope and limits of the PKPA were considered by the Supreme Court in *Thompson v. Thompson* (1988). In its finding, the Court affirmed the significance of the PKPA. The Court explained that the UCCJA, drafted to address the problem of jurisdictional conflicts concerning custody disputes, had not proved fully effective, because a number of states had, at the time the PKPA was enacted, failed to enact the UCCJA or to enact it with modification. The PKPA thus provided for nationwide enforcement of custody orders made in accordance with the terms of the UCCJA (S. E. Friedman, 1992).

Child Support

Section 15 of the Uniform Parentage Act (Bureau of National Affairs, Inc., 1976) sum-marizes major factors to be considered by judges in deciding on child support awards:

> In determining the amount to be paid by a parent for support of the child and the period during which the duty of support is owed, a court enforcing the obligation of support shall consider all relevant facts, including:
>
> (1) the needs of the child;
> (2) the standard of living and circumstances of the parents;
> (3) the relative financial means of the parents;
> (4) the earning ability of the parents;
> (5) the need and capacity of the child for education, including higher education;
> (6) the age of the child;
> (7) the financial resources and earning ability of the child;
> (8) the responsibility of the parents for the support of others; and
> (9) the value of services contributed by the custodial parent.

Child support awards remain in effect until a child reaches the age of majority. Complete and continued follow-through on payment of support obligations, however, represents a major problem. This is particularly the case when the parent making support payments remarries and becomes obligated to provide support to a second family. Generally, support obligations can be enforced through either civil or criminal contempt proceedings. Contempt proceedings call for the parent seeking support payments to show that the supporting parent has not complied with the support order and that this failure was intentional and without justification (Harp, 1982). Given evidence of willful contempt, the amount of money owed must be proved. The court will then order some method of repayment and pronounce a penalty of a fine and/or jail sentence.

Ruback (1984) suggested that, although imposing a fine is an available remedy, it makes little sense if a defaulting parent could not make the original support payment. Neither is it sensible to put the offender in jail, where he or she will be unable to earn the money needed to pay the support and will be costing the state money, in addition to the money the state might have to pay to support the family. Of course, these latter caveats are likely to become secondary in circumstances in which a supporting parent arrogantly refuses, overtly or covertly, to comply with a court order. Aimed at motivating rather than seeking revenge, a judicial penalty may be most appropriate.

In cases in which a supporting parent has remarried and has taken on obligations to a second family, it is not always clear whether obligations to the first family should be reduced because of the new obligations to the children of the second family. The courts have generally not found such changes in circumstances to justify a reduction in previously ordered child support awards (Ruback, 1984). Furthermore, many state courts maintain priority for the children of a first marriage, although it has been strongly suggested that all the children involved should be considered on an equal basis (Krause, 1982).

Most states enforce support obligations ordered in another state. The primary means of enforcing out-of-state support obligations is the Uniform Reciprocal Enforcement of Support Act (URESA) and its later revision, the Revised Uniform Reciprocal Enforcement of Support Act (RURESA). All of the states have adopted URESA or RURESA in some form. Under the provisions of this act, the parent claiming support can bring an action in a court in his or her state of residence. The action is then forwarded to a court located in the supporting parent's home state, under whose law the case is tried. The case is heard and a judgment rendered and enforced in this second court. Monies collected under the judgment are sent to the first court and disbursed to the claimant.

The federal government is also involved in the problem of nonpayment of child support by a parent who resides in a different state or whose whereabouts are unknown. Under legislation passed in 1975 and amended in 1984, the Office of Child Support Enforcement operates as an agency within the Department of Health and Human Services. This agency assists states to find absentee parents, establish paternity, and obtain child support from the absent individuals.

LEGAL ACTIONS BETWEEN PARENTS AND CHILDREN

Historically, the law has failed to recognize civil suits by minor children against their parents for personal injuries wrongfully inflicted (Stack, 1993; Vance, 1995). This prohibition was generally referred to as the "parent–child immunity doctrine." The Washington Supreme Court, ruling in *Roller v. Roller* (1905), addressed the public policy undergirding the parent–child immunity doctrine:

> The rule of law prohibiting suits between parent and child is based upon the interest that society has in preserving harmony in the domestic relations, an interest which has been manifested since the earliest organization of civilized government, an interest inspired by the universally recognized fact that the maintenance of harmonious and proper family relations is conducive to good citizenship, and therefore works to the welfare of the state.

Despite this long-standing legal assumption that parents act in the best interests of their children, statistical data collection has revealed increasingly that this assumption often is contradicted. The spiraling amount of sexual abuse and incest cases, for example, clearly confirms this (Kaslow, 1990a). The result has been a progressive erosion of the parent–child immunity doctrine. Courts have acknowledged that absolute parental immunity may not be justifiable in all circumstances (S. E. Friedman, 1992).

A case frequently cited relative to the erosion of the parent–child immunity doctrine is *Chaffin v. Chaffin* (1964). In ruling on this case, the Oregon Supreme Court stated:

> Each parent, in the rearing of the child, is required under the law to provide maintenance and guidance for that child, and, so long as that parental duty is performed, the family unity is maintained and the parent is entitled to the custody of the child. This family unity the law recognizes and protects against invasion insofar as the parents' duties are concerned. It is only when a parent acts to cause a child to become or when a child becomes a "dependent" or "delinquent" child that the law recognizes a breach of parental duty that will deprive the parent of custody of the child.
>
> Necessarily then, a parent in performing his duties of providing support, discipline and education to his children must have wide discretion. Wealth or poverty, physical strength or weakness, wisdom or mental incapacity are not in themselves criteria for fixing guidelines by which the law judges the performance of parental duties.
>
> Physical, mental or financial weakness may cause parents to provide what many a reasonable man would consider substandard maintenance, guidance, education and recreation for their children, and in many instances to provide a family home which is not reasonably safe as a place of abode. But it would be clearly wrong to permit the minor child to hold the parent liable for these intended injuries.

The Court then concluded that ordinary negligence would not override the parent–child immunity doctrine; something "crueler" was required:

> We conclude that an act by a parent, whether described as willful or malicious or wanton, which will pierce the veil of parental immunity, is an act which is done with an intention to injure the child or is of such a cruel nature in and of itself as to evidence not a reasonably normal parental mind, but an evil mind, *malo animo.* That a negligent act which, although intentionally done, does not disclose an evil mind, but merely a willingness to take great risk in the face of conditions that should warn a reasonably prudent person that there is likelihood of injury is insufficient.

A 1988 Virginia case, *Samantha Baskin v. Peter Baskin,* highlights not only the potential liability a parent faces but also the damages that may arise as a result thereof. In this case, an 11-year-old girl obtained a judgment against her father in the amount of $300,000 for his excessive use of discipline. The girl had attempted to intervene to stop her parents fighting. In response, her father dragged her upstairs by her hair, pounded her on the back, and slapped her across the face several times.

SUMMARY

Family law matters account for over 50% of civil law filings in this country (Hennessey, 1980). Families are increasingly turning to the legal system for help in their problem-solving processes. Part of this willingness can be explained by the confidence expressed toward that system. Yet this often tends to be a false confidence, frequently shattered within the confines of the adversarial system of legal actions. Judges and attorneys now are realizing that many of the problems presented to them fall within the province of mental health rather than the law (Ruback, 1982). Thus, marriage and family therapists are being called on to assist legal professionals more frequently.

More pressing from marriage and family therapists' perspective, however, is the need of their clients to understand and prepare for potential legal interventions into their personal problem-solving processes. For therapeutic efforts to be effective, questions of psycholegal interface must be addressed. As is evident in this chapter, family law encompasses a number of extensive and fluctuating topics. It is vital that marriage and family therapists gain some knowledge in family law to adequately assert themselves, and therefore allow their clients to do so in this regard.

The following is a list of recommended resources for marriage and family therapists. Chapter 10 provides several case examples and critiques that show how family law issues affect therapeutic experience.

RECOMMENDED RESOURCES

Areen, J. (1978). *Cases and materials on family law.* Mineola, NY: Foundation Press.

Friedman, S. E. (1992). *The law of parent–child relationships: A handbook.* Chicago: American Bar Association.

Green, S., & Long, J. V. (1985). *Marriage and family agreements.* Colorado Springs, CO: Shepard's/McGraw-Hill.

Kramer, D. T. (1994). *Legal rights of children* (2nd ed.). New York: McGraw-Hill.

Krause, H. D. (1977). *Family law in a nutshell.* St. Paul, MN: West Publishing.

Krauskopf, J. (1983). *Marital and non-marital contracts.* Chicago: American Bar Association.

Sack, S. M. (1987). *The complete legal guide to marriage, divorce, custody, & living together.* New York: McGraw-Hill.

Legal Considerations

Marriage and family therapists need to understand the basic legal issues that affect their professional practices. They also need to learn when to seek the advice of attorneys. This chapter is structured to make marriage and family therapists more aware of the legal environment in which they function. Case illustrations involving guiding legal principles are presented and explained with reference to leading laws and cases. There is no effort, however, to present an exhaustive analysis of all relevant laws and cases. Practicing attorneys may have need for all such cases, but marriage and family therapists do not.

A variety of legal issues are presented in the cases in this section. We caution readers that the differences in individual state law may affect the actions of marriage and family therapists, depending on the state in which they are practicing. In addition, these cases can contain complex issues, especially since related laws and court case findings are changing. New laws are passed, regulations change, courts are persuaded by novel legal arguments, and the Supreme Court can declare a policy or law unconstitutional. Therefore, no writing related to the law is a final, definitive word at the time of its publication or a substitute for competent legal advice when specific considerations arise.

Knowing when to ask for legal advice is important. Marriage and family therapists need to be able to distinguish among ethical, professional judgment, and legal issues.

Ethical issues require the application of ethical principles that do not also include legal issues that require the advice of an attorney. An example of an ethical issue without legal implications is when a marriage and family therapist tries to determine whether or not to accept a couple for counseling because the therapist is associated with the couple in some other way, such as going to the same church, having children in the same school classroom, or belonging to the same civic organization.

Professional judgment issues require marriage and family therapists to apply their knowledge to particular therapy situations and then make important professional decisions. When marriage and family therapists are trying to determine whether particular clients are at risk for suicide, for example, they are dealing with professional judgment issues.

Legal issues exist for marriage and family therapists when the therapists cannot come to a conclusion regarding particular issues unless they know the law. An example of a legal issue is a situation in which a marriage and family therapist receives a subpoena for therapy records from an attorney representing the wife, and the husband does not want the records disclosed. In situations like this, marriage and family therapists must seek independent legal advice and follow the advice they receive.

When faced with ethical and professional judgment issues, the best course of action for marriage and family therapists is to review written materials such as ethical codes and advice from noted authorities on the issue to determine if answers to their questions can be found there. If not, the next step should be to confer with their direct administrative supervisors for advice and support. Finally, consulting with peers who have the same knowledge, training backgrounds, and work settings can be a great help in resolving ethical and professional judgment dilemmas. Proof of such consultations, such as written documentation, is very useful if the final decisions of the therapists ever lead to negative results or are questioned later by an ethics panel or a court.

When marriage and family therapists need advice on legal issues, it is essential that the advice come from attorneys rather than from other marriage and family therapists (Remley & Herlihy, 2005). Employed marriage and family therapists should pose any legal questions they have to their direct administrative supervisors. The supervisors then have an obligation either to obtain the legal advice for the therapists and relate the information to them, or to give the therapists direct access to an attorney who represents the employer. In rare instances when the best interests of therapists are in conflict with their employers, such as when supervisors are directing therapists to perform illegal activities, then therapists should consult independent attorneys.

Marriage and family therapists who are in private practice have no alternative when they need legal advice except to pay for it from lawyers in private practice (Remley & Herlihy, 2005). Some professional liability insurance policies or professional association memberships provide limited legal consultation services that might be utilized, but in most cases, therapists in private practice will have to pay for legal advice they receive. It is best for marriage and family therapists to develop relationships with attorneys before problems arise. The best attorneys for private practice marriage and family therapists are those who represent other mental health professionals in the community because they already understand legal issues such as privileged communication, duty to warn intended victims, reporting suspected child abuse, and other important mental health issues that have legal implications.

Once administrators have passed legal advice obtained from lawyers to therapists, an employer's attorneys have given therapists advice, or private attorneys have provided advice to therapists, the legal directives must be followed. Of course, therapists should give attorneys full information and even express their views regarding a particular situation. In the end, however, therapists must follow the legal advice they are given even if they do not like it. If legal advice obtained is wrong or is flawed, the attorneys who gave the advice will be legally responsible for any harm experienced by therapists as a result of the bad advice. If legal advice is obtained and not followed, therapists will not have the support of their attorneys if they have to later defend themselves against allegations of wrongdoing.

| **CASE 1** | *Ethics and the Law* |

Dr. D., a marriage and family therapist, is visited by a process server, who hands him a subpoena issued by an attorney representing the husband of a couple he had seen in therapy. Therapy had been prematurely terminated by the couple at the husband's insistence some months earlier. The couple has now separated and is waging a bitter battle over the custody of their two children. The subpoena directs Dr. D. to appear at the attorney's office in 10 days, with all files and notes about treatment of both the husband and wife. In contacting the wife to apprise her of the subpoena, she explicitly states to Dr. D. her desire to maintain the confidentiality of the session records.

Considerations

The potential for conflict between the ethical principles and practice guidelines of marriage and family therapists and the law (local, state, and federal) is ever present. Such conflicts are manifestations of the temporal and cultural relativity of ethical codes (Mappes, Robb, & Engels, 1985) as well as the fact that laws and the regulations that aid in their implementation are often written in ways that do not take into account the nuances or complexities of marriage and family therapy practice (Bennett et al., 1990). Strict compliance with the spirit and letter of one's professional code of ethics provides no certainty of freedom from legal difficulties. Diligent adherence to their professional code of ethics may, in fact, directly lead marriage and family therapists into legal quagmires.

Clients' rights of access to their files constitutes one particular area of potential conflict between marriage and family therapists' ethics and the law. It is critical that marriage and family therapists recognize that there are both ethical and legal reasons to maintain accurate records and a corresponding duty to keep such records confidential. Marriage and family therapists must be reminded, however, that circumstances may arise when these records may be required to be disclosed to clients or third parties (Hopkins & Anderson, 1990).

The majority of marriage and family therapists will, like Dr. D., work with couples who are considering, currently involved in, or may at a later time enter divorce and/or child custody proceedings. Ethically, and under most state laws, clients are entitled to their records. Therefore, if Dr. D.'s client were seen as an individual and the client requested that treatment records be provided to his or her attorney, Dr. D. would be acting legally and ethically in accommodating the request. A dilemma arises, however, when a marriage and family therapist has worked with a couple or family and only one party authorizes a release of the records.

In most states, privileged communication statutes would not apply to this situation, because privilege is waived when two persons are counseled at the same time. In other states, privilege laws specifically cover relationships between marriage and family therapists and couples or family members (Knapp & VandeCreek, 1987). In situations such as this one, marriage and family therapists must seek and obtain legal advice from an attorney who represents the therapist or the agency for which the therapist works (Boughner & Logan, 1999; Remley & Herlihy, 2005).

The *AAMFT Code of Ethics* is quite clear in calling for each member of the couple or family to agree to a waiver; without a waiver from each family member, a therapist cannot disclose information received from any family member. Many marriage and family therapists take a position that they should defy a court order to release client records if all family members have not waived their right to keep the records confidential; they believe that such a release would violate their ethical responsibility to clients to maintain confidentiality. Remley (1990) responded to this position:

> Although counselors certainly should protest such orders, refusing to comply will result in the counselor being held in contempt of court and either fined or imprisoned. Legally, the client should be the one protesting such orders, not the counselor. Judges do not allow contrary ethical standards of a profession to interfere with provisions of the law. Our laws of discovery state that litigants should have access to all information relevant to a case being litigated. When a court order is issued in our society, it supersedes any professional rule to the contrary. When citizens believe laws are wrong, they should become involved in the legislative process to have them changed. Counselors do not have the option of defying laws when they do not agree with them. (pp. 166–167)

The *AAMFT Code of Ethics* is also clear, however, in noting certain exceptions to the dictate that therapists not disclose client confidences. The first noted exception is "as mandated by law." A court order to make records available would constitute such a mandate.

Conclusions

Of primary importance in this case, given the information presented, are two points: (a) Dr. D. does not have both the husband's and the wife's waiver to release the records, and (b) Dr. D. has received a subpoena, not a court order. The second point is possibly more crucial to consider in responding to the current dilemma. A subpoena is not a court order. A subpoena is simply an order filed with the court by an attorney requesting information or testimony. The order to appear in a subpoena must be followed. A court order is a directive by the court to comply and also must be followed (Stevens-Smith & Hughes, 1993). It is recommended that marriage and family therapists always consult with their own or their employer's attorney to determine if a subpoena is valid and to obtain advice on how to proceed (Remley & Herlihy, 2005; Woody, 1988).

At this point, Dr. D. has only received a subpoena. The following guidelines extracted by Arthur and Swanson (1993) from M. A. Fisher (1991) and Remley (1991) would be most apt for Dr. D. to first consider in responding to the subpoena:

1. Determine if the client wants the subpoenaed information disclosed. Ensure that he or she fully understands all the ramifications of such disclosure.
2. If the client does not wish the information to be released or the therapist believes that disclosure may not be in the client's best interests, the therapist should

recommend that the client consult his or her own attorney. The attorney may agree to withdraw his or her subpoena or file a motion to quash a subpoena issued by an opposing legal counsel. Such motions are generally based upon arguments of privilege protection or relevancy to the pending case. Occasionally, a motion to quash may be partially successful, with a judge agreeing to view the information in private to determine if the records are admissible.

3. If concerns remain, seek legal advice from your own independent attorney or from your employer's attorney regarding available appropriate alternatives.

4. Do not simply defy a subpoena. Take definite legal steps through the client's attorney or by securing personal legal counsel.

Given these suggestions, Dr. D. might first contact both the husband and the wife and discuss the potential ramifications of disclosure with each of them, particularly the husband. Perhaps the session records will not serve the husband as well as he might imagine; they might even display him in a poorer light than his wife relative to the custody issue. Should the husband still request that the records be disclosed (and the wife maintain her position that they not be disclosed), Dr. D. should recommend to the wife that she speak to her attorney about the subpoena. If the wife's attorney is unable to have the subpoena quashed, Dr. D. should show up at the time and place the subpoena establishes and bring his own lawyer to the proceeding and follow the advice his lawyer gives him. Should a judge specifically order that the records be produced, Dr. D. will be required to provide the records despite not having the wife's waiver to do so. Dr. D. would be both legally and ethically mandated to do so.

Several concluding points to consider in this case include the following:

1. Subpoenas typically identify the date, place, and time to appear or present records. This is frequently flexible. A telephone call to schedule a more convenient time is common. It is best to have your own personal attorney make such requests.

2. Some therapists maintain private or unofficial notes, separate from official records. Although this practice is acceptable, it does not shield the notes from a subpoena for records (Arthur & Swanson, 1993). Further, the failure to produce all records (including private notes), if so specified by a subpoena, may subject a therapist to contempt of court charges. In addition, should the therapist testify that all records have been furnished, he or she could be charged with perjury, a criminal offense (Remley, 1990).

3. Copies of subpoenaed records and notes should be made. Originals should be retained if at all possible.

4. Never alter or destroy a document that has been subpoenaed. The potential negative consequences of such an action cannot be understated (Stevens-Smith & Hughes, 1993).

5. A therapist subpoenaed to testify will be testifying as a lay witness. This type of witness, also referred to as a factual or general witness, is only responsible to report his or her professional impression of what occurred in the past and should refrain from giving any professional opinions (Remley, 1991).

CASE 2	*Divorce Mediation*

A marriage and family therapist, Mary E., had observed all too often the negative results for families traveling through the emotional grinder of divorce and child custody court battles. Having read about divorce mediation as a potentially more positive alternative, she considered seeking training for the purpose of offering this service as a part of her practice. In discussing this pursuit with several attorneys, however, questions of significant concern arose for her. "Isn't divorce basically a legal process involving the application of legal rules and principles to the facts of the parties' lives?" she wondered. "If so, then how appropriate is it for a marriage and family therapist to offer such services?"

Considerations

The basic issue confronting Mary E. is her belief that divorce is first and foremost a legal event. It has become increasingly evident over the past decade that mental health professionals are taking a more active role in helping families resolve the personal and financial issues incidental to divorce. In doing this, they have found themselves moving into an area once occupied exclusively by attorneys. Marlow (1985), an attorney, argued that viewing divorce as a legal event ignores the fact that it is more importantly a personal event in a family's life. His major points are summarized in the following paragraphs as an alternative for Mary E.'s perspective.

In What Real Sense Is Divorce a Legal Event?
The decision to divorce, like the decision to marry, can be viewed as primarily a personal rather than a legal decision. Many couples seek premarital counseling from marriage and family therapists; very infrequently do they consult attorneys when deciding to marry (unless legal rights and obligations between them are created). If the parties treat such matters as personal at the time of their marriage, deciding on them without resorting to legal counsel, it seems reasonable to suppose that they can continue to do so when divorcing. This does not imply that there are no legal implications whatsoever, simply that personal aspects of the event should take precedence.

What Has Prevented This "Personal Event" Concept of Divorce from Becoming the Dominant View?
Marlow (1985) asserted that the idea that divorcing parties must seek legal counsel, first to determine their legal rights and then to protect those rights—that this is a prerequisite to any resolution of their dispute—is a myth. Many mediators and lawyers insist, however, that attorneys must be a part of divorce mediation if it is to be fair and withstand any later legal challenges (N. J. Foster & Kelly, 1996; Gangel-Jacob, 1997). The divorce process mistakenly has been represented to be more than the resolution of a dispute between a couple; divorcing couples are erroneously perceived to be unable to protect their respective rights and obligations without resorting to the law.

How Does the Law Offer This Protection?

For example, a husband is told by his wife that she is considering divorce and has consulted an attorney. He immediately assumes that his wife and her attorney are planning to get him for everything they can (a reasonable assumption, given the adversarial structure of the legal system). These concerns are further fed by the fact that legal ethics demand that he and his wife cannot be represented by the same attorney; she meets with her attorney "in confidence." To protect himself, he too retains an attorney and thus feeds the adversarial cycle. This phenomenon is referred to as a self-fulling prophecy in psychology.

Doesn't a Divorcing Family Need Attorneys to Advise Them of Their Legal Rights?

Again, the very idea that the determination of the couple's respective legal rights is an issue in the divorce is more myth than fact. This myth has stemmed from a failure to distinguish between two types of laws. The first type is usually constitutional in nature and guarantees such rights as voting, free speech, and practicing the religion of one's choice. Such laws can appropriately be labeled *legal rights*. The second type of laws, however, includes those laws that regulate society's conduct or simply resolve personal disputes. Although these laws may embody society's conception of what is fair and appropriate at any given time, to speak of them as legal rights is to endow them with exaggerated significance.

Most people want their disagreements to be resolved in a fair manner, to represent what is just. The rules that society adopts in the form of laws to resolve disputes between people are just "rules" and no more. Legal rules are applied by society, not because they do justice, but because they are a means of ending disputes that parties are unable to end themselves. The prevailing belief, although a mistaken one, is that divorcing families must use a dispute resolution procedure that emanates from traditional legal regulation, whether they need this regulation or not. That couples may ultimately be required to resort to the law and the application of legal rules to resolve personal disputes does not change them into legal disputes. They remain personal problems that are still best resolved by relevant personal decision-making strategies, not necessarily by the application of legal rules.

Are There Times When Legal Rules Should Legitimately Take Priority in a Divorce Dispute?

Primary legal intervention is relevant in one situation: If one or both partners seek to use the agreement to divorce as a means for venting hurt and anger rather than as a vehicle to resolve their mutual problems, it is best done within a legal structure. If one partner seeks to discredit the other from what is rightfully his or hers, then quite obviously both need to be apprised of legal rules and equally may need to have those rules applied to their dispute.

There is an important point to further consider, however. Families in the process of divorce generally have little accurate understanding of why and how they have gotten to this point in their lives. Frequently both partners tend to idealize themselves as victims; they want the other to pay and look to the divorce agreement as the vehicle to accomplish this. Divorce offers an opportunity to help them put their pasts behind them and to get on with the important business of their future. Divorce agreements that seek to correct past wrongs, whether real or imagined, block this potential opportunity.

Conclusions

Divorce, like marriage, is an important transitional event in the life of a family. As such, it concerns issues that are primarily personal and not legal. What the law only offers is a procedure for resolving a family's dispute if all other dispute resolution mechanisms fail. Given this fact, and contrary to a self-perpetuating myth, the law has little to contribute to the resolution of disputes among members of divorcing families.

After consulting with attorneys on the relevance of divorce mediation for the practice of a marriage and family therapist, Mary E. saw that the mental health community has not overstepped its boundaries and entered into the legal world in assisting divorcing families to resolve their disputes through mediation. Rather, the legal profession has for years taken mostly personal decisions in the lives of divorcing families and, by the blanket imposition of legal rules and principles, converted them into legal problems.

Mary E. can equally assert that divorce mediation represents more than an alternative procedure to help families resolve issues in a less destructive manner. She can affirm a view of divorce as a personal, not a legal, problem to which mediation represents a better means of dispute resolution. What keeps divorcing families from resolving their disagreements is their fear, hurt, and anger; the adversarial procedures inherent in legal rules almost guarantee an exacerbation of these feelings. If families are to experience a psychological as well as a legal divorce, they must be helped to put these destructive emotions into proper perspective and resolve them.

Mary E. might be more accurate in generally viewing divorce mediation based on her own understanding of family functioning. The specialized training she is considering will add to her understanding by offering pragmatic procedures to aid divorcing families making concrete decisions after they have been helped with their emotional confusion.

CASE 3
                                Liability in Crisis Counseling

Lou was a 16-year-old who had been seen together with his parents in family therapy for a few sessions over a year ago. Therapy was initiated originally because Lou had been experiencing problems with regard to peer pressure to engage in drug use. The family prematurely terminated therapy efforts after some early positive changes. More recently, feeling alienated, Lou had turned to drugs to alleviate his anxiety and provide himself with a greater sense of belonging. Paradoxically, he developed a barbiturate dependency, creating depression and feelings of isolation. After an especially hostile interchange with his parents over his drug use, Lou, in a hysterical frenzy, telephoned the therapist, crying that he was going to kill himself. The therapist remembered Lou and attempted to calm him, but Lou responded negatively, perceiving the therapist as preaching to him like his parents. The therapist had taken Lou's call between sessions and had someone waiting to see him. Feeling rushed, impatient with Lou, and not accurately perceiving Lou's desperation, the therapist lashed out at Lou, telling him to "grow up," whereupon Lou hung up. Feeling further rejected, Lou took an overdose of barbiturates and died. Later that day, feeling guilty about his response to the situation, the therapist called Lou's parents, hoping he might get the family to come in for further therapy. The parents were enraged that the therapist had reacted in a way that added to their son's problems. They accused the therapist of "killing" their son and filed suit against the therapist, claiming negligence that resulted in wrongful death.

Considerations

The law of negligence, which comprises a large part of the law of torts, includes various kinds of wrongful acts that result in injury or damages. As a general rule, liability for negligence will accrue if one person causes damage to another through a breach of duty owed to that person. To hold a therapist liable in a tort action for negligence, the court must find the following:

1. A duty was owed by the therapist to the client; that a therapist–client relationship had been established.
2. The duty was breached; that the therapist's conduct fell below an acceptable standard of care.
3. There was a sufficient legal causal connection between the breach of duty and the client's injury.
4. There was an actual injury sustained by the client.

As there had been a previous therapist–client relationship, the first major inquiry in the present case seeks to determine if the therapist's conduct fell below an acceptable standard of care. Concurrently, does the fact that this was a "crisis or emergency" situation have additional bearing on the issue? What standard of care does the law require of therapists in such special situations?

Fischer and Sorenson (1985) quoted former Supreme Court justice Oliver Wendell Holmes, Jr., in this regard: "Detached reflection can not be expected in front of an uplifted knife" (p. 48). What Holmes sought to convey is that in emergency situations, the same degree of care and thoughtful action cannot be expected as would be in ordinary affairs. This principle particularly applies to telephone crisis counseling when the therapist does not typically have real control over the client or the situation. The guiding legal principle in such situations has tended to be this: A person is responsible for harm to another only if failure to exercise reasonable care increases the risk of harm to that other person (Negligence §1, 2000). A failure in crisis counseling requires that the therapist reject the client's cry for help in a way indicating that the therapist did not exercise reasonable care in doing so. If the therapist so acted, the next major question to consider would be whether such action by the therapist had indeed increased the risk of harm to the client (B. Gross, 2005).

Conclusions

Clearly, a crisis was at hand when the therapist received Lou's phone call. Lou was in an extremely distraught emotional state. It might still be argued his emotional state was not sufficiently dangerous that, considered alone, it could be construed as the cause of his death. It could be asserted, however, that the last straw for Lou was the therapist's rejection of his cry for help. Taken in that light, the therapist not only may have failed to alleviate an impending crisis, but he also may have actually made it worse.

An added factor in the therapist's scope of liability was the fact that Lou had been a client and the therapist was aware of his problems. Because the therapist was better informed about Lou's situation than a professional Lou might have selected from the telephone book, a higher standard of care could be expected. The presumption is that increased knowledge about a situation renders an increased capability to give real assistance. As a result, it is possible that a court might find that the therapist's actions did constitute negligence that resulted in wrongful death. On the other hand, additional facts in this case could lead to a different result.

CASE 4	

Informed Consent?

David K. has developed an approach to group couples' therapy that includes a number of touching activities that he has found to help couples understand the importance of their primary and friendship relationships. The activities require couples to massage their partners and other group members, to physically embrace a third member of the group in some instances, and to spend substantial amounts of time in sessions holding hands with, embracing, and standing close enough to touch the bodies of members other than their partners. David has found that his approach is very effective in helping couples strengthen their commitment to each other. However, he has also discovered that if he describes the activities in his sessions in detail, very few people participate. As a result, he now advertises his workshops as "experiences that help couples appreciate their partners and be in touch with themselves and others." Recently, a couple participated in David's therapy experience. The wife had an affair with another group member, left her husband, and told her husband that she had discovered how unhappy she was in her marriage as a result of David's therapy. The husband has sued David, claiming that David never disclosed the nature of the physical contact in David's therapy sessions, that he would have never signed up for therapy with David if he had known what would happen there, and that his wife left him because of David's approach to therapy and David's failure to disclose the therapeutic approach before he agreed to participate.

Considerations

Basic to all treatment is professionals' and clients' discussion of the nature of the problem and possible treatments for it. Before treatment begins, the client must consent to it, thus giving the therapist power to act (Kaplan & Culkin, 1995). Two notable cases are relevant in this regard. In the 1957 case of *Salgo v. Leland Stanford, Jr., University Board of Trustees*, tort liability was established for the failure of a physician to explain the risks and benefits of a medical procedure. The court declared that not all risks need to be explained, but that the practitioner should use discretion in explaining risks based on each person's mental and emotional status. Initiation of the doctrine of informed consent has been attributed to the 1960 case of *Nathanson v. Kline*. Negligence in informing the client of possible risks was the basis for the tort liability. Further, this case changed the standard for assessing liability from the "reasonable person doctrine" to the doctrine of deviation from the standard of conduct of a reasonable and prudent medical doctor of the same school of practice as the defendant under similar circumstances (H. H. Foster, 1978; J. Katz, 1977). This distinction between the "reasonable person" and "reasonable medical doctor" standards was an important one for establishing evidence and proof in a malpractice action. The conduct of a marriage and family therapist is measured against the standard of the average, reasonable person who is a marriage and family therapist (i.e., the average, reasonable person who has superior knowledge and skills as a result of training and experience and whose knowledge and skills are commonly possessed by members in good standing of the profession).

Consent to act is simply willingness that treatment can occur and will prevent liability in a tort. Consent is manifested by words or actions that a "reasonable person" would understand to be consent. Silence or inaction have been held to be consent in cases in which a reasonable person would have spoken if he or she objected. In legal actions seeking damages, the principle of informed consent of the person damaged will ordinarily void liability for intentional interference with a person or property (Prosser, 1971). Typically, consent is usually implied in clients' initiation of therapy. Such a general consent may, however, have no legal force if a client had no opportunity to compare the risks of participating in therapy with the dangers of forgoing it (Dooley, 1977).

Systemically oriented marriage and family therapists maintain the assumption that any procedures they employ may have an impact well beyond the identified client. The work they might do with individual clients is likely to affect not only the client but also those persons in contact with him or her. The legal requirement of obtaining informed consent before beginning actual treatment applies, however, only to those persons who have direct contact with the therapist. Furthermore, *legally adequate consent* of those in direct contact with the therapist has been defined as "consent by a person who has the following characteristics: legal capacity, comprehension of information and voluntary agreement" (Bray et al., 1985, p. 54). *Legal capacity* means that the person giving consent is of minimum legal age and has not been adjudicated as incompetent to manage his or her affairs. *Comprehension of information* means that the person giving consent must have been given information relating to the risks and the benefits of the procedure, the risks of forgoing the procedure, and the procedures available as an alternative to the proposed treatment (Applebaum, Lidz, & Meisel, 1987; Bray et al., 1985).

The type and amount of information to discuss with clients have been subjects of controversy for some time (Behnke & Saks, 1998; Berner, 1998; *Canterbury v. Spence*, 1972). Clients want information about their therapists and perceive those who provide details about themselves and their procedures as more expert and trustworthy than those who do not (Braaten et al., 1993; Handler, 1990; Hendrick, 1998; Walter & Handelsman, 1996). T. R. Johnson (1965) suggests that the only potential risks that need to be disclosed are those that would cause the client to forgo therapy. Yet Oppenheim (1968) argues for the disclosure of any risk that might influence, however slightly, the clients' decision to accept therapy. In general, therapists need not disclose every risk. In deciding what risks to discuss with clients, therapists should balance clients' desires and the right to make their own decisions regarding therapy with the therapist's own desire to withhold information about potential risks when disclosure might harm a client's well-being. Achieving this balance calls for an exercise of professional judgment that is an exception to the basic principle of disclosure of all potential risks (Waltz & Scheuneman, 1969). Waltz and Scheuneman expressed their belief that the ideal informed consent rule calls for risks to be disclosed when a client would find them important in deciding whether or not to consent to therapy. In resolving the question of what to disclose, the therapist can apply the standard of the reasonable person who finds himself or herself in the position of the client. The value of the "Professional Disclosure Statement" presented in Chapter 3 is most relevant regarding this. Touch in the process of therapy is a particularly controversial issue (Mor, 2005), and certainly clients should give their informed consent before any touching takes place (Knapp & VandeCreek, 2006).

Given the legal requirements for informed consent, it has been recommended to ensure proof of such procedures by having clients sign a form during an initial session, indicating that appropriate information was provided and consent is thus given for treatment (R. J. Cohen, 1979; Glosoff, 1997; Haas & Malouf, 1995; Weinrach, 1989; Welfel, 1998). An example of such a form is the "Therapeutic Contract," also discussed in Chapter 3. Failure to obtain informed consent leaves therapists liable and subject to legal action. The proof required to show consent when not in written form is unclear. In many cases, practitioners have been asked to prove that the client consented, and in others, the issue of consent was so vital to the case that the lack of consent must be proved by the client (Prosser, 1971).

Conclusions

Three possible legal actions can be taken in cases of informed consent. The first and most common is negligence. In this instance, the failure to make a complete disclosure can result in a judgment of negligent practice (*Cobbs v. Grant*, 1972). The second potential legal action is battery. If the client's bodily integrity is invaded without consent, battery occurs. Cases of this nature are characterized by absence of informed consent and do not require proof of negligence. The reasoning of this rule is that, had the client known about the risks involved, he or she would not have agreed to the procedure. A third type of possible liability is breach of contract. If a marriage and family therapist guarantees that a certain treatment will "cure" the client and it does not, the therapist is liable for breach of contract (Slovenko, 1978). As in battery complaints, proof is not needed, because it is in the domain of contractual law and not a breach of tort liability.

In the present case, the husband can complain of negligence and breach of contract, in that David never secured the husband's informed consent to the treatment the husband and wife received in the couples' therapy sessions. In addition, the husband might argue that battery occurred, in that the husband never specifically agreed to the touching that took place in the sessions. The husband might point to his wife's leaving the marriage as damages that were a specific result of David's negligent provision of therapy services.

David's defense to these charges of wrongdoing might be that touching exercises were explained to participants before they occurred, that no clients were forced to participate, and that the lack of any objection constituted consent. David might also argue that the wife's decision to leave her husband was based on factors other than the therapy sessions and that the therapy sessions were not the cause of the breakup of the marriage.

Whether or not the negligence suit against David would prevail would depend on additional facts of the case and the response of a judge or jury to hearing the facts. Cases like this could be decided either way.

CASE 5	*Criminal Liability*

Melissa J. is a novice marriage and family therapist employed by a community-funded child guidance clinic. Cindy is a 15-year-old client whom Melissa has been seeing because of family conflicts. Cindy's parents were recently divorced, and she was having problems coping with their breakup. Neither parent was willing to participate in therapy with their daughter, seeing her concerns as "things she needs to work out on her own." Cindy confides to Melissa that she and her boyfriend had stolen a car during the past weekend. They still have the car. Having no one else to turn to, Cindy asks Melissa's help in returning the car to the owner without involving the police.

Considerations

Marriage and family therapists such as Melissa J. who work with minors can encounter situations that might cause the therapist to incur criminal liability. Therapists must be aware of areas of possible danger. Three particular areas to consider include reporting known crimes, contributing to the delinquency of a minor, and being an accessory to a crime before or after the fact (Fischer & Sorenson, 1985).

Reporting Known Crimes

Private citizens have no legal duty to report crimes they know about. Persons cannot attempt to conceal criminal activity, assist a criminal in avoiding prosecution, or refuse to answer questions regarding crimes. They do not have to tell anyone about crimes they have observed or know about, however.

Based on the same principle, marriage and family therapists generally do not have to report criminal activities that clients report in therapy sessions. But, if therapists determine that clients are a danger to themselves or to others, therapists must take actions to prevent harm. As a result, a determination of danger to self or others would require a marriage and family therapist to report the criminal activity of a client, not the criminal activity itself. In addition, marriage and family therapists are prohibited from purposefully concealing crimes from authorities or assisting clients in avoiding being discovered or arrested. If a privileged communication statute protects the relationship with the client, but a legal exception exists to privilege, then a marriage and family therapist would be required to repeat to authorities information they learned from a client related to criminal activities. Statutes vary by state.

Contributing to the Delinquency of a Minor

Each state defines the meaning of "minor" for purposes of its own laws. Although there are variations among states, a *minor* is generally defined as a youth subject to the control of a parent or guardian or under a specified age (usually 16). Likewise, individual states have their own laws concerning what constitutes contributing to the delinquency of a minor. There are several common elements, however. The generally cited purposes of such laws are to protect minors from the negative influence of adults who might lead them astray and to prevent conduct that would lead to delinquency. Massachusetts law provides a typical illustration, stating in part that:

> Any person who shall be found to have caused, induced, abetted, encouraged or contributed toward the waywardness or delinquency of a child, or to have acted in any way tending to cause or induce such waywardness or delinquency, may be punished by a fine of not more than five hundred dollars or by imprisonment for not more than one year, or both. (Massachusetts General Laws, ch. 119, §63)

Contributing to the delinquency of a minor is frequently associated by the general public with sexual interactions. The law identifies a much broader range of actions that might adversely affect the welfare of the public or the healthy development of a minor. Consequently, the meaning of contributing to the delinquency of a minor could encompass a wide variety of behaviors that injure the morals, health, or welfare of minors, or encourage their participation in activities that would lead to such injury.

Fischer and Sorenson (1985) offer case examples of therapists found facing a charge of contributing to the delinquency of a minor:

- The therapist who chaperoned a school-sponsored weekend trip and helped students procure beer and wine for the cookout.
- The therapist who chaperoned a Friday evening party and was aware that several youths were smoking marijuana but did nothing about it.

Even though there may be no intention to commit a crime, a marriage and family therapist could still be found guilty of contributing to the delinquency of a minor in either of these situations. In general, for a person to be guilty of a crime, there must be a concurrence of an act and an intent. The law generally requires *mens rea* (guilty intent) for an act to be a crime. For example, if a pedestrian is hit by an out-of-control car because of a tire blowout, the driver has not committed a crime. If it can be proved that the driver intentionally sought to run down a pedestrian, a crime would have been committed.

In cases involving delinquency, however, individual states differ with regard to proof of guilty intent. Some states require proof of guilty intent, and others do not require the presence of such intent. It is important that marriage and family therapists know the specific provisions in the laws of their respective states to adequately address activities that might be construed by their state courts as contributing to the delinquency of a minor.

Accessory to a Crime

Marriage and family therapists can be in a difficult position if their clients discuss either a plan to commit a crime or a crime they have already committed. Therapists' duty to protect probable victims of a dangerous crime supersedes any claim of confidentiality or privilege. Therapists' obligations are fairly clear in such instances. There is less clarity, however, when a client seeks a therapist's help after a crime has been committed.

Not all crimes involve danger to persons; some crimes are against property. For example, a client might confide a plan to destroy some equipment or a building related to racist or antireligious activities. The mere knowledge that a crime will occur, if there is no special duty to prevent it, does not incur guilt. However, if a therapist accompanied a client to the scene of a crime with knowledge that it likely will be committed or assisted a client in getting away after committing the crime, he or she would become culpable in the eyes of the law (Fischer & Sorenson, 1985). Any person who aids in the commission of a crime, even if he or she is not present when it takes place, may be as guilty as the instigator or may be charged as an accessory before the fact, depending on the laws of the particular state.

An accessory after the fact is generally a person who, knowing that a crime was committed, receives, relieves, comforts, or assists the perpetrator or somehow aids the perpetrator in escaping arrest or punishment. Thus:

1. A crime must have been committed.
2. The accessory must know that the perpetrator committed the crime.
3. The accessory must harbor or protect the perpetrator.

If, during a session, the therapist learns that the client committed a crime, and if, thereafter, the therapist helps the client hide or otherwise offers protection from law enforcement authorities or assists the client in escaping detection, the therapist may be guilty of being an accessory to a crime after the fact (Fischer & Sorenson, 1985).

It is important to note that there may be differences relative to whether the crime is a felony or misdemeanor. Common law identifies no accessory to the commission of a misdemeanor. Individual states, however, may create such a category.

Conclusions

Marriage and family therapists who act with a reasonable degree of care should have few occasions to be concerned about criminal liability. This is not to say, however, that marriage and family therapists are immune from criminal prosecution. Intentional actions or even some careless, unintentional behaviors may constitute contributing to the delinquency of a minor or being an accessory to a crime. Burgum and Anderson (1975) described an illustrative case relating to criminal liability of a school counselor that somewhat parallels Melissa J.'s situation:

> A boy in the custody of a juvenile court had developed a good relationship with his school counselor. The boy, with two companions, robbed a service station and then, realizing the gravity of his actions, went to the counselor for help. The counselor convinced the boy that he should turn himself in to the police. It was late at night, however, so they agreed he would go to the police the next day. Meanwhile, the counselor committed a series of acts that made him an accessory to a felony. He denied to the police that the boy was in his home. He gave the boy money, which was found in the youth's possession when he tried to skip town the next morning rather than reporting to the police. The counselor would have been well-advised to have reported the matter to the boy's juvenile court representative and/or the police. Instead, he inadvertently helped the boy avoid arrest.

The facts of this case indicate that the school counselor was clearly an accessory after the fact: (a) a crime was committed; (b) the counselor knew that the boy committed the crime; and (c) the counselor harbored and protected the boy from police.

In Melissa J.'s case, the best course of action would be for her to convince Cindy to inform one or both of her parents about the car theft. Melissa should tell Cindy to follow her parents' advice in handling the situation. In the event Cindy refused to tell her parents, Melissa should inform one or both parents of the theft over Cindy's objection. By ensuring that one or both of Cindy's parents are informed of the car theft by either having Cindy tell or by Melissa telling them herself, Melissa will have turned the situation over to the parents and transferred responsibility to one or both parents. Only if the parents are incapable of handling the situation in a reasonable or appropriate manner should Melissa tell anyone of the situation beyond the parents.

CASE 6	*Parental Rights and FERPA*

Aaron M. is a marriage and family therapist who regularly receives referrals from public school personnel. He works with families in which the children are experiencing emotional difficulties affecting their ability to perform adequately in the classroom. His common practice has been to provide written reports to the referral source (with the child's and parents' permission) at regular intervals and on completion of therapy efforts.

The Kent family was initially referred to the therapist because their 13-year-old son David was displaying significant acting out behaviors with both peers and school personnel. In consultation with David's teacher, the school guidance counselor suspected that David was having these behaviors modeled at home and thus the referral was made to Aaron M. The therapist structured the therapy so that total family sessions would be alternated weekly with individual sessions for David (primarily because the parents were unable to participate every week because of their work schedules). In discussing the therapist's latest report with the parents, David's teacher made particular reference to the therapist's notation that "David perceives his parents' general hostility toward each other as the way all people are." The parents became incensed, as they had not heard their son say this in their presence, assumed that he had done so during an individual session, and demanded that Aaron M. share all information from the individual sessions. The therapist politely declined, explaining the therapeutic need to allow David the opportunity to feel safe in sharing himself. The parents sought the aid of their attorney, who telephoned the therapist requesting that the parents be allowed to review the therapist's session records, citing the Family Educational Rights and Privacy Act (FERPA), which is sometimes referred to as the Buckley Amendment.

Considerations

It has long been common practice among mental health personnel to clearly mark or otherwise indicate that all client notes, reports, letters, and charts are "confidential." Access to or communication of the materials generally is shared only with relevant professionals directly concerned with the client. Thus, such materials are typically not intended to be seen or used by clients themselves. Many marriage and family therapists believe that such materials could be subject to misinterpretation and misunderstanding by clients and therefore could possibly have negative or harmful effects.

The Family Educational Rights and Privacy Act of 1974 (FERPA, or The Buckley Amendment, 20 U.S.C. §1232g) and the regulations promulgated for its implementation guarantee to parents and to "eligible students" (18 and over) certain rights with regard to the inspection and dissemination of educational records. Because it is a federal law, it applies to all school districts and schools that receive federal financial assistance through the U.S. Department of Education. Since most private and parochial schools receive federal assistance in some form, they generally are governed by FERPA also. Although state departments of education or private schools, at least theoretically, could decide not to accept federal money, the guarantees of FERPA are not really rights in the fullest sense. As one court noted however, FERPA is not necessarily binding on a particular school district, but because federal funding might otherwise be discontinued, the court enforced the provisions of the law (*Sauerkof v. City of New York*, 1981). Pragmatically, FERPA does create rights for parents and students, that most, if not all, schools will be responsible for ensuring (Fischer & Sorenson, 1985). Furthermore, this law is consistent with legislative trends in several other areas and thus grants legal support to persons (parents') right to know and to challenge personal and evaluative material maintained by various agents of society (McGuire & Borowy, 1978).

The minimum requirements of FERPA call for the adoption of policies and practices that meet the following criteria (*Final Regulations*, 1976):

1. Parents and eligible students be informed of their rights.
2. Parents and eligible students be permitted to review educational records, request changes, request a hearing if changes are disallowed, and add their own statements by way of explanation, if necessary.
3. Ensure that the institution does not give out personally identifiable information without prior written, informed consent of a parent or eligible student.
4. Maintain and allow parents and eligible students to see the institution's record of disclosures.
5. Facilitate parents' and eligible students' access to records by providing information on the types of educational records and the procedures for gaining access to them.

Education records under the law are defined as those records that (a) are directly related to the student, and (b) are maintained by the educational agency or institution or by a party acting for that agency or institution (*Final Regulations*, 1976). Although educational records that must be made available on parents' request include a wide variety of materials, some exceptions are especially relevant to the present case. One record not subject to disclosure is that made by a relevant professional remaining in "the sole possession of the maker thereof" and is not "accessible or revealed to any other individual except a substitute" (*Final Regulations*, 1976). The legislative history of FERPA makes clear that educational records do not include the "personal files of psychologists, counselors, or professors if these files are entirely private and not available to other individuals" (120 Cong. Rec. 27, 36555, 1974). However, Senator James Buckley, for whom the law is named, stated that this "memory aids" exception was not intended to allow either regular school personnel or a variety of substitutes to "rotate through courses and classes . . . for the purpose of effectively gaining access to another's notes and evaluations" (120 Cong. Rec. 31, 41381, 1974). This is reinforced by the definition of the term *substitute:* "An individual who performs on a temporary basis the duties of the individual who made the record and does not refer to an individual who permanently succeeds the maker of the record in his or her position" (*Final Regulations*, 1976).

Conclusions

Parental rights are an important issue in this situation. Generally, a therapist's legal obligations are to a parent or guardian, rather than to a client, when a client is below the age of 18 (Orton, 1997). The clients (or in this case, the parents of a client) do have a legal right to see records kept by a therapist related to the therapist's treatment (Application of Striegel, 1977; Claim of Gerkin, 1980; *People v. Cohen,* 1977). Although the parents do not have a legal right to the records under FERPA (as is explained below), they would have a legal right to the records if they were to pursue their rights through court proceedings. So, while Aaron M. might "politely decline" to give copies of his records regarding David's treatment to David's parents upon their demand, the parents do have a legal right to the records and could pursue this legal right through their attorney. Even though FERPA does not provide access to the records, general legal principles regarding patient access to health care records do.

What constitutes eligible educational records is an additional issue in this case. The definition hinges not so much on the nature of the material as on the primary purposes of the material and who may have access to it. Aaron M.'s personal session notes probably would be excluded from the definition of educational records, provided he prepares and maintains them solely for his own purposes; for example, the session notes themselves are not available to the referral source to review. The letters communicating feedback to the referral source are a different matter. Materials accessible to other personnel (i.e., the referral source) would be considered part of David's educational record and must be made available to his parents on their request.

One path that David's parents do have access to, however, regards the contents of the therapist's report. Several provisions in the law guarantee the right to challenge information that parents or eligible students believe is "inaccurate or misleading or violates the privacy or other rights of the student" (Family Rights and Privacy Act, 1997). If the school personnel decline to change the records, there is a further right to a hearing, where parents or eligible students are allowed to bring an attorney or other representative. If, after this hearing, the school still declines to change the record, the complaining party is permitted to add a statement to the record explaining the disagreement. The school is then obliged to give out this explanation any time the part of the record it refers to is disclosed to anyone, including other school personnel.

CASE 7

The Premarital Agreement

Jan and Howard have lived together for the past 11 months. Both are divorced and have children by previous marriages. Jan's daughter lives with her and Howard. Howard's son and daughter live with their mother. The couple initiated therapy efforts to attempt to work out several problems they are experiencing between themselves and Jan's daughter. A dominant difficulty revolves around Jan's guilt feelings over the "negative" role model she sees herself as providing by living with Howard without benefit of formal marriage. Howard clearly states his love for and desire to marry Jan, but equally identifies his fear that, should the marriage fail, he would be overwhelmed if he had to pay support for Jan and any children they might have, in addition to the support he pays his first wife and two children. The issue of a premarital agreement to circumvent this concern is raised.

Considerations

The number of marriages between persons previously married is steadily increasing. For this and other reasons, it is becoming more common for couples contemplating remarriage to attempt to forestall any future problems by creating a premarital agreement. Despite a lengthy legal history of premarital agreements, however, there is still substantial uncertainty as to the enforceability of all, or a portion, of the provisions of such agreements (Belcher & Pomeroy, 1998). Furthermore, there has been a significant lack of uniformity in the treatment of these agreements among the various states. The problems caused by this uncertainty and nonuniformity are exacerbated even more by the mobility of today's population. Nevertheless, this reflects spontaneous and reflexive responses to various factual circumstances at different times rather than basic policy differences among states (Bureau of National Affairs, Inc., 1984).

Accordingly, the Uniform Premarital Agreement Act was adopted by the National Conference of Commissioners on Uniform State Laws in 1983 and was approved by the American Bar Association in 1984. The act was established to provide a model for state governing bodies to conform to modern social policy, providing sufficient certainty yet flexibility to accommodate different circumstances. Its derivation from a consensus of state laws suggests it is a utilitarian model for the purposes of the present case.

Comprised of 13 sections, the act is relatively limited in scope. Section 1 defines a premarital agreement as "an agreement between prospective spouses made in contemplation of marriage and to be effective upon marriage" (Bureau of National Affairs, Inc., 1984). Section 2 requires that a premarital agreement be in writing and signed by both parties. Section 3 provides an illustrative list of those matters that may be properly dealt with in a premarital agreement. Section 4 states that the premarital agreement becomes effective on the marriage of the parties. Sections 1, 2, and 4 in particular establish significant parameters. The act does not deal with agreements between persons who live together but who do not marry or contemplate marriage. Nor does the act provide for postmarital, separation, or oral agreements.

Section 5 prescribes the manner in which a premarital agreement might be amended or revoked. Section 6 is the key operative of the act and sets forth the conditions under which a premarital agreement is not enforceable. Such an agreement is not enforceable if the party against whom enforcement is sought proves that he or she did not enter the agreement voluntarily or that the agreement was one-sided, oppressive, or unfair when it was entered. Also, the agreement is not enforceable if, before the agreement was entered, he or she (a) did not have access to a fair and reasonable disclosure of the property or financial obligations of the other party; (b) did not voluntarily and explicitly waive, in writing, any right to the disclosure of property or financial obligations; and (c) did not have, or reasonably could not have had, an adequate knowledge of the property and financial obligations of the other party. Even if these conditions are not proved, if a provision of a premarital agreement modifies or eliminates spousal support, and that modification or elimination causes a party to be eligible for public assistance should a future separation or divorce occur, the court is authorized to order the other party to provide support to the extent necessary to avoid that eligibility (Bureau of National Affairs, Inc., 1984).

Sections 7 and 8 address more tangential issues. Section 7 provides for very limited enforcement when a marriage is subsequently determined to be void. Section 8 tolls any statute of limitations applicable to an action asserting a claim for relief under a premarital agreement during the parties' marriage. Sections 9 through 13 simply address minor points such as the act's "short title," "time of taking effect," and "repeal."

Of the greatest relevance to the present case is Section 3, relating to areas of contract in a premarital agreement. These include the following points:

1. Rights and obligations of each party in any of either or both the property whenever and wherever acquired or located.
2. The right to buy, sell, use, transfer, exchange, abandon, lease, consume, expend, assign, create a security interest in, mortgage, encumber, dispose of, or otherwise manage and control property.
3. Disposition of property upon separation, marital dissolution, death, or the occurrence of any other such event.
4. Modification or elimination of spousal support.
5. The making of a will, trust, or other arrangement to carry out the provisions of the agreement.
6. Ownership rights in and disposition of a death benefit from a life insurance policy.
7. Choice of law governing construction of the agreement.
8. Any other matter, including personal rights and obligations, not in violation of public policy or a statute imposing a criminal penalty.
9. The right of a child to support may not be adversely affected by a premarital agreement. (Bureau of National Affairs, Inc., 1984).

Conclusions

Section 3 of the Uniform Premarital Agreement Act permits parties to contract in a premarital agreement on any matter listed and any other matter not in violation of public policy or imposing a criminal penalty. Point 4 specifically deals with spousal support obligations.

It is important to remember that this act is a model advanced by the National Conference of Commissioners on Uniform State Laws and the American Bar Association for states to adopt. States have differed on whether a premarital agreement may or may not control the issue of spousal support. Some states have not permitted a premarital agreement to control this issue (e.g., Iowa: *In re Marriage of Winegard*, 1979; Wisconsin: *Fricke v. Fricke*, 1950). The more common and growing trend, however, has been to permit premarital agreements to govern this matter if such agreements and the circumstances of their execution satisfy certain standards (e.g., Colorado: *Newman v. Newman*, 1982; Connecticut: *Parniawski v. Parniawski*, 1976; Massachusetts: *Osborne v. Osborne*, 1981). Thus, it is likely that the couple in the present case, Jan and Howard, might enter into a premarital agreement, eliminating spousal support should their marriage ultimately end in divorce.

Point 9, by contrast, makes clear that any premarital agreement may not adversely affect what would otherwise be this couples' obligation to children born of their marriage. This latter point of concern will not be resolved through any premarital agreement.

CASE 8	*Privileged Communications*

A couple had been seeing a therapist for marital discord during the fourth year of their marriage. The couple met with the therapist for five conjoint sessions. During these sessions, the husband was open in sharing his self-perceived faults. The wife was rather guarded. The wife's lack of commitment to the therapy created a context in which the couple was unable to accommodate their differences and thus led to a decision to divorce. Now, some months after the last session with them, the therapist receives a subpoena to appear in court to testify relative to the custody of the couple's daughter. In contacting both parties, who are now living separately, the therapist learns that the wife's attorney is requesting to have the therapist testify to what her husband had shared about himself. The therapist is requested by the husband to keep what he had stated confidential, recognizing that revealing it might adversely affect his custody chances.

Considerations

According to common law, courts should have broad access to evidence. Citizens should present their evidence to the court because all of society benefits from the proper administration of justice. Privileged communication laws run contrary to common law in this respect because they exclude evidence from the courts (*Harvard Law Review*, 1985). Yet the need for a therapist–client privilege is an obvious one. Successful therapy efforts require the establishment of trust between therapists and clients. Fear of potential disclosure before a court would obviously deter many persons from seeking needed treatment, impair the course of therapy, or foster premature termination when issues of risk arose (H. H. Foster, 1976; Kennedy, 1973).

State legislatures have consequently enacted privileged communication laws to protect consumers of psychotherapy. The application of such privileges vary from state to state or even within the same state according to the professional training or credentials of the therapist. Generally speaking, however, courts tend to strictly interpret privileged communication laws. The traditional view holds that the statutes must specify any exception to the common-law duty to provide testimony to the court. The privilege has existed only for clients of professionals specifically named in the statutes. Hence, the definition of the terms *psychologist, social worker, marriage and family therapist*, or *counselor* in statutes will determine if a specific therapist is included. In the absence of a statute, courts have tended to refuse to extend the privilege (e.g., social workers: *State v. Driscoll*, 1972; unlicensed psychologists: *State v. Vickers*, 1981).

Several states extend privileges to associates working under the direction of a protected professional. For example, a Wisconsin law has held that the privilege extends to persons "who are participating in the diagnosis and treatment under the direction of the . . . psychologist" (*Wisconsin Statutes Annotated*, 1981–1982). This would cover marriage and family therapists, social workers, unlicensed psychologists, and other relevant professionals working with the protected therapist. Of course, the courts have the discretion of interpreting the words "under the direction" (Knapp & VandeCreek, 1985). Furthermore, the privilege applies only to psychotherapy and not to court-ordered evaluations. When the court orders parents to undergo psychiatric or psychological evaluation, the results are always available to the court (e.g., *New Mexico ex rel. Human Services Department v. Levario*, 1982). The failure of parents to comply has severely damaged their position in court (e.g., *In re Marriage of Gove*, 1977).

Courts have always valued the welfare of children very highly and attempt to include all testimony that may help them make a proper placement in custody cases. Usually, courts value the welfare of children more than the privacy of their parents (H. H. Foster, 1978). Unless a statute clearly protects the privacy rights of parents, courts tend to rule in favor of admitting testimony. The ruling judge in *Atwood v. Atwood* (1976) reflected this most explicitly in writing: "Regardless of the desires of the parents in making an award of custody, the polar star is to determine what is for the best interest of the child."

Even in the presence of a privileged communication statute, the court may obtain a therapist's testimony in four ways:

1. A client may waive the privilege and permit testimony in court.
2. The court may nullify the privilege for communications made in the presence of third parties.
3. The wording of the state statutes may allow for waiver of the privilege in certain cases.
4. The privilege may be waived if clients introduce their mental condition into the court proceedings.

Knapp and VandeCreek (1985) offer an analysis of each of these waivers.

Client Waiver

Traditionally, the right to waive the privilege belongs to the client. The therapist has no independent right to invoke the privilege against the wishes of the client. Other interested parties, including payers for the therapy of another, have no right to the privilege. For example, in *Bieluch v. Bieluch* (1983), a father tried to prevent the testimony of a psychologist who was treating his wife and children. Although the father had paid for many of the sessions, he was not allowed to invoke the privilege, because he had no professional relationship with the therapist.

The waiver may be implied or expressed. In an *implied waiver*, the actions of the client imply that the communications were not confidential. For example, in *In re Fred J.* (1979), a mother requested that two psychiatrists examine her children and report the findings to a social service agency. In a later custody hearing, the court concluded that the psychiatrists' evaluations were not privileged because the reports had been divulged earlier to the agency. In an *expressed waiver*, the client explicitly allows the testimony of the therapist. Waivers are absolute; the client may not selectively agree that only one portion of communications be open and another portion withheld.

Third-Party Waiver

Most privileged communication controversies have dealt with situations in which only one person was the client. There have been substantially fewer cases in which families or couples were being treated together and disagreement about the waiver emerged in court. No consistent principles have been established as a result. In a number of jurisdictions, however, the privilege has been waived in such cases, not because one party or the other controls the waiver, but because the presence of a third person in therapy was alleged to indicate that the communications were not intended to be confidential or privileged.

The privilege has thus been waived or maintained according to a court's interpretation of the "third-party rule." Common-law tradition holds that the presence of third parties suggests that communications were not intended to be confidential. This rule is obviously reasonable when applied to casual conversations made in public places. Not so obvious, however, is its applicability to communications made during therapy in the presence of a marital partner or family members (Meyer & Smith, 1977).

The application of the third-party rule has tended to depend on the wording of specific state statutes. For example, a Delaware statute states that "A communication is 'confidential' if not intended to be disclosed to third persons except persons present to further the interests of the patient in the consultation . . . including members of the patient's family" (*Delaware Rules of Evidence*, 1981). When the statutes fail to specify any rule for family psychotherapy, some courts have ruled on therapist–client privilege using the attorney–client model (DeKraai & Sales, 1982). Communications between therapists and clients are placed on the same legal ground as communication between attorneys and clients. According to this model, when two or more persons consult the same attorney about a common matter, communications made by them are not privileged among themselves (Witnesses, §190, 1976). Applying this principle, the Arizona Supreme Court ruled in *Hahman v. Hahman* (1981) that the communications made to a psychologist by a husband and wife were not privileged.

In other states, court decisions have reflected a mixture of findings. Some courts upheld the privilege when parents have been present in therapy with their children (*Grosslight v. Superior Court*, 1977) and when spouses have been seen together (*Yaron v. Yaron*, 1975). Some courts have, however, held otherwise and waived the privilege because a spouse was present (Herrington, 1979). In summary, no consistent judicial trend has emerged in this area. When there is no protective legislation, the ruling depends on the interpretation of the court and/or on the unique circumstances of the case (Knapp & VandeCreek, 1985).

Statutory Waiver

The most common statutory waiver relating to child custody cases is when suspected child abuse is a factor in the proceedings. Almost all states have child abuse reporting laws that waive the privilege in court cases that arise out of reports of suspected child abuse.

A number of states have waiver rules that apply particularly to child custody cases. A Massachusetts law, for example, has specifically allowed a waiver if the judge, on a hearing in chambers, "determines that the psychotherapist has evidence bearing significantly on the patient's ability to provide suitable custody, and that it is more important to the welfare of the child that the communications be disclosed than the relationship between the patient and psychotherapist be protected" (*Massachusetts General Laws*, 1980).

Several other states, including New York, New Hampshire, and Virginia, have allowed judges to waive the privilege when they believe that the interests of justice outweigh clients' need for privacy (DeKraai & Sales, 1982). New York state courts have specified, however, that the privilege may not "cavalierly be ignored or lightly cast aside" (*Perry v. Fiumano*, 1978). To permit the waiver, the mental health of parents must be raised as a relevant issue in a child's placement, and it must be proved that this information is unavailable from other sources (*State ex rel. Hickox v. Hickox*, 1978). Also, the courts must attempt to look for a less intrusive means of acquiring the information, such as requesting that the parents undergo an evaluation, or by viewing relevant records in the privacy of the judge's chambers to first determine their relevance to the case.

Mental Health as a Condition Waiver

Clients waive the privilege when they enter their mental health into the proceedings. States have disagreed, though, on whether or not the mental condition of parents should be entered automatically into litigation in child custody cases. Most states have held that the privilege is maintained and the mental condition of parents does not enter automatically in such cases (e.g., Florida: *Kristensen v. Kristensen*, 1981; Michigan: *Matter of Atkins*, 1982; Texas: *Gillespie v. Gillespie*, 1982).

Courts in Kentucky (*Atwood v. Atwood*, 1976) and Delaware (*Shipman v. Division of Social Services*, 1981), however, have ruled that parents automatically enter their mental health into litigation in child custody cases. In the *Atwood* case, the mother had been awarded custody of her three children. She remarried and later obtained therapy with her children and new husband. Her first husband then sought custody. The Kentucky Supreme Court refused to exclude the testimony of the therapist, concluding that custody investigations needed to be extensive and accurate and that the mental condition of the parties involved must be considered an issue.

Conclusions

The same issues that were discussed in Case 1 exist in this case. The application of privilege varies greatly according to the wording of state statutes, the common-law traditions within each state, and the interpretations made by courts; prime illustrations are found in the *Atwood* and *Shipman* cases. The decisions in these cases were binding only in Kentucky and Delaware, respectively. Most states will not automatically waive privilege in child custody cases. It is impossible to do justice to the myriad nuances of laws among the states with a specific response to the facts in this particular case. Consequently, the therapist in question must of necessity consult a local attorney.

Depending on the state in which they practice, most marriage and family therapists are likely to find themselves operating under a patchwork of existing laws and judicial interpretations. As discussed in Case 1 in this chapter, therapists subpoenaed to court to provide testimony that they believe could ultimately harm a child or family or that represents an unreasonable waiver of privilege need not passively submit to the subpoena. Instead, through their own attorney, they may ask the court to pursue a less intrusive means of acquiring the information. They may suggest that the judge require a court-ordered examination. Or, if the therapist's records are deemed important, the attorney for the therapist can request that the judge screen the records privately in chambers before allowing them into the court proceedings. Obviously, there are no guarantees that the court will be amenable to an attorney's proposals. Nonetheless, such initiatives may create a context in which judges will be able to balance the need for information in court more prudently with the need to protect the confidentiality of therapeutic efforts.

CASE 9

Legal Responsibility of Clinical Supervisors

One state's licensure for marriage and family therapy requires that unlicensed graduates of marriage and family therapy training programs complete two years of clinically supervised postdegree experience. Part of the position agreement for entry-level therapists at a Family Services Agency is that they receive regular supervision by the senior-level therapist at the agency. The designated supervisor has not been able to provide what he considers to be adequate supervision, however. He has had to leave two entry-level therapists mainly on their own with rather difficult caseloads. The staff members at the agency are all overloaded; the supervisor is feeling overburdened by his supervisory responsibility in addition to his regular heavy caseload. Thus, quality supervision time is rare. The supervisor is preparing to bring the situation to the agency's Board of Directors and seeks to identify his legal liability as one justification for a reduced client caseload so he can adequately attend to his supervisory responsibilities.

Considerations

Recent years have seen a gradual and profoundly important change in the attitudes of clients toward helping professionals. Clients have become more consumer-oriented with respect to accountability; this has become a critical concept for both marriage and family therapists and supervisors. From the supervisory standpoint, the legal doctrine of *respondeat superior* (also known as vicarious liability) has consequently become of significant relevance (Christie, Meeks, Pryor, & Sanders, 1997; Cohen, 1979). According to this doctrine, someone in a position of authority or responsibility, such as a clinical supervisor, is responsible for acts of those individuals under his or her supervision. Stated another way, supervisors are ultimately legally responsible for the welfare of clients seen in therapy by their supervisees (Cormier & Bernard, 1982; Snider, 1985).

There are a number of implications inherent in this principle as applied to clinical supervision. The first demands that supervisors ensure that supervision actually occurs and that meetings are documented (Harrar, VandeCreek, & Knapp, 1990; Welfel, 1998). Supervisors must avoid delegating all responsibility to a supervisee because negligence may occur. Therefore, a supervisor must be familiar with each case of every supervisee. This can be established by conducting (and documenting) that face-to-face contacts with supervisees regularly take place.

It is important that supervisors observe the actual work of supervisees through audiotapes, videotapes, or observations rather than relying exclusively on the supervisees' reports of their own work (Navin, Beamish, & Johanson, 1995). Cormier and Bernard (1982) reported an attorney's advice that supervisors also conduct one face-to-face meeting with each supervisee's clients sometime during the initial stages of therapy. Such a contact allows clients the opportunity to meet the supervisor and discover how their therapist is being supervised. This information can assist clients in providing informed consent to their therapist for his or her services. Also, a face-to-face contact with clients allows supervisors to gain additional information about them and the possible management of their cases, and can help the supervisor better determine the amount of supervision needed. Slovenko (1980) restated a comment made by the attorney in the *Tarasoff* (1974) case appropriate to consider in this regard:

> It is my view that if the supervisor of the clinic had personally examined the patient Poddar and made an independent decision that the patient Poddar was not dangerous to himself or his victim, Tatiana Tarasoff, there would be no cause of action based on foreseeability. However, the supervisor never saw the patient Poddar and ignored the medical records developed by his staff. (p. 468)

Thus, it may be of significant importance from a legal standpoint for supervisors to make contact with supervisees' clients.

Van Hoose and Kottler (1985) identified failure to supervise a therapist working with a disturbed client as one of the leading causes of psychological malpractice suits. The supervisor is legally responsible to know when supervisees are insufficiently prepared to deal with certain situations and need assistance. Knowledge that a supervisee is having difficulties in working with particular clients may call for closer supervision, co-therapy, or possibly reassigning the case to a more experienced person.

A further implication of the *respondeat superior* doctrine addresses supervisees' competence to provide adequate services. Some formal assessment of competence should be conducted prior to assuming an independent caseload. If a supervisor has reservations about a supervisee's clinical abilities, supervision should not be agreed on until remedial training activities are undertaken and completed and/or the supervisor seeks to protect himself or herself from liability by stating reservations about the supervisee in writing to relevant parties (Cormier & Bernard, 1982).

Finally, the *respondeat superior* doctrine also suggests certain responsibilities supervisors have to clients to ensure appropriate referral and termination procedures. Dawidoff (1973) noted that supervisors are liable if treatment is terminated or a referral is made without due cause. Referrals and terminations must be handled in a way that meets the recognized standard of care.

Although the *respondeat superior* doctrine creates legal liability for the supervisor, the supervisee is not necessarily absolved. Clients have the option of bringing action against the supervisor, the supervisee, or all parties. R. J. Cohen (1979), for example, reported the case of a supervisee, who away from the formal clinical setting and without the supervisor's knowledge, allegedly engaged in sexual relations with a client. Under the doctrine of *respondeat superior*, a lawsuit was brought against the supervisor rather than the supervisee. The plaintiff claimed that the supervisor was negligent by allowing an unlicensed person, not competent of providing due care, to treat her.

In a contrasting case, a supervisee rather than the supervisor was sued for failure to more closely monitor a client who committed suicide. The supervisee, a student intern, was found to be negligent (*Eady v. Alter*, 1976). Exactly who is named as defendant in such cases obviously depends on the circumstances, setting, alleged acts, plaintiff, and perhaps above all, who is seen as having the most to lose (Cormier & Bernard, 1982).

Conclusions

Slovenko's (1980) warning that "litigation involving supervisors may be the 'suit of the future' " (p. 468) can be addressed best by ensuring that supervisors are well informed and conscientious. The supervisor in the present case should assert the need for regularly scheduled supervision based on a careful assessment of the needs of both the supervisees and their clients. The amount and frequency of the supervision can be determined most accurately by a thorough knowledge of the supervisees' strengths and deficits, as well as the difficulties likely to be presented by their caseloads. The supervisor should be careful to document how supervision is scheduled and what occurs during supervisory sessions.

Beyond this, the supervisor must actually provide the supervision. Negligence is based on the idea that the professional has departed from what is considered acceptable in terms of the standards of the profession. Consultation with professionals in similar situations and with professional association standards can provide a recommended minimum; anything above that can take place as warranted by the results of the supervisor's assessments.

A supervisor should consider professional liability insurance. The agency might provide such coverage, but few do. It is important to identify in advance of purchase, however, what a policy actually covers. Occasionally, policies will not cover damages from either negligent supervision or acts of supervisees with less than a master's degree.

Finally, if the supervisor is not able to provide adequate supervision, or if some undesirable consequences befall clients being seen by a supervisee, the supervisor must take appropriate action. Although an important goal of providing supervised practice is to produce more effective practitioners, the supervisor must protect his or her own welfare, and most importantly, the welfare of clients.

CASE 10

Insurance Fraud?

During their initial session with a newly licensed marriage and family therapist in private practice, a couple asks the therapist if her services are covered by their health insurance. The therapist requests that they bring a copy of their policy manual to the next session for her to review. The couple forgets to bring the policy manual not only at the next session, but also at the following session. It is only after the fourth session that the therapist is able to review the policy's provisions, which allow for individual psychotherapy on an outpatient basis for a maximum of 20 sessions within one calendar year; the manual specifically states that marital therapy is not covered. One of the couple's primary stressors is financial problems. The therapist submits a claim for reimbursement for individual psychotherapy and is reimbursed by the insurance company for the alleged services.

Considerations

Third-party reimbursement and managed health care dilemmas (Bittner, Bialek, Nathiel, Ringwald, & Tupper, 1999; Bonnington, Crawford, et al., 1996; Huber, 1995) can generate a complex set of issues for marriage and family therapists, particularly in early experiences. Third-party reimbursement involves an individual (or his or her employer) who has purchased an insurance policy to cover specific medical or psychiatric conditions. By accepting third-party reimbursement, providers (i.e., the marriage and family therapist in this case) agree to provide whatever documentation an insurance company deems necessary to substantiate treatment (Fong & Sherrard, 1990).

Intentionally reporting to an insurance company that a condition was present and/or was treated when in fact either the condition was not present or the treatment noted was not actually administered is considered fraud (Remley & Herlihy, 2005). Abuse of health insurance through fraudulent claims is prohibited by law. Uncovering such fraudulent actions could result in an insurance company filing civil suit for recovery of funds misspent, as well as the insurance company requesting that criminal action be brought by appropriate legal authorities. Furthermore, the relevant state licensing board might be contacted and sanctions could be imposed on a therapist's license to practice, or the license possibly could be revoked entirely (Stevens-Smith & Hughes, 1993).

The law identifies five elements as necessary to be present for fraud to have occurred (*Case Notes*, 1985–1986):

1. There is concealment or false representation of a material fact.
2. This concealment or false representation is reasonably calculated to deceive.
3. There is an intent to deceive.
4. There is, in fact, deception.
5. The deception results in damage to the injured party.

Conclusions

It is not difficult for most marriage and family therapists to empathize with the therapist in this case. She is newly licensed and in private practice. Her training has been steeped with assertions about the value of marriage and family therapy. It is obviously frustrating that this couple identifies financial problems as a major stressor, that they have insurance coverage ostensibly to limit the negative impact of such a stressor, and yet the coverage does not directly apply. Despite this, the laws are relatively clear in this regard, and the marriage and family therapist here must abide by them.

Considering the elements required by law to be present for fraud, it seems likely the marriage and family therapist in this case is acting in a fraudulent manner under the law: (a) She is falsely representing a material fact in that marital, not individual psychotherapy is the treatment; (b) the false representation is calculated to deceive the insurance company so that the treatment falls under its coverage; (c) there is an intent to deceive for purposes of being reimbursed; (d) there is, in fact, a deception in that the reimbursement forms were submitted to the insurance company; and (e) the deception has resulted in damage to the insurance company in that it reimbursed for specific treatment that had not occurred.

Stevens-Smith and Hughes (1993), in discussing the issue of insurance fraud, noted three areas they described as practiced but forbidden: (a) claiming that a covered provider (e.g., psychiatrist or psychologist) is providing services when a different person is actually doing so, (b) ignoring the requirement of an accurate diagnosis by giving most or all clients the same diagnosis, and (c) intentionally waiving the clients' share of a stated fee while reporting the full fee amount to an insurance company. Stevens-Smith and Hughes (1993) cautioned therapists who consider "bending the rules" to carefully contemplate the potential long-term legal and ethical consequences of their actions before doing so.

Professional Issues in Marriage and Family Therapy

Professionalism . . . an attitude that motivates individuals to be attentive to the image and ideals of their particular profession.

(VanZandt, 1990, p. 243)

CHAPTER 11

Professional Identity as a Marriage and Family Therapist

Chapters 11 and 12 of our text are devoted to examining professional issues in the practice of marriage and family therapy. As with our previous discussions concerning cultural, value, ethical, and legal issues, these final chapters will consider contemporary professional issues that are likely to change over time. Additionally, our intention is to be selective rather than exhaustive in addressing professional concerns.

You may recall our discussion in Chapter 1 about how our psychosocial identity emerges from a variety of socio-cultural influences. In many ways, our professional identity develops in the same manner, being shaped by educational, supervisory, collegial, and similar influences we encounter. Additionally, the layers of personal, professional, and institutional values we discussed in Chapter 2 converge to affect our professional identity in unique and dynamic ways throughout our professional lives.

Professional identity is an evolutionary process for emerging marriage and family therapists. A survey on developmental stages necessary for achieving a competent sense of self as a family therapist was conducted by Kral and Hines (1999). They found empirical support for Friedman and Kaslow's (1986) six-stage developmental model for identity development as a competent family therapist, noting the entire process takes approximately five years.

In stage 1, anticipation, new therapists learn they will be working with clients and supervisors. In stage 2, dependency, novice therapists depend on supervisors for answers. In stage 3, new therapists demonstrate continued dependence on supervisors for answers, with some movement toward independence. Stage 4 marks a major transition and is characterized by new therapists taking charge of therapy sessions; this leads to stage 5, which involves therapists developing a sense of independence and identity. The last stage is characterized by a sense of calm and congeniality. From these findings, one can note that identity development as a marriage and family therapist takes times and is generally sequential in nature.

This developmental sequencing of professional identity has not always been viewed as a part of marriage and family therapy. In fact, the advent of marriage and family therapy was initially viewed as simply another means of treating problems and was not radically different from individual approaches (M. P. Nichols & Schwartz, 2001). Thus, identifying oneself as a marriage and family therapist in the beginning days of the profession did not require a radical change in identity for those who practiced it from any previous therapeutic identity they embraced. The individual was still the client, although treated in a couple or family setting (Okun & Rappaport, 1980). Marital partners, for example, were seen separately to deal with their individual concerns. This perspective and way of working emanated from the dominant epistemological perspective of the time, which was linear in nature.

However, marriage and family therapy changed in the late 1960s and 1970s (Atwood, 1992; W. C. Nichols, 1992). It became and remains a new way of defining and working through a problem. The "client" was not the individual alone, and the "problem" was not confined to the individual, either, but included the client's marital, familial, or social context. This more comprehensive concept called for a redefinition of fundamental beliefs, as well as an expanded epistemology to consider the dynamics of evolving systems, not simply the vicissitudes of individual rights (L'Abate, 1982). Marriage and family approaches generally give attention to relationship dynamics in diagnosis and share similar therapeutic goals (Gladding, 1998b; Liddle, 1991b; Olson, Russell, & Sprenkle, 1980). They are primarily systemic in their epistemological perspective. You will recall the criticisms of the systemic epistemology from Chapter 2 and that some contemporary models of practice (e.g., narrative approaches, etc.) reflect a synthesis of systemic and individual perspectives. Still, the contextual complexity of its origins is preserved in contemporary marriage and family therapy practices.

Despite the epistemological shifts associated over time with the practice of marriage and family therapy, we are more than what we do. Professional identity involves more than an array of techniques or models. Professional identity is reflected in our professional affiliations, our educational and supervisory experiences, our credential status (e.g., state licensure), and our development through research, continuing education, and intraprofessional relationships and service. We would also reiterate our earlier statement that professional identity is unique and dynamic in nature, meaning that no specific formula of actions or points in time can offer requisite tests for verifying one's professional identity. For example, many who identify themselves as marriage and family therapists have multiple professional memberships or multiple licensures along with varied educational backgrounds and varied research agendas. We begin our discussion of the influences upon our professional development by considering the continuing debate relative to whether marriage and family therapy is a profession or a professional specialty.

PROFESSION OR PROFESSIONAL SPECIALIZATION?

Marriage and family therapy initially was and continues to be considered by some as an area of specialization within other professional disciplines. This view is reflected vividly in the professional association membership of practitioners espousing marriage and family therapy. Many therapists who practice marriage and family therapy subscribe their allegiance to the American Association for Marriage and Family Therapy (AAMFT). However, many others identify primarily with professional associations representing psychiatry, psychology, social work, and counseling: the American Psychiatric Association, the American Psychological Association, the National Association of Social Workers, and the American Counseling Association (Atwood, 1992). These latter groups maintain that marriage and family therapy is a therapeutic modality, a professional specialization, within psychiatry, psychology, social work, or counseling. This is a continuing and important debate, because the way marriage and family therapy is conceptualized influences the practice of the profession (Canfield & Locke, 1991). A graphic depiction of the various perspectives on this issue is shown in Figure 11–1.

Marriage and Family Therapy as a Separate and Distinct Profession

Those who believe marriage and family therapy is a separate and distinct profession stress that it has clearly acquired those characteristics that are hallmarks of a profession unto itself (Winkle, Piercy, & Hovestadt, 1981). Ard and Ard (1976) were among the earliest to assert this position by noting:

> Marriage and family counseling is a profession . . . with a scientific body of knowledge, some relevant theory, a code of ethics, and some specific techniques. (p. xv)

FIGURE 11–1   Relationship of Family Therapy to Other Mental Health Professions

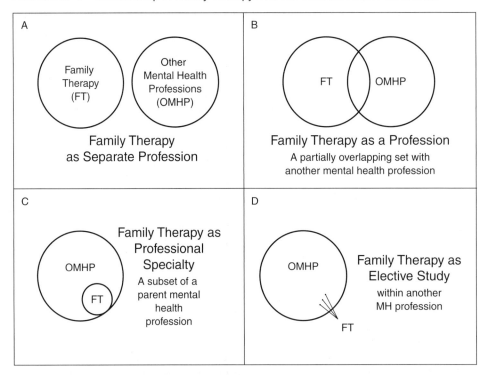

Note. From "Family Therapy as a Profession or Professional Specialty: Implications for Training," by D. L. Fenell and A. J. Hovestadt, 1986, *Journal of Psychotherapy and the Family, 1* (4). © Copyright 1986. Reprinted with permission.

Since the late 1970s, this view and the data supporting it have significantly broadened. Northey (2002) reported on a national survey of 534 AAMFT clinical members. This effort was undertaken to examine possible changes that had evolved in the characteristics and practices of marriage and family therapists in comparison with findings reported by Doherty and Simmons (1996). Specifically, Northey noted an increase from 68% to 80% in the number of respondents who reported licensure as marriage and family therapists. Additionally, he reported an increase from 60.6% to 73% of respondents who indicated that marriage and family therapy was their primary professional identification. These findings support a view of separate and distinct professional identity, to the point that Northey concluded, "the field has matured" (p. 492). Other evidence of this maturity has been noted; for example, as of July 2005, 47 states had established licensure for marriage and family therapy. Additionally, "freedom of choice" legislation in some circumstances mandates specifically that marriage and family therapists are considered to be on a par with other mental health providers in terms of third-party reimbursement for services.

Those who voice the opinion that marriage and family therapy is a distinct profession see marriage and family therapy as an independently identifiable entity, a "peer" to psychiatry, psychology, social work, and counseling. The growth in membership and influence of the AAMFT and the development of educational and training standards and formal accreditation of programs promoting to these standards is one indication that marriage and family therapy is a distinct profession. Legislative efforts creating governmental recognition as well as research demonstrating the efficacy of marriage and family therapy as a profession are additional indicators of its distinction (Bowers, 1992a). As Haley (1984) asserted:

> The issue of whether to organize the family therapy field has been resolved. This organization [AAMFT] has accomplished that. . . . All of us face the accomplished fact that the field is organized and ready for the benefits that follow to those who belong to the club. A certain point is reached, as in nuclear fission, when the outcome is inevitable. As therapists join an organization and are licensed, other therapists must do the same to compete. The supervisors and teachers come under pressure to be properly approved, or their trainees cannot share in the financial benefits of membership. (p. 12)

Shields, Wynne, McDaniel, and Gawinski (1994) offered the observation that marriage and family therapy had lost much of its influence as a separate profession because of its departure from a multidisciplinary paradigm. In this respect, they stated, "The AAMFT needs to continue strongly to support the interdisciplinary nature of the family therapy field, in addition to supporting the 'bread-and-butter' issues of MFT as a professional discipline" (p. 135). In response to these authors, Hardy (1994) emphasized the elements of Wilensky's (1964) model of professionalization as relevant for viewing marriage and family therapy as a separate profession. Hardy summarized the Wilensky framework by suggesting that for a profession to be recognized for its autonomy and authority, it must:

> (a) find a technical base, (b) assert an exclusive jurisdiction, (c) link both skills and jurisdiction of training, and (d) convince the public that its services are uniquely trustworthy. (p. 140)

From this perspective, Hardy disagreed with Shields et al. (1994) by contending that "the multidisciplinary paradigm is a major deterrent to the field's developmental evolution toward becoming a distinct and autonomous profession" (p. 140). Hardy further noted that the evidence of meeting the Wilensky criteria for professionalization were present in developments such as accredited graduate and postgraduate training programs, specialized knowledge for the field from both quantitative and qualitative research, regulatory legislation for state licensure, and distinctive affiliation via membership in AAMFT. Hardy concluded by noting "current and future generations of family therapists must do exactly what the founders did—define themselves, rather than being defined by others" (p. 143). Hardy even suggested that specialties within the field may emerge over time, such as "specialties associated with larger systems and interdisciplinary cooperation—specialties associated with family units and family process . . . and specialties associated with sociocultural issues" (p. 142). Such specialties could only exist as subsets of a larger and distinct field.

Thus, evidence that marriage and family therapy is a separate professional field emerges through accomplishments such as distinct professional affiliations, distinct statutory recognition in licensure, a distinct body of research, and distinct pragmatic considerations in practice. Each of these items will be considered more fully in later sections of this chapter.

Marriage and Family Therapy as a Professional Specialization

Those who view marriage and family therapy as a professional specialization hold that marriage and family therapy is a special way of providing mental health service but not a profession in and of itself. They point out that the prevailing majority of professionals practicing marriage and family therapy received their education as psychiatrists, psychologists, social workers, counselors, ministers, or nurses. They also note the fact that these practitioners maintain membership in well-established professional associations having a distinct identity (not in marriage and family therapy organizations). Furthermore, members of these associations clearly identify marriage and family therapy as a professional specialization through division membership within their parent association (e.g., Division 43—Family Psychology within the American Psychological Association; the International Association of Marriage and Family Counselors within the American Counseling Association).

Introducing additional ambiguity into this overall debate is the fact that the AAMFT, although advocating marriage and family therapy as a separate and distinct profession, has prided itself and continues to pride itself on its multidisciplinary membership (Bowers, 1992a). This fact was revealed vividly in a 1988 survey of training directors and clinical members of AAMFT that found that only slightly more than half (51.8%) "believed that marital and family therapy should be treated as a separate discipline" (Keller, Huber, & Hardy, 1988, p. 304). Likewise, most professional journals that focus on marriage and family therapy, including *Family Process* (the oldest), are interdisciplinary in editorship, authorship, and subscribership. In this respect, the position advanced by Hardy (1994) concerning a multidisciplinary view as a detriment to professional autonomy could be validated.

Bowers (1992a) suggested that the "marketability" of marriage and family therapy is an important element in its evolution as an identifiable profession:

> In the last decade, MFT has become a much more marketable service. As it has gained more acceptance, others, with relatively little history in defining or promulgating standards for the field, have begun to claim it in some way as their own—arguing, in effect, that no independent

discipline of MFT exists. How these tensions are resolved, regarding both standards and "ownership" of the field, will be largely determinative of the identity and scope of MFT in the next generation. (p. 18)

Despite significant advances in professional and consumer recognition, evidence exists to counter a view of marriage and family therapy as a separate profession. As we will note later in this chapter, marriage and family therapy licensure is a significant indicator of professional status. Some states employ a composite framework for this licensure, however, collapsing MFT licensure with other licensure distinctions such as licensed social worker, licensed professional counselor, and other professions. An amalgam such as that portrayed in composite licensure could challenge the view of marriage and family therapy as a separate profession. Additionally, one might argue that such a development strengthens the argument advanced by Shields et al. (1994) that multidisciplinary affiliation is necessary to avoid the marginalization of marriage and family therapy.

Is Balance Possible?

Following from these divergent viewpoints, one might ask about "both-and" as an option for the dilemma of professional identity. For many, the issue of "profession versus specialization" is a significant matter of professional identity. For them, this litmus test is a critical point of origin for therapists, supervisors, and trainers. For others, the point may be less substantive, since the epistemological framework upon which the earliest stages of the debate were founded can exist in either category. An ironic observation has been offered by Fraenkel (2005):

> One thing is clear: because we were studying systems, many of us operated under the delusion that we were somehow immune to them. After its glorious adolescence, our movement was buffeted by forces weak and strong at every level—by internal challenges; by the limitations of our own models; by changes in the time-and-money microsystems of individual families; and by the political and economic shifts in the therapeutic economy and in the wider world.

Fraenkel (2005) further noted "Thus, in the mental health galaxy, family therapy has traced a path from supernova to average star." Still, regardless of its "star status," marriage and family therapy demands notice within the "professional galaxy." Fraenkel reminds us, however, that just as couples and families exist in relational systems, so do professions.

Yet what about marriage and family therapy's membership in the mental health system? Again commenting on the observations of Shields et al. (1994), Hardy (1994) stated:

> I do not share the authors' distress regarding family therapy trainees' dearth of exposure to psychopharmacology, individual assessments, biological bases of behavior, DSM, and so forth. . . . Instead, I believe that the attention devoted to these issues speaks to the field's clarity regarding its technical base. (p. 140)

Hardy further predicted that "The field will advance to the point where it can reject the notion that the establishment of pathology-driven diagnostic categories for families is integral to its legitimacy and survival" (p. 141). Similarly, McIntyre, a past president of the AAMFT, observed, "At this admittedly early date, I predict that the biggest changes in DSM-V—in a decade or so—will be in the area of personality disorders and family or systems (relationship) diagnoses" (1993, p. 3). At this time, such developments have not yet been realized fully for diagnostic frameworks.

Although such observations certainly merit consideration, our discussion in Chapter 6 regarding issues such as managed mental health care and DSM diagnosis emphasizes the institutional framework in which the contemporary practice of marriage and family therapy exists. Eschewing any individual orientation as reductionistic and antithetical to marriage and family therapy may be poorly received in the larger mental health system.

And what about the "political and economic shifts in the therapeutic economy and in the wider world" noted by Fraenkel (2005)? Over two decades ago, W. C. Nichols, Bardill, Everett, Figley, and Clark served on the AAMFT task force on recognition, regulation, and legitimization of marital and family therapy. Their unpublished 1984 report indicated that the major issue for attaining professional recognition concerned "organizing and influencing the politician and social systems of the society" (p. 15). Their comments were similar to those observations offered by Fraenkel (2005). Additionally, this report stated "There have been, and seemingly continue to be, rather naïve assumptions abounding that once regulation is secured, third-party reimbursement for services will follow. Nothing could be farther from the truth" (p. 13). In the ensuing decades, such prophetic observations still appear to be relevant. From this perspective, the external validation of marriage and family therapy as a separate field appears to be mixed.

Commenting on the statements proffered by Shields et al. (1994), H. Anderson (1994) authored an article entitled "Rethinking Family Therapy: A Delicate Balance." In this work, Anderson stated emphatically, "Individual and family do not have to be competing constructs" (p. 147). She further observed that a balance must be struck in attending to internal and external issues of professional identity. In many ways, Anderson's commentary mirrors our discussion in Chapter 2 concerning the integration of personal, professional, and institutional layers of values. At the personal and professional layers, one may embrace a view of distinction concerning marriage and family therapy that may not be accepted, even partially, by various elements of the institutional layer of values (e.g., managed mental health care agencies, local practice setting, DSM diagnostic categories, academic program, etc.). Thus, the internal focus on both the individual therapist as well as specific organizations or groups (e.g., AAMFT) still must be balanced with the external realities of institutional recognition. Otherwise, as Sprenkle (1994) observed about the comments from Shields et al. (1994), "they believe that today we run the risk of so removing ourselves from the traditional mental health disciplines that we will be left talking only to ourselves" (p. 115).

As a final thought, you will recall our discussion in Chapter 1 concerning the unique convergence of socio-cultural influences for the psychosocial identity of each individual. Similar inferences can be drawn concerning the unique convergence of personal, professional, and institutional influences in the "professional identity" of each individual marriage and family therapist. To some, multiple memberships in professional groups may be heresy; to others, such a decision may be a matter of interest and diversity. To some, multiple licensures may be viewed as pandering; to others, such a decision may be a matter of economic reality. To some, support for legislative initiatives by bodies such as the AAMFT Political Action Committee is a matter of professional citizenship; for others, such an effort may be weighed on the basis of personal benefit only. In this respect, H. Anderson's (1994) admonition to find balance appears to be the key element for each individual marriage and family therapist. We recommend that readers consider these thoughts concerning professional identity as we examine issues of professional affiliation, licensure, research, and selected pragmatic matters in the practice of marriage and family therapy.

PROFESSIONAL AFFILIATION

One criterion that identifies a profession is that it is self-regulating. Established professions are identified as such because they have developed standards and policies that, to some degree, control entry into the profession, prescribe training standards, and establish procedures and requirements for membership and practice. Professions develop ethical codes that outline standards of service, prescribe members' appropriate relationships to each other and the general public, and identify proper and improper practice. As you consider the following discussion about the importance of professional affiliation, pay attention to the interrelatedness between factors such as: (a) graduate and postgraduate education, (b) accreditation, (c) supervised experience, (d) eligibility and distinctions in membership, and (e) credentials. You will notice that elements of these factors combine in unique ways to affect one's competence and identity as a marriage and family therapist. Accreditation affects education; education affects supervised experience; supervised experience affects membership eligibility, as does education; and all are factors in securing credentials. In the same circular and contextual ways in which marriage and family therapy is practiced, affiliation is interrelated with other aspects of professionalism.

These procedures for self-regulation in professional affiliation differ from licensure, which is reflective of statutory recognition within a state jurisdiction as a right to practice coupled with external regulations to protect public consumers. Thus, *professional affiliation* concerns ethical propriety, professional advocacy, and service, whereas licensure concerns legal status and governmental oversight. We note this distinction because, during their early years of professional identity development, some marriage and family therapists may be confused about the function of a licensure board and think of it as an advocate for the profession, which is actually the role of professional organizations. In fact, many states even prohibit members of state licensure boards from lobbying for legislative changes proposed by the board in order to avoid the appearance of professional advocacy or a conflict of interest. More discussion on licensure follows in the next section of this chapter.

As a final introductory comment, we offer a terse yet revealing statement from H. Anderson (1994): "Family therapy is no longer exclusively a North American phenomenon" (p. 146). As you will see, evidence of the international and pluralistic nature of a "smaller world" is reflected in the various professional groups we will discuss.

The AAMFT is the organization that highlights marriage and family as a separate and distinct profession. It is described along with three associations that recognize and promote marriage and family therapy as a professional specialization: the American Family Therapy Academy (AFTA), Division 43—Family Psychology of the American Psychological Association, and the International Association of Marriage and Family Counselors (IAMFC), a division of the American Counseling Association.

American Association for Marriage and Family Therapy

The American Association for Marriage and Family Therapy (AAMFT) had its beginnings in 1942. Originally called the American Association of Marriage Counselors, it was renamed the American Association of Marriage and Family Counselors in 1970 and then in 1979 became the American Association for Marriage and Family Therapy. During most of its existence, the AAMFT has consisted primarily of psychiatrists, social workers, psychologists, and counselors who received degrees in their own specific discipline and then sought master's or doctoral training in marriage and family therapy (W. C. Nichols, 1992). As marriage and family therapy came to be promoted as a separate and distinct profession and relevant training programs at universities were established, an increasing number of members began to receive terminal degrees specifically in marriage and family therapy (Kosinski, 1982). As of August 2005, the AAMFT reported a membership of over 23,000 therapists, practitioners, educators, researchers, and students in the United States and throughout the world. Other overview information about the organization can be found at http://www.aamft.org/index_nm.asp

The AAMFT has historically assumed multiple and diverse initiatives within the field, across other disciplines, and in legislative and other advocacy efforts. The AAMFT also sponsors the Commission on Accreditation for Marriage and Family Therapy Education (COAMFTE). The commission serves under a broad mandate from the AAMFT Board of Directors to set standards for and accredit graduate and postdegree clinical training programs in marriage and family therapy. The commission is composed of nine members, seven of whom are professional members and two of whom are public members. The following represent some of the primary ways in which the commission accomplishes this purpose (Commission on Accreditation for Marriage and Family Therapy Education, 1997):

- Establishes criteria and standards for accreditation.
- Provides guidance to programs, preparing self-study reports for candidacy, accreditation, or for renewal of accreditation.
- Appoints site visit teams, schedules and conducts visits, as well as considers and evaluates the report of visiting teams.
- Arranges for review and appeal when a program challenges its accreditation status.
- Accredits training programs in marriage and family therapy.
- Maintains contact with programs relative to their accreditation status and takes note of substantive changes in programs that might affect accreditation.
- Conducts special inquiries into unusual or critical conditions that may develop in an accredited program.
- Endeavors to stimulate and promote continued improvement of educational programs.

In 1978, the COAMFTE gained official recognition as an accrediting agency for graduate degree and postdegree clinical training programs in marriage and family therapy by the U.S. Office of Education, Department of Health, Education, and Welfare. Since that time, the U.S. Department of Education has continued its recognition of the commission (Commission on Accreditation for Marriage and Family Therapy Education, 1997). Additionally, the commission has also been recognized officially by the Council for Higher Education Accreditation (CHEA), a nongovernmental organization for quality control and diversity assurance in American postsecondary education. Finally, the

COAMFTE works cooperatively with the Association of Marital and Family Therapy Regulatory Boards (AMFTRB) as well as with individual state licensure and certification boards to assist in defining minimum national educational requirements for competent practice as a marriage and family therapist. In many ways, the AAMFT's support for accredited specialized education through the commission and its curricular standards serves as a foundational aspect of professional unity and distinction. These and related facts about the COAMFTE can be found at http://www.aamft. org/about/coamfte/ aboutcoamfte.asp.

From its inception, the AAMFT has been active in promoting rigorous standards for gaining and maintaining professional affiliation. Many different membership categories are available within the AAMFT. These categories include:

> *Affiliate Membership*—A nonclinical category for those who want to remain abreast of professional issues and concerns in marriage and family therapy but are not pursuing licensure or any clinical-level membership in the AAMFT.
>
> *Student Membership*—A category for students currently enrolled in graduate or postgraduate study with an expectation to secure licensure or Clinical Membership.
>
> *Associate Membership*—A category for postgraduates engaged in supervised clinical experience required for licensure as well as Clinical Membership.
>
> *Clinical Membership*—A category for independent recognition and practice as a marriage and family therapist, typically eligible for state licensure.

Clinical Membership calls for the completion of a master's or doctoral degree from a regionally accredited educational institution or an equivalent course of study. This has been interpreted to mean the completion of a course of study substantially equivalent to the courses reflected in the COAMFTE minimum academic standards and comprising the following (AAMFT, 1990):

- *Marital and Family Studies* (three courses minimum): Family development and family interaction patterns across the life cycle of the individual as well as the family.
- *Marital and Family Therapy* (three courses minimum): Family therapy methodology; family assessment; treatment and intervention methods; overview of major clinical theories of marital and family therapy.
- *Human Development* (three courses minimum): Human development; personality theory; human sexuality; psychopathology; behavior-pathology.
- *Professional Studies* (one course minimum): Professional socialization and the role of the professional organization; legal responsibilities and liabilities; independent practice and interprofessional cooperation; ethics; family law.
- *Research* (one course minimum): Research design; methods and statistics; research in marital and family studies and therapy.
- *Clinical Practicum* (1 year, 300 hours): Fifteen hours per week, approximately 8 to 10 hours in face-to-face contact with individuals, couples, and families for the purpose of assessment, diagnosis, and treatment.

This course of study can be completed while or after obtaining a master's or doctoral degree. Individuals who have completed a graduate degree from a program accredited by the COAMFTE are considered to have met all educational requirements for Clinical Membership in AAMFT by virtue of their completed degree.

Supervised experience is a hallmark of professionalism in any discipline. Although academic work is immensely valuable as a knowledge base for graduate education, supervised experience in both academic and postgraduate frameworks distinguishes knowledge from competence. As we noted in Chapter 3, an interrelationship exists between competence and due care for clients, making supervised experience an ethical obligation for the profession and for the individual therapist. Concurrent with a focus on maintaining high standards for membership, the AAMFT has emphasized the importance of quality training and supervision opportunities in marriage and family therapy. In this respect, the institutional layer of values from the professional organization serves the professional and personal layers of values for the individual therapist.

To this end, the AAMFT Board of Directors established standards for marriage and family therapy supervision in 1971. The Commission on Supervision (now the Supervision Committee), established in 1983, regulates requirements for Approved Supervisor designation within the AAMFT. The Approved Supervisor is one who has received advanced recognition for clinical skills, special training, and experience in the supervision of prospective marriage and family therapists, and who meets the highest standards of clinical education and practice. Approved Supervisors are recognized as competent to provide supervision to students and Associate Members of the AAMFT as they seek to fulfill their Clinical Member requirements. Additionally, Approved Supervisors serve as supervisory mentors to those pursuing Approved Supervisor status with the AAMFT.

Three tracks are available to gain an Approved Supervisor designation, each with specific requirements (American Association for Marriage and Family Therapy, Supervision Committee, 1997). Depending on their qualifications, individuals may select from the following:

- The *Standard Track* is for marriage and family therapists with limited or no experience as a supervisor.
- The *COAMFTE–Accredited Doctorate Track* is for those who are currently enrolled in doctoral programs accredited by the AAMFT COAMFTE.
- The *Advanced Track* is for individuals with extensive experience in marriage and family therapy, training, and supervision.

The majority of individuals applying for the Approved Supervisor designation do so under the Standard Track (American Association for Marriage and Family Therapy, 1997). The major requirements for this track include the following:

- Accumulated 2,000 hours of post–master's degree marriage and family therapy experience.
- Earned a qualifying graduate degree in a mental health discipline from a regionally accredited institution.
- Have Clinical Membership in AAMFT or demonstrate equivalency.
- Provided at least 180 hours of marriage and family therapy supervision over a minimum period of 18 months and a maximum of 2 years.
- Received at least 36 hours of supervision from an AAMFT–Approved Supervisor within 18 months to 2 years.

- Completed a one-semester graduate course in marriage and family therapy supervision (at least 30 contact hours) or the equivalent.
- Provided at least 3,000 hours of post–master's degree marriage and family therapy over a minimum of 3 years by the time of application for the Approved Supervisor designation.

A summary of these and additional requirements for AAMFT Approved Supervisors can be found at http://www.aamft.org/membership/approved%20supervisor/as_responsibilities.asp.

Clinical Membership in AAMFT calls for two calendar years of supervised professional work experience in marital and family therapy. This experiential requirement is in addition to the supervised clinical practice secured as part of the academic requirements. It requires at least 1,000 hours of direct clinical contact with couples and families and 200 hours of supervision of that work, at least 100 of which must be in individual supervision. Also, this supervision must be provided by AAMFT–Approved Supervisors or supervisors acceptable to the AAMFT Membership Committee. Individuals who have completed programs accredited by the COAMFTE may be credited with all clinical contact and supervision completed during their program, provided they have met the aforementioned requirements. Written endorsement by two Clinical Members of the AAMFT attesting to suitable qualities of personal maturity and integrity for the conduct of marriage and family therapy are also necessary to complete the basic Clinical Membership requirements. Complete requirements for the Clinical Evaluative Application Process can be found at http://www.aamft.org/resources/application_tree/closing/closingpageclinicalevaluative.htm.

Practitioners who hold a state-issued marriage and family therapy license or certificate recognized by the AAMFT Board of Directors and have earned a graduate degree recognized by their state for the licensure or certification also meet the educational and clinical experience qualifications for Clinical Membership. This alternative route to qualifying for Clinical Membership is assisted by the adoption of the language of the Model Marriage and Family Therapy Licensure Act (AAMFT, 1992a) by many states. This act is discussed in a later section of this chapter; it emphasizes the minimum supervision requirements for AAMFT Clinical Membership along with the minimum educational content embraced by the COAMFTE.

The COAMFTE's accrediting role is uncommon among bodies recognized by the Department of Education in that it accredits not only university-based degree-granting programs but also "free-standing" postdegree training centers (Shalett & Everett, 1981). These postdegree programs play a unique role in offering an alternative entry into the marriage and family profession. Ordinarily, the master's degree program is recognized as the entry level into the profession by providing broad theoretical knowledge, basic applied skills, and professional attitudes. The doctoral degree is viewed as offering mastery of further comprehensive theory, advanced supervised practice, basic skills and practice in research, and potential experience in teaching and supervision. The postdegree programs have traditionally offered intensive supervised practice with ongoing didactic seminars for individuals who have already attained allied clinical degrees and are seeking specialized training in marriage and family therapy. As of February 2006, 58 master's degree programs (3 Canadian), 2 educational specialist degree programs, 21 doctoral degree programs, and 17 postdegree clinical training institutes (4 Canadian) had been awarded accreditation or were candidates for accreditation by the COAMFTE. These programs are listed in Table 11–1. For the latest update on program accreditation, consult the AAMFT Web site at http://www.aamft.org/cgi-shl/TWServer.exe/Run:COALIST.

TABLE 11–1 COAMFTE Accredited and Candidacy Status Programs

Alabama
Auburn University (MS)
Dr. Thomas Smith
Director—MFT Program
Human Development and Family Studies
203 Spidle Hall
Auburn, AL 36849
Phone: (334) 844-4478
Fax: (334) 844-1924
Email: smitht8@auburn.edu
Website: http://www.humsci.auburn.edu/hdfs/mft.html
Program Accredited: Masters
Renewal Date: January 31, 2012

California
Loma Linda University (MS)
Dr. Mary Moline
Program Coordinator
MFT Program
Dept. of Counseling and Family Sciences
Loma Linda, CA 92350
Phone: (909) 558-4547
Fax: (213) 397-4542
Email: mmoline@mft.llu.edu
Website: http://www.llu.edu/llu/grad/mfam/
Program Accredited: Masters
Renewal Date: January 31, 2012

California
Alliant International University (MA)
Dr. Scott Woolley
Director, MFT Graduate Programs
Irvine, Orange County Location
2500 Michelson Dr. Bldg. 400
Irvine, CA 92612-1548
Phone: (858) 635-4772
Fax: (949) 833-3507
Email: swooley@alliant.edu
Website: http://www.alliant.edu/cspp/mft
Program Accredited: Masters
Renewal Date: January 27, 2007

California
Alliant International University(Psy.D.)
Dr. Scott Woolley

Director, MFT Program
Irvine, Orange County Location
2500 Michelson Dr. Bldg. 400
Irvine, CA 92612-1548
Phone: (949) 833-2651
Fax: (949) 833-3507
Email: swooley@alliant.edu
Website: http://www.alliant.edu/cspp/mft
Program Accredited: Doctoral
Renewal Date: January 27, 2007

California
San Diego, University of (MA)
Dr. Todd M. Edwards
Associate Professor and Director
Marital and Family Therapy Program
5998 Alcala Park
San Diego, CA 92110-2492
Phone: (619) 260-5963
Fax: (619) 260-6826
Email: tedwards@sandiego.edu
Website: http://www.sandiego.edu/mft
Program Accredited: Masters
Renewal Date: July 31, 2010

California
Loma Linda University (Ph.D.)
Dr. Carmen Knudson-Martin
Program Director
Dept of Counseling and Family Science
Griggs Hall Room 202
Loma Linda, CA 92350
Phone: (909) 824-4935
Email: cknudsonmartin@mft.llu.edu
Website: http://www.llu.edu/llu/grad/mfam/
Program Accredited: Doctoral
Renewal Date: January 31, 2012

California
Alliant International University (MA)
Dr. Scott Woolley
Director, MFT Graduate Programs
San Diego Location (Main Campus)
10455 Pomerado Road
San Diego, CA 92131-1799

TABLE 11–1   *Continued*

Phone: (858) 635-4772
Fax: (858) 635-4585
Email: swoolley@alliant.edu
Website: http://www.alliant.edu/cspp/mft
Program Accredited: Masters
Renewal Date: January 31, 2007

California
San Diego State University (MS)
Dr. Linda Terry
Program Director
Dept of Counseling and School Psychology
5500 Campanile Drive
San Diego, CA 92182-1179
Phone: (619) 594-7455
Fax: (619) 594-7025
Email: lterry@mail.sdsu.edu
Website: http://edweb.sdsu.edu/csp/programs/mft
Program Candidacy: Masters
Renewal Date: July 31, 2009

California
Alliant International University (Psy.D.)
Dr. Scott Woolley
Director, MFT Graduate Programs
San Diego Location (Main Campus)
10455 Pomerado Road
San Diego, CA 92131
Phone: (858) 635-4772
Fax: (858) 635-4585
Email: swoolley@alliant.edu
Website: http://www.alliant.edu/cspp/mft
Program Accredited: Doctoral
Renewal Date: January 31, 2007

California
Southern California Counseling (PDI)
Ms. Maggie Shelton
Program Director
5615 West Pico Boulevard
Los Angeles, CA 90019
Phone: (323) 937-1344
Fax: (323) 937-3487
Email: nsteiny@sccc-la.org
Program Accredited: Post-Degree
Renewal Date: January 31, 2010

Colorado
Family Therapy/Play Therapy Inst. (PDI)
Dr. Reo Leslie
Program Director
12101 East 2nd Ave. Suite 101

Aurora, CO 80011
Phone: (720) 859-0464
Fax: (720) 859-2970
Email: Leslieinstitute@cs.com
Program Candidacy: Post-Degree
Renewal Date: July 31, 2006

Colorado
Colorado State University (MS)
Dr. Toni Zimmerman
Associate Professor
Department of Marriage and Family
Therapy
Human Development and Family Studies
Fort Collins, CO 80523
Phone: (970) 491-6922
Fax: (970) 491-7975
Email: zimmerman@cahs.colostate.edu
Website: http://www.colostate.edu
Program Accredited: Masters
Renewal Date: January 31, 2012

Colorado
Denver Family Institute (PDI)
Mr. James Thomas
Program Director
7200 East Hampden Avenue
Suite 301
Denver, CO 80224
Phone: (303) 756-3340
Fax: (303) 758-6140
Email: denverfamilyinstitute@msn.com
Website: http://www.denverfamily institute.org
Program Accredited: Post-Degree
Renewal Date: January 31, 2007

Connecticut
Fairfield University (MA)
Dr. Rona Preli
Program Director
Grad. School of Educ/Allied Professions
North Benson Road
Fairfield, CT 06430
Phone: (203) 254-4000
Fax: (203) 254-4119
Email: rpreli@fair1.fairfield.edu
Website: http://www.fairfield.edu/gseap.xml
Program Accredited: Masters
Renewal Date: July 31, 2006

Connecticut
Connecticut, University of (MA)
Dr. Teresa McDowell

(Continued)

TABLE 11–1   *Continued*

Program Director
School of Family Studies
U-2058, 348 Mansfield Road
Storrs, CT 06269
Phone: (860) 486-4721
Fax: (860) 486-3452
Email: Teresa.McDowell@Uconn.edu
Website: http://www.familystudies.uconn.edu/mft
Program Accredited: Masters
Renewal Date: July 31, 2006

Connecticut
Saint Joseph College (MA)
Dr. Catherine Kikoski
MFT Chair
MFT Program
1678 Asylum Avenue
West Hartford, CT 06117
Phone: (860) 231-5324
Fax: (860) 231-5774
Email: ckikoski@sjc.edu
Website: http://www.sjc.edu/department_page
Program Accredited: Masters
Renewal Date: July 31, 2011

Connecticut
Central Connecticut State University (MS)
Dr. Ralph S. Cohen
MFT Program Director
1615 Stanley Street
Department of Counseling & Family Therapy
New Britain, CT 06050-4010
Phone: (860) 832-2122
Fax: (860) 832-2145
Email: cohenr@mail.ccsu.edu
Website: http://www.ccsu.edu/couns
Program Accredited: Masters
Renewal Date: January 31, 2009

Connecticut
Southern Connecticut State University (MS)
Ms. Barbara Lynch
Program Director
MFT Program Davis Hall Room 020
501 Crescent Street
New Haven, CT 06515
Phone: (203) 392-6414
Fax: (203) 392-6441
Email: ej52@aol.com
Website: http://www.scsu.ctstateu.edu/cat
Program Accredited: Masters
Renewal Date: July 31, 2009

Connecticut
Connecticut, University of (Ph.D.)
Dr. Teresa McDowell
Program Director
School of Family Studies
U-58, 348 Mansfield Road
Storrs, CT 06269
Phone: (860) 486-3452
Fax: (860) 486-8883
Email: Teresa.McDowell@Uconn.edu
Website: http://www.familystudies.uconn.edu/mft
Program Accredited: Doctoral
Renewal Date: July 31, 2006

Florida
Nova Southeastern University (Ph.D.)
Dr. Tommie Boyd
Program Director
SHSS Dept. of Family Therapy
3301 College Avenue
Fort Lauderdale, FL 33314
Phone: (954) 262-3022
Fax: (954) 262-3968
Email: tommie@nsu.nova.edu
Website: http://www.nova.edu/ssss/FT/
Program Accredited: Doctoral
Renewal Date: July 31, 2010

Florida
Nova Southeastern University (MA)
Dr. Tommie Boyd
Assistant Professor of Family Therapy
SHSS Dept. of Family Therapy
3301 College Avenue
Fort Lauderdale, FL 33314
Phone: (954) 262-3022
Fax: (954) 262-3968
Email: tommie@nsu.nova.edu
Website: http://www.nova.edu/ssss/FT/
Program Accredited: Masters
Renewal Date: July 31, 2008

Florida
Florida State University (Ph.D.)
Dr. Robert Lee
Program Director
Interdiv. Doctoral Prog in Fam. Therapy
240 Sandels Building,
Tallahassee, FL 32306-1491
Phone: (850) 644-3217
Fax: (850) 644-3439

TABLE 11–1 *Continued*

Email: relee@fsu.edu
Website: http://www.chs.fsu.edu/fcs/mft/
Program Accredited: Doctoral
Renewal Date: July 31, 2011

Georgia
Valdosta State University (MS)
Dr. Kate Warner
Program Director
1500 North Patterson St.
Valdosta, GA 31698
Phone: (229) 293-6264
Email: kwarner@valdosta.edu
Website: http://www.valdosta.edu/mft/
Program Candidacy: Masters
Renewal Date: January 31, 2007

Georgia
Georgia, University of (Ph.D.)
Dr. Jerry Gale
Director of MFT Program
Dept of Child and Family Development
MFT Program, Dawson Hall
Athens, GA 30602
Phone: (706) 542-8435
Fax: (706) 542-4489
Email: jgale@fcs.uga.edu
Website: http://www.fcs.uga.edu/cfd/mft.html
Program Accredited: Doctoral
Renewal Date: July 31, 2009

Georgia
Mercer University (MFT)
Dr. Lee Bowen
Director—MFT Program
Dept of Psych and Behavioral Sci—MFT
655 1st Street
Macon, GA 31207
Phone: (478) 301-2208
Fax: (478) 301-5337
Email: bowen_ld@mercer.edu
Website: http://medicine.mercer.edu/programs/
Program Accredited: Masters
Renewal Date: January 31, 2009

Illinois
Northern Illinois University (MS)
Dr. Lin Shi
Program Director
School of Family, Consumer and Nutri. Sci
Wirtz 152
DeKalb, IL 60115
Phone: (815) 753-6349

Fax: (815) 753-1321
Email: lshi@niu.edu
Website: http://www.fcns.niu.edu/html/
smft.html
Program Accredited: Masters
Renewal Date: January 31, 2009

Illinois
Family Institute at Northwestern Univ. (MS)
Mr. William Russell
Program Director—MSMFT Program
618 Library Place
Evanston, IL 60201
Phone: (847) 733-4300
Fax: (847) 733-0390
Email: W-Russell@northwestern.edu
Website: http://www.family-institute.org
Program Accredited: Masters
Renewal Date: January 31, 2012

Indiana
Purdue University (Ph.D.)
Dr. Doug Sprenkle
Program Director
MFT Program
1200 West State Street
West Lafayette, IN 47907
Phone: (765) 494-2952
Fax: (765) 494-0503
Email: sprenkled@aol.com
Website: http://www.cfs.purdue.edu/mft/
Program Accredited: Doctoral
Renewal Date: January 31, 2007

Indiana
Purdue University-Calumet (MS)
Dr. Joseph Wetchler
Professor of Marriage and Family Therapy
Marriage and Family Therapy Program
Department of Behavioral Sciences
Hammond, IN 46323-2094
Phone: (219) 989-2319
Fax: (219) 989-2777
Email: wetchler@calumet.purdue.edu
Website: http://www.calumet.purdue.
edu/mftp/
Program Accredited: Masters
Renewal Date: July 31, 2011

Indiana
Christian Theological Seminary (MA)
Dr. Suzanne Coyle
Program Director

(Continued)

TABLE 11–1 *Continued*

1000 West 42nd Street
Indianapolis, IN 46208
Phone: (317) 924-5205
Fax: (317) 931-2393
Email: scoyle@cts.edu
Website: http://www.cts.edu/Catalog/degree
Program Accredited: Masters
Renewal Date: July 31, 2011

Iowa

Iowa State University (Ph.D.)
Dr. Ronald Werner-Wilson
Professor
Dept of Human Develop and Family Studies
4380 Palmer Building, Suite 1321
Ames, IA 50011-1030
Phone: (515) 294-8671
Email: rwwilson@iastate.edu
Website: http://www.fcs.iastate.edu/hdfs/
Program Accredited: Doctoral
Renewal Date: July 31, 2006

Kansas

Friends University (MS)
Dr. Daniel Lord
Program Director
2100 University Street
Wichita, KS 67213
Phone: (316) 295-5602
Fax: (316) 295-5115
Email: dlord@friends.edu
Website: http://www.friends.edu
Program Accredited: Masters
Renewal Date: January 31, 2012

Kansas

Friends University—Lenexa Site (MS)
Dr. Christopher Habben
MSFT Lenexa Site Director
8207 Melrose Drive
Lenexa, KS 66214
Phone: (913) 233-8716
Fax: (913) 233-8275
Email: chabben@friends.edu
Website: http://www.friends.edu
Program: Masters
Renewal Date: January 31, 2006

Kansas

Kansas State University (Ph.D.)
Dr. Mark White
Program Director
Family Studies and Human Services

MFT Program, Justin Hall
Manhattan, KS 66506
Phone: (785) 532-1487
Fax: (785) 532-5505
Email: mwhite@humec.ksu.edu
Website: http://www.ksu.edu/humec/fshs/
Program Accredited: Doctoral
Renewal Date: January 31, 2009

Kansas

Kansas State University (MA)
Dr. Mark White
Associate Professor
Family Studies and Human Services
MFT Program—303 Justin Hall
Manhattan, KS 66506
Phone: (785) 532-1487
Fax: (785) 532-6523
Email: mwhite@humec.ksu.edu
Website: http://www.ksu.edu/humec/fshs/
Program Accredited: Masters
Renewal Date: January 31, 2009

Kentucky

Kentucky, University of (MS)
Dr. Kay Bradford
Program Director
MFT Program—Dept of Family Studies
319-A Funkhouser Building
Lexington, KY 40506-0054
Phone: (859) 257-5454
Fax: (859) 257-4095
Email: kbrad@uky.edu
Website: http://www.uky.edu/HES/
gwbrock/mftprog/
Program Accredited: Masters
Renewal Date: January 31, 2007

Kentucky

Louisville Presbyterian Theol. Sem. (MA)
Dr. James Hyde
Interim Director—MFT Program
Marriage and Family Therapy Program
1044 Alta Vista Road
Louisville, KY 40205
Phone: (502) 345-1955
Fax: (502) 895-1096
Email: jhyde@lpts.edu
Website: http://www.lpts.edu/education/
mamftf.html
Program Accredited: Masters
Renewal Date: July 31, 2010

TABLE 11–1 *Continued*

Kentucky
Louisville, University of (MSSW)
Dr. Sally St. George
Program Director
FT Program; Kent School of Social Work
University of Louisville
Louisville, KY 40292
Phone: (502) 852-2520
Fax: (502) 852-4598
Email: sastge01@gwise.louisville.edu
Website: http://www.louisville.edu/kent/family/
Program Accredited: Masters
Renewal Date: January 31, 2009

Kentucky
Louisville, University of (PDI)
Dr. Sally St. George
Associate Professor
Family Therapy Program
Kent School of Social Work
Louisville, KY 40292
Phone: (502) 852-2520
Fax: (502) 852-4598
Email: dan.wulff@louisville.edu
Website: http://www.louisville.edu/kent/family/
Program Accredited: Post-Degree
Renewal Date: January 31, 2011

Louisiana
Louisiana Monroe, University of (MA)
Dr. Lamar Woodham
Program Director
Marriage and Family Therapy Program
306 Strauss Hall
Monroe, LA 71209-0280
Phone: (318) 362-3008
Fax: (318) 343-2345
Email: woodham@ulm.edu
Website: http://www.ulm.edu/~mft/mft.html
Program Accredited: Masters
Renewal Date: January 31, 2008

Louisiana
Louisiana Monroe, University of (Ph.D.)
Dr. Lamar Woodham
Program Director
Marriage and Family Therapy
306 Strauss Hall
Monroe, LA 71209-0280
Phone: (318) 362-3008
Fax: (318) 343-2345
Email: woodham@ulm.edu

Website: http://www.ulm.edu/~mft/mft.html
Program Candidacy: Doctoral
Renewal Date: January 31, 2007

Maryland
Maryland, University of (MS)
Dr. Norm Epstein
Professor of Family Studies
Department of Family Studies
Marie Mount Hall 1210-C
College Park, MD 20742
Phone: (301) 405-4013
Fax: (301) 314-9161
Email: ne4@umail.umd.edu
Website: http://www.gradschool.umd.edu
Program Accredited: Masters
Renewal Date: July 31, 2006

Massachusetts
Massachusetts Boston, University of (M.Ed.)
Dr. Gonzalo Bacigalupe
Program Director
Grad. College of Education, Fam. Therapy
100 Morrissey Boulevard
Boston, MA 02125-3393
Phone: (617) 287-7631
Fax: (617) 287-7664
Email: gonzalo.bacigalupe@umb.edu
Website: http://www.familytherapy.umb.edu/
Program Accredited: Masters
Renewal Date: July 31, 2009

Michigan
Michigan State University (Ph.D.)
Dr. Marsha Carolan
Program Director, Associate Professor
Department of Family and Child Ecology
107 Human Ecology
East Lansing, MI 48824-1030
Phone: (517) 353-5248
Fax: (517) 432-3320
Email: carolan@msu.edu
Website: http://www.fce.msu.edu/
Program Accredited: Doctoral
Renewal Date: January 31, 2009

Michigan
Michigan State University (MA)
Dr. Marsha Carolan
Program Director, Assistant Professor
Department of Family and Child Ecology
107 Human Ecology

(Continued)

TABLE 11–1 *Continued*

East Lansing, MI 48824-1030
Phone: (517) 353-5248
Fax: (517) 432-3320
Email: carolan@msu.edu
Website: http://www.fce.msu.edu/
Program Accredited: Masters
Renewal Date: January 31, 2009

Minnesota
Minnesota, University of (Ph.D.)
Dr. William Doherty
MFT Director
Family Social Science, MFT Program
290 McNeal Hall, 1985 Buford Avenue
St. Paul, MN 55108
Phone: (612) 625-1900
Fax: (612) 625-4227
Email: bdoherty@che.umn.edu
Website: http://fsos.che.umn.edu/graduat
Program Accredited: Doctoral
Renewal Date: January 31, 2009

Mississippi
Reformed Theological Seminary (MA)
Dr. James B. Hurley
Professor of Marriage and Family Therapy
5422 Clinton Boulevard
Jackson, MS 39209-3099
Phone: (601) 923-1630
Fax: (601) 923-1634
Email: jhurley@rts.edu
Website: http://www.rts.edu/degrees/ma/
Program Accredited: Masters
Renewal Date: January 31, 2009

Mississippi
Southern Mississippi, University of (MS)
Dr. Patricia Sims
Associate Professor
MFT Program
118 College Drive, Box 5035
Hattiesburg, MS 39406-5035
Phone: (601) 266-4679
Fax: (601) 266-4680
Email: pat.sims@usm.edu
Website: http://www.usm.edu/
childandfamilystudies
Program Accredited: Masters
Renewal Date: July 31, 2010

Missouri
Forest Institute of Psychology (PDI)
Dr. Jennifer Baker

Director
2885 West Battlefield Road
Springfield, MO 65807
Phone: (417) 877-9699
Fax: (417) 823-3442
Email: jbaker@forest.edu
Website: http://www.forest.edu
Program Accredited: Post-Degree
Renewal Date: January 31, 2011

Nebraska
Nebraska Lincoln, University of (MS)
Dr. Richard Bischoff
Assistant Professor
MFT Program, College of Home Economics
110 Ruth Leverton Hall
Lincoln, NE 68583-0801
Phone: (402) 472-5801
Fax: (402) 472-9170
Email: rbischoff2@unl.edu
Website: http://cehs.unl.edu/fcs/grad/
marriage.shtml
Program Accredited: Masters
Renewal Date: January 31, 2011

New Hampshire
New Hampshire, University of (MS)
Dr. Barbara Frankel
Associate Professor of Family Studies
Dept. of Family Studies—Pettee Hall
55 College Road, Room 202
Durham, NH 03824
Phone: (603) 862-2134
Fax: (603) 862-3271
Email: family.studies@unh.edu
Website: http://www.unh.edu/family-studies
Program Accredited: Masters
Renewal Date: July 31, 2005

New Hampshire
Antioch New England Graduate School (MA)
Dr. Janie Long
Director—MFT Program
Marriage and Family Therapy Program
40 Avon Street
Keene, NH 03431
Phone: (603) 357-3122
Fax: (603) 357-0718
Email: jlong@antiochne.edu
Website: http://www.antiochne.edu/ap/
Program Accredited: Masters
Renewal Date: January 31, 2011

TABLE 11–1 *Continued*

New Jersey
Seton Hall University (Ed.S.)
Dr. Robert Massey
Program Director
Dept of Profess Psych and Family Therapy
400 South Orange Ave.
South Orange, NJ 07079
Phone: (973) 761-9450
Fax: (973) 275-2188
Email: masseyro@shu.edu
Website: http://education.shu.edu/ppft
Program Accredited: Masters
Renewal Date: July 31, 2008

New York
Blanton-Peale Institute (PDI)
Dr. Janet Foy
Chair
3 West 29th St., 5th Floor
New York, NY 10001
Phone: (212) 725-7850
Fax: (212) 689-3212
Email: jfoy@blantonpeale.org
Website: http://www.blantonpeale.org
Program Accredited: Post-Degree
Renewal Date: January 31, 2010

New York
Rochester, University of (PDI)
Dr. Pieter leRoux
Program Director
Intensive Family Therapy Program
Dept of Psychiatry; 300 Crittenden Blvd.
Rochester, NY 14642
Phone: (585) 275-2532
Fax: (585) 271-7706
Email: pieter_leroux@urmc.rochester.edu
Website: http://www.urmc.rochester.edu/smd/psych/
educ_train/family/index.cfm
Program Accredited: Post-Degree
Renewal Date: July 31, 2010

New York
Syracuse University (Ph.D.)
Dr. Jonathan Sandberg
Program Director
College of Human Development
426 Ostrom Ave.
Syracuse, NY 13244-1250
Phone: (315) 443-9403
Fax: (315) 443-4062
Email: jgsandbe@syr.edu
Website: http://hshp.syr.edu/schools/mft/

Program Accredited: Doctoral
Renewal Date: July 31, 2007

New York
Syracuse University (MA)
Dr. Jonathan Sandberg
Director—MFT Program
College of Human Services and Hlth Prof
426 Ostrom Ave.
Syracuse, NY 13244-1250
Phone: (315) 443-9403
Fax: (315) 443-4062
Email: jgsandbe@syr.edu
Website: http://hshp.syr.edu/schools/mft/
Program Accredited: Masters
Renewal Date: July 31, 2007

New York
Rochester, University of (MS)
Dr. Pieter leRoux
Clinical Assoc. Professor
Dept. of Psychiatry, Family Therapy Prog.
300 Crittenden Blvd.
Rochester, NY 14642
Phone: (585) 275-2532
Fax: (585) 271-7706
Email: pieter_leroux@urmc.rochester.edu
Website: http://www.urmc.rochester.edu/smd/psych/
educ_train/family/index.cfm
Program Accredited: Masters
Renewal Date: July 31, 2010

New York
Iona College (MA)
Dr. Bob Burns
Program Director
715 North Ave.
New Rochelle, NY 10801-1890
Phone: (914) 633-2073
Fax: (914) 637-7710
Email: rburns@iona.edu
Website:
Program Candidacy: Masters
Renewal Date: July 31, 2009

North Carolina
East Carolina University (MS)
Dr. Wayne Hill
Program Director
M.F.T. Program
Dept. of Child Devel and Family Relations
Greenville, NC 27858-4353
Phone: (252) 328-1681
Fax: (252) 328-5418

(Continued)

TABLE 11–1   *Continued*

Email: hodgsonj@mail.ecu.edu
Website: http://www.ecu.edu/hes/cdfrmftMS.htm
Program Accredited: Masters
Renewal Date: January 31, 2010

North Carolina
Appalachian State University (MA)
Dr. Jon Winek
Coordinator—MFT Program
MFT Program
Dept. of Human Devel
   and Psych Counseling
Boone, NC 28608
Phone: (828) 262-2055
Fax: (828) 262-2128
Email: winekjl@appstate.edu
Website: http://www.hpc.appstate.edu/MFT/
MFT.html
Program Accredited: Masters
Renewal Date: July 31, 2011

North Dakota
North Dakota State University (MS)
Dr. Thomas Carlson
Interim Director—MFT Program
Child Development
   and Family Sci/MFT
P.O. Box 5057
Fargo, ND 58105-5057
Phone: (701) 231-8279
Fax: (701) 231-9645
Email: tom.carlson@ndsu.nodak.edu
Website: http://www.ndsu.nodak.
edu/ndsu/jdeal/cdfs/
Program Accredited: Masters
Renewal Date: January 31, 2008

Ohio
Akron, University of (Ph.D.)
Dr. Patricia Parr
Program Director
MFT, Dept. of Counseling
   and Special Ed.
127 Carroll Hall
Akron, OH 44325-5007
Phone: (330) 972-8151
Fax: (330) 972-5292
Email: pparr@uakron.edu
Website: http://www.uakron.edu/edcouns/
marriage.htm
Program Accredited: Doctoral
Renewal Date: July 31, 2010

Ohio
Ohio State University (Ph.D.)
Dr. Suzanne Bartle-Haring
Program Director
College of Human Ecology
1787 Neil Avenue
Columbus, OH 43210
Phone: (614) 292-5685
Fax: (614) 292-4365
Email: SBartle-Haring@HEC.OHIO-STATE.EDU
Website: http://www.hec.ohio-state.edu/hdfs
Program Accredited: Doctoral
Renewal Date: January 31, 2007

Ohio
Akron, University of (MS)
Dr. Patricia Parr
Progam Director
Dept. of Counseling and Spec. Ed.
127 Carroll Hall
Akron, OH 44325-5007
Phone: (330) 972-8151
Fax: (330) 972-5292
Email: pparr@uakron.edu
Website: http://www.uakron.edu/edcouns/
marriage.htm
Program Accredited: Masters
Renewal Date: July 31, 2010

Oklahoma
Oklahoma State University (MS)
Dr. Charles Hendrix
Director—MFT Specialization
MFT Program, Dept. of HDFS
233 Human Environmental Science
Stillwater, OK 74078-0337
Phone: (405) 744-5057
Fax: (405) 744-2800
Email: charles.hendrix@okstate.edu
Website: http://ches.okstate.edu/
Program Accredited: Masters
Renewal Date: January 31, 2009

Oregon
Oregon, University of (M.Ed.)
Dr. John Miller
Program Director
MFT Spec—College of Education
5251 University of Oregon
Eugene, OR 97403-5251
Phone: (541) 346-5501
Fax: (541) 346-6778

TABLE 11–1   *Continued*

Email: jkmiller@uoregon.edu
Website: http://education.uoregon.edu/mft
Program Accredited: Masters
Renewal Date: July 31, 2009

Pennsylvania

Drexel University (PDI)
Dr. Marlene Watson
Program Director
Couple and Family
    Therapy Program
1505 Race Street; 10th floor, mail stop #905
Philadelphia, PA 19102-1192
Phone: (215) 762-6930
Fax: (215) 762-6933
Email: marlene.f.watson@drexel.edu
Website: http://www.mcphu.edu/shp/gradprogs
Program Accredited: Post-Degree
Renewal Date: July 31, 2011

Pennsylvania

New Family Institute of Philadelphia (PDI)
Mrs. Rhoda Shralow
Director
824 Dover Road
Wynnewood, PA 19096
Phone: (610) 642-8075
Fax: (610) 642-4122
Email: shralowrr@comcast.net
Program Accredited: Post-Degree
Renewal Date: January 31, 2006

Pennsylvania

Council for Relationships (PDI)
Dr. Kenneth Covelman
Director of Training
4025 Chestnut Street, 1st Floor
Philadelphia, PA 19104
Phone: (215) 382-6680
Fax: (215) 386-1743
Email: kcovelman@councilforrelationships.org
Website: http://www.pcfr.org
Program Accredited: Post-Degree
Renewal Date: January 31, 2007

Pennsylvania

Philadelphia Child & Fam. The. Trng. Ctr.
Dr. Marion Lindblad-Goldberg
Center Director
Part-Time Intensive Program
P.O. Box 4092
Philadelphia, PA 19118-8092
Phone: (215) 242-0949

Email: marionlg@philafamily.com
Website: http://www.philafamily.com
Program Accredited: Post-Degree
Renewal Date: July 31, 2011

Pennsylvania

Seton Hill University (MS)
Dr. Susan Cooley
Program Director
Seton Hill Dr.
Greensburg, PA 15601
Phone: (724) 838-7816
Fax: (724) 830-1295
Email: cooley@setonhill.edu
Website: http://www.setonhill.edu
Program Candidacy: Masters
Renewal Date: January 31, 2009

Pennsylvania

Drexel University (MA)
Dr. Marlene F. Watson
Program Director
Couple and Family Therapy
245 North 15th Street; Mail Stop #905
Philadelphia, PA 19102-1192
Phone: (215) 762-6930
Fax: (215) 762-6933
Email: marlene.f.watson@drexel.edu
Website: http://www.mcphu.edu/
shp/gradprogs
Program Accredited: Masters
Renewal Date: July 31, 2011

Rhode Island

Rhode Island, University of (MS)
Dr. Jerome Adams
Prof. of Human Devel. & Family Studies
MFT Program—Transition Center
Lower College Road
Kingston, RI 02881
Phone: (401) 874-2440
Fax: (401) 874-4020
Email: jadams@mail.uri.edu
Website: http://www.uri.edu
Program Accredited: Masters
Renewal Date: January 31, 2007

South Carolina

Converse College (Ed.S.)
Dr. Pamela Clark
Program Director
508 East Main Street
Spartanburg, SC 29302-0006

(Continued)

TABLE 11–1 *Continued*

Phone: (864) 577-2038
Fax: (864) 596-9221
Email: pam.clark@converse.edu
Program Accredited: Masters
Renewal Date: January 31, 2012

South Carolina
WestGate Training & Consult. Network (PDI)
Dr. Jim Rentz
Executive Director & Program Director
167 Alabama Street
Spartanburg, SC 29302
Phone: (864) 583-1010
Fax: (864) 582-6361
Email: jrentz@westgatetcn.org
Program Accredited: Post-Degree
Renewal Date: January 31, 2009

Texas
Houston Clear Lake, University of (MA)
Dr. Linda Bell
Program Director
Behavioral Sciences Program
2700 Bay Area Boulevard
Houston, TX 77058-1098
Phone: (281) 283-3394
Fax: (281) 283-3397
Email: belllinda@cl.uh.edu
Website: http://hsh.cl.uh.edu/family_therapy
Program Accredited: Masters
Renewal Date: July 31, 2009

Texas
St. Marys University (MA)
Dr. Randall Lyle
Graduate Program Director
Family Life Center
One Camino Santa Maria
San Antonio, TX 78228-8539
Phone: (210) 436-3226
Fax: (210) 431-6886
Email: rlyle@stmarytx.edu
Website: http://www.stmarytx.edu/grad/counseling
Program Accredited: Masters
Renewal Date: July 31, 2010

Texas
Texas Tech University (Ph.D.)
Dr. Roy Bean
Director, MFT Program
Dept. of Applied and Professional Studies

P.O. Box 41162
Lubbock, TX 79409-1162
Phone: (806) 742-5050
Fax: (806) 742-5033
Email: roy.bean@ttu.edu
Website: http://www.hs.ttu.edu/mft/
Program Accredited: Doctoral
Renewal Date: January 31, 2010

Texas
St. Marys University (Ph.D.)
Dr. Randall Lyle
Program Director
Family Life Center
One Camino Santa Maria
San Antonio, TX 78228-8539
Phone: (210) 436-3226
Email: rlyle@stmarytx.edu
Website: http://www.stmarytx.edu/grad/counseling
Program Accredited: Doctoral
Renewal Date: July 31, 2010

Texas
Abilene Christian University (MFT)
Dr. Jackie Halstead
Director—Marriage and Family Institute
Department of Marriage and Family Therapy
P.O. Box 8444
Abilene, TX 79699
Phone: (325) 674-3778
Fax: (325) 674-3749
Email: halsteadj@acu.edu
Website: http://www.bible.acu.edu/mft
Program Accredited: Masters
Renewal Date: July 31, 2011

Utah
Utah State University (MS)
Dr. Scot Allgood
Director—MFT Program
Marriage and Family Therapy Program
2700 Old Main Hill
Logan, UT 84322-2700
Phone: (435) 797-7433
Fax: (435) 797-7432
Email: scot.allgood@usu.edu
Website: http://www.usu.edu/mft
Program Accredited: Masters
Renewal Date: July 31, 2007

Utah
Brigham Young University (Ph.D.)
Dr. Robert Stahmann

TABLE 11–1 *Continued*

Program Director
Marriage and Family Therapy Program
274 TLRB—BYU
Provo, UT 84602-8614
Phone: (801) 422-6508
Fax: (801) 422-5782
Email: robert_stahmann@byu.edu
Website: http://mft.byu.edu
Program Accredited: Doctoral
Renewal Date: January 31, 2010

Utah
Brigham Young University (MS)
Dr. Robert Stahmann
Program Director
240 TLRB—BYU
Department of Family Sciences
Provo, UT 84602
Phone: (801) 378-6508
Fax: (801) 378-5782
Email: rfs@ucs-exch.byu.edu
Website: http://mft.byu.edu
Program Accredited: Masters
Renewal Date: January 31, 2010

Virginia
Virginia Tech University Blacksburg (Ph.D.)
Dr. Scott Johnson
Program Director
840 University City Blvd.
Suite 1
Blacksburg, VA 24061-0515
Phone: (540) 231-7201
Fax: (540) 231-7209
Email: swj@vt.edu
Website: http://www.familytherapy.vt.edu
Program Accredited: Doctoral
Renewal Date: July 31, 2009

Virginia
Virginia Tech University Falls Church (MS)
Dr. Sandra Stith
Director—MFT Program
Dept. of Human Development
7054 Haycock Rd., Room 202-F
Falls Church, VA 22043-2311
Phone: (703) 538-8462
Fax: (703) 538-8465
Email: sstith@vt.edu
Website: http://www.nvgc.vt.edu/mft
Program Accredited: Masters
Renewal Date: January 31, 2007

Washington
Pacific Lutheran University (MA)
Dr. Charles York
Department Chair
Department of Marriage & Family Therapy
Tacoma, WA 98447
Phone: (253) 535-7599
Email: yorkcd@plu.edu
Website: http://www.plu.edu/~mftcntr/
home.htm
Program Accredited: Masters
Renewal Date: January 31, 2012

Washington
Seattle Pacific University (MS)
Dr. Claudia Grauf-Grounds
MFT Program Chair
Marriage and Family Therapy Program
3307 Third Ave. West
Seattle, WA 98119-1997
Phone: (206) 281-2632
Fax: (206) 281-2695
Email: claudiagg@spu.edu
Website: http://www.spu.edu/depts/pfc/mft/
Program Accredited: Masters
Renewal Date: July 31, 2008

Wisconsin
Family Therapy Training Institute (PDI)
Dr. Ann Starr
Program Director
PO Box 080440
Milwaukee, WI 53208-0440
Phone: (414) 342-4560
Fax: (414) 342-5326
Email: ann_starr@aurora.org
Program Accredited: Post-Degree
Renewal Date: January 31, 2012

Wisconsin
Wisconsin Stout, University of (MS)
Dr. Bruce Kuehl
Program Director
Marriage and Family Therapy Program
College of Human Development
Menomonie, WI 54751
Phone: (715) 232-2404
Fax: (715) 232-2356
Email: kuehlb@uwstout.edu
Website: http://www.uwstout.edu/
programs/msmft/

(Continued)

TABLE 11–1 *Continued*

Program Accredited: Masters
Renewal Date: January 31, 2009

Canada
Alberta
Calgary Health Region (PDI)
Dr. Maureen Leahey
Program Director
Family Therapy Training Program, 1st Fl.
Cnl Belcher Hospital, 1213 4th St. SW
Calgary, AB T2R OX7
Phone: (403) 943-2440
Fax: (403) 943-2441
Email: maureen.leahey@calgaryhealthregion.ca
Website: http://www.calgaryhealthregion.ca
Program Accredited: Post-Degree
Renewal Date: January 31, 2011

Manitoba
Winnipeg, University of (MMFT)
Ms. Marilyn Boyd
Program Director
Aurora Family Therapy Center
515 Portage Avenue
Winnipeg, MB R3B 2E9
Phone: (204) 786-9252
Fax: (204) 772-2547
Email: m.boyd@uwinnipeg.ca
Website: http://aurora.uwinnipeg.ca
Program Accredited: Masters
Renewal Date: January 31, 2012

Ontario
Interfaith Pastoral Counseling Ctr. (PDI)
Dr. John Schneider
Program Director
151 Frederick Street, 3rd Floor
Kitchener, ON N2H 2M2
Phone: (519) 743-6781
Fax: (519) 743-0610
Email: johnschneiderjr@interfaithmft.on.ca

Program Accredited: Post-Degree
Renewal Date: July 31, 2009

Ontario
Guelph, University of (MS)
Dr. Anna Dienhart
Program Director
Dept. of Family Relations and Applied
Couple and Family Therapy Center
Guelph, ON NIG 2W1
Phone: (519) 824-4120
Fax: (519) 823-7819
Email: adienhar@uoguelph.ca
Program Accredited: Masters
Renewal Date: July 31, 2011

Quebec
Argyle Institute of Human Relations (PDI)
Ms. Maria Alejos
Program Director
Marriage and Family Therapy Program
4115 Sherbrooke St. W., 5th Floor
Montreal, PQ H3Z 1K9
Phone: (514) 932-3254
Fax: (514) 931-8754
Email: argyle.mftprogram@bellnet.ca
Website: http://www.argyleinstitute.org
Program Accredited: Post-Degree
Renewal Date: January 31, 2009

Quebec
Jewish General Hospital-(PDI)
Dr. Sharron Bond
Program Director
Couple and Family Therapy Training Prog
4333 Chemin de la Cote Ste. Catherine
Montreal, PQ H3T 1E4
Phone: (514) 340-8210
Fax: (514) 340-7507
Email: reantill@icfp.jgh.mcgill.ca
Program Accredited: Post-Degree
Renewal Date: July 31, 2011

Shalett and Everett (1981) asserted that the accreditation process provides needed links with licensure in the profession. In their view, licensure basically functions to offer the public minimal protection against untrained practitioners; it identifies minimal qualifications for the practitioner but neither ensures competency nor addresses the quality of the individual education and training. Shalett and Everett identified accreditation as the primary way to establish standards for practitioners' educational and training experiences, because licensure is essentially meaningless in the absence of accreditation. The AAMFT has been recognized as the focal point for the marriage and family therapy profession by several states whose licensing boards have incorporated major aspects of AAMFT membership standards and its Commission on Accreditation's program standards into their licensing laws. Furthermore, the AAMFT's methods of giving credentials have provided recognition for practitioners in those states with no licensure, particularly with regard to insurance reimbursement for services.

In summary, one can note the interrelatedness between specified requirements reflected in accredited educational programs, a prescribed academic curriculum, explicit supervised experience, selective membership, and state licensure that emerges through professional affiliation with the AAMFT. In this regard, such an organization epitomizes the view of marriage and family as a unique and specialized professional field. Such a view is reflected in Quadrant A of Figure 11–1.

American Family Therapy Academy

The American Family Therapy Academy (AFTA) was founded in 1977 by a small group of mental health professionals who were active during the early years when marriage and family therapy was emerging. Its stated objectives at that time included the following:

1. Advancing family therapy as a science that regards the entire family as the unit of study.
2. Promoting research and professional education in family therapy and allied fields.
3. Making information about family therapy available to practitioners in other fields of knowledge and to the public.
4. Fostering cooperation among those concerned with medical, psychological, social, legal, and other aspects of the family, and those involved in the science and practice of family therapy. (Sauber, L'Abate, & Weeks, 1985, p. 180)

There are five categories of membership in the AFTA: Clinical–Teacher, Researcher, Family Scholar and Larger Systems Practitioner, Distinguished, and International. AFTA members represent a wide variety of disciplines, though all share a common and confirmable commitment to study of family life. Membership requirements are as follows:

Clinical–Teacher: A terminal professional degree or its equivalent in a mental health field; five years of postdegree clinical experience working with families; five years of postdegree experience teaching family therapy; verification of good standing with a state/provincial regulatory body; and letters of recommendation from three AFTA members.

Researcher: An advanced degree in social/behavioral sciences; research in the family field deemed significant by the membership committee; verification of good standing with a state/provincial regulatory body; and letters of recommendation from three AFTA members.

Family Scholar and Larger Systems Practitioner: A terminal degree subject to evaluation by the membership committee; five years of postdegree experience working in family policy analysis, family advocacy, family history, family law, program development, or similar areas; verification of good standing with a state/provincial regulatory body; and letters of recommendation from three AFTA members.

Distinguished: Offered by the AFTA Board to those making distinguished contributions relevant to the family field.

International: equivalent to Clinical–Teacher, Researcher, or Distinguished categories based on the evaluation of the membership committee.

Membership requirements and related information about AFTA can be found at http://afta.org/meminfo/criteria.html.

Perhaps the greatest benefit to AFTA members is the networking opportunities for dialogue and cross-fertilization among highly skilled professionals with a variety of specialty backgrounds (Kaslow, 1990b). In a framework much like a think tank, AFTA's annual meeting brings together professionals to address a variety of clinical, research, and teaching topics. Similarly, the biennial Clinical Research Conference offers a unique opportunity for theme-focused symposia, open to both AFTA members and other health professionals. The AFTA "Early Career Membership Pilot Project" also has been established as an opportunity for professionals with two years of postgraduate experience to affiliate with AFTA in the emerging years of their professional lives.

In 1981, a joint liaison committee of representatives from the AAMFT and the AFTA was formed to take up the issue of the respective roles of the two organizations within the profession. The AFTA was identified as an academy of advanced professionals interested in the exchange of ideas; the AAMFT retained its recognition as an organization for providing credentials to marriage and family therapists (W. C. Nichols, 1992). This finding was particularly important in sustaining the prominence of the AAMFT in its attempts to spearhead licensure and other legislative efforts for the field. In many ways, this finding was reflective of our earlier notation from H. Anderson (1994) concerning balance in professional identity and affiliation.

Family Psychology (Division 43 of the American Psychological Association)

Family Psychology was established as Division 43 within the American Psychological Association (APA) in 1984. The division emerged in response to the desire of a significant number of psychologists seeking to maintain their professional identity as psychologists while pursuing family therapeutic practices (Kaslow, 1990b). When the division was formed, a new designation, *family psychologist,* reconnected these professionals with their original discipline and replaced the hyphenated model of professional identity they had been using: *psychologist-family therapist* (Liddle, 1987). To a great degree, this reaffiliation had to do with a return to professional values that endorse the role of a scientific base in clinical practice (i.e., the scientist–practitioner model of training and practice in psychology).

To become a division member, one must hold membership in the APA. From the perspective of this group, marriage and family therapy represents one clinical approach of family psychology (Liddle, 1992). In 1989, the American Board of Professional Psychology (ABPP) voted to recognize Family Psychology as its seventh specialty, due to the efforts of Division 43 members. Recognition by ABPP offers family psychologists the opportunity to gain advanced certification, the "Diplomate in Family

Psychology." The major requirements for achieving this designation include (Specialty Boards: Family, 1992):

1. A doctoral degree meeting the standards of the APA for doctoral training.
2. A minimum of 1,500 hours of supervised training in an organized psychological service setting, completed in no more than two years.
3. Three graduate courses or their equivalent, two graduate clinical practicum courses or their equivalent, and continuing education and supervision, all in family psychology.
4. A minimum of five years postdoctoral work, three years of which must have been supervised.
5. Licensure as a psychologist in the state where one practices.

Once a candidate has met these requirements, he or she must complete a work sample. The work sample is offered to demonstrate proficiency in one's primary professional activities as a family psychologist. A 3- to 4-hour oral examination using the work sample as a springboard is then conducted to assess evaluation and intervention skills, ability to articulate a theoretical position, scientific/professional knowledge, ethics, and knowledge of current professional issues. A live consultation with a family or couple is a further component of the oral examination. Further information about this credential can be found on the APA Division 43 Web site at http://www.apa.org/divisions/div43/about.html.

Discussions about whether marriage and family therapy is a separate and distinct professional field or a specialization within a professional field are reflected in the perspective promoted by the AAMFT versus Division 43 of the APA, respectively. As we noted in Figure 11–1 of this chapter, those who hold that marriage and family therapy is an autonomous discipline might view membership in another organization (e.g., the APA) as affiliation with a peer professional organization. By contrast, those who believe that marriage and family therapy is a specialization within a larger discipline might view membership in a "parent" organization (e.g., the APA) as one's professional base from which other specialty subsets of that base may be pursued. Such a view is reflected in Quadrant C of Figure 11–1. From this vantage point, achieving professional balance may be considerably more challenging for the individual marriage and family therapist.

International Association of Marriage and Family Counselors

The International Association of Marriage and Family Counselors (IAMFC) initially began as an interest group of 143 members within the American Association for Counseling and Development in 1986. This early group was made up of professionals with varied academic backgrounds who maintained interest in and involvement with issues facing couples and families. In 1989, the IAMFC was chartered as a division of the American Association for Counseling and Development (now the American Counseling Association). As of August 2005, there were over 2,300 members in the IAMFC (http://www.iamfc.com/).

The IAMFC goals and purposes included (A Brief History of IAMFC, 1992):

Promote ethical practices in marriage and family counseling/therapy; encourage research in marriage and family counseling/therapy; share knowledge and emphasize adherence to the highest quality training of marriage and family counselors/therapists; provide a forum for dialogue on relevant issues related to marriage and family counseling/therapy; examine ways to intervene in systems; help couples and families cope more successfully with life challenges; and use counseling knowledge and systemic methods to ameliorate the problems confronting marriages and families. (p. 6)

To become a member of the IAMFC, one may join directly or join as a part of being a member of the American Counseling Association (ACA). Membership categories for IAMFC are as follows: (a) Professional, (b) Regular, (c) New Professional, (d) Student, and (e) Retired. All membership categories other than Regular membership feature educational and experiential requirements.

The IAMFC has promoted training standards in marriage and family counseling and therapy through the American Counseling Association–sponsored Council for Accreditation of Counseling and Related Programs (CACREP). These standards have been used in accrediting entry- and doctoral-level educational programs (CACREP, 2001). "The philosophical stance taken by CACREP and ACA is that marriage and family counseling graduates must have a foundation in basic counseling skills, in conjunction with or prior to training in marriage and family therapy" (R. L. Smith, Stevens-Smith, Carlson, & Frame, 1996, p. 328). Whereas COAMFTE requires a minimum of 45 semester hours for an accredited master's program, the CACREP-accredited marital, couple, and family therapy program requires a minimum of 60 semester hours comprised of the following curricular content areas:

Professional Identity
Social and Cultural Diversity
Human Growth and Development
Lifestyle and Career Development
Helping Relationships
Group Work
Assessment
Research and Program Evaluation
Theoretical Foundations of Marital, Couple, and Family Counseling/Therapy
Contextual Dimensions of Marital, Couple, and Family Counseling/Therapy
Knowledge and Skill Requirements for Marital, Couple, and Family Counselor/
    Therapists
Supervised Practicum (100-hour minimum)
Supervised Internship (600-hour minimum)

The IAMFC also has established a credential in marriage and family counseling and therapy through the National Academy of Certified Family Therapists (NACFT), an affiliate of the IAMFC. "According to the NACFT, family therapy certification purports to: (a) promote accountability and visibility and help recognize the practice of family therapy, (b) identify family therapists who have met standards to the public and to professional peers, (c) advocate among groups and agencies actively involved in managed care, (d) encourage the continuing professional growth and development of individuals practicing in marriage and family counseling and therapy, and (e) ensure a national standard" (R. L. Smith et al., 1996, p. 330). The IAMFC Web site states that this certificate has been "recognized by many agencies across the country and included in several of the State Licensure Laws in Marriage and Family Therapy," though "certification is not a substitute for individual state licensure" (see http:// www.natlacad.4t.com/).

Requirements for certification feature five options for eligibility. These options rely on various combinations of professional certification, licensure, professional membership, or specialized graduate education and are summarized below:

> *Option One:* Nationally Certified Counselor, Licensed Professional Counselor, Licensed Social Worker, or Licensed Psychologist
>
> *Option Two:* Licensed Marriage and Family Therapist
>
> *Option Three:* AAMFT Clinical Membership
>
> *Option Four:* Graduate of a COAMFTE-accredited program or a CACREP-accredited program in Marriage, Couple, and Family Counseling/Therapy
>
> *Option Five:* Master's-level graduate in Counseling, Psychology, Counseling Psychology, Social Work, Family Therapy or a closely related field

Additional documentation of course work or supervised experience may be required for various eligibility options, and two letters of endorsement also must be submitted. Nationally Certified Family Therapists (NCFTs) are certified for 6 years and require 144 clock hours of continuing education for renewal of a certificate.

In some ways, the IAMFC may represent the most varied amalgam of perspectives on professional identity. It exists as a specialty division of a larger professional group (i.e., the ACA), it promotes the training standards of an autonomous accrediting body (i.e., CACREP), it supports a national credentialing body (i.e., the NACFT) that draws its constituency from a variety of other professional educational/affiliate backgrounds, and it endorses a national certificate (i.e., NCFT) that is distinct from any statutory authority to empower a professional right to practice. In other ways, however, the IAMFC and the NACFT may be viewed as representing a point of commonality among multiple professional perspectives and groups. Such a view could be reflected with multiple overlapping circles in a manner similar to Quadrant B of Figure 11–1.

STATE LICENSURE AND MARRIAGE AND FAMILY THERAPY

Established professions are self-regulating, and through self-regulation they gain public acceptance and respectability. However, professions are also regulated through legal processes assigning licensure as a symbol of competence to practice the profession. Statute law in all states controls the practice of medical and legal professionals. Since the 1970s, the licensing of psychologists, clinical social workers, counselors, and marriage and family therapists has aroused intense professional interest among and between distinct licensed practitioners. R. L. Smith et al. (1996) maintained that while licensure has become synonymous with professionalism, there is no evidence in the professional research literature that licensure ensures quality services. Nevertheless, as J. W. Davis (1981) stated:

> Licensure . . . seems to furnish an objective positive personal identification ("I am a member of a legally recognized, and therefore valuable, group in our society"). There is reflected public agreement that a licensed person must possess unusual, scarce skills to qualify for licensure. The status by association with institutions wielding the power of social control—that is, to other licensed professionals and to government itself—cannot be overlooked. (p. 84)

Licensure is a statutory process of an agency of government, usually of a state, which legally prescribes the qualifications of those who engage in a given occupation or profession and usually limits the use of a particular title or the practice of the profession (R. L. Smith et al., 1996). In most states with licensing laws, unlicensed practitioners are subject to legal penalties should they misrepresent themselves as licensees. Thus, licensure can restrict entry into the profession, and those denied entry but who persist in their activities can be prosecuted (J. W. Davis, 1981).

Fretz and Mills (1980) identified five major premises supporting licensure efforts:

1. Licensure is designed to protect the public by establishing minimum standards of service. Fretz and Mills (1980) contend that consumers would be harmed by the absence of such standards; incompetent practitioners would have the potential to cause long-term, negative consequences. This position was developed by B. N. Phillips (1982):

   > For all that can be said about legal constraints on practice, one thing is most important. Their purpose is to promote the public's welfare by improving and maintaining the quality of training and practice, maximizing benefits-to-cost service delivery outcomes, and protecting the public from gross incompetence. (p. 924)

2. Licensure is designed to protect the public from ignorance about mental health services. Fretz and Mills (1980) based this assumption on the belief that consumers in need of mental health services typically do not know how to choose an appropriate practitioner or how to judge the quality of services rendered.
3. Licensure increases the likelihood that practitioners will be more competent and their services better distributed and thus more available.
4. Licensure upgrades a profession. Fretz and Mills proposed that a licensed profession will have more practitioners committed to improving and maintaining the highest standards of excellence.
5. Licensing allows a profession to define for itself what it will and will not do. Accordingly, a profession is assumed to be more independent, because other professions or the courts cannot specify its functions.

Corey et al. (1998) concurred with this last point, in particular noting the general perception that licensure enhances a profession and is a sign of maturity for individual licensees as well as a professional discipline.

State licensure can contribute to safeguarding consumers' welfare as well as promoting professional identity and enhancement. It is not without its critics, however. For example, Gill (1982) questioned how licensure leads to more informed consumers. To emphasize this point, he observed that the general public appears to persist in its ignorance of differences among licensed mental health professionals, such as psychologists, social workers, and counselors. Rinas and Clyne-Jackson (1988) noted the increase of malpractice suits and the increase in mental health licenses as evidence that licensure does not guarantee consumer welfare. In fact, these authors even suggested that quackery actually may increase as licensure restricts access to practice.

J. W. Davis (1981) maintained that licensing is designed to create and preserve a "union shop" that works more as a monopoly than as a protection for the public from misrepresentation and incompetence. Bertram (1983) asserted more self-serving interests are inherent in licensure, stating: "Let us be clear, this is not an issue of competence, ethics, or morality. What we are dealing with is turf" (p. 7). Corey et al. (1998)

likewise decried the potential of licensure for promoting professional jealousy and competition, stating that "the process of licensing often contributes to professional specializations' pitting themselves against one another" (p. 279).

Still, the creation of licensure for a profession represents a right to practice and an aspect of fair trade for qualified individuals. Statutory content of licensure laws typically compel either a licensure board or a governmental agency to establish and apply minimum educational, experiential, and competency standards (often by examination) prior to the issuance of a license to an individual. Professional licenses typically require recipients to renew their licensure status, usually through continuing education or similar requirements, to verify awareness of contemporary issues and techniques needed to retain competence.

Most licensure laws specifically indicate that licensure exists to establish jurisdiction over licensees in order to protect public consumers. As we noted earlier in this chapter, licensure differs from professional affiliation in that the former concerns regulated practice, whereas the latter concerns professional initiatives. Consequently, licensure boards and agencies exist to ensure competent and due care for clients rather than to advocate or represent issues for professional groups. This gatekeeping function for licensees is established in licensure legislation to empower either an autonomous board (consisting of professional and nonprofessional members) or a governmental agency (e.g., Department of Health) in a state or jurisdiction.

Most licensure laws have periodic reviews by legislative committees. This process is designed as a deliberate act of review concerning the need for the license, the viability of the license, the successful management and oversight of licensees by the regulatory body or agency, and similar aspects of review. Feedback is typically sought by a sample of licensees and consumers. An aspect of such reviews is that the statutory language for the license is often open to revision, and so lobbying efforts by either professionals licensed under the statutes or others seeking to influence the content of the statutes may attempt to persuade elected officials to revise the law. Such circumstances can result in suggested changes ranging from helpful to disruptive. Consequently, professional groups such as the AAMFT often become involved in lobbying efforts to sustain the stringency and uniqueness of licensure for the profession. For this reason, many licensure boards are reluctant to seek statutory revisions outside of periodic legislative reviews, since such efforts open the law to unwanted and possibly harmful revisions.

One significant distinction in the nature of licensure legislation is whether the licensure establishes a unique designation or *title*, or a unique array of actions or *practices*. This distinction is known as "title law" versus "practice law." To illustrate the functional difference between these two types of licensure law, consider a situation in which a man represents himself to the public as a "marriage and family developmental specialist." He schedules a session for a married couple, conducts an intake, creates a family genogram for each spouse, develops a hypothesis about the nature of their presenting concerns, gives a homework assignment to the couple, charges a fee for his service, schedules an appointment for the next week, and writes a case note that includes a notation to consider a consultation with a psychiatrist about the husband. He has a master's degree in sociology, he has taken two marriage and family studies classes, and he has done extensive reading on marriage and family therapy using online resources. Is he acting illegally in a state with marriage and family licensure? In a state with title law, the designation or title of "Licensed Marriage and Family Therapist" may be the primary, possibly the *only*, matter over which the licensure board has jurisdictional authority, meaning it could only protect the public relative to the *designation* this practitioner uses to identify himself. Since the man did not represent himself using the term "Licensed Marriage and Family Therapist," he may be legally beyond the reach of the licensure board. In a state with practice law, however, the array of activities in which he engaged, *regardless of the title he employed*, is specified in the statute, and the board has jurisdiction to protect the public relative to the *behaviors*. In this respect, the man is engaging in the practice of marriage and family therapy, and the licensure board has the authority to pursue legal means to halt his practice. The AAMFT has always advocated for practice laws as a means of public protection.

The history of most professional licensure laws includes an initial brief period of access to licensure, sometimes with lessened restrictiveness in educational or experiential requirements. This period is often known as "grandparenting," in which persons meeting minimum initial requirements are licensed to create an initial core of licensees. The asset of grandparenting options for the early life of a licensure law is that it serves to establish a viable group of professionals. By contrast, the liability of grandparenting is that it frequently licenses persons who, at a later point in time, might not meet the minimum requirements to qualify for licensure. The AAMFT has historically advocated for stringency equivalent to Clinical Membership in grandparenting for licensees.

Despite some early criticisms, it seems that licensure has become a fixture within marriage and family therapy practice. As of August 2005, state legislation creating licensure specifically for marriage and family therapy had been enacted in 47 states and the District of Columbia, with active plans currently being considered to introduce such legislation in other states.

The initial wave of legislation that allowed the licensing of marriage and family therapists was passed during the 1960s. California was the first state, passing its law in 1963. Michigan followed in 1966, and New Jersey in 1968. Utah passed its law in 1973, Nevada in 1976, and Georgia in 1976. Georgia's licensure law was "sunsetted" out of existence through legislative review. However, a new law was enacted in 1984 (Bowers, 1992b). Throughout the 1980s and into the 1990s, the number of states that have licensing laws regulating marriage and family therapy has increased significantly. As of August 2005, the following states had laws defining licensure requirements for marriage and family therapists:

Alabama	Illinois	Missouri
Alaska	Indiana	Nebraska
Arizona	Iowa	Nevada
Arkansas	Kansas	New Hampshire
California	Kentucky	New Jersey
Colorado	Louisiana	New Mexico
Connecticut	Maine	New York
District of Columbia	Maryland	North Carolina
Florida	Massachusetts	North Dakota
Georgia	Michigan	Ohio
Hawaii	Minnesota	Oklahoma
Idaho	Mississippi	Oregon

Pennsylvania	Tennessee	Virginia
Rhode Island	Texas	Washington
South Carolina	Utah	Wisconsin
South Dakota	Vermont	Wyoming

Significant diversity, however, can be found in the legislation enacted across licensure states. Sporakowski (1982) referred to many of the licensure laws regulating marriage and family therapy as a "hodgepodge," given the variety of assumptions and definitions on which they appear to have been based. Corey et al. (1984) noted several of the partial definitions that have existed in state licensure laws:

> Marriage and family counseling is that service performed with individuals, couples, or groups wherein interpersonal relationships between spouses or members of a family are examined for the purpose of achieving more adequate, satisfying, and productive marriage and family adjustments. (California)
>
> Marriage and family counseling also includes premarital counseling, predivorce and post-divorce counseling, and family counseling. It consists of the application of principles, methods and techniques of counseling and psychotherapeutic techniques for the purpose of resolving psychological conflict, modifying perception and behavior, altering old attitudes and establishing new ones in the area of marriage and family life. (Georgia)
>
> Marriage and family counseling consists of the application of established principles of learning, motivation, perception, thinking, emotional, marital and sexual relationships and adjustments by persons trained in psychology, social work, psychiatry, or marital counseling. (Nevada) (pp. 165–166)

Not only definitions but also essential terminology differs by jurisdiction. For example, not all of the states with licensure regulating marriage and family therapy refer specifically to *therapy* and *therapists*. Sporakowski (1982) suggested that this appears to be as much a result of a states rights' attitude in legislatures as an attempt by states to meet the individual needs of their citizens. He further asserted that other states' lack of legislation is directly related to the issue of the emergence of marriage and family therapy as a distinct profession. Support from the various other major mental health professions has fluctuated. In some states, "omnibus" legislation has been enacted so that marriage and family therapists are licensed along with social workers, mental health counselors, school psychologists, art therapists, and/or other mental health professions within the same law. Such legislation often leads to the establishment of "composite licensure boards," composed of public members as well as members representing the various disciplines authorized under the legislature. Such boards differ in composition and complexity in comparison to "autonomous" or "discipline-specific" licensure boards, which are often composed of public members along with practitioners and educators from the specific discipline for which the license exists. The AAMFT has historically favored discipline-specific legislation and licensure boards.

In other states over the years, other major mental health professions have been resistant to the anticipated intrusion into what they perceive as their service domains. In these latter states, legislation licensing marriage and family therapists has either been opposed or attempts have been made to regulate marriage and family therapy directly or indirectly through another profession's licensure law (Bowers, 1992b). In these instances, professional groups have sought to strengthen licensure laws in a gradual manner through statutory modifications during legislative reviews. In considering these types of issues, one must remember that the establishment of a licensure law is a political process concerning a professional designation. Thus, the developmental process related to licensure (e.g., outgrowing grandparenting, switching from title law to practice law, etc.) may not correspond to the professional identity sought at its inception.

Sporakowski (1982) noted three significant issues that marriage and family therapists should be knowledgeable about regarding state licensure: (a) what and who are covered, (b) what the requirements are to qualify for licensure, and (c) how the licensure process works. In an attempt to provide a focus for uniformity among state marriage and family licensure laws, the AAMFT drafted a model regulatory code in 1979 and has subsequently revised it several times. Given the diversity that exists among laws enacted by different states, excerpts from this model act, the Model Marriage and Family Therapy Licensure Act, are used to highlight major points within each of these three issues.

Licensure Coverage

Most licensure legislation negatively defines the boundaries of practice by identifying prohibitions and exemptions. For example, the Model Marriage and Family Therapy Licensure Act (American Association for Marriage and Family Therapy, 1992a) identified the following "Prohibited Acts" and "Exemptions" in sections 4 and 5, respectively:

Prohibited Acts. Except as specifically provided elsewhere in this Act, commencing on January 1, 19_____, no person who is not licensed under this act shall:

A. advertise the performance of marriage and family therapy or counseling service by him or her; or
B. use a title or description such as "marital or marriage therapist, counselor, advisor or consultant," "marital or marriage and family therapist, counselor advisor, or consultant," or any other name, style, or description denoting that the person is a marriage and family therapist; or
C. practice marriage and family therapy.

Exemptions.

A. A person shall be exempt from the requirements of this Act:
  (1) If the person is practicing marriage and family therapy as part of his duties as an employee of:
    (a) a recognized academic institution, or a federal, state, county, or local governmental institution or agency while performing those duties for which she or he was employed by such an institution, agency, or facility;
    (b) an organization which is nonprofit and which is determined by the Board to meet community needs while performing those duties for which he or she was employed by such an agency; or
  (2) If the person is a marriage and family therapy intern or person preparing for the practice of marriage and family therapy under qualified supervision in a training institution or facility or supervisory arrangement recognized and approved by the Board, provided she or he is designated by such titles as "marriage and family therapy intern," "marriage therapy intern," "family therapy intern," or others, clearly indicating such training status; or
  (3) If the person has been issued a temporary permit by the Board to engage in the activity for which licensure is required.

B. Nothing in this Act shall be construed to prevent qualified members of other professional groups as defined by the Board, including but not necessarily limited to clinical social workers, psychiatric nurses, psychologists, physicians, or members of the clergy, from doing or advertising that they perform work of a marriage and family therapy nature consistent with the accepted standards of their respective professions. Provided, however, no such persons shall use the title or description stating or implying that they are marriage and family therapists or marriage and family counselors or that they are licensed as marriage and family therapists or marriage and family counselors. (pp. 2–3)

Similar prohibitions and exemptions exist in most states' licensure laws. One particular point of contention in this regard, however, has related to other licensed mental health professionals claiming to practice marriage and family therapy. In such instances, individuals practicing within the guidelines of another professional license have typically been exempted as long as they do not claim to be or practice as a marriage and family therapist. Essentially, such legislation represents respect for other professions and the right for qualified *and licensed* peer professionals to engage in regulated practice.

Qualifications

Those states regulating marriage and family therapy all require that the prospective licensee possess a minimum of a master's degree in marriage and family therapy, social work, pastoral counseling, or relevant qualifications in behavioral sciences such as psychology or sociology. Some states have enacted requirements beyond the master's degree as an academic minimum, some states have narrowed the scope of the academic degree, and some states have simply specified a curricular content for applicants. For these and related issues, our earlier discussion of the interrelatedness between the AAMFT and the COAMFTE becomes particularly relevant. Few states would disqualify a licensure applicant who has graduated with the entry-level (i.e., master's) degree from a COAMFTE-accredited program or who has secured Clinical Membership in the AAMFT.

In addition to these academic qualifications, states differ in their requirements for postgraduate supervised experience. Qualifications in this sphere of licensure regulations may be quite varied in terms of number of years, number of hours, full-time employment status, and supervision-to-service ratio hours (e.g., 1 hour of supervision for every 10 hours of direct service to clients). Most states require that the majority of clinical experience be gained under supervision.

The Model Marriage and Family Therapy Licensure Act (American Association for Marriage and Family Therapy, 1992a) identified the following education and experience requirements in section 11:

1. Educational requirements: a Master's degree or a Doctoral degree in marriage and family therapy from a recognized educational institution, or a graduate degree in an allied field from a recognized educational institution and graduate level coursework which is equivalent to a Master's degree in marriage and family therapy, as determined by the Board.
2. Experience requirements: successful completion of two calendar years of work experience in marriage and family therapy under qualified supervision following receipt of a qualifying degree. (p. 6)

An important concern relating to the second item above is the definition of "qualified supervision." Only "an individual who has been recognized by the Board as an approved supervisor" (p. 2) can provide the necessary supervision to a potential licensee. Thus, it is incumbent on a potential licensee to ascertain early on that his or her supervision will be provided by an approved supervisor. Some states specify the AAMFT–Approved Supervisor status or its equivalent must be held by supervisors, but others may not be so specific. Some states require a preapproved plan of supervision, and others may not. While engaged in supervised practice, most states offer a certificate or license with a qualifier such as "Associate" to distinguish the supervisee from those who hold licenses for independent practice.

Because of the proliferation and variety of marriage and family therapy licensure, the Association of Marital and Family Therapy Regulatory Boards (AMFTRB) emerged as a body for collaboration and exchange among boards or delegates responsible for enacting licensure regulation. As noted in our earlier discussion about professional affiliation, the AMFTRB has worked cooperatively with the AAMFT and the COAMFTE concerning regulatory issues. This convergence of purpose has introduced measures of uniformity among licensure states, although concerns related to relocating one's practice and securing licensure in a new state—*portability* issues—can present a difficult proposition, particularly in states with omnibus or composite licensure statutes, or in instances in which a licensee is "grandparented" as a licensee based on less stringent standards. Essentially, meeting the minimum academic and supervision qualifications for licensure in one state is not always interchangeable with other states. Of the many initiatives currently under consideration among member bodies of AMFTRB, portability is one of substantial interest.

The Licensure Process

As we have indicated, state laws typically require prospective licensees to file a formal application, supplying letters of recommendation, giving proof of their academic credentials, and documenting hours of supervised experience. Many also request that applicants complete a written or oral examination or both. The Model Marriage and Family Therapy Licensure Act (American Association for Marriage and Family Therapy, 1992a), for example, specifies that applicants for licensure pass a written or oral examination that includes "questions in such theoretical and applied fields as the Board deems most suitable to test an applicant's knowledge and competence to engage in the practice of marriage and family therapy" (p. 6).

The AMFTRB has developed and provides the Examination in Marital and Family Therapy (EMFT) to assist licensure boards and agencies in evaluating the extent to which applicants possess the knowledge for entry-level professional practice. This multiple-choice examination may be used in conjunction with oral examinations or may serve as the only examination employed by a licensure board or agency. The specific practice domains assessed by the EMFT are:

Domain 01—The Practice of Marital and Family Therapy
Domain 02—Assessing, Hypothesizing, and Diagnosing
Domain 03—Designing and Conducting Treatment
Domain 04—Evaluating Ongoing Process and Terminating Treatment
Domain 05—Maintaining Ethical, Legal, and Professional Standards

For additional information concerning the EMFT or other aspects of the AMFTRB, readers may access their Web site at http://www.amftrb.org.

After successful completion of all requirements, the applicant is awarded a license. Maintenance of the license normally depends on paying renewal fees and obtaining the requisite hours of continuing education before renewal. Continuing education must be relevant to the profession for which license renewal is sought and approved by the state regulatory body governing professional license renewal (Psychological Services Act, 1983).

In addition to conducting applicant reviews and renewals, licensure boards and agencies are responsible for gatekeeping functions for licensees regarding public welfare. In this regard, investigation and adjudication of complaints is another duty of boards and agencies. A license may be suspended or revoked for a variety of reasons that are typically defined within the legislation creating the license. Frequent violations cited include fraud or deceit practiced on the regulatory board, conviction of a crime, abuse of chemical substances, and unethical behavior. It is the responsibility of licensed individuals as well as the general public to identify and report these violations. In some cases, a "friendly remonstrance" is considered sufficient remedy unless violations are repeated, represent blatant departures from accepted practice, or involve criminal acts (Sporakowski, 1982).

The adjudication process for licensure hearings in most states bears some resemblance to the Decision Tree illustrated in Chapter 7. This similarity is particularly true in terms of due process procedures. Such hearings, however, are legal actions on behalf of public protection. Violation of the licensing law itself normally results in a remedial action with possible fines. Of course, associated criminal violations could garner more serious legal action and consequences. Federal regulations require that any formal action taken against a licensee be registered with the National Practitioner Data Bank-Healthcare Integrity and Protection Data Bank (http://www.npdb-hipdb.com). This national database is accessible to professionals, managed care groups, and state agencies that need to verify the licensure history of a person to prevent an instance in which someone may try to relocate to another state and acquire a new license without disclosing his or her past violations.

In summary, we note that licensure can be a significant aspect of professional identity. As we have discussed, however, licensure represents both professional and regulatory perspectives on the practice of marriage and family therapy, meaning that both convergence and divergence can emerge from these dual perspectives. Practitioners who have: (a) qualified for licensure by graduating from a COAMFTE-accredited institution (or its equivalent), (b) passed the EMFT, (c) received supervision from an AAMFT Approved Supervisor, and (d) been granted practice rights as a "Licensed Marriage and Family Therapist" by autonomous regulatory board can appreciate the multiple intersections of a separate professional status similar to Quadrant A of Figure 11–1. By contrast, practitioners licensed through combinations of: (a) omnibus licensure and composite boards, (b) multiple options for meeting academic requirements, (c) grandparenting, (d) supervision from professionals from other disciplines, and (e) examinations other than the EMFT could view their status as a licensee as more reflective of the other quadrants of Figure 11–1 in terms of professional identity. Future issues related to licensure probably will include attention to licensure portability and efforts to determine the applicable licensure laws for the practice of on-line or e-therapy, as we discussed previously in Chapter 6. The specific requirements for licensure as a marriage and family therapist may vary from state to state. In seeking a license, prospective licensees should contact the appropriate state professional regulatory agency for information about licensure laws and application requirements.

RELATED ASPECTS OF PROFESSIONAL IDENTITY

The training that marriage and family therapists receive prepares them to employ a systematic integrated theoretical perspective and an adequate repertoire of intervention strategies. They can select and tailor treatment plans for their clients. Although at times these treatment tasks require attending to significant roadblocks, the competently trained clinician is ready to do so. However, many marriage and family therapists have a limited awareness of the array of choices they have when they make nonclinical professional decisions.

In this section, we address some related issues of professional identity issues facing marriage and family therapists. Specifically, we will discuss the relevance of research, professional growth through continuing education, and the importance of maintaining intraprofessional relationships and service as nonclinical but significant aspects of professional identity for marriage and family therapists.

Research: Examining and Refining Professional Identity

Liddle (1991a) described research in marriage and family therapy as a topic influencing "how we see ourselves and how others view us" (p. 327). More recently, Wampler (2005) observed, "Like diet and exercise, research is one of the field's most visible items on our list of 'ought to do,' 'need to do more,' 'heavy cost if we don't,' and 'ain't it awful,' accompanied by the usual finger-pointing as to whom to blame" (p. 1). A mere five years after its organizational founding, the AAMFT in 1947 established the nonprofit Research and Education Foundation with the mission of promoting the well-being of families through initiatives in research, education, and policy (see http://www.aamft.org/membership/duespaymentformfoundation.htm). Thus, as a professional organization, the AAMFT sought to supplement its constituency interest in therapy with a mission of *inquiry.*

Cavell and Snyder (1991) drew on the analogy of safeguards imposed by the U.S. Food and Drug Administration before authorizing use of a new drug by licensed physicians in asserting the importance of research for promoting the practice and professional identity of marriage and family therapy:

> Clear demonstration of the drug's efficacy is required, under carefully controlled conditions, with delineation of potential hazards or unwanted effects, before conclusions may be drawn regarding the generalizability of treatment effectiveness for specific symptoms across divergent patient populations. How many of us would give our informed consent to some pharmacologic intervention based on an intensive case-study of the drug's efficacy with one patient (or one group of patients) under one unique set of conditions? Yet this is precisely the situation in which we often place clients . . . typically without providing (or even possessing) documentation regarding generalizability of treatment effects. (p. 170)

Despite a history of over 60 years, marriage and family therapy had been characterized previously by some as still being in an early stage of conceptual development buoyed by empirical support (Bednar, Burlingame, & Masters, 1988; Liddle, 1991b; Liddle, Gurman, Pinsof, & Roberto, 1990). Bednar et al. (1988) were particularly critical in this regard. They pointed to the imprecise definition of family therapy's basic concepts in comparison to other forms of psychotherapy. They also cited the idiosyncratic development of most family therapy models as contributing to a lack of standardization within the field, thus inhibiting basic accountability efforts. Sprenkle and Moon (1996) went further by stating that "the field remains vulnerable because of its lack of attention to developing a solid foundation of research on the process and outcomes of family therapy" (p. 3). In an article entitled, "Family Therapy—Professional Endeavor or Successful Religion?" Werry (1989) characterized family therapy as "a rather sad sack relying for its status on assertion, self-congratulation, guruism and denigration of alternatives" (p. 380).

In reviewing the contemporary context of research in marriage and family therapy, however, M. P. Nichols and Schwartz (2001) argued that despite a lack of specificity within the field, sufficient research studies support the overall effectiveness of systems-oriented marriage and family therapy. Their summary of major reviews of marriage and family therapy research (e.g., Dewitt, 1987; Gurman & Kniskern, 1978; Jacobson & Bussod, 1983; Pinsof & Wynne, 1995) concluded that (a) systems-oriented family therapy is based on concepts, assumptions, and procedures that differ from traditional forms of psychotherapy; (b) family therapy is a useful treatment for a variety of problems; (c) family therapy is at least as effective as other forms of psychotherapy; and (d) further research directed at the process of family therapy and the mechanisms through which change occurs is needed. More recently, Nichols and Schwartz (2004) offered some rather provocative observations about the difficulties in marriage and family therapy research.

> Although the field has emphasized the need to make research relevant for clinicians, perhaps the problem in the research–practice gap has to do with the framing of the issue. For instance, should all research be directly relevant to the practice of therapy? Doubtful. Research and practice are two contexts of remarkable diversity . . . (for research) this information is reported in terms of groups of individuals, whereas therapists work in terms of individual cases that may or may not be similar to those in outcome studies. (p. 419)

Such comments clearly emphasize the need to determine the extent to which marriage and family therapy research addresses obstacles in conceptual paradigms and reconciles empirical and applied initiatives.

A variety of factors may converge to affect research efforts for the field. For example, Hawley and Gonzalez (2005) surveyed COAMFTE-accredited institutions and reported they could only identify 109 full-time faculty in research-oriented programs (i.e., doctoral programs plus master's programs requiring thesis research). Such a scarcity of academic professionals would appear to be relevant in considering the empirical efforts in the field. Additionally, the need to integrate research and clinical training in graduate study is critical for emerging marriage and family therapy practitioners, both for inquiry and professional identity (Hodgson, Johnson, Ketring, Wampler, & Lamson, 2005).

Liddle (1992) proposed 10 key considerations for strengthening the research–clinical practice connection in marriage and family therapy, and in doing so, enhancing the professional identity of marriage and family therapy within the mental health community and to the public in general. These include the following:

1. Clearer guidelines incorporating and translating content from both basic and applied research into clinical work need to be developed.
2. Research findings need to better inform clinicians in particular population-, age-, and problem-specific situations (i.e., individual case circumstances).
3. The results of current research efforts need to be critically examined and alternatives generated as applicable, instead of engaging in extremist debates that serve primarily political and ideological masters rather than enhancing the knowledge base.
4. Traditional research methods are applicable to family therapy studies in appreciating context and interaction (i.e., systemic processes) and need to be maintained and used, even though some maintain that there is insufficient consistency between systemic theories and traditional research frameworks.
5. Productive, mutual influencing between the clinical practice and research domains needs to become a priority of supervisors and teachers in marriage and family therapy training programs.
6. Additional models that effectively demonstrate the research–practice and theory interconnection, as well as the benefits that can generate from such interaction, need to be promoted.
7. Additional vehicles are needed to demonstrate how the research and practice divide can be decreased. For example, the *Clinician's Research Digest*, a publication of the APA, provides detailed abstracts of research reports with a notable focus suggesting how findings can affect practice.
8. Marriage and family therapists need to identify a research–training–practice framework to serve as a clear orienting force for itself, somewhat akin to the scientist–practitioner model within psychology.
9. Each individual marriage and family therapist needs to strive to be multidimensional in his or her personal practice model so as to more readily incorporate new information and adopt new processes, especially as they relate to case conceptualization decision making.
10. Marriage and family therapy needs to actively promote an attitude and values supportively connecting the research and practice realms.

Considerations such as these were particularly significant for the last decade and remain into the 21st century. Inquiry into the effectiveness of therapy approaches has been a continuous and challenging vigil since the early days of the field. Such efforts are fueled by both professional curiosity and institutional pressure (e.g., managed care agencies) to determine efficient and preferred outcomes. However, two rather notable observations have been offered concerning mainstays of classical marriage and family therapy: the Bowenian model and the Symbolic-Experiential model. Regarding the Bowenian model, Miller, Anderson, and Keala (2004) stated, "Although there is emerging evidence validating some of Bowen's basic theoretical propositions, there is still a glaring lack of clinical process and outcome research that has tested the effectiveness of Bowens' model of therapy" (p. 463). Similarly, Mitten and Connell (2004) observed, "This is the first study to identify core variables of symbolic-experiential therapy" (p. 474). Given that these classical models are examined in many graduate marriage and family therapy programs and may even be employed by some contemporary practitioners, the fact that such statements are offered in the fourth decade of their existence makes the discerning reader stop to think: Could the conceptual nature of these models be such that operational clarity will continue to be elusive? If so, does this imply a duality about empirical and applied research that cannot be reconciled? On the other hand, cognitive-behavior interventions in couple and family therapy have been shown to be successful in a variety of circumstances. Still, Cognitive-Behavioral Couple Therapy (CBCT) and Cognitive-Behavioral Family Therapy (CBFT):

> have not been recognized consistently in the family therapy field, because of what appears to be a persistently narrow view of the model as focused on cognition, micro-level behavior responses rather than meaningful macro-level patterns in family interaction, and linear causal processes. . . . However, developments in CBCT and CBFT more fully capture circular processes that involve cognitive, affective, and behavioral factors, macro-level patterns and themes in family interaction, and influences of broader contextual factors. (Dattillo & Epstein, 2005, p. 10)

Such comments suggest that the interplay of empirical and applied research need not be reductionistic nor indefinitely closed to scrutiny simply because of traditional veneration afforded a theoretical model. Rather, persistent efforts to integrate these two intentions in meaningful ways appears to be a destination along the route to viewing research as a component of professional identity for marriage and family therapists.

H. Anderson (1994) offered some challenging comments about the purposes of research. Specifically, she noted that research for the sake of inquiry and learning has been and will continue to be meaningful. However, she also observed "I favor research wholeheartedly. I agree it legitimizes and is necessary for political positioning and economic viability" (p. 149). Such a statement reflects the significance of managed mental health care (MMHC) as a contemporary force affecting research in marriage and family therapy as well as other mental health fields. In this respect, Shields et al. (1994) noted the importance of cost-effectiveness in family therapy. Similarly, Northey (2005) discussed "evidence-based treatments" or EBTs, noting "The goal of promoting EBT models is predicated on the belief that patient care will improve with the use of EBTs" (p. 100). Though patient care continues to be a focal point of contemporary mental health care, the political and economic implications of cost-effectiveness have given rise to research as an aspect of cost-containment in MMHC. Such concerns have been addressed previously in Chapter 6. The purposes of expanding knowledge and addressing economic realities are not antithetical to one another, but they can have divergent effects on individual marriage and family therapy researchers.

A second contemporary force affecting marriage and family research is the continuing awareness of family diversity. Recently, two special edition of the *Journal of Marital and Family Therapy* (2004, Volumes 30, Numbers 3 and 4) addressed the significant implications of research with diverse families. As we noted in Chapter 1, the significance of culture, ethnicity, and race cannot be underestimated in attempting to understand and serve contemporary couples and families. Turner and Weiling (2004) observed that marriage and family research has reflected greater sensitivity to families of color:

> Although some of this research has focused directly on marriage and family service delivery, much, if not most, has focused on more basic aspects of family research. However, these important findings have enormous implications for family therapists, and there is a great need for the psychotherapy community to better understand this new research and the ensuing implications for how we better engage and accommodate families of color in therapy. (p. 255)

From this perspective, culturally sensitive marriage and family therapists can come to realize the complexity and importance of research that recognizes the distinctions in the personal layer of values and traditions between and among diverse family groups. In this respect, an "agenda of standardization" that drives some evidence-based therapy efforts for outcome research in an era of MMHC *must* be steadied by respect for group and even individual differences among contemporary couples and families. Research in pursuit of generalizable results at all costs is, at best, ill-conceived, and at most, repressive. In either case, myopia in a research agenda would likely weaken the sense of professional identity emerging from research efforts by marriage and family therapists.

Liddle (1992) quoted C. M. Anderson (1986) in summarizing the importance of research for promoting the professional identity of marriage and family therapy:

> As a field, we must address the issue of what constitutes acceptable evidence of efficacy and how we go about obtaining it. It is absolutely vital that the field of family therapy develop a respect for research, knowledge of basic research methods, and the requirements of scientific inquiry. Without this knowledge and respect, the field of family therapy will not continue to develop and will not receive the support it requires from academic institutions, governmental policies or funding agencies. This does not mean that we all must do research, nor that we need to use empirical methods that do not reflect systems thinking. It does mean, however, that we all must be able to evaluate ourselves and our colleagues, using strict research criteria, or we will be no different from psychoanalysts whose work has become increasingly discounted rather than accepted. In the world of increased emphasis on cost effectiveness and decreased resources, unless we can offer proof of efficacy, acceptable to the scientific community, we will eventually cease to exist. (p. 353)

We would also note that "evaluating ourselves and our colleagues" is associated with personal and professional layers of values that primarily concern standards for due care and competence, as we discussed earlier in Chapter 4. Although such foci may be evident in the institutional layer of values regarding research, additional agendas reflecting political and economic concerns may be of equal or greater importance for agencies managing the financial burdens of mental health care. Thus, the individual marriage and family therapist is once again faced with the need to establish balance in terms of the meaning of research as a matter of professional identity.

Continuing Education: Sustaining and Renewing Professional Identity

The continuing education of professionals in all fields has become a matter of great and pragmatic concern. In earlier times, the basic information employed in practicing a profession, whether medicine, law, theology, or the like, was relatively stable and could be mastered by a student in the course of a reasonable training period. The application of this knowledge was then largely a matter of professional skill and diligent experience. Changes in professions were gradual and relatively easily incorporated by practicing professionals during their careers.

One of the most impressive developments in contemporary as well as professional life during the last century has been the dramatic increase in knowledge and information. Scientific and technological developments make it virtually impossible for a professional to rely on initial training in a field for any significant part of a career (L. Walker, 1981). As Vitulano and Copeland (1980) observed with regard to the health care professions in particular:

> First, the knowledge base for these professions is increasing at an astonishing rate. . . . One must continue to learn or suffer from professional obsolescence. Second, the enormous ethical responsibilities of our practice demand the highest standards. Licensure or certification solely at the beginning of one's career merely identifies a minimum standard for professional practice, not the ideal toward which one should strive. Third, lifetime education should constitute an important goal of the training and practice of the health professions. Fourth, a proactive commitment to the maintenance of competency over time would help maintain public confidence in the profession. (p. 891)

Students graduating from most professional programs must immediately begin a program of continuing education and development to have any chance of survival in their chosen field. Should they fail to do so, by the end of 3 years (in most professions), their functioning would become substandard; by the end of 5 years, that functioning would become seriously compromised; and, by the end of 10 years, they would be totally incompetent (L. Walker, 1981). Continuing education is even a necessity in the field of professional ethics: "No amount of initial training will replace the need for ongoing training and review of . . . codes of ethics because codes are regularly revised" (K. Jordan & Stevens, 1999, p. 174).

Professional organizations have responded to this potential dilemma by sponsoring and supporting continuing education efforts. They have further posited this pragmatic issue as an ethical responsibility as well, placing it within their ethical codes. For example, the *AAMFT Code of Ethics* (American Association for Marriage and Family Therapy, 2001) states in Subprinciple 3.1: "Marriage and family therapists pursue knowledge of new developments and maintain competence in marriage and family therapy through education, training, or supervised experience."

To assist members in keeping abreast of new developments, professional organizations such as the AAMFT, Division 43 of the APA (Family Psychology), and the IAMFC all sponsor regularly published newsletters and journals. These include *Family Therapy Magazine* and the *Journal of Marital and Family Therapy* by the AAMFT; *The Family Psychologist* and the *Journal of Family Psychology* by Division 43 of the APA (Family Psychology), and the *IAMFC Newsletter* and *The Family Journal: Counseling and Therapy for Couples and Families* by the IAMFC. A number of other well-established journals and newsletters (e.g., *Family Process, American Journal of Family Therapy,* etc.) devoted to marriage and family therapy offer articles and news of important developments in the field as well.

The aforementioned professional organizations also sponsor state, regional, and national conferences (Division 43—Family Psychology and the IAMFC, primarily within their parent associations) as well as training workshops, publication of monographs and books, and the production of videotapes. Furthermore, they encourage their members to engage in continuing education opportunities sponsored by other professionally recognized groups that are relevant to marriage and family therapy. These are all part of a necessary and ongoing process of continuing education and professional development to encourage competent, high-quality provision of services.

As noted previously, the primary professional organizations of marriage and family therapy practitioners support the concept of continuing education. All these organizations promote professional continuing education as a voluntary process, however. Acceptable continuing education activities are required for a variety of professional categories. For example, continuing education is required to sustain Approved Supervisor status with the AAMFT. Similarly, continuing education is required to sustain national certification by the NACFT. Typically, marriage and family therapists who are state licensed are required to complete certain continuing education activities to renew and thus maintain their licenses. The concept of mandatory continuing education (MCE) for licensed mental health professionals has its detractors who question whether it is necessary, let alone whether it can be structured in a manner that will actually improve the quality of services being offered. For example, Corey et al. (1998) cautioned that although physical attendance can be required to earn MCE credit, there is no way to ensure intellectual or emotional involvement by every MCE course participant. The knowledge that is absorbed and integrated into practice may be much less than a certificate of attendance indicates.

A variety of options exists in addition to in-person attendance for continuing education activities. On-line or technology assisted educational activities have become particularly popular among active professionals. Even a cursory review of the professional publications noted earlier in this section will reveal on-line opportunities for knowledge-based or skill-based continuing education. Of a similar nature are off-site Webcast or videoconferencing seminars, which provide an effective and efficient means of accessing continuing education and professional development. Offered at training sites (e.g., universities, professional institutes, etc.) or even as ancillary options at conferences, these technology-enhanced methods of instruction are often attractive to practitioners who want to enhance their knowledge and skills but are unable to afford the expense of travel and lodging, not to mention lost revenue from multiple days away from their practices. Similarly, many academic institutions are utilizing interactive video delivery for both graduate-level classes and continuing education activities. The options for technology-based professional learning and development have become a mainstay for contemporary continuing education.

Wilcoxon and Archer (1997) also described a unique approach to continuing education as well as professional networking: a consortium model for professional development. These authors described a framework combining academicians and practitioners convening on a monthly basis in a local setting for continuing education and professional networking. The benefits described in this framework were: (a) affordability, (b) practitioner-focused modules, (c) a regular group of local participants, (d) a formalized educational format (sometimes including homework between meetings or selected texts for discussion), and (e) minimal disruption to the practice week, since monthly meetings were typically scheduled on Friday afternoons.

In considering all health and allied health professionals together, L. E. Phillips (1987) reported that 70% of professionals in states with MCE approve of the requirement, and more approve of it after its implementation than before. This observation would be consistent with Schwallie's (2005) statements about the necessity of continuing professional education as a factor in assuring sustained competency for licensed practitioners. Concerning this matter, she stated:

> Continuing education and standards for continuing professional competency of licensed MFTs who are already established in MFT practice are other key issues for regulatory boards. Regulators recognize that it is not only critical for MFTs to assume personal accountability to stay abreast of changes in statutes and rules affecting their practice in their states, but also to be aware of and integrate new evidence based strategies and attitudes about treatment that benefit clients' well being. (p. 26)

VandeCreek, Knapp, and Brace (1990) argued convincingly for mandatory continuing education. Based on a thorough review of the literature in this area, they proposed several specific factors that appear to promote optimal MCE:

- Practitioners should be able to fulfill requirements through a variety of activities so as to take account of the diversity of interests and professional responsibilities.
- All continuing education activities should include a method for objectively showing that learning has occurred (e.g., pre- and posttests of knowledge, audio or video demonstration of skills, copies of client records—appropriately disguised—to demonstrate new learning).
- Continuing education should emphasize enhancing existing skills as well as new knowledge.

In summary, VandeCreek et al. (1990) concluded that, essentially, MCE needs to connect continuing education activities to professional practice if it is to be pragmatically purposeful. One primary means of doing so—emanating from their previously noted proposals for promoting optimal MCE—is to require licensees to document specifically how their completed continuing education activities are supposed to improve their performance of identifiable professional services. Whether mandatory or voluntary, these conclusions seem wise counsel for all marriage and family therapists to consider in enhancing their professional development.

Intraprofessional Relationships and Service: Expanding and Enriching Professional Identity

Mental health professionals are part of the upper strata of the social structure of U.S. society. Their status is partly due to the fact that they are among the best-educated members of society. However, their status is also partly due to their assumption of responsibility for public welfare. Such responsibility begins with a commitment to ethical principles that support social values such as *justice* and *autonomy*. Such aims may even lead to social activism on the part of professionals. For example, the AAMFT has stated this position clearly in its promotional materials. In a broader sense, the AAMFT is concerned not simply with the profession of marriage and family therapy but also with people—the needs and problems they face in relationships, whether they are now married, have been married, or may somehow be affected by marriage in our society. The AAMFT is also concerned with the institution of marriage itself—its strengths and weaknesses, its changing patterns, its role in the lives of all people. The AAMFT firmly supports a position that this most important and intimate of human relations demands increased advocacy, research, and education at all levels, and that the professional marriage and family therapist must take the lead to ensure that these needs are met (American Association for Marriage and Family Therapy, 2000).

Similarly, the AAMFT advocates for nontraditional family structures and relationships, especially for those who may be marginalized or even oppressed by cultural or institutional insensitivity. Such aims naturally extend to dialogue and exchanges on an international scale concerning similarities and differences in support of individuals, couples, and families.

Another facet of this responsibility for the public good includes the preservation and enhancement of one's professional position as well as the profession itself (Bayles, 1981). In our earlier discussion concerning professional affiliation, we presented information concerning the professional standards, rigorous reviews, and personal–professional benefits associated with professional affiliation. Essentially, these comments concerned *what professional affiliation gives to its members.* However, affiliation also involves *what members give to the profession.* Service to a large-scale mission represents a form of "professional citizenship" that strengthens our identity as marriage and family therapists. We become more than just ourselves; we become peers and colleagues pursuing an agenda of equity, wellness, and fulfillment for our clients, ourselves, and society at large. In this way, our intraprofessional relationships and service assists in enhancing our professional identity. State, regional, national, and international professional organizations provide support, facilitate development, bring together colleagues with similar interests, offer opportunities for active participation in leadership roles, disseminate information, and generally provide a regular forum for intraprofessional communications. Both at the state/regional and national levels, opportunities for intraprofessional communications are available for active participation in relevant associational affairs and through contact via professional journals, newsletters, and meetings.

A somewhat underappreciated aspect of intraprofessional relationships and service is its place in the developmental nature of professional identity. As a form of "professional generativity," such interactions often yield opportunities for mentor–protégé relationships in which seasoned marriage and family therapists impart wisdom and advice for emerging and eager professionals. We would all do well to recognize that we must *learn history* before we can *make history,* and that once made, we should *share history* with subsequent generations of professionals. In this respect, intraprofessional relationships and service are a key aspect of continuity for the field.

On a narrower, more local level, regular intraprofessional relationships and service with colleagues also is critical for maintaining personal–professional wellness and preventing burnout. Such concerns reflect the even more immediate and pragmatic needs related to one's "personal–professional wellness." Professional burnout is a phenomenon that has been the topic of numerous publications and has received tremendous attention at professional conferences and continuing education endeavors. Burnout is a state of physical, emotional, and mental exhaustion frequently associated with intense involvement with people over long periods. Burnout is particularly critical for professionals working in the mental health field. With so much emphasis on giving to others, there is often not enough focus on giving to oneself (Corey et al., 1998). Regular intraprofessional communications are one major means of preventing or remediating burnout, and they fulfill other professional duties as well. For one to be truly in "private practice" is to destine oneself to become a victim of burnout, often because of professional isolation. "Independent practice" has been suggested as a healthier alternative—active networking with colleagues, referral sources, and cooperating and functioning as a team member within the community system (L. R. Peterson, 1992). It is an essential means of keeping oneself fresh and excited as a marriage and family therapist. This issue will be examined more fully in Chapter 12.

SUMMARY

During the past six decades, marriage and family therapy has developed from an interdisciplinary and nondistinct foundation of ideas to the recognized status of a profession. The theory, research, practice, and organization of marriage and family therapy have undergone a dramatic evolution that has increasingly delineated it as a separate entity—a peer within the major mental health disciplines. Many individuals who originally studied traditional professions have pursued further training and now identify themselves distinctly as marriage and family therapists. Many others, although they still maintain their original professional identities, clearly specify marriage and family as their area of professional specialization.

With this evolution there has been an equally astonishing increase in those who have taken membership not only in that organization that highlights marriage and family as a separate and distinct profession, the American Association for Marriage and Family Therapy (AAMFT), but also in those associations that recognize and promote marriage and family therapy as a professional specialization: the American Family Therapy Association (AFTA), Division 43—Family Psychology of the American Psychological Association (APA), and the International Association of Marriage and Family Counselors (IAMFC) of the American Counseling Association (ACA).

With this rise in professional association membership has come an equally impressive rise in the legislative recognition of marriage and family therapy through the enactment of licensing laws. Therapists can no longer practice whatever they wish under the guise of an unregulated profession. Accountability is now firmly established as an active part of marriage and family therapy practice. As of August 2005, state legislation creating licensure specifically for marriage and family therapy had been enacted in 47 states (including the District of Columbia) with active plans to introduce such legislation present in other states.

Maintenance of professional credibility is a multidimensional process involving active participation in one's professional development as well as actions to enhance the status and support base of the profession through research, continuing education, and intraprofessional relationships and service. These are not separate processes. Rather, they are an interrelated series of activities that foster professional identity as a marriage and family therapist. In our final chapter, we will offer opportunities to consider specific situations and questions arising from identifying oneself professionally as a marriage and family therapist.

CHAPTER 12

Contemporary Professional Issues

Chapter 11 presented a discussion of the predominant elements of professional identity affecting marriage and family therapists. As the professional practice of marriage and family therapy has grown from a radical new approach to an established force within mainstream mental health, many questions and challenges have naturally arisen concerning other related professional issues. In a format similar to the manner in which Chapters 7 and 10 of our text highlighted selected ethical and legal considerations with case studies, this chapter is devoted to an examination of selected professional issues in marriage and family therapy. As we noted previously, an issue is often an "issue" because multiple options and interpretations exist for a troublesome circumstance. Thus, measured professional judgment is often required to resolve dilemmas involving such issues. Otherwise, a rule or law governs one's behavior, sometimes making the issue more about compliance than judgment.

Just as with ethical and legal issues, marriage and family therapists should consider *application* and *precedent* when making decisions related to professional issues. In terms of application, most professional issues evolve into *practice* issues. For example, considering the professional issue of advertising as a topical discussion in a graduate-level seminar class is primarily an intellectual exercise. However, an independent practitioner faces a variety of applied considerations in making decisions about the form and content of a public announcement of services. The aspects of such decisions are not simply cerebral; they are substantive. In this respect, a form of "professional alchemy" merges values, intuition, knowledge, experience, and identity into a decision with practical application for the therapist facing this professional issue.

Precedents have been discussed at length in the previous examinations of ethical and legal issues affecting marriage and family therapists. For ethical and legal issues, reliance on codified statements from professional organizations, regulatory agencies, and bodies of legal work can yield broad precepts (e.g., *beneficence*) or narrow instructions (e.g., no sexual relationships with clients). As we will see, some professional issues can be resolved by relying on these codified statements. However, some professional issues are not addressed with specificity in code or law. For example, professional rules to address an unexpected interruption in the practice of a marriage and family therapist or closing an office are either broad (e.g., make arrangements, no abandonment, etc.) or derivative (e.g., examine business law). In such cases, the precedents employed by other practitioners or recommended in professional sources can be particularly relevant. Wilcoxon (1987) distinguished such precedents as reflecting either *customary* practices or *suggested* practices to which the therapist can refer. Customary practices are those that are typically employed or are employed with some frequency by other professionals. For example, customary practice by a therapist closing an office might include referring clients to a local colleague, securing written authorization in anticipation of a request for clinical records, and possibly meeting with some clients and the referral to assist in the transition. A precedent of this type can offer a template for the therapist who is planning to conclude his or her career in a professional and caring manner. However, such specific instructions are often not codified in professional statements such as ethical standards or legal decisions. By contrast, suggested practices come from reliable professional sources such as journals, juried presentations at professional meetings, and similar channels. Suggested practices are particularly assistive for emerging professional issues, since the lack of precedent in actual decisions may be so limited that a customary approach has not yet been established. In many ways, customary and suggested practices are a form of professional lore and tradition, often learned in supervision and mentoring relationships.

As we will see, professional issues also often involve people (e.g., teachers, probation officers, physicians, managed care representatives, etc.) or procedures (e.g., licensure statutes, HIPAA, nonreimbursable DSM categories, etc.) associated with other systems tangential or parallel to the practice of marriage and family therapy. In this respect, our discussion in Chapter 2 regarding the *professional* and *institutional* layers of values can be particularly significant in one's practice decisions. To further complicate the picture, as we discussed in Chapter 6, the ubiquitous nature of technology as a medium for transfer and storage of information in contemporary mental health care has introduced a consideration that cannot be ignored by even the most well-intentioned practitioner.

A final overarching professional issue for marriage and family therapists is the continuing need for sensitivity to human diversity in all practice decisions. As we will see in the coming discussion, some institutional layer values minimize, if not ignore, the very concerns that permeate the standards of due care and competent practice by marriage and family therapists. In fact, one metaview of such situations is that they represent a "cultural clash" at the professional or institutional layers of values.

In its early development, marriage and family therapy was vulnerable to demands that it prove itself (W. C. Nichols, 1992). In seeking to do so, defensive claims were advanced purporting the essence of marriage and family therapy theory and practice (i.e., systemic epistemology) to be a panacea for all ills. As we discussed in Chapter 2, however, a variety of critiques have arisen concerning the systemic viewpoint. Responding to these questions and challenges has led to the need for that early systemic epistemology to evolve in order to maintain its relevance for the conceptual and applied work of marriage and family therapists. However, the relevance of a systemic view must continue beyond an insular intraprofessional debate between "professional family members." If a contemporary systemic epistemology that embraces equity and diversity, while respecting individuality, is to have an impact upon larger mental health practices and legislation, it must develop in a manner that can coexist with other perspectives while maintaining its roots in a contextual view of relationships. Such development need not be adversarial or combative in nature.

You may recall our discussion about the process of *valuing* in Chapter 1. In this discussion, valuing was described as a means by which exchanges between systems, containing elements of multiple subsystems, can be negotiated in a synergistic manner that can be evolutionary and beneficial to all. Though this discussion concerned the relationship within the therapy system, its tenets are relevant for marriage and family therapists interacting with other systems. Such negotiation and valuing has allowed marriage and family therapists to maintain the importance of an epistemology that recognizes the benefits of understanding the shapes and patterns of interaction while simultaneously augmenting and deepening that understanding by finding relevance with peer professions.

Although the roots of marriage and family therapy can be traced to Freud, the profession did not receive formal recognition until the 1970s. In that decade, the American Association of Marriage Counselors changed its name first to the American Association of Marriage and Family Counselors and later to the American Association for Marriage and Family Therapy (AAMFT). The 1970s also saw the advent of state licensing laws regulating the profession's practice. This trend continued in the 1980s, along with focused energies on becoming a political force at state and national levels. The 1990s saw continuing refinement of the systemic epistemology and its meaning in a world linked by technology, impacted by managed care, and often divided by insensitivity and oppression. Similar agendas and concerns have continued into the 21st century. When compared with some longer-standing professions such as medicine and law, marriage and family therapy is in its adolescence. However, as practitioners in a vibrant and recognized mental health discipline, marriage and family therapists also often face complex and perplexing professional issues. This chapter features questions about pragmatic professional issues along with discussions about reasonable considerations and actions one may employ in addressing those issues.

QUESTION 1   *Evolving Epistemology in Actual Practice*

As a marriage and family therapist, I recognize the importance of conceptualizing clients' issues as residing in systems. I also recognize the importance of respecting the place of the individual in the system. How can I best put this evolving epistemology into actual practice and work with individuals in sessions as well as with the larger family system?

Response

Experienced marriage and family therapists' employment of a systemic epistemology is not reflected by who is in the room, but rather, by how many persons are involved in the therapist's thinking about the problem. Historically, the work of marriage and family therapists has encompassed a wide variation of ideas about who should actually be seen in sessions. Napier and Whitaker (1978) insisted that convening the entire system was a critical element of the Battle for Structure. By contrast, Kaslow (1986) noted that requiring the presence of others or even a waiver from others in order to pursue individual work reflected an "intrusion on individuality, privacy, and selfhood" (p. 264).

In our discussion of the critique of systemic epistemology in Chapter 2, you will recall one element of commentary concerned the loss of self and individualism. Although many cultures value a form of acquiescence into group identity and benefit, not all do. For some clients, the importance of self-exploration is not a selfish indulgence but a necessary element in their personal development. Sometimes, such an opportunity is a necessary preliminary step prior to participating in larger-scale change. Formats of this type are not inconsistent with many postmodern approaches to change. Still, one of the professional hallmarks of marriage and family therapy is the *conceptualization* of problems in a systemic framework.

As we noted earlier, the application aspect of a professional issue concerns one's practice. For example, from our discussion of on-line therapy in Chapter 6, the e-therapist may be "thinking systemically" while interacting with only one client. Similarly, as we discussed in Chapter 4, a marriage and family therapist may be working with one spouse as a strategy for ultimately engaging both spouses for marital therapy. In these and other cases, one significant ethical consideration emerges for this professional issue: the work with the individual should feature *beneficence* (for good) and *fidelity* (for truthfulness). In essence, the work with an individual, while maintaining a systemic perspective, must be truly initiated for the good of the individual client, rather than as a simple "holding pattern" until other members of the system are engaged.

Although it is generally accepted that family therapy is the treatment of choice for marital or family conflict, many therapists use individual sessions as a part of ongoing family efforts (M. P. Nichols, 1987a, 1987b). Berman (1982) suggested several ways that individual sessions can be incorporated within a systemic framework: first as a part of the diagnostic/planning process and then as a part of ongoing treatment.

Diagnosis/Planning

Alliance Issues

Conjoint or family sessions allow a clear focus on the system but may make it difficult for the therapist to gain the confidence of individual members. Having more than two persons in the room permits a reduction in therapist–individual relationship intensity. For some clients, this approach may be a matter of pacing their vulnerability with others, which could have a cultural origin.

Individual sessions can serve to intensify therapist–individual client relationship of trust that many believe deepens clients' commitment to the therapy. For example, Brock and Barnard (1999) indicated that the therapeutic engagement of a minimally committed family member can be enhanced in this manner. However, as we noted in Chapter 4, therapists must take care in balancing such alliances in a manner that would not lead to bias or triangulation.

History Taking

Marital partners and family members can profit from learning or reviewing each other's history, often adding considerably to it. However, histories taken individually may be quite different from histories taken when a marital partner or family member is present. A client may omit crucial information because of guilt or embarrassment.

In individual sessions, the recall process is often facilitated when a client does not have to worry about whether a spouse, parent, or child is recording potentially shameful incidents for future reference. On a more pragmatic level, individual sessions to do family-of-origin work are ideal when regularly scheduled conjoint or family sessions are difficult to coordinate (Brock & Barnard, 1999).

Assessing a Client's Manner of Acting Apart from the System

Systems can significantly contribute to a channeling of their members' behaviors. Rigid systems often can promote highly polarized and role-specific interactions among members when assembled together. A startling therapeutic event is the change that frequently occurs in persons apart from their family.

Direct knowledge of clients' alternative behavioral repertoires is an invaluable therapeutic awareness. Individual sessions can foster this awareness. As we discussed in Chapter 5, in instances of intimate partner violence, individual sessions may be a requirement for purposes of assessment and planning.

Ventilation/Rehearsal

Many clients enter therapy so furiously angry that they are unable to express anything else. To help these clients rehearse more effective ways of relating, it is frequently beneficial to allow some time for ventilating feelings without spouses or other family members present. The therapist can then suggest alternative ways for the client to act. Likewise, if a client is massively afraid of confronting a spouse or family member alone at home, it may help to first practice adaptive responses without feeling the pressure of the other person present. Individual sessions can facilitate this type of constructive skill building (Falloon, 1991).

As a note of caution in this regard, Stith et al. (2004) indicated that any conjoint interactions with intact couples in which intimate partner violence has occurred that could agitate the victimizer should be avoided. Rather, these authors advocated for the use of group work with aggressive partners as the better setting for such situations.

Secrets

Many clients have significant difficulty directly sharing certain past or present feelings and beliefs with marital partners and family members. Such "secrets" can seriously hinder therapy efforts. Individual sessions can provide a context in which disclosure of relevant secrets is facilitated. Therapists who are aware of relevant, though unshared, marital or family information may find themselves in the difficult position of how to use it. In essence, they may find themselves in a coalition with a family member (Brendel & Nelson, 1999).

Remember our previous discussion in Chapter 4 concerning the distinctions Vangelisti (1994) offered about family secrets. Specifically, these distinctions concerned: (a) *taboo topics*, which could concern embarrassing or liablous actions (e.g., extramarital affairs, illegalities, etc.), (b) *rule violations*, which could concern departures from accepted social norms (e.g., sexual activity, underage drinking, etc.), and (c) *conventional secrets*, which could concern conversational topics members would prefer to remain private (e.g., religion, academic difficulties, etc.). Further, Farber and Hall (2003) indicated that cultural norms and traditions also may affect clients' willingness to address secrets within any or all of these categories.

No easy solutions are available in such situations; potential directions depend on the particular information and context. Thus, marriage and family therapists need to have strategies for handling secrets *before* they are revealed—for example, helping the client sort out how the secret could be revealed to those who have a need to know. Regardless, a therapist who is not privy to this kind of information may spend months doing unprofitable therapy with a couple while one marital partner is carrying on an affair, for example, or planning to pursue a divorce. In this respect, the use of individual sessions for *expressing* secrets should be distinguished from the use of individual sessions for *conspiring* about secrets. The former could be a meaningful approach to the process of change, whereas the latter could create inequities in therapy relationships.

For each of the previous categories, Berman (1982) asserted that individual work, with a systemic perspective, could be useful in planning and diagnosing for initiating therapy. However, he also noted that individual work can be considered coincidental to therapy involving partners or multiple family members. Refer to Chapter 4 to review the various positions therapists may take in handling secrets with couples or family members.

Individual Sessions During Ongoing Therapy

Individual Issues

Contemporary postmodern approaches to marriage and family therapy place a premium on the respect of individual realities of each member of a family. However, one or more members of a marital or family system may be so involved in their own internal conflicts, transition issues, or irrational beliefs that efforts directed at altering their perceptions and behaviors consumes a sizeable amount of time during sessions. Although the system in some way helps to generate or support individual concerns, it may be more efficient, and ultimately more effective, to spend one or more individual sessions in a concerted effort to diminish that client's internal conflicts so that work on couple or family goals can proceed with less conflict.

Certain developmental times during the family life cycle are particularly appropriate circumstances for individual sessions, such as when an offspring enters young adulthood where individuation–separation issues and inner–outer conflict are pronounced (C. A. Carter, 1987; B. A. Carter & McGoldrick, 2005). Other more chronic concerns (e.g., family-of-origin issues, delayed grieving, etc.) also may persist for an individual that can stymie systemic progress. As a *therapy* matter, including individual sessions concurrent with couple or family sessions may have great merit. As was noted in Chapter 6, however, therapists should also beware of the *business* matters of managed mental health care (MMHC) restrictions or policies that might impact success for systemic concerns by exhausting allowable resources for individual concerns.

Missing Puzzle Pieces

Occasionally, information may be deliberately withheld or simply not shared early in therapy. Individual sessions offer an opportunity for enhanced awareness.

For example, imagine that a family had been participating in weekly therapy sessions for almost four months with no apparent progress toward agreed-on goals. The therapist requested a second set of individual interviews. During her individual session, the eldest daughter reveals that she learned she was pregnant shortly after therapy began but had been unable to tell her parents and brother. Although management of secrets from individual sessions would have been addressed beforehand by the therapist, significant information such as an unplanned pregnancy could certainly offer new and vital information for the therapist. Additionally, such information may alter the focus and intended goals for therapy.

Sexual Dysfunction

Certain issues of a more intimate nature often lend themselves particularly well to individual sessions. For example, sexual difficulties can frequently be addressed more comfortably in a brief series of individual sessions with a therapist who is well trained in human sexuality.

Although most sexual education with partners should be undertaken with both present, it is sometimes more productive to pursue some educational efforts in private. Additionally, the need for referral for medical concerns may become more readily apparent for the therapist as well as the client(s).

Strategic and Structural Maneuvers

Individual sessions are a valuable means of unbalancing. The therapist can use them to give clients private tasks and the like and thereby reduce overinvolvement or reorder alliances. However, Berman (1982) cautioned that before seeing marital partners or family members alone, therapists should discuss the proposed sessions with all members of the system together. Members of the system should be made aware that they may experience some concern or mistrust regarding what was shared outside their presence. The rationale for individual sessions should be explained as well as all aspects of confidentiality (or lack of confidentiality) to be in effect for such session.

Although the use of individual sessions in the diagnostic/planning process is a matter of clinical preference, movement to individual sessions during ongoing therapy can be a choice significantly facilitated by several common indicators: (a) therapy has not been progressing for some period of time, (b) the therapist senses that a hidden agenda is blocking therapy efforts, and (c) a client requests private time (this last indicator calls for careful clinical judgment to balance the possibility of manipulation, i.e., creating an unbalanced alliance versus trust in a client's sense of what is necessary).

Other Approaches to Blending Systemic and Individual Work

In addition to the suggestions offered by Berman, others have advocated a "think systems" approach for circumstances involving work with individual members of the system. For example, May and Church (1999) observed, "Many family therapists today recognize the limits of traditional family therapies with their emphasis on the dynamics that occur within the family. They call for the need to expand our work with families to include the societal context in which families live" (p. 51). In this respect, these authors advocated for the use of community resources for families *as well as individuals*, such as networks (e.g. churches, neighbors, etc.) and kinships (e.g., extended families) as resources for individuals to address concerns that could then be brought into conjoint sessions with other members. Similarly, Sherman (1999) supported the use of extended family members as an emergent "self-help group" for nuclear families and individual members. In this way, he noted that the multigenerational nature of extended families, coupled with a self-help group framework, would be consistent with "social construction theory so that the new self-help system is encouraged to develop new, more constructive interpretations of reality" for individuals and the nuclear family (p. 72).

In both the approach advocated by May and Church (1999) and that advocated by Sherman (1999), the ecological emphasis on "individual-in-context" features an appreciation for selfhood while also introducing resources available to those individuals that would not threaten the integrity and purpose of systemic therapy. In these ways, the critique of systemic epistemology concerning loss of self noted in Chapter 2 is respected and addressed.

QUESTION 2 *Marriage and Family Therapy Interventions with Other Systems*

My understanding of systemic dynamics so far emphasized the roles, relationships, rules, and balance of forces operating within marital and family systems. As a marriage and family therapist, I am recognized for my work with couples and families. How might my marital and family understandings and interventions be applied in working with other systems?

Response

As we noted in the response to the previous question, marriage and family therapy from a systemic perspective is not a method but, rather, a viewpoint. It is a clinical orientation applicable to the problems of all systems, not just marital and family systems. For example, a systemic perspective has been extended quite naturally to the school context by a number of practitioners (Colapinto, 1988; Fine & Holt, 1983; Hinkle & Wells, 1995). An individual school is a part of a larger school system, with a hierarchy of faculty, staff, and administrative roles and relationships. Within an individual school, each classroom likewise has a subsystem characterized by the same roles, relationships, rules, and balances of forces operating within couple and family systems.

The following points and case illustration adapted from Fine (1985) provide an overview of what the application of a systemic perspective within a school setting can mean for marriage and family therapists serving as consultants:

1. There is no standard operating procedure for a systemic perspective. The perspective is just that—a perspective—a mental frame of reference for viewing function and dysfunction.
2. A systemic perspective views behavior contextually and in interaction terms: What happens when a student does . . . ? What precedes undesirable behaviors? How does the host system contribute to generating and escalating these behaviors? Understanding characteristic sequences of undesirable events presents the means for disrupting them and enacting desirable options.

3. A systemic perspective is concerned with the "fit" of students within the system, for example, the classroom. Do the present instructional components of the classroom match or clash with a student's learning style and developmental readiness to engage in certain learning and socialization experiences? These understandings offer the opportunity for modifying classroom variables such as seating, pace, and content of instruction; number and complexity of assignments; nature of teacher–student interactions; specific teacher control techniques; and more.

4. The systemic perspective recognizes that standard operating procedures in a situation may be exacerbating a problem and, in fact, may have defined the problem. Relevant examples include the use of certain labels that represent static views of students and teachers that, in turn, establish an expectation that influences interactions.

5. A systemic perspective is cognizant that systems overlap and thus can influence each other, and that systems seek stability and may resist change as a result of homeostatic forces attempting to exert control. Because students live in multiple systems, one system might seek to influence the other to assume a particular stance. For example, parents who regularly complain to a teacher that their child refuses to listen can project this expectation into the school situation where that behavior may not be a predominant concern. Should the teacher come to accept this view of the student, the two systems become destructively aligned.

Another illustration further clarifies the applicability of a systemic perspective within a school setting:

John was a physically large, mildly retarded 14-year-old who had just completed a year of training in a residential rehabilitation facility because of a history of emotional acting out. Shortly after John enrolled in a primarily self-contained classroom in public school, his teacher became very concerned. In refusing to do a number of tasks he found frustrating, John had pounded his desk and glared menacingly at the teacher. Given John's institutional background and sheer bulk, his teacher feared being attacked.

The consultant, a marriage and family therapist who worked regularly with the schools, was called on for assistance. A review of John's background revealed no instances of physical acting out. It was decided to interpret John's actions to his teacher and other school personnel in a manner that would reduce their anxiety and offer a functional way of working with John's disruptive outbursts. His aggressive stance was defined as "the way he's learned to act to keep away persons who might make frustrating demands of him." In essence, John's emotional outbursts were reframed as poor coping strategies.

Meeting with the teacher and other involved school personnel for several sessions (some of which included John), the consultant assured everyone involved that John had never displayed any instances of physical aggression except some minor "normal" scuffles with peers that had occurred more than four years previously. The consultant sought enactments among all present to reinforce the reframing of John's behavior as "faulty social learnings." Within this reframing, efforts and successes at teaching more adaptive interaction skills to John were highlighted. The therapist used simple diagramming to show how behaviors and reactions were related and to illustrate what was occurring among John, the teacher, and other classmates and school personnel. John, in interaction with his teacher, received training in how to verbalize his frustration to the teacher more adaptively. The teacher was trained to facilitate and reinforce the new behavior.

In summary, the consultant framed the situation in a way that changed the perception of the problem's severity and identified more adaptive roles for John, the teacher, and other school personnel. In effect, the consultant identified society as the "persecutor," John as the "victim," and the school as the "rescuer." This facilitated movement toward a positive "let's help each other" relationship between John and the school personnel, with the society in which John had previously learned his poor coping strategies as the "villain." This way of systemically triangulating relationships represented a constructive shift from the school personnel's initial view that they were being victimized by both society and by John.

Although this response has addressed marriage and family therapy understandings and interventions within a school setting, similar successes have been evidenced in other settings. One emergent opportunity for employing a systemic view has been marriage and family therapy within the world of business (Cole, 1992).

A meaningful discussion of systemic principles of therapy applicable to other systems would be incomplete without reinforcing two previously mentioned principles: institutional values and cultural sensitivity. Recall from Chapter 2 the discussion about personal, professional, and institutional layers of values. Although an "institution" does not "hold values," its gatekeepers typically adopt and implement policies and procedures to accomplish the established mission of the agency or institution. Such missions lead agency representatives to develop and promote institutional values. One might posit that families certainly have "institutional values" that typically reflect a collective position of its members. Such values are typically influenced by the local custom and an aggregate of "personal values" for the group, however. Additionally, the legitimate power of a family or even a community is typically more localized than a larger-scale system such as a school system or a managed care agency.

In many instances, systems of service and care for others employ a rule structure for systemic balance based on compliance and standardization. Thus, conformity may be an overarching institutional value. For these and many more systems, compliance is a rule-governed, homeostatic aspect of interaction. As such, "success" is often related to conformity. However, many culturally insensitive systems (even those with benevolent social agendas) may in fact be oppressive and inattentive to individual/group differences. Such an outcome may be in direct opposition to the personal and professional values held by a marriage and family therapist serving a couple or family. In many ways, to encounter institutional values of some systems is to experience a "cultural schism" or conflict, since the paradigms and missions of therapy may run counter to those of institutions or agencies affecting therapy. Thus, a marriage and family therapist who wants to utilize experience and expertise with systemic interventions must be sensitive to the "culture" of institutional values operating in nontherapy systems. As we will see in the next question, aspects of our values and those of others permeate the professional issues faced by marriage and family therapists.

I recognize that as a marriage and family therapist I need to acknowledge the influential power my values may have on a couple or family, and that I should attend to the transactions over values that occur between us. However, I find it difficult at times to ascertain if or when I should actively seek to influence a couple's or family's values. Are there guidelines to consider in encountering and managing such situations?

Response

Negotiations about values are held at different levels of abstraction and application. Consider a situation with a troubled married couple. The therapist's values might range from the notion that "marital partners should love each other" (general principle), to "this man should love his wife" (specific principle), or to "in these circumstances, this man should demonstrate love for his wife in this particular manner" (operational application). The more abstract the value level, the more likely agreement may emerge between therapist and couple or family. Agreement is also more likely to occur if the therapist and couple or family share similar personal, socioeconomic, and cultural backgrounds, especially concerning reference points such as gender equity, religion, lawfulness, and similar issues. The closer interactions move to operational applications of a value, or the greater the background differences between therapist and couple or family, the greater the probability that different values will be involved.

The model of therapy, the characteristics of clients, and the personal and professional styles of therapists all influence the level of involvement a therapist has in addressing a couple's or family's values. As a general rule, Aponte (1985) recommended that "the therapist should attempt to exercise no more influence over the family's values than is required adequately to address the family's problems" (p. 335). In expounding this basic premise, Aponte differentiated between *structure, function,* and *values.* He identified these three elements as formative constructs in a social system, a social system being an aggregate of people who join in patterned structures to carry out a function or array of functions in accord with a standard of values. Aponte further described four situations (with case examples) in which a change in a family's values would be essential to therapeutic change. These situations are described in the following sections.

Values Conflicts as a Source of Dysfunction

Aponte (1985) contended that when a conflict between members of a family or between a family and its community is a significant force in the dysfunction being addressed in therapy, a change in values is essential to therapeutic success. He noted examples, such as marital dysfunction, when partners are in conflict because they come from different cultural, racial, religious, ethnic, or socioeconomic backgrounds, or when a minority family has problems living in a community in which there is discrimination against the minority (e.g., same-gender couple, etc.). As Boszormenyi-Nagy and

Sparks (1973) also noted, the loyalty to one's family of origin can substantively affect values to the point of discord between couples.

Conflicting values may serve simply as a superficial distraction from deeper emotional issues. Family members may present a values conflict as their principal concern to avoid confronting emotional forces embedded in a structural conflict. Aponte (1985) noted the example of family conflict in which an adolescent and parent may present a conflict over values about dress style, but the more significant struggle really may be based on tension over the emerging emotional independence, a developmental outgrowth of an adolescent's increasing separation from the family. Although emotional issues may represent the primary source of the family problem, the values conflict, although secondary, may sufficiently influence the predominant problem to demand the therapist's attention.

Incompatible Values, Functions, and Structures

Addressing a possible change in values is in order when a family's values are incompatible with the function the family intends to carry out or the structures through which it is to operate. This lack of fit between the values of the family and its functions or structures most commonly emerges from evolutionary changes in the family or its social circumstances.

Aponte (1985) offered the example of a family in which the parents cannot interact intimately within their marital dyad, reflecting an overriding value of centering family interactions on the children. Essentially, the preferred functional role for these adults is that of "parent" rather than "partner" in their demonstration of love and protection. As the children mature and move away from home, however, this priority no longer serves as an adequate structure or function by which to organize the parents' relationship with each other. Thus, the value of love for children is incompatible with functions and structures available to the parents in demonstrating their love. In some instances, expressions of this value to children living elsewhere become intrusive or even contentious.

Underdeveloped Values

A change in family values is relevant to therapy efforts if a family or its members have not developed the values needed to guide the evolution of structures necessary to deal with functional issues. For example, an underorganized family not only lacks structure but also lacks a well-elaborated, cohesive, and flexible framework of values. In other words, an indefinite value may exist in a family, causing conflict between members attempting to functionally demonstrate that value or create a structure that allows for its expression.

Consider the example of a family with an underdeveloped value concerning social activism. For some members, this value may be expressed in personal contemplation or dialogue with others about hatred and oppression, whereas for others it may be expressed in giving money, joining local activist groups, and securing support from influential politicians and public leaders. Unless there is great respect and tolerance for differences in the expression of this commonly held value among the family members, the likelihood of tension and conflict concerning its expression is quite high. The development of a value framework influences how well organized the structure of a family's relationships will be around the demonstration of that value. A family that has primitive, inconsistent, conflicting, or rigid values will find it difficult to effectively establish functional relationships among its members.

Disagreement over the Therapeutic Process

Value change represents a more complex issue in the therapeutic process. A family and therapist struggle to seek agreement on the values framework for addressing the family's dysfunction. Consider the following example:

> A therapist sought supervision in a case in which a couple with two children was working to face the husband's ongoing affair with another woman. The therapy had consisted primarily of technical assistance offered to aid the couple's decision-making process. These efforts had become stalled. The therapist was unable to incorporate the family's underlying emotional issues into this framework. The therapist lacked a framework of values to define and direct his approach for working with the couple's emotional struggle. An exploration of the therapist's own family revealed a father who had carried on a long-term affair with his mother's knowledge while the therapist was a child. The therapist had been made part of the family's conspiracy of silence by sharing a number of recreational outings with the father and his woman friend and being cautioned to keep quiet about the outings. Furthermore, problems concerning relationships in the therapist's current life were occasioned by the infidelities of a lover and the therapist's consequent inability to establish an enduring, exclusive committed relationship with anyone. The therapist was unable to decide what fidelity could be expected in a love relationship or marriage. The therapist (as well as the couple) had no personal reference point from which to organize the confusion of the couple being treated about their respective expectations of marital fidelity. Moreover, the therapist, who had not adequately dealt with personally relevant childhood conflicts, did not even think to consider the effect of the client-father's infidelity on the couple's young children. Without a values framework forged out of a resolution of personal life experiences, the therapist was approaching the family's dilemma without a means to guide interventions. The therapist obviously needed a clear set of values before he could guide the couple in efforts to resolve their conflict.

This example reflects the difficulties of value transactions when the framework for discussion is unclear or unshared among those in the therapeutic relationship. In this particular example, the *therapist's* experiences and values contributed to therapy being stalled. In such instances, options such as supervision, consultation, co-therapy, and even personal therapy would be viable possibilities.

Unshared value frameworks are one source of difficulties between client/system and therapist. However, one substantive difference between the therapist and the client/system is that the client(s) may address only the personal layer of values, but the therapist must address the personal *as well as professional* layers of values. Our previous discussion in Chapters 2 and 3 concerning the interface between values and ethical precepts is reflected in the idea of *virtue ethics* (i.e., "Who do I want to be?") rather than *principle ethics* (i.e., "What do I want to do?"). In some instances, the professional values of a virtuous marriage and family therapist forces an examination of client values, possibly to the extent of attempting to alter those values. Consider the following two examples:

Case 1

A conflicted married couple has sought therapy for their dwindling commitment to one another. Among the many difficulties they face is uncertainty in sustained employment for the husband (a specialist in working outdoors with concrete, which is highly dependent on good weather). In one session, the couple presents a united front with a newly realized purpose in their relationship. They report that they attended a tent revival over the weekend and were moved to agree to adopt a severely disabled and mentally retarded child as a sign of their faith. The therapist is uncertain about how to proceed.

Case 2

A troubled married couple has begun therapy concerning their continued financial difficulties. The husband is in a managerial position with a local company, the wife is not employed outside the home, and they have no children. In their second session, the therapist queries about their frequent offhand comments about gambling, to which they respond that it is simple entertainment. Upon further inquiry, the therapist begins to explore the possibility of a gambling addiction on the part of the husband, to which the husband replies, "What we really need is better paying jobs and we're here for you to help us come up with the best strategies. Also, I think it's about time for my wife to look for a job." The wife immediately says, "I think that's exactly what we want to do." The therapist views this circumstance as one fraught with enabling and denial.

For each of these cases, the ethical principles of *autonomy* (i.e., self-determination) and *fidelity* (i.e., truthfulness) are important, and somewhat competing, considerations for a virtuous practitioner. Additionally, most experienced marriage and family therapists have learned to accept the fact that clients make unwise choices, often regrettable and occasionally without the prospect of recovery.

In Case 1, the therapist may feel the need to explore the possible hazards and multiple obstacles facing this couple. The difficulty arises from what may be perceived as an attack on the couples' expression of faith. Although the therapist certainly should respect their right to autonomy, it is also important for the therapist to address the personal and professional value of honesty. From Aponte's (1985) distinctions, this effort may not be toward amending the *value* held by the couple but, rather, may work to change the *function* and *structure* of that value.

In Case 2, the therapist may also feel compelled to respect the *autonomy* of the clients to value an increase in their income level. In this case, however, respect for autonomy without the veracity of confrontation over the *function* of the expressed value (i.e., to avoid dealing with a gambling addiction) would violate the professional value for fidelity. Providing accurate information, an informed professional opinion, or even an alternate viewpoint do not equate with client exploitation or imposition of values; they are virtuous professional obligations about the functions and structures of those values. Such circumstances can be further complicated by cultural traditions or short-term crises. In summary, we would note that the very essence of marriage and family therapy involves transactions of values between client and therapist. Such a role should always be respected and vigilantly scrutinized.

Addressing Ambivalence

As a marriage and family therapist seeking to act responsibly in clarifying my own values and assisting clients to do similarly, I am frequently confronted by ambivalence in myself and my clients. I recognize that at best, such ambivalence is nonproductive and at worst, promotes the disintegration and destruction of relationships. How might I address this ambivalence?

Response

Marital and family therapists often hear the following types of statements from clients: "I know I don't want a divorce, but I still can't get motivated enough to do what is needed to make the marriage better," or "We know our sex life is not great and want to make it better, but we can't seem to get together no matter how hard we try." Therapists might be making similar statements to themselves as well: "I know that this couple needs to discontinue their extramarital affairs if they are going to significantly improve their marital relationship, but I'm not sure it's my place to impose my personal value on them." These statements reflect an ambivalence that keeps the speaker stuck midway between two points, simultaneously attracted toward and pushing away from each point.

Bergin (1991) asserted that values collaboration is critical to successful therapy outcomes. He offered the following:

> During treatment, therapists must make important decisions about how to enhance clients' functioning. . . . At these decision points, therapist, client, and concerned others should collaborate in arriving at the goals toward which change is directed. (p. 396)

For values collaboration to take place as proposed by Bergin, marriage and family therapists need to be able to provide both themselves and their clients with a framework that can be used for probing the bases for their actions. Without such a framework, continued ambivalence will tend to sap available energy and prevent commitment or concerted movement toward more adaptive options. Furthermore, in interactions between therapists and clients, or within marital or family systems, decision making tends to shift to nonambivalent members, forcing ambivalent members to take reactive and defensive positions. In effect, ambivalent members abdicate decision-making powers and become bystanders or victims instead of active participants.

Accepting the basic concept that actions reflect values—that at any given time, people are doing what is aligned with their most cherished beliefs—calls for a framework based on values analysis. Hof and Dwyer (1982) offered such a framework and suggested that persons can perceive (or can be helped to perceive) what is most important to them and how that can affect what they actually do. In their analysis of behavior as a function of values, Hof and Dwyer outlined five conditions that must be fulfilled if persons are to engage in certain actions.

1. People must have some minimal perception of self-confidence. Although the level or intensity of confidence can vary significantly, there still must be some minimal

confidence, or fear of failure will lead to avoidance of action or predestined attempts to fail. For example, the marriage and family therapist who plans to confront a couple regarding the effects of extramarital affairs must believe that such a confrontation ultimately will result in greater commitment by the couple to their relationship and will consequently lead to greater satisfaction. Furthermore, the therapist must have the self-discipline to follow through and further assist the couple to fully examine the confronted issue.

2. People must perceive some values fulfillment, at least as potentially available. Rarely is attention directed at any action unless there is the belief it could potentially deliver values fulfillment. The therapist must have some sense of the importance of personal values that would find fulfillment through the couple's enhanced marital interaction.

3. People must perceive a reasonable probability that values fulfillment will be delivered. The perception of some relevant, substantial values is not enough by itself. Again, following the example, the therapist must perceive that confronting the couple's extramarital affairs will, very likely, deliver values fulfillment to the therapist.

4. People's perception of the costs to be paid by engaging in the behavior—values fulfillment to be given up—must be acceptable relative to the perception and probability of alternative values fulfillment. A behavior with a high cost in terms of value fulfillment means that a person would lose a great deal of fulfillment by engaging in the proposed behavior. On the other end of the cost continuum are behaviors that have a low cost, in that a person would lose very little, if any, fulfillment when engaging in this behavior.

5. People's perceptions of the risks to other values involved in the behavior must be acceptable relative to their perceptions and probability of alternative values fulfillment. Not only are there perceptions of costs in all behavior changes, but there are also perceptions of risks. For example, a risk is believed to have a probability of less than 1 of occurring. It is therefore less definite and is only a possible consequence of engaging in the proposed behavior. The therapist may have only a vague sense that something unknown may happen, or may worry about the possibility of the couple's rejection, premature termination from therapy, and other concerns.

To the extent that it can be seen as a function of values fulfillment, behavior constitutes the following equation:

$$\text{Behavior} = \text{confidence} + \text{value fulfillment} \times \text{probability of value fulfillment} - \text{cost} + \text{risk}$$

A therapist can think of clients as being in a process of continual calculation concerning this equation, often at a subconscious level. With regard to a proposed behavior change, if the equation results in a negative or neutral conclusion, no change will take place. If it is positive, the behavior change will occur. Current behavior is always the product of a positive result. Any change in behavior requires a change in the amount or intensity of one or more of the five conditions until the end result of the calculation is pushed onto the positive side. In the end, if there is no change in behavior, current behavior is perceived to better serve values fulfillment.

Hof and Dwyer (1982) further offered several areas for exploration and intervention for each of the five conditions. A list of these categories and an illustrative example with a couple in therapy follow:

1. Confidence
   a. Gathering more facts and information.
   b. "Testing the water," successive approximation to build confidence.
   c. Asking others to assess competence.
   d. Sharing with others for self-reinforcement and obtaining reinforcement from others.
   e. Practice and rehearsal.
2. Conception of values fulfillment
   a. Inventorying values to determine which might be positively affected by a behavior change.
   b. Interviewing others about their values fulfillment.
3. Probability of values fulfillment
   a. Trying out aspects of the new behavior that are likely to offer the most immediate values fulfillment.
   b. Trying out the new behavior in contexts that are most likely to be supportive to values fulfillment.
   c. Providing self-reward at preset milestones.
   d. Seeking information on the success rate of others who have engaged in the new behavior.
4. Perception of cost
   a. Careful planning to assess and reduce costs.
   b. Experimenting to assess and reduce costs.
   c. Placing an upper limit on costs that would be incurred before quitting.
   d. Realizing the option of backing out is always available.
5. Perception of risks
   a. Planning and taking appropriate precautions to reduce risks.
   b. Sharing risks whenever possible.
   c. Learning from experience; experimenting to reduce risks.
   d. Assessing the worst that could happen and what that might mean to overall values fulfillment.

We offer the following illustration as an application of the risk–benefit equation of a values analysis:

A couple with two children entered therapy with the intention of ending their marital relationship. It was soon evident that although the physical relationship change could be made rather easily, some factors were causing ambivalence, thereby inhibiting the decision-making process and blocking action. The values analysis construction was presented to the couple, emphasizing the relevance of the five conditions, each of which was then considered separately:

1. Does the couple have the self-confidence regarding the task confronting them? Answer: Yes. Both partners were intelligent, self-responsible individuals. Both had achieved individual career success and were professionally well established.

Clearly, both had had to make significant decisions and act on them in their professional lives. They also recognized that they would survive physically and emotionally if divorced and agreed that joint custody of the children would actually allow them to be more effective parents. So, the question that remained was: If they have the self-confidence needed to change, what is preventing them from changing?

2. Does the couple perceive values fulfillment in the proposed change? Again, the answer is yes. Exploration of their original marital "contract" indicated an early need by the wife to be taken care of by her husband as her family of origin had done. This dependency stance had since become aversive to her. She perceived divorce as enabling her to pursue and more fully achieve the personal fulfillment the independence in her career had provided her. The husband had made clear his need to be "the head of the household" from his family of origin and sought to maintain a situation in which that need could continue to find satisfaction. His wife's desire for greater personal independence blocked his need. Divorce with potential remarriage to a partner more able to satisfy this need represented a clear values fulfillment. The question that remained was: If they see values fulfillment, why do they not actively pursue change?

3. Does the couple believe they will find values fulfillment, that positive benefits would accrue to them if they made a decision and acted on it? When pressed regarding the quality of their lives apart from each other, both maintained the belief that they would develop the quality of life and find values fulfillment more easily if they ended their marriage. Both were finding such fulfillment only in professional endeavors at present because of their contrasting personal needs. Freedom to pursue more accommodating personal relationships would allow increased personal values fulfillment. The question again became: If they believe that they will achieve values fulfillment by changing their situation, why do they not act to change it?

4. Does the couple perceive the cost of enacting the behavior change, and do the perceived benefits sufficiently outweigh the costs to move them toward the stated values fulfillment? Again, yes. Perceived costs (what would actually be given up in terms of values fulfillment if the behavior change is undertaken) included selling their current residence and having to move, some reduced income, loss of extended in-law family contacts, and guilt for creating a broken home for their children. These costs were perceived as being inevitable and were therefore direct costs of pursuing a divorce. Each of these costs was examined in depth; for example, their guilt resulted from a clear breach of values that led them to believe that "children need both parents present." They did, however, present an understanding that these values were changing and needed to be balanced by the negative effects on the children of remaining unhappy and frequently frustrated with their marriage. The guilt was framed as appropriate, but not as necessarily crippling or debilitating. The question still remained: If they perceive the costs of the behavior change, and the cost/benefit ratio is in favor of the perceived benefits, what is preventing change from occurring?

5. Does the couple perceive the risks of engaging in the desired behavior change, and do the benefits sufficiently outweigh the risks to enable them to move

toward actively pursuing the behavior change? Once more, a clear yes. Risks (values fulfillment that might be blocked, but with a perceived probability of less than 1) were noted as possible loss of children if either decided to seek single custody, and loss of what little satisfaction they had in their marriage if other relationships were unable to produce greater satisfaction. The loss of the children was unlikely because both agreed on joint custody. Because their present satisfaction in their marriage was so low, it was not a very powerful deterrent to action. The question that remained was: If they perceive the risks of engaging in the behavior change and the risk/benefit ratio is in favor of the perceived benefits, why is no change actively being pursued?

The values analysis as undertaken and completed indicated that barriers to movement were not sufficient to deter the couple from taking the desired action. Yet ambivalence still prevailed. The therapist considered the possibility or probability that, although the five conditions were satisfied on an intellectual level in the present situation, perhaps one or both of them were not satisfied at a subconscious level. A review of the process with the couple again proved that this was the case. Condition 4 represented a sustained and strongly held value about family life. Both partners had long ago learned and continually had been other- and self-reinforced in the belief that "children need two parents." Thus, only two options were being considered with regard to parenting: immediate presence as equaling love and caring, and nonimmediate presence through divorce as equaling rejection.

Identifying these beliefs and the early learning experiences that led to their formation did not result in instantaneous resolution of the couple's ambivalence. However, it did lead to an agreement to seek resolution in this area through therapy efforts that ultimately led to satisfaction of this fourth condition and the originally desired behavior change—divorce.

One notable source of possible variance for the values equation is the extent to which it is uniformly applicable across cultures. N. R. Hill and Crews (2005) observed that, in many instances, culturally based values are not equivalent, even to the extent of tolerating cost and risk to such issues as personal improvement or even personal safety. These authors have noted "Different cultural groups espouse different values and perceptions related to what is healthy and normal. . . . Failure to attend to the cultural context creates the possibility of misdiagnosis and inappropriate conceptualization of the clinical issue" (p. 179). Similarly, ambivalence may be reflective of cultural preferences for the pace of change rather than resistance to the change itself. In an era of managed mental health care, the rapidity of change expressed as an institutional value could even be perceived as oppression toward conformity, possibly casting the issue as one of cultural pride in the face of repression rather than therapeutic resistance or indifference.

As a different expression of culturally based ambivalence, Western culture tends to promote expectations of "fast service with minimal inconvenience." Some have even suggested the market for on-line forms of therapy has been bolstered by such an ideology. Thus, clients' ambivalence could be related to their inconvenience and a methodical approach to change as an aspect of "value fulfillment" rather than deeper psychological issues. As with most value-related concerns, the values associated with client ambivalence can be complex.

QUESTION 5	*Professional Advertising*

I am moving from my position in a publicly funded agency to pursue an independent practice as a marriage and family therapist. I know that in the past advertising by the professions was discouraged, but today it is acceptable with conditions. I recognize the importance of advertising in building and maintaining my practice and I am concerned about proceeding appropriately. Are there issues relative to advertising my practice that I should be particularly aware of?

Response

Almost all companies and individuals who provide a product or service to the public advertise their goods and services. Traditionally, however, most professions have severely restricted their members with regard to advertising. The notion behind such restrictions was that professionals are devoted to public service rather than making money. Thus, the prevailing thought was that advertising would change the image of a profession and undermine public confidence in professionals. Yet because advertising is the standard means by which consumers learn about available services and products, such restrictions tended to prevent average citizens from having equal access to professional help (Bayles, 1981).

In 1977, the Supreme Court declared that the "ban on advertising" promoted by professional organizations was restraint of trade. The practice of a profession such as medicine, dentistry, accounting, psychology, and marriage and family therapy is considered a business as well as a profession and is, therefore, subject to the same regulation as other businesses (Bruce, 1990). In an effort to come to terms with these new realities about professional advertising, the AAMFT initially developed its Standards on Public Information and Advertising (American Association for Marriage and Family Therapy, 1982). The 1985 and subsequent revisions of the *AAMFT Code of Ethics* have incorporated a specific principle addressing "Advertising." Principle 8—Advertising (American Association for Marriage and Family Therapy, 2001) is shown in Figure 12–1.

In 1988, the AAMFT retained the George Alban Company of San Jose, California, to coordinate all orders for the AAMFT trademark (name and logo) and trademark (name only) in telephone directories (i.e., the *Yellow Pages*) in the United States and Canada. This arrangement was continued until 1998 and ensured that only authorized Clinical Members of the association advertised under the AAMFT name and logo and did so in a manner consistent with its ethical principles. This practice also gave all eligible members of the association equal access to participate in advertising at a cost no more than that typically charged by representatives of local directories. In 1998, a new AAMFT Clinical Member logo, shown in Figure 12–2, was issued along with guidelines for its use (American Association for Marriage and Family Therapy, 1998). The new clinical logo program replaced the George Alban Company program and allowed Clinical Members of AAMFT more flexibility.

With regard to newspaper or similar media advertising, two popular formats for mental health services are the announcement advertisement and the public service message (Kissell, 1983). Figures 12–3 and 12–4, respectively, illustrate an announcement advertisement and public service message.

FIGURE 12–1   Principle 8. Advertising

---

8. Advertising

Marriage and family therapists engage in appropriate informational activities, including those that enable the public, referral sources, or others to choose professional services on an informed basis.

8.1 Marriage and family therapists accurately represent their competencies, education, training, and experience relevant to their practice of marriage and family therapy.

8.2 Marriage and family therapists ensure that advertisements and publications in any media (such as directories, announcements, business cards, newspapers, radio, television, Internet, and facsimiles) convey information that is necessary for the public to make an appropriate selection of professional services. Information could include: (a) office information, such as name, address, telephone number, credit card acceptability, fees, languages spoken, and office hours; (b) qualifying clinical degree (see subprinciple 8.5); (c) other earned degrees (see subprinciple 8.5) and state or provincial licensures and/or certifications; (d) AAMFT clinical member status; and (e) description of practice.

8.3 Marriage and family therapists do not use names that could mislead the public concerning the identity, responsibility, source, and status of those practicing under that name, and do not hold themselves out as being partners or associates of a firm if they are not.

8.4 Marriage and family therapists do not use any professional identification (such as a business card, office sign, letterhead, Internet, or telephone or association directory listing) if it includes a statement or claim that is false, fraudulent, misleading, or deceptive.

8.5 In representing their educational qualifications, marriage and family therapists list and claim as evidence only those earned degrees: (a) from institutions accredited by regional accreditation sources recognized by the United States Department of Education, (b) from institutions recognized by states or provinces that license or certify marriage and family therapists, or (c) from equivalent foreign institutions.

8.6 Marriage and family therapists correct, wherever possible, false, misleading, or inaccurate information and representations made by others concerning the therapist's qualifications, services, or products.

8.7 Marriage and family therapists make certain that the qualifications of their employees or supervisees are represented in a manner that is not false, misleading, or deceptive.

8.8 Marriage and family therapists do not represent themselves as providing specialized service unless they have the appropriate education, training, or supervised experience.

Note. From *AAMFT Code of Ethics.* AAMFT can make further revision at any time, as the Association deems necessary. Reprinted from the *AAMFT Code of Ethics,* Copyright 2001, American Association for Marriage and Family Therapy. Reprinted with permission.

As presented, the *AAMFT's Code of Ethics* on advertising provides broad guidelines for marriage and family therapists. These guidelines indicate what AAMFT members should and should not do. The following simplified checklist incorporates major aspects of Principle 8 into additional elements to which practitioners should attend (Ridgewood Financial Institute, Inc., 1984):

- Only facts, not opinions, should be stated. Facts represented should obviously be truthful, but also, their accurate meanings should be easily understood by the average layperson.

FIGURE 12–2 Logos of the American Association of Marriage and Family Therapy: Corporate Logos (left and center) and Member Logo (right)

Note. From *AAMFT Code of Ethics,* Copyright 1998, American Association for Marriage and Family Therapy. Reprinted with permission.

- Past performance results should be avoided. It is almost impossible through advertising media to adequately explain all the relevant and important variables.
- There should be no guarantees about the outcomes of therapy. Even the best of therapeutic services are ultimately uncertain, and thus explicit or implicit guarantees cannot be assured.
- Be cautious about appeals based on fear. The use of brash or extravagant statements in seeking business could mislead and potentially harm laypersons, particularly those who are emotionally vulnerable.
- Fee information demands special care. It is very difficult to adequately provide complete and accurate enough information through advertising sources to avoid misleading, if not deceiving, an uninformed layperson. If a set fee is advertised for a special service, it obviously should be strictly adhered to.
- Do not use misleading names, titles, or practice descriptors. Any information that could give an erroneous impression about identity, responsibilities, status, or improperly imply a link to any group should be scrupulously avoided.

To offer further response to Question 5, we offer two relevant case examples and their accompanying analysis using Principle 8 of the *AAMFT Code of Ethics* (American

FIGURE 12–3 An Announcement Advertisement

> Jane Krandell, Ph.D.
>
> Announces the opening of her office for the practice of marriage and family therapy. I am particularly interested in providing consultation and treatment services to couples and families where substance abuse is a concern.
>
> Saturday and evening hours. 1st Avenue, Ocala, Florida 32217, 369–4390.

Note. From *Private Practice for the Mental Health Clinician* (unpaged), by S. Kissel, 1983, Gaithersburg, MD: Aspen Publishers. Copyright 1983 by Aspen Publishers. Adapted by permission.

FIGURE 12–4   A Public Service Message

Views on Family Health

By Jane Krandell, Ph.D.

FACTS ABOUT CHILDREN'S EMOTIONAL PROBLEMS

Emotional problems, unlike certain physical ailments, may take years to develop to the point where symptoms cause concern and worry to the individual. The symptoms are indicators of too-heavy burdens, stresses, and conflicts. What are some of these signs for children? Mental health experts agree that the following are *possible* danger signals:

- Prolonged periods of unhappiness without apparent cause.
- Refusal to accept school or parental authority.
- Persistent avoidance of school.
- Excessive fears which are upsetting and interfere with normal functioning.
- Poor achievement in school subjects.
- Returning to activities associated with infancy, such as frequent (and not occasional) bedwetting, soiling, head-banging, thumb sucking, and little ability to tolerate frustration.

If too many of these signals are present, a consultation with your family physician, clergy person, school counselor, or a mental health expert such as a marriage and family therapist may be helpful.

A public service message with the aim of promoting more satisfying family home environments from the office of Jane Krandell, Ph.D., Marriage and Family Therapist, 1st Avenue, Ocala, Florida 32217.

Phone: 369-4390

Note. From *Private Practice for the Mental Health Clinician* (unpaged), by S. Kissel, 1983, Gaithersburg, MD: Aspen Publishers. Copyright 1983 by Aspen Publishers. Adapted by permission.

Association for Marriage and Family Therapy, 2001). For the first case example, we note the following:

> A marriage and family therapist joining a private partnership relocated from another state. The local licensing regulations required an endorsement of the therapist's out-of-state license by the state's Department of Professional Regulation. The therapist allowed the partner to place an advertisement in the telephone book and send out announcements indicating licensure as a marriage and family therapist before completion of the endorsement process.

Both the therapist and partner violated ethical principles in this case. The therapist's approval of the premature telephone book advertisement and announcements represented a direct violation of Subprinciples 8.1, 8.4, 8.6, and 8.7. The therapist not only sanctioned an inaccurate representation of present licensure status but also made no attempt to correct the inaccurate information being disseminated by the partner when the partner presented intentions to do so. The partner's actions represented a particularly flagrant violation of Subprinciple 8.7 in knowingly misrepresenting the qualifications of the therapist. Impatience preempted professionally ethical practice in this instance. For the second case example, we offer the following:

> An announcement was mailed out by two partners in independent practice. The brochure described the types of services available, including marriage and family therapy and educational diagnostic services. No information indicating any distinction between the partners was included, although only one had training and licensure as a marriage and family therapist. The other, a school psychologist, had training and relevant licensure in educational diagnosis.

The brochure in this case violated Subprinciples 8.1, 8.2, and 8.4, because it misled the public in implying the marriage and family therapist was qualified to offer educational diagnostic services and the school psychologist was competent to offer marriage and family therapy services.

The AAMFT Code of Ethics provides extensive information about advertising considerations, but marriage and family therapists also should be vigilant in examining and incorporating any restrictions or requirements deriving from their licensure. For example, if a statute or administrative code concerning state licensure indicates that one may advertise only a "specialty" or "specialization" in a particularly modality or format (e.g., custody evaluations, play therapy, etc.) based on recognition by the licensing agency, the licensee could inadvertently come to be in violation of a code with an advertisement listing specializations that have not been validated by the licensure board or agency. This issue is based on legality rather than competence. If a licensee has the clinical competence to *practice* a unique specialty but is not legally authorized to *advertise* that specialty without securing the proper sanction by the licensure authority, she or he may encounter problems. This circumstance becomes even more complicated for those with multiple licenses.

R. S. Leslie (2004) observed that advertising specialty expertise actually may serve to raise the standard of due care to which a licensed marriage and family therapist is held, thus increasing one's vulnerability for legal suit. Even the use of the phrase "practice limited to" could be interpreted as an indirect means of claiming specialty skills. Leslie (2004) also noted that marriage and family therapists should attend closely to other aspects of codified restriction in statutes or licensure regulations concerning public representation and advertisement. For example, the use of the generic term "psychotherapy" or "psychotherapist" may be inappropriate or illegal, depending on the laws and regulations for a licensure state. He concluded by noting that no exhaustive list exists to specify all information that should be included or excluded in an advertisement. In situations of uncertainty, securing legal counsel or a consultation with the licensure board or agency would be wise.

As a final matter, the professional layer of values associated with customary practices offers some precedent for the tastefulness of advertising. For example, an e-therapist employing "pop-up" advertising represents marriage and family therapy in an unprofessional or even amateurish manner. Soliciting former clients for testimonials is both exploitive and pandering. Classified ads, "weekend specials," or unique rates are demeaning and undignified. Marriage and family therapists should realize that, in many ways, the advertisement of *their* practice serves as an advertisement of the *field*. Our comments on this question have addressed issues related to advertising a professional practice to sustain its success. The following question concerns instances of interruption of one's practice as a marriage and family therapist.

QUESTION 6	*Practice Interruptions*

I recently established an independent practice as a marriage and family therapist and suddenly found myself having to undergo an operation followed by a three-week hospital recovery stay. This significant interruption in my practice caught me completely off guard. Are there any suggested professional guidelines for handling such unexpected circumstances?

Response

Any absence, even one created by responding to another client's emergency, may appear to some clients as insufficient professional "caring," or at the extreme, as abandonment. No one can control all aspects of their life. Emergencies and unanticipated circumstances inevitably arise. As professional mental health providers, marriage and family therapists should plan for these exigencies. Additionally, marriage and family therapists also should recognize the importance of maintaining personal wellness in conjunction with enhancing professional development and plan for expected interruptions in providing therapeutic services such as vacations and travel to continuing education activities.

Bennett et al. (1990) recommended strategies to prepare for therapeutic interruptions, both emergencies and longer-term absences.

Planning for Emergencies

1. Arrange for another marriage and family therapist to stand in (as appropriate) during emergency situations.
2. Be sure that a substitute is fully qualified both in training and awareness of the special needs of clients he or she may be called on to see to deliver the necessary services.
3. Fully inform clients about how emergencies are handled as part of their orientation to therapy. Obtain clients' written consent to provide information to anyone who might serve as a substitute therapist in an emergency. This consent is best gained at the onset of therapy in the form of a general release covering emergencies.
4. Discuss with clients the potential for emergencies in their lives as well as in the therapist's life. Agree on provisions for emergencies that clients may experience (e.g., what number/whom to telephone).
5. Periodically provide a reminder (e.g., verbal, or printed on an appointment card) of emergency policy.

Planning for Longer-Term Absences

1. Arrange for coverage by another marriage and family therapist who is experienced in areas pertinent to the needs of clients he or she may see. Adequately orient this therapist to these cases.
2. Prepare clients before prolonged absences. Within reason, explain the absence and identify how long it will probably last.

3. Explain to clients the procedures they should follow during the absence.
4. On returning, meet with the substitute therapist and fully address any contacts he or she had with clients.
5. Address any relevant matters having occurred with the substitute therapist with clients immediately on reinitiating sessions with them.

Some reasons for emergencies and absences can be positive ones for the marriage and family therapist (e.g., childbirth, vacation, etc.). However, no matter how positive for the therapist, the consequence of an interruption in therapy can be a painful and upsetting experience for some clients, either before a planned absence or upon returning from an emergency. By contrast, if the emergency or absence is the result of a positive life event, some clients may view the experience as uplifting, which could potentially enhance the therapeutic process. For those clients who are upset, be prepared for their unhappiness and work to encourage discussion of the issue in a constructive context within therapy (Bennett et al., 1990).

Absences Due to Impairment or Incapacitation

Our discussion of the interrelated nature of competence and due care in Chapter 3 concerned the *ability* of the therapist to provide services to clients as well as the *obligations* to utilize that ability within the standard of due care and practice associated with the profession (see Figure 3-1, p. 62). In tandem, these dual and complementary components of professionalism are minimal expectations for any therapist agreeing to serve individuals, couples, or families.

As previously discussed in Chapter 3, however, instances of impairment or incapacitation may occur, chronically or acutely, that may interrupt the practice of a marriage and family therapist. The suggestions noted earlier in this section related to emergencies and long-term absences are certainly applicable to such circumstances. However, an emergency interruption of practice for situations such as life transitions (e.g., births, deaths, etc.) or vacations differs appreciably from a situation involving impairment or incapacitation in one glaring way: The therapist's competence or capacity for due care may be in question. In this respect, the therapist must take the significant step of evaluating his or her ability to provide competent due care to clients.

For example, a therapist who has addressed a chemical addiction through an inpatient stay, followed by an intensive out-patient program, cannot reasonable expect to return to practice without establishing appropriate oversight for the protection of his or her clients. Such oversight may include supervision, co-therapy, regular case consultation and review, or similar procedures. Some therapists in this situation may also make a decision to refer clients presenting with addiction-related concerns. As a final point, therapists returning to their practices under such circumstances should consider the possibility of revealing the nature of their absence to their clients as a matter of full disclosure. In licensure states with impairment programs, such actions may be mandatory prior to returning to licensed practice.

Discontinuing a Practice

As with most professionals, marriage and family therapists often reach a point in their careers when they decide to discontinue their professional practice. Whether for health reasons, a new career path, or a preferred change of pace and lifestyle, the decision to close an independent practice or leave a group practice is one made by many practitioners.

Discontinuing a practice in a mental health profession is quite different from closing other businesses. Clients are not simply consumers or customers; they are persons with whom therapists have shared intimate and confidential details. Though business-related details are an element of therapy practices, marriage and family therapists do not deal in commodities or products; they deal in relationships. Consequently, discontinuing a practice is not a simple matter of "selling a business" to another practitioner.

Think back to our discussion of informed consent in Chapter 3. In that discussion, we noted the importance of preparing clients for the obstacles and stresses that could reasonably be anticipated throughout the course of therapy. In this way, clients can know the risks as well as the potential benefits of therapy prior to or at the beginning of therapy. This customary approach is consistent with the *AAMFT Code of Ethics* (2001) regarding client consent. A decision to discontinue a practice is neither an emergency nor a planned long-term absence interrupting service to clients. Rather, it is a conclusion and, just like a pending absence or even a referral to another practitioner, it represents an opportunity to demonstrate care to clients as well as professionalism on behalf of peers. This is not to say that clients must consent to the retirement or departure of a therapist. However, clients should have notice and therapists should reasonably anticipate possible obstacles or concerns in the course of discontinuing a practice. Some customary professional procedures for discontinuing a practice might involve the following:

1. Provide reasonable notice to current clients about the closure, including a referral to a qualified colleague. Referral considerations could also involve exchange of confidential records.
2. Give attention to storage of client records to maintain confidentiality as well as to gain access in the event of requests for information. This concern is particularly important if one is leaving a group practice rather than an independent practice, since colleagues' files are mingled and the files of the retiring or departing colleague may easily be overlooked.
3. Devote similar attentiveness to electronic records and other confidential materials.
4. Give formal notification of the pending closure to other agencies, local colleagues, and managed care personnel. This may be done in a public announcement as well as in a formal letter.
5. In using public notices to announce one's pending retirement/departure, therapists should be prepared for the possibility of inquiries or requests from former clients regarding records, referrals, or related issues.
6. In group practices, the retiring/departing therapist may have developed copyright materials or software that should be addressed as a business asset. As such, care should be taken not to interrupt the therapy of clients served by those remaining in the practice through actions such as removing materials, deleting software, or similar measures.
7. Consider the logistics of ending one's professional status also. Professional memberships may need attention (particularly if a "retiree rate" is available). Address the possible need to discontinue liability insurance. If it is available as an option, consider inactivating one's licensure rather than simply allowing the license to expire, particularly if returning to licensure status at a later time would

require requalifying under current regulations. Other logistical concerns may include concluding promised reports for a professional committee, informing peers in a divisional interest group of the planned departure, or requesting replacement on a task force.

The analogy to therapy is comparable: For successful therapy, one must begin well; for successful termination, one must conclude well. Thus, for a marriage and family therapist planning to discontinue practice, intentionality is important for a successful transition.

Other Related Items

In instances of an interruption in practice, whether for an emergency, a planned long-term hiatus, or a departure from the profession, our first concern is for the welfare of clients, both in terms of continued care and protection. Even short-term practice interruptions have implications for those other than clients, however.

As we discussed in Chapter 11, a common procedure in the licensure process is supervised postgraduate practice under the supervision of an experienced licensee. In such arrangements, most prelicensed therapists have an "associate" or similar designation, signifying the licensure board or agency has placed the supervisor in a gatekeeper role for consumer oversight. Such a status is significant in many ways, not the least of which is to ensure due care and competence on the part of the supervisee. In essence, the associate is "practicing off the license" of the supervisor. In instances of even emergency interruptions to practice, interruptions to supervision and oversight may occur. The ultimate jeopardy for such situations concerns client care, although attention to the concerns of the associate licensee is also highly compelling. In planned interruptions, the supervisor must be diligent in making arrangements with colleagues, other supervisors, and possibly even the licensure board or agency to ensure that all issues are addressed appropriately. In a similar manner, therapists with Approved Supervisor status with AAMFT may be serving as mentors or overseers for supervisors-in-training and should attend to their overseer duties prior to an anticipated interruption or as soon as possible in an emergency interruption.

Other examples of practice interruptions may not be related to the actions of the therapist per se, but the actions of others. For example, interruption in service based on a managed care mental health agency stipulation about a maximum number of therapy sessions represents an interruption in therapy. Although this may be more of a clinical issue than a professional issue, the management of the client's case, the procedures of interaction with the agency, and the methods of re-engaging the client for therapy are all professional considerations for the therapist.

A more difficult circumstance of practice disruption attributable to the actions of others is the death of a professional colleague in a group practice. In such instances, great care must be devoted to disclosing this event to current clients, and deliberate planning should be undertaken to address requests from former clients, affiliated agencies (e.g., insurance companies, etc.), official agencies or agents (e.g., courts, probation officers, etc.), and other stakeholders. In situations of the death of a local colleague who is not part of a group practice, local peers would be well advised to secure the advice of legal counsel for suggestions about how they can assist clients and others without inadvertently violating confidentiality. The added complexity of family members requesting access to the office or practice site of the deceased should be addressed with sensitivity tempered by attention to confidentiality. Schwitzgebel and Schwitzegebel (1980) even noted that some practitioners will establish a "professional will" to delineate issues such as how specific clients should be contacted and even those who should be advised against attending a funeral or memorial service.

In conclusion, the realities of interrupting or concluding a therapy practice are of nearly equal, though different, importance as those of sustaining a therapy practice. Our next question addresses business concerns related to the practice of marriage and family therapy.

QUESTION 7 *Business-Oriented Details*

Since entering independent practice as a marriage and family therapist, I have become attuned to the ongoing attention needed to business-oriented details. A major example and area of concern in this regard has been clients who have fallen behind in their payments of fees and/or who have terminated therapy and failed to pay for those services already rendered. The typical business often resolves such situations by either absorbing the losses, by taking action against the debtor through a collection agency, or by using other legal alternatives such as obtaining an attorney to attempt collection or bring suit. But as a marriage and family therapist, a professional person with whom clients have entered a complex confidential relationship, should I consider myself a "typical creditor" who possesses these options for action?

Response

Obviously, the professional practice of marriage and family therapy requires attention to business-oriented details if the therapist is to survive financially. Because of the professional nature of the "business," however, extraordinary ethical and legal considerations must be considered, particularly with regard to employing external services to collect delinquent accounts.

Ethically, the question involves deciding if the referral of a delinquent account to a collection service constitutes a breach of confidentiality. The *AAMFT Code of Ethics* (American Association for Marriage and Family Therapy, 2001) states the following regarding confidentiality:

> Marriage and family therapists have unique confidentiality concerns because the client in a therapeutic relationship may be more than one person. Therapists respect and guard confidences of each individual client.

More specifically, however, the *AAMFT Code of Ethics* offers the following from Subprinciple 7.3:

> Marriage and family therapists give reasonable notice to clients with unpaid balances of their intent to seek collection by agency or legal recourse. When such action is taken, therapists will not disclose clinical information.

An initial question emerges as to whether the referral of a client's name to a collection service may be interpreted as a breach of confidence. One could readily dispute the contention that disclosing a client's name (and other relevant information such as address and phone number) constitutes a betrayal of confidences conveyed in the clinical relationship. Traditionally, however, there has been a consensus that clients have control over who knows that they have sought therapy (Pressman, 1979). Thus, clients' names could be viewed as a protected confidence of the therapeutic relationship.

Fortunately, within the *AAMFT Code of Ethics*, using a collection agency clearly may be ethical if the therapist, before the initiation of therapy, provides the client with full knowledge of the financial conditions of the therapeutic relationship. The client can then decide from the outset whether or not to enter therapy under these conditions.

Informed consent of clients at the beginning of therapy would therefore seem to settle any possible ethical concerns. If a client had not been properly informed of pertinent financial conditions, a warning that an account may be released (e.g., after the therapy had begun and a debt was incurred) could be a paper tiger and, if acted on, an ethical violation. In other words, warning clients that they had better pay their bills or else a collection service will be brought in would be unethical if the therapist lacked consent to release the relevant information from the outset of therapy.

The release of information by marriage and family therapists to a collection service is quite different from the release of material to facilitate a third-party payment. In the case of third-party payments, clients usually are aware of the information that will be released, because most will bring claim forms to the therapist or will have to sign forms so that reimbursement can be directed to the therapist. In most cases, clients encourage such a release of information to defray personal financial costs. However, clients still must be provided with adequate information to allow informed consent on their behalf.

Although some of the possible ethical ramifications of employing an external collection service may be arguable, much clearer consequences for marriage and family therapists are evident in considering potential legal vulnerability. A legal complaint against a marriage and family therapist may result from a fee dispute. If harassment by collection agencies retained by a marriage and family therapist occurs, the legal situation may become especially troublesome. Bennett et al. (1990) stated that use of a collection agency increases the risk of malpractice litigation, particularly if clients fail to pay for services they felt were unsatisfactory, unhelpful, or incompetent.

Clients terminate therapy and leave unpaid bills for numerous reasons. Some clients may be financially overextended and may place greater priority on the payment of other accounts. Others may view the therapy efforts as not having been helpful, thus negating their financial obligation. Such clients may view the use of a collection service as harassment even when they gave their informed consent at the onset of therapy, and attempts to obtain payment from such clients could result in their bringing suit against the therapist. The therapist may be falsely accused of a variety of charges, some of which may result in a difficult legal defense. Legal expert Cohen (1979) explicitly suggested, "One thing doctors should never do, however, is routinely turn accounts over to collection agencies. Collection agencies can be coarse in their treatment of patients, and they might push patients thinking about litigation into actually contacting an attorney" (p. 273).

Again, Bennett et al. (1990) affirmed Cohen's admonition and suggest attempting to negotiate a payment plan or some such strategy, and suggested that using a collection agency should only be considered as a last resort.

Two significant developments have emerged since these observations were offered by Cohen (1979) and Bennett et al. (1990): (a) the phenomenal increase in the use of technology for storage and retrieval of personal and confidential information, and (b) the implementation of the Health Insurance Portability and Accountability Act (HIPAA) of 1996. The enhanced capability of third parties (e.g., collection agencies) to retrieve stored electronic data or to contact persons with delinquent accounts has created opportunities for intrusion with the possibility of unintended effects for both clients and therapists. One can only imagine the possible consequences for former clients who are bombarded multiple times daily with e-mail messages from a collection agency concerning unpaid balances with a practicing marriage and family therapist. What if such contacts were sent to workplaces where they can be accessed by others? A host of traumas is possible if electronic means such as these are used by an agency attempting to secure unpaid fees. Additionally, HIPAA legislation was introduced specifically to address the electronic storage *and distribution* of confidential medical and related client information. The potential implications of an unintended federal offense traceable to the initiative of a therapist are obvious. Again, the *AAMFT Code of Ethics* is specific about the prohibition of the release of "clinical" information to collection agencies.

The ultimate pragmatic argument may be that a marriage and family therapist has as much right as any other businessperson to take action against debtors. Such an argument notes that clients enter an implied contract at the outset of therapy; services have a price, and clients are obligated to pay for services rendered. Taken alone, this argument is undeniably true, yet it may only hold true in settings other than therapy.

Faustman (1982) recommended that the best means of avoiding the potential ethical and legal problems created by resorting to collection services is to use billing strategies that prevent delinquent payments. He proposed requiring payment at the time of the visit, a practice common among other professionals (e.g., physicians, dentists). The acceptance of credit cards also provides immediate payment. Credit card receipts can be filled out so the confidential nature of clients' therapeutic status is ensured (e.g., listing therapy as "services rendered" and avoiding information relating to the practice of marriage and family therapy). Using extended payment plans in cases of financial hardship offers another avenue to avoid nonpayment of fees. Such procedures are also not uncommon in instances of clients and care providers (i.e., therapists) who deal with managed mental health care agencies. In many ways, these approaches have evolved into customary practices for marriage and family therapy as well as other mental health-related professions.

In summary, although external collection services constitute one source of debt collection, a therapist must consider the potential legal risks and proceed with extreme caution when pursuing financial action against clients, particularly those who might have conveyed dissatisfaction regarding the quality or nature of therapy. When such action is taken, clients should have been properly informed at the start of therapy that external collection services are employed by the therapist when necessary and subsequently offered their informed consent to continue in therapy given this caveat.

Independent Practice in a Rural Area

I am presently employed in an urban community mental health center and I am considering moving to a small community that has no marriage and family therapist in residence. My training and experiences have been in more urban settings. What can I expect in developing an independent practice in a small town?

Response

Information about independent mental health providers in small communities is scarce. The majority of potentially relevant professional literature has focused on practitioners employed by community mental health centers in rural areas. However, many issues regarding the independent practice of marriage and family therapy in small communities do bear a strong resemblance to those raised by rural community mental health workers, and a review of the professional literature in this area may prove fruitful.

Sobel (1984) raised a number of professional issues considered relevant to small-town practice from the viewpoint of a psychologist. These same issues are applicable to a marriage and family therapist seeking a similar situation and are summarized in the following paragraphs.

Generalist vs. Specialist

Urban-based practices allow marriage and family therapists to specialize, because other therapists are available to deliver a full complement of services to the population. Small-town practice does not typically support specialization. For example, consider a therapist who specializes in marital therapy practicing in a community that sees adolescent drug abuse as its major mental health problem. Although the marriage and family therapist may perceive adolescent drug abuse as primarily precipitated by dysfunctional marital relationships of parents, centering a practice on marital therapy would probably fail because the community's defined need is not being met. If the therapist were to initially establish a practice to work with adolescent drug abuse and demonstrate success to the community, however, the therapist's credibility would increase, and he or she could bring greater attention to marital dyads and develop a more direct demand for such services.

Previous discussions in our text have cautioned about the importance of marriage and family therapists practicing within the scope of their competence. Ethical as well as legal ramifications could emerge from a *beneficent* and *nonmaleficent* urge to assist troubled clients in an underserved rural setting by attempting to employ techniques or address presenting problems for which the therapist is unskilled. Certainly, the concept of due care is related to such a decision. However, J. K. Miller (2005) observed that a delicate balance exists between competency and innovation. Additionally, as we noted in Chapter 11, one's competence can grow stale without continued development. Though rural settings may have a scarcity of options for referral, reasonable extensions of the skills of a therapist are not a professional novelty. The key to such efforts, whether in rural or urban settings, is adequate supervision and training, which may be accessible via graduate study, workshops, or even technology.

Community Agencies and Organizations

Involvement with community agencies and organizations is important for any independent practitioner, particularly from the standpoint of generating and maintaining referral sources. In a small-town setting, a marriage and family therapist will need to pursue an extraordinary involvement. Although one does not usually perceive independent practitioners as taking a major role in community education, the therapist in a smaller community must give consideration to such a role. Residents need to be educated about the identification of relevant problems and the availability of treatment resources. Thus, involvements with religious, professional, and social organizations become a regular part of the therapist's practice, though it is usually on a pro bono basis. Work within the schools is a particularly valuable service and source of referrals.

We would also remind readers of our discussion in Chapter 6 concerning multiple relationships on the part of marriage and family therapist. Immersing oneself into a small rural community creates wonderful opportunities for a marriage and family therapist. However, care should also be taken to balance such opportunities with the necessity for professional boundaries.

Professional Impact on Personal Privacy

The marriage and family therapist in a small town will probably live in the community. Thus, unlike in a larger urban setting, some personal privacy is lost. The expectations of neighbors as well as other community people may call for the therapist to maintain a "professional image" at all times so that his or her credibility and practice do not suffer. Sensitivity to the community's standards is critical. In many ways, local customs and expectations, regardless of how unfair they may be for a professional manner, reflect the cultural norms of the community. An obvious benefit is the esteem afforded the therapist.

Whether as an independent practitioner or an employee in a rural mental health agency, a significant professional issue is the careful and thorough orientation of the professional support staff affiliated with one's practice. Such concerns are uniformly important regardless of whether a therapist practices in an urban or rural setting, but the likelihood of practice personnel being members of the local community means that elements of the "professional image" will also be extended to them. In a manner similar to the marriage and family therapist, balancing community involvement with professional boundaries and confidentiality is a must for support staff in rural settings.

Funding Dilemmas

Small towns are likely to have fewer funding resources than urban communities. The financial resources of residents themselves and the general community revenues that often serve as a source of fees for marriage and family therapists in independent practice will be more limited. Innovative therapeutic practice (e.g., multiple family therapy) as well as innovative business practice (e.g., bartering) may even be considered. However, in such cases, the therapist should take care to respect the guidelines in the *AAMFT Code of Ethics* (2001).

Qualifying as a provider for managed mental health care can sometimes be easier in some rural settings, particularly for federally mandated coverage related to military or governmental benefits. Therapists should examine such options in their initial exploration of possible location to such communities. Additionally, grant support for state or federal projects, sometimes through affiliation with hospitals, schools, or the legal system, also can create options for practitioners willing to partner with outside agencies. Finally, some therapists may consider supplementing their in-office practice with on-line therapy services extending beyond the local community. As we discussed in Chapter 6, special care should be exercised when venturing into this arena.

Professional Isolation

Independent practice can lead to professional isolation. The isolation of the marriage and family therapist is likely to be much greater in a small community than in urban areas. Peer consultation is not readily available. The therapist must rely on personal resources to keep abreast of new developments as well as creatively consider innovative interventions. Again, the use of technology may be particularly beneficial for exchanges with colleagues.

Potentially the most frustrating isolation issue may be the lack of a full complement of mental health services within the community. The therapist often may be confronted with the decision of whether to refuse treatment or to deliver a service that is not the treatment of choice.

Continuing Professional Development

Closely tied to the issue of professional isolation is the increased need for continuing education. Needing to assume more of a generalist role calls for working with a wide diversity of presenting problems. To be successful, the therapist needs an eclectic orientation to provide the widest breadth of services possible. Thus, continuing education is critical.

Given the paucity of library resources and limited access to conferences, lectures, and seminars, a multifaceted program is recommended. Subscriptions to relevant professional journals and the regular purchase of appropriate books constitute necessary business expenses. However, utilization of on-line resources for formal credits or informal learning has become so commonplace that it verges on being a necessary business expense for contemporary practitioners as well. Attendance at workshops, seminars, and professional meetings must be worked into a therapist's schedule even if significant travel is required. Therapists within a reasonable distance of each other, such as a 2- to 3-hour drive, might arrange monthly or bimonthly meetings to discuss professional issues and topics to maintain and enhance clinical skills. Such an arrangement using a consortium model was discussed in Chapter 11.

Hovestadt, Fenell, and Canfield (2002) reported that six major characteristics were evident when examining effective MFT service providers in rural mental health settings. These six characteristics were: (a) effective skills in marriage and family therapy (e.g., clinical flexibility, varied approaches, understanding, professionalism, etc.); (b) rural community understanding, appreciation, and participation; (c) personal characteristics and flexibility (e.g., use of home-based as well as office-based therapy, use of natural helpers and kin, ability to cope with out-of-office social contacts with clients, willingness to be on call, etc.); (d) generalist skills with a nonspecific foundation (i.e., eclectic approach to handling clinical practice); (e) education, training, and experience as an MFT; and (f) utilizing formal and informal community resources. These findings support a view that the practice of marriage and family therapy in rural settings requires certain skills and characteristics that are unique for such locales.

In summary, the decision by a marriage and family therapist to establish an independent practice or affiliate with a mental health center in a rural setting is fraught with benefits and obstacles. As with any practice locale, however, the deliberate and attentive therapist can anticipate some difficulties and respond in an informed manner for others. In many ways, marriage and family therapists practicing in rural settings are under close scrutiny because of their "professional celebrity" status. In our next discussion, we examine the concerns a therapist may face by becoming a public professional figure.

QUESTION 9   *Being a "Public" Marriage and Family Therapist*

As my practice has expanded and my expertise within the community has become more well known, I have received an increasing number of invitations to be interviewed for the newspaper, appear as a guest on radio, and speak at local gatherings. I feel that I have represented myself well as a professional marriage and family therapist. Knowing what I now know, however, I question how prepared a novice therapist might be for such situations. What are the significant concerns one should consider in becoming more visible in media and other public forums?

Response

The importance of being well prepared if one is to assume the role of a "public" marriage and family therapist has been strongly asserted within the professional literature. For example, Harkaway (1989) proposed that "Therapists should think twice before they decide to feed the talk-show lion" (p. 3). Yet, she further noted that if experienced therapists do not present marriage and family therapy professionally to the public, the task will be left to less-experienced novices, who are likely to be less well suited to the task.

Bennett et al. (1990) offered a list of suggestions for being a "public" psychologist. Adaptations of these suggestions are offered here for being a "public" marriage and family therapist:

1. All "advice" should be scientifically valid.
2. Be especially sensitive to the possibility that information provided to consumers may be misunderstood or misused. Do not assume that the audience will either understand or take the time to understand what is being said.
3. Avoid offering advice or information in any area in which your training or experience are insufficient.
4. Clearly state the limitations of any information provided.
5. Always prepare carefully for live presentations. Recognize that nervousness, the pressures of a radically different environment, the presence of an audience, and other factors can contribute to confusion and possible misstatements. Become familiar with the presentation, interview, or broadcast setting in advance, if at all possible.

6. During live presentations, especially those involving questions and answers, take time to think before speaking. Avoid becoming emotional when faced with conflict or contentious issues.

7. Avoid representing theory as fact or beliefs held by some marriage and family therapists as being held by the profession as a whole. Be objective with regard to controversial topics, or provide the names of colleagues who can speak to the other side of the issue.

8. Be fully aware of what is being said as well as how it is being said. Define terms and use lay language to enhance audience understanding.

9. If documents or films are being produced from the presentation, be clear on editing policies and the opportunity to participate in that process.

10. Be especially sensitive to the limitations of evaluating and providing appropriate diagnoses to consumers by radio, television, telephone, or newspaper articles and books. Always consider the implications of any instructions or advice offered without adequate rehearsal and follow-up.

11. Screen callers and media participants to protect those who should not have such exposure. Develop and maintain referral procedures to qualified professionals.

In addition to these items, marriage and family therapists engaged in public discourses should carefully scrutinize the purpose of any media presentation they are invited to make, when and how it will be presented, and the kind of audience that will be addressed. As therapists, we are inclined to think in terms of "client" welfare. Participants in media-sponsored events are not "clients," however, and this distinction should be made vividly clear at the outset using a disclaimer or similar statement. Other disclaimer items might include statements clearly indicating that: (a) the purpose of the activity is to educate and inform, (b) care will be taken to retain client confidentiality in any comments offered in the activity, and (c) the activity is not an opportunity to secure a "second opinion" or to second-guess a peer professional.

Requests for public presentations and interviews are quite common for professionals elected or appointed to leadership positions in professional organizations. In such capacities, leaders should remember that their invitation to such events is an opportunity to represent the organization, rather than for personal advancement or promotion. To do otherwise is unprofessional and exploitive of the trust extended to the leader by his or her professional constituency. In advocating for the field of marriage and family therapy, speakers should also take great care not to engage in "turf wars" or professional undercutting of other fields, since such acts only harm the public faith in all professionals.

A speaking opportunity or an interview with a television or newspaper reporter is the more conventional type of public address. However, marriage and family therapists should not underestimate the "public" nature of statements offered in either synchronous or asynchronous forms of on-line media. In an era of instant information, ill-considered remarks in an on-line format can quickly become public information, usually without many of the safeguards or controls one might wish to have in place.

Public marriage and family therapists should learn about the sponsor of any presentation and should never accept any invitation unless the sponsor's reliability and respectability can be ensured. They should assume that their comments are being recorded and may be replayed at a later time. Finally, no matter how much pressure is exerted or the possibility of favorable exposure, marriage and family therapists should only agree to address or speak about issues for which they are well qualified and prepared (Bennett et al., 1990).

QUESTION 10   *Optimally Serving Oneself and One's Clients*

I am presently employed as a marriage and family therapist in a large community mental health center where my caseload consists of an array of distressed and complicated family circumstances. The paperwork alone feels overwhelming most of the time. I'm beginning to question if I can ever work hard enough to keep offering optimal professional services and yet still take care of myself and my own family responsibilities. I am not a perfectionist and I am not prone to overreacting. Still, I have concerns about my own well-being and how, if I am not attentive, I may become jaded, cynical, or simply indifferent.

Response

Several points are relevant to consider in serving oneself as well as one's clients optimally as a marriage and family therapist. First and foremost, it is critical that therapists recognize that the more clients they serve, the greater the potential for stress becomes. Comparatively, family-oriented service providers, such as marriage and family therapists, have a high likelihood of experiencing excessive job stress. As a second issue, it is important to consider one's initial motivation for becoming a marriage and family therapist. Individuals enter the mental health professions for a variety of reasons, some of which are healthier than others (Gladding, 2000). The marriage and family therapist who enters the profession to help others primarily because of unresolved issues in his or her own family of origin or the therapist who has an excessive need to be needed are likely candidates to become overinvolved with client families to the neglect of themselves and their own families.

Guy (1987) noted that the work of being a therapist has the potential for both positive and negative impact on one's family life. On the positive side, marriage and family therapists can become more aware of the importance of their spouses and families in helping them experience meaning and fulfillment in life. They may even take more time to interact with family members because of their increased awareness of the value these persons play in their lives.

On the negative side, marriage and family therapists can feel they have exhausted their emotions after a day at the office, and that they do not have the time or interest to interact meaningfully with their own family members. Consequently, they may retreat into themselves and separate from those who could emotionally and physically nourish them.

Finding a balance between work and personal and family life is critical if marriage and family therapists want to maintain their ability to function optimally, both personally and professionally. "Poor counselor self-care is associated with the potential for ethical breaches, reduced self-monitoring, emotional vulnerability, and impaired judgment (Frame, 1999, p. 110). Thus, it is important to heed the advice of Brock and Barnard (1999):

> Therapists engaged in family-based treatment, particularly those who work with families in acute distress, are well advised to continually attend to their own needs to prevent acute distress. (p. 176)

Ways for marriage and family therapists to achieve a balance between their personal/family and professional life include the following:

1. Have a lifestyle that accurately reflects personal and professional values. All too often, some marriage and family therapists profess values they do not live by. For instance, they may advise families to spend more together time while they themselves live at the office instead of blocking out reasonable time periods for personal and family interactions.
2. Teach and supervise other therapists as a way of serving oneself and the profession. Through teaching and supervising other therapists, understanding and empathy for oneself and one's own circumstances are increased (Kottler, 1990).
3. Confront the source(s) of stress. The source may be anything from one's supervisor to one's caseload. The important point is to investigate the roots of the stressor, not just any manifest symptoms. In such a scenario, marriage and family therapists can change the system through environmental structuring or different personal interactions. It is critical for the therapist to gain greater power over his or her circumstances and not continue feeling victimized or helpless (Kottler, 1990).
4. Look for humor. Although the events that marriage and family therapists face daily are not funny, and are often very serious, there is humor to be found sometime during almost every day. The healing power of small doses of humor can diminish stress considerably (Pittman, 1995).

The graduate curriculum of most any marriage and family therapy program features multiple discussions about the family life cycle. This roadmap offers insight into the developmental stressors and benchmarks encountered by many families. In a similar fashion, the "professional life cycle" of a marriage and family therapist features developmental stressors and benchmarks. We join professional organizations while in school; we complete our graduate studies; we become entry-level associate licensees and ultimately transition into independent licensure; we become professional advocates, sometimes even leaders, in our professional affiliations; we become supervisors and mentors; and we conclude our practices. Throughout this process, attending to our personal wellness is a must.

In our discussion about virtue ethics in Chapter 2, we addressed the distinction between "Who am I?" and "What do I do?" In addressing this issue, Protinsky and Coward (2001) authored an article entitled "Developmental Lessons of Seasoned Marital and Family Therapists: A Qualitative Investigation." They reported, "The most important outcome of this study was identifying the synthesis of personal and professional selves as a highly significant developmental process for experienced MFTs" (p. 381). In accomplishing this outcome, their findings revealed the need for: (a) balancing and self nurturing, and (b) family-of-origin work. These authors specifically indicated that the latter finding "may be a major factor setting MFTs apart from other therapists" (p. 380). This effort seems particularly important in that if much of the vigor for successfully progressing through the "professional life cycle" comes from deriving satisfaction as a marriage and family therapist, guarding against stress and burnout is essential. Otherwise, why choose such a demanding line of work?

There are many ways to promote and maintain optimal personal/family and professional well-being, just as there are many ways that contribute to its deterioration. For some, addressing business details is self-care; for others, personal therapy is self-care; for still others, increased intraprofessional relationships and service is self-care. Marriage and family therapists, regardless of their work setting, must be active in pursuit of wellness. Surrounding oneself with a healthy balance of personal/family and professional activities and intentionally employing coping strategies to deal with stressful events are keys to enjoying one's work and family. As with therapy efforts, it is essential to recognize that mental, physical, familial, and professional health are all processes that require continuous monitoring and occasional modification.

CLOSING THOUGHTS AND A VIEW TO THE HORIZON

As we conclude our text, we note that our efforts have been to examine selected ethical, legal, and professional issues related to the practice of marriage and family therapy. Our intention has been to be neither exhaustive nor definitive in this task. We grounded our discussion with an initial examination of the substantive influence of values and diversity upon the practice dilemmas and decisions faced by therapists, and we have emphasized these influences throughout our discussions. Our focus has been on a mix of classically critical issues (e.g., confidentiality, legal duties, multiple relationships, competence, etc.) and emergent contemporary issues (e.g., technology, HIPAA and related legislation, managed mental health care, being a "public" marriage and family therapist, etc.).

The future for marriage and family therapists likely holds many unanticipated developments. However, we believe that some significant challenges and opportunities are being defined currently and will unfold more fully in the near future. At the risk of suggesting that we can see into the future, we believe the horizon offers a glimpse of developments such as:

1. Greater utilization of technology for therapy purposes.
2. Heightened consumer awareness and legislative success in consumer choice within managed mental health care.
3. Case law decisions concerning AIDS/HIV disclosures as well as parameters for marriage and family therapists involving end-of-life decisions.
4. Evolution and revision of HIPAA and similar governmental regulation to enhance client confidentiality.
5. Professional activism to address licensure issues such as scope of practice, oversight of interstate therapy services via technology, and licensure portability.
6. Careful review of and possible accreditation by COAMFTE for on-line graduate programs.

7. Burgeoning offers for practitioners to outsource practice-related tasks.
8. Even greater emphasis on internationalism in the efforts professional associations such as the AAMFT.
9. Increased attention to the nature of marriage and family therapy with evolving models and frameworks for "marriage" and "family."
10. Heightened awareness of and new avenues for research and intervention involving aging family members with the retirement of "baby boomers" and family dynamics related to military deployment and return.

The field of marriage and family therapy is vibrant yet still developing, holding great promise and opportunity for its practitioners. We encourage your vigilant and careful attention to the various ethical, legal, and professional issues you will face as you pursue your careers.

References

120 Cong. Rec. 27, 36533 (1974).

120 Cong. Rec. 31, 41381 (1974).

Abelson, R., & Nielson, K. (1967). History of ethics. In P. Edwards (Ed.), *The encyclopedia of philosophy: Vol. 3* (pp. 188–223). New York: Macmillan.

Abroms, G. M. (1978). The place of values in psychotherapy. *Journal of Marriage and Family Counseling, 4,* 3–17.

Allen, J., & Curran, J. (1988). Prevention of AIDS and HIV infection: Needs and priorities for epidemiologic research. *American Journal of Public Health, 78,* 381–386.

Alsager v. District Court of Polk County, Iowa, 406 F. Supp. 10. (1975).

American Association for Marriage and Family Therapy. (1982). *Standards on public information and advertising.* Washington, DC: Author.

American Association for Marriage and Family Therapy. (1985). *Master series: James and Mary Ramo.* Washington, DC: Author.

American Association for Marriage and Family Therapy. (1990). *AAMFT membership requirements.* Washington, DC: Author.

American Association for Marriage and Family Therapy. (1992a). *The model marriage and family therapy licensure act.* Washington, DC: Author.

American Association for Marriage and Family Therapy. (1992b). *Procedures for handling ethical matters.* Washington, DC: Author.

American Association for Marriage and Family Therapy. (1997). *Approved supervisor designation: Standards and responsibilities.* Washington, DC: Author.

American Association for Marriage and Family Therapy. (1998, August/September). Guidelines for use of the new AAMFT clinical member logo. *Family Therapy News, 29,* 18–20.

American Association for Marriage and Family Therapy. (1999, April/May). Therapy by e-mail. *Family Therapy News, 29,* 3.

American Association for Marriage and Family Therapy. (2000). AAMFT overview. Retrieved August 14, 2005, from http://www.aamft.org/index.nm.asp

American Association for Marriage and Family Therapy. (2001). *AAMFT code of ethics.* Washington, DC: Author.

American Association for Marriage and Family Therapy. (2005). *AAMFT code of ethics.* Washington, DC: Author. Retrieved March 1, 2005, from http://www.aamft.org/resources/lrmplan/ethics/ethicscode2001.asp

American Association for Marriage and Family Therapy, Supervision Committee. (1999). *Introduction to the approved supervisor designation.* Retrieved December 19, 1999, from http://www.aamft.org/membership/approved%20supervisor/as_app_checklist.asp

American Counseling Association. (2005). *Code of ethics and standards of practice.* Alexandria, VA: Author.

American Psychiatric Association. (1980). *Diagnostic and statistical manual of mental disorders* (3rd ed.). Washington, DC: Author.

American Psychiatric Association. (1987). *Diagnostic and statistical manual of mental disorders* (Rev. 3rd ed.). Washington, DC: Author.

American Psychiatric Association. (2000). *Diagnostic and statistical manual of mental disorders—Text revised* (Rev. 4th ed.). Washington, DC: Author.

American Psychological Association. (1981). *Ethical standards of psychologists* (Rev. ed.). Washington, DC: Author.

American Psychological Association. (1987). *Casebook on ethical principles of psychologists.* Washington, DC: Author.

American Psychological Association (2000). Guidelines for psychotherapy with lesbian, gay, and bisexual clients. *American Psychologist, 55*(2), 1440–1451.

American Psychological Association. (2002). *Ethical principles of psychologists and code of conduct.* Washington, DC: Author.

Anderson, B. S., & Hopkins, B. R. (1996). *The counselor and the law* (4th ed.). Alexandria, VA: American Counseling Association.

Anderson, C. M. (1986). The all-too-short trip from positive to negative connotation. *Journal of Marital and Family Therapy, 12,* 351–354.

Anderson, C. M. (1995). *Flying solo.* New York: Norton.

Anderson, C. M., Reiss, D. J., & Hogarty, G. E. (1986). *Schizophrenia and the family.* New York: Guilford.

Anderson, H. (1994). Rethinking family therapy: A delicate balance. *Journal of Marital and Family Therapy, 20*(2), 145–149.

Anderson, H., & Goolishian, H. (1988). Human systems as linguistic systems: Evolving ideas about the implications of theory and practice. *Family Process, 27,* 371–393.

Andolfi, M., Angelo, C., Menghi, P., & Nicolo-Corigliano, M. (1983). *Beyond the family mask. Therapeutic change in rigid family systems.* New York: Brunner/Mazel.

Annas, G. (1978, December). Who to call when the doctor is sick. *Hasting Center Report,* 18–20.

Aponte, H. J. (1985). The negotiation of values in therapy. *Family Process, 24,* 323–338.

Applebaum, P. S. (2002). Privacy in psychiatric treatment: Threats and responses. *American Journal of Psychiatry, 159*(11), 1809–1819.

Appelbaum, P. S., Lidz, C. W., & Meisel, A. (1987). *Informed consent: Legal theory and clinical practice.* New York: Oxford University Press.

Appleson, G. (1982). More patients suing their psychiatrists. *American Bar Association Journal, 68,* 1353–1354.

Application of Striegel, 92 Misc.2d 113, 399 N.Y.S.2d 584 (1977).

Ard, B. N., & Ard, C. (Eds.). (1976). *Handbook of marriage counseling* (2nd ed.). Palo Alto, CA: Science and Behavior Books.

Areen, J. (1978). *Cases and materials on family law.* Mineola, NY: Foundation Press.

Arthur, G. L., & Swanson, C. D. (1993). *Confidentiality and privileged communication.* Alexandria, VA: American Counseling Association.

Atkinson, D. R., Morten, G., & Sue, D. W. (1998). *Counseling American minorities: A cross-cultural perspective* (5th ed.). Dubuque, IA: Brown.

Atwood, J. D. (1992). The historical aspects of marriage and family therapy. In J. D. Atwood (Ed.), *Family therapy* (pp. 5–28). Chicago: Nelson-Hall.

Atwood v. Atwood, 550 S.W.2d 465 (Ky. 1976).

Baehr v. Lewis, 852 P2d 44 (Haw. 1993), remanded sub.nom. Baehr v. Miike, No. 91-1394, 1996 L 694235 (Haw. Cir. Ct. Dec. 3, 1996) order aff'd, 950 P.2d 1234 (1997).

Bagarozzi, G. A., & Giddings, C. W. (1983). Conjugal violence: A critical review of current research and clinical practices. *American Journal of Family Therapy, 11,* 3–12.

Baier, K. (1958). *The moral point of view.* Ithaca, NY: Cornell University Press.

Baltimore, M. L. (2000). Ethical considerations in the use of technology for marriage and family counselors. *Family Journal, 8*(4), 390–394.

Barry, V. C. (1982). *Moral aspects of health care.* Pacific Grove, CA: Brooks/Cole.

Baruth, L. G., & Manning, M. L. (2003). *Multicultural counseling and psychotherapy: A lifespan perspective* (3rd ed.). Upper Saddle River, NJ: Merrill/Prentice Hall.

Bateson, G. (1977). The birth of a matrix or double bind and epistemology. In M. Berger (Ed.), *Beyond the double bind.* New York: Brunner/Mazel.

Bateson, G. (1979). *Mind and nature: A necessary unity.* New York: Bantam.

Bayles, M. D. (1981). *Professional ethics.* Belmont, CA: Wadsworth.

Beauchamp, T. L., & Childress, J. F. (1994). *Principles of biomedical ethics* (4th ed). New York: Oxford University Press.

Beauchamp, T. L., & Childress, J. F. (2001). *Principles of biomedical ethics* (5th ed). New York: Oxford University Press.

Beck, J., & Baxter, P. (1998). The violent patient. In L. E. Lifson & R. I. Simon (Eds.), *The mental health practitioner and the law* (pp. 153–165). Cambridge, MA: Harvard University Press.

Becker, R. F. (1997). *Scientific evidence and expert testimony handbook: A guide for lawyers, criminal investigators and forensic specialists.* Springfield, IL: Charles C. Thomas.

Becvar, D. S., Becvar, R. J., & Bender, A. E. (1982). First let us do no harm. *Journal of Marital and Family Therapy, 8,* 385–392.

Bednar, R. L., Burlingame, G. M., & Masters, K. S. (1988). Systems of family treatment: Substance or semantics? *Annual Review of Psychology, 39,* 401–434.

Behnke, S. H., & Saks, E. R. (1998). Therapeutic jurisprudence: Informed consent as a clinical indication for the chronically suicidal patient with borderline personality disorder. *Loyola of Los Angeles Law Review, 31,* 945–982.

Belcher, D. I., & Pomeroy, L. O. (1998). For richer, for poorer: Strategies for premarital agreements. *Probate and Property, 12,* 54–59.

Bellotti v. Baird (II), 443 U.S. 622 (1979).

Benke, S. (1998). *The essentials of California mental health law: A straightforward guide for clinicians of all disciplines.* New York: Norton.

Bennett, B. E., Bryant, B. K., VandenBos, G. R., & Greenwood, A. (1990). *Professional liability and risk management.* Washington, DC: American Psychological Association.

Beresin, E.V. (2004). Experiences as protégé and mentor. *Psychiatric Times, 21*(9), 59–63.

Bergantino, L. A. (1978). A theory of imperfection. *Counselor Education and Supervision, 17,* 286–292.

Bergin, A. E. (1985). Proposed values for guiding and evaluating counseling and psychotherapy. *Counseling and Values, 29,* 99–115.

Bergin, A. E. (1991). Values and religious issues in psychotherapy and mental health. *American Psychologist, 46,* 394–403.

Berman, E. M. (1982). The individual interview as a treatment technique in conjoint therapy. *American Journal of Family Therapy, 10,* 27–37.

Berner, M. (1998). Informed consent. In L. E. Lifson & R. I. Simon (Eds.), *The mental health practitioner and the law* (pp. 23–43). Cambridge, MA: Harvard University Press.

Bernstein, B. E. (1982). Ignorance of the law is no excuse. In J. C. Hansen & L. L'Abate (Eds.), *Values, ethics, legalities and the family therapist* (pp. 87–102). Rockville, MD: Aspen.

Berry v. Moensch, 8 Utah 2d 191, 331 P2d 814 (1958).

Bersoff, D. N. (1995). *Ethical conflicts in psychology.* Washington, DC: American Psychological Association.

Bersoff, D. N. (Ed.) (1999). *Ethical conflicts in psychology* (2nd ed.). Washington, DC: American Psychological Association.

Bersoff, D. N. (Ed.) (2003). *Ethical conflicts in psychology* (3rd ed.). Washington, DC: American Psychological Association.

Bersoff, D., & Jain, M. (1980). A practical guide to privileged communication for psychologists. In G. Cooke (Ed.), *The role of the forensic psychologist.* Springfield, IL: Charles C. Thomas.

Bertram, B. (1983). A threat to licensure. *American Mental Health Counselors Association News, 6*(6), 1, 7.

Besharov, D. J. (1982). Representing abused and neglected children: When protecting children means seeking the dismissal of court proceedings. *Journal of Family Law, 20,* 217–239.

Betancourt, M. (1997). *What to do when love turns violent: A practical resource for women in abusive relationships.* New York: HarperCollins.

Bevan, E. & Higgins, D. J. (2002). Is domestic violence learned? The contribution of five forms of child maltreatment to men's violence and adjustment. *Journal of Family Violence, 17,* 223–246.

Bieluch v. Bieluch, 462 A2d 1060 (Conn. 1983).

Bird, G., & Sporakowski, M. J. (1992). *Taking sides: Clashing views on controversial issues in family and personal relationships.* Guilford, CT: Dushkin.

Bird, G., & Sporakowski, M. J. (1997). *Taking sides: Clashing views on controversial issues in family and personal relationships* (3rd ed.). Guilford, CT: Dushkin.

Bissell, L. (1983). Alcoholism in physicians. *Postgraduate Medicine, 74*(1), 177–187.

Bittner, S., Bialek, E., Nathiel, S., Ringwald, J., & Tupper, M. (1999). An alternative to managed care: A "guild" model for the independent practice of psychotherapy. *Journal of Marital and Family Therapy, 25,* 99–111.

Black, D. W., Yates, W. R., & Andreasen, N. C. (1988). Schizophrenia, schizophreniform disorder, and delusional (paranoid) disorders. In J. A. Talbott, R. E. Hales, & S. C. Yudofsky (Eds.), *The American psychiatric press textbook of psychiatry* (pp. 110–139). Washington, DC: American Psychiatric Press.

Black, M., & Joffe, W. A. (1978). A lawyer/therapist team approach to divorce. *Conciliation Courts Review, 16,* 1–5.

Black's Law Dictionary (4th ed.). (1968). St. Paul, MN: West Publishing.

Black's Law Dictionary (8th ed.). (2004). St. Paul, MN: West Publishing.

Blades, J. (1984, March). Mediation: An old art revitalized. *Mediation Quarterly,* pp. 146–193.

Blasi, A. (1980). Bridging moral cognition and moral action: A critical review of the literature. *Psychological Bulletin, 88,* 1–42.

Bograd, M. (1984). Family systems approaches to wife battering: A feminist critique. *American Journal of Orthopsychiatry, 54,* 558–568.

Bograd, M. (1986). Holding the line: Confronting the abusive partner. *The Family Therapy Networker, 10*(4), 44–47.

Bograd, M. (1999). Strengthening domestic violence theories: Intersection of race, class, sexual orientation, and gender. *Journal of Marital and Family Therapy, 25,* 275–290.

Bograd, M., & Mederos, F. (1999). Battering and couple therapy: Universal screening and selection of treatment modality. *Journal of Marital and Family Therapy, 25,* 291–312.

Bonnington, S. B., Crawford, R. L., Curtis, T., & Watts, R. (1996). Family ethics: Managed care limits on third-party payment. *Family Journal: Counseling and Therapy for Couples and Families, 4,* 239–241.

Bonnington, S. B., McGrath, P., & Martinek, S. A. (1996). The fax of the matter: The electronic transfer of confidential material. *Family Journal: Counseling and Therapy for Couples and Families, 4,* 155–156.

Borys, D. S. (1988). *Dual relationships between therapist and client: A national survey of clinicians' attitudes and practices.* Unpublished doctoral dissertation, University of California, Los Angeles.

Boszormenyi-Nagy, I. (1974). Ethical and practical implications of intergenerational family therapy. *Psychotherapy and Psychosomatics, 24,* 261–268.

Boszormenyi-Nagy, I., & Sparks, G. (1973). *Invisible loyalties.* Hagerstown, MD: Harper & Row.

Boszormenyi-Nagy, I., & Ulrich, D. N. (1981). Contextual family therapy. In A. S. Gurman & D. P. Kniskern (Eds.), *Handbook of family therapy* (pp. 159–186). New York: Brunner/Mazel.

Boughner, S. R., & Logan, J. P. (1999). Robert H. Woody: Legal issues in couple and family counseling. *The Family Journal: Counseling and Therapy for Couples and Families, 7,* 302–310.

Bourne, P. G. (1982). Ethical problems of therapists in government and industry. In M. Rosenbaum (Ed.), *Ethics and values in psychotherapy: A guidebook* (pp. 385–402). New York: Free Press.

Bowen, M. (1978). *Family therapy in clinical practice.* New York: Jason Aronson.

Bowers, M. (1992a). Politics, power, and prestige: The emergence of the profession. *Family Therapy News, 23*(5), 5, 18.

Bowers, M. (1992b). *Regulating the profession.* AAMFT 1992 leadership conference proceedings. Washington, DC: American Association for Marriage and Family Therapy.

Braaten, E. E., & Handelsman, M. M. (1997). Client preferences for informed consent information. *Ethics and Behavior, 74,* 311–328.

Braaten, E. E., Otto, S., & Handelsman, M. M. (1993). What do people want to know about psychotherapy? *Psychotherapy, 30,* 565–570.

Brady v. Hopper, 570 F.Supp. 1333 (D. Colo. 1983); aff'd, 751 F.2d 329 (10th Cir. 1984).

Brandt, R. (1959). *Ethical theory.* Upper Saddle River, NJ: Prentice Hall.

Bray, J. H., Shepherd, J. N., & Hays, J. R. (1985). Legal and ethical issues in informed consent to psychotherapy. *American Journal of Family Therapy, 13,* 50–60.

Brendel, J. M., & Nelson, K. W. (1999). The stream of family secrets: Navigating the islands of confidentiality and triangulation involving family therapists. *Family Journal: Counseling and Therapy for Couples and Families, 7,* 112–117.

Bricklin, B., & Halbert, M. H. (2004). Can child custody data be generated scientifically? Part I. *The American Journal of Family Therapy, 32,* 119–138.

A Brief History of IAMFC. (1992). *IAMFC Newsletter,* p. 6.

Britton, P. J. (2000). Staying on the roller coaster with clients: Implications of the new HIV/AIDS medical treatments for counseling. *Journal of Mental Health Counseling, 22*(1), 85–95.

Broadhurst, D. D. (1979). *The educator's role in the prevention and treatment of child abuse and neglect.* Washington, DC: National Center on Child Abuse and Neglect, U. S. Department of Health, Education and Welfare.

Brock, G. W. (1998). *Ethics casebook.* Washington, DC: American Association for Marriage and Family Therapy.

Brock, G. W., & Barnard, C. P. (1999). *Procedures in marriage and family therapy* (3rd ed.). Upper Saddle River, NJ: Prentice Hall.

Brodsky, S. L., & Robey, A. (1972). On becoming an expert witness: Issues of orientation and effectiveness. *Professional Psychology, 3,* 173–176.

Bromberg, W. (1979). *The uses of psychiatry and the law.* Westport, CT: Quorum.

Brown, H. I. (1977). *Perception, theory and commitment.* Chicago: University of Chicago Press.

Brown, J. (2004). Shame and domestic violence: Treatment perspectives for perpetrators from self psychology and affect theory. *Sexual and Relationship Therapy, 19,* 39–57.

Brown, R., & Strozier, M. (2004). Resisting abuse at what cost? The impact of mandated reporting laws on the process and content of therapy. *Contemporary Family Therapy: An International Journal, 27,* 193–212.

Bruce, D. K. (1990). Ethicism, advertising, and restraint of trade. *The Family Psychologist, 6*(2), 23.

Bryan, J. F., Barnett, T., Hester, K, & Relyea, C. (2003). A social identity perspective on the relationship between perceived organizational support and organizational commitment. *Journal of Social Psychology, 143*(6), 789–792.

Budman, S. (1989, August). *Training experienced clinicians to do brief treatment—silk purses into sow's ears.* Paper presented at the 97th Annual Convention of the American Psychological Association, New Orleans, LA.

Budman, S. H., & Gurman, A. S. (1988). *Theory and practice of brief therapy.* New York: Guilford.

Bullock, C. (2003). Low income parents victimized by child protective services. *American University Journal of Gender, Social Policy & the Law, 11,* 1023. Retrieved on February 21, 2006 from http://www.wcl.american.edu/journal/genderlaw/1_1/bullock.pdf?rd=1

Bureau of National Affairs, Inc. (1976). *Uniform parentage act.* Washington, DC: Author.

Bureau of National Affairs, Inc. (1982). *Uniform marriage and divorce act.* Washington, DC: Author.

Bureau of National Affairs, Inc. (1984). *Uniform premarital agreement act.* Washington, DC: Author.

Burgum, F., & Anderson, S. (1975). *The counselor and the law.* Washington, DC: American Personnel and Guidance Association.

Burkemper, E. M. (2002). Family therapists' ethical decision-making processes in two duty-to-warn situations. *Journal of Marital and Family Therapy, 28*(2), 203–212.

Butcher, J. N., Rouse, S. V., & Perry, J. N. (1998). Assessing resistance to psychological treatment.

Measurement and Evaluation in Counseling and Development, 31, 95–188.

Buttell, F. P. (2001). Moral development among court-ordered batterers: Evaluating the impact of treatment. *Research on Social Work Practice, 11*(2), 93–102.

Buttell, F. P., & Carney, M. M. (2004). A multidimensional assessment of a batter treatment program: An alert to a problem? *Research on Social Work Practice, 14*(2), 93–102.

Caban v. Mohammed, 441 U.S. 380 (1979).

Cambien, J. (1989). Reality in psychotherapy. *Journal of Family Psychology, 3,* 29–38.

Canfield, B., & Locke, D. W. (1991, Summer). Are we addressing the right problem? *IAMFC News letter,* pp. 1, 4.

Canterbury v. Spence, 464 F.2d 772 (D.C. Cir 1972).

Carl, D., & Jurkovic, G. J. (1983). Agency triangles: Problems in agency–family relationships. *Family Process, 22,* 441–451.

Carney, M. M., & Buttell, F. P. (2004). A multidimensional evaluation of a treatment program for female batterers: A pilot study. *Research on Social Work Practice, 14,* 249–259.

Carter, B. (1986). Success in family therapy. *Family Therapy Networker, 10*(4), 16–22.

Carter, B. A., & McGoldrick, M. (Eds.). (2005). *The expanded family life cycle* (4th ed.). Needham Heights, MA: Allyn & Bacon.

Carter, C. A. (1987). Some indications for combining individual and family therapy. *American Journal of Family Therapy, 15,* 99–110.

Case Notes. (1985–1986). *Journal of Family Law, 24,* 552–558.

Castro, K., Lifson, A., White, C., Bush, T., Chamberland, M., Lekatsas, A., & Jaffe, H. (1988). Investigations of AIDS patients with no previously identified risk factors. *Journal of the American Medical Association, 262,* 1338–1342.

Caudill, O. B., Jr. (1999, June/July). The technology trap. *Family Therapy News, 30,* 20–22.

Cavell, T. A., & Snyder, D. K. (1991). Iconoclasm versus innovation: Building a science of family therapy. *Journal of Marital and Family Therapy, 17,* 167–171.

Centers for Disease Control. (1989). First 100,000 cases of acquired immunodeficiency syndrome—United States. *Journal of the American Medical Association, 262,* 1453–1456.

Centers for Disease Control. (1999). *Division of HIV/AIDS Prevention: Basic statistics—cumulative cases.* Washington, DC: Author. Retrieved June 11, 1999, from http://www.cdc.gov/hiv/stats/cumulati.htm

Centers for Disease Control. (2003). *Incidence, Prevalence, and Consequences of Intimate Partner Violence Against Women in the United States.* Retrieved June 7, 2005, from http://www.cdc.gov/ncipc/pub-res/ipv_cost/03_incidence.htm

Chaffin v. Chaffin, 239 Or. 374, 397 P.2d 771 (1964).

Chaimowitz, G., Glancy, G., & Blackburn, J. (2000). The duty to warn and protect—impact on practice. *Canadian Journal of Psychiatry, 45,* 899–904.

Chang, H., & Saunders, D. G. (2002). Predictors of attrition in two types of group programs for men who batter. *Journal of Family Violence, 17,* 273–293.

Chemerinsky, E. (1979). Defining the "best interests": Constitutional protections in involuntary adoptions. *Journal of Family Law, 18,* 79–113.

Chenneville, T. (2000). HIV, confidentiality, and duty to protect: A decision-making model. *Professional Psychology: Research and Practice, 31,* 661–671.

Christiansen, L. L., & Miller, R. B. (2001). Marriage and family therapists evaluate managed mental health care: A qualitative inquiry. *Journal of Marital and Family Therapy, 27* (4), 509–514.

Christie, G. C., Meeks, J. E., Pryor, E. S., & Sanders, J. (1997). *Cases and materials on the law of torts* (3rd ed.). St. Paul, MN: West Publishing.

Christie, G. C., Meeks, J. E., Pryor, E. S., & Sanders, J. (2004). *Cases and materials on the law of torts* (4th ed.). St. Paul, MN: West Publishing.

Christopher, J. C. (1996). Counseling's inescapable moral visions. *Journal of Counseling and Development, 75,* 17–25.

Claim of Gerkin, 106 Misc.2d 643, 434 N.Y.S.2d 607 (1980).

Clark, H. H., Jr. (1968). *The law of domestic relations.* St. Paul, MN: West Publishing.

Clark, H. H., Jr. (1974). *Cases and problems on domestic relations.* St. Paul, MN: West Publishing.

Cleary, E. W. (Ed.). (1972). *McCormick's handbook of law evidence* (2nd ed.). St: Paul, MN: West.

COAMFTE Accredited and Candidacy Status Programs. (1992). *AAMFT Accreditation News, 2*(1), program listing.

Cobbs v. Grant. 8 Cal., 3d 229, 502 P.2d 1 (1972).

Cobia, D. C., & Boes, S. R. (2000). Professional disclosure statements and formal plans for supervision: Two strategies for minimizing the risk of ethical conflicts in post-master's supervision. *Journal of Counseling and Development, 78*(3), 293–297.

Cohen, J. A. (2003). Managed care and the evolving role of the clinical social worker in mental health. *Social Work, 48*(1), 34–44.

Cohen, R. J. (1979). *Malpractice: A guide for mental health professionals.* New York: Free Press.

Cohen, R. J., & Mariano, W. E. (1982). *Legal guidebook in mental health.* New York: The Free Press.

Coker, J. K., Jones, W. P., Staples, P. A., & Harbach, R. L. (2002). Cybersupervision in the first practicum: Implications for research and practice. *Guidance and Counseling, 18*(1), 33–39.

Colapinto, J. (1988). Avoiding a common pitfall in compulsory school referrals. *Journal of Marital and Family Therapy, 14,* 89–96.

Cole, P. M. (1992). Family systems business: A merger at last. *Family Therapy News, 23*(2), 29.

Coleman, M. (2003). Behind managed care's courtship of clinical social workers. *Behavioral Health Management, 23*(6), 36–38.

Combrinck-Graham, L. (1986). Coercion and therapy. *The Family Therapy Networker, 10*(4), 69.

Commission on Accreditation for Marriage and Family Therapy Education. (1997). *Manual on accreditation.* Washington, DC: Author. Available from http://www.aamft.org/about/accred.htm

Commission on Accreditation for Marriage and Family Therapy Education. (2005). *Manual on accreditation.* Washington, DC: Author. Retrieved on May 9, 2005, from http://www.aamft.org/about/COAMFTE/manual.asp

Condoms for prevention of sexually transmitted diseases. (1988). *Journal of the American Medical Association, 259*, 1925–1927.

Connell, M. J. (1981). Property division and alimony awards: A survey of statutory limitations on judicial discretion. *Fordham Law Review, 50*, 415–449.

Constantine, M. G., Heather, L. J., & Laing, J-C. (2001). Examining multicultural competencies and race-related attitudes among white marital and family therapists. *Journal of Marital & Family Therapy, 27*(3), 353–362.

Coogler, O. J. (1978). *Structured mediation in divorce settlement.* Lexington, MA: Heath.

Corey, G., Corey, M. S., & Callanan, P. (1984). *Issues and ethics in the helping professions* (2nd ed.). Pacific Grove, CA: Brooks/Cole.

Corey, G., Corey, M. S., & Callanan, P. (1993). *Issues and ethics in the helping professions* (4th ed.). Pacific Grove, CA: Brooks/Cole.

Corey, G., Corey, M. S., & Callanan, P. (1998). *Issues and ethics in the helping professions* (5th ed.). Pacific Grove, CA: Brooks/Cole.

Corey, G., Corey, M. S., & Callanan, P. (2003). *Issues and ethics in the helping professions* (6th ed.). Pacific Grove, CA: Brooks/Cole.

Cormier, L. S., & Bernard, J. M. (1982). Ethical and legal responsibilities of clinical supervisors. *Personnel and Guidance Journal, 60*, 486–490.

Costa, L., & Altekruse, M. (1994). Duty-to-warn guidelines for mental health counselors. *Journal of Counseling and Development, 72*(4), 346–351.

Costello, C. Y. (2004). Changing clothes: Gender inequality and professional socialization. *NASW Journal, 16*(2), 138–156.

Cottone, R. R. (1988). Epistemological and ontological issues in counseling: Implications of social systems theory. *Counseling Psychology Quarterly, 1*, 357–365.

Cottone, R. R. (1991). Counselor roles according to two counseling world views. *Journal of Counseling and Development, 69*, 398–401.

Cottone, R. R., & Greenwell, R. J. (1992). Beyond linearity and circularity: Deconstructing social systems theory. *Journal of Marital and Family Therapy, 18*, 167–177.

Cottone, R. R., & Tarvydas, V. M. (1998). *Ethical and professional issues in counseling.* Upper Saddle River, NJ: Prentice Hall.

Cottone, R. R., & Tarvydas, V. M. (2003). *Ethical and professional issues in counseling* (2nd ed.). Upper Saddle River, NJ: Prentice Hall.

Council for Accreditation of Counseling and Related Educational Programs (2001). *CACREP accreditation manual: 2001 standards.* Alexandria, VA: Author.

Covan, E. D. (2000). Revisiting the relationship between elder modelers and their protégés. *Sociological Perspectives, 43*(7) 7–21.

Coyne, J. C., & Anderson, B. J. (1989). The "psychosomatic family" reconsidered II: Recalling a defective model and looking ahead. *Journal of Marital and Family Therapy, 15*, 139–148.

Cruchfield, C. F. (1981). Nonmarital relationships and their impact on the institution of marriage and the traditional family structure. *Journal of Family Law, 19*, 247–261.

Cummings, N. (1985, August). *Therapist–patient sex: Search for a solution to a systems problem.* Symposium presented at the annual meeting of the American Psychological Association, Los Angeles.

Danginger, P. R., Patterson, W., & Welfel, E. R. (2001). The impact of managed care on mental health counselors: A survey of perceptions, practices, and compliance with ethical standards. *Journal of Mental Health Counseling, 23*(2), 137–150.

Danis, F. S., & Lockhart, L. (2003). Domestic violence and social work education: What do we know, what do we need to know? *Journal of Social Work Education, 39*, 215–225.

Darom, D. (1988). Freedom and commitment: Values and issues in humanistic education. *Journal of Humanistic Education and Development, 26*, 98–108.

Datillo, F. M., & Epstein, N. B. (2005). Introduction to the special section. *Journal of Marital and Family Therapy, 31*(1), 7–14.

Daubner, E. V., & Daubner, E. S. (1970). Ethics and counseling decisions. *Personnel and Guidance Journal, 48*, 433–442.

Davis, J. W. (1981). Counselor licensure: Overkill? *Personnel and Guidance Journal, 60*, 83–85.

Davis, L. (1991). *Allies in healing.* New York: Harper Perennial.

Davis v. Lhim, 430 Mich. 326 (1988).

Dawidoff, D. J. (1973). *The malpractice of psychiatrists.* Springfield, IL: Charles C. Thomas.

Day, D. (1977). Termination of parental rights statutes and void for vagueness doctrine: A successful attack on the *parens patriae* rationale. *Journal of Family Law, 16*, 213.

Day, S. X., & Schneider, P. L. (2002). Psychotherapy using distance technology: A comparison of face-to-face, video, and audio treatment. *Journal of Counseling Psychology, 49*, 499–504.

Defense of Marriage Act, Pub. L. No. 104-199, 110 Stat. 2419; codified at 1 U.S.C. § 7, 28 U.S.C. § 1738c (1996).

DeKraai, M. B., & Sales, B. D. (1982). Privileged communications of psychologists. *Professional Psychology, 13*, 372–388.

Delaware Rules of Evidence, 503 (1981).

DelCampo, R. L., & Anderson, A. S. (1992). Court-ordered family mediation: A brief overview. *Topics in Family Psychology and Counseling, 1*(2), 72–77.

Dell, P. (1982). Beyond homeostasis: Toward a concept of coherence. *Family Process, 21*, 21–41.

Dell, P. (1983). From pathology to ethics. *The Family Therapy Networker 7*(6), 29–31, 64.

Denkowski, K. M., & Denkowski, G. C. (1982). Client–counselor confidentiality: An update of rationale, legal status, and implications. *Personnel and Guidance Journal, 60*, 371–375.

Denton, W. H. (1989). DSM-III-R and the family therapist: Ethical considerations. *Journal of Marital and Family Therapy, 15*, 367–377.

Denton, W. H. (1990). A family systems analysis of DSM-III-R. *Journal of Marital and Family Therapy, 16*, 113–125.

Denton, W. H. (1996). Problems encountered in reconciling individual and relational diagnoses. In F. W. Kaslow (Ed.), *Handbook of relational diagnosis and dysfunctional family patterns* (pp. 35–45). New York: Wiley.

Denton, W. H., Patterson, J. E., & Van Meir, E. S. (1997). Use of the DSM in marriage and family therapy programs: Current practices and attitudes. *Journal of Marital and Family Therapy, 23*, 81–86.

DePauw, M. E. (1986). Avoiding ethical violations: A timeline perspective for individual counseling. *Journal of Counseling and Development, 64*, 303–305.

Dermer, S. B., Hemesath, C. W., & Russell, C. S. (1998). A feminist critique of solution-focused therapy. *American Journal of Family Therapy, 26*, 239–251.

De Shazer, S. (1999). *Patterns of brief family therapy: An ecosystem approach*. New York: Guilford.

Deutsch, M. (1973). *The resolution of conflict*. New Haven, CT: Yale University Press.

Dewitt, K. N. (1987). The effectiveness of family therapy: A review of outcome research. *Archives of General Psychiatry, 35*, 549–561.

Diamond, J. (2000). *Narrative means to sober ends: Treating addiction and its aftermath*. New York: Guilford.

Dincin, J., Selleck, V., & Streicker, S. (1978). Restructuring parental attitudes: Working with parents of the adult mentally ill. *Schizophrenia Bulletin, 4*, 597–608.

Doe v. Bolton. Rehearing denied, 410 U.S. 959 (1973).

Doherty, W. J. (1992). Values and ethics in family therapy. In M. T. Burke & J. G. Miranti (Eds.), *Ethical and spiritual values in counseling* (pp. 75–80). Alexandria, VA: Association for Religious and Values Issues in Counseling.

Doherty, W. J., & Simmons, D.S. (1996). Clinical practice patterns of marriage and family therapists: A national survey of therapists and their clients. *Journal of Marital and Family Therapy, 22*, 9–25.

Dooley, J. A. (1977). Malpractice: Professional liability and the law. *Professional Psychology, 9*, 467–477.

Doss, B. D., Atkins, D. C., & Christensen, A. (2003). Who's dragging their feet? Husbands and wives seeking marital therapy. *Journal of Marital and Family Therapy, 29*, 165–177.

Douthwaite, G. (1979). *Unmarried couples and the law*. Indianapolis: Smith.

Downing, N. E., & Roush, K.L. (1985). From passive acceptance to active commitment: A model of feminist identity for women. *Counseling Psychologist, 13*, 695–709.

Draguns, J. G. (1989). Dilemmas and choices in cross-cultural counseling: The universal versus the culturally disjunctive. In P. B. Pedersen, J. G. Draguns, J. Lonner, & J. E. Trimble (Eds.), *Counseling across the cultures* (3rd ed., pp. 1–21). Honolulu: University of Hawaii Press.

Duncan, D. M., & Watts, R. E. (1999). Counseling and the Internet. In P. Stevens (Ed.), *Ethical casebook for the practice of marriage and family counseling* (pp. 159–170). Alexandria, VA: American Counseling Association.

Eady v. Alter, 380 N.Y.S. 2d 737 (New York, 1976).

Early, T. M., & Hulse, D. (1986). Humanizing a technological society: Ethical implications for the counselor. *Journal of Counseling and Development, 64*, 334–337.

Edwards, J. K., & Bess, J. M. (1998). Developing effectiveness in the therapeutic use of self. *Clinical Social Work Journal, 26*(1), 89–105.

Efran, J., & Lukens, M. (1985). The world according to Humberto Maturana. *The Family Therapy Networker 9*(3), 22–28, 72–75.

Ehrensaft, M. K., & Vivian, D. (1996). Spouses' reasons for not reporting existing physical aggression as a marital problem. *Journal of Family Psychology, 10*, 443–453.

Ehrlich, J. S. (2003). Grounded in the reality of their lives: Listening to teens who make the abortion decision without involving their parents. *Berkeley Women's Law Journal, 18*, 61.

Eisikovits, Z. C., Edleson, J. L., Guttmann, E., & Sela-Amit, M. (1991). Cognitive styles and socialized attitudes of men who batter: Where should we intervene? *Family Relations, 40*, 72–77.

Elias, M. (1988, August 15). Many lie about AIDS risk. *USA Today*, p. D–1.

Elkins, D. (1990, June). On being spiritual without necessarily being religious. *Association for Humanistic Psychology Perspective*, 4–5.

Emerson, S., & Markos, O. A. (1996). Signs and symptoms of the impaired counselor. *Journal of Humanistic Education and Development*, *34*(3), 108–117.

Engelberg, S. L. (1985). General counsel's report: Ethics committee's procedures outlined. *Family Therapy News*, *16*(2), 16.

Erickson, G. D. (1988). Against the grain: Decentering family therapy. *Journal of Marital and Family Therapy*, *14*, 225–236.

Erickson, S. H. (1998). Counseling a couple with AIDS. *Family Journal: Counseling and Therapy for Couples and Families*, *6*, 223–225.

Eskridge, W. N., Jr. (1993). A history of same-sex marriage. *Virginia Law Review*, *79*, 1419–1514.

Ethics Committee of the American Psychological Association. (1988). Trends in ethics cases, common pitfalls, and published resources. *American Psychologist*, *43*, 564–572.

Evans, J. (1983). The treatment specialist: An emerging role for counselors within the criminal court system. *Personnel and Guidance Journal*, *61*, 349–351.

Everstine, L., Everstine, D. S., Heymann, G. M., True, R. H, Frey, D. H., Johnson, H. G., & Seiden, R. H. (1980). Privacy and confidentiality in psychotherapy. *American Psychologist*, *9*, 828–840.

Fall, K. A., & Lyons, C. (2003). Ethical considerations of family secret disclosure and post-session safety management. *The Family Journal*, *11*, 281–285.

Falloon, I. R. H. (1991). Behavioral family therapy. In A. S. Gurman & D. P. Kniskern (Eds.), *Handbook of family therapy:* Volume II (pp. 65–133). New York: Brunner/Mazel.

Family Educational Rights and Privacy Act of 1974, 20 U.S.C.A. § 1232g.

Family Rights and Privacy Act, 20 U.S.C.A. § 1232g (West, 1997).

Farber, B. A., & Hall, D. (2003). Disclosure to therapists: What is and is not discussed in psychotherapy. *Journal of Clinical Psychology*, *58*, 359–371.

Faustman, W. O. (1982). Legal and ethical issues in debt collection strategies of professional psychologists. *Professional Psychology*, *13*, 208–214.

Featherstone, V. (1996). A feminist critique of family therapy. *Counseling Psychology Quarterly*, *9*, 15–24.

Feldman, L. (1990). *Multi-dimensional family therapy.* New York: Guilford Press.

Felstiner, W. L., & Williams, L. A. (1978). Mediation as an alternative to criminal prosecution. *Law and Human Behavior*, *2*, 223–244.

Felthous, A. R. (1999). The clinician's duty to protect third parties. *The Psychiatric Clinics of North America*, *22*, 42–49.

Fenell, D. L., & Hovestadt, A. J. (1986). Family therapy as a profession or professional specialty: Implications for training. *Journal of Psychotherapy and the Family*, *1*, 25–40.

Ferraro, K. J., & Johnson, J. M. (1983). How women experience battering: The process of victimization. *Social Problems*, *30*, 325–339.

Fieldsteel, N. D. (1982). Ethical issues in family therapy. In M. Rosenbaum (Ed.), *Ethics and values in psychotherapy: A guidebook* (pp. 258–268). New York: Free Press.

Final Regulations: Family Educational Rights and Privacy Act. (1976). *Federal Register*, *41*, 24670–24675.

Fine, M. J. (1985). Intervention from a systems-ecological perspective. *Professional Psychology: Research and Practice*, *16*, 262–270.

Fine, M. J., & Holt, P. (1983). Intervening with school problems: A family systems perspective. *Psychology in the Schools*, *20*, 59–66.

Fischer, L., & Sorenson, G. P. (1985). *School law for counselors, psychologists, and social workers.* New York: Longman.

Fish, V. (1990). Introducing causality and power into family therapy theory: A correction to the systemic paradigm. *Journal of Marital and Family Therapy*, *16*, 21–37.

Fisher, L., Anderson, A., & Jones, J. E. (1981). Types of paradoxical interventions and indications/contraindications for use in clinical practice. *Family Process*, *20*, 25–35.

Fisher, M. A. (1991). *Ethical issues in clinical practice under Virginia law: A clinical psychology handbook.* Charlottesville, VA: Author.

Flax, M. (1977). *Couples therapy in battering relationships.* Paper presented at Colorado Women's College Conference of Battered Women, Denver.

Folberg, J. (1984). Custody overview. In J. Folberg (Ed.), *Joint custody and shared parenting* (pp. 3–10). Washington, DC: Bureau of National Affairs, Inc.

Folberg, J., & Graham, M. (1979). Joint custody of children following divorce. University of California, *Davis Law Review*, *12*, 523–581.

Fong, M. L., & Sherrard, P. A. D. (1990). Ethical dilemmas in marketing counseling services. In B. Herlihy & L. B. Golden, *Ethical standards casebook* (pp. 127–136). Alexandria, VA: American Association for Counseling and Development.

Foos, J. A., Ottens, A. J., & Hill, L. K. (1991). Managed mental health: A primer for counselors. *Journal of Counseling and Development*, *69*, 332–336.

Ford, C. G. (2001). *Ethical reasoning in the mental health professions.* Boca Raton: CRC Press.

Foss, L. L., & Warnke, M. A. (2003). Fundamentalist Protestant Christian women: Recognizing cultural and gender influences on domestic violence. *Counseling and Values, 48*(1), 14–24.

Foster, H. H. (1976). An overview of confidentiality and privilege. *Journal of Psychiatry and the Law, 4*, 393–401.

Foster, H. H. (1978). Informed consent of mental patients. In W. E. Barton & C. J. Sanborn (Eds.), *Law and the mental health professions: Friction at the interface.* New York: International Universities.

Foster, N. J., & Kelly, J. B. (1996). Divorce mediation: Who should be certified? *University of San Francisco Law Review, 30*, 665–680.

Fowers, B. J., & Wenger, A. (1997). Are trustworthiness and fairness enough? Contextual family therapy and the good family. *Journal of Marital and Family Therapy, 23*, 153–169.

Fraenkel, P. (2005, May/June). Whatever happened to family therapy? It may be in better shape than you think. *Psychotherapy Networker.* Retrieved July 5, 2005, from http://www.psychotherapynetworker.org

Frame, M. W. (1997). The ethics of counseling via the Internet. *Family Journal: Counseling and Therapy for Couples and Families, 5*, 328–330.

Frame, M. W. (1999). The impaired counselor. In P. Stevens (Ed.), *Ethical casebook for the practice of marriage and family counseling* (pp. 103–112). Alexandria, VA: American Counseling Association.

Framo, J. L. (1981). The integration of marital therapy with sessions with family of origin. In A. Gurman & D. Kniskern (Eds.), *Handbook of family therapy* (pp. 133–158). New York: Brunner/Mazel.

Fraser, J. S. (1984). Paradox and orthodox: Folie à deux. *Journal of Marital and Family Therapy, 10*, 361–372.

Freed, D. J., & Foster, H. H. (1981). Divorce in the fifty states: An overview. *Family Law Quarterly, 14*, 229–284.

Freeman, J., & Combs, G. (1996). *Narrative therapy: The social construction of preferred realities.* New York: Norton.

Freeman, S. J., Engels, D. W., & Altekruse, M. K. (2004). Foundations for ethical standards and codes: The role of moral philosophy and theory in ethics. *Counseling and Values, 48*(3), 163–174.

Freeny, M. (1995). Do the walls have ears? *Family Therapy Networker, 19* (5), 36–39, 41, 43, 65.

Fretz, B. R., & Mills, D. H. (1980). *Licensing and certification of psychologists and counselors.* San Francisco: Jossey-Bass.

Fricke v. Fricke, 42 N.W. 2d 500 (Wis. 1950).

Friedman, D., & Kaslow, N. (1986). The development of professional identity in psychotherapists: Six stages in the supervision process. In F. W. Kaslow (Ed.), *Supervision and training models, dilemmas and challenges* (pp. 29–50). New York: Haworth.

Friedman, S. E. (1992). *The law of parent–child relationships: A handbook.* Chicago: American Bar Association.

Fulcher, J. A. (2002). Domestic violence and the rights of women in Japan and the United States. *Human Rights: Journal of the Section of Individual Rights and Responsibilities, 29*(3), 16–18.

Fulero, S. M. (1988). *Tarasoff:* 10 years later. *Professional Psychology: Research and Practice, 19*, 184–190.

Gangel-Jacob, P. (1997, August). Without lawyers, mediation sacrifices justice. *Trial, 33*, 45–50.

Garcia, J. G., Cartwright, B., Winston, S. M., & Borzuchowska, B. (2003). A transcultural integrative model for ethical decision making in counseling. *Journal of Counseling and Development, 81*, 268–278.

Gardner, R. (1989). *Family evaluation in child custody mediation, arbitration and litigation.* Cresskill, NJ: Creative Therapeutics.

Geller, J. A., & Wasserstrom, J. (1984). Conjoint therapy for the treatment of domestic violence. In A. R. Roberts (Ed.), *Battered women and their families: Intervention strategies and treatment programs.* New York: Springer.

Gelles, R. J., & Maynard, P. E. (1987). A structural family systems approach to intervention in cases of domestic violence. *Family Relations, 36*, 270–275.

Gergen, K. (1991). *The saturated self.* New York: Basic Books.

Gerlock, A. A. (2001). Relationship mutuality: Why is it important in batterers' rehabilitation? *Journal of Interpersonal Violence, 16*, 768–784.

Giblin, P., & Chan, J. (1995). A feminist perspective. *Family Journal: Counseling and Therapy for Couples and Families, 3*, 234–238.

Gill, S. J. (1982). Professional disclosure and consumer protection in counseling. *Personnel and Guidance Journal, 60*, 443–446.

Gillespie v. Gillespie, 631 S.W. 2d 592 (Tex. App. 1982).

Ginsberg, B. (2004). *Tarasoff* at thirty: Victim's knowledge shrinks the psychotherapist's duty to warn and protect. *Journal of Contemporary Health Law and Policy, 21*, 1.

Gladding, S. T. (1998a). *Counseling as an art: The creative arts in counseling* (2nd ed.). Alexandria, VA: American Counseling Association.

Gladding, S. T. (1998b). *Family therapy: History, theory, and practice* (2nd ed.). Upper Saddle River, NJ: Prentice Hall.

Gladding, S. T. (2000). *Counseling: A comprehensive profession* (4th ed.). Upper Saddle River, NJ: Prentice Hall.

Gladding, S. T. (2001). *The counseling dictionary: Concise definitions of frequently used terms.* Upper Saddle River, NJ: Prentice Hall.

Gladding, S. T. (2002). *Family therapy: History, theory, and practice* (3rd ed.). Upper Saddle River, NJ: Prentice Hall.

Gladding, S. T. (2004). *Counseling: A comprehensive profession* (5th ed.). Upper Saddle River, NJ: Prentice Hall.

Gladding, S. T. (2005). *Counseling as an art: The creative arts in counseling* (3rd ed.). Alexandria, VA: American Counseling Association.

Glaser, B., & Kirschenbaum, H. (1980). Using values clarification in counseling settings. *Personnel and Guidance Journal, 58,* 569–574.

Glendon, M. A. (1976). Marriage and the state: The washing away of marriage. *Virginia Law Review, 62,* 663–720.

Glendon, M. A. (1980). Modern marriage law and its underlying assumptions: The new marriage and the new property. *Family Law Quarterly, 13,* 441–460.

Glosoff, H. L. (1997). Multiple relationships in private practice. In B. Herlihy & G. Corey (Eds.), *Boundary issues in counseling* (pp. 114–120). Alexandria, VA: American Counseling Association.

Glosoff, H. L., Herlihy, B., & Spence, E. D. (2000). Privileged communication in the counselor–client relationship. *Journal of Counseling and Development, 78,* 454–462.

Golden, L., & Schmidt, S. J. (1998). Unethical practice as perceived by mental health professionals: The next generation. *Counseling and Values, 42,* 166–170.

Goldner, V. (1999). Morality and multiplicity: Perspectives on the treatment of violence in intimate life. *Journal of Marital and Family Therapy, 25,* 325–336.

Gomez v. Perez, 409 U.S. 535 (1973).

Gondolf, E. (2002). *Batterer intervention systems: Issues, outcomes, and recommendations.* Thousand Oaks, CA: Sage.

Goodyear, R. K., Crego, C. A., & Johnston, M. W. (1992). Ethical issues in the supervision of student research: A study of critical incidents. *Professional Psychology Research and Practice, 23,* 203–210.

Gould, J. W. (1998). *Conducting scientifically crafted child custody evaluations.* Thousand Oaks, CA: Sage.

Graham, D., Rawlings, E., & Rimini, N. (1988). Survivors of terror: Battered women, hostages and the Stockholm syndrome. In K. Yllo & M. Bograd (Eds.), *Female perspectives on wife abuse* (pp. 217–233). Newbury Park, CA: Sage.

Gray, L. A., & Harding, A. I. (1988). Confidentiality limits with clients who have the AIDS virus. *Journal of Counseling and Development, 66,* 219–223.

Green, S., & Long, J. V. (1985). *Marriage and family agreements.* Colorado Springs, CO: Shephard's/McGraw-Hill.

Green, S. L., & Hansen, J. C. (1989). Ethical dilemmas faced by family therapists. *Journal of Marital and Family Therapy, 15,* 149–158.

Greene, K., & Bogo, M. (2002). The different faces of intimate violence: Implications for assessment and treatment. *Journal of Marital and Family Therapy, 28,* 455–466.

Greenspun, W. (2000). Embracing the controversy: A metasystemic approach to the treatment of domestic violence. In P. Papp (Ed.), *Couples on the fault line: New directions for therapists* (pp. 152–175). New York: Guilford.

Gross, B. (2005). Death throes: Professional liability after client suicide. *Annals of the American Psychological Association, 8,* 34–35.

Gross, S. J. (1977). Professional disclosure: An alternative to licensure. *Personnel and Guidance Journal, 55,* 586–588.

Grosslight v. Superior Court of Los Angeles County, 72 Cal. App. 3d 502, 140 Cal. Rptr. 278 (1977).

Grumet, B. R. (1988). The standard of care: Legal considerations in protocols and standing orders. *HMO, 2,* 20–23.

Grunebaum, H. (1984). Comments on Terkelsen's "Schizophrenia and the family: II. Adverse effects of family therapy." *Family Process, 23,* 421–428.

Guernsey, T. F. (1981). The psychotherapist–patient privilege in child placement: A relevancy analysis. *Villanova Law Review, 26,* 955–966.

Guggenheim, P. D. (1979, March). The juvenile offender. *Bulletin, Area 11, American Psychiatric Association.*

Guillette, W. (1979). Is psychotherapy insurable? *National Association of Private Psychiatric Hospitals Journal, 9,* 30–32.

Gulliver, P. H. (1979). *Disputes and negotiations: A cross-cultural perspective.* New York: Academic Press.

Gumper, L. L., & Sprenkle, D. H. (1981). Privileged communication in therapy: Special problems for the family and couples therapist. *Family Process, 20,* 11–23.

Gurman, A. S. (1978). Contemporary marital therapies: A critique and comparative analysis of psychoanalytic, behavioral and systems theory approaches. In T. J. Paolino & B. S. McCrady (Eds.), *Marriage and marital therapy: Psychoanalytic, behavioral, and systems theory perspectives* (pp. 445–566). New York: Brunner/Mazel.

Gurman, A. S., & Kniskern, D. P. (1978). Deterioration in marital and family therapy: Empirical, clinical and conceptual issues. *Family Process, 17,* 3–20.

Gurman, A. S., & Kniskern, D. P. (1981). Family therapy outcome research. Knowns and unknowns. In A. S. Gurman & D. P. Kniskern (Eds.), *Handbook of family therapy* (pp. 742–776). New York: Bruner/Mazel.

Gurman, A. S., & Kniskern, D. P. (1991). *Handbook of family therapy*: Volume II. New York: Brunner/Mazel.

Guy, J. D. (1987). *The personal life of the psychotherapist*. New York: Wiley.

H. L. v. Matheson, 450 U.S. 398 (1981).

Haas, L. J., & Cummings, N. A. (1991). Managed outpatient mental health plans: Clinical, ethical, and practical guidelines for participation. *Professional Psychology: Research and Practice, 22,* 45–51.

Haas, L. J., & Malouf, J. L. (1995). *Keeping up the good work: A practitioner's guide to mental health ethics* (2nd ed.). Sarasota, FL: Professional Resource Exchange.

Haas, L. J., & Malouf, J. L. (2005). *Keeping up the good work: A practitioner's guide to mental health ethics* (4th ed.). Sarasota, FL: Professional Resource Exchange.

Hagan, M. A. (1997). *Whores of the court: The fraud of psychiatric testimony and the rape of American justice*. New York: Regan Books.

Hahman v. Hahman, 628 P.2d 984 (Ariz. App. 1981).

Hahn, R. A., & Kleist, D. M. (2000). Divorce mediation: Research and implications for family and couples counseling. *Family Journal: Counseling and Therapy for Couples and Families, 8,* 165–171.

Haley, J. (1971). *Changing families: A family therapy reader*. New York: Grune & Stratton.

Haley, J. (1976). *Problem-solving therapy: New strategies for effective family therapy*. San Francisco: Jossey-Bass.

Haley, J. (1984). Marriage or family therapy. *The American Journal of Family Therapy, 12*(2), 3–14.

Haley, J. (1987). The disappearance of the individual. *The Family Therapy Networker, 11*(2), 39–40.

Halleck, S. L. (1976). Another response to "Homosexuality: The ethical challenge." *Journal of Consulting and Clinical Psychology, 44,* 167–170.

Hammond, J. M. (1981). Children, divorce, and you. *Learning, 9,* 83–89.

Handel, W. W., & Sherwyn, B. A. (1982). Surrogate parenting. *Trial, 18,* 57–60, 77.

Handler, J. F. (1990). *Law and the search for community*. Philadelphia: University of Pennsylvania Press.

Hardy, K. V. (1994). Marginalization or development?; A response to Shields, Wynne, McDaniel, and Gawinski. *Journal of Marital and Family Therapy, 20*(2), 139–143.

Hardy, K. V., & Laszloffy, T. A. (1992). Training racially sensitive family therapists: Context, content, and contact. *Families in Society, 73,* 364–370.

Hare-Mustin, R. T. (1980). Family therapy may be dangerous for your health. *Professional Psychology, 11,* 935–938.

Hare-Mustin, R. T., Marecek, J., Kaplan, A. G., & Liss-Levinson, N. (1979). Rights of clients, responsibilities of therapists. *American Psychologist, 34,* 3–16.

Harkaway, J. (1989). Circus maximus. *The Family Therapy Networker, 13*(2), 3, 42–46, 78–79.

Harp, B. S., Jr. (1982). Post judgement proceedings. In *Program materials for seminars on family law practice*. Athens, GA: Institute of Continuing Legal Education in Georgia.

Harrar, W. R., VandeCreek, L., & Knapp, S. (1990). Ethical and legal aspects of clinical supervision. *Professional Psychology: Research and Practice, 21,* 37–41.

Harvard Law Review. (1985). Developments in privileged communications. *Harvard Law Review, 98,* 1450–1605.

Haslam, D. R., & Harris, S. M. (2004). Informed consent documents of marriage and family therapists in private practice: A qualitative analysis. *American Journal of Family Therapy, 32,* 359–375.

Hassouneh-Phillips, D., & Curry, M. A. (2002). Abuse of women with disabilities: State of the science. *Rehabilitation Counseling Bulletin, 45*(2), 96–105.

Hawley, D. R., & Gonzalez, C. (2005). Publication patterns of faculty in Commission on Accreditation for Marriage and Family Therapy Education programs. *Journal of Marital and Family Therapy, 31*(1), 89–98.

Haynes, J. (1978). Divorce mediation: A new role. *Journal of Social Work, 23,* 5–9.

Haynes, J. (1981). *Divorce mediation: A practical guide for therapists and counselors*. New York: Springer.

Hedlund v. Superior Court, 34 Cal. 3d 695, 669 p. 2d 41 (1983).

Heinlen, K. T., Welfel, E. R., Richmond, E. N., & Rak, C. F. (2003). The scope of WebCounseling: A survey of services and compliance with NBCC standards for the ethical practice of WebCounseling. *Journal of Counseling and Development, 81,* 61–70.

Held, B. S. (1990). What's in a name? Some confusions and concerns about constructivism. *Journal of Marital and Family Therapy, 16,* 179–186.

Helms, J. E. (1990). *Black and white racial identity: Theory, research, and practice*. Westport, CT: Greenwood.

Henderson, G. (2000). Race in America. *National Forum, 82*(2), 12–15.

Hendrick, S. S. (1988). Counselor self-disclosure. *Journal of Counseling and Development, 66,* 419–424.

Hendrickson, R. M. (1982). Counselor liability: Does the risk require insurance coverage? *Personnel and Guidance Journal, 61,* 205–207.

Hendrickson, R. M., & Mangum, R. S. (1978). *Governing board and administrator liability*. (ERIC Higher Education Research Report No. 9).

Henggeler, S., & Borduin, C. (1990). *Family therapy and beyond: A multisystemic approach to treating the behavior problems of children and adolescents*. Pacific Grove, CA: Brooks/Cole.

Hennessey, E. F. (1980). Explosion in family law litigation: Challenges and opportunities for the bar. *Family Law Quarterly, 14*, 187–201.

Henning, K., Jones, A., & Holdford, R. (2003). Treatment needs of women arrested for domestic violence. *Journal of Interpersonal Violence, 18*, 838–857.

Henry, M. (1994). Legal implications of in vitro fertilization with donor eggs: A research guide. *Legal Reference Services Quarterly, 13* (2), 5–34.

Heppner, M. (1978). Counseling the battered wife: Myths, facts and decisions. *Personnel and Guidance Journal, 56*, 522–525.

Herlihy, B. (1996). When a colleague is impaired: The individual counselor's response. *Journal of Humanistic Education and Development, 34*, 156–157.

Herlihy, B., & Corey, G. (1992). *Dual relationships in counseling*. Alexandria, VA: American Counseling Association.

Herlihy, B., & Corey, G. (1996). *ACA ethical standards casebook* (5th ed.). Alexandria, VA: American Counseling Association.

Hernandez, H. (1989). *Multicultural education: A teacher's guide to content and practice*. Upper Saddle River, NJ: Merrill/Prentice Hall.

Herrington, B. S. (1979). Privilege denied in joint therapy. *Psychiatric News, 14*(1), 1–9.

High, L. (2005). Personal communication.

Hill, M. R. (2001). Family therapists and religious communities: Negotiating dual relationships. *Family Relations, 50*, 199–209.

Hill, N. R., & Crews, J. A. (2005). The application of an ethical lens to the issue of diagnosis in marriage and family counseling. *The Family Journal, 13*(2), 176–180.

Hines, P. M., & Hare-Mustin, R. T. (1978). Ethical concerns in family therapy. *Professional Psychology, 9*, 165–171.

Hinkle, J. S., & Wells, M. (1995). *Family counseling in the schools*. Greensboro, NC: ERIC/CASS.

Hirschfeld, R. M. A., & Goodwin, F. K. (1988). Mood disorders. In J. A. Talbott, R. E. Hales, & S. C. Yudofsky (Eds.), *The American psychiatric press textbook of psychiatry*. Washington, DC: American Psychiatric Press.

Hoare, C. H. (1991). Psychosocial identity development and cultural others. *Journal of Counseling and Development, 70*, 45–53.

Hodgson, J. L., Johnson, L. N., Ketring, S. A., Wampler, R., & Lamson, A. L. (2005). Integrating research and clinical training in marriage and family therapy training programs. *Journal of Marital and Family Therapy, 31*(1), 75–88.

Hof, L., & Dwyer, C. E. (1982). Overcoming ambivalence through the use of values analysis. *The American Journal of Family Therapy, 10*(1), 17–26.

Hoffman, L. (1981). *Foundations of family therapy*. New York: Basic.

Hoffman, L., & Long, L. (1969). A systems dilemma. *Family Process, 8*, 211–234.

Holmes, J. (1996). Values in psychotherapy. *American Journal of Psychotherapy, 50*, 259–273.

Holtzworth-Munroe, A., & Stuart, G. L. (1994). Typeologies of male batterers: Three subtypes and the differences among them. *Psychological Bulletin, 116*, 476–497.

Holtzworth-Munroe, A., Meechan, J. C., Herron, K., Rehman, U., & Stuart, G. (2000). Testing the Holtzworth-Munroe and Stuart (1994) Batterer Typology. *Journal of Consulting and Clinical Psychology, 68*, 1000–1019.

Honos-Webb, L., & Leitner, L. M. (2001). How using the DSM causes damage: A client's report. *Journal of Humanistic Psychology, 41*(4), 36–56.

Hopkins, B. R., & Anderson, B. S. (1990). *The counselor and the law*. Alexandria, VA: American Counseling Association.

Hovestadt, A. J., Fenell, D. L., & Canfield, B. S. (2002). Characteristics of effective providers of marital and family therapy in rural mental health settings. *Journal of Marital and Family Therapy, 28*(2), 225–232.

Huber, C. H. (1995). Counselor responsibility within managed mental health care. *Family Journal: Counseling and Therapy for Couples and Families, 3*, 42–44.

Huber, C. H. (1996). Facilitating disclosure of HIV-positive status to family members. *Family Journal: Counseling and Therapy for Couples and Families, 4*, 53–55.

Huber, C. H. (1998). Time-limited counseling, invisible rationing, and informed consent. *Family Journal, 6*, 325–328.

Hulnick, H. R. (1977). Counselor: Know thyself. *Counselor Education and Supervision, 17*, 69–72.

Hundert, E. M. (1987). A model for ethical problem solving in medicine, with practical applications. *American Journal of Psychiatry, 144*, 839–846.

Hunter, L. (2005). Introduction. *Family Court Review, 43*, 191.

Hunter, N. D. (1991). Marriage, law, and gender: A feminist inquiry. *Law and Sexuality, 1*, 9–22.

Huntley, D. K., & Konetsky, C. D. (1992). Healthy families with adolescents. *Topics in Family Psychology and Counseling, 1*(1), 62–71.

Huston, K. (1984). Ethical decisions in treating battered women. *Professional Psychology: Research and Practice, 15*, 822–832.

Ibrahim, F. A. (1985). Human rights and ethical issues in the use of advanced technology. *Journal of Counseling and Development, 64*, 134–135.

Imber-Black, E. (1988). *Families and larger systems: A family therapist's guide through the labyrinth*. New York: Norton.

In re Adams, 174 Ill. App. 3d 595, 528 N. E. 2d 1075 (1988) rev'd and remanded, 133 Ill. 2d 437, 551 N. E. 2d 635 (1990).

In re Carrafa, 77 Cal. App. 3d 788, 143 Cal. Rptr. 848 (1978).

In re Fred J., 89 Cal. App. 3d 168, 152 Cal. Rptr. 327 (1979).

In re Marriage of Gove, 572 P.2d 458 (Ariz. App. 1977).

In re Marriage of Kovash, 858 P.2d 351 (Mont. 1993).

In re Marriage of Winegard, 278 N.W.2d 505 (Iowa, 1979).

In re Roger B., 84 Ill. 2d 323, 418 N.E.2d 751 (1981).

International Association of Marriage and Family Counselors (IAMFC). (2005). Ethical code for the International Association of Marriage and Family Counselors. *Family Journal: Counseling and Therapy for Couples and Families, 1,* 73–77.

Ivey, A. E., D'Andrea, M., Ivey, M. B., & Simek-Morgan, L. (2002). *Theories of counseling and psychotherapy: A multicultural perspective* (5th ed.). Boston: Allyn & Bacon.

Jablonski v. United States, 712 F.2d 391 (9th Cir. 1983).

Jacobson, N. S., & Bussod, N. (1983). Marital and family therapy. In M. Herson, A. E. Kazdin, & A. S. Bellack (Eds.), *The clinical psychology handbook.* New York: Pergamon.

Jacobson, N. S., & Margolin, G. (1979). *Marital therapy: Strategies based on social learning and behavior exchange principles.* New York: Brunner/Mazel.

Janeway, E. (1980). *Powers of the weak.* New York: Knopf.

Jantsch, E. (1980). *The self-organizing universe: Scientific and human implications of the emerging paradigm of evolution.* New York: Pergamon.

Jencius, M., & Sager, D. E. (2001). The practice of marriage and family counseling in cyberspace. *Family Journal, 9,* 295–302.

Johnson, M. P. (1995). Patriarchal terrorism and common couple violence: Two forms of violence against women. *Journal of Marriage and the Family, 57,* 283–294.

Johnson, M. P., & Ferraro, K. (2000). Research on domestic violence in the 1990s: Making distinctions. *Journal of Marriage and the Family, 62,* 948–963.

Johnson, T. R. (1965). Medical malpractice—Doctrines of *res ipsa loquitur* and informed consent. *University of Colorado Law Review, 37,* 182–195.

Jones, K. D. (1999). Ethics in publication. *Counseling and Values, 43,* 99–105.

Jones, S. R., & McEwen, M. K. (2000). A conceptual model of multiple dimensions of identity. *Journal of College Student Development, 41,* 405–413.

Jones, W. T., Sontag, F., Beckner, M. O., & Fogelin, R. J. (Eds.). (1977). *Approaches to ethics* (3rd ed.). New York: McGraw-Hill.

Jordan, A. E., & Meara, N. M. (1990). Ethics and the professional practice of psychologists: The role of virtues and principles. *Professional Psychology: Research and Practice, 21,* 107–114.

Jordan, K., & Stevens, P. (1999). Revising the ethics code of the IAMFC—A training exercise for counseling psychology and counselor education students. *Family Journal: Counseling and Therapy for Couples and Families, 7,* 170–175.

Jory, B., Anderson, D., & Greer, C. (1997). Intimate justice: Confronting issues of accountability, respect, and freedom in treatment for abuse and violence. *Journal of Marital and Family Therapy, 23,* 399–419.

Jurkovic, G. J. (1997). *Lost childhoods: The plight of the parentified child.* San Francisco: Brunner/Mazel.

Kahle, P. A., & Robbins, J. M. (2003). *The power of spirituality in therapy: Integrating spiritual and religious beliefs in mental health practice.* New York: Haworth.

Kain, C. D. (1988). To breach or not to breach: Is that the question? A response to Gray and Harding. *Journal of Counseling and Development, 66,* 224–225.

Kanani, D., & Regehr, C. (2003). Clinical, ethical, and legal issues in e-therapy. *Families in Society, 84*(2), 155–163.

Kaplan, D. (1999). Models of ethical decision making in marriage and family counseling. In P. Stevens (Ed.), *Ethical casebook for the practice of marriage and family counseling* (pp. 3–16). Alexandria, VA: American Counseling Association.

Kaplan, D., & Culkin, M. (1995). Family ethics: Lessons learned. *Family Journal: Counseling and Therapy for Couples and Families, 3,* 335–338.

Kaplan, H., Sager, C., & Schiavi, R. (1986). Editorial: Preventing the spread of AIDS. *Journal of Sex and Marital Therapy, 12,* 159–164.

Karpel, M. A. (1980). Family secrets: I. Conceptual and ethical issues in the relational context: II. Ethical and practical considerations in therapeutic management. *Family Process, 19,* 295–306.

Karpel, M. A., & Strauss, E. S. (1983). *Family evaluation.* New York: Gardner.

Kaschak, E. (2001). Intimate betrayal: Domestic violence in lesbian relationships. *Women and Therapy, 23,* 1–6.

Kaslow, F. W. (1986). Commentary: Individual therapy focused on marital problems. *American Journal of Family Therapy, 14,* 264.

Kaslow, F. W. (1990a). Children who sue parents: A new form of family homicide. *Journal of Marital and Family Therapy, 16,* 151–163.

Kaslow, F. W. (1990b). *Voices in family psychology.* Newbury Park, CA: Sage.

Kass, A. (1990). *Mediation* (VHS recording). Albuquerque, NM: Second Judicial District.

Kasturirangan, A., & Williams, E. N. (2003). Counseling Latina battered women: A qualitative study of the Latina perspective. *Journal of Multicultural Counseling and Development, 31*(3), 162–179.

Katz, J. (1977). Informed consent—A fairy tale? Law's vision. *University of Pittsburgh Law Review, 39,* 137–174.

Katz, S. N. (1981). *Child snatching: The legal response to the abduction of children.* Chicago: American Bar Association.

Kausch, O., & Resnick, P. J. (1998). The assessment of violence in the workplace and its legal ramifications. In F. Flach (Ed.), *Malpractice risk management in psychiatry* (pp. 332–246). New York: Hatherleigh.

Kavanaugh, P. B. (1989, March–April). People v. Cavaiani: Cavaiani wins. *Michigan Psychologist,* 8.

Kazen, B. A. (1977). *When father wants custody: A lawyer's view.* Austin: State Bar of Texas.

Keary, A. O. (1985). Criminal law and procedure. In N. T. Sidney (Ed.), *Law and ethics: A guide for the health professional* (pp. 63–102). New York: Human Sciences.

Keefe, R. H., Hall, M. L., & Corvo, K. N. (2002). Providing therapy when managed care organizations deny reimbursement: Are private practitioners and their clients taking the fall? *Social Work in Health Care, 36*(2), 49–65.

Kegeles, T., Catania, J., & Coates, T. (1988). Intentions to communicate positive HIV antibodies status to sex partners [Letter to the Editor]. *Journal of the American Medical Association, 259,* 216–217.

Keim, J. (2000). Strategic family therapy: The Washington school. In A. M. Horne (Ed.), *Family counseling and therapy* (3rd ed., pp. 170–207). Itasca, IL: F. E. Peacock.

Keith-Spiegel, P., & Koocher, G. P. (1998). *Ethics in psychology: Professional standards and cases* (2nd ed.). New York: Oxford University Press.

Keller, J. F., Huber, J. R., & Hardy, K. V. (1988). Accreditation: What constitutes appropriate marriage and family therapy education? *Journal of Marital and Family Therapy, 14,* 297–305.

Kelly, G. (1955). *The psychology of personal constructs.* New York: Norton.

Kemp, A. (1998). *Abuse in the family.* Pacific Grove, CA: Brooks/Cole.

Kempin, F. (1982). *Historical introduction to Anglo-American law* (2nd ed.). St. Paul, MN: West Publishing.

Kennedy, C. (1973). The psychotherapists' privilege. *Washburn Law Review, 12,* 297–315.

Kessler, S. (1978). *Creative conflict resolution: Mediation.* Atlanta: National Institute for Professional Training.

Kidder, R. M. (1995). *How good people make tough choices.* New York: Fireside.

Kier, F. J., & Molinari, V. (2004). Do-it-yourself testing for mental illness: Ethical issues, concerns and recommendations. *Professional Psychology: Research and Practice, 35,* 261–268.

Kimberly, J. A., Serovich, J. M., & Greene, K. (1995). Disclosure of HIV-positive status: Five women's stories. *Family Relations, 44,* 316–322.

Kissel, S. (1983). *Private practice for the mental health clinician.* Rockville, MD: Aspen.

Kitchener, K. S. (1984a). Ethics in counseling psychology: Distinctions and directions. *Counseling Psychologist, 12,* 15–18.

Kitchener, K. S. (1984b). Intuition, critical evaluation, and ethical principles: The foundation for ethical decisions in counseling psychology. *Counseling Psychologist, 12,* 43–55.

Kitchener, K. S. (1985). Ethical principles and ethical decisions in student affairs. In H. J. Canon & R. D. Brown (Eds.), *Applied ethics: Tools for practitioners.* San Francisco: Jossey-Bass.

Kitchener, K. S. (1986). Teaching applied ethics in counselor education: An integration of psychological processes and philosophical analysis. *Journal of Counseling and Development, 64,* 306–310.

Kitchener, K. S. (1988). Dual role relationships: What makes them so problematic. *Journal of Counseling and Development, 67,* 217–221.

Kitchener, K. S. (1992). Posttherapy relationships: Ever or never? In B. Herlihy & G. Corey (Eds.), *Dual relationships in counseling* (pp. 145–148). Alexandria, VA: American Association for Counseling and Development.

Kitchener, K. S., & Harding, S. S. (1990). Dual role relationships. In B. Herlihy & L. B. Golden (Eds.), *AACD Ethical standards casebook* (4th ed., pp. 146–154). Alexandria, VA: American Counseling Association.

Kluckhohn, F., & Strodtbeck, F. L. (1961). *Variations in value orientation.* Evanston, IL: Row, Peterson.

Knapp, S., & VandeCreek, L. (1982). *Tarasoff:* Five years later. *Professional Psychology, 13,* 511–516.

Knapp, S., & VandeCreek, L. (1985). Psychotherapy and privileged communications in child custody cases. *Professional Psychology: Research and Practice, 16,* 398–407.

Knapp, S., & VandeCreek, L. (1987). *Privileged communications in the mental health professions.* New York: Van Nostrand Reinhold.

Knapp, S., & VandeCreek, L. (1990). Application of the duty to protect HIV-positive patients. *Professional Psychology: Research and Practice, 21,* 161–166.

Knapp, S. J., & VandeCreek, L. D. (2006). Multiple relationships and professional boundaries. In S. J. Knapp & L. D. VandeCreek (Eds.), *Practical ethics for psychologists: A positive approach* (pp. 75–97). Washington, DC: American Psychological Association.

Knapp, S., VandeCreek, L., & Zirkel, P. A. (1985). Legal research techniques: What the psychologist needs to know. *Professional Psychology: Research and Practice, 16*, 363–372.

Knudson-Martin, C. (1997). The politics of gender in family therapy. *Journal of Marital and Family Therapy, 23*, 421–437.

Knudson-Martin, C. (2001). Women and mental health: A feminist family systems approach. In M. MacFarlane (Ed.), *Family therapy and mental health: Innovations in theory and practice* (pp. 331–359). New York: Haworth Press.

Knudson-Martin, C. (2002, July/August). Feminism in MFT: Where has it led us. *Family Therapy Magazine*, 28–31.

Kosinski, F. A. (1982). Standards, accreditation, and licensure in marriage and family therapy. *Personnel and Guidance Journal, 60*, 350–352.

Kottler, J. A. (1990). *On being a therapist*. San Francisco: Jossey-Bass.

Kottler, J. A. (2003). *On being a therapist* (3rd ed.). San Francisco: Jossey-Bass.

Kottler, J. A., & Hazler, R. J. (1996). Impaired counselors: The dark side brought to light. *Journal of Humanistic Education & Development, 34*(3), 98–107.

Kovacs, K. E. (1995). Recognizing gay and lesbian families: Marriage and parental rights. *Law and Sexuality, 5*, 513–539.

Kral, R., & Hines, M. (1999). A survey on developmental stages in achieving a competent sense of self as a family therapist. *The Family Journal, 7*, 102–111.

Kramer, D. T. (1994). *Legal rights of children* (2nd ed.). New York: McGraw-Hill.

Krause, H. D. (1977). *Family law in a nutshell*. St. Paul, MN: West Publishing.

Krause, H. D. (1982). Child support enforcement: Legislative tasks for the early 1980's. *Family Law Quarterly, 15*, 349–370.

Krauskopf, J. (1983). *Marital and non-marital contracts*. Chicago: American Bar Association.

Kristensen v. Kristensen, 406 So. 2d 1210 (Fla. 5th DCA 1981).

Krugman, S. (1986). Challenging tradition: Sometimes violence is a way of life. *The Family Therapy Networker, 10*(4), 41–43.

Kurilla, V. (1998). Multicultural counseling perspectives: Culture specificity and implications in family therapy. *Family Counseling: Counseling and Therapy for Couples and Families, 6*, 207–211.

Kurri, K., & Wahlstrom, L. (2001). Dialogical management of morality in domestic violence counseling. *Feminism and Psychology, 11*, 187–209.

L'Abate, L. (1982). Introduction. In J. C. Hansen & L. L'Abate (Eds.), *Values, ethics, legalities and the family therapist* (pp. xv–xvi). Rockville, MD: Aspen.

Laird, J. (2000). Gender in lesbian relationships: Cultural, feminist, and constructionist reflections. *Journal of Marital and Family Therapy, 26*(4), 455–467.

Laliotis, D. A., & Grayson, J. H. (1985). Psychologist heal thyself: What is available for the impaired psychologist? *American Psychologist, 40*, 84–89.

Lamb, D. H., Clark, C., Drumheller, P., Frizzell, K., & Surrey, L. (1989). Applying *Tarasoff* to AIDS-related psychotherapy issues. *Professional Psychology: Research and Practice, 20*, 37–43.

Lane, P. J., & Spruill, J. (1980). To tell or not to tell: The psychotherapist's dilemma. *Psychotherapy: Theory, Research, and Practice, 17*, 202–209.

Langsley, D. C., & Kaplan, D. M. (1968). *The treatment of families in crisis*. New York: Grune & Stratton.

Larson v. Larson, 24 Ill. App.2d 467, 192 N.E.2d 594 (1963).

Lavori, N. (1976). *Living together, married or single: Your legal rights*. New York: Harper & Row.

Lawless, L. L., Ginter, E. J., & Kelly, K. R. (1999). Managed care: What mental health counselors need to know. *Journal of Mental Health Counseling, 21*, 50–66.

Lebow, J. (1992). Systemically evaluating custody disputes. *Family Therapy News, 23*(2), 15.

Lee, M. Y., Uken, A., & Sebold, J. (2004). Accountability for change: Solution-focused treatment with domestic violence offenders. *Family and Society, 85*, 463–477.

Lee, S. B. (2003). Working with Korean-American families: Multicultural hermeneutics in understanding and dealing with marital domestic violence. *American Journal of Family Therapy, 31*(3), 159–179.

Leedy v. Hartnett, 510 F.Supp. 1125 (M.D. Penn. 1981).

Lehr v. Robertson, 463 U.S. 248 (1983).

Leslie, L. A., & Clossick, M. L. (1996). Sexism in family therapy: Does training in gender make a difference? *Journal of Marital and Family Therapy, 22*, 253–265.

Leslie, R. S. (2004). Advertising—Selected legal and ethical issues. *Family Therapy Magazine, 3*(6), 48–50.

Liddle, H. A. (1987). Family psychology: The journal, the field. *Journal of Family Psychology, 1*, 5–22.

Liddle, H. A. (1991a). Empirical values and the culture of family therapy. *Journal of Marital and Family Therapy, 17*, 327–348.

Liddle, H. A. (1991b). Training and supervision in family therapy: A comprehensive and critical analysis. In A. S. Gurman & D. P. Kniskern (Eds.), *Handbook of family therapy: Volume II* (pp. 638–697). New York: Brunner/Mazel.

Liddle, H. A. (1992). Family psychology: Progress and prospects of a maturing discipline. *Journal of Family Psychology, 5*, 249–263.

Liddle, H. A., Gurman, A. S., Pinsof, W. M., & Roberto, L. G. (1990, October). *What's wrong with family therapy?* Symposium conducted at the annual meeting of the American Association of Marriage and Family Therapy, Washington, DC.

Lifson, L. E., & Simon, R. I. (Eds.). (1998). *The mental health practitioner and the law*. Cambridge, MA: Harvard University Press.

Linton, R. (1945). *The science of man in the world crisis*. New York: Columbia University Press.

Loving v. Virginia, 388 U.S. 1 (1967).

Lyddon, W. J., & Adamson, L. A. (1992). Worldview and counseling preference: An analogue study. *Journal of Counseling and Development, 71,* 41–47.

Mabe, A. R., & Rollin, S. A. (1986). The role of a code of ethical standards in counseling. *Journal of Counseling and Development, 64,* 294–297.

MacDonald, J. M. (1969). *Psychiatry and the criminal* (2nd ed.). Springfield, IL: Charles C. Thomas.

Mace, D. R. (1976). Marital intimacy and the deadly love-anger cycle. *Journal of Marriage and Family Counseling, 2,* 131–137.

MacGillivray, I.K. (2000). Educational equity for gay, lesbian, bisexual, transgendered, and queer/questioning students: The demands of democracy and justice for America's schools. *Education and Urban Society, 32,* 303–323.

Madanes, C. (1980). Protection, paradox, and pretending. *Family Process, 19,* 73–85.

Madanes, C. (1983). Strategic therapy of schizophrenia. In W. R. McFarlane (Ed.), *Family therapy in schizophrenia*. New York: Guilford.

Madonna, J. M. (1986). A treatment of a case of marital abuse. *American Journal of Family Therapy, 14,* 235–246.

Maheu, M. M., & Gordon, B. L. (2000). Counseling and therapy on the Internet. *Professional Psychology: Research and Practice, 31*(5), 84–90.

Mahmoud, V. (1996). African American Muslim families. In M. McGoldrick, J. Giordano, & J. K. Pearce (Eds.), *Ethnicity and family therapy* (2nd ed.) (pp. 112–128). New York: Guilford.

Mahoney, M. M. (2005). Forces shaping the law of cohabitation for opposite sex couples. *Journal of Law and Family Studies, 7,* 135.

Malcolm, J. C. (1988). *Treatment choices and informed consent*. Springfield, IL: Charles C. Thomas.

Mappes, D. C., Robb, G. P., & Engels, D. W. (1985). Conflicts between ethics and the law in counseling and psychotherapy. *Journal of Counseling and Development, 64,* 246–252.

Margolin, G. (1982). Ethical and legal considerations in marriage and family therapy. *American Psychologist, 7,* 788–801.

Marlow, L. (1985). Divorce mediation: Therapists in the legal world. *The American Journal of Family Therapy, 13,* 3–10.

Marvin v. Marvin, 18 Cal. 3d 660, 134 Cal. Rptr.815, 557 P.2d 106 (1976).

Maslow, A. H. (1959). *New knowledge in human values*. New York: Harper & Row.

Massachusetts General Laws, ch. 119, § 63 (West Supp. 1980).

Massachusetts General Laws Annotated, ch. 233 § 20B (e) (West Supp. 1980).

Mathias, B. (1986). Lifting the shade on family violence. *The Family Therapy Networker, 10*(4), 20–29.

Matter of Atkins, 316 NW. 2d 477 (Mich. App. 1982).

Maturana, H. R. (1978). Biology of language: Epistemology of reality. In G. A. Miller & E. Lenneberg (Eds.), *Psychology and biology of language and thought*. New York: Academic.

May, K. M. (1998). A feminist and multicultural perspective in family therapy. *Family Journal: Counseling and Therapy for Couples and Families, 6,* 123–124.

May, K. M., & Church, N. L. (1999). Families and communities: Building bridges. *The Family Journal, 7*(1), 51–53.

McCarthy, P., & Sugden, S. (1995). A practical guide to informed consent in clinical supervision. *Counselor Education and Supervision, 35*(2), 130–139.

McCarty v. McCarty, 101 S. Ct. 2728 (1981).

McCloskey, L. A., Treviso, M., Scionti, T., & Posson, G. D. (2002). A comparative study of battered women and their children in Italy and the United States. *Journal of Family Violence, 17*(1), 53–75.

McCrady, B. S. (1989). The distressed or impaired professional: From retribution to rehabilitation. *Journal of Drug Issues, 19,* 337–349.

McCullough, M. E., Worthington, E. L, Maxey, J. L., & Rachal, K. C. (1997). Gender in the context of supportive and challenging religious counseling interventions. *Journal of Counseling Psychology, 44,* 80–88.

McG Mullen, R., & Carroll, M. (1983). The battered-woman syndrome: Contributing factors and remedial interventions. *American Mental Health Counselors Association Journal, 5,* 31–38.

McGoldrick, M., & Carter, B. (2001). Advances in coaching: Family therapy with one person. *Journal of Marital and Family Therapy, 27,* 281–300.

McGoldrick, M., Giordano, J., Pearce, J. K., & Giordano, J. (1996). *Ethnicity and family therapy* (2nd ed.). New York: Guilford.

McGoldrick, M., Giordano, J., Pearce, J. K., & Giordano, J. (2005). *Ethnicity and family therapy* (3rd ed.). New York: Guilford.

McGrath, P, Browning, F., Martinek, S., Beck, E., & Culkin, M. (Eds.). (1995). Family ethics: Dual relationships. *Family Journal: Counseling and Therapy for Couples and Families, 3,* 142–144.

McGuire, J. M., & Borowy, T. D. (1978). Confidentiality and the Buckley-Pell amendment: Ethical and legal considerations for counselors. *Personnel and Guidance Journal, 56,* 554–557.

McIntosh, D. M., & Cartaya, C. Y. (1992). Pychotherapist as clairvoyant: Failing to predict and warn. *Defense Counsel Journal, 59,* 569–573.

McIntosh v. Milano, 403 A.2d 500 (N.J. 1979).

McIntyre, J. (1993, June). Some highlights of APA's Annual Meeting. *Psychiatric News, 28*(12), 3.

McKenzie, D. J. (1978). The setting up of a family court counseling system in Australia. *Conciliation Courts Review, 16,* 23–30.

McLaughlin, B. (1999). Planned Parenthood of the Blue Ridge v. Camblos: Further impediment to a minor's right to abortion. *Thomas Jefferson Law Review, 21,* 147–164.

McLellan, B. (1999). The prostitution of psychotherapy: A feminist critique. *British Journal of Guidance and Counseling, 27,* 325–338.

McRae, M. B., Thompson, D. A., & Cooper, S. (1996). Black churches as therapeutic groups. *Journal of Multicultural Counseling and Development, 27,* 207–220.

Melito, R. (1988). Combining individual psychodynamics with structural family therapy. *Journal of Marital and Family Therapy, 14,* 29–43.

Melton, G. B. (1988). Ethical and legal issues in AIDS-related practice. *American Psychologist, 43,* 941–947.

Meyer, R., & Smith, S. (1977). A crisis in group therapy. *American Psychologist, 32,* 638–643.

Meyerstein, I., & Todd, J. C. (1980). On the witness stand: The family therapist and expert testimony. *The American Journal of Family Therapy, 8*(4), 43–51.

Middleton, R. A., Rollins, C. W., & Harley, D. A. (1999). The historical and political context of the civil rights of persons with disabilities. *Journal of Multicultural Counseling and Development, 27,* 105–120.

Miller, J. K. (2005). The question of competence. *Family Therapy Magazine, 4*(4), 28–31.

Miller, R. B., Anderson, S., & Keala, D. K. (2004). Is Bowen theory valid? A review of basic research. *Journal of Marital and Family Therapy, 30*(4), 453–466.

Miller, T. W., Veltkamp, L. J., Lane, T., Bilyeu, J., & Elzie, N. (2002). Care pathway guides for assessment and counseling for domestic violence. *The Family Journal, 10*(1), 41–49.

Mills, T. (1985). The assault on the self: Stages in coping with battering husbands. *Qualitative Sociology, 8,* 103–123.

Milne, A. (1978). Custody of children in a divorce process. A family self-determination model. *Conciliation Courts Review, 16,* 1–10.

Minuchin, S. (1974). *Families and family therapy.* Cambridge, MA: Harvard University Press.

Minuchin, S., & Fishman, H. C. (1981). *Family therapy techniques.* Cambridge, MA: Harvard University Press.

Mitten, T. J., & Connell, G. M. (2004). The core variables of Symbolic-Experiential Therapy: A qualitative study. *Journal of Marital and Family Therapy, 30*(4), 467–478.

Mnookin, R. (1973). Foster care in whose best interest? *Harvard Educational Review, 43,* 599–638.

Mnookin, R. H., & Weisberg, D. K. (1995). *Child, family and state: Problems and materials on children and the law.* Boston: Little, Brown.

Mnookin, R. H., & Weisberg, D. K. (2000). *Child, family and state: Problems and materials on children and the law* (4th ed.). Boston: Little, Brown.

Monahan, J. (1993). Limiting therapists exposure to *Tarasoff* liability: Guidelines for risk containment. *American Psychologist, 48,* 242–250.

Mor, B. (2005). The space between love and not touching in psychotherapy. *American Journal of Psychotherapy, 59,* 42–60.

Morreim, E. H. (1988). Cost containment: Challenging fidelity and justice. *Hastings Center Report, 18,* 20–25.

Morrison, J. K., Layton, B., & Newman, J. (1982). Ethical conflict in clinical decision making: A challenge for family therapists. In J. C. Hansen & L. L'Abate (Eds.), *Values, ethics, legalities and the family therapist* (pp. 75–86). Rockville, MD: Aspen.

Mowrer, O. H. (Ed.). (1967). *Morality and mental health.* Chicago: Rand McNally.

Mulvey, E. P., Reppucci, N. D., & Weithorn, L. A. (1984). Mental health, law, and children. In N. D. Reppucci, L. A. Weithorn, E. P. Mulvey, & J. Monahan (Eds.), *Children, mental health, and the law* (pp. 15–24). Beverly Hills: Sage.

Nagy, T. F. (2000). *Ethics in plain English: An illustrative casebook for psychologists.* Washington, DC: American Psychological Association.

Napier, A. Y., & Whitaker, C. (1978). *The family crucible.* New York: Harper & Row.

Nastasi, B. (2004 July 26). Personal communication.

Nathanson v. Kline. 186 Kan. 393, 350 P.2d 1093 (1960) affirmed on rehearing, 187 Kan. 186, 354 P.2d 1093 (1960).

National Association of Social Workers. (1999). *Code of ethics* (Rev. ed.). Silver Springs, MD: Author.

National Board for Certified Counselors, Inc. (2001). *The Practice of Internet Counseling.* Retrieved June 7, 2005, from http://www.nbcc.org/ethics/web ethics.htm

National Gay and Lesbian Task Force. (2005). *Ways to protect same sex relationships: A comparison.* Los Angeles: Author. Retrieved November 15, 2005, from http://www.thetaskforce.org/downloads/MarriageDifferences.pdf

Navin, S., Beamish, P., & Johanson, G. (1995). Ethical practices of field-based mental health counselor supervisors. *Journal of Mental Health Counseling, 17,* 243–253.

Negligence § 1. (2000). American Jurisprudence 2d, 57A, 63.

Nelson, K. W., & Jackson, S. A. (2003). Professional counselor identity and development: A qualitative study of Hispanic student interns. *Counselor Education & Supervision, 43,* 2–15.

Nelson, L. J., Clark, H. W., Goldman, R. L., & Schore, J. E. (1989). Taking the train to a world of strangers:

Health care marketing and ethics. *Hastings Center Report, 19,* 36–43.

Neukrug, E., Lovell, C., & Parker, R. J. (1996). Employing ethical codes and decision-making models: A developmental process. *Counseling and Values, 40,* 98–106.

Newman, R., & Bricklin, P. M. (1991). Parameters of managed mental health care: Legal, ethical, and professional guidelines. *Professional Psychology: Research and Practice, 22,* 26–35.

Newman v. Newman, 653 P.2d 728 (Colo Sup. Ct. 1982).

New Mexico Center for Dispute Resolution. (1990). *Parent–child mediation training manual.* Albuquerque, NM: Parent–Child Mediation Training Institute.

New Mexico ex. rel. Human Services Department v. Levario, 649 P.2d 510 (N.M. Ct. App. 1982).

Nichols, M. P. (1987a). The individual in the system. *The Family Therapy Networker, 11*(2), 33–38, 85.

Nichols, M. P. (1987b). *The self in system: Expanding the limits of family therapy.* New York: Brunner/Mazel.

Nichols, M. P., & Schwartz, R. C. (2001). *Family therapy: Concepts and methods* (5th ed.). Boston: Allyn & Bacon.

Nichols, M. P., & Schwartz, R. C. (2004). *Family therapy: Concepts and methods* (6th ed.). Boston: Allyn & Bacon.

Nichols, W. C. (1986). Understanding family violence: An orientation for family therapists. *Contemporary Family Therapy, 8,* 188–201.

Nichols, W. C. (1992). *The AAMFT: Fifty years of marital and family therapy.* Washington: American Association for Marriage and Family Therapy.

Nichols, W. C., Bardhill, D. R., Everett, C., Figley, C., & Clark, T. E. (1984). *A report from task force on recognition, regulation, and legitimization of marital and family therapy.* Unpublished report, AAMFT: Washington, DC.

Nickelson, D. W. (1998). Telehealth and the evolving health care system: Strategic opportunities for professional psychology. *Professional Psychology: Research and Practice, 29,* 527–535.

Norcross, J. C., Alford, B. A., & DeMichele, J. T. (1992). The future of psychotherapy: Delta data and concluding observations. *Psychotherapy, 29,* 150.

Northey, Jr., W. F. (2002). Characteristics and clinical practices of marriage and family therapists: A national survey. *Journal of Marital and Family Therapy, 28*(4), 487–494.

Northey, Jr., W. F. (2005). Studying marriage and family therapists in the 21st century: Methodological and technological issues. *Journal of Marital and Family Therapy, 31*(1), 99–106.

Nozick, R. (1968). Moral complications and moral structure. *Natural Law Forum, 13,* 1–50.

O'Dell, M. (2003). Intersecting worldviews: Including versus imposing spirituality in therapy. *Family Therapy Magazine, 2*(4), 26–30.

Office of Civil Rights. (2005). Medical privacy—National standards that protect the privacy of personal health information. Washington, DC: United States Department of Health and Human Services. Retrieved November 19, 2005, from http://www.hhs.gov/ocr/hipaa/

Okun, B. F., & Rappaport, L. J. (1980). *Working with families: An introduction to family therapy.* North Scituate, MA: Duxbury.

Olson, D. H., Russell, C. S., & Sprenkle, D. H. (1980). Marital and family therapy: A decade review. *Journal of Marriage and the Family, 42,* 973–993.

Oppenheim, C. L. (1968). Valid consent to medical treatment: Need the patient know? *Duquesne Law Review, 4,* 450–577.

Orlando, F. A. (1978). Conciliation programs: Their effect on marriage and family life. *Florida Bar Journal, 52,* 218–221.

Orton, G. L. (1997). *Strategies for counseling with children and their parents.* Pacific Grove, CA: Brooks/Cole.

Osborne v. Osborne, 428 N.E. 2d 810 (Mass. 1981).

O'Shea, M., & Jessee, E. (1982). Ethical, value, and professional conflicts in systems therapy. In J. C. Hansen & L. L'Abate (Eds.), *Values, ethics, legalities and the family therapist* (pp. 1–22). Rockville, MD: Aspen.

Owens, K., & King, M. C. (1999). Genomic views of human society. *Science, 291,* 1219–1220.

Packer, P. (1988, October 3). Let's put a stop to the "insurance diagnosis." *Medical Economics,* 19–28.

Painter, S., & Dutton, D. (1985). Patterns of emotional bonding in battered women: Traumatic bonding. *International Journal of Women's Studies, 8,* 363–375.

Pais, S., Piercy, F., & Miller, J. (1998). Factors related to family therapists' breaking confidence when clients disclose high-risks-to-HIV/AIDS sexual behaviors. *Journal of Marital and Family Therapy, 24,* 457–473.

Palmer, N., & Kaufman, M. (2003). The ethics of informed consent: Implications for multicultural practice. *Journal of Ethnic and Cultural Diversity in Social Work, 12,* 1–27.

Papp, P. (1984). The creative leap. *The Family Therapy Networker, 8*(5), 20–29.

Parniawski v. Parniawski, 359 A.2d 719 (Conn. 1976).

Patten, C., Barnett, T., & Houlihan, D. (1991). Ethics in marital and family therapy: A review of the literature. *Professional Psychology: Research and Practice, 22,* 171–175.

Pearson, B., & Piazza, N. (1997). Classification of dual relationships in the helping professions. *Counselor Education and Supervision, 37,* 89–99.

Pearson, J., & Thoennes, H. (1982). Mediation and divorce: The benefits outweigh the costs. *Family Advocate, 4*(3), 25–32.

Peck v. Counseling Service of Addison County, Inc., 499 A. 2d 422 (Vt. 1985).

Pedersen, P. (1994). *A handbook for developing multicultural awareness* (2nd ed.). Alexandria, VA: American Counseling Association.

Pedersen, P. (1996). The importance of both similarities and differences in multicultural counseling: Reaction to C. H. Patterson. *Journal of Counseling and Development, 74,* 236–237.

Pell, E. R. (1979). A theory of imperfection: An imperfect theory? *Counselor Education and Supervision, 19,* 54–59.

People v. Cohen, 98 Misc.2d 874, 414 N.Y.S.2d 642 (1977).

Perry v. Fiumano, 403 N.Y.S.2d 382 (1978).

Peterman, L. M., & Dixon, C. G. (2003). Domestic violence between same-sex partners: Implications for counseling. *Journal of Counseling and Development, 81*(1), 40–48.

Peterson, K. S. (1999, June 29). Criticism, new ideas pull marital therapists asunder. *USA Today,* D1–D2.

Peterson, L. R. (1992). Practice pointers. *Family Therapy News, 23*(2), 21.

Petrashek v. Petrashek, 232 Neb. 212, 440 N.W. 2d 220 (1989).

Pfeiffer, S., & Tittler, B. (1983). Utilizing the multidisciplinary team to facilitate a school–family systems orientation. *School Psychology Review, 12,* 168–173.

Phillips, B. N. (1982). Regulation and control in psychology: Implications for certification and licensure. *American Psychologist, 37,* 919–936.

Phillips, L. E. (1987). Thoughts on improving mandatory continuing education. *Lifelong Learning Forum, 4,* 1–2.

Phinney, J. S. (2000). Identity formation across cultures: The interaction of personal, societal, and historical change. *Human Development, 43,* 27–32.

Physicians, surgeons, and other healers § 99. (2000). *American Jurisprudence 2d, 61,* 241–242.

Piercy, F. P., & Sprenkle, D. H. (1983). Ethical, legal and professional issues in family therapy: A graduate level course. *Journal of Marital and Family Therapy, 9,* 393–401.

Pinsof, W. M., & Wynne, L. C. (Eds.). (1995). The effectiveness of marital and family therapy [Special issue]. *Journal of Marital and Family Therapy, 21.*

Pittman, F. (1985). Gender myths. *Family Therapy Networker, 9*(6), 24–33.

Pittman, F. (1995). Turning tragedy into comedy. *Family Therapy Networker, 19*(6), 36–40.

Planned Parenthood Association v. Ashcroft, 462 U.S. 476, 103 S.Ct. 2517, 76 L.Ed. 2d 733 (1983).

Planned Parenthood of the Blue Ridge v. Camblos, 155 F3d 352 (4th Cir. 1998).

Planned Parenthood of Central Missouri v. Danforth, 428 U.S. 52 (1976).

Polikoff, N. C. (1993). We will get what we ask for: Why legalizing gay and lesbian marriage will not "dismantle the legal structure of gender in every marriage." *Virginia Law Review, 79,* 1535–1550.

Pomerantz, A. M. (2000). What if prospective clients knew how managed care impacts psychologists' practice and ethics? An exploratory study. *Ethics and Behavior, 10,* 159–171.

Ponterotto, J. G. (1991). The nature of prejudice revisited: Implications for counseling intervention. *Journal of Counseling and Development, 70,* 216–224.

Pope, K. S., & Vasquez, M. J. T. (1999). *Ethics in psychotherapy and counseling: A practical guide for psychologists* (2nd ed.). San Francisco: Jossey-Bass.

Posner v. Posner, 233 So.2d 381 (Fla. 1979).

Poston, W. S. C. (1990). The biracial identity development model: A needed addition. *Journal of Counseling and Development, 69,* 152–155.

Pressman, R. M. (1979). *Private practice: A guide for the independent mental health practitioner.* New York: Gardner.

Prosser, W. (1971). *Handbook of the law of torts.* St. Paul, MN: West Publishing.

Prosser, W. L., Wade, J. W., & Schwartz, V. E. (1988). *Cases and materials on torts* (8th ed.). Westbury, NY: Foundation Press.

Protinsky, H., & Coward, L. (2001). Developmental lessons of seasoned marital and family therapists: A qualitative investigation. *Journal of Marital and Family Therapy, 27*(3), 375–384.

Psychological Services Act, Florida Statutes, Chapter 490 (1983).

Purtilo, R., & Sorrel, J. (1986). The ethical dilemmas of a rural physician. *Hastings Center Report, 16,* 24–28.

Reamer, F. G. (1992). The impaired social worker. *Social Work, 37,* 165–171.

Redekop, F. (1995). The "problem" of Michael White and Michael Foucault. *Journal of Marital and Family Therapy, 21,* 309–318.

Reed, J. M. (1985). The origin and functions of American law. In N. T. Sidney (Ed.), *Law and ethics: A guide for the health professional* (pp. 1–10). New York: Human Sciences Press.

Reen v. Reen, 8 Fam. L. Rep. 2193 (Mass. 1981).

Reeve, D. (2000). Oppression within the counseling room. *Disability and Society, 15,* 669–682.

Remley, T. P. (1990). Counseling records: Legal and ethical issues. In B. Herlihy & L. B. Golden (Eds.), *Ethical standards casebook* (pp. 162–169). Alexandria, VA: American Counseling Association.

Remley, T. P. (1991). *Preparing for court appearances.* Alexandria, VA: American Association for Counseling and Development.

Remley, T. P., Jr., & Herlihy, B. (2001). *Ethical, legal, and professional issues in counseling.* Upper Saddle River, NJ: Prentice Hall.

Remley, T. P., & Herlihy, B. (2005). *Ethical, legal, and professional issues in counseling* (2nd ed.). Upper Saddle River, NJ: Merrill/Prentice Hall.

Reppucci, N. D., Weithorn, L. A., Mulvey, E. P., & Monahan, J. (Eds.). (1984). *Children, mental health and the law.* Beverly Hills: Sage.

Rest, J. R. (1982, February). A psychologist looks at the teaching of ethics. *Hastings Center Report,* pp. 29–36.

Rest, J. R. (1983). Morality. In J. Flavell & E. Markman (Eds.), *Cognitive development* (Vol. 4). New York: Wiley.

Rice, M. E., & Harris, G. T. (1995). Psychopathy, schizophrenia, alcohol abuse, and violent recidivism. *International Journal of Law and Psychiatry, 18,* 333–342.

Richards, P. S., Rector, J. M., Tjeltveit, A. C. (1999). Values, spirituality, and psychotherapy. In W. R. Miller (Ed.), *Integrating spirituality in treatment: Resources for practitioners* (pp. 133–160). Washington, DC: American Psychological Association.

Richardson, L. M., & Austad, C. S. (1991). Realities of mental health practice in managed-care settings. *Professional Psychology: Research and Practice, 22,* 52–59.

Richman, J. (1979). Family therapy of attempted suicide. *Family Process, 18,* 131–142.

Ridgewood Financial Institute, Inc. (1984). *Psychotherapy finances: Guide to private practice.* Ho-Ho-Kus, NJ: Author.

Riemer-Reiss, M. L. (2000). Utilizing distance technology for mental health counseling. *Journal of Mental Health Counseling, 22,* 189–204.

Riley, P., Hartwell, S., Sargent, G., & Patterson, J. E. (1997). Beyond law and ethics: An interdisciplinary course in family law and family therapy. *Journal of Marital and Family Therapy, 23,* 461–476.

Rinas, J., & Clyne-Jackson, T. (1988). *Professional conduct and legal concerns in mental health practice.* Norwalk, CT: Appleton & Lange.

Roberts, A. R. (1996). *Helping battered women: New perspectives and remedies.* New York: Oxford University Press.

Robinson, A. (2002). "There's a stranger in this house:" African American lesbians and domestic violence. *Women and Therapy, 25,* 125–137.

Robinson, T. L. (2005). *The convergence of race, ethnicity, and gender: Multiple identities in counseling* (2nd ed.). Upper Saddle, NJ: Pearson/Prentice Hall.

Roe v. Wade, 410 U.S. 113 (1973).

Rohrbaugh, M., Tennen, H., Press, S., & White, L. (1981). Compliance, defiance, and therapeutic paradox: Guidelines for strategic use of paradoxical interventions. *American Journal of Orthopsychiatry, 5,* 454–467.

Rokeach, M. (1968). A theory of organization and change within value-attitude systems. *Journal of Social Issues, 24,* 13–33.

Rokeach, M. (1973). *The nature of human values.* New York: Macmillan.

Roller v. Roller, 37 Wash. 242, 79 P. 788 (1905).

Rosen, C. E. (1977). Why clients relinquish their right to privacy under sign-away pressures. *Professional Psychology, 8,* 17–24.

Rosen, K. H., Matheson, J. L., Stith, S. M., McCollum, E. E., & Locke, L. D. (2003). Negotiated time-out: A de-escalation tool for couples. *Journal of Marital and Family Therapy, 29,* 291–298.

Rosenberg, M. S., & Hunt, R. D. (1984). Child maltreatment: Legal and mental health issues. In N. D. Reppucci, L. A. Weithorn, E. P. Mulvey, & J. Monahan (Eds.), *Children, mental health, and the law* (pp. 79–102). Beverly Hills: Sage.

Rowe, W., Bennett, S. K., & Atkinson, D. R. (1994). White racial identity models: A critique and alternative proposal. *Counseling Psychologist, 22,* 129–146.

Ruback, R. B. (1982). Issues in family law: Implications for therapists. In J. C. Hansen & L. L'Abate (Eds.), *Values, ethics, legalities and the family therapist* (pp. 103–124). Rockville, MD: Aspen.

Ruback, R. B. (1984). Family law. In R. H. Woody & Associates (Eds.), *The law and the practice of human services* (pp. 113–154). San Francisco: Jossey-Bass.

Ryder, R., & Hepworth, J. (1990). AAMFT ethical code: "Dual relationships." *Journal of Marital and Family Therapy, 16,* 127–132.

Sack, S. M. (1987). *The complete legal guide to marriage, divorce, custody, & living together.* New York: McGraw-Hill.

Salgo v. Leland Stanford, Jr., University Board of Trustees. 154 Cal. App. 2d 560, 317 P.2d 170 (1957).

Samantha Baskin v. Peter Baskin, No. 77368, Fairfax City. Ct., VA (1988).

Sanders, J. D. (2004). Obtaining useful parenting evaluations in cases involving third parties. *American Journal of Family Law, 18,* 161–166.

Satir, V. (1972). *Peoplemaking.* Palo Alto, CA: Science and Behavior Books.

Sauber, S. R., L'Abate, L., & Weeks, G. R. (1985). *Family therapy: Basic concepts and terms.* Rockville, MD: Aspen.

Sauerkof v. City of New York, 438 N.Y.S 2d 982 (Sup Ct. 1981).

Saunders, D. (1984). Helping husbands who batter. *Social Casework, 65,* 347–353.

Saunders, D. (1988). Other "truths" about domestic violence: A reply to McNeely and Robinson-Simpson. *Social Work, 33,* 179–183.

Sayette, M. A., & Mayne, T. J. (1990). Survey of current clinical and research trends in clinical psychology. *American Psychologist, 45,* 1263–1266.

Scalise, J. J. (2000). The ethical practice of marriage and family therapy. In A. M. Horne (Ed.), *Family counseling and therapy* (pp. 565–596). Itasca, IL: F. E. Peacock.

Schlossberger, E., & Hecker, L. (1996). HIV and family therapists' duty to warn: A legal and ethical analysis.

Journal of Marital and Family Therapy, 22, 27–40.

Schoyer, N. L. (1980). Divorce and the pre-school child. *Childhood Education, 57,* 2–7.

Schultz, B. (1982). *Legal liability in psychotherapy.* San Francisco: Jossey-Bass.

Schwallie, L. (2005). Core competencies and marriage and family therapy regulatory activity. *Family Therapy Magazine,* July–August, 24–27.

Schwartz, R. (1987). Our multiple selves. *The Family Therapy Networker, 11*(2), 24–31, 80–83.

Schwartz, S. H. (1977). Normative influences on altruism. In L. Berkowitz (Ed.), *Advances in experimental social psychology* (Vol. 10). New York: Academic.

Schwitzgebel, R. K. (1975). A contractual model for the protection of the rights of institutionalized mental patients. *American Psychologist, 30,* 815–820.

Schwitzgebel, R. K. (1976). Treatment contracts and ethical self-determination. *Clinical Psychologist, 29*(3), 5–7.

Schwitzgebel, R. L., & Schwitzgebel, R. K. (1980). *Law and psychological practice.* New York: Wiley.

Scott, E. (1984). Adolescents' reproductive rights: Abortion, contraception, and sterilization. In N. D. Reppucci, L. A. Weithorn, E. P. Mulvey, & J. Monahan (Eds.), *Children, mental health, and the law* (pp. 125–150). Beverly Hills: Sage.

Searight, H. R., & Openlander, P. (1984). Systemic therapy: A new brief intervention model. *Personnel and Guidance Journal, 62,* 387–391.

Selvini-Palazzoli, N., Boscolo, L., Cecchin, G., & Prata, G. (1978). *Paradox and counterparadox.* New York: Jason Aronson.

Selvini-Palazzoli, N., Boscolo, L., Cecchin, G., & Prata, G. (1980). The problem of the referring person. *Journal of Marriage and Family Therapy, 6,* 3–10.

Serovich, J. M., & Mosack, K. E. (2000). Training issues for supervisors of marriage and family therapists working with persons living with HIV. *Journal of Marital and Family Therapy, 26,* 103–111.

Seymour, W. R. (1982). Counselor/therapist values and therapeutic style. In J. C. Hansen & L. L' Abate (Eds.), *Values, ethics, legalities and the family therapist* (pp. 41–60). Rockville, MD: Aspen.

Shah, S. (1969). Privileged communications, confidentiality, and privacy. *Professional Psychology, 1,* 56–69.

Shah, S. (1970). Privileged communications, confidentiality, and privacy: Privileged communications. *Professional Psychology, 1,* 159–164.

Shalett, J. S., & Everett, C. A. (1981). Accreditation in family therapy education: Its history and role. *The American Journal of Family Therapy, 9*(4), 82–84.

Shapiro, R. (1984). Therapy with violent families. In S. Saunders, A. M. Anderson, C. A. Hart, & G. M. Rubenstein (Eds.), *Violent individuals and families: A handbook for practitioners.* Springfield, IL: Charles C. Thomas.

Shapiro, R. (1986). Passing the buck: Too often family therapists steer clear of violent cases. *The Family Therapy Networker, 10*(4), 48, 64–66.

Sharman, A. (2001). Healing the wounds of domestic abuse: Improving the effectiveness of feminist therapeutic interventions with immigrant and racially visible women who have been abused. *Violence Against Women, 7,* 1405–1429.

Shea, T. E. (1985). Finding the law: Legal research and citation. In N. T. Sidney (Ed.), *Law and ethics: A guide for the health professional* (pp. 411–424). New York: Human Sciences.

Sheffield, D. S. (1998). Counselor impairment: Moving toward a concise definition and protocol. *Journal of Humanistic Education and Development, 37,* 96–107.

Sherman, R. (1999). Organizing the extended family as a self-help group. *The Family Journal, 7*(1), 71–74.

Shields, C. G., Wynne, L. C., McDaniel, S. H., & Gawinski, B. A. (1994). The marginalization of family therapy: A historical and continuing problem. *Journal of Marital and Family Therapy, 20*(2), 117–138.

Shipman v. Division of Social Services, 442 A. 2d 101 (Del. Fam. Ct. 1981).

Shrybman, J., & Halpern, W. I. (1979, March). *The mental health clinician's day in court.* Workshop presented at the Rochester Mental Health Center, Rochester, NY.

Shulte, J. M. (1990). The morality of influencing in counseling. *Counseling and Values, 34,* 103–118.

Sidley, N. T. (Ed.). (1985). *Law and ethics: A guide for the health professional.* New York: Human Sciences.

Sidley, N. T., & Petrila, J. P. (1985). On being involved personally in a lawsuit, as a plaintiff, expert witness, or defendant. In N. T. Sidley (Ed.), *Law and ethics: A guide for the health professional* (pp. 351–378). New York: Human Sciences.

Siegel, M. (1979). Privacy, ethics, and confidentiality. *Professional Psychology, 10,* 249–258.

Silber, D. E. (1976). Ethical relativity and professional psychology. *Clinical Psychologist, 29,* 3–5.

Silva, A., Leong, G., & Weinstock, R. (1989). An HIV-infected psychiatric patient: Some clinicolegal dilemmas. *Bulletin of the American Academy of Psychiatry and Law, 17,* 33–43.

Simola, S. K., Parker, K. C. H., & Froese, A. P. (1999). Relational V-code conditions in a child and adolescent population do warrant treatment. *Journal of Marital and Family Therapy, 25,* 225–236.

Simon, R. (1997). Fearsome foursome: An interview with the women's project. *Family Therapy Networker, 21*(6), 58–68.

Sims v. Sims, 243 Ga. 276, 253 S.E. 2d 763 (1979).

Skowron, E. A., Holmes, S. E., & Sabatelli, R. M. (2003). Deconstructing differentiation: Self-regulation, interdependent relating, and well-being in adulthood. *Contemporary Family Therapy, 25*(1), 111–129.

Slovenko, R. (1973). *Psychiatry and law.* Boston: Little, Brown.

Slovenko, R. (1978). Psychotherapy and informed consent: A search in judicial regulation. In W. E. Barton & C. J. Sanborn (Eds.), *Law and the mental health professions: Friction at the interface.* New York: International Universities.

Slovenko, R. (1980). Legal issues in psychotherapy supervision. In A. K. Hess (Ed.), *Psychotherapy supervision.* New York: Wiley.

Sluzki, C. E. (1978). Marital therapy from a systems theory perspective. In T. J. Paolino, Jr., & B. S. McCrady (Eds.), *Marriage and marital therapy: Psychoanalytic, behavioral and systems theory perspectives* (pp. 366–394). New York: Brunner/Mazel.

Smith, J. A., & Smith, A. H. (2000). Dual relationships and professional integrity: An ethical dilemma case for a family counselor as clergy. *Family Journal, 9,* 438–444.

Smith, R. L. (1999). Client confidentiality in marriage and family counseling. In P. Stevens (Ed.), *Ethical casebook for the practice of marriage and family counseling* (pp. 83–92). Alexandria, VA: American Counseling Association.

Smith, R. L., Stevens-Smith, P., Carlson, J., & Frame, M. W. (1996). Marriage and family therapy: Critique of accreditation, certification, and licensure. *Family Journal: Counseling and Therapy for Couples and Families, 4,* 327–336.

Smith, S. M., Rosen, K. H., McCollum, E. E., & Thomsen, C. J. (2004). Treating intimate partner violence within intact couple relationships: Outcomes of multi-couple versus individual couple therapy. *Journal of Marital and Family Therapy, 30,* 305–318.

Smith, T. S., McGuire, J. M., Abbott, D. W., & Blau, B. I. (1991). Clinical ethical decision making: An investigation of the rationales used to justify doing less than one believes one should. *Professional Psychology: Research and Practice, 22,* 235–239.

Sneyd, R. (2000, April 26). Gay civil unions bill awaits Vermont governor's pen. *The Times-Picayune, 94,* A-10.

Snider, P. D. (1985). The duty to warn: A potential issue of litigation for the counseling supervisor. *Counselor Education and Supervision, 25,* 66–73.

Sobel, S. B. (1984). Independent practice in child and adolescent psychotherapy in small communities: Personal, professional, and ethical issues. *Psychotherapy, 21,* 110–117.

Sodowsky, G. R., & Johnson, P. (1994). Worldviews: Culturally learned assumptions and values. In P. Pedersen & J. C. Carey (Eds.), *Multicultural counseling in schools: A practical handbook* (pp. 59–79). Boston: Allyn & Bacon.

Sophie, J. (1985/1986). A critical examination of stage theories of lesbian identity development. *Journal of Homosexuality, 12,* 39–51.

Sosna v. Iowa, 419 U.S. 393 (1975).

Specialty Boards: Family. (1992). *The Diplomate, 12*(1), 14–15.

Sperling, M. B., & Sack, A. (2002). Psychodynamics and managed care: The art of the impossible? *American Journal of Psychotherapy, 56,* 362–378.

Sperry, L. (1989). Contemporary approaches to brief psychotherapy: A comparative analysis. *Individual Psychology: The Journal of Adlerian Theory, Research, and Practice, 45,* 3–25.

Sporakowski, M. J. (1982). The regulation of marital and family therapy. In J. C. Hansen & L. L'Abate (Eds.), *Values, ethics, legalities and the family therapist* (pp. 125–143). Rockville, MD: Aspen.

Sprenkle, D. H. (1994). Editor's introduction. *Journal of Marital and Family Therapy, 20*(2), 115–116.

Sprenkle, D. H., & Moon, S. M. (1996). Toward pluralism in family therapy research. In D. H. Sprenkle & S. M. Moon (Eds.), *Research methods in family therapy* (pp. 3–19). New York: Guilford.

Stack, C. R. (1993). Should children be allowed to sue their parents? *Human Rights, 20*(2), 2.

Stadler, H. A. (1986). To counsel or not to counsel: The ethical dilemma of dual relationships. *Journal of Counseling and Human Service Professionals, 1,* 134–140.

Stadler, H. H. (1986). Making hard choices: Clarifying controversial ethical issues. *Counseling and Human Development, 19,* 1–10.

Stadler, H. H. (1990). Confidentiality. In B. Herlihy & L. B. Golden (Eds.), *AACD ethical standards casebook* (4th ed.) (pp. 177–187). Alexandria, VA: American Association for Counseling and Development.

Stanley v. Illinois, 406 U.S. 645 (1972).

Stanton, M. D. (1981). Strategic approaches to family therapy. In A. S. Gurman & D. P. Kniskern (Eds.), *Handbook of family therapy* (pp. 361–402). New York: Brunner/Mazel.

State ex rel. Hickox v. Hickox, 410 N.Y.S 2d 81 (1978).

State v. Driscoll, 193 N.W. ed 851 (Wisconsin, 1972) 50 ALR 3d 544 (1973).

State v. Vickers, 633 P 2d 315 (Ariz. 1981).

Stensrud, R., & Stensrud, K. (1981). Counseling may be hazardous to your health: How we teach people to feel powerless. *Personnel and Guidance Journal, 59,* 300–304.

Stern, D. T. (2000). The development of professional character in medical students. *Hastings Center Report, 30*(4), 26–30.

Stevens, P. (Ed.). (1999). *Ethical casebook for the practice of marriage and family counseling.* Alexandria, VA: American Counseling Association.

Stevens-Smith, P. (1997a). A case of individual rights versus the common good: "Right versus right." *Family Journal: Counseling and Therapy for Couples and Families, 5,* 250–252.

Stevens-Smith, P. (1997b). Of cyberspace, managed care, and family counseling: Entering the 21st century. *Family Journal: Counseling and Therapy for Couples and Families, 5,* 53–55.

Stevens-Smith, P., & Hughes, M. M. (1993). *Legal issues in marriage and family counseling.* Alexandria, VA: American Counseling Association.

Stith, S. M., Rosen, K. H., & McCullum, E. E. (2002). Developing a manualized couples treatment for domestic violence: Overcoming challenges. *Journal of Marital and Family Therapy, 28*(1), 21–26.

Stith, S. M., Rosen, K. H., McCullum, E. E., & Thomsen, C. J. (2004). Treating intimate partner violence within intact couple relationships: Outcomes of multi-couple versus individual couple therapy. *Journal of Marital & Family Therapy, 30,* 305–318.

Strickman, L. P. (1982). Marriage, divorce and the Constitution. *Family Law Quarterly, 15,* 259–348.

Strong, L. D. (1992). Freedom of choice legislation passes in Connecticut. *Family Therapy News, 23*(4), 1, 25.

Strupp, H. H., Hadley, S. W., & Gomes-Schwartz, B. (1977). *Psychotherapy for better or worse: The problem of negative effects.* New York: Jason Aronson.

Stuart, R. B. (1980). *Helping couples change: A social learning approach to marital therapy.* New York: Guilford.

Stude, E. W., & McKelvey, J. (1979). Ethics and the law: Friend or foe? *Personnel and Guidance Journal, 57,* 453–456.

Sue, D. W. (1978). Worldviews and counseling. *Personnel and Guidance Journal, 56,* 458–462.

Sue, D. W., Carter, R. T., Casas, J. M., Fouad, N. A., Ivey, A. E., Jensen, M., LaFromgoise, T., Manese, J. E., Ponterotto, J. G., and Vazquez-Nuttal, E. (1998). *Multicultural counseling competencies: Individual and organizational development.* Thousand Oaks, CA: Sage.

Sue, D. W., & Sue, D. (1999). *Counseling the culturally different: Theory and practice* (3rd ed.). New York: Wiley.

Swanson, J. L. (1979). Counseling directory and consumer's guide: Implementing professional disclosure and consumer protection. *Personnel and Guidance Journal, 58,* 190–193.

Swanson, J. W. (1993). Alcohol abuse, mental disorder, and violent behavior. *Alcohol Health and Research World, 2,* 123–132.

Symonds, A. (1979). Violence against woman: The myth of masochism. *American Journal of Psychotherapy, 33,* 161–173.

Taggart, M. (1982). Linear versus systemic values. Implications for family therapy. In J. C. Hansen & L. L'Abate (Eds.), *Values, ethics, legalities and the family therapist* (pp. 23–40). Rockville, MD: Aspen.

Taggart, M. (1989). Epistemological equality as the fulfillment of family therapy. In M. McGoldrick, C. Anderson, & F. Walsh (Eds.), *Women in families: A framework for family therapy.* New York: Norton.

Tarasoff v. Board of Regents of the University of California, 13 Cal. 3d 177, 529 P.2d 553 (1974), vacated, 17 Cal. 3d 425, 551 P2d 334 (1976).

Taylor, R. E. (2004). Not being an "expert" expert: Four ways an expert can falter before even speaking a word. *American Journal of Family Law, 18,* 119–138.

Teismann, M. W. (1980). Convening strategies in family therapy. *Family Process, 19,* 393–400.

Terkelsen, K. G. (1983). Schizophrenia and the family: II. Adverse effects of family therapy. *Family Process, 22,* 191–200.

Terkelsen, K. G. (1984). Response by Kenneth G. Terkelsen, M. D. *Family Process, 23,* 425–428.

Theodore, P. S., & Basrow, S. A. (2000). Heterosexual masculinity and homophobia: A reaction. *Journal of Homosexuality, 40*(2), 31–48.

Thomas, A. J. (1998). Ethical mandates for multicultural sensitivity for family counseling. *Family Journal: Counseling and Therapy for Couples and Families, 6,* 49–51.

Thompson, R. A., Tinsley, B. R., Scalora, M. J., & Parke, R. D. (1989). Grandparents' visitation rights: Legalizing the ties that bind. *American Psychologist, 44,* 1217–1222.

Thompson v. County of Alameda, 167-Cal. Rptr. 70 (1980).

Thompson v. Thompson, 484 U.S. 174 (1988).

Thompson-Schneider, D. (1997). The arc of history: Or, the resurrection of feminism's sameness/difference dichotomy in the gay and lesbian marriage debate. *Law and Sexuality, 7,* 1–30.

Thoreson, R., Nathan, P., Skorina, J., & Kilburg, R. (1983). The alcoholic psychologist: Issues, problems, and implications for the profession. *Professional Psychology: Research and Practice, 14,* 670–684.

Tippins, T. M., & Wittmann, J. P. (2005). Empirical and ethical problems with custody recommendations: A call for clinical humility and judicial vigilance. *Family Court Review, 43,* 193.

Torres, A., Forest, J., & Eisman, S. (1980). Telling parents. Clinic policies and adolescents' use of family planning and abortion services. *Family Planning Perspectives, 11,* 284–292.

Toulmin, S. (1950). *An examination of the place of reason in ethics.* Cambridge, England: Cambridge University.

Trimble v. Gordon, 430 U.S. 762 (1977).

Troiden, R. R. (1989). The formation of homosexual identities. *Journal of Homosexuality, 17,* 43–73.

Turner, W. L., & Wieling, E. (2004). Introduction to the special section: Implications of research with diverse families. *Journal of Marital and Family Therapy, 30*(3), 255–256.

Tymchuk, A. J., Drapkin, R., Major-Kingsley, S., Ackerman, A. B., Coffman, E. W., & Baum, M. S. (1982). Ethical decision making and psychologists' attitudes and training in ethics. *Professional Psychology, 13,* 412–421.

U.S. Advisory Board on Child Abuse and Neglect. (1990). *Child abuse and neglect: Critical first steps in response to a national emergency* (No. 017-092-00104-5). Washington, DC: U.S. Government Printing Office.

U.S. Bureau of the Census. (1981). *Statistical abstract of the United States.* Washington, DC: Government Printing Office.

Van Hoose, W. H. (1980). Ethics and counseling. *Counseling and Human Development, 13*(1), 1–12.

Van Hoose, W. H., & Kottler, J. A. (1985). *Ethical and legal issues in counseling and psychotherapy* (2nd ed.). San Francisco: Jossey-Bass.

Vance, G. A. (1995). Rock-a-bye lawsuit: Can a baby sue the hand that rocked the cradle? *The John Marshall Law Review, 28,* 429–469.

VandeCreek, L., Knapp, S., & Brace, K. (1990). Mandatory continuing education for licensed psychologists: Its rationale and current implementation. *Professional Psychology: Research and Practice, 21,* 135–140.

Vangelisti, A. L. (1994). Family secrets: Forms, functions and correlates. *Journal of Social and Personal Relationships, 11,* 113–135.

Vangelisti, A. L., Caughlin, J. P., & Timmerman, L. (2001). Criteria for revealing family secrets. *Communication Monographs, 68,* 1–27.

van Knipper, D., & van Schie, E. C. M. (2000). Foci and correlates of organizational identification. *Journal of Occupational and Organizational Psychology, 73,* 137–148.

VanZandt, C. E. (1990). Professionalism: A matter of personal initiative. *Journal of Counseling and Development, 68,* 243–245.

Vasquez, M. J. T. (1991). Sexual intimacies with clients after termination: Should a prohibition be explicit? *Ethics and Behavior, 1,* 45–61.

Vatcher, C., & Bogo, M. (2001). The feminist/emotionally focused therapy practice model: An integrated approach for couple therapy. *Journal of Marital and Family Therapy, 27,* 69–83.

Vitiello, M. (1999). How imperial is the Supreme Court? An analysis of Supreme Court abortion doctrine and popular will. *University of San Francisco Law Review, 34,* 49–98.

Vitulano, L. A., & Copeland, B. A. (1980). Trends in continuing education and competency demonstration. *Professional Psychology, 11,* 891–897.

von Weizsacker, E., & von Weizsacker, C. (1974). *Offene systeme I: Beitrage zur zeitstruktur von information, entropie und evolution.* Stuttgart, West Germany: Klett.

Vroom, P. (1983). The anomalous profession: Bumpy going in the divorce mediation movement. *The Family Therapy Networker, 7*(3), 38–42.

Wachtel, E. F. (1979). Learning family therapy: The dilemmas of an individual therapist. *Journal of Contemporary Psychotherapy, 10,* 122–135.

Wald, M. S. (1975). State intervention on behalf of "neglected" children: A search for realistic standards. *Stanford Law Review, 27,* 985–1040.

Wald, M. S. (1976). State intervention on behalf of "neglected" children: Standards for removal of children from their homes, monitoring the status of children in foster care, and termination of parental rights. *Stanford Law Review, 28,* 625–706.

Wald, M. S. (1982). State intervention on behalf of endangered children: A proposed legal response. *Child Abuse and Neglect, 6,* 3–45.

Walker, C. E. (1981). Continuing professional development. In C. E. Walker (Ed.), *Clinical practice of psychology.* New York: Pergamon.

Walker, L. (1979). *The battered woman.* New York: Harper Colophon.

Walker, L. (1981). Battered women: Sex roles and clinical issues. *Professional Psychology, 12,* 81–90.

Walker, L. (1984). *The battered woman syndrome.* New York: Springer.

Wall, J. E. (2004). Assessment and technology—Allies in educational reform: An overview of issues for counselors and educators. *Measurement and Evaluation in Counseling and Development, 37*(2), 112–128.

Walter, M. I., & Handelsman, M. M. (1996). *Informed consent for mental health interactional patterns, pathologies and paradoxes.* New York: Norton.

Walters, M., Carter, B., Papp, P., & Silverstein, O. (1988). *The invisible web: Gender patterns in family relationships.* New York: Guilford.

Walther, D. L. (2005). Confidentiality broadly defined. *American Journal of Family Law, 19,* 1–2.

Walton, T. (1996). *Splitting the baby.* Palo Alto, CA: Internet Attorney. Retrieved November 15, 2005, from http://www.netatty.com/articles/parent.html

Waltz, J. R., & Scheuneman, T. W. (1969). Informed consent to therapy. *Northwestern University Law Review, 64,* 628–650.

Wampler, K. S. (2005). Editorial: Research (again). *Journal of Marital and Family Therapy, 31*(1), 1–2.

Watts, A. (1961). *Psychotherapy east and west.* New York: Random House.

Watts, R. E. (1999). Confidentiality and the duty to report: A case study. *Family Journal: Counseling and Therapy for Couples and Families, 7,* 64–66.

Watzlawick, F., Beavin, J. H., & Jackson, D. D. (1967). Pragmatics of human communications: A study of counseling: Effects of information specificity on clients' ratings of counselors. *Journal of Mental Health Counseling, 18,* 253–262.

Watzlawick, P., Weakland, J. H., & Fish, R. (1974). *Change: Principles of problem formation and problem resolution.* New York: Norton.

Wear, S. (1999). Enhancing clinician provision of informed consent and counseling: Some pedagogical strategies. *Journal of Medicine and Philosophy, 24,* 34–43.

Weber v. Aetna Casualty & Surety Co., 406 U.S. 164 (1972).

Webster v. Reproductive Health Services, 109 S. Ct. 3040 (1989).

Weidman, A. (1986). Family therapy with violent couples. *Social Casework, 67,* 211–218.

Weikel, W. J., & Hughes, P. R. (1993). *The counselor as an expert witness.* Alexandria, VA: American Counseling Association.

Weinrach, S. G. (1989). Guidelines for clients of private practitioners: Committing the structure to print. *Journal of Counseling and Development, 67,* 299–300.

Weiss, R. S. (1979). Issues in the adjudication of custody when parents separate. In G. Levinger & O. C. Moles (Eds.), *Divorce and separation.* New York: Basic.

Welfel, E. R. (1998). *Ethics in counseling and psychotherapy.* Pacific Grove, CA: Brooks/Cole.

Welfel, E. R., & Lipsitz, N. E. (1984). The ethical behavior of professional psychologists. *Counseling Psychologist, 12*(3), 31–43.

Wentzel, L., & Ross, M. A. (1983). Psychological and social ramifications of battering: Observations leading to a counseling methodology for victims of domestic violence. *Personnel and Guidance Journal, 61,* 423–428.

Werry, J. S. (1989). Family therapy: Professional endeavor or successful religion? *Journal of Family Therapy, 11,* 377–382.

Weyrauch, W. O., & Katz, S. N. (1983). *American family law in transition.* Washington, DC: Bureau of National Affairs, Inc.

Whetsone, B. (2002, July/August). Papp and Pittman: Reflections on gender. *Family Therapy Magazine,* 10–13.

Whitaker, C., & Keith, D. (1981). Symbolic-experiential family therapy. In A. S. Gurman & D. Kniskern (Eds.), *Handbook of family therapy* (pp. 187–225). New York: Brunner/Mazel.

White, M. (1993). Deconstruction and therapy. In S. Gilligan & R. Price (Eds.), *Therapeutic conversations* (pp. 22–61). New York: Norton.

White, M., & Epstein, D. (1990). *Narrative means to therapeutic ends.* New York: Norton.

Widiger, T. A., & Rorer, L. G. (1984). The responsible psychotherapist. *American Psychologist, 39,* 503–515.

Wilcoxon, S. A. (1986). One-spouse marital therapy: Is informed consent necessary? *American Journal of Family Therapy, 14,* 265–270.

Wilcoxon, S. A. (1987). Client consent in departures from customary and suggested treatment formats. *American Mental Health Counselors Association Journal, 9*(2), 77–83.

Wilcoxon, S. A. (2004, July). *Brief therapy: A multicultural perspective.* Paper presentation at the annual conference of the International School Psychology Association. University of Exeter, UK.

Wilcoxon, S. A., & Archer, G. D. (1997). Professional development and training: A consortium model. *Journal of Mental Health Counseling, 19,* 191–198.

Wilcoxon, S. A., & Fenell, D. (1983). Engaging the non-attending spouse in marital therapy through the use of therapist-initiated written communication. *Journal of Marital and Family Therapy, 9,* 199–203.

Wilcoxon, S. A., & Fenell, D. (1986). Linear and paradoxical letters to the non-attending spouse: A comparison of engagement rates. *Journal of Marital and Family Therapy, 12,* 191–193.

Wilcoxon, S. A., & Puleo, S. G. (1992). Professional development needs of mental health counselors: Results of a national survey. *Journal of Mental Health Counseling, 14,* 185–187.

Wilensky, H. (1964, June). The professionalization of everyone? *American Journal of Sociology, 70,* 137–157.

Willbach, D. (1989). Ethics and family therapy: The case management of family violence. *Journal of Marital and Family Therapy, 15,* 43–52.

Williams, C. (1999). Ethical considerations in multicultural family counseling. In P. Stevens (Ed.), *Ethical casebook for the practice of marriage and family counseling* (pp. 124–132). Alexandria, VA: American Counseling Association.

Williams, R. M. (1968). Values. In E. Sills (Ed.), *International encyclopedia of the social sciences* (pp. 1–38). New York: Macmillan.

Wilson, G. F. (1985). Ethical and legal aspects of peer review. In J. M. Hamilton (Ed.), *Psychiatric peer review: Prelude and promise* (pp. 194–217). Washington, DC: American Psychiatric Press.

Winborn, B. B. (1977). Honest labeling and other procedures for the protection of consumers of counseling. *Personnel and Guidance Journal, 56,* 206–209.

Winkle, C. W., Piercy, F. P., & Hovestadt, A. J. (1981). A curriculum for graduate-level marriage and family therapy education. *Journal of Marital and Family Therapy, 7,* 201–210.

Wisconsin Statutes Annotated, 905.04 (1981–1982 Supp.).

Witmer, J. M. (1978). Professional disclosure in licensure. *Counselor Education and Supervision, 18,* 71–73.

Witnesses §190 (1976). *American Jurisprudence, 2d.*

Wohlman, B., & Stricker, G. (1983). *Handbook of family and marital therapy.* New York: Plenum Press.

Wolf-Smith, J. H., & LaRossa, R. (1992). After he hits her. *Family Relations, 41,* 324–329.

Woody, R. H. (1988). *Fifty ways to avoid malpractice.* Sarasota, FL: Professional Resource Exchange.

Woody, R. H., & Associates. (1984). *The law and the practice of human services.* San Francisco: Jossey-Bass.

Woody, R. H., & Mitchell, R. E. (1984). Understanding the legal system and legal research. In R. H. Woody & Associates (Eds.), *The law and the practice of human services* (pp. 1–38). San Francisco: Jossey-Bass.

Wylie, M. S. (1989). Looking for fence posts. *Family Therapy Networker, 13*(2), 22–33.

Wylie, M. S. (1995). Diagnosing for dollars? *Family Therapy Networker, 19*(3), 23–26, 28–33, 65–69.

Yaron v. Yaron, 372 N.Y.S.2d 518 (1975).

Zablocki v. Redhail, 434 U.S. 374 (1978).

Zajonc, R. B. (1980). Feeling and thinking: Preferences need no inferences. *American Psychologist, 35,* 151–175.

Zibert, J., Engels, D. W., Kern, C. W., & Durodoye, B. A. (1998). Ethical knowledge of counselors. *Counseling and Values, 43,* 34–48.

Zimet, C. N. (1989). The mental health care revolution: Will psychology survive? *American Psychologist, 44,* 703–708.

Zimmerman, J., & Dickerson, V. (1996). *If problems talked: Adventures in narrative therapy.* New York: Guilford.

Ziskin, J. (1995). *Coping with psychiatric and psychological testimony, Vols. I, II, & III* (5th ed.). Los Angeles, CA: Law and Psychology Press.

Name Index

Huntley, D. K., 14
Huston, K., 48, 128, 129, 133

Ibrahim, F. A., 37, 142
Imber-Black, E., 24
Ivey, A. E., 3, 31
Ivey, M. B., 3, 31

Jackson, D. D., 103
Jackson, S. A., 33
Jacobson, N. S., 94, 339
Jain, M., 67
Janeway, E., 135
Jantsch, E., 12
Jencius, M., 37, 143
Jessee, E., 87, 99, 104, 106, 108,
    112, 113
Joffe, W. A., 225
Johanson, G., 295
Johnson, G. H., 75
Johnson, J. M., 130
Johnson, L. N., 339
Johnson, M. P., 110, 123, 124, 128
Johnson, T. R., 281
Johnston, M. W., 172
Jones, A., 125
Jones, J. E., 112
Jones, K. D., 172
Jones, S. R., 6, 7
Jones, W. P., 140
Jones, W. T., 43
Jordan, A. E., 43, 44
Jordan, K., 148
Jory, B., 125
Jurkovic, G. J., 111, 116, 117,
    118, 119

Kahle, P. A., 6, 29
Kain, C. D., 168
Kanani, D., 143
Kaplan, A. G., 72
Kaplan, D., 3, 64, 72, 280
Kaplan, D. M., 107
Kaplan, H., 170
Karpel, M. A., 17, 18, 19, 20, 88,
    90, 91, 92
Kaschak, E., 126
Kaslow, F. W., 82, 102, 268, 326, 351
Kaslow, N., 300
Kass, A., 226
Kasturirangan, A., 126, 127
Katz, J., 281
Katz, S. N., 246, 247, 249, 258, 266
Kaufman, M., 72, 76, 77, 93
Kausch, O., 211
Kavanaugh, P. B., 218
Kazen, B. A., 265
Keala, D. K., 340

Keary, A. O., 206
Keefe, R. H., 156
Kegeles, T., 167
Keim, J., 112
Keith, D., 34
Keith-Spiegel, P., 51, 59, 159
Keller, J. F., 304
Kelly, J. B., 224, 276
Kelly, K. R., 151
Kemp, A., 107, 136
Kennedy, C., 291
Kern, C. W., 45
Kessler, S., 225
Ketring, S. A., 339
Kidder, R. M., 48, 59, 131
Kier, F. J., 139
Kilburg, R., 62
Kimberly, J. A., 168, 172
King, M.C., 4
Kirschenbaum, H., 10
Kissel, S., 219, 367, 369, 370
Kitchener, K. S., 48, 49, 59, 132,
    159, 163, 164, 165
Kleist, D. M., 224
Kluckholn, F., 3
Knapp, S., 70, 204, 206, 274, 292,
    293, 295, 345
Knapp, S. J., 169, 170, 282
Kniskern, D. P., 102, 108, 339
Knudson-Martin, C., 4, 27, 28,
    102, 106
Konetsky, C. D., 14
Koocher, G. P., 51, 59, 159
Kottler, J. A., 45, 62, 234, 296, 385
Kovacs, K. E., 245
Kral, R., 300
Kramer, D. T., 266
Krause, H. D., 246, 249, 251, 252,
    261, 262, 263, 264, 268
Krugman, S., 135
Kurri, K., 124, 127, 131, 132

L'Abate, L., 11, 116, 301, 325
Laing, J-C., 4, 23
Laird, J., 4, 110
Laliotis, D. A., 62
Lamb, D. H., 169
Lamson, A. L., 339
Lane, P. J., 212
Lane, T., 131
Langsley, D. C., 107
LaRossa, R., 133
Laszloffy, T. A., 148
Lavori, N., 248
Lawless, L. L., 151
Lebow, J., 220
Lee, M. Y., 155
Lee, S. B., 126

Leitner, L. M., 148
Leong, G., 172
Leslie, L. A., 27
Leslie, R. S., 371
Liddle, H. A., 301, 326, 338, 340, 342
Lidz, C. W., 281
Lifson, L. E., 234
Linton, R., 3
Lipsitz, N. E., 49
Liss-Levenson, N., 72
Locke, D. W., 302
Locke, L. D., 107
Lockhart, L., 123, 125, 127
Logan, J. P., 274
Long, L., 117, 118
Lovell, C., 45
Lyddon, W. J., 6
Lyons, C., 91

Mabe, A. R., 1, 44
MacDonald, J. M., 226
Mace, D. R., 109
MacGillivray, I. K., 5
Madanes, C., 96, 115
Madonna, J. M., 136
Maheu, M. M., 141
Mahmoud, V., 6
Mahoney, M. M., 248
Malcolm, J. C., 234
Malouf, J. L., 282
Mangum, R. S., 235
Manning, M. L., 3, 4, 5, 6, 9–10, 87
Mappes, D. C., 273
Marecek, J., 72
Margolin, G., 16, 54, 66, 80, 82, 83,
    84, 89, 91, 93, 94, 95, 98, 103
Markos, O. A., 62
Marlow, L., 276
Martinek, S., 158
Martinek, S. A., 145
Maslow, A. H., 9
Masters, K. S., 339
Matheson, J. L., 107
Mathias, B., 135
Maturana, H. R., 15
Maxey, J.L., 4
May, K. M., 28, 125, 354, 355
Maynard, P. E., 136
McCarthy, P., 72
McCloskey, L. A., 125, 126
McCollough, M. E., 4
McCollum, E. E., 28, 107, 131
McCrady, B. S., 62
McDaniel, S. H., 303
McEwen, M. K., 6, 7
McG Mullen, R., 128, 129
McGoldrick, M., 4, 32, 107, 353
McGrath, P., 145, 158

Subject Index